Human Rights and Justice

International Documents

To My Wife

Ratna

Human Rights and Justice

International Documents

Wg Cdr (Dr) U C Jha (Retd)

Vij Books India Pvt Ltd
2/19, Ansari Road, Daryaganj, New Delhi

Published by

Vij Books India Pvt Ltd
(Publishers, Distributors & Importers)
2/19, Ansari Road, Darya Ganj
New Delhi - 110002
Phones: 91-11-43596460, 91-11- 65449971
Fax: 91-11-30126465
e-mail : vijbooks@rediffmail.com

ISBN: 978-93-80177-32-8

Price in India: ₹ 1950/-
Price outside India: US $ 65.00

Printed in India
at Narula Printers , New Delhi

HUMAN RIGHTS AND JUSTICE

International Documents

CHAPTERS

Contents

PREFACE

The international human rights movement got a shot in the arm when the United Nations General Assembly adopted the Universal Declaration of Human Rights (UDHR) on 10 December 1948. The UDHR expresses the "common understanding of the peoples of the world concerning the inalienable and inviolable rights of all members of the human family and constitutes an obligation for the members of the international community." Though the UDHR is only a declaration rather than a legally binding treaty, most international lawyers accept that substantial parts of the UDHR now enjoy the status of binding rules of customary international law, that is to say, non-treaty law generated through consistent practice accompanied by a sense of legal obligation.

Nine core, legally binding, international human rights treaties have been promulgated under the auspices of the United Nations (UN) since the adoption of the UDHR. The ratification of these treaties by a majority of the States has given concrete expression to their universality.[1] In addition, various declarations, principles and resolutions passed by the UN bodies have further strengthened human right norms. The other relevant sources of international law beyond treaties and custom are "general principles" derived from the domestic or international legal systems, and so-called *jus cogens*, or peremptory norms from which no derogation is permitted.

The prerequisite for human rights to be enforceable as domestic legal rights is a domestic legal system based on the rule of law. The principle of the rule of law can thus also be described as an overarching principle in the field of human rights protection because,

---

[1] The nine core international human rights treaties are: the International Convention on the Elimination of All Forms of Racial Discrimination (ICERD) (173 State Parties as on 30 June 2010), the International Covenant on Civil and Political Rights (ICCPR) (165 State Parties), the International Covenant on Economic, Social and Cultural Rights (ICESCR) (160 State Parties), the Convention on the Elimination of All Forms of Discrimination against Women (CEDAW) (186 State Parties), the Convention against Torture and Other Cruel, Inhuman or Degrading Treatment or Punishment (CAT) (146 State Parties), the Convention on the Rights of the Child (CRC) (193 State Parties), the International Convention on the Protection of the Rights of All Migrant Workers and Members of Their Families (ICRMW) (42 State Parties), the International Convention for the Protection of All Persons from Enforced Disappearance (not yet in force) (18 State Parties), and the Convention on the Rights of Persons with Disabilities (CRPD) (80 State Parties).

where it does not exist, respect for human rights becomes illusory. The rule of law is a principle of governance in which all persons, institutions and entities, public and private, including the State itself, are accountable to laws that are publicly promulgated, equally enforced and independently adjudicated, and which are consistent with international human rights norms and standards. It requires measures to ensure adherence to the principles of supremacy of the law, equality before the law, accountability to the law, fairness in the application of the law, separation of powers, participation in decision-making, legal certainty, avoidance of arbitrariness, and procedural and legal transparency. Justice is an ideal of accountability and fairness in the protection and vindication of rights and the prevention and punishment of wrongs. Its administration involves certain formal judicial and informal/ customary/traditional mechanisms.

A strong and impartial judiciary is a cornerstone of access to justice. The judiciary's roles and functions vary from one jurisdiction to another. However, they share the same basic principles in the settlement of disputes, interpretation of laws, and constitutional checks on the exercise of power by the executive and legislative branches of government. Judicial independence is crucial for an effective judiciary.

International human rights law lays down obligations which States are bound to respect. By becoming parties to international treaties, States assume obligations and duties under international law to respect, to protect and to fulfil human rights. The obligation to respect means that States must refrain from interfering with or curtailing the enjoyment of human rights. The obligation to protect requires States to protect individuals and groups against human rights abuses. The obligation to fulfil means that States must take positive action to facilitate the enjoyment of basic human rights. The State has the duty to provide effective remedies against human rights violations, to investigate and reveal the truth about human rights violations, to bring perpetrators of gross human rights violations to justice, and to provide reparation to victims. Victims of gross human rights violations have a right to truth, a right to justice and a right to reparation.

This book is divided into 14 chapters. Chapter 1 is introductory. It discusses the concepts of human rights and dwells upon the international bill of rights and the administration of justice. Chapter 2 contains international documents relating to the duties and responsibilities of the officials related with the administration of justice—judges, prosecutors, lawyers and enforcement officers. The international documents dealing with the right of prisoners have been covered in Chapter 3, while those relating to children have been included in Chapter 4. Chapter 5 of the book deals with international documents relating to women.

Chapter 6 contains the full text of The UN Convention on the Rights of Persons with Disabilities and its Optional Protocol. It was adopted on 13 December 2006. There were 82 signatories to the Convention, 44 signatories to the Optional Protocol, and 1ratification of the Convention. This is the highest number of signatories in history to a UN Convention on its opening day. It is the first comprehensive human rights treaty of the 21st century and is the first human rights convention to be open for signature by regional integration organizations. Chapter 7 contains international conventions relating to the abolition of apartheid, racial discrimination, slavery and forced labour. The international law of human rights, which is applicable both in times of peace and in times of emergency and armed conflict, absolutely prohibits torture. Chapter 8 of the book is devoted to conventions against torture and enforced disappearance; and principles for effective investigations in the cases of alleged torture.

It is recognized universally that the right to life is the most fundamental and basic of human rights. In Chapter 9, the principles relating to the prevention and investigation of extra-legal, arbitrary and summary executions have been covered. The 1991 UN Manual on the investigation of arbitrary and summary executions has been included in the chapter, which also enumerates the safeguards guaranteeing protection of the rights of those facing the death penalty..

International humanitarian law (IHL) is a set of international rules, which are specifically intended to solve humanitarian problems directly arising from international or non-international armed conflicts. Chapter 10 covers relevant provisions of IHL treaties, whereas Chapter 11 contains safeguards under the Rome Statute of the International Criminal Court and its rules of procedure and evidence. It also includes the convention on the prevention of genocide and principles relating to crimes against humanity.

The armed forces the world over are governed by a special code of conduct. It is necessary that such a special code be based on international standards relating to the right to a fair trial. Chapter 12 includes draft principles governing the administration of justice through military tribunals. Chapter 13 of provides a brief account of the three regional conventions on rights, and principles and guidelines on the right to a fair trial and legal assistance in Africa.

It is important for States to provide appropriate and effective mechanisms for the society as a whole and, in particular, for the relatives of the victims, to know the truth regarding gross violations of human rights and serious violations of IHL. The victims also have a right to an effective remedy and to reparation. Chapter 14 contains documents relating to reparation for victims of violations of IHL and human rights law.

I am thankful to Ms Medha and Ms Chandana for their editorial assistance. I am also grateful to Vij Books India Pvt Ltd for taking great pains to shape the book.

-U C Jha

CHAPTER 1

HUMAN RIGHTS AND JUSTICE: AN INTRODUCTION

Generally speaking, human rights are those rights which allow an individual the freedom to live a dignified and secure life of her/his choice. They include rights related to the safety of person; the right to be free from coercion; the right to social benefits, rest and leisure; and the right to basic education. They are, in fact, universal legal guarantees protecting individuals and groups against actions which interfere with fundamental freedoms and human dignity. The concept of human rights is founded on the ancient doctrine of natural rights based on natural law. It evolved from the desire of people to seek laws that would be binding on human authorities and that would protect them from the shortcomings and tyranny of ruling powers. It is thought that these rights are anterior to the development of political societies and have been universally applicable among all peoples of all ages and of all religions. Hence, they are superior to the rights created by human authorities.

In the system based on Roman law, dignity was seen as a right of personality and status, and criminal and civil remedies were frequently provided if dignity in this sense was infringed. In his famous oration *On the Dignity of Man*, published in 1486, Pico della Mirandola argued that at the root of Man's dignity is the ability to choose to be what he wants to be, and that this is a gift from God. 'It is given to him to have that which he chooses and to be that which he wills.'

'Human rights' have been defined in numerous ways in the modern era.

- Basic Rights for all humans independent of the nationality.
- Human rights are those rights which are held by all human beings.
- Human rights are moral rights held equally by all human beings, unconditionally and unalterably.

- Human rights are rights inherent to all human beings, whatever our nationality, place of residence, sex, national or ethnic origin, colour, religion, language, or any other status.

- The basic rights and freedoms, to which all humans are entitled, often held to include the right to life and liberty, freedom of thought and expression, and equality before the law.

- The conditions and expectations to which every person, by virtue of his or her existence as a human being, is entitled.

- These are the rights that every human being automatically qualifies for at birth. They cannot be denied because of the colour of one's skin, religion, age or other personal factors. Central to the concept of human rights is the protection of human dignity....

- An individual's statutory right to equal treatment and free from discrimination prohibited by statute and which, generally, provides a civil remedy to provide compensation or to punish such discrimination when it is reported.

- Human rights comprise a universal moral right, something which all people, everywhere, at all times ought to have, something of which no one may be deprived without grave affront to justice, something which is owing to every human being simply because one is human.

- Human rights as those minimal rights which every individual must have against the State or other public authority by virtue of his being a member of the human family, irrespective of any other consideration.

- Human rights means the rights relating to life, liberty, equality, and dignity of the individual guaranteed by the Constitution or embodied in the International Covenants and enforceable by courts in India.[1]

However varied may be the terms of these definitions, they generally focus upon the idea that human rights apply to all human beings because they are human beings, and thereby, distinguish human rights from other rights, such as legal, contractual and conventional. Human rights are based on a theory that takes for its starting point the human dignity[2] of individuals

---

[1] Section 2 (1) (d) of the Protection of Human Rights Act, 1993. Therefore, so far as India is concerned, only enforceable rights embodied in the Constitution are human rights.

[2] The Protection of Human Rights Act, 1993, refers to the 'dignity of the individual'. However, none of the human rights

and their entitlement to have certain basic freedoms respected and basic needs satisfied. They form a set of minimum prerequisites for leading a 'good life'. Also, all human rights and fundamental freedoms 'derive from the inherent dignity of the human person', and not from the State or any other external authority. There are two related premises here, that these rights are not assigned by any authority, and therefore may not be taken away by such an authority and that they belong to every person by virtue of their being human.

While human rights are founded on moral principles and are conceived of in terms of inherence, universality and indivisibility, they are, at core, (legal) guarantees against actions and omissions.[3] As with all rights, human rights embody duties, providing a legal framework of entitlements and obligations; each right implies a claim holder (an individual or a group) and a duty bearer (generally a state). Human rights have the following inherent characteristics: (i) They focus on the dignity of the human being, (ii) They protect individuals and groups, (iii) They are universal, (iv) They are equal and interdependent, (v) They are internationally guaranteed, (vi) They are legally protected, (vii) They obligate States and State actors, and (viii) They cannot be waived or taken away.

The following list gives a few examples of conduct that offends or denigrates the dignity of an individual or a group.

- Statements that demean and humiliate individuals or groups because of their origin, status, religion or beliefs
- Denial of the capacity of a person to assert claims to basic rights
- Punishment of a detained person by psychological or physical means that are meant to humiliate or ridicule their beliefs, origins or way of life
- Implying that members of certain groups are inferior
- Restrictions on opportunities and means to maintain family life

---

contd/-

documents define the term 'dignity'. The Webster Twentieth Century dictionary (1959) gives various meanings of the term as: 'worthiness', 'nobility', 'honour', 'the degree of worth', and 'self-respect'. The root of the word may throw some light on its meaning. The word originated from the Latin word '*dignitas*', which means 'worth'. One meaning of dignity is 'intrinsic worth'. Thus, when the United Nation's Charter refers to the 'dignity and worth' of the human person, it uses two synonyms for the same concept. The other instruments speak of 'inherent dignity', an expression that is close to 'intrinsic worth'.

[3] UNDP, *A Human Rights Approach to Development – Primer for Development Practitioners* (Amparo Tomas), August 2003, p. 1.

- Denial of educational or employment opportunities to a person or a group of persons
- Deprivation of basic needs
- Abuse by officials, especially of persons suffering from infirmities
- Insensitivity in medical treatment or hospital care

Human Rights in Ancient India

It is often claimed by Western scholars that the concept of human rights law is a product of European civilization. In reality, the roots of human rights law can be traced back to ancient Indian and other ancient civilizations. It is said in the Rig Veda: "There is one race; of human beings". The validity of different traditions and religions, indeed of the path to truth, was respected in ancient India under the principle *sarva dharma saman*.

An ancient text runs thus: "I seek no kingdom, nor heaven nor rebirth, but I wish that all living beings be spared of the manifold pains and distress." An individual in ancient India existed as a citizen of the State, and in that capacity he had both rights and obligations. These rights and duties were expressed in terms of duties (*dharma*)—duties to oneself, to one's family, to fellow men, to the society and to the world at large.

The Buddhist doctrine of non-violence in deed and thought is a humanitarian doctrine *par excellence*, dating back to the third century BC. Both Buddhism and Jainism emphasized the principles of equality and non-violence. They preached compassion for all human beings and acknowledged the rights of the downtrodden. They spoke of protecting plants and animals since every creature has life and is sensitive to pain and pleasure. Jainism defined 'sin' as a violation of, and encroachment on, others' right to life. This was perhaps the first time in human history that a right to life was laid down as a right to be respected.

In ancient India, the first and the foremost duty of the king was to protect his people. Protection of the people consisted in meeting internal threats as well as external aggression. Gautama prescribed that the special responsibility of the king was to protect all beings and to award just punishments. He was to protect the *varnas* and *ashrams* according to the rule of *sastra* and to bring them to the path of their proper duties when they swerved from it. Vashistha stated that protection was a life-long *sutra* to serve which the king had to give up fear and softness of heart.

It was also the duty of the king to make provisions for education, public health, medical attendance, insurance against unemployment, and for the care of orphans, widows and the old. An extremely high ideal was placed on the king by Kautilya in the *Arthashastra.* He proclaimed that "In the happiness of the subject lies the happiness of the king, in their welfare lies his welfare, the good of the king does not consist in what is pleasing to himself but what is pleasing to the subjects." He called upon the king to support the destitute, the disabled, and so on, and to provide them with medicines, lodging, food and clothing according to their requirements.

A discussion on human rights in ancient India cannot be complete without reference to King Ashoka. His most significant contribution was his totally anti-war perspective. Wars have been justified by rulers throughout history. Ashoka stands out as an exception. His attitude to war is recorded in his 13th major rock edict. This rock edict is the oldest anti-war statement and should be treated as one of the oldest human rights documents.

1.1 THE UNITED NATIONS

The United Nations (UN) is an international organization founded in 1945[4] after the Second World War by 51 countries committed to maintaining international peace and security, developing friendly relations among nations and promoting social progress, better living standards and human rights. Due to its unique international character, and the powers vested in its founding Charter, the UN can take action on a wide range of issues, and provide a forum for its 192 Member States to express their views, through the General Assembly, the Security Council, the Economic and Social Council and other bodies and committees.

Although best known for peacekeeping, peace-building, conflict prevention and humanitarian assistance, there are many other ways the United Nations and its System (specialized agencies, funds and programmes) affect our lives and make the world a better place. The Organization works on a broad range of fundamental issues, from sustainable development, environment and refugees protection, disaster relief, counter terrorism, disarmament and non-proliferation, to promoting democracy, human rights, gender equality and the advancement of women, governance, economic and social development and international health, clearing landmines, expanding food production, and more, in order to achieve its goals and coordinate efforts for a safer world for this and future generations.

---

[4] The UN officially came into existence on 24 October 1945 upon ratification of the Charter by the five permanent members of the Security Council —France, the Republic of China, the Soviet Union, the United Kingdom and the United States —and by a majority of the other 46 signatories.

The United Nations Charter and Human Rights

The Charter, signed on 26 June 1945, set out three main goals for the nascent organization: to prevent future wars by fostering peace and security; to promote social and economic progress; and to define and protect the rights and freedoms of every human being regardless of race, sex, language or religion. The Preamble of the UN Charter and the provisions safeguarding basic human rights and fundamental freedoms are as follows.

PREAMBLE

We the Peoples of the United Nations determined to save succeeding generations from the scourge of war, which twice in our lifetime has brought untold sorrow to mankind, and **to reaffirm faith in fundamental human rights, in the dignity and worth of the human person, in the equal rights of men and women and of nations large and small,** and to establish conditions under which justice and respect for the obligations arising from treaties and other sources of international law can be maintained, and to promote social progress and better standards of life in larger freedom...,

Article 1

The Purposes of the United Nations are:

3. To achieve international cooperation in solving international problems of an economic, social, cultural, or humanitarian character, and in promoting and encouraging **respect for human rights and for fundamental freedoms for all without distinction as to race, sex, language, or religion**.

Article 13

1. The **General Assembly** shall initiate studies and make recommendations for the purpose of:

b. promoting international cooperation in the economic, social, cultural, educational, and health fields, and assisting in the **realization of human rights and fundamental freedoms for all without distinction as to race, sex, language, or religion.**

Article 55

With a view to the creation of conditions of stability and well-being which are necessary for peaceful and friendly relations among nations based on respect for the principle of equal rights and self-determination of peoples, the **United Nations shall promote:**

C. **universal respect for, and observance of, human rights and fundamental freedoms for all without distinction as to race, sex, language, or religion**.

Article 62

1. The **Economic and Social Council** may.......

2. ...... make recommendations for the purpose of **promoting respect for, and observance of, human rights and fundamental freedoms for all**.

Article 68

The **Economic and Social Council** shall set up commissions in economic and social fields and for the **promotion of human rights**, and such other commissions as may be required for the performance of its functions.

Article 76

The **basic objectives** of the trusteeship system, in accordance with the Purposes of the United Nations laid down in Article 1 of the present Charter, shall be:

c. **to encourage respect for human rights and for fundamental freedoms for all without distinction as to race, sex, language, or religion**, and to encourage recognition of the interdependence of the peoples of the world.

One of the most important consequences of incorporating human rights clauses in the UN Charter was to internationalize human rights. After the adoption of the UN Charter, many countries incorporated similar provisions in their constitutions with a view to protecting the dignity and worth of human beings. The members of the United Nations are under legal obligation to act in accordance with provisions of the Charter. It is their duty to respect and observe fundamental human rights and freedoms.

International cooperation in promoting and encouraging respect for the human rights and fundamental freedoms of all is one of the purposes of the United Nations, as outlined in Article 1 of its Charter. According to Articles 56 and 55(c) read in conjunction, United Nations Member States have a legal obligation "to take joint and separate action in co-operation with the Organization for the achievement of universal respect for, and observance of, human rights and fundamental freedoms for all without distinction as to race, sex, language, or religion". This important legal duty conditions Member States' participation in the United Nations human rights programme. Thus, since the founding of the Organization in 1945, human rights have been the business of every Member State, every constituent body, every programme and agency, and every staff member of the United Nations.

UN Bodies Involved in Protection of Human Rights

Today virtually all UN bodies and specialized agencies, including the World Bank and the International Monetary Fund, are undertaking efforts to incorporate the promotion or protection of human rights into their programmes and activities. The Economic and Social Council (ECOSOC) and the General Assembly have been entrusted with the responsibility of monitoring human rights activities. The ECOSOC provides the input on which the General Assembly acts. In practical terms, however, the main cogs in the organization's human rights machinery are the Human Rights Council and its Advisory Committee. In addition, the Committee on Human Rights established under the International Covenant on Civil and Political Rights provides information relating to the human rights issues to the ECOSOC.

The General Assembly

Since the promotion of human rights is listed as one of the important purposes of the UN, all the principal organs have an obligation to assist the UN in the accomplishment of this task. However, the Charter places primary responsibility on the General Assembly and on the ECOSOC under its authority.

The General Assembly has various committees to deal with all the matters covered by the Charter of the United Nations. Issues relating to human rights are primarily debated by its Third Committee (Social, Humanitarian and Cultural Committee). Nevertheless, decisions taken by the other main committees may also have an impact on human rights issues. The Sixth Committee participates in the standard-setting process regarding these issues.

The Universal Declaration of Human Rights, both International Covenants on Human Rights, and all other United Nations human rights treaties were adopted by the General Assembly. The activities of the General Assembly in the field of human rights may be categorized as follows.

1. Substantive human rights issues
2. Violations of human rights on a large scale
3. Drafting conventions or declarations
4. Organizational matters

The agenda of the various committees of the General Assembly varies from session to session. For example, the agenda of the Third Committee during the 56th session in 2001, included the following issues: (i) Implementation of human rights instruments; (ii) Human rights situations relating to violations on a large scale; (iii) Implementation of and follow-up to the Vienna Declaration; (iv) Report of the United Nations Commissioner for Human Rights; (v) Promotion and protection of the rights of children; (vi) Elimination of racism and racial discrimination; and (vii) Rights of people to self-determination.

The resolutions adopted by the General Assembly (in connection with human rights) reflect not only the assessment of the Third Committee but also recommendations by the international community as a whole, specifically by governments, components of the United Nations, and non-governmental organizations. Most of the General Assembly resolutions are adopted by its Third Committee without a vote. However, country-specific resolutions need a vote because consensus is generally impossible. The Third Committee may also create working groups to handle its agenda.

Acting under its general mandate, the General Assembly created, in 1993, the post of the United Nations High Commissioner for Human Rights with special responsibility for the human rights activities of the United Nations, under the aegis of the UN Secretary-General. The first UN High Commissioner for Human Rights was appointed in 1994.

The Economic and Social Council

As already mentioned, the promotion and protection of human rights are among the main functions of the ECOSOC. In this context, the ECOSOC undertakes the following tasks.

- Making recommendations for promoting respect for and observance of human rights and fundamental freedoms for all
- Preparing draft conventions to be submitted to the General Assembly
- Convening international conferences on subjects within its competence
- Considering the reports of bodies like the Commission on Human Rights, Human Rights Committee and Committee on Economic, Social and Cultural Rights

The ECOSOC is the primary coordinating organ of the United Nations in the economic and social spheres. It has set up various commissions to deal with matters relating to these fields, for example, the Commission on Human Rights and the Commission on the Status of Women. These commissions report to the ECOSOC annually, prepare relevant draft decisions and recommendations as well as draft conventions and declarations. Resolutions of commission that have financial implications need to be approved by the ECOSOC before implementation. Some other commissions established by the ECOSOC are the Commission on Crime Prevention and Criminal Justice, the Commission on Sustainable Development, and the Commission for Social Development.

The ECOSOC also decides on the consultative status of non-governmental organizations (NGOs). This is important because NGOs help to promote UN human rights in various ways.

The Commission on Human Rights

Article 68 of the UN Charter provided for the establishment of a Commission on Human Rights, which was created in 1946. The Commission was successful in launching the vision of an international Bill of Human Rights consisting of the Universal Declaration of Human Rights (UDHR), the International Covenant on Civil and Political Rights (ICCPR) and the International Covenant on Economic Social and Cultural Rights (ICESCR). At that time only a few expected this organization to play a more dynamic role in subsequent years. Although the Commission remained an auxiliary body of the ECOSOC, it came a long way from being a small body of experts representing various countries. Initially composed of 18 Member States, the Commission, at the time of its dissolution, had 53 members.

The composition of the Commission was based on the principle of regional balance. Keeping in mind the geographical distribution of the members, the seats in the Commission were divided as follows.[5]

African Group	Asian Group	Eastern European Group	Latin and Caribbean Group	Western European and other Groups
15	12	5	11	10

The Commission played a pivotal role in UN activities in the field of human rights. Its mandate ranged from participation in monitoring the setting of standards, to guiding the implementation of human rights and providing technical assistance. The Commission submitted proposals, recommendations and information to the ECOSOC, helping it coordinate United

[5] This distribution of seats was determined in 1990, when the membership increased by ten. This arrangement gave better representation to African and developing countries.

Nations activities in the field of human rights. The Commission had three responsibilities: (i) coordinating the activities of various UN human rights organs and bodies; (ii) addressing thematic human rights issues; and (iii) dealing with country-specific human rights situations.

From the late 1990s, the Commission dedicated one meeting for a Special Dialogue on an annual theme decided by the UN General Assembly. Some subjects of these Special Dialogues were "Tolerance and Respect", "Poverty and Enjoyment of Human Rights" and the "Rights of the Child". To conclude such discussions on thematic issues or on country-specific situations, the Commission adopts a resolution.

Standard-setting: This has been one of the central functions of the Commission on Human Rights, which has been the main UN body responsible for drafting international human rights standards and related procedural norms. The treaties and declarations drafted by the Commission are forwarded through the ECOSOC to the General Assembly for final adoption.

Country situations: If a human rights situation in a country was on the Commission's agenda, the delegation of the country could join the consultation or refuse to participate in the process or object to the consideration of human rights situation in its country through a formal 'no action motion'. The Commission was also empowered by the ECOSOC to call special sessions to deal with large-scale human rights emergencies in a country. It held emergency sessions in the case of the former Yugoslavia (1992), Rwanda (1994), East Timor (1999), and the Palestinian people (2000).

The ECOSOC empowered the Commission on Human Rights to establish two sub-commissions: the Sub-Commission on Freedom of Information and of the Press and the Sub-Commission on the Prevention of Discrimination against and Protection of Minorities. Both these sub-commissions were created in 1947. The mandate of the first expired in 1952. The Commission was empowered to establish working groups to draft human rights treaties or declarations concerning human rights standards, for example the Working Group on the Right to Development.

The Sub-Commission on the Promotion and Protection of Human Rights: This sub-commission was formerly known as the Sub-Commission on the Prevention of Discrimination against and Protection of Minorities. It had 26 members, seven from Africa, five from Asia, five from Latin America and the Caribbean, three from Eastern Europe and six from Western European and other states. The Sub-Commission's agenda included the following issues.

1. Violation of human rights and fundamental freedoms

2. Administration of justice
3. Economic, social and cultural rights
4. Prevention of discrimination
5. Other human rights issues

The Commission on Human Rights provided the institutional framework for drafting most of the human rights treaties and international declarations. It helped in developing human rights standards, including the Universal Declaration of Human Rights and the International Covenants on Human Rights. Debates in the Commission contributed to the broadening of the UN agenda concerning human rights. The Commission also responded to major human rights violations in different regions of the world and provided a platform for victims to approach the international community. The Commission developed special procedures for examining issues and situations of gross violations of human rights. It met for the last time in March 2006, at its sixty-second session. Its normative and standard-setting achievements form the foundation for the procedures of the Human Rights Council.

The Human Rights Council

The Human Rights Council was created by the UN General Assembly on 15 March 2006 with the main purpose of addressing situations of human rights violations and making recommendations in this regard.[6] Based in Geneva, the Council is an inter-governmental body within the UN system made up of representatives of 47 States and responsible for strengthening the promotion and protection of human rights around the globe. Keeping in mind the principle of regional balance, the seats in the Council are divided as follows.

African States	Asian States	Eastern European States	Latin American & Caribbean States	Western Europe & other States
13	13	6	8	7

The UN General Assembly shall review the status of the Council within five years (due in 2011). The Council is responsible for promoting universal respect for the protection of all human rights and fundamental freedoms for all, without distinction of any kind and in a fair and equal manner. It is supposed to address situations of violations of human rights, including

[6] The Human Rights Council was established by the UN General Assembly Resolution 60/251 of 03 April 2006.

gross and systematic violations, and make recommendations thereon. It is also meant to promote the effective coordination and the mainstreaming of human rights within the United Nations system. The Council has the following agenda:

(a) Promoting human rights education and learning as well as advisory services, technical assistance and capacity-building, to be provided in consultation with and with the consent of Member States concerned;

(b) Serving as a forum for dialogue on thematic issues on all human rights;

(c) Making recommendations to the General Assembly for the further development of international law in the field of human rights;

(d) Promoting the full implementation of human rights obligations undertaken by States and follow-up to the goals and commitments related to the promotion and protection of human rights emanating from United Nations conferences and summits;

(e) Undertaking a universal periodic review, based on objective and reliable information, of the fulfilment by each State of its human rights obligations and commitments in a manner which ensures universality of coverage and equal treatment with respect to all States; the review shall be a cooperative mechanism, based on an interactive dialogue, with the full involvement of the country concerned and with consideration given to its capacity-building needs; such a mechanism shall complement and not duplicate the work of treaty bodies; the Council shall develop the modalities and necessary time allocation for the universal periodic review mechanism within one year after the holding of its first session;

(f) Contributing, through dialogue and cooperation, towards the prevention of human rights violations and responding promptly to human rights emergencies;

(g) Assuming the role and responsibilities of the Commission on Human Rights relating to the work of the Office of the United Nations High Commissioner for Human Rights;

(h) Working in close cooperation in the field of human rights with Governments, regional organizations, national human rights institutions and civil society;

(i) Making recommendations with regard to the promotion and protection of human rights; and

(j) Submitting an annual report to the General Assembly.

The Human Rights Council, in resolution No. 13/30 adopted at its 14th session in April 2010, has urged the States to protect children from all forms of sexual violence and abuse by all those who work with and for children, including those in educational, care and detention settings, as well as government officials, such as the police, law enforcement authorities and employees and officials in detention centres or welfare institutions. It has also asked the States to ensure the meaningful participation of children in all matters and decisions affecting their lives by eliciting their views, and by giving due importance to these views in accordance with their age and maturity, including in all administrative and judicial proceedings. The States are to ensure that disability-, gender- and age-appropriate assistance is provided to enable the active and equal participation of all children.

The Council, in resolution No. 11 on the right to truth, adopted at its ninth session, recognized the importance of respecting and ensuring the right to truth so as to contribute to ending impunity and to promote and protect human rights. It encouraged States to consider establishing specific judicial mechanism and, where appropriate, truth and reconciliation commissions to complement the judicial system to investigate and address gross violations of human rights and serious violations of international humanitarian law.

In resolution No. 10, on transitional justice, adopted at its ninth session, the Council welcomed the importance and urgency of national and international efforts to restore justice and the rule of law in conflict and post-conflict situations and, where relevant, in the context of transitional processes. It underlined the need for the rights of victims as well as accused persons to be respected in accordance with international standards.

Human Rights Council Advisory Committee

The Advisory Committee is a subsidiary body of the Human Rights Council. It replaced the Sub-Commission on the Promotion and Protection of Human Rights of the Commission on Human Rights, and functions as a think tank for the Council, focusing mainly on studies and research-based advice in a manner and form requested by the Council. While unable to adopt resolutions or decisions, or to establish subsidiary bodies without the Council's authorization, the Advisory Committee can make suggestions to the Council: (i) to enhance its own procedural efficiency; and (ii) to further research proposals within the scope of its work. The Advisory Committee consists of 18 experts drawn proportionally from the five UN regional groups (Africa, Asia, Eastern Europe, Latin America and the Caribbean, and Western Europe and others). Members serve in their personal capacity for three-year terms and are eligible for re-election only once. The Advisory Committee meets twice each year for a total of up to 10 working days, and can hold additional ad hoc sessions with the Council's approval.

The Security Council

The Security Council aims to build a world in which peace would be maintained on the basis of respect for human rights, and political, economic and social progress and justice. The world community looks to the Council to use its good offices to uphold international norms of human rights. This is more so because the Security Council has dealt with violations of human rights and has adopted a series of decisions to bring to justice those accused of grave breaches of human rights. However, the Security Council has not always been able to live up to the expectations of the international community.

Article 24 of the United Nations Charter confers on the Security Council the 'responsibility for the maintenance of international peace and security'. For many years, the Security Council refrained from intervening in issues of violations of human rights, due to the controversial nature of international relations. In those days, human rights issues were usually referred to as humanitarian problems. During the Cold War the Security Council tended to avoid human rights disputes other than apartheid in South Africa. The situation changed gradually in the 1990s. In the recent past, the Security Council has dealt with many issues pertaining to human rights violations and war crimes. It authorized the use of military force in Somalia, the former Yugoslavia, Rwanda, Haiti and East Timor, and sponsored a number of peacekeeping missions. It also established international criminal tribunals for Rwanda (ICTR) and Yugoslavia (ICTY); and a Special Court for Sierra Leone (SCSL).[7]

Now human rights abuses are recognized as one of the root causes of armed conflicts, and the protection of human rights is considered to be one of the essential elements of peace-making and peace-building. Hence, the Security Council's decisions frequently address human rights issues and peace accords supported by the Security Council contain references to human rights. On 13 December 2005, the Government of the Republic of Lebanon requested the United Nations to establish a tribunal of an international character to try all those who are alleged responsible for the attack of 14 February 2005 in Beirut that killed the former Lebanese Prime Minister Rafiq Hariri and 22 others. Pursuant to Security Council resolution 1664 (2006), the United Nations and the Lebanese Republic negotiated an agreement on the establishment of the Special Tribunal for Lebanon.

---

[7] The Special Court for Sierra Leone was set up jointly by the Government of Sierra Leone and the United Nations. It is mandated to try those who bear the greatest responsibility for serious violations of international humanitarian law and Sierra Leonean law committed in the territory of Sierra Leone since 30 November 1996.

In discharging its duties, the Security Council acts on behalf of the members in accordance with the purpose and principles of the UN. The members of the UN agree to accept and carry out the decisions of the Security Council.

(A) Threat to Peace, Breaches of Peace and Acts of Aggression: The Security Council is mandated to determine the existence of any threat to peace, breach of peace, or act of aggression. It may indicate provisional measures, apply economic sanctions, or take such other actions as may be necessary to maintain international peace and security.

(B) Advancing Human Rights: The maintenance of peaceful relations within, as well as among countries facilitates the enjoyment, promotion and protection of human rights. The connection between the maintenance of international peace and security and human rights has been explored in reports prepared for the UN Sub-Commission on the Promotion and Protection of Human Rights.

(C) Settlement of Conflicts: The Council has dealt with many conflicts and disputes concerned with the right to self-determination, the principles of equality and non-discrimination, the rights of minorities and gross violations of human rights. It has dealt with threats to international peace and security posed by apartheid in South Africa, for example, and with gross human rights violations, such as the Sharpeville massacre in South Africa in 1960.

(D) Internal Conflicts: The Security Council has also taken account of the growing number of internal conflicts involving gross violations of human rights. Many of these internal conflicts/ ethnic clashes had an international dimension and resulted in large-scale migrations, creating social and economic pressure on neighbouring countries and threatening peace and stability in those countries.

Human Rights Issues and the Security Council

The Security Council has, on many occasions, intervened/come out in favour of the highest standards of human rights. In 1998, deeply concerned about the discrimination against girls and women and other violations of human rights in Afghanistan, the Council asked the parties to the conflict to comply with their obligations under international law. It also intervened in cases of alleged violations of human rights in Zaire, Liberia, Burundi, Croatia, Guinea Bissau and Albania. It established the International Criminal Tribunal for the former Yugoslavia and the International Tribunal for Rwanda for the trial of cases related to gross violations of human rights and of genocide.

Some situations that the Security Council could become engaged in are as follows.

- Those which entail threats to, or breaches of, international peace and security
- Those which involve a breakdown of governmental authority in a country
- Those which entail the flaunting of the authority of the United Nations
- Those which involve a high magnitude of human suffering or crimes against humanity
- Where a government so requests
- Where the conscience of the international community is shocked

The competence of the Security Council in dealing with violations of human rights has gained growing acceptance through practice. The Security Council is not meant to duplicate the role of the human rights organs or to supplant them. It is meant to complement and support them and to take action in situations where the exercise of its authority could bring protection to those at risk – such as the deployment of preventive peace-keepers or observers or the deployment of protection forces. The importance given to human rights issues by the Secretary General and the Security Council has inspired not only an increased number of UN resolutions, but also the deployment of peacekeeping missions, and the institution of peace-building initiatives, such as truth missions and war crime tribunals.

The Office of the High Commissioner for Human Rights (OHCHR)

With the increased awareness of human rights issues and the growing tendencies of the states to invoke human rights as integral to foreign policy decisions, the expectations upon the UN human rights system have increased in the last two decades. The UN Secretary General's report submitted to the General Assembly in September 2002 highlighted the importance of the United Nation's work on human rights and the need to build upon achievements while simultaneously strengthening the human rights structure of the organization. The General Assembly, in December 1993 passed resolution 48/141, establishing the Office of the High Commissioner for Human Rights (OHCHR) as the umbrella and coordinating body for all of the UN human rights machinery. OHCHR is guided in its work by the mandate provided by the General Assembly in resolution 48/141, the Charter of the United Nations, the Universal Declaration of Human Rights and subsequent human rights instruments, the Vienna Declaration and Programme of Action the 1993 World Conference on Human Rights, and the 2005 World Summit Outcome Document.

The mission of the OHCHR is to work for the protection of all human rights for all people; to help empower people to realize their rights; and to assist those responsible for upholding such rights in ensuring that they are implemented. In carrying out its mission OHCHR will:

- Give priority to addressing the most pressing human rights violations, both acute and chronic, particularly those that put life in imminent peril;
- Focus attention on those who are at risk and vulnerable on multiple fronts;
- Pay equal attention to the realization of civil, cultural, economic, political, and social rights, including the right to development; and
- Measure the impact of its work through the substantive benefit that is accrued, through it, to individuals around the world.

Operationally, OHCHR works with governments, legislatures, courts, national institutions, civil society, regional and international organizations, and the United Nations system to develop and strengthen capacity, particularly at the national level, for the protection of human rights in accordance with international norms. Institutionally, OHCHR is committed to strengthening the United Nations human rights programme and to providing it with the highest quality support. OHCHR is committed to working closely with its United Nations partners to ensure that human rights form the bedrock of the work of the United Nations.

The mandate of the OHCHR includes preventing human rights violations, securing respect for all human rights, promoting international cooperation to protect human rights, coordinating related activities throughout the United Nations, and strengthening and streamlining the United Nations system in the field of human rights. In addition to its mandated responsibilities, the Office leads efforts to integrate a human rights approach within all work carried out by United Nations agencies. The OHCHR has actively engaged in human rights promotion and protection systems at the national, regional and global levels including participation in the Human Rights Council and the United Nations Treaty body process[8].

---

[8] There are eight human rights treaty bodies that monitor implementation of the core international human rights treaties: (i) Human Rights Committee (CCPR), (ii) Committee on Economic, Social and Cultural Rights (CESCR), (iii) Committee of the Elimination of Racial Discrimination (CERD), (iv) Committee on the Elimination of Discrimination Against Women (CEDAW), (v) Committee Against Torture (CAT) & Optional Protocol to the Convention Against Torture (OPCAT) – Sub Committee on Prevention of Torture (SPT), (vi) Committee on the Rights of the Child (CRC), (vii) Committee on Migrant Workers (CMW), and (viii) Committee on the Rights of Persons with Disability (CRPD).

Specialized Agencies

The General Assembly, in its resolution of 1978 recognized that some of the specialized agencies, especially the International Labour Organization (ILO), United Nations Educational, Scientific and Cultural Organization (UNESCO), World Health Organization (WHO), United Nations Children's Fund (UNICEF), and Food and Agriculture Organization (FAO) had developed procedures and programmes for the promotion of human rights within their fields of competence. The work of these agencies has significantly complemented the work done by the human rights organs of the UN.

1. The International Labour Organization. The ILO was established in 1919 as an autonomous institution associated with the League of Nations. Its preamble stated that universal peace "can be established only if it is based upon social justice", that unjust conditions of labour imperilled the peace and harmony of the world; and that an improvement in such conditions was urgently required. The ILO is concerned with economic and social rights, such as the right to work, the right to the enjoyment of just and favourable conditions of work, the right to form and join trade unions of one's choice, the right to social security, and the right to an adequate standard of living; and with civil and political rights, such as freedom of expression, freedom of association and the right to peaceful assembly. The ILO implements the principles of its constitution by laying down standards, by supervising their application and by assisting governments to achieve its objectives. The primary way in which the ILO has worked to improve labour conditions and human rights in the workplace has been through setting of international standards, based on the general consensus of its members. These standards are embodied in ILO conventions, declarations and recommendations.

2. The Food and Agriculture Organization. The Food and Agriculture Organization was the first of the specialized agencies to be established. Among the functions of the FAO described in Article 1 of its Constitution, are the collection, analysis, interpretation and dissemination of information relating to nutrition, food and agriculture; the promotion of national and international action to improve education and administration relating to nutrition, food and agriculture; and the furnishing of technical assistance to governments in these fields.

3. The United Nations Educational, Scientific and Cultural Organization. The purpose of UNESCO, as stated in Article 1 of its Constitution, is to contribute to peace and security by promoting collaboration among the nations through education, science and culture in order to further universal respect for justice, for the rule of law and for the human rights and fundamental freedoms which are affirmed for the peoples of the world, without distinction of race, sex, language or religion, by the Charter of the United Nations. To achieve these aims, UNESCO

establishes standards and supervises their application; gathers and disseminates information of educational, scientific or cultural interest; provides advisory services and technical assistance in the establishment of educational, scientific and cultural institutions; organizes congresses and symposia; and provides subsidies to certain non-governmental organizations.

UNESCO has adopted a number of international instruments aimed at the promotion of human rights, including the Convention against Discrimination in Education, adopted on 14 December 1960. A Protocol to this Convention, instituting a Conciliation and Good Offices Commission for seeking settlement of any dispute which may arise between Sate parties to the Convention was adopted in 1962. In addition, the Declaration on Fundamental Principles concerning the Contribution of the Mass Media to Strengthening Peace and Understanding, to the Promotion of Human Rights and to Countering Racialism, Apartheid and Incitement to War was adopted on 22 November 1978. UNESCO has also issued the Declaration on Race and Racial Prejudices, which was adopted on 27 November 1978.

4. World Health Organization (WHO). The constitution of the WHO was adopted in 1946 by the International Health Conference, called for the purpose by the ECOSOC. The objective of the WHO as stated in Article 1 of its constitution is "the attainment by all peoples of the highest possible level of health". The preamble defines health as, "a state of complete physical, mental and social well-being and not merely the absence of disease or infirmity".

The WHO concept of technical cooperation has replaced the idea of technical assistance, which was based on a donor-recipient relationship and on time-bound assistance. Technical cooperation for health implies true partnership to attain national health goals that have been defined by a country, and that can be sustained and developed further by the country when the involvement of the WHO or other member States is no longer required. In view of the WHO such technical cooperation facilitates self-reliant health development.

Although the WHO has not adopted an international instrument in the field of human rights, it played an important role in the preparation of principles of medical ethics relevant to the role of health personnel, particularly physicians, in the protection of prisoners and detainees against torture and other cruel, inhuman or degrading treatment or punishment, adopted by the General Assembly in 1982.

5. The United Nations Children's Fund (UNICEF). UNICEF was established on 11 December 1946 by the United Nations to meet the emergency needs of children in post-war Europe and China.[9]

[9] Its full name was the United Nations International Children's Emergency Fund (UNICEF). In 1950, its mandate was broadened to address the long-term needs of children and women in developing countries everywhere. UNICEF became a permanent part of the United Nations system in 1953, when its name was shortened to the United Nations Children's Fund. However, it retained its original acronym 'UNICEF'.

It works towards the attainment of sustainable human development goals adopted by the world community and the realization of the vision of peace and social progress enshrined in the Charter of the United Nations.

It is mandated by the General Assembly to advocate for the protection of children's rights, to help meet their basic needs and to expand their opportunities to reach their full potential. It is guided by the Convention on the Rights of the Child and strives to establish children's rights as enduring ethical principles and international standards of behaviour. It is committed to ensuring special protection for the most disadvantaged children - victims of war, disasters, extreme poverty, all forms of violence and exploitation and those with disabilities. UNICEF responds in emergencies to protect the rights of children. It has promoted equal rights of women and girls and supported their full participation in the political, social, and economic development of their communities.

1.2 UNIVERSAL DECLARATION OF HUMAN RIGHTS (UDHR)

After the United Nations came into being, the General Assembly, at its first session in 1946, considered a Cuban draft "Declaration of Fundamental Human Rights and Freedoms". It asked the ECOSOC to get it evaluated by its newly constituted Commission on Human Rights as it was engaged in the preparation of an "international bill of rights". The need for such a bill was strongly felt for the following reasons:

a. The UN Charter does not define human rights. Without a clear definition, the obligation of States remains unclear and undefined.

b. The provisions of the Charter do not themselves provide for effective guarantee for the implementation of human rights by States. It does not clarify how States can be made accountable to the UN for such implementation.

c. The international standards of implementation and the function and powers of the international monitoring system were required to be clarified.

Therefore, an elaborate treaty with binding and enforceable international obligations of States in respect of human rights was envisaged. The rights drafted and recommended by the Commission of Human Rights to the General Assembly through the ECOSOC comprised the first instalment of an international bill of rights. The statement of rights was adopted on 10 December 1948 by the United Nations in the form of the Universal Declaration of Human Rights (UDHR).[10]

[10] In the beginning, different views were expressed about the form the bill of rights should take. The Drafting Committee decided to prepare two documents: one in the form of a declaration, which would set forth general principles or standards of human rights; the other in the form of a convention, which would define specific rights and their limitations.

The preamble of the UDHR bears ample testimony to the fact that it was the first response of the international community to the terrible experience it had gone through during the two World Wars. It notes that, "disregard and contempt for human rights have resulted in barbarous acts which have outraged the conscience of mankind". It emphasizes that, "recognition of the inherent dignity and of equal and inalienable rights of all members of human family is the foundation of freedom, justice and peace in the world". It also stresses that a common understanding of the human rights and freedoms enshrined in the UN Charter, "is of greatest importance for the full realization of the pledge".

Salient Features of the UDHR

The UDHR contains 30 articles. Articles 1 and 2 deal with the right of equality in dignity and right against discrimination based on race, colour, sex, language, religion, national or social origin, property, etc.

Articles 3-9, 12-18 guarantee the civil rights of an individual, such as the right to life, liberty and security of person; prohibition of slavery; prohibition of torture or cruel, inhuman and degrading treatment or punishment; the right to recognition as a person before the law; equality before law and equal protection of law; right against arbitrary arrest, detention or exile; the right to seek asylum; the right to freedom of thought and religion; the right to privacy; the right to family; freedom of movement; and the right to nationality.

Articles 10 and 11 deal with procedural rights, i.e. the right to a fair and public hearing by an impartial tribunal, and the right to be presumed innocent until proved guilty according to law.[11] Articles 19-21 protect the right to freedom of opinion and expression; the right to freedom

Accordingly, the Committee transmitted to the Commission on Human Rights draft articles of an international declaration and an international convention on human rights. At its second session, in December 1947, the Commission decided to apply the term "International Bill of Human Rights" to the series of documents in preparation and established three working groups: one on the declaration, one on the convention (which it renamed "covenant") and one on implementation. The Commission revised the draft declaration at its third session, in May/June 1948, taking into consideration comments received from Governments. It did not have time, however, to consider the covenant or the question of implementation. The declaration was therefore submitted through the Economic and Social Council to the General Assembly, meeting in Paris. By its resolution 217 A (III) of 10 December 1948, the General Assembly adopted the Universal Declaration of Human Rights as the first of these projected instruments.

[11] Article 10: Everyone is entitled in full equality to a fair and public hearing by an independent and impartial tribunal, in the determination of his rights and obligations and of any criminal charge against him. Article 11: 1. Everyone charged with a penal offence has the right to be presumed innocent until proved guilty according to law in a public trial at which he has had all the guarantees necessary for his defence. 2. No one shall be held guilty of any penal offence on account of any act or omission which did not constitute a penal offence, under national or international law, at the time when it was committed. Nor shall a heavier penalty be imposed than the one that was applicable at the time the penal offence was committed.

of peaceful assembly and association; the right to vote; and the right to equal access to public service.

Articles 22-27 grant individuals certain minimal economic, social and cultural rights, such as the right to social security, the right to work and choice of employment, the right to just and favourable conditions of work; the right to education; the right to leisure and minimum standards of living; and cultural rights.

Articles 28-30 are of general application and have a bearing upon the entire Declaration. Article 29 (1) deals with the duties of the individual; and Article 29 (2) and (3) state: 'in the exercise of his rights and freedoms, everyone shall be subject only to such limitations as are determined by law; and these rights and freedoms may in no case be exercised contrary to the purposes and principles of the United Nations.

In sum, the UDHR and various treaties (also called "covenants" and "conventions"), declarations, guidelines and bodies of principles elaborated by the United Nations and by regional organizations guarantee the following rights to all human beings.

> The right to life; freedom from torture and cruel, inhuman or degrading treatment or punishment; freedom from arbitrary arrest or detention; the right to a fair trial; freedom from discrimination; the right to equal protection of the law; freedom from arbitrary interference with privacy, family, home or correspondence; freedom of association, expression, assembly and movement; the right to seek and enjoy asylum; the right to a nationality; freedom of thought, conscience and religion; the right to vote and take part in government; the right to just and favourable work conditions; the right to adequate food, shelter, clothing and social security; the right to health; the right to education; the right to property; the right to participate in cultural life; and, the right to development.

Though the UDHR is not a legally binding document *per se*, the principles contained therein are now considered to be legally binding on States either as customary international law, general principles of law, or as fundamental principles of humanity.

Significance of the UDHR

When the General Assembly adopted the UDHR, it was only intended to be, "a common standard of achievement for all peoples of nations". However, 62 years after its adoption, the Declaration remains the single most important normative instrument ever adopted by the United Nations for the following reasons.

1. It is the first international statement of human rights. An international committee under the auspices of the United Nations Commission of Human Rights drafted it. The world community through the General Assembly endorsed it.

2. It is a comprehensive instrument. It covers civil and political, as well as social, economic and cultural rights. It thus represents the coming together of differing political approaches to human rights. It also recognizes the importance of duties.

3. Though not legally binding, the UDHR has acquired a legally binding character in two ways:

   (a) It has come to be regarded as an elaboration of the provisions on human rights in the UN Charter.

   (b) It has had a far-reaching influence on the Constitutions of the States that have come into existence after 1948.

4. The UDHR has become binding in its own right. It is accepted as part of general or customary international law, as representing the consensus of the international community and has been referred to in the jurisprudence of national and international tribunals.

5. Its norms have been given legal effect in various instruments like: (a)The International Covenant on Economic, Social and Cultural Rights (ICESCR), 1966 and its Optional Protocol of 2009; (b) The International Covenant on Civil and Political Rights (ICCPR), 1966 and its two Optional Protocols (i) First Optional Protocol relating to communications from individuals claiming to be victims of violations of any of the rights set forth in the ICCPR, and (ii) Second Optional Protocol aiming at the abolition of the death penalty, 1991; and (c) The UN Convention Against Torture and Other Cruel, Inhuman or Degrading Treatment or Punishment, 1984.

6. The UDHR, ICESCR and ICCPR together constitute the International Bill of Rights. These Covenants were followed by specialized instruments for refugees, women, children, migrant workers, and for indigenous people. The task of formulating more detailed and specific standards on the basis of the UDHR is not yet complete.

7. The UDHR has led to the evolution of various regional arrangements for the protection of human rights. The most advanced of these is the European Convention of Human Rights. The American Convention on Human Rights, 1969, and The African Charter on Human and Peoples' Rights, 1986 also acknowledge its influence.

8. Several countries have established regular procedures for the enforcement of human rights. At the international level, there are monitoring bodies, which help to interpret the legal provisions under most of the international conventions on human rights.

9. There has been a considerable change in the character or emphasis of these rights since 1948. The shift is now towards social justice, economic rights and an orientation towards groups like migrants, refugees and ethnic minorities. This shift represents an enlargement in the scope of the rights available under the UDHR.

10. The rights contained in the UDHR are the basis for social and political mobilization. They have facilitated the rise of NGOs and social movements, and networking across the world, with human rights providing their agenda and legitimacy. There is now a general acceptance of the legitimacy of human rights.

The International Court of Justice, in its dictum in the case concerning hostages in Tehran, clearly invoked "the fundamental principles enunciated in the ... Declaration" as being legally binding on Iran, in particular with regard to the wrongful deprivation of liberty and the imposition of "physical constraint in conditions of hardship".[12] The Indian judiciary has recognized the importance of the UDHR and has been giving effect to its provisions in letter and spirit while interpreting the constitution and the law.[13]

1.3 INTERNATIONAL COVENANT ON CIVIL AND POLITICAL RIGHTS (ICCPR)

The United Nations' efforts to translate the moral standards of the UDHR into legally binding principles led to the drafting and ratification of the two major human rights treaties. These are

---

[12] *United States Diplomatic and Consular Staff in Tehran (United States of America v. Iran), Judgment, ICJ Reports 1980* , p. 42, para. 91.

[13] In *Minerva Mills v. Union of India* AIR 1980 SC 178, the Supreme Court noted the various dimensions of the UDHR. In *Maneka Gandhi v. Union of India* A. 1978 SC 597, a bench of seven judges relied on Article 13(2) of the UDHR and held that although the freedom to go abroad was not specifically named in the Constitution of India as a fundamental right under Article 19, it was included in the right to personal liberty guaranteed by Article 21. In *Randhir Singh v. Union of India* A. 1982 SC 879, the Court relied on Article 23 of the UDHR and Article 14 of the Indian Constitution and held that everyone without any discrimination had a right to equal pay for equal work. In *Attorney General of India v Lachma Devi* A. 1986 SC 467, the Court relied on Article 5 of the UDHR, which says that no one shall be subjected to torture or cruel, inhuman or degrading treatment, and set aside the execution of the death sentence, which was to be carried out in public. In *D K Basu v. State of WB* (1997) 1 SCC 416, the Supreme Court came down heavily against custodial torture. Relying on Article 5 of the UDHR, it commented, "Custodial torture is a naked violation of human dignity ... it is a calculated assault on human dignity and whenever human dignity is wounded, civilization takes a step backwards — the flag of humanity must on each such occasion fly half mast."

the International Covenant on Civil and Political Rights (ICCPR), and the International Covenant on Economic, Social and Cultural Rights (ICESCR). While the Commission on Human Rights was drafting these two Covenants, many States from Asia and Africa became members of the United Nations. Their priorities were economic, social and cultural rights, rather than the civil and political rights emphasized by the developed countries. Therefore, the ECOSOC and the UN General Assembly finally decided to formulate two treaties – one to provide for civil and political rights, and the other for economic, social and cultural rights. The UN General Assembly adopted the ICCPR and ICESCR on 16 December 1966, and they came into force in 1976 when the required number of States, 35 in all, ratified and became parties to these Covenants.

Civil and Political Rights

Civil rights cover the right to the protection of physical integrity, procedural due process rights, and right against discrimination. Political rights enable one to participate meaningfully in the political process of one's society and include rights such as freedom of expression, assembly, and association, and the right to vote. The ICCPR is divided into six major Parts. Parts I and II set out a series of provisions generally applicable to all the rights described in the Covenant. Part III is the "backbone" of the Covenant, elaborating the substantive individual rights. The final Parts deal with the establishment of the Human Rights Committee, the Committee's monitoring functions and a variety of technical matters.

The first two parts, comprising Articles 1 to 5, cover important aspects of the Covenant and may be described as provisions of an overarching or structural nature.[14] Part I comprises Article 1, which guarantees the right of self-determination. This right differs from the other rights in that it is a right expressly ascribed to "peoples" rather than to individuals. It is also the only right that is common to both Covenants, as Article 1 of the ICESCR is identical. While the precise contours under international law of the right of self-determination remain in a state of flux, it can safely be taken that a precondition for a full and genuine expression of self-determination on the part of a people is the enjoyment by its members in whole measure of the rights contained in the Covenant.

Part II comprises articles 2 through 5. Article 2 is one of the fundamental cornerstones of the Covenant. It provides that a State party must respect and ensure the rights of the Covenant

---

[14] The preambles and articles 1, 3 and 5 of the two International Covenants are almost identical. The preambles recall the obligation of States under the Charter of the United Nations to promote human rights; remind the individual of his responsibility to strive for the promotion and observance of those rights; and recognize that, in accordance with the Universal Declaration of Human Rights, the ideal of free human beings enjoying civil and political freedom and freedom from fear and want can be achieved only if conditions are created whereby everyone may enjoy his civil and political rights, as well as his economic, social and cultural rights.

to all persons within its jurisdiction. With some exceptions, such as the right to vote, these rights extend not only to citizens but to all persons in the State's territory, and must be respected without discrimination. If necessary, legislation should be enacted to properly guarantee these rights. The States parties are required to provide remedies to persons whose rights under the Covenant are breached.

The Human Rights Committee, in its jurisprudence, has interpreted this right as the requirement for a forum to be available to hear an allegation of a violation of a Covenant right when it is "sufficiently well founded to be arguable under the Covenant". Commonly, it is the courts and administrative authorities that provide these remedies. Without this right to enforce a Covenant right before the domestic authorities by way of remedy, the actual substantive rights of the Covenant would be deprived of practical effect.

There are three obligations imposed by treaties on a State party. The first obligation is to respect human rights, which requires Governments to refrain from violating these rights. This is often called a "negative" obligation, or an obligation not to engage in a particular act or practice. The classic example being that a State must refrain from an act of torture or arbitrary deprivation of life. The second obligation, to protect the enjoyment of the rights, goes further: the State party must not only refrain from violating an individual's rights itself, but it must also protect an individual from a violation of his or her rights by third parties, be they private individuals, corporations, or other non-State actors. This may require positive action by the State party, for example by establishing an appropriate legislative and policy framework and devoting sufficient resources to their effective implementation. Thirdly, a State party must promote or fulfil an individual's rights by taking the required steps to create a conducive environment within which the rights can be fully realized. This again is a "positive" obligation which may require a State party to take substantial steps, including the allocation of appropriate resources to satisfy its obligations under the treaty.[15]

Article 2, paragraph 3 provides:

> Each State Party to the present Covenant undertakes:
>
> (a) To ensure that any person whose rights or freedoms as herein recognized are violated shall have an effective remedy, notwithstanding that the violation has been committed by persons acting in an official capacity;

---

[15] For example, with respect to the ICCPR, a State party must provide legal aid to persons "where the interests of justice so require" under Article 14, paragraph 3 (d), and prevent overcrowding in prisons so as to comply with the guarantee in Article 10, paragraph 1, of humane conditions of detention for prisoners.

(b) To ensure that any person claiming such a remedy shall have his right thereto determined by competent judicial, administrative or legislative authorities, or by any other competent authority provided for by the legal system of the State, and to develop the possibilities of judicial remedy;

(c) To ensure that the competent authorities shall enforce such remedies when granted.

Article 3 of the Covenant provides for the equal right of men and women to the enjoyment of Covenant rights. As the Committee's jurisprudence has evolved, Article 26 in Part III of the Covenant, which provides for equality before the law and equal protection of the law without discrimination, including on the basis of sex, has been interpreted to encompass the same protection, however, the importance of this question to the framers of the Covenant may be seen by virtue of its location in the first Part of the Covenant.

Article 4 of the Covenant recognizes that exceptional situations affecting a State party may make the guarantee of some rights difficult or impossible, at a practical level, for a temporary period of time. However, it clearly sets out the strictly permissible boundaries for suspending or derogating from certain rights, in order to foreclose the possibility of any abuses.[16] The threshold condition is that there must exist a public emergency, officially proclaimed, which threatens the life of the nation.

The Human Rights Committee can, and does, question, in appropriate cases, whether this basic requirement has been satisfied when a State decides to derogate from its obligations under the Covenant. Even if such a situation does exist, the measures taken must be "strictly required by the exigencies of" the relevant crisis. This is a high standard, the respect for which a State party may be required to demonstrate to the Committee's satisfaction. In addition, regardless of the situation, there are some rights, including the rights to life and to be protected from torture, which may not be derogated from in any circumstances. These rights are listed in paragraph 2 of Article 4. Part II of the Covenant concludes with Article 5, a general protective provision stating that nothing in the Covenant confers the right to limit or destroy any of its provisions, and that a State party whose domestic law provides greater protections than those contained in the Covenant may not use that as an excuse to restrict or derogate from the fundamental rights contained in the Covenant.

---

[16] The State is not permitted, under any circumstances, to violate or derogate from certain rights right to life, freedom from torture, freedom from slavery, freedom from civil prison, right against *ex post fact* criminal law, right to recognition as a person before law, and the right to freedom of thought, conscience and religion. These rights are considered the minimum fundamental rights which should remain guaranteed to the individual at all times and a State has no excuse to abridge, limit, or deny them to its people.

Part III lists the substantive rights and fundamental freedoms guaranteed by the treaty. These are the articles that are commonly invoked by individuals alleging that their rights under the Covenant have been violated, although the provisions of Part I may also be invoked and may lend support to their interpretation. Articles 6 to 11 may be regarded as the core provisions for the protection of the life, liberty and physical security of the individual. Article 6, paragraph states: "Every human being has the inherent right to life. This right shall be protected by law. No one shall be arbitrarily deprived of his life."[17] These provisions also stipulate the narrow confines within which the death penalty may legitimately be imposed by States parties that have not abolished it. Specific prohibitions are set out concerning torture, unauthorized medical experimentation, slavery and forced labour. The rights of a person in the context of deprivation of liberty, commonly by arrest, and in detention are also covered here. Articles 12 and 13 deal with the liberty of movement and the freedom to leave any country including one's own, and contains particular rules applicable to the expulsion of aliens.

Articles 14 to 16 deal with how a person must be treated by the judicial process. Article 14 of the ICCPR states:

> 1. All persons shall be equal before the courts and tribunals. In the determination of any criminal charge against him, or of his rights and obligations in a suit at law, everyone shall be entitled to a fair and public hearing by a competent, independent and impartial tribunal established by law. The press and the public may be excluded from all or part of a trial for reasons of morals, public order (ordre public) or national security in a democratic society, or when the interest of the private lives of the parties so requires, or to the extent strictly necessary in the opinion of the court in special circumstances where publicity would prejudice the interests of justice; but any judgement rendered in a criminal case or in a suit at law shall be made public except where the interest of juvenile persons otherwise requires or the proceedings concern matrimonial disputes or the guardianship of children.
>
> 2. Everyone charged with a criminal offence shall have the right to be presumed innocent until proved guilty according to law.

---

[17] Certain human rights are never derogable. Among them are the right to life, prohibition of torture or cruel, inhuman or degrading treatment or punishment, prohibition of slavery and servitude and the prohibition of retroactive criminal laws. The definition of the term'right to life' is evolving and expanding. For example, European Court of Human Rights (in Application No 23452/94; 28 October 1998) stated that the right to life, under Article 2 (1) of the European Convention included the obligation to put in place "effective criminal law provisions to deter the commission of offences against the person backed up by law enforcement machinery for the prevention, suppression and sanctioning of breaches of such provisions".

3. In the determination of any criminal charge against him, everyone shall be entitled to the following minimum guarantees, in full equality:

(a) To be informed promptly and in detail in a language which he understands of the nature and cause of the charge against him;

(b) To have adequate time and facilities for the preparation of his defence and to communicate with counsel of his own choosing;

(c) To be tried without undue delay;

(d) To be tried in his presence, and to defend himself in person or through legal assistance of his own choosing; to be informed, if he does not have legal assistance, of this right; and to have legal assistance assigned to him, in any case where the interests of justice so require, and without payment by him in any such case if he does not have sufficient means to pay for it;

(e) To examine, or have examined, the witnesses against him and to obtain the attendance and examination of witnesses on his behalf under the same conditions as witnesses against him;

(f) To have the free assistance of an interpreter if he cannot understand or speak the language used in court;

(g) Not to be compelled to testify against himself or to confess guilt.

4. In the case of juvenile persons, the procedure shall be such as will take account of their age and the desirability of promoting their rehabilitation.

5. Everyone convicted of a crime shall have the right to his conviction and sentence being reviewed by a higher tribunal according to law.

6. When a person has by a final decision been convicted of a criminal offence and when subsequently his conviction has been reversed or he has been pardoned on the ground that a new or newly discovered fact shows conclusively that there has been a miscarriage of justice, the person who has suffered punishment as a result of such conviction shall be compensated according to law, unless it is proved that the non-disclosure of the unknown fact in time is wholly or partly attributable to him.

7. No one shall be liable to be tried or punished again for an offence for which he has already been finally convicted or acquitted in accordance with the law and penal procedure of each country.

Article 14 guarantees the right to a fair trial in both criminal and civil cases. It sets out the rights to equality before the courts and to fair adjudication of claims before courts and tribunals, and lists a series of additional protections applicable to criminal trials. Article 15 prohibits retrospective criminal punishment, while Article 16 states simply that everyone has the right to be recognized as a person before the law.

Articles 17 to 22 set out fundamental freedoms to be enjoyed without unjustified external interference. Article 17 addresses the right to privacy, Article 18 freedom of thought and religion, Article 19 freedom of opinion and expression (subject to the prohibitions in Article 20 of advocacy of war or of national, racial or religious hatred), Article 21 the right to peaceful assembly and Article 22 freedom of association, including through trade unions.

Articles 23 and 24 recognize the particular role of the family unit and addresses issues of marriage and the rights of children. Article 25 stands alone as the major right to political participation in the Covenant, outlining the rights to vote and to be elected at genuine periodic elections by universal suffrage and secret ballot as well as the rights to take part in public affairs and to have equal access to the public service.

Together with Articles 2 and 14, Article 26 is a fundamental provision of the Covenant. It sets out the rights to equality before the law and to equal protection of the law, with a wide guarantee of non-discrimination. The Human Rights Committee has taken a broad view of this provision, relating it to all provisions of law, rather than simply the terms of the Covenant. Thus, if a State party confers a particular benefit of any kind on a person or group of persons, it must be accorded in a non-discriminatory fashion. Distinctions drawn by law must be based upon reasonable and objective grounds.

Part III of the Covenant concludes with article 27, which guarantees persons belonging to ethnic, religious or linguistic minorities the right, in community with other members of the group, to enjoy and practice their own culture, religion or language. While nominally expressed as an individual right, this provision, by definition, may best be understood as a group right protecting a community of individuals.

Restrictions on Rights

A number of the rights described in Part III are expressly set out as being subject to restrictions or limitations, commonly where provided by law and necessary for specific enumerated purposes. Articles 17, 18, 19, 21, 22 and 25 expressly permit some form of restriction or limitation. A State party may choose to limit or restrict one of these rights within the limits prescribed, without its amounting to a violation of the right in question. Other rights, notably those lending protection against "arbitrary" action on the part of the State, implicitly recognize as permissible certain reasonable measures taken by the State.

Some ICCPR rights are absolute. Examples of such rights are Article 7, which prohibits torture, inhuman and degrading treatment, or punishment; and Article 8 (1), which prohibits slavery. A State cannot impose limits on seven absolute rights listed in the ICCPR unless it has entered a valid derogation under Article 4, or has entered a valid reservation. All the rights, except the seven irreducible minimum rights (Articles 6, 7, 8 (paragraphs 1 and 2), 11, 15, 16 and 18), can be denied by a state to its people during public emergency. However, this is subject to the following conditions: (1) The public emergency must be of such a nature as to threaten the life of the nation; (2) It must be officially proclaimed; (3) The limitations on the rights must only be to the extent strictly required by the exigencies of the situation; (4) They must not be in conformity with other obligations of the State under international law, and (5) They must not be discriminatory, solely on the ground of race, colour, sex, language, religion or social origin.

In any case, the permissible limits are neither wide nor generous, and certainly do not permit a State party to void a certain right of practical meaning. While imposing limits on rights, the burden of justification lies with the State party to show, including to the Human Rights Committee, that the limitations satisfy the tests of legality, necessity, reasonableness and legitimate purpose. A right claimed by one person may have to be balanced against a right claimed by another. For example, it may be consistent with a child's right to protection under Article 24, for the child to be removed from an abusive domestic environment, even though such a separation from the family may appear contrary to the parents' right, under Article 23, to the protection of the family unit.

The State invoking the powers of derogation must "immediately inform" other States, about the scope and extent of such derogation. It must also inform them after the withdrawal of such restriction on rights as it can only be of temporary character. As soon as the state of public emergency ends, the limitations on rights must also end.

The other method by which rights may be restricted is by reservation. A reservation is a formal declaration lodged by a State at the time it becomes party to a treaty that it declines to apply one or more provisions, either in whole or in part, in its jurisdiction. In contrast to some other treaties, the Covenant is silent on the effect of reservations. A reservation may be entered subject to the general rule of international law, as expressed in the Vienna Convention on the Law of Treaties, that it may not be inconsistent with the object and purpose of the treaty. The traditional indicator of whether a reservation is acceptable is the reaction of other States parties, which may submit objections to a reservation lodged by another State party.

Monitoring and Technical Aspects of the Covenant

The remaining Parts of the Covenant establish the Human Rights Committee as the treaty's monitoring body. Part IV, covering Articles 28 to 45, is related to the establishment of the Committee and provides for its functions and procedures. Part V of the Covenant, in articles 46 and 47, includes savings provisions with respect to various organs of the United Nations. Articles 48 to 53, comprising the final Part VI, contain standard treaty provisions concerning the mechanics for becoming a party, notifications and amendments. Article 50 provides that the Covenant's provisions extend to all parts of a federal State without limitation or exception. This is important in the case of States in which domestic law reserves exclusive competence in certain areas to state or provincial rather than federal authorities. In such cases, the federal authorities, representing a State party before the Committee, must take such measures as may be necessary to ensure that the Covenant is fully applicable within its territory and that the necessary remedies for violations are available. In this sense, Article 50 is a restatement of the well-known principles of international law whereby a State's international responsibility is engaged by the acts and omissions of its authorities at all levels, whether national, provincial or local, and its domestic law does not excuse a breach of a treaty obligation.

The Two Optional Protocols to ICCPR

The first Optional Protocol is procedural and provides a mechanism for the Committee to receive and consider individual complaints alleging a violation of the Covenant, i.e., of the substantive rights contained in Part III, if appropriate, in conjunction with the provisions of Parts I and II. As is evident from the name, the Protocol is not compulsory, but once a State party to the Covenant also becomes a party to the Protocol, any person subject to the jurisdiction of the State party may lodge a written complaint with the Human Rights Committee (subject to any permissible reservations). This is not limited to nationals, or to persons within a State's territory, but extends to all persons who are directly subject to a State's exercise of power through its authorities. Thus, for example, a national of a State party residing abroad who has been denied a passport by that State is authorized to bring a claim to the HR Committee.

Articles 1, 2, 3 and 5 of the Protocol set out a series of admissibility requirements, explicit and implicit, which a complaint must satisfy before its substance, or merits, can be considered. Article 4 of the Protocol lists the basic procedural requirements for the treatment of a complaint. Under Article 6, the Committee reports annually to the General Assembly on its activities concerning complaints, while Articles 7 through 14 contain largely standard savings and technical provisions on the mechanics of becoming a party, notification, amendment, denunciation and the like. Article 10, like the parent Covenant, provides that the Protocol too extends without exception to all parts of federal States. Article 12 allows a State party to denounce the Optional Protocol.

The Second Optional Protocol is aimed at the abolition of the death penalty. Its single substantive provision, Article 1, states directly that no person within a State party's jurisdiction shall be executed, and that each State party shall take all necessary measures to abolish the death penalty. Article 2 permits, subject to certain procedural requirements, only one reservation, namely one reserving the death penalty in time of war pursuant to a conviction for a most serious crime of a military nature committed in wartime. Article 6 provides that these provisions are non-derogable and, as substantive provisions, apply as additional provisions to the Covenant.

Articles 3 to 5 apply to the Protocol the same reporting and State complaint procedures that have been discussed with respect to the Covenant, as well as complaints lodged under the Optional Protocol. The remaining Articles 7 to 11 set out the usual treaty mechanics dealing with its entry into force and amendments.

1.4 INTERNATIONAL COVENANT ON ECONOMIC, SOCIAL AND CULTURAL RIGHTS (ICESCR)

The ICESCR contains a preamble and 31 articles divided into five parts. Of these, 10 articles are directly related to rights, while the rest deal with implementation procedure and subsequent amendments. The preamble, which is almost identical to that of the ICCPR, clearly places the Covenant in the context of the UN Charter. It recalls the human rights obligations imposed on the States by the Charter, and notes that they form the basis of freedom, justice and peace in the world.

Self-Determination

Part 1 of the Covenant comprises solely of Article 1. It proclaims the right of all peoples to self determination, including the right to freely pursue their economic, social and cultural development and to dispose of their natural wealth and resources. The three paragraphs of Article 1 set out the different perspectives of self-determination. Paragraph 1 covers what is normally considered political self-determination under which all people have the right to determine their political status and freely pursue their economic, social and cultural development. This entails both the external dimensions of self-determination and internal self-determination. Paragraph 2 concerns economic self-determination under which people may dispose of their natural wealth and resources for their own ends. Paragraph 3 establishes a solidarity position on self-determination, as all State parties to the Covenant are to promote and respect the exercise of the right to self-determination.

State Obligations

Part II of the Covenant (Articles 2-5), outlines the general clauses that apply to all the substantive provisions in Part III, including clauses relating to general obligations [Article 2 (1)], nondiscrimination [Article 2 (2)], equal rights for men and women [Article 3], and general limitations [Articles 4 and 5]. No provision is made in the ICESCR for derogation from the rights in times of public emergency. Article 2(1) could be described as the heart of the ICESCR. It describes the duties incumbent upon State parties in the realization of the rights contained in the Covenant. As the terms of Article 2(1) clarify, the full realization of the rights has to be achieved in a progressive manner.

Article 2(1) can be best explained as incorporating a mixture of two types of obligations—those that need immediate fulfillment and others which can be fulfilled over time. Article 6, for example, provides for the right to work and requires steps to be taken towards the achievement of full employment, and at the same time it safeguards fundamental political and economic freedoms of the individual. Additionally, to the extent that the rights within the Covenant are not capable of being fulfilled immediately, States are required to undertake certain obligations of conduct with a view to their progressive achievement. For example, while Article 12 provides for the recognition of the right to health, paragraph 2 of the article outlines the steps to be taken, including *inter alia,* for the "prevention, treatment, and control of epidemic, endemic, occupational, and other diseases".

The most striking feature of the Covenant as a human rights guarantee is the nature of the obligations undertaken by the State as regards the implementation of the rights. Unlike the other human rights instruments, Sates are not required to guarantee the rights immediately, but may implement them over time, depending upon the availability of necessary resources. The full realization of some of the rights presumes the availability of sufficient economic resources.

Economic, Social and Cultural Rights

Part III (Articles 6 -15) of the ICESCR constitutes the heart of the covenant. The rights recognized under the Covenant are:

Article 6: Right to Work

Article 7: Right to the enjoyment of just and favourable conditions of work, fair wages and safe and healthy conditions of work

Article 8: Right to form and join a trade union of one's choice

Article 9: Right to social security

Article 10: Right to family, including the right to protection of motherhood and childhood

Article 11: Right to an adequate standard of living, food, clothing and housing; and to continuous improvement of living conditions

Article 12: Right to physical and mental health

Article 13: Right to education

Article 14: Compulsory free primary education

Article 15: Right to take part in cultural life and benefits of science and technology

There is a substantial overlap between the substantive provisions of the two Covenants. Both Covenants proclaim the right to self-determination [Article 1 of the ICESCR and Article 1 of the ICCPR]. Both prohibit discrimination on various grounds [Article 2(2) of ICESCR and Article 2(1) of the ICCPR]. Both protect the right to join trade unions [Article 8 of the ICESCR and Article 22 of the ICCPR]. The ICESCR places certain limitations on the exercise of the rights recognized by it. Many of these limitations flow from the very nature of the rights and the problems involved in their implementation. For instance, since the full realization of the rights contained in it would require a high level of economic development, the developing countries are allowed to determine to what extent they would guarantee these rights, "with due regard to human rights and their national economy" [Article 2(1)]. The States are permitted to impose limitations upon the economic, social and cultural rights, subject to two conditions: (i) that the limitations must be "compatible with the nature of these rights" and (ii) that they must be imposed "solely for the purpose of promoting the general welfare in a democratic society" (Article 4). This does not mean that the State or any group or person may engage in any activity that destroys these rights [Article 5(1)].

Implementation System under the ICESCR

During the drafting of the Covenant, there was considerable disagreement on the nature of the implementation procedure that should accompany the substantive articles. Three forms of supervision were mooted: supervision through a petition procedure; supervision by specialized agencies; and supervision by an expert committee set up for that purpose. It was finally provided in Article 17 of the ICESCR that State parties are required to submit reports "in stages", in accordance with a programme to be established by the ECOSOC after consultation with the State parties and the specialized agency concerned.

Part IV of the Covenant outlines the main elements of the system of supervision. Unlike the ICCPR, it does not provide for the receipt of individual or State complaints, but envisages a system [Article 16] in which states are required to submit periodic reports to the UN on measures adopted and progress made in achieving the rights in the Covenant. They may additionally indicate the factors and difficulties affecting the degree of fulfilment of the obligations. Such reports are to be submitted to the Secretary-General, who is required to transmit copies of these to the ECOSOC for consideration and copies of relevant parts of the reports to the specialized agencies. It has been provided in Article 19 of the Covenant that the ECOSOC may also transmit the State reports to the Human Rights Council "for study and general recommendations and for information". Provision has also been made for the involvement of the UN and the specialized agencies, such as the Commission on the Status of Women, UNDP, UNICEF, World Bank and IMF, which are entitled to submit reports to the ECOSOC on matters falling within the scope of their activities. Any recommendation submitted by the Human Rights Council is open to comment by the specialized agencies and the State Parties (Article 20).

The ECOSOC may "from time to time" submit to the General Assembly reports and recommendations of a general nature, together with a summary of the information received from the Sate parties and the specialized agencies (Article 21). It may also bring to the attention of other organs of the United Nations or specialized agencies concerned with furnishing technical assistance, any matter arising out of the reports that may help those bodies in deciding, each within its fiend of competence, on the advisability of the international measures likely to contribute to the effective implementation of the Covenant (Article 22).

In 1988, the ECOSOC laid down the implementation procedure for the rights under the Covenant. It created a three-stage, biennial reporting process with a cycle of six years. In the first stage, the States were required to submit reports on the rights covered by Articles 6 to 9. Two years later, the States would be required to report on Articles 10 to 12, and two years after that on Articles 13 to 15. The reports were to be forwarded by the Secretary-General to the ECOSOC. A 'sessional working group' was created by the ECOSOC for the consideration of these reports. The functioning of the 'sessional working group' was later criticized on the grounds that the examination of the reports was superficial and not in accordance with duly established standards or procedure. The working group reports were purely procedural, giving little indication of the substance of the State reports or the discussions on these reports. They did not indicate any conclusions or recommendations. The general dissatisfaction with the effectiveness of the working group led to the creation of a truly independent committee of experts.

The Committee on Economic, Social and Cultural Rights

The Committee on Economic, Social and Cultural Rights was created in 1985 by the ECOSOC Resolution 1985/17. The Committee has 18 members, who are experts with recognized competence in the field of human rights. The members of the Committee serve in their personal capacity and are elected by the ECOSOC by secret ballot from a list of nominees submitted by Sate parties. In the selection of members, due consideration is given to equitable geographical distribution and to the representation of different forms of social and legal systems. To this end, 15 seats are equally distributed among the regional groups, while the additional three seats are allocated in accordance with the increase in the total number of State parties per regional group. The regular term of office of the members is 4 years. The expertise of the members is of importance not only in as far as it relates to the ability of the committee to assess the State reports, but also in that it lends to the credibility of the committee in the eyes of the State parties.

The reporting obligations under the ICESCR (Part IV) are designed primarily to assist each State party in fulfilling its obligations under the Covenant. In addition, it provides a basis on which the ECOSOC, assisted by the committee, can discharge its responsibilities for monitoring the measures taken by State parties to promote social and cultural rights in accordance with the provisions of the Covenant. It would be incorrect to assume that reporting is only a procedural matter to satisfy each State party's formal obligation to report to the international monitoring body.

Part IV of the Covenant provides that nothing in the Covenant should be interpreted "as impairing the inherent right of all people to enjoy and utilize fully and freely their natural wealth and resources". The intention of this provision appears to be to ensure that the developed states do not interfere excessively (by means of the supervision system) in the utilization of natural resources by the developing countries. Part V contains the final provision relating to the modalities of ratification and entry into the Covenant.

Optional Protocol to ICESCR

In 2004, the members of the United Nations came together, in the form of a working-group, to discuss the possibility of an Optional Protocol to ICESCR. In June 2006, the first session of the

Human Rights Council (replacing the UN Commission on Human Rights) finally decided to authorize a working-group to begin actual negotiations on the text of an Optional Protocol. On December 10, 2008, on the 60th Anniversary of the Universal Declaration of Human Rights, the United Nations adopted the Optional Protocol to the ICESCR.

The Optional Protocol is important because it provides victims of economic, social and cultural (ESC) rights violations who are not able to get an effective remedy in their domestic legal system with an avenue to get redress. As such, it corrects the longstanding imbalance in the protection of economic, social and cultural rights which were earlier marginalized. Such an international complaint mechanism will help develop the content of ESC rights and the obligations of States related to these rights, as well as give guidance to national courts and human rights institutions. Victims of violations of ESC rights can utilize the procedure only after their State has ratified the Optional Protocol.

The Optional Protocol provides for the possibility of so-called "interim measures" by providing that the Committee may transmit to the State party concerned for its urgent consideration a request that it take such interim measures to avoid possible irreparable damage to the victims of the alleged violations. The Optional Protocol also creates an inquiry procedure, setting out that if the Committee receives reliable information indicating grave or systematic violations of the Covenant, the Committee shall invite that State Party to cooperate in the examination of the information and to this end to submit observations with regard to the information concerned. The inquiry may include a visit to the territory of the State Party concerned. The Optional Protocol requires that States take all appropriate measures to ensure that individuals under their jurisdiction are not subjected to any form of ill-treatment or intimidation as a consequence of communicating with the Committee pursuant to the Optional Protocol.

International Bill of Human Rights

The international human rights movement was strengthened when the United Nations General Assembly adopted of the Universal Declaration of Human Rights on 10 December 1948. Drafted as "a common standard of achievement for all peoples and nations", the Declaration for the first time in human history spelt out basic civil, political, economic, social and cultural rights that all human beings should enjoy. It has over time been widely accepted as the fundamental norm of human rights that everyone should respect and protect. The UDHR, together with the ICCPR and its two Optional Protocols, and the ICESCR and its Optional Protocol, form the so-called International Bill of Human Rights.

1.5 THREE GENERATIONS OF HUMAN RIGHTS

Some human rights commentators have classified human rights into 'three generations of rights' reflecting the different historical periods in which these rights emerged.

First-Generation Rights

First-generation rights are civil and political rights associated with the liberal movement in the eighteenth century, e.g. the right to freedom from arbitrary arrest, freedom of assembly or freedom of conscience and expression, as well as freedom from torture. They presuppose a duty of non-interference on the part of government towards individuals. They primarily require forbearance or non-interference on the part of the State and impose a duty on it to refrain from interfering with individual choice.

Second-Generation Rights

Second-generation rights evolved in the twentieth century.[18] These guarantee the economic and social rights and require affirmative government action for their realization. These rights are often referred to as group rights or collective rights (contradicts previous sentence which speaks of individuals), in that they pertain to the well-being of the whole society. In contrast with first-generation rights, which have been perceived as individual entitlements, second-generation rights are held and exercised by all the people collectively or by specific subsets of people. Examples of second-generation rights include the right to education, employment, social security, health, food, and an adequate standard of living. Both first- and second-generation rights are embodied in the ICCPR and the ICESCR.

---

[18] The second generation of rights refers to economic, social and cultural rights which were included in the USSR Constitution 1904 as the right to work, to leisure, to maintenance in old age and sickness, right to education and freedom of association. The notion of such rights found its way into the Universal Declaration of Human Rights, 1948 and constituted the subject-matter of the International Covenant on Economic, Social and Cultural Rights, 1966. Economic, social and cultural rights were also incorporated, as (non-justiciable), "Directive Principles of State Policy" first, in the Constitution of Spain 1932, Constitution of Irish Republic 1937, the 1948 Constitution of Burma, the 1950 Constitution of India, the 1950 Constitution of Indonesia, the 1960 Constitution of Ghana and lately, the 1979 and 1999 Constitutions of the Federal Republic of Nigeria. The "Directive Principles of State Policy" which still remain as non-justiciable rights in most countries in Africa have been entrenched as enforceable rights in the enterprising Basic Law of the Federal Republic of Germany.

Third-Generation Rights

The end of the twentieth century saw the emergence of third-generation rights.[19] Rooted in Article 28 of the UDHR, these have also been termed "development rights" or "solidarity rights". Third- generation rights are based on holistic community interests although they reflect both individual and collective interests. It follows from this, that they also have a broader range of corresponding duties, which may vest not only in a State party to a particular instrument, but more broadly, in the larger global community. Third-generation rights are usually termed 'group rights' or 'people's rights', e.g. the right to self determination; the right to development; the right to a safe, healthy and ecologically balanced environment, the right to inter-generational equity and the right to peace.

Third-generation rights fall under two categories. The first category is seen to reflect a "revolution of expectation" in the developing world and its demand for a global redistribution of power, wealth and resources, and includes the right to self-determination (political, economic, social and cultural), the right to economic and social development, and the right to participate in and benefit from the common heritage of mankind (progress in science and information, cultural traditions and sites and monuments). The second category relates more to areas in which the nation state falls short (and thus implies duties that may fall on the wider international community). These rights include the right to peace, the right to a clean, healthy and sustainable environment, and the right to humanitarian disaster relief and the right of groups of people to cultural, political and economic development. While these rights may not have a long or established pedigree, their importance should not be underestimated. Proponents of these rights emphasize that they will reinforce and strengthen the existing human rights, enhancing their effectiveness and making them more relevant to both governments and individuals.

---

[19] During the last two decades, a new category of rights emerged, which is commonly referred to as "third generation rights" and which was first conceptionalized by Karel Vasak in his inaugural address to the Tenth Study Session of the International Institute of Human Rights, Strasbourg, France in 1979. These rights include: the right to peace, the right to development of disadvantaged sections of political community or, in the international context of developing countries, the right to nature conservation and to a clean and healthy environment, the right to share in the common heritage of humankind and so on. The third generation rights have the following attributes among others: First, the beneficiaries of these rights are no longer confined to individuals. The rights are now collectively perceived either in the sense of humanity as a whole, a particular political community or a distinct section of the population within the body politic. Second, the third generation rights cannot be adequately protected within the confines of municipal bills of rights and their effective implementation consequently requires international cooperation. For instance, agitations and campaigns against Female Genital Mutilation being practised in various ethnic groups can no longer be confined to individual and personal efforts but a matter of international concern.

There is now also talk of a fourth generation of rights linked mostly to issues of intergenerational justice or the rights of future generations.

1.6 JUSTICE

The term 'justice' has been defined differently not only by different societies, but even within a single society. There are numerous adjectives which are connected with different kinds of justice: distributive, retributive, compensatory, natural, judicial, administrative, procedural, and so on. However, here we are concerned with retributive justice, which is a theory of criminal justice wherein punishments are justified on the grounds that the criminal has created an imbalance in the social order that must be addressed by action against the criminal. Punishment, according to this theory, is expected to act as a deterrent and is justified to the extent that it is fair and just. In general, while deciding on punishments, one must take into account relevant criteria, such as the seriousness of the crime and the intent of the criminal, and discount irrelevant criteria, such as race, religion and sex.

Retributive justice demands the infliction of some kind of suffering on the wrongdoer. The suffering may be the deprivation of wealth, liberty or even life. While punishment *per se* is considered to be bad, it becomes good if it brings about greater good. Another term associated with justice is 'compensation'. It refers to the extent to which people are fairly compensated for their injuries by those who have injured them. Just compensation is proportional to the loss inflicted on a person.

Access to justice is a basic human right, as well as an indispensable means of combating poverty and preventing and resolving conflict. Access to justice means much more than improving an individual's access to courts, or guaranteeing legal representation. It has to do with creating a sustainable environment with equal access to justice and requires different types of institutions and various actors, such as the police, the courts, prosecutors, social workers, prison officials, community leaders, paralegals, traditional councils and other local arbitrators.

Law and justice are two distinct concepts. They are inter-related but each has a distinct sphere of its own. The whole aim of law is an approximation of an ideal justice. Justice is the legitimate end of law. Justice must necessarily precede law because people conceived of law because they wanted justice. We cannot expect security in a society or a state where justice is denied to the people and they suffer from a sense of injustice. Thus, justice is necessary for ensuring peace and security in a society. A society's system of law must be such as to impose moral duties and obligations on all its members and be regulated by justice. It must at least uphold such basic human rights as the right to life and security, right to personal property, and elements of the rule of law, as well as the right to a certain liberty of conscience and freedom of association.

The United Nations and its subsidiary bodies have promoted a wide range of specialized human rights instruments which encourage States to ensure adequate domestic practices in the administration of justice. It is the primary responsibility of the States to secure the protection of human rights by ensuring that they are protected by domestic laws. While incorporating various international treaties into domestic laws, the States must keep in mind that human rights are 'universal', 'indivisible', 'interdependent' and 'interrelated'. The Proclamation of Tehran, adopted by a United Nations international conference on human rights in 1968 is unambiguous in this regard:

> Since human rights and fundamental freedoms are indivisible, the full realization of civil and political rights without the enjoyment of economic, social and cultural rights is impossible. The achievement of lasting progress in the implementation of human rights is dependent upon sound and effective national and international policies of economic and social development.

A series of international human rights treaties and other instruments adopted since 1945 have conferred legal status on inherent human rights and developed the body of international human rights. Instruments have been adopted at the regional level to give expression to the particular human rights concerns of the region and provide for specific mechanisms of protection. Most States have also adopted constitutions and other laws which formally protect basic human rights. While international treaties and customary law form the backbone of international human rights law, declarations, guidelines and principles adopted at the international level contribute to its understanding, implementation and development. Respect for human rights requires the establishment of the rule of law at the national and international levels. It would be relevant to quote UN Secretary-General Kofi Annan: "Since respect for human rights is central to the legitimacy of the State order, human rights should be nurtured locally by branches of government, national human rights institutions and civil society." A justice system can be weakened by:[20]

- Long delays; prohibitive costs of using the system; lack of available and affordable legal representation, that is reliable and has integrity; abuse of authority and powers, resulting in unlawful searches, seizures, detention and imprisonment; and weak enforcement of laws and implementation of orders and decrees

---

[20] Access to Justice, UNDP Document, 9 March 2004.

- Severe limitations in existing remedies provided either by law or in practice (Most legal systems fail to provide remedies that are preventive, timely, non-discriminatory, adequate, just and deterrent.)
- Gender bias and other barriers, such as inadequacies in existing laws which fail to protect women, children, the poor and other disadvantaged people
- Lack of *de facto* protection, especially for women, children, and prisoners or inmates of centres of detention
- Lack of adequate information about what is supposed to exist under the law, what prevails in practice, and limited popular knowledge of rights
- Lack of adequate legal aid systems
- Limited public participation in reform programmes
- Excessive number of laws
- Formalistic and expensive legal procedures (in criminal and civil litigation and in administrative board procedures)
- Avoidance of the legal system due to economic reasons, fear, or a sense of futility of purpose

International human rights law lays down obligations which States are bound to respect. By becoming parties to international treaties, States assume obligations and duties under international law to respect, protect and fulfil human rights. The obligation to respect human rights means that States must refrain from interfering with or curtailing the enjoyment of human rights. The obligation to protect these rights requires States to protect individuals and groups against human rights abuses. The obligation to fulfil human rights means that States must take positive action to facilitate the enjoyment of basic human rights. Governments need to develop capacities to ensure that the rights of people, specially disadvantaged people, are recognized within the scope of justice systems. Legal protection of disadvantaged groups can be enhanced through: (i) ratification of treaties and their implementation in domestic law; (ii) national legislation; and (iii) implementation of rules and regulations and administrative orders.

International human rights law also lays down obligations of governments to act in certain ways or to refrain from certain acts. With regard to the administration of justice, the State has an obligation to establish laws and systems sufficient to deter and respond to attacks on individuals. On the other hand, laws must not go so far as to deny individual rights, including due process rights. Indeed, once accused of a criminal offence, an individual benefits from rights-based procedural and substantive safeguards. In this context, the State must establish a balance that ensures both the freedom and the protection of the individual as well as public safety and well-being. For the administration of justice, this balance can be considered at three levels: (i) with respect to what should, or should not be a criminal offence; (ii) with respect to criminal justice penalties; and (iii) in the criminal justice process.[21]

The Commission on Human Rights, in its resolution on 'Democracy and the Rule of Law'[22] has called upon States to make continuous efforts to strengthen the rule of law and promote democracy by (i) upholding the separation of powers by legislative, judicial and other institutions; (ii) guaranteeing that no individual or public or private institution is above the law; and (iii) respecting equal protection under the law. The States must ensure that the administration of justice is free from any form of discrimination. In order to avoid any arbitrariness, sufficient degree of legal certainty and predictability is provided in the application of the law. The military remains accountable to democratically elected civilian Government; and military courts or special tribunals are independent, competent and impartial, and that such courts or tribunals apply established procedures of due process of law and guarantees of a fair trial, in accordance with international obligations. The States must encourage the continuous training of public servants, military personnel, parliamentary experts, lawyers, judges at all levels and the staff of the courts, as appropriate to their area of responsibility, on international standards and jurisprudence in the field of human rights, in particular with respect to legal aspects and procedures related to the equality under the law.

A number of United Nations conventions, principles and declarations as well as regional conventions dealing with human rights and the administration of justice have been included in the subsequent chapters of the book. Although these documents set out international standards and provide international mechanisms for the protection of human rights, the primary responsibility for the protection and promotion of human rights rests with each individual

---

[21] Use and Application of United Nations Standards and norms in Crime Prevention and Criminal Justice, Commission on Crime Prevention and Criminal Justice; E/CN.15/2010/1.Vienna, 17-21 May April 2010.

[22] 2005/32, adopted on 19 April 2005.

[23] The general rule of interpretation is contained in Article 31 of the 1969 Vienna Convention on the Law of Treaties (Vienna Convention), whose provisions are commonly considered to be declaratory of customary international law. Article 31 provides that a "treaty shall be interpreted in good faith in accordance with the ordinary meaning to be given to the terms of the treaty in their context and in the light of its object and purpose," and taking into account, inter alia, "any subsequent practice in the application of the treaty which establishes the agreement of the parties regarding its interpretation."

state. State parties to international treaties, therefore, must incorporate and interpret the terms of such treaties in a dynamic manner.[23]

The chapters in the book have been organized to provide easy reference based on the status of the victim. In order to avoid bulkiness, only relevant portions of documents relating to the protection of human rights and the administration of justice have been included.

CHAPTER 2

ADMINISTRATION OF JUSTICE: OFFICIALS

Comments: The Vienna Declaration and Programme of Action, adopted by the World Conference on Human Rights in Vienna on 25 June 1993, declared: "The administration of justice, including law enforcement and prosecutorial agencies and, especially, an independent judiciary and legal profession in full conformity with applicable standards contained in international human rights instruments, are essential to the full and non-discriminatory realization of human rights and indispensable to the processes of democracy and sustainable development (paragraph 27)."

A country's judicial system is, therefore, central to the protection of human rights and the preservation of the rule of law. Judges, lawyers and prosecutors play a major role in the administration of justice. They have a duty to ensure that victims of human rights violations are protected and perpetrators of human rights abuses are suitably punished. The judiciary is also responsible for ensuring that the executive and the legislature respect international human rights and the rule of law.

The independence of the judiciary is addressed in the Basic Principles of the Independence of the Judiciary. This instrument requires that the independence of the judiciary be guaranteed by national law and prohibits the inappropriate and unwarranted interference with the judicial process. It also obligates States to provide adequate resources to enable the judiciary to properly perform its functions, and sets forth principles for the selection, training and conditions of service and discipline of the judiciary. The Basic Principles on the Role of Lawyers requires governments to ensure that efficient procedures and responsive mechanisms for equal access to lawyers are provided, including the provision of sufficient funding and other resources for legal services to the poor and other disadvantaged persons. The Guidelines on the Role of Prosecutors identify the responsibility of prosecutors in protecting human dignity and upholding human rights and ensuring due process. The Guidelines also strictly separate judicial functions from the office of the prosecutor. Requirements of law enforcement officials, including military authorities that exercise police powers, are set out in the Code of Conduct for Law Enforcement Officials. It requires officers of the law to uphold the human rights of all persons and to provide particular assistance to those who, by reason of personal, economic, social or other emergencies, are in need of immediate aid.

2.1 BASIC PRINCIPLES ON THE IDEPENDENCE OF JUDICIARY, 1985[1]

Whereas in the Charter of the United Nations the peoples of the world affirm, inter alia , their determination to establish conditions under which justice can be maintained to achieve international co-operation in promoting and encouraging respect for human rights and fundamental freedoms without any discrimination,

Whereas the Universal Declaration of Human Rights enshrines in particular the principles of equality before the law, of the presumption of innocence and of the right to a fair and public hearing by a competent, independent and impartial tribunal established by law,

Whereas the International Covenants on Economic, Social and Cultural Rights and on Civil and Political Rights both guarantee the exercise of those rights, and in addition, the Covenant on Civil and Political Rights further guarantees the right to be tried without undue delay,

Whereas frequently there still exists a gap between the vision underlying those principles and the actual situation,

Whereas the organization and administration of justice in every country should be inspired by those principles, and efforts should be undertaken to translate them fully into reality,

Whereas rules concerning the exercise of judicial office should aim at enabling judges to act in accordance with those principles,

Whereas judges are charged with the ultimate decision over life, freedoms, rights, duties and property of citizens,

Whereas the Sixth United Nations Congress on the Prevention of Crime and the Treatment of Offenders, by its resolution 16, called upon the Committee on Crime Prevention and Control to include among its priorities the elaboration of guidelines relating to the independence of judges and the selection, professional training and status of judges and prosecutors,

---

[1] Adopted by the Seventh United Nations Congress on the Prevention of Crime and the Treatment of Offenders held at Milan from 26 August to 6 September 1985 and endorsed by General Assembly resolutions 40/32 of 29 November 1985 and 40/146 of 13 December 1985.

Whereas it is, therefore, appropriate that consideration be first given to the role of judges in relation to the system of justice and to the importance of their selection, training and conduct,

The following basic principles, formulated to assist Member States in their task of securing and promoting the independence of the judiciary should be taken into account and respected by Governments within the framework of their national legislation and practice and be brought to the attention of judges, lawyers, members of the executive and the legislature and the public in general. The principles have been formulated principally with professional judges in mind, but they apply equally, as appropriate, to lay judges, where they exist.

Independence of the judiciary

1. The independence of the judiciary shall be guaranteed by the State and enshrined in the Constitution or the law of the country. It is the duty of all governmental and other institutions to respect and observe the independence of the judiciary.

2. The judiciary shall decide matters before them impartially, on the basis of facts and in accordance with the law, without any restrictions, improper influences, inducements, pressures, threats or interferences, direct or indirect, from any quarter or for any reason.

3. The judiciary shall have jurisdiction over all issues of a judicial nature and shall have exclusive authority to decide whether an issue submitted for its decision is within its competence as defined by law.

4. There shall not be any inappropriate or unwarranted interference with the judicial process, nor shall judicial decisions by the courts be subject to revision. This principle is without prejudice to judicial review or to mitigation or commutation by competent authorities of sentences imposed by the judiciary, in accordance with the law.

5. Everyone shall have the right to be tried by ordinary courts or tribunals using established legal procedures. Tribunals that do not use the duly established procedures of the legal process shall not be created to displace the jurisdiction belonging to the ordinary courts or judicial tribunals.

6. The principle of the independence of the judiciary entitles and requires the judiciary to ensure that judicial proceedings are conducted fairly and that the rights of the parties are respected.

7. It is the duty of each Member State to provide adequate resources to enable the judiciary to properly perform its functions.

Freedom of expression and association

8. In accordance with the Universal Declaration of Human Rights, members of the judiciary are like other citizens entitled to freedom of expression, belief, association and assembly; provided, however, that in exercising such rights, judges shall always conduct themselves in such a manner as to preserve the dignity of their office and the impartiality and independence of the judiciary.

9. Judges shall be free to form and join associations of judges or other organizations to represent their interests, to promote their professional training and to protect their judicial independence.

Qualifications, selection and training

10. Persons selected for judicial office shall be individuals of integrity and ability with appropriate training or qualifications in law. Any method of judicial selection shall safeguard against judicial appointments for improper motives. In the selection of judges, there shall be no discrimination against a person on the grounds of race, colour, sex, religion, political or other opinion, national or social origin, property, birth or status, except that a requirement, that a candidate for judicial office must be a national of the country concerned, shall not be considered discriminatory.

Conditions of service and tenure

11. The term of office of judges, their independence, security, adequate remuneration, conditions of service, pensions and the age of retirement shall be adequately secured by law.

12. Judges, whether appointed or elected, shall have guaranteed tenure until a mandatory retirement age or the expiry of their term of office, where such exists.

13. Promotion of judges, wherever such a system exists, should be based on objective factors, in particular ability, integrity and experience.

14. The assignment of cases to judges within the court to which they belong is an internal matter of judicial administration.

Professional secrecy and immunity

15. The judiciary shall be bound by professional secrecy with regard to their deliberations and to confidential information acquired in the course of their duties other than in public proceedings, and shall not be compelled to testify on such matters.

16. Without prejudice to any disciplinary procedure or to any right of appeal or to compensation from the State, in accordance with national law, judges should enjoy personal immunity from civil suits for monetary damages for improper acts or omissions in the exercise of their judicial functions.

Discipline, suspension and removal

17. A charge or complaint made against a judge in his/her judicial and professional capacity shall be processed expeditiously and fairly under an appropriate procedure. The judge shall have the right to a fair hearing. The examination of the matter at its initial stage shall be kept confidential, unless otherwise requested by the judge.

18. Judges shall be subject to suspension or removal only for reasons of incapacity or behaviour that renders them unfit to discharge their duties.

19. All disciplinary, suspension or removal proceedings shall be determined in accordance with established standards of judicial conduct.

20. Decisions in disciplinary, suspension or removal proceedings should be subject to an independent review. This principle may not apply to the decisions of the highest court and those of the legislature in impeachment or similar proceedings.

2.2 THE BANGALORE PRINCIPLES OF JUDICIAL CONDUCT, 2002[2]

Preamble

WHEREAS the Universal Declaration of Human Rights recognizes as fundamental the principle that everyone is entitled in full equality to a fair and public hearing by an independent and impartial tribunal, in the determination of rights and obligations and of any criminal charge.

WHEREAS the International Covenant on Civil and Political Rights guarantees that all persons shall be equal before the courts, and that in the determination of any criminal charge or of rights and obligations in a suit at law, everyone shall be entitled, without undue delay, to a fair and public hearing by a competent, independent and impartial tribunal established by law.

WHEREAS the foregoing fundamental principles and rights are also recognized or reflected in regional human rights instruments, in domestic constitutional, statutory and common law, and in judicial conventions and traditions.

---

[2] The Bangalore Draft Code of Judicial Conduct 2001 adopted by the Judicial Group on Strengthening Judicial Integrity, as revised at the Round Table Meeting of Chief Justices held at the Peace Palace, The Hague, November 25-26, 2002.

WHEREAS the importance of a competent, independent and impartial judiciary to the protection of human rights is given emphasis by the fact that the implementation of all the other rights ultimately depends upon the proper administration of justice.

WHEREAS a competent, independent and impartial judiciary is likewise essential if the courts are to fulfil their role in upholding constitutionalism and the rule of law.

WHEREAS public confidence in the judicial system and in the moral authority and integrity of the judiciary is of the utmost importance in a modern democratic society.

WHEREAS it is essential that judges, individually and collectively, respect and honour judicial office as a public trust and strive to enhance and maintain confidence in the judicial system.

WHEREAS the primary responsibility for the promotion and maintenance of high standards of judicial conduct lies with the judiciary in each country.

AND WHEREAS the United Nations Basic Principles on the Independence of the Judiciary are designed to secure and promote the independence of the judiciary, and are addressed primarily to States.

THE FOLLOWING PRINCIPLES are intended to establish standards for ethical conduct of judges. They are designed to provide guidance to judges and to afford the judiciary a framework for regulating judicial conduct. They are also intended to assist members of the executive and the legislature, and lawyers and the public in general, to better understand and support the judiciary. These principles presuppose that judges are accountable for their conduct to appropriate institutions established to maintain judicial standards, which are themselves independent and impartial, and are intended to supplement and not to derogate from existing rules of law and conduct which bind the judge.

Value 1:

INDEPENDENCE

Principle: Judicial independence is a pre-requisite to the rule of law and a fundamental guarantee of a fair trial. A judge shall therefore uphold and exemplify judicial independence in both its individual and institutional aspects.

Application:

1.1 A judge shall exercise the judicial function independently on the basis of the judge's assessment of the facts and in accordance with a conscientious understanding of the law, free of any extraneous influences, inducements, pressures, threats or interference, direct or indirect, from any quarter or for any reason.

1.2 A judge shall be independent in relation to society in general and in relation to the particular parties to a dispute which the judge has to adjudicate.

1.3 A judge shall not only be free from inappropriate connections with, and influence by, the executive and legislative branches of government, but must also appear to a reasonable observer to be free therefrom.

1.4 In performing judicial duties, a judge shall be independent of judicial colleagues in respect of decisions which the judge is obliged to make independently.

1.5 A judge shall encourage and uphold safeguards for the discharge of judicial duties in order to maintain and enhance the institutional and operational independence of the judiciary.

1.6 A judge shall exhibit and promote high standards of judicial conduct in order to reinforce public confidence in the judiciary which is fundamental to the maintenance of judicial independence.

Value 2:

IMPARTIALITY

Principle: Impartiality is essential to the proper discharge of the judicial office. It applies not only to the decision itself but also to the process by which the decision is made.

Application:

2.1 A judge shall perform his or her judicial duties without favour, bias or prejudice.

2.2 A judge shall ensure that his or her conduct, both in and out of court, maintains and enhances the confidence of the public, the legal profession and litigants in the impartiality of the judge and of the judiciary.

2.3 A judge shall, so far as is reasonable, so conduct himself or herself as to minimise the occasions on which it will be necessary for the judge to be disqualified from hearing or deciding cases.

2.4 A judge shall not knowingly, while a proceeding is before, or could come before, the judge, make any comment that might reasonably be expected to affect the outcome of such proceeding or impair the manifest fairness of the process. Nor shall the judge make any comment in public or otherwise that might affect the fair trial of any person or issue.

2.5 A judge shall disqualify himself or herself from participating in any proceedings in which the judge is unable to decide the matter impartially or in which it may appear to a reasonable observer that the judge is unable to decide the matter impartially. Such proceedings include, but are not limited to, instances where:

2.5.1 the judge has actual bias or prejudice concerning a party or personal knowledge of disputed evidentiary facts concerning the proceedings;

2.5.2 the judge previously served as a lawyer or was a material witness in the matter in controversy; or

2.5.3 the judge, or a member of the judge's family, has an economic interest in the outcome of the matter in controversy:

Provided that disqualification of a judge shall not be required if no other tribunal can be constituted to deal with the case or, because of urgent circumstances, failure to act could lead to a serious miscarriage of justice.

Value 3:

INTEGRITY

Principle: Integrity is essential to the proper discharge of the judicial office.

Application:

3.1 A judge shall ensure that his or her conduct is above reproach in the view of a reasonable observer.

3.2 The behaviour and conduct of a judge must reaffirm the people's faith in the integrity of the judiciary. Justice must not merely be done but must also be seen to be done.

Value 4:

PROPRIETY

Principle: Propriety, and the appearance of propriety, are essential to the performance of all of the activities of a judge.

Application:

4.1 A judge shall avoid impropriety and the appearance of impropriety in all of the judge's activities.

4.2. As a subject of constant public scrutiny, a judge must accept personal restrictions that might be viewed as burdensome by the ordinary citizen and should do so freely and willingly. In particular, a judge shall conduct himself or herself in a way that is consistent with the dignity of the judicial office.

4.3. A judge shall, in his or her personal relations with individual members of the legal profession who practise regularly in the judge's court, avoid situations which might reasonably give rise to the suspicion or appearance of favouritism or partiality.

4.4 A judge shall not participate in the determination of a case in which any member of the judge's family represents a litigant or is associated in any manner with the case.

4.5 A judge shall not allow the use of the judges residence by a member of the legal profession to receive clients or other members of the legal profession.

4.6 A judge, like any other citizen, is entitled to freedom of expression, belief, association and assembly, but in exercising such rights, a judge shall always conduct himself or herself in such a manner as to preserve the dignity of the judicial office and the impartiality and independence of the judiciary.

4.7 A judge shall inform himself or herself about the judge's personal and fiduciary financial interests and shall make reasonable efforts to be informed about the financial interests of members of the judge's family.

4.8 A judge shall not allow the judge's family, social or other relationships improperly to influence the judge's judicial conduct and judgment as a judge.

4.9 A judge shall not use or lend the prestige of the judicial office to advance the private interests of the judge, a member of the judge's family or of anyone else, nor shall a judge convey or permit others to convey the impression that anyone is in a special position improperly to influence the judge in the performance of judicial duties.

4.10 Confidential information acquired by a judge in the judge's judicial capacity shall not be used or disclosed by the judge for any other purpose not related to the judge's judicial duties.

4.11 Subject to the proper performance of judicial duties, a judge may:

4.11.1 write, lecture, teach and participate in activities concerning the law, the legal system, the administration of justice or related matters;

4.11.2 appear at a public hearing before an official body concerned with matters relating to the law, the legal system, the administration of justice or related matters;

4.11.3 serve as a member of an official body, or other government commission, committee or advisory body, if such membership is not inconsistent with the perceived impartiality and political neutrality of a judge; or

4.11.4 engage in other activities if such activities do not detract from the dignity of the judicial office or otherwise interfere with the performance of judicial duties.

4.12 A judge shall not practise law whilst the holder of judicial office.

4.13 A judge may form or join associations of judges or participate in other organizations representing the interests of judges.

4.14 A judge and members of the judge's family, shall neither ask for, nor accept, any gift, bequest, loan or favour in relation to anything done or to be done or omitted to be done by the judge in connection with the performance of judicial duties.

4.15 A judge shall not knowingly permit court staff or others subject to the judge's influence, direction or authority, to ask for, or accept, any gift, bequest, loan or favour in relation to anything done or to be done or omitted to be done in connection with his or her duties or functions.

4.16 Subject to law and to any legal requirements of public disclosure, a judge may receive a token gift, award or benefit as appropriate to the occasion on which it is made provided that such gift, award or benefit might not reasonably be perceived as intended to influence the judge in the performance of judicial duties or otherwise give rise to an appearance of partiality.

Value 5:

EQUALITY

Principle: Ensuring equality of treatment to all before the courts is essential to the due performance of the judicial office.

Application:

5.1 A judge shall be aware of, and understand, diversity in society and differences arising from various sources, including but not limited to race, colour, sex, religion, national origin, caste, disability, age, marital status, sexual orientation, social and economic status and other like causes ("irrelevant grounds").

5.2 A judge shall not, in the performance of judicial duties, by words or conduct, manifest bias or prejudice towards any person or group on irrelevant grounds.

5.3 A judge shall carry out judicial duties with appropriate consideration for all persons, such as the parties, witnesses, lawyers, court staff and judicial colleagues, without differentiation on any irrelevant ground, immaterial to the proper performance of such duties.

5.4 A judge shall not knowingly permit court staff or others subject to the judge's influence, direction or control to differentiate between persons concerned, in a matter before the judge, on any irrelevant ground.

5.5 A judge shall require lawyers in proceedings before the court to refrain from manifesting, by words or conduct, bias or prejudice based on irrelevant grounds, except such as are legally relevant to an issue in proceedings and may be the subject of legitimate advocacy.

Value 6:

COMPETENCE AND DILIGENCE

Principle: Competence and diligence are prerequisites to the due performance of judicial office.

Application:

6.1 The judicial duties of a judge take precedence over all other activities.

6.2 A judge shall devote the judge's professional activity to judicial duties, which include not only the performance of judicial functions and responsibilities in court and the making of decisions, but also other tasks relevant to the judicial office or the court's operations.

6.3 A judge shall take reasonable steps to maintain and enhance the judge's knowledge, skills and personal qualities necessary for the proper performance of judicial duties, taking advantage for this purpose of the training and other facilities which should be made available, under judicial control, to judges.

6.4 A judge shall keep himself or herself informed about relevant developments of international law, including international conventions and other instruments establishing human rights norms.

6.5 A judge shall perform all judicial duties, including the delivery of reserved decisions, efficiently, fairly and with reasonable promptness.

6.6 A judge shall maintain order and decorum in all proceedings before the court and be patient, dignified and courteous in relation to litigants, jurors, witnesses, lawyers and others with whom the judge deals in an official capacity. The judge shall require similar conduct of legal representatives, court staff and others subject to the judge's influence, direction or control.

6.7 A judge shall not engage in conduct incompatible with the diligent discharge of judicial duties.

IMPLEMENTATION

By reason of the nature of judicial office, effective measures shall be adopted by national judiciaries to provide mechanisms to implement these principles if such mechanisms are not already in existence in their jurisdictions.

DEFINITIONS

In this statement of principles, unless the context otherwise permits or requires, the following meanings shall be attributed to the words used:

"Court staff" includes the personal staff of the judge including law clerks.

"Judge" means any person exercising judicial power, however designated.

"Judge's family" includes a judge's spouse, son, daughter, son-in-law, daughter-in-law, and any other close relative or person who is a companion or employee of the judge and who lives in the judge's household.

"Judge's spouse" includes a domestic partner of the judge or any other person of either sex in a close personal relationship with the judge.

Explanatory Note

In preparing a draft code of judicial conduct in accordance with the directions set out above, reference was made to several existing codes and international instruments including, in particular, the following:

(a) The Code of Judicial Conduct adopted by the House of Delegates of the American Bar Association, August 1972.

(b) Declaration of Principles of Judicial Independence issued by the Chief Justices of the Australian States and Territories, April 1997.

(c) Code of Conduct for the Judges of the Supreme Court of Bangladesh, prescribed by the Supreme Judicial Council in the exercise of power under Article 96(4)(a) of the Constitution of the People's Republic of Bangladesh, May 2000.

(d) Ethical Principles for Judges, drafted with the cooperation of the Canadian Judges Conference and endorsed by the Canadian Judicial Council, 1998.

(e) The European Charter on the Statute for Judges, Council of Europe, July 1998.

(f) The Idaho Code of Judicial Conduct 1976.

(g) Restatement of Values of Judicial Life adopted by the Chief Justices Conference of India, 1999.

(h) The Iowa Code of Judicial Conduct.

(i) Code of Conduct for Judicial Officers of Kenya, July 1999.

(j) The Judges' Code of Ethics of Malaysia, prescribed by the Yang di-Pertuan Agong on the recommendation of the Chief Justice, the President of the Court of Appeal and the Chief Judges of the High Courts, in the exercise of powers conferred by Article 125(3A) of the Federal Constitution of Malaysia, 1994.

(k) The Code of Conduct for Magistrates in Namibia.

(l) Rules Governing Judicial Conduct, New York State, USA.

(m) Code of Conduct for Judicial Officers of the Federal Republic of Nigeria.

(n) Code of Conduct to be observed by Judges of the Supreme Court and of the High Courts of Pakistan.

(o) The Code of Judicial Conduct of the Philippines, September 1989.

(p) The Canons of Judicial Ethics of the Philippines, proposed by the Philippines Bar Association, approved by the Judges of First Instance of Manila, and adopted for the guidance of and observance by the judges under the administrative supervision of the Supreme Court, including municipal judges and city judges.

(q) Yandina Statement: Principles of Independence of the Judiciary in Solomon Islands, November 2000.

(r) Guidelines for Judges of South Africa, issued by the Chief Justice, the President of the Constitutional Court, and the Presidents of High Courts, the Labour Appeal Court, and the Land Claims Court, March 2000.

(s) Code of Conduct for Judicial Officers of Tanzania, adopted by the Judges and Magistrates Conference, 1984.

(t) The Texas Code of Judicial Conduct.

(u) Code of Conduct for Judges, Magistrates and Other Judicial Officers of Uganda, adopted by the Judges of the Supreme Court and the High Court, July 1989.

(v) The Code of Conduct of the Judicial Conference of the United States.

(w) The Canons of Judicial Conduct for the Commonwealth of Virginia, adopted and promulgated by the Supreme Court of Virginia, 1998.

(x) The Code of Judicial Conduct adopted by the Supreme Court of the State of Washington, USA, October 1995.

(y) The Judicial (Code of Conduct) Act, enacted by the Parliament of Zambia, December 1999.

(z) Draft Principles on the Independence of the Judiciary ("Siracusa Principles"), prepared by a committee of experts convened by the International Association of Penal Law, the International Commission of Jurists, and the Centre for the Independence of Judges and Lawyers, 1981.

(aa) Minimum Standards of Judicial Independence adopted by the International Bar Association, 1982.

(bb) United Nations Basic Principles on the Independence of the Judiciary, endorsed by the UN General Assembly, 1985.

(cc) Draft Universal Declaration on the Independence of Justice ("Singhvi Declaration") prepared by Mr L.V. Singhvi, UN Special Rapporteur on the Study on the Independence of the Judiciary, 1989.

(dd) The Beijing Statement of Principles of the Independence of the Judiciary in the Lawasia Region, adopted by the 6th Conference of Chief Justices, August 1997.

(ee) The Latimer House Guidelines for the Commonwealth on good practice governing relations between the Executive, Parliament and the Judiciary in the promotion of good governance, the rule of law and human rights to ensure the effective implementation of the Harare Principles, 1998.

(ff) The Policy Framework for Preventing and Eliminating Corruption and Ensuring the Impartiality of the Judicial System, adopted by the expert group convened by the Centre for the Independence of Judges and Lawyers, February 2000.

2.3 GUIDELINES ON THE ROLE OF PROSECUTORS, 1990[3]

Whereas in the Charter of the United Nations the peoples of the world affirm, inter alia, their determination to establish conditions under which justice can be maintained, and proclaim as one of their purposes the achievement of international cooperation in promoting and encouraging respect for human rights and fundamental freedoms without distinction as to race, sex, language or religion,

Whereas the Universal Declaration of Human Rights enshrines the principles of equality before the law, the presumption of innocence and the right to a fair and public hearing by an independent and impartial tribunal,

Whereas frequently there still exists a gap between the vision underlying those principles and the actual situation, Whereas the organization and administration of justice in every country should be inspired by those principles, and efforts undertaken to translate them fully into reality,

Whereas prosecutors play a crucial role in the administration of justice, and rules concerning the performance of their important responsibilities should promote their respect for and compliance with the above-mentioned principles, thus contributing to fair and equitable criminal justice and the effective protection of citizens against crime,

---

[3] U.N. Doc. A/CONF.144/28/Rev.1 at 189 (1990).

Whereas it is essential to ensure that prosecutors possess the professional qualifications required for the accomplishment of their functions, through improved methods of recruitment and legal and professional training, and through the provision of all necessary means for the proper performance of their role in combating criminality, particularly in its new forms and dimensions,

Whereas the General Assembly, by its resolution 34/169 of 17 December 1979, adopted the Code of Conduct for Law Enforcement Officials, on the recommendation of the Fifth United Nations Congress on the Prevention of Crime and the Treatment of Offenders,

Whereas in resolution 16 of the Sixth United Nations Congress on the Prevention of Crime and the Treatment of Offenders, the Committee on Crime Prevention and Control was called upon to include among its priorities the elaboration of guidelines relating to the independence of judges and the selection, professional training and status of judges and prosecutors, Whereas the Seventh United Nations Congress on the Prevention of Crime and the Treatment of Offenders adopted the Basic Principles on the Independence of the Judiciary, subsequently endorsed by the General Assembly in its resolutions 40/32 of 29 November 1985 and 40/146 of 13 December 1985,

Whereas the Declaration of Basic Principles of Justice for Victims of Crime and Abuse of Power, recommends measures to be taken at the international and national levels to improve access to justice and fair treatment, restitution, compensation and assistance for victims of crime,

Whereas, in resolution 7 of the Seventh Congress the Committee was called upon to consider the need for guidelines relating, inter alia, to the selection, professional training and status of prosecutors, their expected tasks and conduct, means to enhance their contribution to the smooth functioning of the criminal justice system and their cooperation with the police, the scope of their discretionary powers, and their role in criminal proceedings, and to report thereon to future United Nations congresses,

The Guidelines set forth below, which have been formulated to assist Member States in their tasks securing and promoting the effectiveness, impartiality and fairness of prosecutors in criminal proceedings, should be respected and taken into account by Governments within the framework of their national legislation and practice, and should be brought to the attention of prosecutors, as well as other persons, such as judges, lawyers, members of the executive and the legislature and the public in general. The present Guidelines have been formulated principally with public prosecutors in mind, but they apply equally, as appropriate, to prosecutors appointed on an ad hoc basis.

Qualifications, selection and training

1. Persons selected as prosecutors shall be individuals of integrity and ability, with appropriate training and qualifications.

2. States shall ensure that:

(a) Selection criteria for prosecutors embody safeguards against appointments based on partiality or prejudice, excluding any discrimination against a person on the grounds of race, colour, sex. Language, religion, political or other opinion, national, social or ethnic origin, property, birth, economic or other status, except that it shall not be considered discriminatory to require a candidate for prosecutorial office to be a national of the country concerned;

(b) Prosecutors have appropriate education and training and should be made aware of the ideals and ethical duties of their office, of the constitutional and statutory protections for the rights of the suspect and the victim, and of human rights and fundamental freedoms recognized by national and international law.

Status and conditions of service

3. Prosecutors, as essential agents of the administration of justice, shall at all times maintain the honour and dignity of their profession.

4. States shall ensure that prosecutors are able to perform their professional functions without intimidation, hindrance, harassment, improper interference or unjustified exposure to civil, penal or other liability.

5. Prosecutors and their families shall be physically protected by the authorities when their personal safety is threatened as a result of the discharge of prosecutorial functions.

6. Reasonable conditions of service of prosecutors, adequate remuneration and, where applicable, tenure, pension and age of retirement shall be set out by law or published rules or regulations.

7. Promotion of prosecutors, wherever such a system exists, shall be based on objective factors, in particular professional qualifications, ability, integrity and experience, and decided upon in accordance with fair and impartial procedures.

Freedom of expression and association

8. Prosecutors like other citizens are entitled to freedom of expression, belief, association and assembly. In particular, they shall have the right to take part in public discussion of matters concerning the law, the administration of justice and the promotion and protection of human rights and to join or form local, national or international organizations and attend their meetings, without suffering professional disadvantage by reason of their lawful action or their membership in a lawful organization. In exercising these rights, prosecutors shall always conduct themselves in accordance with the law and the recognized standards and ethics of their profession.

9. Prosecutors shall be free to form and join professional associations or other organizations to represent their interests, to promote their professional training and to protect their status.

Role in criminal proceedings

10. The office of prosecutors shall be strictly separated from judicial functions.

11. Prosecutors shall perform an active role in criminal proceedings, including institution of prosecution and, where authorized by law or consistent with local practice, in the investigation of crime, supervision over the legality of these investigations, supervision of the execution of court decisions and the exercise of other functions as representatives of the public interest.

12. Prosecutors shall, in accordance with the law, perform their duties fairly, consistently and expeditiously, and respect and protect human dignity and uphold human rights, thus contributing to ensuring due process and the smooth functioning of the criminal justice system.

13. In the performance of their duties, prosecutors shall:

(a) Carry out their functions impartially and avoid all political, social, religious, racial, cultural, sexual or any other kind of discrimination;

(b) Protect the public interest, act with objectivity, take proper account of the position of the suspect and the victim, and pay attention to all relevant circumstances, irrespective of whether they are to the advantage or disadvantage of the suspect;

(c) Keep matters in their possession confidential, unless the performance of duty or the needs of justice require otherwise;

(d) Consider the views and concerns of victims when their personal interests are affected and ensure that victims are informed of their rights in accordance with the Declaration of Basic Principles of Justice for Victims of Crime and Abuse of Power.

14. Prosecutors shall not initiate or continue prosecution, or shall make every effort to stay proceedings, when an impartial investigation shows the charge to be unfounded.

15. Prosecutors shall give due attention to the prosecution of crimes committed by public officials, particularly corruption, abuse of power, grave violations of human rights and other crimes recognized by international law and, where authorized by law or consistent with local practice, the investigation of such offences.

16. When prosecutors come into possession of evidence against suspects that they know or believe on reasonable grounds was obtained through recourse to unlawful methods, which constitute a grave violation of the suspect's human rights, especially involving torture or cruel, inhuman or degrading treatment or punishment, or other abuses of human rights, they shall refuse to use such evidence against anyone other than those who used such methods, or inform the Court accordingly, and shall take all necessary steps to ensure that those responsible for using such methods are brought to justice.

Discretionary functions

17. In countries where prosecutors are vested with discretionary functions, the law or published rules or regulations shall provide guidelines to enhance fairness and consistency of approach in taking decisions in the prosecution process, including institution or waiver of prosecution.

Alternatives to prosecution

18. In accordance with national law, prosecutors shall give due consideration to waiving prosecution, discontinuing proceedings conditionally or unconditionally, or diverting criminal cases from the formal justice system, with full respect for the rights of suspect(s) and the victim(s). For this purpose, States should fully explore the possibility of adopting diversion schemes not only to alleviate excessive court loads, but also to avoid the stigmatization of pre-trial detention, indictment and conviction, as well as the possible adverse effects of imprisonment.

19. In countries where prosecutors are vested with discretionary functions as to the decision whether or not to prosecute a juvenile, special considerations shall be given to the nature and gravity of the offence, protection of society and the personality and background of the juvenile. In making that decision, prosecutors shall particularly consider available alternatives to prosecution under the relevant juvenile justice laws and procedures. Prosecutors shall use their best efforts to take prosecutory action against juveniles only to the extent strictly necessary.

Relations with other government agencies or institutions

20. In order to ensure the fairness and effectiveness of prosecution, prosecutors shall strive to cooperate with the police, the courts, the legal profession, public defenders and other government agencies or institutions.

Disciplinary proceedings

21. Disciplinary offences of prosecutors shall be based on law or lawful regulations. Complaints against prosecutors which allege that they acted in a manner clearly out of the range of professional standards shall be processed expeditiously and fairly under appropriate procedures. Prosecutors shall have the right to a fair hearing. The decision shall be subject to independent review.

22. Disciplinary proceedings against prosecutors shall guarantee an objective evaluation and decision. They shall be determined in accordance with the law, the code of professional conduct and other established standards and ethics and in the light of the present Guidelines. Observance of the Guidelines

23. Prosecutors shall respect the present Guidelines. They shall also, to the best of their capability, prevent and actively oppose any violations thereof.

24. Prosecutors who have reason to believe that a violation of the present Guidelines has occurred or is about to occur shall report the matter to their superior authorities and, where necessary, to other appropriate authorities or organs vested with reviewing or remedial power.

2.4 CODE OF CONDUCT FOR LAW ENFORCEMENT OFFICIALS, 1979[4]

Article 1

Law enforcement officials shall at all times fulfil the duty imposed upon them by law, by serving the community and by protecting all persons against illegal acts, consistent with the high degree of responsibility required by their profession.

---

[4] Adopted by the UN General Assembly resolution 34/169 of 17 December 1979.

Commentary:

(a) The term "law enforcement officials", includes all officers of the law, whether appointed or elected, who exercise police powers, especially the powers of arrest or detention.

(b) In countries where police powers are exercised by military authorities, whether uniformed or not, or by State security forces, the definition of law enforcement officials shall be regarded as including officers of such services.

(c) Service to the community is intended to include particularly the rendition of services of assistance to those members of the community who by reason of personal, economic, social or other emergencies are in need of immediate aid.

(d) This provision is intended to cover not only all violent, predatory and harmful acts, but extends to the full range of prohibitions under penal statutes. It extends to conduct by persons not capable of incurring criminal liability.

Article 2

In the performance of their duty, law enforcement officials shall respect and protect human dignity and maintain and uphold the human rights of all persons.

Commentary:

(a) The human rights in question are identified and protected by national and international law. Among the relevant international instruments are the Universal Declaration of Human Rights, the International Covenant on Civil and Political Rights, the Declaration on the Protection of All Persons from Being Subjected to Torture and Other Cruel, Inhuman or Degrading Treatment or Punishment, the United Nations Declaration on the Elimination of All Forms of Racial Discrimination, the International Convention on the Elimination of All Forms of Racial Discrimination, the International Convention on the Suppression and Punishment of the Crime of Apartheid , the Convention on the Prevention and Punishment of the Crime of Genocide, the Standard Minimum Rules for the Treatment of Prisoners and the Vienna Convention on Consular Relations.

(b) National commentaries to this provision should indicate regional or national provisions identifying and protecting these rights.

Article 3

Law enforcement officials may use force only when strictly necessary and to the extent required for the performance of their duty.

Commentary:

(a) This provision emphasizes that the use of force by law enforcement officials should be exceptional; while it implies that law enforcement officials may be authorized to use force as is reasonably necessary under the circumstances for the prevention of crime or in effecting or assisting in the lawful arrest of offenders or suspected offenders, no force going beyond that may be used.

(b) National law ordinarily restricts the use of force by law enforcement officials in accordance with a principle of proportionality. It is to be understood that such national principles of proportionality are to be respected in the interpretation of this provision. In no case should this provision be interpreted to authorize the use of force which is disproportionate to the legitimate objective to be achieved.

(c) The use of firearms is considered an extreme measure. Every effort should be made to exclude the use of firearms, especially against children. In general, firearms should not be used except when a suspected offender offers armed resistance or otherwise jeopardizes the lives of others and less extreme measures are not sufficient to restrain or apprehend the suspected offender. In every instance in which a firearm is discharged, a report should be made promptly to the competent authorities.

Article 4

Matters of a confidential nature in the possession of law enforcement officials shall be kept confidential, unless the performance of duty or the needs of justice strictly require otherwise.

Commentary:

By the nature of their duties, law enforcement officials obtain information which may relate to private lives or be potentially harmful to the interests, and especially the reputation, of others. Great care should be exercised in safeguarding and using such information, which should be disclosed only in the performance of duty or to serve the needs of justice. Any disclosure of such information for other purposes is wholly improper.

Article 5

No law enforcement official may inflict, instigate or tolerate any act of torture or other cruel, inhuman or degrading treatment or punishment, nor may any law enforcement official invoke superior orders or exceptional circumstances such as a state of war or a threat of war, a threat to national security, internal political instability or any other public emergency as a justification of torture or other cruel, inhuman or degrading treatment or punishment.

Commentary:

(a) This prohibition derives from the Declaration on the Protection of All Persons from Being Subjected to Torture and Other Cruel, Inhuman or Degrading Treatment or Punishment, adopted by the General Assembly, according to which: "[Such an act is] an offence to human dignity and shall be condemned as a denial of the purposes of the Charter of the United Nations and as a violation of the human rights and fundamental freedoms proclaimed in the Universal Declaration of Human Rights [and other international human rights instruments]."

(b) The Declaration defines torture as follows:

". . . torture means any act by which severe pain or suffering, whether physical or mental, is intentionally inflicted by or at the instigation of a public official on a person for such purposes as obtaining from him or a third person information or confession, punishing him for an act he has committed or is suspected of having committed, or intimidating him or other persons. It does not include pain or suffering arising only from, inherent in or incidental to, lawful sanctions to the extent consistent with the Standard Minimum Rules for the Treatment of Prisoners."

(c) The term "cruel, inhuman or degrading treatment or punishment" has not been defined by the General Assembly but should be interpreted so as to extend the widest possible protection against abuses, whether physical or mental.

Article 6

Law enforcement officials shall ensure the full protection of the health of persons in their custody and, in particular, shall take immediate action to secure medical attention whenever required.

Commentary:

(a) "Medical attention", which refers to services rendered by any medical personnel, including certified medical practitioners and paramedics, shall be secured when needed or requested.

(b) While the medical personnel are likely to be attached to the law enforcement operation, law enforcement officials must take into account the judgement of such personnel when they recommend providing the person in custody with appropriate treatment through, or in consultation with, medical personnel from outside the law enforcement operation.

(c) It is understood that law enforcement officials shall also secure medical attention for victims of violations of law or of accidents occurring in the course of violations of law.

Article 7

Law enforcement officials shall not commit any act of corruption. They shall also rigorously oppose and combat all such acts.

Commentary:

(a) Any act of corruption, in the same way as any other abuse of authority, is incompatible with the profession of law enforcement officials. The law must be enforced fully with respect to any law enforcement official who commits an act of corruption, as Governments cannot expect to enforce the law among their citizens if they cannot, or will not, enforce the law against their own agents and within their agencies.

(b) While the definition of corruption must be subject to national law, it should be understood to encompass the commission or omission of an act in the performance of or in connection with one's duties, in response to gifts, promises or incentives demanded or accepted, or the wrongful receipt of these once the act has been committed or omitted.

(c) The expression "act of corruption" referred to above should be understood to encompass attempted corruption.

Article 8

Law enforcement officials shall respect the law and the present Code. They shall also, to the best of their capability, prevent and rigorously oppose any violations of them. Law enforcement officials who have reason to believe that a violation of the present Code has occurred or is about to occur shall report the matter to their superior authorities and, where necessary, to other appropriate authorities or organs vested with reviewing or remedial power.

Commentary:

(a) This Code shall be observed whenever it has been incorporated into national legislation or practice. If legislation or practice contains stricter provisions than those of the present Code, those stricter provisions shall be observed.

(b) The article seeks to preserve the balance between the need for internal discipline of the agency on which public safety is largely dependent, on the one hand, and the need for dealing with violations of basic human rights, on the other. Law enforcement officials shall report violations within the chain of command and take other lawful action outside the chain of command only when no other remedies are available or effective. It is understood that law enforcement officials shall not suffer administrative or other penalties because they have reported that a violation of this Code has occurred or is about to occur.

(c) The term "appropriate authorities or organs vested with reviewing or remedial power" refers to any authority or organ existing under national law, whether internal to the law enforcement agency or independent thereof, with statutory, customary or other power to review grievances and complaints arising out of violations within the purview of this Code.

(d) In some countries, the mass media may be regarded as performing complaint review functions similar to those described in subparagraph (c) above. Law enforcement officials may, therefore, be justified if, as a last resort and in accordance with the laws and customs of their own countries and with the provisions of article 4 of the present Code, they bring violations to the attention of public opinion through the mass media.

(e) Law enforcement officials who comply with the provisions of this Code deserve the respect, the full support and the co-operation of the community and of the law enforcement agency in which they serve, as well as the law enforcement profession.

2.5 BASIC PRINCIPLES ON THE USE OF FORCE AND FIREARMS BY LAW ENFORCEMENT OFFICIALS, 1990[5]

Whereas the work of law enforcement officials[6] is a social service of great importance and there is, therefore, a need to maintain and, whenever necessary, to improve the working conditions and status of these officials,

Whereas a threat to the life and safety of law enforcement officials must be seen as a threat to the stability of society as a whole,

Whereas law enforcement officials have a vital role in the protection of the right to life, liberty and security of the person, as guaranteed in the Universal Declaration of Human Rights and reaffirmed in the International Covenant on Civil and Political Rights,

Whereas the Standard Minimum Rules for the Treatment of Prisoners provide for the circumstances in which prison officials may use force in the course of their duties,

Whereas article 3 of the Code of Conduct for Law Enforcement Officials provides that law enforcement officials may use force only when strictly necessary and to the extent required for the performance of their duty,

Whereas the preparatory meeting for the Seventh United Nations Congress on the Prevention of Crime and the Treatment of Offenders, held at Varenna, Italy, agreed on elements to be considered in the course of further work on restraints on the use of force and firearms by law enforcement officials,

Whereas the Seventh Congress, in its resolution 14, inter alia, emphasizes that the use of force and firearms by law enforcement officials should be commensurate with due respect for human rights,

Whereas the Economic and Social Council, in its resolution 1986/10, section IX, of 21 May 1986, invited Member States to pay particular attention in the implementation of the Code to the

---

[5] Adopted by the Eighth United Nations Congress on the Prevention of Crime and the Treatment of Offenders, Havana, Cuba, 27 August to 7 September 1990.

[6] In accordance with the commentary to article 1 of the Code of Conduct for Law Enforcement Officials, the term "law enforcement officials" includes all officers of the law, whether appointed or elected, who exercise police powers, especially the powers of arrest or detention. In countries where police powers are exercised by military authorities, whether uniformed or not, or by State security forces, the definition of law enforcement officials shall be regarded as including officers of such services.

use of force and firearms by law enforcement officials, and the General Assembly, in its resolution 41/149 of 4 December 1986, inter alia, welcomed this recommendation made by the Council,

Whereas it is appropriate that, with due regard to their personal safety, consideration be given to the role of law enforcement officials in relation to the administration of justice, to the protection of the right to life, liberty and security of the person, to their responsibility to maintain public safety and social peace and to the importance of their qualifications, training and conduct,

The basic principles set forth below, which have been formulated to assist Member States in their task of ensuring and promoting the proper role of law enforcement officials, should be taken into account and respected by Governments within the framework of their national legislation and practice, and be brought to the attention of law enforcement officials as well as other persons, such as judges, prosecutors, lawyers, members of the executive branch and the legislature, and the public.

General provisions

1. Governments and law enforcement agencies shall adopt and implement rules and regulations on the use of force and firearms against persons by law enforcement officials. In developing such rules and regulations, Governments and law enforcement agencies shall keep the ethical issues associated with the use of force and firearms constantly under review.

2. Governments and law enforcement agencies should develop a range of means as broad as possible and equip law enforcement officials with various types of weapons and ammunition that would allow for a differentiated use of force and firearms. These should include the development of non-lethal incapacitating weapons for use in appropriate situations, with a view to increasingly restraining the application of means capable of causing death or injury to persons. For the same purpose, it should also be possible for law enforcement officials to be equipped with self-defensive equipment such as shields, helmets, bullet-proof vests and bullet-proof means of transportation, in order to decrease the need to use weapons of any kind.

3. The development and deployment of non-lethal incapacitating weapons should be carefully evaluated in order to minimize the risk of endangering uninvolved persons, and the use of such weapons should be carefully controlled.

4. Law enforcement officials, in carrying out their duty, shall, as far as possible, apply non-violent means before resorting to the use of force and firearms. They may use force and firearms only if other means remain ineffective or without any promise of achieving the intended result.

5. Whenever the lawful use of force and firearms is unavoidable, law enforcement officials shall:

(a) Exercise restraint in such use and act in proportion to the seriousness of the offence and the legitimate objective to be achieved;

(b) Minimize damage and injury, and respect and preserve human life;

(c) Ensure that assistance and medical aid are rendered to any injured or affected persons at the earliest possible moment;

(d) Ensure that relatives or close friends of the injured or affected person are notified at the earliest possible moment.

6. Where injury or death is caused by the use of force and firearms by law enforcement officials, they shall report the incident promptly to their superiors, in accordance with principle 22.

7. Governments shall ensure that arbitrary or abusive use of force and firearms by law enforcement officials is punished as a criminal offence under their law.

8. Exceptional circumstances such as internal political instability or any other public emergency may not be invoked to justify any departure from these basic principles.

Special provisions

9. Law enforcement officials shall not use firearms against persons except in self-defence or defence of others against the imminent threat of death or serious injury, to prevent the perpetration of a particularly serious crime involving grave threat to life, to arrest a person presenting such a danger and resisting their authority, or to prevent his or her escape, and only when less extreme means are insufficient to achieve these objectives. In any event, intentional lethal use of firearms may only be made when strictly unavoidable in order to protect life.

10. In the circumstances provided for under principle 9, law enforcement officials shall identify themselves as such and give a clear warning of their intent to use firearms, with sufficient time for the warning to be observed, unless to do so would unduly place the law enforcement

officials at risk or would create a risk of death or serious harm to other persons, or would be clearly inappropriate or pointless in the circumstances of the incident.

11. Rules and regulations on the use of firearms by law enforcement officials should include guidelines that:

(a) Specify the circumstances under which law enforcement officials are authorized to carry firearms and prescribe the types of firearms and ammunition permitted;

(b) Ensure that firearms are used only in appropriate circumstances and in a manner likely to decrease the risk of unnecessary harm;

(c) Prohibit the use of those firearms and ammunition that cause unwarranted injury or present an unwarranted risk;

(d) Regulate the control, storage and issuing of firearms, including procedures for ensuring that law enforcement officials are accountable for the firearms and ammunition issued to them;

(e) Provide for warnings to be given, if appropriate, when firearms are to be discharged;

(f) Provide for a system of reporting whenever law enforcement officials use firearms in the performance of their duty.

Policing unlawful assemblies

12. As everyone is allowed to participate in lawful and peaceful assemblies, in accordance with the principles embodied in the Universal Declaration of Human Rights and the International Covenant on Civil and Political Rights, Governments and law enforcement agencies and officials shall recognize that force and firearms may be used only in accordance with principles 13 and 14.

13. In the dispersal of assemblies that are unlawful but non-violent, law enforcement officials shall avoid the use of force or, where that is not practicable, shall restrict such force to the minimum extent necessary.

14. In the dispersal of violent assemblies, law enforcement officials may use firearms only when less dangerous means are not practicable and only to the minimum extent necessary. Law enforcement officials shall not use firearms in such cases, except under the conditions stipulated in principle 9.

Policing persons in custody or detention

15. Law enforcement officials, in their relations with persons in custody or detention, shall not use force, except when strictly necessary for the maintenance of security and order within the institution, or when personal safety is threatened.

16. Law enforcement officials, in their relations with persons in custody or detention, shall not use firearms, except in self-defence or in the defence of others against the immediate threat of death or serious injury, or when strictly necessary to prevent the escape of a person in custody or detention presenting the danger referred to in principle 9.

17. The preceding principles are without prejudice to the rights, duties and responsibilities of prison officials, as set out in the Standard Minimum Rules for the Treatment of Prisoners, particularly rules 33, 34 and 54.

Qualifications, training and counselling

18. Governments and law enforcement agencies shall ensure that all law enforcement officials are selected by proper screening procedures, have appropriate moral, psychological and physical qualities for the effective exercise of their functions and receive continuous and thorough professional training. Their continued fitness to perform these functions should be subject to periodic review.

19. Governments and law enforcement agencies shall ensure that all law enforcement officials are provided with training and are tested in accordance with appropriate proficiency standards in the use of force. Those law enforcement officials who are required to carry firearms should be authorized to do so only upon completion of special training in their use.

20. In the training of law enforcement officials, Governments and law enforcement agencies shall give special attention to issues of police ethics and human rights, especially in the investigative process, to alternatives to the use of force and firearms, including the peaceful settlement of conflicts, the understanding of crowd behaviour, and the methods of persuasion, negotiation and mediation, as well as to technical means, with a view to limiting the use of force and firearms. Law enforcement agencies should review their training programmes and operational procedures in the light of particular incidents.

21. Governments and law enforcement agencies shall make stress counselling available to law enforcement officials who are involved in situations where force and firearms are used.

Reporting and review procedures

22. Governments and law enforcement agencies shall establish effective reporting and review procedures for all incidents referred to in principles 6 and 11 (f). For incidents reported pursuant to these principles, Governments and law enforcement agencies shall ensure that an effective review process is available and that independent administrative or prosecutorial authorities are in a position to exercise jurisdiction in appropriate circumstances. In cases of death and serious injury or other grave consequences, a detailed report shall be sent promptly to the competent authorities responsible for administrative review and judicial control.

23. Persons affected by the use of force and firearms or their legal representatives shall have access to an independent process, including a judicial process. In the event of the death of such persons, this provision shall apply to their dependants accordingly.

24. Governments and law enforcement agencies shall ensure that superior officers are held responsible if they know, or should have known, that law enforcement officials under their command are resorting, or have resorted, to the unlawful use of force and firearms, and they did not take all measures in their power to prevent, suppress or report such use.

25. Governments and law enforcement agencies shall ensure that no criminal or disciplinary sanction is imposed on law enforcement officials who, in compliance with the Code of Conduct for Law Enforcement Officials and these basic principles, refuse to carry out an order to use force and firearms, or who report such use by other officials.

26. Obedience to superior orders shall be no defence if law enforcement officials knew that an order to use force and firearms resulting in the death or serious injury of a person was manifestly unlawful and had a reasonable opportunity to refuse to follow it. In any case, responsibility also rests on the superiors who gave the unlawful orders.

2.6 BASIC PRINCIPLES ON THE ROLE OF LAWYERS, 1990[7]

Whereas in the Charter of the United Nations the peoples of the world affirm, inter alia , their determination to establish conditions under which justice can be maintained, and proclaim as one of their purposes the achievement of international cooperation in promoting and encouraging respect for human rights and fundamental freedoms without distinction as to race, sex, language or religion,

---

[7] Adopted by the Eighth United Nations Congress on the Prevention of Crime and the Treatment of Offenders, Havana, Cuba, 27 August to 7 September 1990.

Whereas the Universal Declaration of Human Rights enshrines the principles of equality before the law, the presumption of innocence, the right to a fair and public hearing by an independent and impartial tribunal, and all the guarantees necessary for the defence of everyone charged with a penal offence,

Whereas the International Covenant on Civil and Political Rights proclaims, in addition, the right to be tried without undue delay and the right to a fair and public hearing by a competent, independent and impartial tribunal established by law,

Whereas the International Covenant on Economic, Social and Cultural Rights recalls the obligation of States under the Charter to promote universal respect for, and observance of, human rights and freedoms,

Whereas the Body of Principles for the Protection of All Persons under Any Form of Detention or Imprisonment provides that a detained person shall be entitled to have the assistance of, and to communicate and consult with, legal counsel,

Whereas the Standard Minimum Rules for the Treatment of Prisoners recommend, in particular, that legal assistance and confidential communication with counsel should be ensured to untried prisoners,

Whereas the Safeguards guaranteeing protection of those facing the death penalty reaffirm the right of everyone suspected or charged with a crime for which capital punishment may be imposed to adequate legal assistance at all stages of the proceedings, in accordance with article 14 of the International Covenant on Civil and Political Rights,

Whereas the Declaration of Basic Principles of Justice for Victims of Crime and Abuse of Power recommends measures to be taken at the international and national levels to improve access to justice and fair treatment, restitution, compensation and assistance for victims of crime,

Whereas adequate protection of the human rights and fundamental freedoms to which all persons are entitled, be they economic, social and cultural, or civil and political, requires that all persons have effective access to legal services provided by an independent legal profession,

Whereas professional associations of lawyers have a vital role to play in upholding professional standards and ethics, protecting their members from persecution and improper restrictions and infringements, providing legal services to all in need of them, and cooperating with governmental and other institutions in furthering the ends of justice and public interest,

The Basic Principles on the Role of Lawyers, set forth below, which have been formulated to assist Member States in their task of promoting and ensuring the proper role of lawyers, should be respected and taken into account by Governments within the framework of their national legislation and practice and should be brought to the attention of lawyers as well as other persons, such as judges, prosecutors, members of the executive and the legislature, and the public in general. These principles shall also apply, as appropriate, to persons who exercise the functions of lawyers without having the formal status of lawyers.

Access to lawyers and legal services

1. All persons are entitled to call upon the assistance of a lawyer of their choice to protect and establish their rights and to defend them in all stages of criminal proceedings.

2. Governments shall ensure that efficient procedures and responsive mechanisms for effective and equal access to lawyers are provided for all persons within their territory and subject to their jurisdiction, without distinction of any kind, such as discrimination based on race, colour, ethnic origin, sex, language, religion, political or other opinion, national or social origin, property, birth, economic or other status.

3. Governments shall ensure the provision of sufficient funding and other resources for legal services to the poor and, as necessary, to other disadvantaged persons. Professional associations of lawyers shall cooperate in the organization and provision of services, facilities and other resources.

4. Governments and professional associations of lawyers shall promote programmes to inform the public about their rights and duties under the law and the important role of lawyers in protecting their fundamental freedoms. Special attention should be given to assisting the poor and other disadvantaged persons so as to enable them to assert their rights and where necessary call upon the assistance of lawyers.

Special safeguards in criminal justice matters

5. Governments shall ensure that all persons are immediately informed by the competent authority of their right to be assisted by a lawyer of their own choice upon arrest or detention or when charged with a criminal offence.

6. Any such persons who do not have a lawyer shall, in all cases in which the interests of justice so require, be entitled to have a lawyer of experience and competence commensurate with the nature of the offence assigned to them in order to provide effective legal assistance, without payment by them if they lack sufficient means to pay for such services.

7. Governments shall further ensure that all persons arrested or detained, with or without criminal charge, shall have prompt access to a lawyer, and in any case not later than forty-eight hours from the time of arrest or detention.

8. All arrested, detained or imprisoned persons shall be provided with adequate opportunities, time and facilities to be visited by and to communicate and consult with a lawyer, without delay, interception or censorship and in full confidentiality. Such consultations may be within sight, but not within the hearing, of law enforcement officials.

Qualifications and training

9. Governments, professional associations of lawyers and educational institutions shall ensure that lawyers have appropriate education and training and be made aware of the ideals and ethical duties of the lawyer and of human rights and fundamental freedoms recognized by national and international law.

10. Governments, professional associations of lawyers and educational institutions shall ensure that there is no discrimination against a person with respect to entry into or continued practice within the legal profession on the grounds of race, colour, sex, ethnic origin, religion, political or other opinion, national or social origin, property, birth, economic or other status, except that a requirement, that a lawyer must be a national of the country concerned, shall not be considered discriminatory.

11. In countries where there exist groups, communities or regions whose needs for legal services are not met, particularly where such groups have distinct cultures, traditions or languages or have been the victims of past discrimination, Governments, professional associations of lawyers and educational institutions should take special measures to provide opportunities for candidates from these groups to enter the legal profession and should ensure that they receive training appropriate to the needs of their groups.

Duties and responsibilities

12. Lawyers shall at all times maintain the honour and dignity of their profession as essential agents of the administration of justice.

13. The duties of lawyers towards their clients shall include:

> (a) Advising clients as to their legal rights and obligations, and as to the working of the legal system in so far as it is relevant to the legal rights and obligations of the clients;

(b) Assisting clients in every appropriate way, and taking legal action to protect their interests;

(c) Assisting clients before courts, tribunals or administrative authorities, where appropriate.

14. Lawyers, in protecting the rights of their clients and in promoting the cause of justice, shall seek to uphold human rights and fundamental freedoms recognized by national and international law and shall at all times act freely and diligently in accordance with the law and recognized standards and ethics of the legal profession.

15. Lawyers shall always loyally respect the interests of their clients.

Guarantees for the functioning of lawyers

16. Governments shall ensure that lawyers (a) are able to perform all of their professional functions without intimidation, hindrance, harassment or improper interference; (b) are able to travel and to consult with their clients freely both within their own country and abroad; and (c) shall not suffer, or be threatened with, prosecution or administrative, economic or other sanctions for any action taken in accordance with recognized professional duties, standards and ethics.

17. Where the security of lawyers is threatened as a result of discharging their functions, they shall be adequately safeguarded by the authorities.

18. Lawyers shall not be identified with their clients or their clients' causes as a result of discharging their functions.

19. No court or administrative authority before whom the right to counsel is recognized shall refuse to recognize the right of a lawyer to appear before it for his or her client unless that lawyer has been disqualified in accordance with national law and practice and in conformity with these principles.

20. Lawyers shall enjoy civil and penal immunity for relevant statements made in good faith in written or oral pleadings or in their professional appearances before a court, tribunal or other legal or administrative authority.

21. It is the duty of the competent authorities to ensure lawyers access to appropriate information, files and documents in their possession or control in sufficient time to enable lawyers to provide effective legal assistance to their clients. Such access should be provided at the earliest appropriate time.

22. Governments shall recognize and respect that all communications and consultations between lawyers and their clients within their professional relationship are confidential.

Freedom of expression and association

23. Lawyers like other citizens are entitled to freedom of expression, belief, association and assembly. In particular, they shall have the right to take part in public discussion of matters concerning the law, the administration of justice and the promotion and protection of human rights and to join or form local, national or international organizations and attend their meetings, without suffering professional restrictions by reason of their lawful action or their membership in a lawful organization. In exercising these rights, lawyers shall always conduct themselves in accordance with the law and the recognized standards and ethics of the legal profession.

Professional associations of lawyers

24. Lawyers shall be entitled to form and join self-governing professional associations to represent their interests, promote their continuing education and training and protect their professional integrity. The executive body of the professional associations shall be elected by its members and shall exercise its functions without external interference.

25. Professional associations of lawyers shall cooperate with Governments to ensure that everyone has effective and equal access to legal services and that lawyers are able, without improper interference, to counsel and assist their clients in accordance with the law and recognized professional standards and ethics.

Disciplinary proceedings

26. Codes of professional conduct for lawyers shall be established by the legal profession through its appropriate organs, or by legislation, in accordance with national law and custom and recognized international standards and norms.

27. Charges or complaints made against lawyers in their professional capacity shall be processed expeditiously and fairly under appropriate procedures. Lawyers shall have the right to a fair hearing, including the right to be assisted by a lawyer of their choice.

28. Disciplinary proceedings against lawyers shall be brought before an impartial disciplinary committee established by the legal profession, before an independent statutory authority, or before a court, and shall be subject to an independent judicial review.

29. All disciplinary proceedings shall be determined in accordance with the code of professional conduct and other recognized standards and ethics of the legal profession and in the light of these principles.

CHAPTER 3

PRISONERS

Comments: Imprisonment does not deprive a prisoner of every basic right that the ordinary citizen enjoys. Prisoners are human beings and as such they retain their rights even when in prison. This is so because human rights are universal. This means that every person, including a prisoner, has human rights, no matter who he is, where s/he lives or his/her class, race, sex, age, social status, etc. Also, human rights are said to be inalienable. This means that they cannot be taken away from a person, including a prisoner. However, the enjoyment of human rights may be restricted or limited in certain circumstances. Prisoners awaiting trial or people who have been sentenced lose some of their rights, such as freedom of movement, but they retain other rights, such as the right to dignity. Rights that cannot be suspended under any circumstances include the right to human dignity, the right to life (except in countries which have not abolished death penalty in national laws for most serious crimes), the right to equality and freedom from discrimination, and the right not be tortured or treated cruelly or inhumanely.

3.1 UNITED NATIONS: STANDARD MINIMUM RULES FOR THE TREATMENT OF PRISONERS[1]

PRELIMINARY OBSERVATIONS

1. The following rules are not intended to describe in detail a model system of penal institutions. They seek only, on the basis of the general consensus of contemporary thought and the essential elements of the most adequate systems of today, to set out what is generally accepted as being good principle and practice in the treatment of prisoners and the management of institutions.

---

[1] Adopted by the First United Nations Congress on the Prevention of Crime and the Treatment of Offenders, held at Geneva in 1955, and approved by the Economic and Social Council by its resolutions 663 C (XXIV) of 31 July 1957 and 2076 (LXII) of 13 May 1977.

2. In view of the great variety of legal, social, economic and geographical conditions of the world, it is evident that not all of the rules are capable of application in all places and at all times. They should, however, serve to stimulate a constant endeavour to overcome practical difficulties in the way of their application, in the knowledge that they represent, as a whole, the minimum conditions which are accepted as suitable by the United Nations.

3. On the other hand, the rules cover a field in which thought is constantly developing. They are not intended to preclude experiment and practices, provided these are in harmony with the principles and seek to further the purposes which derive from the text of the rules as a whole. It will always be justifiable for the central prison administration to authorize departures from the rules in this spirit.

4. (1) Part I of the rules covers the general management of institutions, and is applicable to all categories of prisoners, criminal or civil, untried or convicted, including prisoners subject to "security measures" or corrective measures ordered by the judge.

(2) Part II contains rules applicable only to the special categories dealt with in each section. Nevertheless, the rules under section A, applicable to prisoners under sentence, shall be equally applicable to categories of prisoners dealt with in sections B, C and D, provided they do not conflict with the rules governing those categories and are for their benefit.

5. (1) The rules do not seek to regulate the management of institutions set aside for young persons such as Borstal institutions or correctional schools, but in general part I would be equally applicable in such institutions.

(2) The category of young prisoners should include at least all young persons who come within the jurisdiction of juvenile courts. As a rule, such young persons should not be sentenced to imprisonment.

Part I

RULES OF GENERAL APPLICATION

Basic principle

6. (1) The following rules shall be applied impartially. There shall be no discrimination on grounds of race, colour, sex, language, religion, political or other opinion, national or social origin, property, birth or other status.

(2) On the other hand, it is necessary to respect the religious beliefs and moral precepts of the group to which a prisoner belongs.

Register

7. (1) In every place where persons are imprisoned there shall be kept a bound registration book with numbered pages in which shall be entered in respect of each prisoner received:

(a) Information concerning his identity;

(b) The reasons for his commitment and the authority therefor;

(c) The day and hour of his admission and release.

(2) No person shall be received in an institution without a valid commitment order of which the details shall have been previously entered in the register.

Separation of categories

8. The different categories of prisoners shall be kept in separate institutions or parts of institutions taking account of their sex, age, criminal record, the legal reason for their detention and the necessities of their treatment. Thus,

(a) Men and women shall so far as possible be detained in separate institutions; in an institution which receives both men and women the whole of the premises allocated to women shall be entirely separate;

(b) Untried prisoners shall be kept separate from convicted prisoners;

(c) Persons imprisoned for debt and other civil prisoners shall be kept separate from persons imprisoned by reason of a criminal offence;

(d) Young prisoners shall be kept separate from adults.

Accommodation

9. (1) Where sleeping accommodation is in individual cells or rooms, each prisoner shall occupy by night a cell or room by himself. If for special reasons, such as temporary overcrowding, it becomes necessary for the central prison administration to make an exception to this rule, it is not desirable to have two prisoners in a cell or room.

(2) Where dormitories are used, they shall be occupied by prisoners carefully selected as being suitable to associate with one another in those conditions. There shall be regular supervision by night, in keeping with the nature of the institution.

10. All accommodation provided for the use of prisoners and in particular all sleeping accommodation shall meet all requirements of health, due regard being paid to climatic conditions and particularly to cubic content of air, minimum floor space, lighting, heating and ventilation.

11. In all places where prisoners are required to live or work,

(a) The windows shall be large enough to enable the prisoners to read or work by natural light, and shall be so constructed that they can allow the entrance of fresh air whether or not there is artificial ventilation;

(b) Artificial light shall be provided sufficient for the prisoners to read or work without injury to eyesight.

12. The sanitary installations shall be adequate to enable every prisoner to comply with the needs of nature when necessary and in a clean and decent manner.

13. Adequate bathing and shower installations shall be provided so that every prisoner may be enabled and required to have a bath or shower, at a temperature suitable to the climate, as frequently as necessary for general hygiene according to season and geographical region, but at least once a week in a temperate climate.

14. All parts of an institution regularly used by prisoners shall be properly maintained and kept scrupulously clean at all times.

Personal hygiene

15. Prisoners shall be required to keep their persons clean, and to this end they shall be provided with water and with such toilet articles as are necessary for health and cleanliness.

16. In order that prisoners may maintain a good appearance compatible with their self-respect, facilities shall be provided for the proper care of the hair and beard, and men shall be enabled to shave regularly.

Clothing and bedding

17. (1) Every prisoner who is not allowed to wear his own clothing shall be provided with an outfit of clothing suitable for the climate and adequate to keep him in good health. Such clothing shall in no manner be degrading or humiliating.

(2) All clothing shall be clean and kept in proper condition. Underclothing shall be changed and washed as often as necessary for the maintenance of hygiene.

(3) In exceptional circumstances, whenever a prisoner is removed outside the institution for an authorized purpose, he shall be allowed to wear his own clothing or other inconspicuous clothing.

18. If prisoners are allowed to wear their own clothing, arrangements shall be made on their admission to the institution to ensure that it shall be clean and fit for use.

19. Every prisoner shall, in accordance with local or national standards, be provided with a separate bed, and with separate and sufficient bedding which shall be clean when issued, kept in good order and changed often enough to ensure its cleanliness.

Food

20. (1) Every prisoner shall be provided by the administration at the usual hours with food of nutritional value adequate for health and strength, of wholesome quality and well prepared and served.

(2) Drinking water shall be available to every prisoner whenever he needs it.

Exercise and sport

21. (1) Every prisoner who is not employed in outdoor work shall have at least one hour of suitable exercise in the open air daily if the weather permits.

(2) Young prisoners, and others of suitable age and physique, shall receive physical and recreational training during the period of exercise. To this end space, installations and equipment should be provided.

Medical services

22. (1) At every institution there shall be available the services of at least one qualified medical officer who should have some knowledge of psychiatry. The medical services should be organized in close relationship to the general health administration of the community or nation. They shall include a psychiatric service for the diagnosis and, in proper cases, the treatment of states of mental abnormality.

(2) Sick prisoners who require specialist treatment shall be transferred to specialized institutions or to civil hospitals. Where hospital facilities are provided in an institution, their equipment,

furnishings and pharmaceutical supplies shall be proper for the medical care and treatment of sick prisoners, and there shall be a staff of suitable trained officers.

(3) The services of a qualified dental officer shall be available to every prisoner.

23. (1) In women's institutions there shall be special accommodation for all necessary pre-natal and post-natal care and treatment. Arrangements shall be made wherever practicable for children to be born in a hospital outside the institution. If a child is born in prison, this fact shall not be mentioned in the birth certificate.

(2) Where nursing infants are allowed to remain in the institution with their mothers, provision shall be made for a nursery staffed by qualified persons, where the infants shall be placed when they are not in the care of their mothers.

24. The medical officer shall see and examine every prisoner as soon as possible after his admission and thereafter as necessary, with a view particularly to the discovery of physical or mental illness and the taking of all necessary measures; the segregation of prisoners suspected of infectious or contagious conditions; the noting of physical or mental defects which might hamper rehabilitation, and the determination of the physical capacity of every prisoner for work.

25. (1) The medical officer shall have the care of the physical and mental health of the prisoners and should daily see all sick prisoners, all who complain of illness, and any prisoner to whom his attention is specially directed.

(2) The medical officer shall report to the director whenever he considers that a prisoner's physical or mental health has been or will be injuriously affected by continued imprisonment or by any condition of imprisonment.

26. (1) The medical officer shall regularly inspect and advise the director upon:

(a) The quantity, quality, preparation and service of food;

(b) The hygiene and cleanliness of the institution and the prisoners;

(c) The sanitation, heating, lighting and ventilation of the institution;

(d) The suitability and cleanliness of the prisoners' clothing and bedding;

(e) The observance of the rules concerning physical education and sports, in cases where there is no technical personnel in charge of these activities.

(2) The director shall take into consideration the reports and advice that the medical officer submits according to rules 25 (2) and 26 and, in case he concurs with the recommendations made, shall take immediate steps to give effect to those recommendations; if they are not within his competence or if he does not concur with them, he shall immediately submit his own report and the advice of the medical officer to higher authority.

Discipline and punishment

27. Discipline and order shall be maintained with firmness, but with no more restriction than is necessary for safe custody and well-ordered community life.

28. (1) No prisoner shall be employed, in the service of the institution, in any disciplinary capacity.

(2) This rule shall not, however, impede the proper functioning of systems based on self-government, under which specified social, educational or sports activities or responsibilities are entrusted, under supervision, to prisoners who are formed into groups for the purposes of treatment.

29. The following shall always be determined by the law or by the regulation of the competent administrative authority:

(a) Conduct constituting a disciplinary offence;

(b) The types and duration of punishment which may be inflicted;

(c) The authority competent to impose such punishment.

30. (1) No prisoner shall be punished except in accordance with the terms of such law or regulation, and never twice for the same offence.

(2) No prisoner shall be punished unless he has been informed of the offence alleged against him and given a proper opportunity of presenting his defence. The competent authority shall conduct a thorough examination of the case.

(3) Where necessary and practicable the prisoner shall be allowed to make his defence through an interpreter.

31. Corporal punishment, punishment by placing in a dark cell, and all cruel, inhuman or degrading punishments shall be completely prohibited as punishments for disciplinary offences.

32. (1) Punishment by close confinement or reduction of diet shall never be inflicted unless the medical officer has examined the prisoner and certified in writing that he is fit to sustain it.

(2) The same shall apply to any other punishment that may be prejudicial to the physical or mental health of a prisoner. In no case may such punishment be contrary to or depart from the principle stated in rule 31.

(3) The medical officer shall visit daily prisoners undergoing such punishments and shall advise the director if he considers the termination or alteration of the punishment necessary on grounds of physical or mental health.

Instruments of restraint

33. Instruments of restraint, such as handcuffs, chains, irons and strait-jackets, shall never be applied as a punishment. Furthermore, chains or irons shall not be used as restraints. Other instruments of restraint shall not be used except in the following circumstances:

(a) As a precaution against escape during a transfer, provided that they shall be removed when the prisoner appears before a judicial or administrative authority;

(b) On medical grounds by direction of the medical officer;

(c) By order of the director, if other methods of control fail, in order to prevent a prisoner from injuring himself or others or from damaging property; in such instances the director shall at once consult the medical officer and report to the higher administrative authority.

34. The patterns and manner of use of instruments of restraint shall be decided by the central prison administration. Such instruments must not be applied for any longer time than is strictly necessary.

Information to and complaints by prisoners

35. (1) Every prisoner on admission shall be provided with written information about the regulations governing the treatment of prisoners of his category, the disciplinary requirements of the institution, the authorized methods of seeking information and making complaints, and all such other matters as are necessary to enable him to understand both his rights and his obligations and to adapt himself to the life of the institution.

(2) If a prisoner is illiterate, the aforesaid information shall be conveyed to him orally.

36. (1) Every prisoner shall have the opportunity each week day of making requests or complaints to the director of the institution or the officer authorized to represent him.

(2) It shall be possible to make requests or complaints to the inspector of prisons during his inspection. The prisoner shall have the opportunity to talk to the inspector or to any other inspecting officer without the director or other members of the staff being present.

(3) Every prisoner shall be allowed to make a request or complaint, without censorship as to substance but in proper form, to the central prison administration, the judicial authority or other proper authorities through approved channels.

(4) Unless it is evidently frivolous or groundless, every request or complaint shall be promptly dealt with and replied to without undue delay.

Contact with the outside world

37. Prisoners shall be allowed under necessary supervision to communicate with their family and reputable friends at regular intervals, both by correspondence and by receiving visits.

38. (1) Prisoners who are foreign nationals shall be allowed reasonable facilities to communicate with the diplomatic and consular representatives of the State to which they belong.

(2) Prisoners who are nationals of States without diplomatic or consular representation in the country and refugees or stateless persons shall be allowed similar facilities to communicate with the diplomatic representative of the State which takes charge of their interests or any national or international authority whose task it is to protect such persons.

39. Prisoners shall be kept informed regularly of the more important items of news by the reading of newspapers, periodicals or special institutional publications, by hearing wireless transmissions, by lectures or by any similar means as authorized or controlled by the administration.

Books

40. Every institution shall have a library for the use of all categories of prisoners, adequately stocked with both recreational and instructional books, and prisoners shall be encouraged to make full use of it.

Religion

41. (1) If the institution contains a sufficient number of prisoners of the same religion, a qualified representative of that religion shall be appointed or approved. If the number of prisoners justifies it and conditions permit, the arrangement should be on a full-time basis.

(2) A qualified representative appointed or approved under paragraph (1) shall be allowed to hold regular services and to pay pastoral visits in private to prisoners of his religion at proper times.

(3) Access to a qualified representative of any religion shall not be refused to any prisoner. On the other hand, if any prisoner should object to a visit of any religious representative, his attitude shall be fully respected.

42. So far as practicable, every prisoner shall be allowed to satisfy the needs of his religious life by attending the services provided in the institution and having in his possession the books of religious observance and instruction of his denomination.

Retention of prisoners' property

43. (1) All money, valuables, clothing and other effects belonging to a prisoner which under the regulations of the institution he is not allowed to retain shall on his admission to the institution be placed in safe custody. An inventory thereof shall be signed by the prisoner. Steps shall be taken to keep them in good condition.

(2) On the release of the prisoner all such articles and money shall be returned to him except in so far as he has been authorized to spend money or send any such property out of the institution, or it has been found necessary on hygienic grounds to destroy any article of clothing. The prisoner shall sign a receipt for the articles and money returned to him.

(3) Any money or effects received for a prisoner from outside shall be treated in the same way.

(4) If a prisoner brings in any drugs or medicine, the medical officer shall decide what use shall be made of them.

Notification of death, illness, transfer, etc.

44. (1) Upon the death or serious illness of, or serious injury to a prisoner, or his removal to an institution for the treatment of mental affections, the director shall at once inform the spouse, if the prisoner is married, or the nearest relative and shall in any event inform any other person previously designated by the prisoner.

(2) A prisoner shall be informed at once of the death or serious illness of any near relative. In case of the critical illness of a near relative, the prisoner should be authorized, whenever circumstances allow, to go to his bedside either under escort or alone.

(3) Every prisoner shall have the right to inform at once his family of his imprisonment or his transfer to another institution.

Removal of prisoners

45. (1) When the prisoners are being removed to or from an institution, they shall be exposed to public view as little as possible, and proper safeguards shall be adopted to protect them from insult, curiosity and publicity in any form.

(2) The transport of prisoners in conveyances with inadequate ventilation or light, or in any way which would subject them to unnecessary physical hardship, shall be prohibited.

(3) The transport of prisoners shall be carried out at the expense of the administration and equal conditions shall obtain for all of them.

Institutional personnel

46. (1) The prison administration shall provide for the careful selection of every grade of the personnel, since it is on their integrity, humanity, professional capacity and personal suitability for the work that the proper administration of the institutions depends.

(2) The prison administration shall constantly seek to awaken and maintain in the minds both of the personnel and of the public the conviction that this work is a social service of great importance, and to this end all appropriate means of informing the public should be used.

(3) To secure the foregoing ends, personnel shall be appointed on a full-time basis as professional prison officers and have civil service status with security of tenure subject only to good conduct, efficiency and physical fitness. Salaries shall be adequate to attract and retain suitable men and women; employment benefits and conditions of service shall be favourable in view of the exacting nature of the work.

47. (1) The personnel shall possess an adequate standard of education and intelligence.

(2) Before entering on duty, the personnel shall be given a course of training in their general and specific duties and be required to pass theoretical and practical tests.

(3) After entering on duty and during their career, the personnel shall maintain and improve their knowledge and professional capacity by attending courses of in-service training to be organized at suitable intervals.

48. All members of the personnel shall at all times so conduct themselves and perform their duties as to influence the prisoners for good by their example and to command their respect.

49. (1) So far as possible, the personnel shall include a sufficient number of specialists such as psychiatrists, psychologists, social workers, teachers and trade instructors.

(2) The services of social workers, teachers and trade instructors shall be secured on a permanent basis, without thereby excluding part-time or voluntary workers.

50. (1) The director of an institution should be adequately qualified for his task by character, administrative ability, suitable training and experience.

(2) He shall devote his entire time to his official duties and shall not be appointed on a part-time basis.

(3) He shall reside on the premises of the institution or in its immediate vicinity.

(4) When two or more institutions are under the authority of one director, he shall visit each of them at frequent intervals. A responsible resident official shall be in charge of each of these institutions.

51. (1) The director, his deputy, and the majority of the other personnel of the institution shall be able to speak the language of the greatest number of prisoners, or a language understood by the greatest number of them.

(2) Whenever necessary, the services of an interpreter shall be used.

52. (1) In institutions which are large enough to require the services of one or more full-time medical officers, at least one of them shall reside on the premises of the institution or in its immediate vicinity.

(2) In other institutions the medical officer shall visit daily and shall reside near enough to be able to attend without delay in cases of urgency.

53. (1) In an institution for both men and women, the part of the institution set aside for women shall be under the authority of a responsible woman officer who shall have the custody of the keys of all that part of the institution.

(2) No male member of the staff shall enter the part of the institution set aside for women unless accompanied by a woman officer.

(3) Women prisoners shall be attended and supervised only by women officers. This does not, however, preclude male members of the staff, particularly doctors and teachers, from carrying out their professional duties in institutions or parts of institutions set aside for women.

54. (1) Officers of the institutions shall not, in their relations with the prisoners, use force except in self-defence or in cases of attempted escape, or active or passive physical resistance to an order based on law or regulations. Officers who have recourse to force must use no more than is strictly necessary and must report the incident immediately to the director of the institution.

(2) Prison officers shall be given special physical training to enable them to restrain aggressive prisoners.

(3) Except in special circumstances, staff performing duties which bring them into direct contact with prisoners should not be armed. Furthermore, staff should in no circumstances be provided with arms unless they have been trained in their use.

Inspection

55. There shall be a regular inspection of penal institutions and services by qualified and experienced inspectors appointed by a competent authority. Their task shall be in particular to ensure that these institutions are administered in accordance with existing laws and regulations and with a view to bringing about the objectives of penal and correctional services.

Part II

RULES APPLICABLE TO SPECIAL CATEGORIES

A. Prisoners under sentence

Guiding principles

56. The guiding principles hereafter are intended to show the spirit in which penal institutions should be administered and the purposes at which they should aim, in accordance with the declaration made under Preliminary Observation 1 of the present text.

57. Imprisonment and other measures which result in cutting off an offender from the outside world are afflictive by the very fact of taking from the person the right of self-determination by

depriving him of his liberty. Therefore the prison system shall not, except as incidental to justifiable segregation or the maintenance of discipline, aggravate the suffering inherent in such a situation.

58. The purpose and justification of a sentence of imprisonment or a similar measure deprivative of liberty is ultimately to protect society against crime. This end can only be achieved if the period of imprisonment is used to ensure, so far as possible, that upon his return to society the offender is not only willing but able to lead a law-abiding and self-supporting life.

59. To this end, the institution should utilize all the remedial, educational, moral, spiritual and other forces and forms of assistance which are appropriate and available, and should seek to apply them according to the individual treatment needs of the prisoners.

60. (1) The regime of the institution should seek to minimize any differences between prison life and life at liberty which tend to lessen the responsibility of the prisoners or the respect due to their dignity as human beings.

(2) Before the completion of the sentence, it is desirable that the necessary steps be taken to ensure for the prisoner a gradual return to life in society. This aim may be achieved, depending on the case, by a pre-release regime organized in the same institution or in another appropriate institution, or by release on trial under some kind of supervision which must not be entrusted to the police but should be combined with effective social aid.

61. The treatment of prisoners should emphasize not their exclusion from the community, but their continuing part in it. Community agencies should, therefore, be enlisted wherever possible to assist the staff of the institution in the task of social rehabilitation of the prisoners. There should be in connection with every institution social workers charged with the duty of maintaining and improving all desirable relations of a prisoner with his family and with valuable social agencies. Steps should be taken to safeguard, to the maximum extent compatible with the law and the sentence, the rights relating to civil interests, social security rights and other social benefits of prisoners.

62. The medical services of the institution shall seek to detect and shall treat any physical or mental illnesses or defects which may hamper a prisoner's rehabilitation. All necessary medical, surgical and psychiatric services shall be provided to that end.

63. (1) The fulfilment of these principles requires individualization of treatment and for this purpose a flexible system of classifying prisoners in groups; it is therefore desirable that such groups should be distributed in separate institutions suitable for the treatment of each group.

(2) These institutions need not provide the same degree of security for every group. It is desirable to provide varying degrees of security according to the needs of different groups. Open institutions, by the very fact that they provide no physical security against escape but rely on the self-discipline of the inmates, provide the conditions most favourable to rehabilitation for carefully selected prisoners.

(3) It is desirable that the number of prisoners in closed institutions should not be so large that the individualization of treatment is hindered. In some countries it is considered that the population of such institutions should not exceed five hundred. In open institutions the population should be as small as possible.

(4) On the other hand, it is undesirable to maintain prisons which are so small that proper facilities cannot be provided.

64. The duty of society does not end with a prisoner's release. There should, therefore, be governmental or private agencies capable of lending the released prisoner efficient after-care directed towards the lessening of prejudice against him and towards his social rehabilitation.

Treatment

65. The treatment of persons sentenced to imprisonment or a similar measure shall have as its purpose, so far as the length of the sentence permits, to establish in them the will to lead law-abiding and self-supporting lives after their release and to fit them to do so. The treatment shall be such as will encourage their self-respect and develop their sense of responsibility.

66. (1) To these ends, all appropriate means shall be used, including religious care in the countries where this is possible, education, vocational guidance and training, social casework, employment counselling, physical development and strengthening of moral character, in accordance with the individual needs of each prisoner, taking account of his social and criminal history, his physical and mental capacities and aptitudes, his personal temperament, the length of his sentence and his prospects after release.

(2) For every prisoner with a sentence of suitable length, the director shall receive, as soon as possible after his admission, full reports on all the matters referred to in the foregoing paragraph. Such reports shall always include a report by a medical officer, wherever possible qualified in psychiatry, on the physical and mental condition of the prisoner.

(3) The reports and other relevant documents shall be placed in an individual file. This file shall be kept up to date and classified in such a way that it can be consulted by the responsible personnel whenever the need arises.

Classification and individualization

67. The purposes of classification shall be:

(a) To separate from others those prisoners who, by reason of their criminal records or bad characters, are likely to exercise a bad influence;

(b) To divide the prisoners into classes in order to facilitate their treatment with a view to their social rehabilitation.

68. So far as possible separate institutions or separate sections of an institution shall be used for the treatment of the different classes of prisoners.

69. As soon as possible after admission and after a study of the personality of each prisoner with a sentence of suitable length, a programme of treatment shall be prepared for him in the light of the knowledge obtained about his individual needs, his capacities and dispositions.

Privileges

70. Systems of privileges appropriate for the different classes of prisoners and the different methods of treatment shall be established at every institution, in order to encourage good conduct, develop a sense of responsibility and secure the interest and co-operation of the prisoners in their treatment.

Work

71. (1) Prison labour must not be of an afflictive nature.

(2) All prisoners under sentence shall be required to work, subject to their physical and mental fitness as determined by the medical officer.

(3) Sufficient work of a useful nature shall be provided to keep prisoners actively employed for a normal working day.

(4) So far as possible the work provided shall be such as will maintain or increase the prisoners, ability to earn an honest living after release.

(5) Vocational training in useful trades shall be provided for prisoners able to profit thereby and especially for young prisoners.

(6) Within the limits compatible with proper vocational selection and with the requirements of institutional administration and discipline, the prisoners shall be able to choose the type of work they wish to perform.

72. (1) The organization and methods of work in the institutions shall resemble as closely as possible those of similar work outside institutions, so as to prepare prisoners for the conditions of normal occupational life.

(2) The interests of the prisoners and of their vocational training, however, must not be subordinated to the purpose of making a financial profit from an industry in the institution.

73. (1) Preferably institutional industries and farms should be operated directly by the administration and not by private contractors.

(2) Where prisoners are employed in work not controlled by the administration, they shall always be under the supervision of the institution's personnel. Unless the work is for other departments of the government the full normal wages for such work shall be paid to the administration by the persons to whom the labour is supplied, account being taken of the output of the prisoners.

74. (1) The precautions laid down to protect the safety and health of free workmen shall be equally observed in institutions.

(2) Provision shall be made to indemnify prisoners against industrial injury, including occupational disease, on terms not less favourable than those extended by law to free workmen.

75. (1) The maximum daily and weekly working hours of the prisoners shall be fixed by law or by administrative regulation, taking into account local rules or custom in regard to the employment of free workmen.

(2) The hours so fixed shall leave one rest day a week and sufficient time for education and other activities required as part of the treatment and rehabilitation of the prisoners.

76. (1) There shall be a system of equitable remuneration of the work of prisoners.

(2) Under the system prisoners shall be allowed to spend at least a part of their earnings on approved articles for their own use and to send a part of their earnings to their family.

(3) The system should also provide that a part of the earnings should be set aside by the administration so as to constitute a savings fund to be handed over to the prisoner on his release.

Education and recreation

77. (1) Provision shall be made for the further education of all prisoners capable of profiting thereby, including religious instruction in the countries where this is possible. The education of illiterates and young prisoners shall be compulsory and special attention shall be paid to it by the administration.

(2) So far as practicable, the education of prisoners shall be integrated with the educational system of the country so that after their release they may continue their education without difficulty.

78. Recreational and cultural activities shall be provided in all institutions for the benefit of the mental and physical health of prisoners.

Social relations and after-care

79. Special attention shall be paid to the maintenance and improvement of such relations between a prisoner and his family as are desirable in the best interests of both.

80. From the beginning of a prisoner's sentence consideration shall be given to his future after release and he shall be encouraged and assisted to maintain or establish such relations with persons or agencies outside the institution as may promote the best interests of his family and his own social rehabilitation.

81. (1) Services and agencies, governmental or otherwise, which assist released prisoners to re-establish themselves in society shall ensure, so far as is possible and necessary, that released prisoners be provided with appropriate documents and identification papers, have suitable s and work to go to, are suitably and adequately clothed having regard to the climate and season, and have sufficient means to reach their destination and maintain themselves in the period immediately following their release.

(2) The approved representatives of such agencies shall have all necessary access to the institution and to prisoners and shall be taken into consultation as to the future of a prisoner from the beginning of his sentence.

(3) It is desirable that the activities of such agencies shall be centralized or co-ordinated as far as possible in order to secure the best use of their efforts.

B. Insane and mentally abnormal prisoners

82. (1) Persons who are found to be insane shall not be detained in prisons and arrangements shall be made to remove them to mental institutions as soon as possible.

(2) Prisoners who suffer from other mental diseases or abnormalities shall be observed and treated in specialized institutions under medical management.

(3) During their stay in a prison, such prisoners shall be placed under the special supervision of a medical officer.

(4) The medical or psychiatric service of the penal institutions shall provide for the psychiatric treatment of all other prisoners who are in need of such treatment.

83. It is desirable that steps should be taken, by arrangement with the appropriate agencies, to ensure if necessary the continuation of psychiatric treatment after release and the provision of social-psychiatric after-care.

C. Prisoners under arrest or awaiting trial

84. (1) Persons arrested or imprisoned by reason of a criminal charge against them, who are detained either in police custody or in prison custody (jail) but have not yet been tried and sentenced, will be referred to as "untried prisoners" hereinafter in these rules.

(2) Unconvicted prisoners are presumed to be innocent and shall be treated as such.

(3) Without prejudice to legal rules for the protection of individual liberty or prescribing the procedure to be observed in respect of untried prisoners, these prisoners shall benefit by a special regime which is described in the following rules in its essential requirements only.

85. (1) Untried prisoners shall be kept separate from convicted prisoners.

(2) Young untried prisoners shall be kept separate from adults and shall in principle be detained in separate institutions.

86. Untried prisoners shall sleep singly in separate rooms, with the reservation of different local custom in respect of the climate.

87. Within the limits compatible with the good order of the institution, untried prisoners may, if they so desire, have their food procured at their own expense from the outside, either through the administration or through their family or friends. Otherwise, the administration shall provide their food.

88. (1) An untried prisoner shall be allowed to wear his own clothing if it is clean and suitable.

(2) If he wears prison dress, it shall be different from that supplied to convicted prisoners.

89. An untried prisoner shall always be offered opportunity to work, but shall not be required to work. If he chooses to work, he shall be paid for it.

90. An untried prisoner shall be allowed to procure at his own expense or at the expense of a third party such books, newspapers, writing materials and other means of occupation as are compatible with the interests of the administration of justice and the security and good order of the institution.

91. An untried prisoner shall be allowed to be visited and treated by his own doctor or dentist if there is reasonable ground for his application and he is able to pay any expenses incurred.

92. An untried prisoner shall be allowed to inform immediately his family of his detention and shall be given all reasonable facilities for communicating with his family and friends, and for receiving visits from them, subject only to restrictions and supervision as are necessary in the interests of the administration of justice and of the security and good order of the institution.

93. For the purposes of his defence, an untried prisoner shall be allowed to apply for free legal aid where such aid is available, and to receive visits from his legal adviser with a view to his defence and to prepare and hand to him confidential instructions. For these purposes, he shall if he so desires be supplied with writing material. Interviews between the prisoner and his legal adviser may be within sight but not within the hearing of a police or institution official.

D. Civil prisoners

94. In countries where the law permits imprisonment for debt, or by order of a court under any other non-criminal process, persons so imprisoned shall not be subjected to any greater restriction or severity than is necessary to ensure safe custody and good order. Their treatment shall be not less favourable than that of untried prisoners, with the reservation, however, that they may possibly be required to work.

E. Persons arrested or detained without charge

95. Without prejudice to the provisions of article 9 of the International Covenant on Civil and Political Rights, persons arrested or imprisoned without charge shall be accorded the same protection as that accorded under part I and part II, section C. Relevant provisions of part II, section A, shall likewise be applicable where their application may be conducive to the benefit of this special group of persons in custody, provided that no measures shall be taken implying that re-education or rehabilitation is in any way appropriate to persons not convicted of any criminal offence.

3.2 UNITED NATIONS: BODY OF PRINCIPLES FOR THE PROTECTION OF ALL PERSONS UNDER ANY FORM OF DETENTION OR IMPRISONMENT, 1988[2]

The General Assembly,

Recalling its resolution 35/177 of 15 December 1980, in which it referred the task of elaborating the draft Body of Principles for the Protection of All Persons under Any Form of Detention or Imprisonment to the Sixth Committee and decided to establish an open-ended working group for that purpose,

Taking note of the report of the Working Group on the Draft Body of Principles for the Protection of All Persons under Any Form of Detention or Imprisonment, which met during the forty-third session of the General Assembly and completed the elaboration of the draft Body of Principles,

Considering that the Working Group decided to submit the text of the draft Body of Principles to the Sixth Committee for its consideration and adoption,

Convinced that the adoption of the draft Body of Principles would make an important contribution to the protection of human rights,

Considering the need to ensure the wide dissemination of the text of the Body of Principles,

1. Approves the Body of Principles for the Protection of All Persons under Any Form of Detention or Imprisonment, the text of which is annexed to the present resolution;

2. Expresses its appreciation to the Working Group on the Draft Body of Principles for the Protection of All Persons under Any Form of Detention or Imprisonment for its important contribution to the elaboration of the Body of Principles;

3. Requests the Secretary-General to inform the States Members of the United Nations or members of specialized agencies of the adoption of the Body of Principles;

---

[2] A/RES/43/173, 9 December 1988.

4. Urges that every effort be made so that the Body of Principles becomes generally known and respected.

ANNEX

Body of Principles for the Protection of All Persons under Any Form of Detention or Imprisonment

Scope of the Body of Principles

These principles apply for the protection of all persons under any form of detention or imprisonment.

Use of terms

For the purposes of the Body of Principles:

(a) "Arrest" means the act of apprehending a person for the alleged commission of an offence or by the action of an authority;

(b) "Detained person" means any person deprived of personal liberty except as a result of conviction for an offence;

(c) "Imprisoned person" means any person deprived of personal liberty as a result of conviction for an offence;

(d) "Detention" means the condition of detained persons as defined above;

(e) "Imprisonment" means the condition of imprisoned persons as defined above;

(f) The words "a judicial or other authority" mean a judicial or other authority under the law whose status and tenure should afford the strongest possible guarantees of competence, impartiality and independence.

Principle 1

All persons under any form of detention or imprisonment shall be treated in a humane manner and with respect for the inherent dignity of the human person.

Principle 2

Arrest, detention or imprisonment shall only be carried out strictly in accordance with the provisions of the law and by competent officials or persons authorized for that purpose.

Principle 3

There shall be no restriction upon or derogation from any of the human rights of persons under any form of detention or imprisonment recognized or existing in any State pursuant to law, conventions, regulations or custom on the pretext that this Body of Principles does not recognize such rights or that it recognizes them to a lesser extent.

Principle 4

Any form of detention or imprisonment and all measures affecting the human rights of a person under any form of detention or imprisonment shall be ordered by, or be subject to the effective control of, a judicial or other authority.

Principle 5

1. These principles shall be applied to all persons within the territory of any given State, without distinction of any kind, such as race, colour, sex, language, religion or religious belief, political or other opinion, national, ethnic or social origin, property, birth or other status.

2. Measures applied under the law and designed solely to protect the rights and special status of women, especially pregnant women and nursing mothers, children and juveniles, aged, sick or handicapped persons shall not be deemed to be discriminatory. The need for, and the application of, such measures shall always be subject to review by a judicial or other authority.

Principle 6

No person under any form of detention or imprisonment shall be subjected to torture or to cruel, inhuman or degrading treatment or punishment.[3] No circumstance whatever may be invoked as a justification for torture or other cruel, inhuman or degrading treatment or punishment.

Principle 7

1. States should prohibit by law any act contrary to the rights and duties contained in these principles, make any such act subject to appropriate sanctions and conduct impartial investigations upon complaints.

---

[3] The term "cruel, inhuman or degrading treatment or punishment" should be interpreted so as to extend the widest possible protection against abuses, whether physical or mental, including the holding of a detained or imprisoned person in conditions which deprive him, temporarily or permanently, of the use of any of his natural senses, such as sight or hearing, or of his awareness of place and the passing of time.

2. Officials who have reason to believe that a violation of this Body of Principles has occurred or is about to occur shall report the matter to their superior authorities and, where necessary, to other appropriate authorities or organs vested with reviewing or remedial powers.

3. Any other person who has ground to believe that a violation of this Body of Principles has occurred or is about to occur shall have the right to report the matter to the superiors of the officials involved as well as to other appropriate authorities or organs vested with reviewing or remedial powers.

Principle 8

Persons in detention shall be subject to treatment appropriate to their unconvicted status. Accordingly, they shall, whenever possible, be kept separate from imprisoned persons.

Principle 9

The authorities which arrest a person, keep him under detention or investigate the case shall exercise only the powers granted to them under the law and the exercise of these powers shall be subject to recourse to a judicial or other authority.

Principle l0

Anyone who is arrested shall be informed at the time of his arrest of the reason for his arrest and shall be promptly informed of any charges against him.

Principle 11

1. A person shall not be kept in detention without being given an effective opportunity to be heard promptly by a judicial or other authority. A detained person shall have the right to defend himself or to be assisted by counsel as prescribed by law.

2. A detained person and his counsel, if any, shall receive prompt and full communication of any order of detention, together with the reasons therefor.

3. A judicial or other authority shall be empowered to review as appropriate the continuance of detention.

Principle 12

1. There shall be duly recorded:

(a) The reasons for the arrest;

(b) The time of the arrest and the taking of the arrested person to a place of custody as well as that of his first appearance before a judicial or other authority;

(c) The identity of the law enforcement officials concerned;

(d) Precise information concerning the place of custody.

2. Such records shall be communicated to the detained person, or his counsel, if any, in the form prescribed by law.

Principle 13

Any person shall, at the moment of arrest and at the commencement of detention or imprisonment, or promptly thereafter, be provided by the authority responsible for his arrest, detention or imprisonment, respectively, with information on and an explanation of his rights and how to avail himself of such rights.

Principle 14

A person who does not adequately understand or speak the language used by the authorities responsible for his arrest, detention or imprisonment is entitled to receive promptly in a language which he understands the information referred to in principle 10, principle 11, paragraph 2, principle 12, paragraph 1, and principle 13 and to have the assistance, free of charge, if necessary, of an interpreter in connection with legal proceedings subsequent to his arrest.

Principle 15

Notwithstanding the exceptions contained in principle 16, paragraph 4, and principle 18, paragraph 3, communication of the detained or imprisoned person with the outside world, and in particular his family or counsel, shall not be denied for more than a matter of days.

Principle 16

1. Promptly after arrest and after each transfer from one place of detention or imprisonment to another, a detained or imprisoned person shall be entitled to notify or to require the competent authority to notify members of his family or other appropriate persons of his choice of his arrest, detention or imprisonment or of the transfer and of the place where he is kept in custody.

2. If a detained or imprisoned person is a foreigner, he shall also be promptly informed of his right to communicate by appropriate means with a consular post or the diplomatic mission of the State of which he is a national or which is otherwise entitled to receive such communication in accordance with international law or with the representative of the competent international organization, if he is a refugee or is otherwise under the protection of an intergovernmental organization.

3. If a detained or imprisoned person is a juvenile or is incapable of understanding his entitlement, the competent authority shall on its own initiative undertake the notification referred to in the present principle. Special attention shall be given to notifying parents or guardians.

4. Any notification referred to in the present principle shall be made or permitted to be made without delay. The competent authority may however delay a notification for a reasonable period where exceptional needs of the investigation so require.

Principle 17

1. A detained person shall be entitled to have the assistance of a legal counsel. He shall be informed of his right by the competent authority promptly after arrest and shall be provided with reasonable facilities for exercising it.

2. If a detained person does not have a legal counsel of his own choice, he shall be entitled to have a legal counsel assigned to him by a judicial or other authority in all cases where the interests of justice so require and without payment by him if he does not have sufficient means to pay.

Principle 18

1. A detained or imprisoned person shall be entitled to communicate and consult with his legal counsel.

2. A detained or imprisoned person shall be allowed adequate time and facilities for consultations with his legal counsel.

3. The right of a detained or imprisoned person to be visited by and to consult and communicate, without delay or censorship and in full confidentiality, with his legal counsel may not be suspended or restricted save in exceptional circumstances, to be specified by law or lawful regulations, when it is considered indispensable by a judicial or other authority in order to maintain security and good order.

4. Interviews between a detained or imprisoned person and his legal counsel may be within sight, but not within the hearing, of a law enforcement official.

5. Communications between a detained or imprisoned person and his legal counsel mentioned in the present principle shall be inadmissible as evidence against the detained or imprisoned person unless they are connected with a continuing or contemplated crime.

Principle 19

A detained or imprisoned person shall have the right to be visited by and to correspond with, in particular, members of his family and shall be given adequate opportunity to communicate with the outside world, subject to reasonable conditions and restrictions as specified by law or lawful regulations.

Principle 20

If a detained or imprisoned person so requests, he shall if possible be kept in a place of detention or imprisonment reasonably near his usual place of residence.

Principle 21

1. It shall be prohibited to take undue advantage of the situation of a detained or imprisoned person for the purpose of compelling him to confess, to incriminate himself otherwise or to testify against any other person.

2. No detained person while being interrogated shall be subject to violence, threats or methods of interrogation which impair his capacity of decision or his judgement.

Principle 22

No detained or imprisoned person shall, even with his consent, be subjected to any medical or scientific experimentation which may be detrimental to his health.

Principle 23

1. The duration of any interrogation of a detained or imprisoned person and of the intervals between interrogations as well as the identity of the officials who conducted the interrogations and other persons present shall be recorded and certified in such form as may be prescribed by law.

2. A detained or imprisoned person, or his counsel when provided by law, shall have access to the information described in paragraph 1 of the present principle.

Principle 24

A proper medical examination shall be offered to a detained or imprisoned person as promptly as possible after his admission to the place of detention or imprisonment, and thereafter medical care and treatment shall be provided whenever necessary. This care and treatment shall be provided free of charge.

Principle 25

A detained or imprisoned person or his counsel shall, subject only to reasonable conditions to ensure security and good order in the place of detention or imprisonment, have the right to request or petition a judicial or other authority for a second medical examination or opinion.

Principle 26

The fact that a detained or imprisoned person underwent a medical examination, the name of the physician and the results of such an examination shall be duly recorded. Access to such records shall be ensured. Modalities therefor shall be in accordance with relevant rules of domestic law.

Principle 27

Non-compliance with these principles in obtaining evidence shall be taken into account in determining the admissibility of such evidence against a detained or imprisoned person.

Principle 28

A detained or imprisoned person shall have the right to obtain within the limits of available resources, if from public sources, reasonable quantities of educational, cultural and informational material, subject to reasonable conditions to ensure security and good order in the place of detention or imprisonment.

Principle 29

1. In order to supervise the strict observance of relevant laws and regulations, places of detention shall be visited regularly by qualified and experienced persons appointed by, and responsible to, a competent authority distinct from the authority directly in charge of the administration of the place of detention or imprisonment.

2. A detained or imprisoned person shall have the right to communicate freely and in full confidentiality with the persons who visit the places of detention or imprisonment in

accordance with paragraph l of the present principle, subject to reasonable conditions to ensure security and good order in such places.

Principle 30

1. The types of conduct of the detained or imprisoned person that constitute disciplinary offences during detention or imprisonment, the description and duration of disciplinary punishment that may be inflicted and the authorities competent to impose such punishment shall be specified by law or lawful regulations and duly published.

2. A detained or imprisoned person shall have the right to be heard before disciplinary action is taken. He shall have the right to bring such action to higher authorities for review.

Principle 31

The appropriate authorities shall endeavour to ensure, according to domestic law, assistance when needed to dependent and, in particular, minor members of the families of detained or imprisoned persons and shall devote a particular measure of care to the appropriate custody of children left without supervision.

Principle 32

1. A detained person or his counsel shall be entitled at any time to take proceedings according to domestic law before a judicial or other authority to challenge the lawfulness of his detention in order to obtain his release without delay, if it is unlawful.

2. The proceedings referred to in paragraph l of the present principle shall be simple and expeditious and at no cost for detained persons without adequate means. The detaining authority shall produce without unreasonable delay the detained person before the reviewing authority.

Principle 33

1. A detained or imprisoned person or his counsel shall have the right to make a request or complaint regarding his treatment, in particular in case of torture or other cruel, inhuman or degrading treatment, to the authorities responsible for the administration of the place of detention and to higher authorities and, when necessary, to appropriate authorities vested with reviewing or remedial powers.

2. In those cases where neither the detained or imprisoned person nor his counsel has the possibility to exercise his rights under paragraph 1 of the present principle, a member of the

family of the detained or imprisoned person or any other person who has knowledge of the case may exercise such rights.

3. Confidentiality concerning the request or complaint shall be maintained if so requested by the complainant.

4. Every request or complaint shall be promptly dealt with and replied to without undue delay. If the request or complaint is rejected or, in case of inordinate delay, the complainant shall be entitled to bring it before a judicial or other authority. Neither the detained or imprisoned person nor any complainant under paragraph 1 of the present principle shall suffer prejudice for making a request or complaint.

Principle 34

Whenever the death or disappearance of a detained or imprisoned person occurs during his detention or imprisonment, an inquiry into the cause of death or disappearance shall be held by a judicial or other authority, either on its own motion or at the instance of a member of the family of such a person or any person who has knowledge of the case. When circumstances so warrant, such an inquiry shall be held on the same procedural basis whenever the death or disappearance occurs shortly after the termination of the detention or imprisonment. The findings of such inquiry or a report thereon shall be made available upon request, unless doing so would jeopardize an ongoing criminal investigation.

Principle 35

1. Damage incurred because of acts or omissions by a public official contrary to the rights contained in these principles shall be compensated according to the applicable rules on liability provided by domestic law.

2. Information required to be recorded under these principles shall be available in accordance with procedures provided by domestic law for use in claiming compensation under the present principle.

Principle 36

1. A detained person suspected of or charged with a criminal offence shall be presumed innocent and shall be treated as such until proved guilty according to law in a public trial at which he has had all the guarantees necessary for his defence.

2. The arrest or detention of such a person pending investigation and trial shall be carried out only for the purposes of the administration of justice on grounds and under conditions and

procedures specified by law. The imposition of restrictions upon such a person which are not strictly required for the purpose of the detention or to prevent hindrance to the process of investigation or the administration of justice, or for the maintenance of security and good order in the place of detention shall be forbidden.

Principle 37

A person detained on a criminal charge shall be brought before a judicial or other authority provided by law promptly after his arrest. Such authority shall decide without delay upon the lawfulness and necessity of detention. No person may be kept under detention pending investigation or trial except upon the written order of such an authority. A detained person shall, when brought before such an authority, have the right to make a statement on the treatment received by him while in custody.

Principle 38

A person detained on a criminal charge shall be entitled to trial within a reasonable time or to release pending trial.

Principle 39

Except in special cases provided for by law, a person detained on a criminal charge shall be entitled, unless a judicial or other authority decides otherwise in the interest of the administration of justice, to release pending trial subject to the conditions that may be imposed in accordance with the law. Such authority shall keep the necessity of detention under review.

General clause

Nothing in this Body of Principles shall be construed as restricting or derogating from any right defined in the International Covenant on Civil and Political Rights.

3.3 UNITED NATIONS STANDARD MINIMUM RULES FOR NON-CUSTODIAL MEASURES, 1990[4]

(The Tokyo Rules)

The General Assembly,

Bearing in mind the Universal Declaration of Human Rights and the International Covenant on Civil and Political Rights, as well as other international human rights instruments pertaining to the rights of persons in conflict with the law,

Bearing in mind also the Standard Minimum Rules for the Treatment of Prisoners, adopted by the First United Nations Congress on the Prevention of Crime and the Treatment of Offenders, and the important contribution of those Rules to national policies and practices,

Recalling resolution 8 of the Sixth United Nations Congress on the Prevention of Crime and the Treatment of Offenders on alternatives to imprisonment,

Recalling also resolution 16 of the Seventh United Nations Congress on the Prevention of Crime and the Treatment of Offenders on the reduction of the prison population, alternatives to imprisonment, and social integration of offenders,

Recalling further section XI of Economic and Social Council resolution 1986/10 of 21 May 1986, on alternatives to imprisonment, in which the Secretary-General was requested to prepare a report on alternatives to imprisonment for the Eighth United Nations Congress on the Prevention of Crime and the Treatment of Offenders and to study that question with a view to the formulation of basic principles in that area, with the assistance of the United Nations institutes for the prevention of crime and the treatment of offenders,

Recognizing the need to develop local, national, regional and international approaches and strategies in the field of non-institutional treatment of offenders and the need to formulate standard minimum rules, as emphasized in the section of the report of the Committee on Crime Prevention and Control on its fourth session, concerning the methods and measures likely to be most effective in preventing crime and improving the treatment of offenders,

Convinced that alternatives to imprisonment can be an effective means of treating offenders within the community to the best advantage of both the offenders and society,

---

[4] A/RES/45/110, 14 December 1990.

Aware that the restriction of liberty is justifiable only from the viewpoints of public safety, crime prevention, just retribution and deterrence and that the ultimate goal of the criminal justice system is the reintegration of the offender into society,

Emphasizing that the increasing prison population and prison overcrowding in many countries constitute factors that create difficulties for the proper implementation of the Standard Minimum Rules for the Treatment of Prisoners,

Noting with appreciation the work accomplished by the Committee on Crime Prevention and Control, as well as by the Interregional Preparatory Meeting for the Eighth United Nations Congress on the Prevention of Crime and the Treatment of Offenders on topic II, "Criminal justice policies in relation to problems of imprisonment, other penal sanctions and alternative measures", and by the regional preparatory meetings for the Eighth Congress,

Expressing its gratitude to the United Nations Asia and Far East Institute for the Prevention of Crime and the Treatment of Offenders for the work accomplished in the development of standard minimum rules for non-custodial measures, as well as to the various intergovernmental and non-governmental organizations involved, in particular, the International Penal and Penitentiary Foundation for its contribution to the preparatory work,

1. Adopts the United Nations Standard Minimum Rules for Non-custodial Measures, contained in the annex to the present resolution, and approves the recommendation of the Committee on Crime Prevention and Control that the Rules should be known as "the Tokyo Rules";

2. Recommends the Tokyo Rules for implementation at the national, regional and interregional levels, taking into account the political, economic, social and cultural circumstances and traditions of countries;

3. Calls upon Member States to apply the Tokyo Rules in their policies and practice;

4. Invites Member States to bring the Tokyo Rules to the attention of, in particular, law enforcement officials, prosecutors, judges, probation officers, lawyers, victims, offenders, social services and non-governmental organizations involved in the application of non-custodial measures, as well as members of the executive, the legislature and the general public;

5. Requests Member States to report on the implementation of the Tokyo Rules every five years, beginning in 1994;

6. Urges the regional commissions, the United Nations institutes for the prevention of crime and the treatment of offenders, specialized agencies and other entities within the United

Nations system, other intergovernmental organizations concerned and non-governmental organizations in consultative status with the Economic and Social Council to be actively involved in the implementation of the Tokyo Rules;

7. Calls upon the Committee on Crime Prevention and Control to consider, as a matter of priority, the implementation of the present resolution;

8. Requests the Secretary-General to take the necessary steps to prepare a commentary to the Tokyo Rules, which is to be submitted to the Committee on Crime Prevention and Control at its twelfth session for approval and further dissemination, paying special attention to the legal safeguards, the implementation of the Rules and the development of similar guidelines at the regional level;

9. Invites the United Nations institutes for the prevention of crime and the treatment of offenders to assist the Secretary-General in that task;

10. Urges intergovernmental and non-governmental organizations and other entities concerned to remain actively involved in this initiative;

11. Requests the Secretary-General to take steps, as appropriate, to ensure the widest possible dissemination of the Tokyo Rules, including their transmission to Governments, interested intergovernmental and non-governmental organizations and other parties concerned;

12. Also requests the Secretary-General to prepare every five years, beginning in 1994, a report on the implementation of the Tokyo Rules for submission to the Committee on Crime Prevention and Control;

13. Further requests the Secretary-General to assist Member States, at their request, in the implementation of the Tokyo Rules and to report regularly thereon to the Committee on Crime Prevention and Control;

14. Requests that the present resolution and the text of the annex be brought to the attention of all United Nations bodies concerned and be included in the next edition of the United Nations publication entitled Human Rights: A Compilation of International Instruments.

ANNEX

United Nations Standard Minimum Rules for Non-custodial Measures (The Tokyo Rules)

I. GENERAL PRINCIPLES

1. Fundamental aims

1.1 The present Standard Minimum Rules provide a set of basic principles to promote the use of non-custodial measures, as well as minimum safeguards for persons subject to alternatives to imprisonment.

1.2 The Rules are intended to promote greater community involvement in the management of criminal justice, specifically in the treatment of offenders, as well as to promote among offenders a sense of responsibility towards society.

1.3 The Rules shall be implemented taking into account the political, economic, social and cultural conditions of each country and the aims and objectives of its criminal justice system.

1.4 When implementing the Rules, Member States shall endeavour to ensure a proper balance between the rights of individual offenders, the rights of victims, and the concern of society for public safety and crime prevention.

1.5 Member States shall develop non-custodial measures within their legal systems to provide other options, thus reducing the use of imprisonment, and to rationalize criminal justice policies, taking into account the observance of human rights, the requirements of social justice and the rehabilitation needs of the offender.

2. The scope of non-custodial measures

2.1 The relevant provisions of the present Rules shall be applied to all persons subject to prosecution, trial or the execution of a sentence, at all stages of the administration of criminal justice. For the purposes of the Rules, these persons are referred to as "offenders", irrespective of whether they are suspected, accused or sentenced.

2.2 The Rules shall be applied without any discrimination on the grounds of race, colour, sex, age, language, religion, political or other opinion, national or social origin, property, birth or other status.

2.3 In order to provide greater flexibility consistent with the nature and gravity of the offence, with the personality and background of the offender and with the protection of society and to avoid unnecessary use of imprisonment, the criminal justice system should provide a wide range of non-custodial measures, from pre-trial to post-sentencing dispositions. The number and types of non-custodial measures available should be determined in such a way that consistent sentencing remains possible.

2.4 The development of new non-custodial measures should be encouraged and closely monitored and their use systematically evaluated.

2.5 Consideration shall be given to dealing with offenders in the community, avoiding as far as possible resort to formal proceedings or trial by a court, in accordance with legal safeguards and the rule of law.

2.6 Non-custodial measures should be used in accordance with the principle of minimum intervention.

2.7 The use of non-custodial measures should be part of the movement towards depenalization and decriminalization instead of interfering with or delaying efforts in that direction.

3. Legal Safeguards

3.1 The introduction, definition and application of non-custodial measures shall be prescribed by law.

3.2 The selection of a non-custodial measure shall be based on an assessment of established criteria in respect of both the nature and gravity of the offence and the personality, the background of the offender, the purposes of sentencing and the rights of victims.

3.3 Discretion by the judicial or other competent independent authority shall be exercised at all stages of the proceedings by ensuring full accountability and only in accordance with the rule of law.

3.4 Non-custodial measures imposing an obligation on the offender, applied before or instead of formal proceedings or trial, shall require the offender's consent.

3.5 Decisions on the imposition of non-custodial measures shall be subject to review by a judicial or other competent independent authority, upon application by the offender.

3.6 The offender shall be entitled to make a request or complaint to a judicial or other competent independent authority on matters affecting his or her individual rights in the implementation of non-custodial measures.

3.7 Appropriate machinery shall be provided for the recourse and, if possible, redress of any grievance related to non-compliance with internationally recognized human rights.

3.8 Non-custodial measures shall not involve medical or psychological experimentation on, or undue risk of physical or mental injury to, the offender.

3.9 The dignity of the offender subject to non-custodial measures shall be protected at all times.

3.10 In the implementation of non-custodial measures, the offender's rights shall not be restricted further than was authorized by the competent authority that rendered the original decision.

3.11 In the application of non-custodial measures, the offender's right to privacy shall be respected, as shall be the right to privacy of the offender's family.

3.12 The offender's personal records shall be kept strictly confidential and closed to third parties. Access to such records shall be limited to persons directly concerned with the disposition of the offender's case or to other duly authorized persons.

4. Saving Clause

4.1 Nothing in the present Rules shall be interpreted as precluding the application of the Standard Minimum Rules for the Treatment of Prisoners, the United Nations Standard Minimum Rules for the Administration of Juvenile Justice (The Beijing Rules), the Body of Principles for the Protection of All Persons under Any Form of Detention or Imprisonment or any other human rights instruments and standards recognized by the international community and relating to the treatment of offenders and the protection of their basic human rights.

II. PRE-TRIAL STAGE

5. Pre-trial dispositions

5.1 Where appropriate and compatible with the legal system, the police, the prosecution service or other agencies dealing with criminal cases should be empowered to discharge the offender if they consider that it is not necessary to proceed with the case for the protection of society, crime prevention or the promotion of respect for the law and the rights of victims. For the purpose of deciding upon the appropriateness of discharge or determination of proceedings, a set of established criteria shall be developed within each legal system. For minor cases the prosecutor may impose suitable non-custodial measures, as appropriate.

6. Avoidance of pre-trial detention

6.1 Pre-trial detention shall be used as a means of last resort in criminal proceedings, with due regard for the investigation of the alleged offence and for the protection of society and the victim.

6.2 Alternatives to pre-trial detention shall be employed at as early a stage as possible. Pre-trial detention shall last no longer than necessary to achieve the objectives stated under rule 5.1 and shall be administered humanely and with respect for the inherent dignity of human beings.

6.3 The offender shall have the right to appeal to a judicial or other competent independent authority in cases where pre-trial detention is employed.

III. TRIAL AND SENTENCING STAGE

7. Social inquiry reports

7.1 If the possibility of social inquiry reports exists, the judicial authority may avail itself of a report prepared by a competent, authorized official or agency . The report should contain social information on the offender that is relevant to the person's pattern of offending and current offences. It should also contain information and recommendations that are relevant to the sentencing procedure. The report shall be factual, objective and unbiased, with any expression of opinion clearly identified.

8. Sentencing dispositions

8.1 The judicial authority, having at its disposal a range of noncustodial measures, should take into consideration in making its decision the rehabilitative needs of the offender, the protection of society and the interests of the victim, who should be consulted whenever appropriate.

8.2 Sentencing authorities may dispose of cases in the following ways:

(a) Verbal sanctions, such as admonition, reprimand and warning;

(b) Conditional discharge;

(c) Status penalties;

(d) Economic sanctions and monetary penalties, such as fines and day-fines;

(e) Confiscation or an expropriation order;

(f) Restitution to the victim or a compensation order;

(g) Suspended or deferred sentence;

(h) Probation and judicial supervision;

(i) A community service order;

(j) Referral to an attendance centre;

(k) House arrest;

(l) Any other mode of non-institutional treatment;

(m) Some combination of the measures listed above.

IV. POST-SENTENCING STAGE

9. Post-sentencing dispositions

9.1 The competent authority shall have at its disposal a wide range of post-sentencing alternatives in order to avoid institutionalization and to assist offenders in their early reintegration into society.

9.2 Post-sentencing dispositions may include:

(a) Furlough and half-way houses;

(b) Work or education release;

(c) Various forms of parole;

(d) Remission;

(e) Pardon.

9.3 The decision on post-sentencing dispositions, except in the case of pardon, shall be subject to review by a judicial or other competent independent authority, upon application of the offender.

9.4 Any form of release from an institution to a non-custodial programme shall be considered at the earliest possible stage.

V. IMPLEMENTATION OF NON-CUSTODIAL MEASURES

10. Supervision

10.1 The purpose of supervision is to reduce reoffending and to assist the offender's integration into society in a way which minimizes the likelihood of a return to crime.

10.2 If a non-custodial measure entails supervision, the latter shall be carried out by a competent authority under the specific conditions prescribed by law.

10.3 Within the framework of a given non-custodial measure, the most suitable type of supervision and treatment should be determined for each individual case aimed at assisting the offender to work on his or her offending. Supervision and treatment should be periodically reviewed and adjusted as necessary.

10.4 Offenders should, when needed, be provided with psychological, social and material assistance and with opportunities to strengthen links with the community and facilitate their reintegration into society.

11. Duration

11.1 The duration of a non-custodial measure shall not exceed the period established by the competent authority in accordance with the law.

11.2 Provision may be made for early termination of the measure if the offender has responded favourably to it.

12. Conditions

12.1 If the competent authority shall determine the conditions to be observed by the offender, it should take into account both the needs of society and the needs and rights of the offender and the victim.

12.2 The conditions to be observed shall be practical, precise and as few as possible, and be aimed at reducing the likelihood of an offender relapsing into criminal behaviour and of increasing the offender's chances of social integration, taking into account the needs of the victim.

12.3 At the beginning of the application of a non-custodial measure, the offender shall receive an explanation, orally and in writing, of the conditions governing the application of the measure, including the offender's obligations and rights.

12.4 The conditions may be modified by the competent authority under the established statutory provisions, in accordance with the progress made by the offender.

13. Treatment process

13.1 Within the framework of a given non-custodial measure, in appropriate cases, various schemes, such as case-work, group therapy, residential programmes and the specialized treatment of various categories of offenders, should be developed to meet the needs of offenders more effectively.

13.2 Treatment should be conducted by professionals who have suitable training and practical experience.

13.3 When it is decided that treatment is necessary, efforts should be made to understand the offender's background, personality, aptitude, intelligence, values and, especially, the circumstances leading to the commission of the offence.

13.4 The competent authority may involve the community and social support systems in the application of non-custodial measures.

13.5 Case-load assignments shall be maintained as far as practicable at a manageable level to ensure the effective implementation of treatment programmes.

13.6 For each offender, a case record shall be established and maintained by the competent authority.

14. Discipline and breach of conditions

14.1 A breach of the conditions to be observed by the offender may result in a modification or revocation of the non-custodial measure.

14.2 The modification or revocation of the non-custodial measure shall be made by the competent authority; this shall be done only after a careful examination of the facts adduced by both the supervising officer and the offender.

14.3 The failure of a non-custodial measure should not automatically lead to the imposition of a custodial measure.

14.4 In the event of a modification or revocation of the non-custodial measure, the competent authority shall attempt to establish a suitable alternative non-custodial measure. A sentence of imprisonment may be imposed only in the absence of other suitable alternatives.

14.5 The power to arrest and detain the offender under supervision in cases where there is a breach of the conditions shall be prescribed by law.

14.6 Upon modification or revocation of the non-custodial measure, the offender shall have the right to appeal to a judicial or other competent independent authority.

VI. STAFF

15. Recruitment

15.1 There shall be no discrimination in the recruitment of staff on the grounds of race, colour, sex, age, language, religion, political or other opinion, national or social origin, property, birth or other status. The policy regarding staff recruitment should take into consideration national policies of affirmative action and reflect the diversity of the offenders to be supervised.

15.2 Persons appointed to apply non-custodial measures should be personally suitable and, whenever possible, have appropriate professional training and practical experience. Such qualifications shall be clearly specified.

15.3 To secure and retain qualified professional staff, appropriate service status, adequate salary and benefits commensurate with the nature of the work should be ensured and ample opportunities should be provided for professional growth and career development.

16. Staff training

16.1 The objective of training shall be to make clear to staff their responsibilities with regard to rehabilitating the offender, ensuring the offender's rights and protecting society. Training should also give staff an understanding of the need to cooperate in and coordinate activities with the agencies concerned.

16.2 Before entering duty, staff shall be given training that includes instruction on the nature of non-custodial measures, the purposes of supervision and the various modalities of the application of non-custodial measures.

16.3 After entering duty, staff shall maintain and improve their knowledge and professional capacity by attending in-service training and refresher courses. Adequate facilities shall be made available for that purpose.

VII. VOLUNTEERS AND OTHER COMMUNITY RESOURCES

17. Public participation

17.1 Public participation should be encouraged as it is a major resource and one of the most important factors in improving ties between offenders undergoing non-custodial measures and the family and community. It should complement the efforts of the criminal justice administration.

17.2 Public participation should be regarded as an opportunity for members of the community to contribute to the protection of their society.

18. Public understanding and cooperation

18.1 Government agencies, the private sector and the general public should be encouraged to support voluntary organizations that promote noncustodial measures.

18.2 Conferences, seminars, symposia and other activities should be regularly organized to stimulate awareness of the need for public participation in the application of non-custodial measures.

18.3 All forms of the mass media should be utilized to help to create a constructive public attitude, leading to activities conducive to a broader application of non-custodial treatment and the social integration of offenders.

18.4 Every effort should be made to inform the public of the importance of its role in the implementation of non-custodial measures.

19. Volunteers

19.1 Volunteers shall be carefully screened and recruited on the basis of their aptitude for and interest in the work involved. They shall be properly trained for the specific responsibilities to be discharged by them and shall have access to support and counselling from, and the opportunity to consult with, the competent authority.

19.2 Volunteers should encourage offenders and their families to develop meaningful ties with the community and a broader sphere of contact by providing counselling and other appropriate forms of assistance according to their capacity and the offenders' needs.

19.3 Volunteers shall be insured against accident, injury and public liability when carrying out their duties. They shall be reimbursed for authorized expenditures incurred in the course of their work. Public recognition should be extended to them for the services they render for the well-being of the community.

VIII. RESEARCH, PLANNING, POLICY FORMULATION AND EVALUATION

20. Research and Planning

20.1 As an essential aspect of the planning process, efforts should be made to involve both public and private bodies in the organization and promotion of research on the non-custodial treatment of offenders.

20.2 Research on the problems that confront clients, practitioners, the community and policy-makers should be carried out on a regular basis. 20.3 Research and information mechanisms should be built into the criminal justice system for the collection and analysis of data and statistics on the implementation of non-custodial treatment for offenders.

21. Policy formulation and programme development

21.1 Programmes for non-custodial measures should be systematically planned and implemented as an integral part of the criminal justice system within the national development process.

21.2 Regular evaluations should be carried out with a view to implementing non-custodial measures more effectively.

21.3 Periodic reviews should be concluded to assess the objectives, functioning and effectiveness of non-custodial measures.

22. Linkages with relevant agencies and activities

22.1 Suitable mechanisms should be evolved at various levels to facilitate the establishment of linkages between services responsible for noncustodial measures, other branches of the criminal justice system, social development and welfare agencies, both governmental and non-governmental, in such fields as health, housing, education and labour, and the mass media.

23. International Cooperation

23.1 Efforts shall be made to promote scientific cooperation between countries in the field of non-institutional treatment. Research, training, technical assistance and the exchange of information among Member States on non-custodial measures should be strengthened, through the United Nations institutes for the prevention of crime and the treatment of offenders, in close collaboration with the Crime Prevention and Criminal Justice Branch of the Centre for Social Development and Humanitarian Affairs of the United Nations Secretariat.

23.2 Comparative studies and the harmonization of legislative provisions should be furthered to expand the range of non-institutional options and facilitate their application across national frontiers, in accordance with the Model Treaty on the Transfer of Supervision of Offenders Conditionally Sentenced or Conditionally Released.

CHAPTER 4

CHILDREN

Comments: Millions of children worldwide are subjected to violence, exploitation and abuse in the family, community, in schools and institutions; and during armed conflict. Millions more, not yet victims, also remain without adequate protection. There are a series of international instruments in relation to children. While some of these are legally binding on states that have ratified them, others, which serve as guidelines still carry the authority of the UN and can be used to support advocacy based on the legally binding instruments. Together, they represent the 'best practice' for a humane, fair, efficient and effective justice system in the context of children. The Convention on the Rights of the Child (CRC) is the most important legal instrument in relation to juvenile justice because it is legally binding on all States, except Somalia and the USA. It defines 'children' as all people under the age of 18. The CRC was designed to look at children as entire human beings. It is complemented by two Optional Protocols, both of which entered into force in 2002: the Optional Protocol on the Involvement of Children in Armed Conflict and the Optional Protocol on the Sale of Children, Child Prostitution and Child Pornography.

In addition to the CRC, there are other instruments specifically addressing child rights. In times of armed conflict, children are also protected by the laws and customs of war, including general provisions relating to civilians, provisions specific to children and, for those children recruited into the armed forces, provisions specific to combatants. The key instruments in this respect are the four Geneva Conventions and their two Additional Protocols.

The Committee on the Rights of the Child in its "General Comments: Children's rights in juvenile justice",[1] has observed that many State parties still have a long way to go in ensuring procedural rights in full compliance with the CRC. The Human Rights Council, in its resolution13/20 on the

[1] No. CRC/C/GC/10 of 25 April 2007.

"Rights of the child: the fight against sexual violence against children", adopted on15 April 2010, has stressed the need to treat all forms of sexual violence and sexual abuse against children as criminal acts, punishable by law, as well as the duty to provide access to just and effective remedies and specialized assistance to victims, including medical, psychological and legal assistance, as well as effective counselling and social services, in a manner that is age-, gender- and disability-sensitive.

4.1 DECLARATION OF THE RIGHTS OF CHILD, 1959[2]

Preamble

Whereas the peoples of the United Nations have, in the Charter, reaffirmed their faith in fundamental human rights and in the dignity and worth of the human person, and have determined to promote social progress and better standards of life in larger freedom,

Whereas the United Nations has, in the Universal declaration of Human Rights, proclaimed that everyone is entitled to all the rights and freedoms set forth therein, without distinction of any kind, such as race, colour, sex, language, religion, political or other opinion, national or social origin, property, birth or other status,

Whereas the child, by reason of his physical and mental immaturity, needs special safeguards and care, including appropriate legal protection, before as well as after birth,

Whereas the need for such special safeguards has been stated in the Geneva Declaration of the Rights of Child of 1924, and recognized in the *Universal Declaration of Human Rights* and in the statutes of specialized agencies and international organizations concerned with the welfare of children,

Whereas mankind owes to the child the best it has to give,

Now therefore,

The General Assembly

Proclaims this *Declaration of the Rights of the Child* to the end that he may have a happy childhood and enjoy for his own good and for the good of society the rights and freedoms herein set forth, and calls upon parents, upon men and women as individuals, and upon voluntary organizations, local authorities and national Governments to recognize these rights and strive

---

[2] UN General Assembly Resolution 1386 (XIV), 14 U.N. GAOR Supp. (No. 16) at 19 UN Doc. A/4354 (1959).

for their observance by legislative and other measures progressively taken in accordance with the following principles:

Principle 1

The child shall enjoy all the rights set forth in this Declaration. Every child, without any exception whatsoever, shall be entitled to these rights, without distinction or discrimination on account of race, colour, sex, language, religion, political or other opinion, national or social origin, property, birth or other status, whether of himself or of his family.

Principle 2

The child shall enjoy special protection, and shall be given opportunities and facilities, by law and by other means, to enable him to develop physically, mentally, morally, spiritually and socially in a healthy and normal manner and in conditions of freedom and dignity. In the enactment of laws for this purpose, the best interests of the child shall be the paramount consideration.

Principle 3

The child shall be entitled from his birth to a name and a nationality.

Principle 4

The child shall enjoy the benefits of social security. He shall be entitled to grow and develop in health; to this end, special care and protection shall be provided both to him and to his mother, including adequate pre-natal and post-natal care. The child shall have the right to adequate nutrition, housing, recreation and medical services.

Principle 5

The child who is physically, mentally or socially handicapped shall be given the special treatment, education and care required by his particular condition.

Principle 6

The child, for the full and harmonious development of his personality, needs love and understanding. He shall, wherever possible, grow up in the care and under the responsibility of his parents, and, in any case, in an atmosphere of affection and of moral and material security; a child of tender years shall not, save in exceptional circumstances, be separated from his mother. Society and the public authorities shall have the duty to extend particular care to children without a family and to those without adequate means of support. Payment of State and other assistance towards the maintenance of children of large families is desirable.

Principle 7

The child is entitled to receive education, which shall be free and compulsory, at least in the elementary stages. He shall be given an education which will promote his general culture and enable him, on a basis of equal opportunity, to develop his abilities, his individual judgement, and his sense of moral and social responsibility, and to become a useful member of society.

The best interests of the child shall be the guiding principle of those responsible for his education and guidance; that responsibility lies in the first place with his parents.

The child shall have full opportunity for play and recreation, which should be directed to the same purposes as education; society and the public authorities, shall endeavour to promote the enjoyment of this right.

Principle 8

The child shall in all circumstances be among the first to receive protection and relief.

Principle 9

The child shall be protected against all forms of neglect, cruelty and exploitation. He shall not be the subject of traffic, in any form.

The child shall not be admitted to employment before an appropriate minimum age; he shall in no case be caused or permitted to engage in any occupation or employment which would prejudice his health or education, or interfere with his physical, mental or moral development.

Principle 10

The child shall be protected from practices which may foster racial, religious and any other form of discrimination. He shall be brought up in a spirit of understanding, tolerance, friendship among peoples, peace and universal brotherhood, and in full consciousness that his energy and talents should be devoted to the service of his fellow men.

4.2 CONVENTION ON THE RIGHTS OF THE CHILD, 1989 [3]

Article 1

For the purposes of the present Convention, a child means every human being below the age of eighteen years unless under the law applicable to the child, majority is attained earlier.

Article 4

States Parties shall undertake all appropriate legislative, administrative and other measures for the implementation of the rights recognized in the present Convention. With regard to economic, social and cultural rights, States Parties shall undertake such measures to the maximum extent of their available resources and, where needed, within the framework of international co-operation.

Article 9

1. States Parties shall ensure that a child shall not be separated from his or her parents against their will, except when competent authorities subject to judicial review determine, in accordance with applicable law and procedures, that such separation is necessary for the best interests of the child. Such determination may be necessary in a particular case such as one involving abuse or neglect of the child by the parents, or one where the parents are living separately and a decision must be made as to the child's place of residence.

2. In any proceedings pursuant to paragraph 1 of the present article, all interested parties shall be given an opportunity to participate in the proceedings and make their views known.

3. States Parties shall respect the right of the child who is separated from one or both parents to maintain personal relations and direct contact with both parents on a regular basis, except if it is contrary to the child's best interests.

4. Where such separation results from any action initiated by a State Party, such as the detention, imprisonment, exile, deportation or death (including death arising from any cause while the person is in the custody of the State) of one or both parents or of the child, that State Party shall, upon request, provide the parents, the child or, if appropriate, another member of the family with the essential information concerning the whereabouts of the absent member(s) of the family unless the provision of the information would be detrimental to the well-being of

---

[3] The Convention on the Rights of the Child was adopted and opened for signature, ratification and accession by General Assembly resolution 44/25 of 20 November 1989. It entered into force 2 September 1990, in accordance with article 49.

the child. States Parties shall further ensure that the submission of such a request shall of itself entail no adverse consequences for the person(s) concerned.

Article 12

1. States Parties shall assure to the child who is capable of forming his or her own views the right to express those views freely in all matters affecting the child, the views of the child being given due weight in accordance with the age and maturity of the child.

2. For this purpose, the child shall in particular be provided the opportunity to be heard in any judicial and administrative proceedings affecting the child, either directly, or through a representative or an appropriate body, in a manner consistent with the procedural rules of national law.

Article 16

1. No child shall be subjected to arbitrary or unlawful interference with his or her privacy, family, home or correspondence, nor to unlawful attacks on his or her honour and reputation.

2. The child has the right to the protection of the law against such interference or attacks.

Article 19

1. States Parties shall take all appropriate legislative, administrative, social and educational measures to protect the child from all forms of physical or mental violence, injury or abuse, neglect or negligent treatment, maltreatment or exploitation, including sexual abuse, while in the care of parent(s), legal guardian(s) or any other person who has the care of the child.

2. Such protective measures should, as appropriate, include effective procedures for the establishment of social programmes to provide necessary support for the child and for those who have the care of the child, as well as for other forms of prevention and for identification, reporting, referral, investigation, treatment and follow-up of instances of child maltreatment described heretofore, and, as appropriate, for judicial involvement.

Article 37

States Parties shall ensure that:

(a) No child shall be subjected to torture or other cruel, inhuman or degrading treatment or punishment. Neither capital punishment nor life imprisonment without possibility of release shall be imposed for offences committed by persons below eighteen years of age;

(b) No child shall be deprived of his or her liberty unlawfully or arbitrarily. The arrest, detention or imprisonment of a child shall be in conformity with the law and shall be used only as a measure of last resort and for the shortest appropriate period of time;

(c) Every child deprived of liberty shall be treated with humanity and respect for the inherent dignity of the human person and in a manner which takes into account the needs of persons of his or her age. In particular, every child deprived of liberty shall be separated from adults unless it is considered in the child's best interest not to do so and shall have the right to maintain contact with his or her family through correspondence and visits, save in exceptional circumstances;

(d) Every child deprived of his or her liberty shall have the right to prompt access to legal and other appropriate assistance, as well as the right to challenge the legality of the deprivation of his or her liberty before a court or other competent, independent and impartial authority and to a prompt decision on any such action.

Article 40

1. States Parties recognize the right of every child alleged as, accused of, or recognized as having infringed the penal law to be treated in a manner consistent with the promotion of the child's sense of dignity and worth, which reinforces the child's respect for the human rights and fundamental freedoms of others and which takes into account the child's age and the desirability of promoting the child's reintegration and the child's assuming a constructive role in society.

2. To this end and having regard to the relevant provisions of international instruments, States Parties shall, in particular, ensure that:

(a) No child shall be alleged as, be accused of, or recognized as having infringed the penal law by reason of acts or omissions that were not prohibited by national or international law at the time they were committed;

(b) Every child alleged as or accused of having infringed the penal law has at least the following guarantees:

(i) To be presumed innocent until proven guilty according to law;

(ii) To be informed promptly and directly of the charges against him or her, and, if appropriate, through his or her parents or legal guardians and to have legal or other appropriate assistance in the preparation and presentation of his or her defense;

(iii) To have the matter determined without delay by a competent, independent and impartial authority or judicial body in a fair hearing according to law, in the presence of legal or other appropriate assistance and, unless it is considered not to be in the best interest of the child, in particular, taking into account his or her age or situation, his or her parents or legal guardians;

(iv) Not to be compelled to give testimony or to confess guilt; to examine or have examined adverse witnesses and to obtain the participation and examination of witnesses on his or her behalf under conditions of equality;

(v) If considered to have infringed the penal law, to have this decision and any measures imposed in consequence thereof reviewed by a higher competent, independent and impartial authority or judicial body according to law;

(vi) To have the free assistance of an interpreter if the child cannot understand or speak the language used;

(vii) To have his or her privacy fully respected at all stages of the proceedings.

3. States Parties shall seek to promote the establishment of laws, procedures, authorities and institutions specifically applicable to children alleged as, accused of, or recognized as having infringed the penal law, and, in particular:

(a) The establishment of a minimum age below which children shall be presumed not to have the capacity to infringe the penal law;

(b) Whenever appropriate and desirable, measures for dealing with such children without resorting to judicial proceedings, providing that human rights and legal safeguards are fully respected.

4. A variety of dispositions, such as care, guidance and supervision orders; counselling; probation; foster care; education and vocational training programmes and other alternatives to institutional care shall be available to ensure that children are dealt with in a manner appropriate to their well-being and proportionate both to their circumstances and the offence.

4.3 OPTIONAL PROTOCOL TO THE CONVENTION ON THE RIGHTS OF THE CHILD ON THE SALE OF CHILDREN, CHILD PROSTITUTUION AND CHILD PORNOGRAPHY, 2000[4]

Article 1

States Parties shall prohibit the sale of children, child prostitution and child pornography as provided for by the present Protocol.

Article 2

For the purposes of the present Protocol:

(a) Sale of children means any act or transaction whereby a child is transferred by any person or group of persons to another for remuneration or any other consideration;

(b) Child prostitution means the use of a child in sexual activities for remuneration or any other form of consideration;

(c) Child pornography means any representation, by whatever means, of a child engaged in real or simulated explicit sexual activities or any representation of the sexual parts of a child for primarily sexual purposes.

Article 3

1. Each State Party shall ensure that, as a minimum, the following acts and activities are fully covered under its criminal or penal law, whether such offences are committed domestically or transnationally or on an individual or organized basis:

(a) In the context of sale of children as defined in article 2:

(i) Offering, delivering or accepting, by whatever means, a child for the purpose of:

a. Sexual exploitation of the child;

b. Transfer of organs of the child for profit;

c. Engagement of the child in forced labour;

---

[4] Adopted and opened for signature, ratification and accession by General Assembly resolution A/RES/54/263 of 25 May 2000, entered into force on 18 January 2002.

(ii) Improperly inducing consent, as an intermediary, for the adoption of a child in violation of applicable international legal instruments on adoption;

(b) Offering, obtaining, procuring or providing a child for child prostitution, as defined in article 2;

(c) Producing, distributing, disseminating, importing, exporting, offering, selling or possessing for the above purposes child pornography as defined in article 2.

2. Subject to the provisions of the national law of a State Party, the same shall apply to an attempt to commit any of the said acts and to complicity or participation in any of the said acts.

3. Each State Party shall make such offences punishable by appropriate penalties that take into account their grave nature.

4. Subject to the provisions of its national law, each State Party shall take measures, where appropriate, to establish the liability of legal persons for offences established in paragraph 1 of the present article. Subject to the legal principles of the State Party, such liability of legal persons may be criminal, civil or administrative.

5. States Parties shall take all appropriate legal and administrative measures to ensure that all persons involved in the adoption of a child act in conformity with applicable international legal instruments.

Article 4

1. Each State Party shall take such measures as may be necessary to establish its jurisdiction over the offences referred to in article 3, paragraph 1, when the offences are committed in its territory or on board a ship or aircraft registered in that State.

2. Each State Party may take such measures as may be necessary to establish its jurisdiction over the offences referred to in article 3, paragraph 1, in the following cases:

(a) When the alleged offender is a national of that State or a person who has his habitual residence in its territory;

(b) When the victim is a national of that State.

3. Each State Party shall also take such measures as may be necessary to establish its jurisdiction over the aforementioned offences when the alleged offender is present in its territory and it

does not extradite him or her to another State Party on the ground that the offence has been committed by one of its nationals.

4. The present Protocol does not exclude any criminal jurisdiction exercised in accordance with internal law.

Article 5

1. The offences referred to in article 3, paragraph 1, shall be deemed to be included as extraditable offences in any extradition treaty existing between States Parties and shall be included as extraditable offences in every extradition treaty subsequently concluded between them, in accordance with the conditions set forth in such treaties.

2. If a State Party that makes extradition conditional on the existence of a treaty receives a request for extradition from another State Party with which it has no extradition treaty, it may consider the present Protocol to be a legal basis for extradition in respect of such offences. Extradition shall be subject to the conditions provided by the law of the requested State.

3. States Parties that do not make extradition conditional on the existence of a treaty shall recognize such offences as extraditable offences between themselves subject to the conditions provided by the law of the requested State.

4. Such offences shall be treated, for the purpose of extradition between States Parties, as if they had been committed not only in the place in which they occurred but also in the territories of the States required to establish their jurisdiction in accordance with article 4.

5. If an extradition request is made with respect to an offence described in article 3, paragraph 1, and the requested State Party does not or will not extradite on the basis of the nationality of the offender, that State shall take suitable measures to submit the case to its competent authorities for the purpose of prosecution.

Article 6

1. States Parties shall afford one another the greatest measure of assistance in connection with investigations or criminal or extradition proceedings brought in respect of the offences set forth in article 3, paragraph 1, including assistance in obtaining evidence at their disposal necessary for the proceedings.

2. States Parties shall carry out their obligations under paragraph 1 of the present article in conformity with any treaties or other arrangements on mutual legal assistance that may exist

between them. In the absence of such treaties or arrangements, States Parties shall afford one another assistance in accordance with their domestic law.

Article 7

States Parties shall, subject to the provisions of their national law:

(a) Take measures to provide for the seizure and confiscation, as appropriate, of:

(i) Goods, such as materials, assets and other instrumentalities used to commit or facilitate offences under the present protocol;

(ii) Proceeds derived from such offences;

(b) Execute requests from another State Party for seizure or confiscation of goods or proceeds referred to in subparagraph (a);

(c) Take measures aimed at closing, on a temporary or definitive basis, premises used to commit such offences.

Article 8

1. States Parties shall adopt appropriate measures to protect the rights and interests of child victims of the practices prohibited under the present Protocol at all stages of the criminal justice process, in particular by:

(a) Recognizing the vulnerability of child victims and adapting procedures to recognize their special needs, including their special needs as witnesses;

(b) Informing child victims of their rights, their role and the scope, timing and progress of the proceedings and of the disposition of their cases;

(c) Allowing the views, needs and concerns of child victims to be presented and considered in proceedings where their personal interests are affected, in a manner consistent with the procedural rules of national law;

(d) Providing appropriate support services to child victims throughout the legal process;

(e) Protecting, as appropriate, the privacy and identity of child victims and taking measures in accordance with national law to avoid the inappropriate dissemination of information that could lead to the identification of child victims;

(f) Providing, in appropriate cases, for the safety of child victims, as well as that of their families and witnesses on their behalf, from intimidation and retaliation;

(g) Avoiding unnecessary delay in the disposition of cases and the execution of orders or decrees granting compensation to child victims.

2. States Parties shall ensure that uncertainty as to the actual age of the victim shall not prevent the initiation of criminal investigations, including investigations aimed at establishing the age of the victim.

3. States Parties shall ensure that, in the treatment by the criminal justice system of children who are victims of the offences described in the present Protocol, the best interest of the child shall be a primary consideration.

4. States Parties shall take measures to ensure appropriate training, in particular legal and psychological training, for the persons who work with victims of the offences prohibited under the present Protocol.

5. States Parties shall, in appropriate cases, adopt measures in order to protect the safety and integrity of those persons and/or organizations involved in the prevention and/or protection and rehabilitation of victims of such offences.

6. Nothing in the present article shall be construed to be prejudicial to or inconsistent with the rights of the accused to a fair and impartial trial.

Article 9

1. States Parties shall adopt or strengthen, implement and disseminate laws, administrative measures, social policies and programmes to prevent the offences referred to in the present Protocol. Particular attention shall be given to protect children who are especially vulnerable to such practices.

2. States Parties shall promote awareness in the public at large, including children, through information by all appropriate means, education and training, about the preventive measures and harmful effects of the offences referred to in the present Protocol. In fulfilling their obligations under this article, States Parties shall encourage the participation of the community and, in particular, children and child victims, in such information and education and training programmes, including at the international level.

3. States Parties shall take all feasible measures with the aim of ensuring all appropriate assistance to victims of such offences, including their full social reintegration and their full physical and psychological recovery.

4. States Parties shall ensure that all child victims of the offences described in the present Protocol have access to adequate procedures to seek, without discrimination, compensation for damages from those legally responsible.

5. States Parties shall take appropriate measures aimed at effectively prohibiting the production and dissemination of material advertising the offences described in the present Protocol.

4.4 UNITED NATIONS STANDARD MINIMUM RULES FOR THE ADMINISTRATION OF JUVENILE JUSTICE, 1985 [5]

(The Beijing Rules)

The General Assembly,

Bearing in mind the Universal Declaration of Human Rights, the International Covenant on Civil and Political Rights and the International Covenant on Economic, Social and Cultural Rights, as well as other international human rights instruments pertaining to the rights of young persons,

Also bearing in mind that 1985 was designated the International Youth Year: Participation, Development, Peace and that the international community has placed importance on the protection and promotion of the rights of the young, as witnessed by the significance attached to the Declaration of the Rights of the Child,

Recalling resolution 4 adopted by the Sixth United Nations Congress on the Prevention of Crime and the Treatment of Offenders, held at Caracas from 25 August to 5 September 1980, which called for the development of standard minimum rules for the administration of juvenile justice and the care of juveniles, which could serve as a model for Member States,

Recalling also Economic and Social Council decision 1984/153 of 25 May 1984, by which the draft rules were forwarded to the Seventh United Nations Congress on the Prevention of Crime and the Treatment of Offenders, through the Interregional Preparatory Meeting, held at Beijing from 14 to 18 May 1984,

---

[5] Adopted by the UN General Assembly resolution 40/33 of 29 November 1985.

Recognizing that the young, owing to their early stage of human development, require particular care and assistance with regard to physical, mental and social development, and require legal protection in conditions of peace, freedom, dignity and security,

Considering that existing national legislation, policies and practices may well require review and amendment in view of the standards contained in the rules,

Considering further that, although such standards may seem difficult to achieve at present in view of existing social, economic, cultural, political and legal conditions, they are nevertheless intended to be attainable as a policy minimum,

1. Notes with appreciation the work carried out by the Committee on Crime Prevention and Control, the Secretary-General, the United Nations Asia and Far East Institute for the Prevention of Crime and the Treatment of Offenders and other United Nations institutes in the development of the Standard Minimum Rules for the Administration of Juvenile Justice;

2. Takes note with appreciation of the report of the Secretary-General on the draft Standard Minimum Rules for the Administration of Juvenile Justice;

3. Commends the Interregional Preparatory Meeting held at Beijing for having finalized the text of the rules submitted to the Seventh United Nations Congress on the Prevention of Crime and the Treatment of Offenders for consideration and final action;

4. Adopts the United Nations Standard Minimum Rules for the Administration of Juvenile Justice recommended by the Seventh Congress, contained in the annex to the present resolution, and approves the recommendation of the Seventh Congress that the Rules should be known as "the Beijing Rules";

5. Invites Member States to adapt, wherever this is necessary, their national legislation, policies and practices, particularly in training juvenile justice personnel, to the Beijing Rules and to bring the Rules to the attention of relevant authorities and the public in general;

6. Calls upon the Committee on Crime Prevention and Control to formulate measures for the effective implementation of the Beijing Rules, with the assistance of the United Nations institutes on the prevention of crime and the treatment of offenders;

7. Invites Member States to inform the Secretary-General on the implementation of the Beijing Rules and to report regularly to the Committee on Crime Prevention and Control on the results achieved;

8. Requests Member States and the Secretary-General to undertake research and to develop a data base with respect to effective policies and practices in the administration of juvenile justice;

9. Requests the Secretary-General and invites Member States to ensure the widest possible dissemination of the text of the Beijing Rules in all of the official languages of the United Nations, including the intensification of information activities in the field of juvenile justice;

10. Requests the Secretary-General to develop pilot projects on the implementation of the Beijing Rules;

11. Requests the Secretary-General and Member States to provide the necessary resources to ensure the successful implementation of the Beijing Rules, in particular in the areas of recruitment, training and exchange of personnel, research and evaluation, and the development of new alternatives to institutionalization;

12. Requests the Eighth United Nations Congress on the Prevention of Crime and the Treatment of Offenders to review the progress made in the implementation of the Beijing Rules and of the recommendations contained in the present resolution, under a separate agenda item on juvenile justice;

13. Urges all relevant organs of the United Nations system, in particular the regional commissions and specialized agencies, the United Nations institutes for the prevention of crime and the treatment of offenders, other intergovernmental organizations and non-governmental organizations to collaborate with the Secretariat and to take the necessary measures to ensure a concerted and sustained effort, within their respective fields of technical competence, to implement the principles contained in the Beijing Rules.

ANNEX

United Nations Standard Minimum Rules for the Administration of Juvenile Justice (Beijing Rules)

Part one

GENERAL PRINCIPLES

1. Fundamental perspectives

1.1 Member States shall seek, in conformity with their respective general interests, to further the well-being of the juvenile and her or his family.

1.2 Member States shall endeavour to develop conditions that will ensure for the juvenile a meaningful life in the community, which, during that period in life when she or he is most susceptible to deviant behaviour, will foster a process of personal development and education that is as free from crime and delinquency as possible.

1.3 Sufficient attention shall be given to positive measures that involve the full mobilization of all possible resources, including the family, volunteers and other community groups, as well as schools and other community institutions, for the purpose of promoting the well-being of the juvenile, with a view to reducing the need for intervention under the law, and of effectively, fairly and humanely dealing with the juvenile in conflict with the law.

1.4 Juvenile justice shall be conceived as an integral part of the national development process of each country, within a comprehensive framework of social justice for all juveniles, thus, at the same time, contributing to the protection of the young and the maintenance of a peaceful order in society.

1.5 These Rules shall be implemented in the context of economic, social and cultural conditions prevailing in each Member State.

1.6 Juvenile justice services shall be systematically developed and coordinated with a view to improving and sustaining the competence of personnel involved in the services, including their methods, approaches and attitudes.

Commentary

These broad fundamental perspectives refer to comprehensive social policy in general and aim at promoting juvenile welfare to the greatest possible extent, which will minimize the necessity of intervention by the juvenile justice system, and in turn, will reduce the harm that may be caused by any intervention. Such care measures for the young, before the onset of delinquency, are basic policy requisites designed to obviate the need for the application of the Rules.

Rules 1.1 to 1.3 point to the important role that a constructive social policy for juveniles will play in the prevention of juvenile crime and delinquency. Rule 1.4 defines juvenile justice as an integral part of social justice for juveniles, while rule 1.6 refers to the necessity of constantly improving juvenile justice, without falling behind the development of progressive social policy for juveniles in general and bearing in mind the need for consistent improvement of staff services. Rule 1.5 seeks to take account of existing conditions in Member States which would cause the manner of implementation of particular rules necessarily to be different from the manner adopted in other States.

2. Scope of the Rules and definitions used

2.1 The following Standard Minimum Rules shall be applied to juvenile offenders impartially, without distinction of any kind, for example as to race, colour, sex, language, religion, political or other opinions, national or social origin, property, birth or other status.

2.2 For purposes of these Rules, the following definitions shall be applied by Member States in a manner which is compatible with their respective legal systems and concepts:

(a) A juvenile is a child or young person who, under the respective legal systems, may be dealt with for an offence in a manner which is different from an adult;

(b) An offence is any behaviour (act or omission) that is punishable by law under the respective legal systems;

(c) A juvenile offender is a child or young person who is alleged to have committed or who has been found to have committed an offence.

2.3 Efforts shall be made to establish, in each national jurisdiction, a set of laws, rules and provisions specifically applicable to juvenile offenders and institutions and bodies entrusted with the functions of the administration of juvenile justice and designed:

(a) To meet the varying needs of juvenile offenders, while protecting their basic rights;

(b) To meet the need of society;

To implement the following rules thoroughly and fairly.

Commentary

The Standard Minimum Rules are deliberately formulated so as to be applicable within different legal systems and, at the same time, to set some minimum standards for the handling of juvenile offenders under any definition of a juvenile and under any system of dealing with juvenile offenders. The Rules are always to be applied impartially and without distinction of any kind.

Rule 2.1 therefore stresses the importance of the Rules always being applied impartially and without distinction of any kind. The rule follows the formulation of principle 2 of the Declaration of the Rights of the Child.

Rule 2.2 defines "juvenile" and "offence" as the components of the notion of the "juvenile offender", who is the main subject of these Standard Minimum Rules (see, however, also rules 3 and 4). It should be noted that age limits will depend on, and are explicitly made dependent on, each respective legal system, thus fully respecting the economic, social, political, cultural and legal systems of Member States. This makes for a wide variety of ages coming under the definition of "juvenile", ranging from 7 years to 18 years or above. Such a variety seems inevitable in view of the different national legal systems and does not diminish the impact of these Standard Minimum Rules. Rule 2.3 is addressed to the necessity of specific national legislation for the optimal implementation of these Standard Minimum Rules, both legally and practically.

3. Extension of the Rules

3.1 The relevant provisions of the Rules shall be applied not only to juvenile offenders but also to juveniles who may be proceeded against for any specific behaviour that would not be punishable if committed by an adult.

3.2 Efforts shall be made to extend the principles embodied in the Rules to all juveniles who are dealt with in welfare and care proceedings.

3.3 Efforts shall also be made to extend the principles embodied in the Rules to young adult offenders.

Commentary

Rule 3 extends the protection afforded by the Standard Minimum Rules for the Administration of Juvenile Justice to cover:

(a) The so-called "status offences" prescribed in various national legal systems where the range of behaviour considered to be an offence is wider for juveniles than it is for adults (for example, truancy, school and family disobedience, public drunkenness, etc.) (rule 3.1);

(b) Juvenile welfare and care proceedings (rule 3.2);

(c) Proceedings dealing with young adult offenders, depending of course on each given age limit (rule 3.3).

The extension of the Rules to cover these three areas seems to be justified. Rule 3.1 provides minimum guarantees in those fields, and rule 3.2 is considered a desirable step in the direction of more fair, equitable and humane justice for all juveniles in conflict with the law.

4. Age of criminal responsibility

4.1 In those legal systems recognizing the concept of the age of criminal responsibility for juveniles, the beginning of that age shall not be fixed at too low an age level, bearing in mind the facts of emotional, mental and intellectual maturity.

Commentary

The minimum age of criminal responsibility differs widely owing to history and culture. The modern approach would be to consider whether a child can live up to the moral and psychological components of criminal responsibility; that is, whether a child, by virtue of her or his individual discernment and understanding, can be held responsible for essentially antisocial behaviour. If the age of criminal responsibility is fixed too low or if there is no lower age limit at all, the notion of responsibility would become meaningless. In general, there is a close relationship between the notion of responsibility for delinquent or criminal behaviour and other social rights and responsibilities (such as marital status, civil majority, etc.).

Efforts should therefore be made to agree on a reasonable lowest age limit that is applicable internationally.

5. Aims of juvenile justice

5. 1 The juvenile justice system shall emphasize the well-being of the juvenile and shall ensure that any reaction to juvenile offenders shall always be in proportion to the circumstances of both the offenders and the offence.

Commentary

Rule 5 refers to two of the most important objectives of juvenile justice. The first objective is the promotion of the well-being of the juvenile. This is the main focus of those legal systems in which juvenile offenders are dealt with by family courts or administrative authorities, but the well-being of the juvenile should also be emphasized in legal systems that follow the criminal court model, thus contributing to the avoidance of merely punitive sanctions. (See also rule 14.)

The second objective is "the principle of proportionality". This principle is well-known as an instrument for curbing punitive sanctions, mostly expressed in terms of just deserts in relation to the gravity of the offence. The response to young offenders should be based on the consideration not only of the gravity of the offence but also of personal circumstances. The individual circumstances of the offender (for example social status, family situation, the harm caused by the offence or other factors affecting personal circumstances) should influence the proportionality of the reactions (for example by having regard to the offender's endeavour to indemnify the victim or to her or his willingness to turn to wholesome and useful life).

By the same token, reactions aiming to ensure the welfare of the young offender may go beyond necessity and therefore infringe upon the fundamental rights of the young individual, as has been observed in some juvenile justice systems. Here, too, the proportionality of the reaction to the circumstances of both the offender and the offence, including the victim, should be safeguarded.

In essence, rule 5 calls for no less and no more than a fair reaction in any given cases of juvenile delinquency and crime. The issues combined in the rule may help to stimulate development in both regards: new and innovative types of reactions are as desirable as precautions against any undue widening of the net of formal social control over juveniles.

6. Scope of discretion

6.1 In view of the varying special needs of juveniles as well as the variety of measures available, appropriate scope for discretion shall be allowed at all stages of proceedings and at the different levels of juvenile justice administration, including investigation, prosecution, adjudication and the follow-up of dispositions.

6.2 Efforts shall be made, however, to ensure sufficient accountability at all stages and levels in the exercise of any such discretion.

6.3 Those who exercise discretion shall be specially qualified or trained to exercise it judiciously and in accordance with their functions and mandates.

Commentary

Rules 6.1, 6.2 and 6.3 combine several important features of effective, fair and humane juvenile justice administration: the need to permit the exercise of discretionary power at all significant levels of processing so that those who make determinations can take the actions deemed to be most appropriate in each individual case; and the need to provide checks and balances in order to curb any abuses of discretionary power and to safeguard the rights of the young offender. Accountability and professionalism are instruments best apt to curb broad discretion. Thus, professional qualifications and expert training are emphasized here as a valuable means of ensuring the judicious exercise of discretion in matters of juvenile offenders. (See also rules 1.6 and 2.2.) The formulation of specific guidelines on the exercise of discretion and the provision of systems of review, appeal and the like in order to permit scrutiny of decisions and accountability are emphasized in this context. Such mechanisms are not specified here, as they do not easily lend themselves to incorporation into international standard minimum rules, which cannot possibly cover all differences in justice systems.

7. Rights of juveniles

7.1 Basic procedural safeguards such as the presumption of innocence, the right to be notified of the charges, the right to remain silent, the right to counsel, the right to the presence of a parent or guardian, the right to confront and cross-examine witnesses and the right to appeal to a higher authority shall be guaranteed at all stages of proceedings.

Commentary

Rule 7.1 emphasizes some important points that represent essential elements for a fair and just trial and that are internationally recognized in existing human rights instruments (See also rule 14.). The presumption of innocence, for instance, is also to be found in article 11 of the Universal Declaration of Human rights and in article 14, paragraph 2, of the International Covenant on Civil and Political Rights.

Rules 14 seq. of these Standard Minimum Rules specify issues that are important for proceedings in juvenile cases, in particular, while rule 7.1 affirms the most basic procedural safeguards in a general way.

8. Protection of privacy

8.1 The juvenile's right to privacy shall be respected at all stages in order to avoid harm being caused to her or him by undue publicity or by the process of labelling.

8.2 In principle, no information that may lead to the identification of a juvenile offender shall be published.

Commentary

Rule 8 stresses the importance of the protection of the juvenile's right to privacy. Young persons are particularly susceptible to stigmatization. Criminological research into labelling processes has provided evidence of the detrimental effects (of different kinds) resulting from the permanent identification of young persons as "delinquent" or "criminal".

Rule 8 stresses the importance of protecting the juvenile from the adverse effects that may result from the publication in the mass media of information about the case (for example the names of young offenders, alleged or convicted). The interest of the individual should be protected and upheld, at least in principle. (The general contents of rule 8 are further specified in rule 2 1.)

9. Saving clause

9.1 Nothing in these Rules shall be interpreted as precluding the application of the Standard Minimum Rules for the Treatment of Prisoners adopted by the United Nations and other human rights instruments and standards recognized by the international community that relate to the care and protection of the young.

Commentary

Rule 9 is meant to avoid any misunderstanding in interpreting and implementing the present Rules in conformity with principles contained in relevant existing or emerging international human rights instruments and standards-such as the Universal Declaration of Human Rights, the International Covenant on Economic, Social and Cultural Rights and the International Covenant on Civil and Political Rights, and the Declaration of the Rights of the Child and the draft convention on the rights of the child. It should be understood that the application of the present Rules is without prejudice to any such international instruments which may contain provisions of wider application. (See also rule 27.)

Part Two

INVESTIGATION AND PROSECUTION

10. Initial contact

10.1 Upon the apprehension of a juvenile, her or his parents or guardian shall be immediately notified of such apprehension, and, where such immediate notification is not possible, the parents or guardian shall be notified within the shortest possible time thereafter.

10.2 A judge or other competent official or body shall, without delay, consider the issue of release.

10.3 Contacts between the law enforcement agencies and a juvenile offender shall be managed in such a way as to respect the legal status of the juvenile, promote the well-being of the juvenile and avoid harm to her or hi m, with due regard to the circumstances of the case.

Commentary

Rule 10.1 is in principle contained in rule 92 of the Standard Minimum Rules for the Treatment of Prisoners.

The question of release (rule 10.2) shall be considered without delay by a judge or other competent official. The latter refers to any person or institution in the broadest sense of the term, including community boards or police authorities having power to release an arrested person. (See also the International Covenant on Civil and Political Rights, article 9, paragraph 3.)

Rule 10.3 deals with some fundamental aspects of the procedures and behaviour on the part of the police and other law enforcement officials in cases of juvenile crime. To "avoid harm" admittedly is flexible wording and covers many features of possible interaction (for example the use of harsh language, physical violence or exposure to the environment). Involvement in juvenile justice processes in itself can be "harmful" to juveniles; the term "avoid harm" should be broadly interpreted, therefore, as doing the least harm possible to the juvenile in the first instance, as well as any additional or undue harm. This is especially important in the initial contact with law enforcement agencies, which might profoundly influence the juvenile's attitude towards the State and society. Moreover, the success of any further intervention is largely dependent on such initial contacts. Compassion and kind firmness are important in these situations.

11. Diversion

11.1 Consideration shall be given, wherever appropriate, to dealing with juvenile offenders without resorting to formal trial by the competent authority, referred to in rule 14.1 below.

11.2 The police, the prosecution or other agencies dealing with juvenile cases shall be empowered to dispose of such cases, at their discretion, without recourse to formal hearings, in accordance with the criteria laid down for that purpose in the respective legal system and also in accordance with the principles contained in these Rules.

11.3 Any diversion involving referral to appropriate community or other services shall require the consent of the juvenile, or her or his parents or guardian, provided that such decision to refer a case shall be subject to review by a competent authority, upon application.

11.4 In order to facilitate the discretionary disposition of juvenile cases, efforts shall be made to provide for community programmes, such as temporary supervision and guidance, restitution, and compensation of victims.

Commentary

Diversion, involving removal from criminal justice processing and, frequently, redirection to community support services, is commonly practised on a formal and informal basis in many legal systems. This practice serves to hinder the negative effects of subsequent proceedings in juvenile justice administration (for example the stigma of conviction and sentence). In many cases, non-intervention would be the best response. Thus, diversion at the outset and without referral to alternative (social) services may be the optimal response. This is especially the case where the offence is of a non-serious nature and where the family, the school or other informal social control institutions have already reacted, or are likely to react, in an appropriate and constructive manner.

As stated in rule 11.2, diversion may be used at any point of decision-making-by the police, the prosecution or other agencies such as the courts, tribunals, boards or councils. It may be exercised by one authority or several or all authorities, according to the rules and policies of the respective systems and in line with the present Rules. It need not necessarily be limited to petty cases, thus rendering diversion an important instrument.

Rule 11.3 stresses the important requirement of securing the consent of the young offender (or the parent or guardian) to the recommended diversionary measure(s). (Diversion to community service without such consent would contradict the Abolition of Forced Labour Convention.) However, this consent should not be left unchallengeable, since it might sometimes be given out of sheer desperation on the part of the juvenile. The rule underlines that care should be taken to minimize the potential for coercion and intimidation at all levels in the diversion process. Juveniles should not feel pressured (for example in order to avoid court appearance) or be pressured into consenting to diversion programmes. Thus, it is advocated that provision should be made for an objective appraisal of the appropriateness of dispositions involving young offenders by a "competent authority upon application". (The "competent authority", may be different from that referred to in rule 14.)

Rule 11.4 recommends the provision of viable alternatives to juvenile justice processing in the form of community-based diversion. Programmes that involve settlement by victim restitution and those that seek to avoid future conflict with the law through temporary supervision and guidance are especially commended. The merits of individual cases would make diversion appropriate, even when more serious offences have been committed (for example first offence, the act having been committed under peer pressure, etc.).

12. Specialization within the police

12.1 In order to best fulfil their functions, police officers who frequently or exclusively deal with juveniles or who are primarily engaged in the prevention of juvenile crime shall be specially instructed and trained. In large cities, special police units should be established for that purpose.

Commentary

Rule 12 draws attention to the need for specialized training for all law enforcement officials who are involved in the administration of juvenile justice. As police are the first point of contact with the juvenile justice system, it is most important that they act in an informed and appropriate manner.

While the relationship between urbanization and crime is clearly complex, an increase in juvenile crime has been associated with the growth of large cities, particularly with rapid and unplanned growth. Specialized police units would therefore be indispensable, not only in the interest of implementing specific principles contained in the present instrument (such as rule 1.6) but more generally for improving the prevention and control of juvenile crime and the handling of juvenile offenders.

13. Detention pending trial

13.1 Detention pending trial shall be used only as a measure of last resort and for the shortest possible period of time.

13.2 Whenever possible, detention pending trial shall be replaced by alternative measures, such as close supervision, intensive care or placement with a family or in an educational setting.

13.3 Juveniles under detention pending trial shall be entitled to all rights and guarantees of the Standard Minimum Rules for the Treatment of Prisoners adopted by the United Nations.

13.4 Juveniles under detention pending trial shall be kept separate from adults and shall be detained in a separate institution or in a separate part of an institution also holding adults.

13.5 While in custody, juveniles shall receive care, protection and all necessary individual assistance-social, educational, vocational, psychological, medical and physical-that they may require in view of their age, sex and personality.

Commentary

The danger to juveniles of "criminal contamination" while in detention pending trial must not be underestimated. It is therefore important to stress the need for alternative measures. By doing so, rule 13.1 encourages the devising of new and innovative measures to avoid such detention in the interest of the well-being of the juvenile.

Juveniles under detention pending trial are entitled to all the rights and guarantees of the Standard Minimum Rules for the Treatment of Prisoners as well as the International Covenant on Civil and Political Rights, especially article 9 and article 10, paragraphs 2 (b) and 3.

Rule 13.4 does not prevent States from taking other measures against the negative influences of adult offenders which are at least as effective as the measures mentioned in the rule.

Different forms of assistance that may become necessary have been enumerated to draw attention to the broad range of particular needs of young detainees to be addressed (for example females or males, drug addicts, alcoholics, mentally ill juveniles, young persons suffering from the trauma, for example, of arrest, etc.).

Varying physical and psychological characteristics of young detainees may warrant classification measures by which some are kept separate while in detention pending trial, thus contributing to the avoidance of victimization and rendering more appropriate assistance.

The Sixth United Nations Congress on the Prevention of Crime and the Treatment of Offenders, in its resolution 4 on juvenile justice standards, specified that the Rules, inter alia, should reflect the basic principle that pre-trial detention should be used only as a last resort, that no minors should be held in a facility where they are vulnerable to the negative influences of adult detainees and that account should always be taken of the needs particular to their stage of development.

Part Three

ADJUDICATION AND DISPOSITION

14. Competent authority to adjudicate

14.1 Where the case of a juvenile offender has not been diverted (under rule 11), she or he shall be dealt with by the competent authority (court, tribunal, board, council, etc.) according to the principles of a fair and just trial.

14.2 The proceedings shall be conducive to the best interests of the juvenile and shall be conducted in an atmosphere of understanding, which shall allow the juvenile to participate therein and to express herself or himself freely.

Commentary

It is difficult to formulate a definition of the competent body or person that would universally describe an adjudicating authority. "Competent authority" is meant to include those who preside over courts or tribunals (composed of a single judge or of several members), including professional and lay magistrates as well as administrative boards (for example the Scottish and Scandinavian systems) or other more informal community and conflict resolution agencies of an adjudicatory nature.

The procedure for dealing with juvenile offenders shall in any case follow the minimum standards that are applied almost universally for any criminal defendant under the procedure known as "due process of law". In accordance with due process, a "fair and just trial" includes such basic safeguards as the presumption of innocence, the presentation and examination of witnesses, the common legal defences, the right to remain silent, the right to have the last word in a hearing, the right to appeal, etc. (See also rule 7.1.)

15. Legal counsel, parents and guardians

15.1 Throughout the proceedings the juvenile shall have the right to be represented by a legal adviser or to apply for free legal aid where there is provision for such aid in the country.

15.2 The parents or the guardian shall be entitled to participate in the proceedings and may be required by the competent authority to attend them in the interest of the juvenile. They may, however, be denied participation by the competent authority if there are reasons to assume that such exclusion is necessary in the interest of the juvenile.

Commentary

Rule 15.1 uses terminology similar to that found in rule 93 of the Standard Minimum Rules for the Treatment of Prisoners. Whereas legal counsel and free legal aid are needed to assure the juvenile legal assistance, the right of the parents or guardian to participate as stated in rule 15.2 should be viewed as general psychological and emotional assistance to the juvenile-a function extending throughout the procedure.

The competent authority's search for an adequate disposition of the case may profit, in particular, from the co-operation of the legal representatives of the juvenile (or, for that matter, some other personal assistant who the juvenile can and does really trust). Such concern can be thwarted if the presence of parents or guardians at the hearings plays a negative role, for instance, if they display a hostile attitude towards the juvenile, hence, the possibility of their exclusion must be provided for.

16. Social inquiry reports

16.1 In all cases except those involving minor offences, before the competent authority renders a final disposition prior to sentencing, the background and circumstances in which the juvenile is living or the conditions under which the offence has been committed shall be properly investigated so as to facilitate judicious adjudication of the case by the competent authority.

Commentary

Social inquiry reports (social reports or pre-sentence reports) are an indispensable aid in most legal proceedings involving juveniles. The competent authority should be informed of relevant facts about the juvenile, such as social and family background, school career, educational experiences, etc. For this purpose, some jurisdictions use special social services or personnel attached to the court or board. Other personnel, including probation officers, may serve the same function. The rule therefore requires that adequate social services should be available to deliver social inquiry reports of a qualified nature.

17. Guiding principles in adjudication and disposition

17.1 The disposition of the competent authority shall be guided by the following principles:

(a) The reaction taken shall always be in proportion not only to the circumstances and the gravity of the offence but also to the circumstances and the needs of the juvenile as well as to the needs of the society;

(b) Restrictions on the personal liberty of the juvenile shall be imposed only after careful consideration and shall be limited to the possible minimum;

(c) Deprivation of personal liberty shall not be imposed unless the juvenile is adjudicated of a serious act involving violence against another person or of persistence in committing other serious offences and unless there is no other appropriate response;

(d) The well-being of the juvenile shall be the guiding factor in the consideration of her or his case.

17.2 Capital punishment shall not be imposed for any crime committed by juveniles.

17.3 Juveniles shall not be subject to corporal punishment.

17.4 The competent authority shall have the power to discontinue the proceedings at any time.

Commentary

The main difficulty in formulating guidelines for the adjudication of young persons stems from the fact that there are unresolved conflicts of a philosophical nature, such as the following:

(a) Rehabilitation versus just desert;

(b) Assistance versus repression and punishment;

(c) Reaction according to the singular merits of an individual case versus reaction according to the protection of society in general;

(d) General deterrence versus individual incapacitation.

The conflict between these approaches is more pronounced in juvenile cases than in adult cases. With the variety of causes and reactions characterizing juvenile cases, these alternatives become intricately interwoven.

It is not the function of the Standard Minimum Rules for the Administration of Juvenile Justice to prescribe which approach is to be followed but rather to identify one that is most closely in consonance with internationally accepted principles. Therefore the essential elements as laid down in rule 17.1, in particular in subparagraphs (a) and (c), are mainly to be understood as practical guidelines that should ensure a common starting point; if heeded by the concerned authorities (see also rule 5), they could contribute considerably to ensuring that the fundamental rights of juvenile offenders are protected, especially the fundamental rights of personal development and education.

Rule 17.1 (b) implies that strictly punitive approaches are not appropriate. Whereas in adult cases, and possibly also in cases of severe offences by juveniles, just desert and retributive sanctions might be considered to have some merit, in juvenile cases such considerations should always be outweighed by the interest of safeguarding the well-being and the future of the young person.

In line with resolution 8 of the Sixth United Nations Congress, rule 17.1 (b) encourages the use of alternatives to institutionalization to the maximum extent possible, bearing in mind the need to respond to the specific requirements of the young. Thus, full use should be made of the range of existing alternative sanctions and new alternative sanctions should be developed, bearing the public safety in mind. Probation should be granted to the greatest possible extent via suspended sentences, conditional sentences, board orders and other dispositions.

Rule 17.1 (c) corresponds to one of the guiding principles in resolution 4 of the Sixth Congress which aims at avoiding incarceration in the case of juveniles unless there is no other appropriate response that will protect the public safety.

The provision prohibiting capital punishment in rule 17.2 is in accordance with article 6, paragraph 5, of the International Covenant on Civil and Political Rights.

The provision against corporal punishment is in line with article 7 of the International Covenant on Civil and Political Rights and the Declaration on the Protection of All Persons from Being Subjected to Torture and Other Cruel, Inhuman or Degrading Treatment or Punishment, as well as the Convention against Torture and Other Cruel, Inhuman or Degrading Treatment or Punishment and the draft convention on the rights of the child.

The power to discontinue the proceedings at any time (rule 17.4) is a characteristic inherent in the handling of juvenile offenders as opposed to adults. At any time, circumstances may become known to the competent authority which would make a complete cessation of the intervention appear to be the best disposition of the case.

18. Various disposition measures

18.1 A large variety of disposition measures shall be made available to the competent authority, allowing for flexibility so as to avoid institutionalization to the greatest extent possible. Such measures, some of which may be combined, include:

(a) Care, guidance and supervision orders;

(b) Probation;

(c) Community service orders;

(d) Financial penalties, compensation and restitution;

(e) Intermediate treatment and other treatment orders;

(f) Orders to participate in group counselling and similar activities;

(g) Orders concerning foster care, living communities or other educational settings;

(h) Other relevant orders.

18.2 No juvenile shall be removed from parental supervision, whether partly or entirely, unless the circumstances of her or his case make this necessary.

Commentary

Rule 18.1 attempts to enumerate some of the important reactions and sanctions that have been practised and proved successful thus far, in different legal systems. On the whole they represent promising opinions that deserve replication and further development. The rule does not enumerate staffing requirements because of possible shortages of adequate staff in some regions; in those regions measures requiring less staff may be tried or developed.

The examples given in rule 18.1 have in common, above all, a reliance on and an appeal to the community for the effective implementation of alternative dispositions. Community-based correction is a traditional measure that has taken on many aspects. On that basis, relevant authorities should be encouraged to offer community-based services.

Rule 18.2 points to the importance of the family which, according to article 10, paragraph l, of the International Covenant on Economic, Social and Cultural Rights, is "the natural and fundamental group unit of society". Within the family, the parents have not only the right but also the responsibility to care for and supervise their children. Rule 18.2, therefore, requires that the separation of children from their parents is a measure of last resort. It may be resorted to only when the facts of the case clearly warrant this grave step (for example child abuse).

19. Least possible use of institutionalization

19.1 The placement of a juvenile in an institution shall always be a disposition of last resort and for the minimum necessary period.

Commentary

Progressive criminology advocates the use of non-institutional over institutional treatment. Little or no difference has been found in terms of the success of institutionalization as compared to non-institutionalization. The many adverse influences on an individual that seem unavoidable within any institutional setting evidently cannot be outbalanced by treatment efforts. This is especially the case for juveniles, who are vulnerable to negative influences. Moreover, the negative effects, not only of loss of liberty but also of separation from the usual social environment, are certainly more acute for juveniles than for adults because of their early stage of development.

Rule 19 aims at restricting institutionalization in two regards: in quantity ("last resort") and in time ("minimum necessary period"). Rule 19 reflects one of the basic guiding principles of resolution 4 of the Sixth United Nations Congress: a juvenile offender should not be incarcerated unless there is no other appropriate response. The rule, therefore, makes the appeal that if a juvenile must be institutionalized, the loss of liberty should be restricted to the least possible degree, with special institutional arrangements for confinement and bearing in mind the differences in kinds of offenders, offences and institutions. In fact, priority should be given to "open" over "closed" institutions. Furthermore, any facility should be of a correctional or educational rather than of a prison type.

20. Avoidance of unnecessary delay

20.1 Each case shall from the outset be handled expeditiously, without any unnecessary delay.

Commentary

The speedy conduct of formal procedures in juvenile cases is a paramount concern. Otherwise whatever good may be achieved by the procedure and the disposition is at risk. As time passes, the juvenile will find it increasingly difficult, if not impossible, to relate the procedure and disposition to the offence, both intellectually and psychologically.

21. Records

21.1 Records of juvenile offenders shall be kept strictly confidential and closed to third parties. Access to such records shall be limited to persons directly concerned with the disposition of the case at hand or other duly authorized persons.

21.2 Records of juvenile offenders shall not be used in adult proceedings in subsequent cases involving the same offender.

Commentary

The rule attempts to achieve a balance between conflicting interests connected with records or files: those of the police, prosecution and other authorities in improving control versus the interests of the juvenile offender. (See also rule 8.) "Other duly authorized persons" would generally include, among others, researchers.

22. Need for professionalism and training

22.1 Professional education, in-service training, refresher courses and other appropriate modes of instruction shall be utilized to establish and maintain the necessary professional competence of all personnel dealing with juvenile cases.

22.2 Juvenile justice personnel shall reflect the diversity of juveniles who come into contact with the juvenile justice system. Efforts shall be made to ensure the fair representation of women and minorities in juvenile justice agencies.

Commentary

The authorities competent for disposition may be persons with very different backgrounds (magistrates in the United Kingdom of Great Britain and Northern Ireland and in regions influenced by the common law system; legally trained judges in countries using Roman law and in regions influenced by them; and elsewhere elected or appointed laymen or jurists, members of community-based boards, etc.). For all these authorities, a minimum training in law, sociology, psychology, criminology and behavioural sciences would be required. This is considered as important as the organizational specialization and independence of the competent authority.

For social workers and probation officers, it might not be feasible to require professional specialization as a prerequisite for taking over any function dealing with juvenile offenders. Thus, professional on-the job instruction would be minimum qualifications.

Professional qualifications are an essential element in ensuring the impartial and effective administration of juvenile justice. Accordingly, it is necessary to improve the recruitment, advancement and professional training of personnel and to provide them with the necessary means to enable them to properly fulfil their functions.

All political, social, sexual, racial, religious, cultural or any other kind of discrimination in the selection, appointment and advancement of juvenile justice personnel should be avoided in order to achieve impartiality in the administration of juvenile justice. This was recommended by the Sixth Congress. Furthermore, the Sixth Congress called on Member States to ensure the fair and equal treatment of women as criminal justice personnel and recommended that special measures should be taken to recruit, train and facilitate the advancement of female personnel in juvenile justice administration.

Part Four

NON-INSTITUTIONAL TREATMENT

23. Effective implementation of disposition

23.1 Appropriate provisions shall be made for the implementation of orders of the competent authority, as referred to in rule 14.1 above, by that authority itself or by some other authority as circumstances may require.

23.2 Such provisions shall include the power to modify the orders as the competent authority may deem necessary from time to time, provided that such modification shall be determined in accordance with the principles contained in these Rules.

Commentary

Disposition in juvenile cases, more so than in adult cases, tends to influence the offender's life for a long period of time. Thus, it is important that the competent authority or an independent body (parole board, probation office, youth welfare institutions or others) with qualifications equal to those of the competent authority that originally disposed of the case should monitor the implementation of the disposition. The composition, powers and functions of the authority must be flexible; they are described in general terms in rule 23 in order to ensure wide acceptability.

24. Provision of needed assistance

24.1 Efforts shall be made to provide juveniles, at all stages of the proceedings, with necessary assistance such as lodging, education or vocational training, employment or any other assistance, helpful and practical, in order to facilitate the rehabilitative process.

Commentary

The promotion of the well-being of the juvenile is of paramount consideration. Thus, rule 24 emphasizes the importance of providing requisite facilities, services and other necessary assistance as may further the best interests of the juvenile throughout the rehabilitative process.

25. Mobilization of volunteers and other community services

25.1 Volunteers, voluntary organizations, local institutions and other community resources shall be called upon to contribute effectively to the rehabilitation of the juvenile in a community setting and, as far as possible, within the family unit.

Commentary

This rule reflects the need for a rehabilitative orientation of all work with juvenile offenders. Co-operation with the community is indispensable if the directives of the competent authority are to be carried out effectively. Volunteers and voluntary services, in particular, have proved to be valuable resources but are at present underutilized. In some instances, the co-operation of ex-offenders (including ex-addicts) can be of considerable assistance.

Rule 25 emanates from the principles laid down in rules 1.1 to 1.6 and follows the relevant provisions of the International Covenant on Civil and Political Rights.

Part Five

INSTITUTIONAL TREATMENT

26. Objectives of institutional treatment

26.1 The objective of training and treatment of juveniles placed in institutions is to provide care, protection, education and vocational skills, with a view to assisting them to assume socially constructive and productive roles in society.

26.2 Juveniles in institutions shall receive care, protection and all necessary assistance-social, educational, vocational, psychological, medical and physical-that they may require because of their age, sex, and personality and in the interest of their wholesome development .

26.3 Juveniles in institutions shall be kept separate from adults and shall be detained in a separate institution or in a separate part of an institution also holding adults.

26.4 Young female offenders placed in an institution deserve special attention as to their personal needs and problems. They shall by no means receive less care, protection, assistance, treatment and training than young male offenders. Their fair treatment shall be ensured.

26.5 In the interest and well-being of the institutionalized juvenile, the parents or guardians shall have a right of access.

26.6 Inter-ministerial and inter-departmental co-operation shall be fostered for the purpose of providing adequate academic or, as appropriate, vocational training to institutionalized juveniles, with a view to ensuring that they do no leave the institution at an educational disadvantage.

Commentary

The objectives of institutional treatment as stipulated in rules 26.1 and 26.2 would be acceptable to any system and culture. However, they have not yet been attained everywhere, and much more has to be done in this respect.

Medical and psychological assistance, in particular, are extremely important for institutionalized drug addicts, violent and mentally ill young persons.

The avoidance of negative influences through adult offenders and the safeguarding of the well-being of juveniles in an institutional setting, as stipulated in rule 26.3, are in line with one of the basic guiding principles of the Rules, as set out by the Sixth Congress in its resolution 4. The rule does not prevent States from taking other measures against the negative influences of adult offenders, which are at least as effective as the measures mentioned in the rule. (See also rule 13.4.)

Rule 26.4 addresses the fact that female offenders normally receive less attention than their male counterparts, as pointed out by the Sixth Congress. In particular, resolution 9 of the Sixth Congress calls for the fair treatment of female offenders at every stage of criminal justice processes and for special attention to their particular problems and needs while in custody. Moreover, this rule should also be considered in the light of the Caracas Declaration of the Sixth Congress, which, inter alia, calls for equal treatment in criminal justice administration, and against the background of the Declaration on the Elimination of Discrimination against Women and the Convention on the Elimination of All Forms of Discrimination against Women.

The right of access (rule 26.5) follows from the provisions of rules 7.1, 10.1, 15.2 and 18.2. Inter-ministerial and inter-departmental co-operation (rule 26.6) are of particular importance in the interest of generally enhancing the quality of institutional treatment and training.

27. Application of the Standard Minimum Rules for the Treatment of Prisoners adopted by the United Nations

27.1 The Standard Minimum Rules for the Treatment of Prisoners and related recommendations shall be applicable as far as relevant to the treatment of juvenile offenders in institutions, including those in detention pending adjudication.

27.2 Efforts shall be made to implement the relevant principles laid down in the Standard Minimum Rules for the Treatment of Prisoners to the largest possible extent so as to meet the varying needs of juveniles specific to their age, sex and personality.

Commentary

The Standard Minimum Rules for the Treatment of Prisoners were among the first instruments of this kind to be promulgated by the United Nations. It is generally agreed that they have had a world-wide impact. Although there are still countries where implementation is more an aspiration than a fact, those Standard Minimum Rules continue to be an important influence in the humane and equitable administration of correctional institutions.

Some essential protections covering juvenile offenders in institutions are contained in the Standard Minimum Rules for the Treatment of Prisoners (accommodation, architecture, bedding, clothing, complaints and requests, contact with the outside world, food, medical care, religious service, separation of ages, staffing, work, etc.) as are provisions concerning punishment and discipline, and restraint for dangerous offenders. It would not be appropriate to modify those Standard Minimum Rules according to the particular characteristics of institutions for juvenile offenders within the scope of the Standard Minimum Rules for the Administration of Juvenile Justice.

Rule 27 focuses on the necessary requirements for juveniles in institutions (rule 27.1) as well as on the varying needs specific to their age, sex and personality (rule 27.2). Thus, the objectives and content of the rule interrelate to the relevant provisions of the Standard Minimum Rules for the Treatment of Prisoners.

28. Frequent and early recourse to conditional release

28.1 Conditional release from an institution shall be used by the appropriate authority to the greatest possible extent, and shall be granted at the earliest possible time.

28.2 Juveniles released conditionally from an institution shall be assisted and supervised by an appropriate authority and shall receive full support by the community.

Commentary

The power to order conditional release may rest with the competent authority, as mentioned in rule 14.1, or with some other authority. In view of this, it is adequate to refer here to the "appropriate" rather than to the "competent" authority.

Circumstances permitting, conditional release shall be preferred to serving a full sentence. Upon evidence of satisfactory progress towards rehabilitation, even offenders who had been deemed dangerous at the time of their institutionalization can be conditionally released whenever feasible. Like probation, such release may be conditional on the satisfactory fulfilment of the requirements specified by the relevant authorities for a period of time established in the decision, for example relating to "good behavior" of the offender, attendance in community programmes, residence in half-way houses, etc.

In the case of offenders conditionally released from an institution, assistance and supervision by probation or other officer (particularly where probation has not yet been adopted) should be provided and community support should be encouraged.

29. Semi-institutional arrangements

29.1 Efforts shall be made to provide semi-institutional arrangements, such as half-way houses, educational s, day-time training centres and other such appropriate arrangements that may assist juveniles in their proper reintegration into society.

Commentary

The importance of care following a period of institutionalization should not be underestimated. This rule emphasizes the necessity of forming a net of semi-institutional arrangements.

This rule also emphasizes the need for a diverse range of facilities and services designed to meet the different needs of young offenders re-entering the community and to provide guidance and structural support as an important step towards successful reintegration into society.

Part Six

RESEARCH, PLANNING, POLICY FORMULATION AND EVALUATION

30. Research as a basis for planning, policy formulation and evaluation

30.1 Efforts shall be made to organize and promote necessary research as a basis for effective planning and policy formulation.

30.2 Efforts shall be made to review and appraise periodically the trends, problems and causes of juvenile delinquency and crime as well as the varying particular needs of juveniles in custody.

30.3 Efforts shall be made to establish a regular evaluative research mechanism built into the system of juvenile justice administration and to collect and analyse relevant data and information for appropriate assessment and future improvement and reform of the administration.

30.4 The delivery of services in juvenile justice administration shall be systematically planned and implemented as an integral part of national development efforts.

Commentary

The utilization of research as a basis for an informed juvenile justice policy is widely acknowledged as an important mechanism for keeping practices abreast of advances in knowledge and the continuing development and improvement of the juvenile justice system. The mutual feedback between research and policy is especially important in juvenile justice. With rapid and often drastic changes in the life-styles of the young and in the forms and dimensions of juvenile crime, the societal and justice responses to juvenile crime and delinquency quickly become outmoded and inadequate.

Rule 30 thus establishes standards for integrating research into the process of policy formulation and application in juvenile justice administration. The rule draws particular attention to the need for regular review and evaluation of existing programmes and measures and for planning within the broader context of overall development objectives.

A constant appraisal of the needs of juveniles, as well as the trends and problems of delinquency, is a prerequisite for improving the methods of formulating appropriate policies and establishing adequate interventions, at both formal and informal levels. In this context, research by independent persons and bodies should be facilitated by responsible agencies, and it may be valuable to obtain and to take into account the views of juveniles themselves, not only those who come into contact with the system.

The process of planning must particularly emphasize a more effective and equitable system for the delivery of necessary services. Towards that end, there should be a comprehensive and regular assessment of the wide-ranging, particular needs and problems of juveniles and an identification of clear-cut priorities. In that connection, there should also be a co-ordination in the use of existing resources, including alternatives and community support that would be suitable in setting up specific procedures designed to implement and monitor established programmes.

4.5 DECLARATION ON SOCIAL AND LEGAL PRINCIPLES RELATING TO THE PROTECTION AND WELFARE OF CHILDREN, WITH SPECIAL REFERENCE TO FOSTER PLACEMENT AND ADOPTION NATIONALLY AND INTERNATIONALLY, 1986 [6]

The General Assembly,

Recalling its resolutions 36/167 of 16 December 1981, 37/115 of 16 December 1982, 38/142 of 19 December 1983 and 39/89 of 13 December 1984, and its decision 40/422 of 11 December 1985,

Taking note of the draft Declaration on Social and Legal Principles relating to the Protection and Welfare of Children, with Special Reference to Foster Placement and Adoption Nationally and Internationally, as submitted by the Economic and Social Council by its resolution 1979/28 of 9 May 1979,

Taking note with appreciation of the work done on this question in the Third and Sixth Committees, as well as the efforts made by Member States representing different legal systems, during the consultations held at Headquarters from 16 to 27 September 1985 and early in the forty-first session, to join in the common endeavour of completing the work on the draft Declaration,

Adopts the Declaration on Social and Legal Principles relating to the Protection and Welfare of Children, with Special Reference to Foster Placement and Adoption Nationally and Internationally, the text of which is annexed to the present resolution.

---

[6] UN General Assembly resolution, A/RES/41/85, 3 December 1986.

ANNEX

Declaration on Social and Legal Principles relating to the Protection and Welfare of Children, with Special Reference to Foster Placement and Adoption Nationally and Internationally

The General Assembly,

Recalling the Universal Declaration of Human Rights, the International Covenant on Economic, Social and Cultural Rights, the International Covenant on Civil and Political Rights, the International Convention on the Elimination of All Forms of Racial Discrimination and the Convention on the Elimination of All Forms of Discrimination against Women,

Recalling also the Declaration of the Rights of the Child, which it proclaimed by its resolution 1386 (XIV) of 20 November 1959,

Reaffirming principle 6 of that Declaration, which states that the child shall, wherever possible, grow up in the care and under the responsibility of his parents and, in any case, in an atmosphere of affection and of moral and material security,

Concerned at the large number of children who are abandoned or become orphans owing to violence, internal disturbance, armed conflicts, natural disasters, economic crises or social problems,

Bearing in mind that in all foster placement and adoption procedures the best interests of the child should be the paramount consideration,

Recognizing that under the principal legal systems of the world, various valuable alternative institutions exist, such as the Kafala of Islamic Law, which provide substitute care to children who cannot be cared for by their own parents,

Recognizing further that only where a particular institution is recognized and regulated by the domestic law of a State would the provisions of this Declaration relating to that institution be relevant and that such provisions would in no way affect the existing alternative institutions in other legal systems,

Conscious of the need to proclaim universal principles to be taken into account in cases where procedures are instituted relating to foster placement or adoption of a child, either nationally or internationally,

Bearing in mind, however, that the principles set forth hereunder do not impose on States such legal institutions as foster placement or adoption,

Proclaims the following principles:

A. GENERAL FAMILY AND CHILD WELFARE

Article 1

Every State should give a high priority to family and child welfare.

Article 2

Child welfare depends upon good family welfare.

Article 3

The first priority for a child is to be cared for by his or her own parents.

Article 4

When care by the child's own parents is unavailable or inappropriate, care by relatives of the child's parents, by another substitute - foster or adoptive - family or, if necessary, by an appropriate institution should be considered.

Article 5

In all matters relating to the placement of a child outside the care of the child's own parents, the best interests of the child, particularly his or her need for affection and right to security and continuing care, should be the paramount consideration.

Article 6

Persons responsible for foster placement or adoption procedures should have professional or other appropriate training.

Article 7

Governments should determine the adequacy of their national child welfare services and consider appropriate actions.

Article 8

The child should at all times have a name, a nationality and a legal representative. The child should not, as a result of foster placement, adoption or any alternative regime, be deprived of his or her name, nationality or legal representative unless the child thereby acquires a new name, nationality or legal representative.

Article 9

The need of a foster or an adopted child to know about his or her background should be recognized by persons responsible for the child's care, unless this is contrary to the child's best interests.

B. FOSTER PLACEMENT

Article 10

Foster placement of children should be regulated by law.

Article 11

Foster family care, though temporary in nature, may continue, if necessary, until adulthood but should not preclude either prior return to the child's own parents or adoption.

Article 12

In all matters of foster family care, the prospective foster parents and, as appropriate, the child and his or her own parents should be properly involved. A competent authority or agency should be responsible for supervision to ensure the welfare of the child.

C. ADOPTION

Article 13

The primary aim of adoption is to provide the child who cannot be cared for by his or her own parents with a permanent family.

Article 14

In considering possible adoption placements, persons responsible for them should select the most appropriate environment for the child.

Article 15

Sufficient time and adequate counselling should be given to the child's own parents, the prospective adoptive parents and, as appropriate, the child in order to reach a decision on the child's future as early as possible.

Article 16

The relationship between the child to be adopted and the prospective adoptive parents should be observed by child welfare agencies or services prior to the adoption. Legislation should ensure that the child is recognized in law as a member of the adoptive family and enjoys all the rights pertinent thereto.

Article 17

If a child cannot be placed in a foster or an adoptive family or cannot in any suitable manner be cared for in the country of origin, inter-country adoption may be considered as an alternative means of providing the child with a family.

Article 18

Governments should establish policy, legislation and effective supervision for the protection of children involved in inter-country adoption. Inter-country adoption should, wherever possible, only be undertaken when such measures have been established in the States concerned.

Article 19

Policies should be established and laws enacted, where necessary, for the prohibition of abduction and of any other act for illicit placement of children.

Article 20

In inter-country adoption, placements should, as a rule, be made through competent authorities or agencies with application of safeguards and standards equivalent to those existing in respect of national adoption. In no case should the placement result in improper financial gain for those involved in it.

Article 21

In inter-country adoption through persons acting as agents for prospective adoptive parents, special precautions should be taken in order to protect the child's legal and social interests.

Article 22

No inter-country adoption should be considered before it has been established that the child is legally free for adoption and that any pertinent documents necessary to complete the adoption, such as the consent of competent authorities, will become available. It must also be established that the child will be able to migrate and to join the prospective adoptive parents and may obtain their nationality.

Article 23

In inter-country adoption, as a rule, the legal validity of the adoption should be assured in each of the countries involved.

Article 24

Where the nationality of the child differs from that of the prospective adoptive parents, all due weight shall be given to both the law of the State of which the child is a national and the law of the State of which the prospective adoptive parents are nationals. In this connection due regard shall be given to the child's cultural and religious background and interests.

4.6 UNITED NATIONS RULES FOR THE PROTECTION OF JUVENILES DEPRIVED OF THEIR LIBERTY, 1990[7]

I. Fundamental perspectives

1. The juvenile justice system should uphold the rights and safety and promote the physical and mental well-being of juveniles. Imprisonment should be used as a last resort.

2. Juveniles should only be deprived of their liberty in accordance with the principles and procedures set forth in these Rules and in the United Nations Standard Minimum Rules for the Administration of Juvenile Justice (The Beijing Rules). Deprivation of the liberty of a juvenile should be a disposition of last resort and for the minimum necessary period and should be limited to exceptional cases. The length of the sanction should be determined by the judicial authority, without precluding the possibility of his or her early release.

3. The Rules are intended to establish minimum standards accepted by the United Nations for the protection of juveniles deprived of their liberty in all forms, consistent with human rights and fundamental freedoms, and with a view to counteracting the detrimental effects of all types of detention and to fostering integration in society.

[7] Adopted by General Assembly resolution 45/113 of 14 December 1990.

4. The Rules should be applied impartially, without discrimination of any kind as to race, colour, sex, age, language, religion, nationality, political or other opinion, cultural beliefs or practices, property, birth or family status, ethnic or social origin, and disability. The religious and cultural beliefs, practices and moral concepts of the juvenile should be respected.

5. The Rules are designed to serve as convenient standards of reference and to provide encouragement and guidance to professionals involved in the management of the juvenile justice system.

6. The Rules should be made readily available to juvenile justice personnel in their national languages. Juveniles who are not fluent in the language spoken by the personnel of the detention facility should have the right to the services of an interpreter free of charge whenever necessary, in particular during medical examinations and disciplinary proceedings.

7. Where appropriate, States should incorporate the Rules into their legislation or amend it accordingly and provide effective remedies for their breach, including compensation when injuries are inflicted on juveniles. States should also monitor the application of the Rules.

8. The competent authorities should constantly seek to increase the awareness of the public that the care of detained juveniles and preparation for their return to society is a social service of great importance, and to this end active steps should be taken to foster open contacts between the juveniles and the local community.

9. Nothing in the Rules should be interpreted as precluding the application of the relevant United Nations and human rights instruments and standards, recognized by the international community, that are more conducive to ensuring the rights, care and protection of juveniles, children and all young persons.

10. In the event that the practical application of particular Rules contained in sections II to V, inclusive, presents any conflict with the Rules contained in the present section, compliance with the latter shall be regarded as the predominant requirement.

II. Scope and application of the rules

11. For the purposes of the Rules, the following definitions should apply:

(a) A juvenile is every person under the age of 18. The age limit below which it should not be permitted to deprive a child of his or her liberty should be determined by law;

(b) The deprivation of liberty means any form of detention or imprisonment or the placement of a person in a public or private custodial setting, from which this person is not permitted to leave at will, by order of any judicial, administrative or other public authority.

12. The deprivation of liberty should be effected in conditions and circumstances which ensure respect for the human rights of juveniles. Juveniles detained in facilities should be guaranteed the benefit of meaningful activities and programmes which would serve to promote and sustain their health and self-respect, to foster their sense of responsibility and encourage those attitudes and skills that will assist them in developing their potential as members of society.

13. Juveniles deprived of their liberty shall not for any reason related to their status be denied the civil, economic, political, social or cultural rights to which they are entitled under national or international law, and which are compatible with the deprivation of liberty.

14. The protection of the individual rights of juveniles with special regard to the legality of the execution of the detention measures shall be ensured by the competent authority, while the objectives of social integration should be secured by regular inspections and other means of control carried out, according to international standards, national laws and regulations, by a duly constituted body authorized to visit the juveniles and not belonging to the detention facility.

15. The Rules apply to all types and forms of detention facilities in which juveniles are deprived of their liberty. Sections I, II, IV and V of the Rules apply to all detention facilities and institutional settings in which juveniles are detained, and section III applies specifically to juveniles under arrest or awaiting trial.

16. The Rules shall be implemented in the context of the economic, social and cultural conditions prevailing in each Member State.

III. Juveniles under arrest or awaiting trial

17. Juveniles who are detained under arrest or awaiting trial ("untried") are presumed innocent and shall be treated as such. Detention before trial shall be avoided to the extent possible and limited to exceptional circumstances. Therefore, all efforts shall be made to apply alternative measures. When preventive detention is nevertheless used, juvenile courts and investigative bodies shall give the highest priority to the most expeditious processing of such cases to ensure the shortest possible duration of detention. Untried detainees should be separated from convicted juveniles.

18. The conditions under which an untried juvenile is detained should be consistent with the rules set out below, with additional specific provisions as are necessary and appropriate, given

the requirements of the presumption of innocence, the duration of the detention and the legal status and circumstances of the juvenile. These provisions would include, but not necessarily be restricted to, the following:

(a) Juveniles should have the right of legal counsel and be enabled to apply for free legal aid, where such aid is available, and to communicate regularly with their legal advisers. Privacy and confidentiality shall be ensured for such communications;

(b) Juveniles should be provided, where possible, with opportunities to pursue work, with remuneration, and continue education or training, but should not be required to do so. Work, education or training should not cause the continuation of the detention;

(c) Juveniles should receive and retain materials for their leisure and recreation as are compatible with the interests of the administration of justice.

IV. The management of juvenile facilities

A. Records

19. All reports, including legal records, medical records and records of disciplinary proceedings, and all other documents relating to the form, content and details of treatment, should be placed in a confidential individual file, which should be kept up to date, accessible only to authorized persons and classified in such a way as to be easily understood. Where possible, every juvenile should have the right to contest any fact or opinion contained in his or her file so as to permit rectification of inaccurate, unfounded or unfair statements. In order to exercise this right, there should be procedures that allow an appropriate third party to have access to and to consult the file on request. Upon release, the records of juveniles shall be sealed, and, at an appropriate time, expunged.

20. No juvenile should be received in any detention facility without a valid commitment order of a judicial, administrative or other public authority. The details of this order should be immediately entered in the register. No juvenile should be detained in any facility where there is no such register.

B. Admission, registration, movement and transfer

21. In every place where juveniles are detained, a complete and secure record of the following information should be kept concerning each juvenile received:

(a) Information on the identity of the juvenile;

(b) The fact of and reasons for commitment and the authority therefor;

(c) The day and hour of admission, transfer and release;

(d) Details of the notifications to parents and guardians on every admission, transfer or release of the juvenile in their care at the time of commitment;

(e) Details of known physical and mental health problems, including drug and alcohol abuse.

22. The information on admission, place, transfer and release should be provided without delay to the parents and guardians or closest relative of the juvenile concerned.

23. As soon as possible after reception, full reports and relevant information on the personal situation and circumstances of each juvenile should be drawn up and submitted to the administration.

24. On admission, all juveniles shall be given a copy of the rules governing the detention facility and a written description of their rights and obligations in a language they can understand, together with the address of the authorities competent to receive complaints, as well as the address of public or private agencies and organizations which provide legal assistance. For those juveniles who are illiterate or who cannot understand the language in the written form, the information should be conveyed in a manner enabling full comprehension.

25. All juveniles should be helped to understand the regulations governing the internal organization of the facility, the goals and methodology of the care provided, the disciplinary requirements and procedures, other authorized methods of seeking information and of making complaints and all such other matters as are necessary to enable them to understand fully their rights and obligations during detention.

26. The transport of juveniles should be carried out at the expense of the administration in conveyances with adequate ventilation and light, in conditions that should in no way subject them to hardship or indignity. Juveniles should not be transferred from one facility to another arbitrarily.

C. Classification and placement

27. As soon as possible after the moment of admission, each juvenile should be interviewed, and a psychological and social report identifying any factors relevant to the specific type and level of care and programme required by the juvenile should be prepared. This report, together with the report prepared by a medical officer who has examined the juvenile upon admission,

should be forwarded to the director for purposes of determining the most appropriate placement for the juvenile within the facility and the specific type and level of care and programme required and to be pursued. When special rehabilitative treatment is required, and the length of stay in the facility permits, trained personnel of the facility should prepare a written, individualized treatment plan specifying treatment objectives and time-frame and the means, stages and delays with which the objectives should be approached.

28. The detention of juveniles should only take place under conditions that take full account of their particular needs, status and special requirements according to their age, personality, sex and type of offence, as well as mental and physical health, and which ensure their protection from harmful influences and risk situations. The principal criterion for the separation of different categories of juveniles deprived of their liberty should be the provision of the type of care best suited to the particular needs of the individuals concerned and the protection of their physical, mental and moral integrity and well-being.

29. In all detention facilities juveniles should be separated from adults, unless they are members of the same family. Under controlled conditions, juveniles may be brought together with carefully selected adults as part of a special programme that has been shown to be beneficial for the juveniles concerned.

30. Open detention facilities for juveniles should be established. Open detention facilities are those with no or minimal security measures. The population in such detention facilities should be as small as possible. The number of juveniles detained in closed facilities should be small enough to enable individualized treatment. Detention facilities for juveniles should be decentralized and of such size as to facilitate access and contact between the juveniles and their families. Small-scale detention facilities should be established and integrated into the social, economic and cultural environment of the community.

D. Physical environment and accommodation

31. Juveniles deprived of their liberty have the right to facilities and services that meet all the requirements of health and human dignity.

32. The design of detention facilities for juveniles and the physical environment should be in keeping with the rehabilitative aim of residential treatment, with due regard to the need of the juvenile for privacy, sensory stimuli, opportunities for association with peers and participation in sports, physical exercise and leisure-time activities. The design and structure of juvenile detention facilities should be such as to minimize the risk of fire and to ensure safe evacuation from the premises. There should be an effective alarm system in case of fire, as

well as formal and drilled procedures to ensure the safety of the juveniles. Detention facilities should not be located in areas where there are known health or other hazards or risks.

33. Sleeping accommodation should normally consist of small group dormitories or individual bedrooms, while bearing in mind local standards. During sleeping hours there should be regular, unobtrusive supervision of all sleeping areas, including individual rooms and group dormitories, in order to ensure the protection of each juvenile. Every juvenile should, in accordance with local or national standards, be provided with separate and sufficient bedding, which should be clean when issued, kept in good order and changed often enough to ensure cleanliness.

34. Sanitary installations should be so located and of a sufficient standard to enable every juvenile to comply, as required, with their physical needs in privacy and in a clean and decent manner.

35. The possession of personal effects is a basic element of the right to privacy and essential to the psychological well-being of the juvenile. The right of every juvenile to possess personal effects and to have adequate storage facilities for them should be fully recognized and respected. Personal effects that the juvenile does not choose to retain or that are confiscated should be placed in safe custody. An inventory thereof should be signed by the juvenile. Steps should be taken to keep them in good condition. All such articles and money should be returned to the juvenile on release, except in so far as he or she has been authorized to spend money or send such property out of the facility. If a juvenile receives or is found in possession of any medicine, the medical officer should decide what use should be made of it.

36. To the extent possible juveniles should have the right to use their own clothing. Detention facilities should ensure that each juvenile has personal clothing suitable for the climate and adequate to ensure good health, and which should in no manner be degrading or humiliating. Juveniles removed from or leaving a facility for any purpose should be allowed to wear their own clothing.

37. Every detention facility shall ensure that every juvenile receives food that is suitably prepared and presented at normal meal times and of a quality and quantity to satisfy the standards of dietetics, hygiene and health and, as far as possible, religious and cultural requirements. Clean drinking water should be available to every juvenile at any time.

E. Education, vocational training and work

38. Every juvenile of compulsory school age has the right to education suited to his or her needs and abilities and designed to prepare him or her for return to society. Such education

should be provided outside the detention facility in community schools wherever possible and, in any case, by qualified teachers through programmes integrated with the education system of the country so that, after release, juveniles may continue their education without difficulty. Special attention should be given by the administration of the detention facilities to the education of juveniles of foreign origin or with particular cultural or ethnic needs. Juveniles who are illiterate or have cognitive or learning difficulties should have the right to special education.

39. Juveniles above compulsory school age who wish to continue their education should be permitted and encouraged to do so, and every effort should be made to provide them with access to appropriate educational programmes.

40. Diplomas or educational certificates awarded to juveniles while in detention should not indicate in any way that the juvenile has been institutionalized.

41. Every detention facility should provide access to a library that is adequately stocked with both instructional and recreational books and periodicals suitable for the juveniles, who should be encouraged and enabled to make full use of it.

42. Every juvenile should have the right to receive vocational training in occupations likely to prepare him or her for future employment.

43. With due regard to proper vocational selection and to the requirements of institutional administration, juveniles should be able to choose the type of work they wish to perform.

44. All protective national and international standards applicable to child labour and young workers should apply to juveniles deprived of their liberty.

45. Wherever possible, juveniles should be provided with the opportunity to perform remunerated labour, if possible within the local community, as a complement to the vocational training provided in order to enhance the possibility of finding suitable employment when they return to their communities. The type of work should be such as to provide appropriate training that will be of benefit to the juveniles following release. The organization and methods of work offered in detention facilities should resemble as closely as possible those of similar work in the community, so as to prepare juveniles for the conditions of normal occupational life.

46. Every juvenile who performs work should have the right to an equitable remuneration. The interests of the juveniles and of their vocational training should not be subordinated to the purpose of making a profit for the detention facility or a third party. Part of the earnings of a

juvenile should normally be set aside to constitute a savings fund to be handed over to the juvenile on release. The juvenile should have the right to use the remainder of those earnings to purchase articles for his or her own use or to indemnify the victim injured by his or her offence or to send it to his or her family or other persons outside the detention facility.

F. Recreation

47. Every juvenile should have the right to a suitable amount of time for daily free exercise, in the open air whenever weather permits, during which time appropriate recreational and physical training should normally be provided. Adequate space, installations and equipment should be provided for these activities. Every juvenile should have additional time for daily leisure activities, part of which should be devoted, if the juvenile so wishes, to arts and crafts skill development. The detention facility should ensure that each juvenile is physically able to participate in the available programmes of physical education. Remedial physical education and therapy should be offered, under medical supervision, to juveniles needing it.

G. Religion

48. Every juvenile should be allowed to satisfy the needs of his or her religious and spiritual life, in particular by attending the services or meetings provided in the detention facility or by conducting his or her own services and having possession of the necessary books or items of religious observance and instruction of his or her denomination. If a detention facility contains a sufficient number of juveniles of a given religion, one or more qualified representatives of that religion should be appointed or approved and allowed to hold regular services and to pay pastoral visits in private to juveniles at their request. Every juvenile should have the right to receive visits from a qualified representative of any religion of his or her choice, as well as the right not to participate in religious services and freely to decline religious education, counselling or indoctrination.

H. Medical care

49. Every juvenile shall receive adequate medical care, both preventive and remedial, including dental, ophthalmological and mental health care, as well as pharmaceutical products and special diets as medically indicated. All such medical care should, where possible, be provided to detained juveniles through the appropriate health facilities and services of the community in which the detention facility is located, in order to prevent stigmatization of the juvenile and promote self-respect and integration into the community.

50. Every juvenile has a right to be examined by a physician immediately upon admission to a detention facility, for the purpose of recording any evidence of prior ill-treatment and identifying any physical or mental condition requiring medical attention.

51. The medical services provided to juveniles should seek to detect and should treat any physical or mental illness, substance abuse or other condition that may hinder the integration of the juvenile into society. Every detention facility for juveniles should have immediate access to adequate medical facilities and equipment appropriate to the number and requirements of its residents and staff trained in preventive health care and the handling of medical emergencies. Every juvenile who is ill, who complains of illness or who demonstrates symptoms of physical or mental difficulties, should be examined promptly by a medical officer.

52. Any medical officer who has reason to believe that the physical or mental health of a juvenile has been or will be injuriously affected by continued detention, a hunger strike or any condition of detention should report this fact immediately to the director of the detention facility in question and to the independent authority responsible for safeguarding the well-being of the juvenile.

53. A juvenile who is suffering from mental illness should be treated in a specialized institution under independent medical management. Steps should be taken, by arrangement with appropriate agencies, to ensure any necessary continuation of mental health care after release.

54. Juvenile detention facilities should adopt specialized drug abuse prevention and rehabilitation programmes administered by qualified personnel. These programmes should be adapted to the age, sex and other requirements of the juveniles concerned, and detoxification facilities and services staffed by trained personnel should be available to drug- or alcohol-dependent juveniles.

55. Medicines should be administered only for necessary treatment on medical grounds and, when possible, after having obtained the informed consent of the juvenile concerned. In particular, they must not be administered with a view to eliciting information or a confession, as a punishment or as a means of restraint. Juveniles shall never be testees in the experimental use of drugs and treatment. The administration of any drug should always be authorized and carried out by qualified medical personnel.

I. Notification of illness, injury and death

56. The family or guardian of a juvenile and any other person designated by the juvenile have the right to be informed of the state of health of the juvenile on request and in the event of any

important changes in the health of the juvenile. The director of the detention facility should notify immediately the family or guardian of the juvenile concerned, or other designated person, in case of death, illness requiring transfer of the juvenile to an outside medical facility, or a condition requiring clinical care within the detention facility for more than 48 hours. Notification should also be given to the consular authorities of the State of which a foreign juvenile is a citizen.

57. Upon the death of a juvenile during the period of deprivation of liberty, the nearest relative should have the right to inspect the death certificate, see the body and determine the method of disposal of the body. Upon the death of a juvenile in detention, there should be an independent inquiry into the causes of death, the report of which should be made accessible to the nearest relative. This inquiry should also be made when the death of a juvenile occurs within six months from the date of his or her release from the detention facility and there is reason to believe that the death is related to the period of detention.

58. A juvenile should be informed at the earliest possible time of the death, serious illness or injury of any immediate family member and should be provided with the opportunity to attend the funeral of the deceased or go to the bedside of a critically ill relative.

J. Contacts with the wider community

59. Every means should be provided to ensure that juveniles have adequate communication with the outside world, which is an integral part of the right to fair and humane treatment and is essential to the preparation of juveniles for their return to society. Juveniles should be allowed to communicate with their families, friends and other persons or representatives of reputable outside organizations, to leave detention facilities for a visit to their and family and to receive special permission to leave the detention facility for educational, vocational or other important reasons. Should the juvenile be serving a sentence, the time spent outside a detention facility should be counted as part of the period of sentence.

60. Every juvenile should have the right to receive regular and frequent visits, in principle once a week and not less than once a month, in circumstances that respect the need of the juvenile for privacy, contact and unrestricted communication with the family and the defence counsel.

61. Every juvenile should have the right to communicate in writing or by telephone at least twice a week with the person of his or her choice, unless legally restricted, and should be assisted as necessary in order effectively to enjoy this right. Every juvenile should have the right to receive correspondence.

62. Juveniles should have the opportunity to keep themselves informed regularly of the news by reading newspapers, periodicals and other publications, through access to radio and television programmes and motion pictures, and through the visits of the representatives of any lawful club or organization in which the juvenile is interested.

K. Limitations of physical restraint and the use of force

63. Recourse to instruments of restraint and to force for any purpose should be prohibited, except as set forth in rule 64 below.

64. Instruments of restraint and force can only be used in exceptional cases, where all other control methods have been exhausted and failed, and only as explicitly authorized and specified by law and regulation. They should not cause humiliation or degradation, and should be used restrictively and only for the shortest possible period of time. By order of the director of the administration, such instruments might be resorted to in order to prevent the juvenile from inflicting self-injury, injuries to others or serious destruction of property. In such instances, the director should at once consult medical and other relevant personnel and report to the higher administrative authority.

65. The carrying and use of weapons by personnel should be prohibited in any facility where juveniles are detained.

L. Disciplinary procedures

66. Any disciplinary measures and procedures should maintain the interest of safety and an ordered community life and should be consistent with the upholding of the inherent dignity of the juvenile and the fundamental objective of institutional care, namely, instilling a sense of justice, self-respect and respect for the basic rights of every person.

67. All disciplinary measures constituting cruel, inhuman or degrading treatment shall be strictly prohibited, including corporal punishment, placement in a dark cell, closed or solitary confinement or any other punishment that may compromise the physical or mental health of the juvenile concerned. The reduction of diet and the restriction or denial of contact with family members should be prohibited for any purpose. Labour should always be viewed as an educational tool and a means of promoting the self-respect of the juvenile in preparing him or her for return to the community and should not be imposed as a disciplinary sanction. No juvenile should be sanctioned more than once for the same disciplinary infraction. Collective sanctions should be prohibited.

68. Legislation or regulations adopted by the competent administrative authority should establish norms concerning the following, taking full account of the fundamental characteristics, needs and rights of juveniles:

(a) Conduct constituting a disciplinary offence;

(b) Type and duration of disciplinary sanctions that may be inflicted;

(c) The authority competent to impose such sanctions;

(d) The authority competent to consider appeals.

69. A report of misconduct should be presented promptly to the competent authority, which should decide on it without undue delay. The competent authority should conduct a thorough examination of the case.

70. No juvenile should be disciplinarily sanctioned except in strict accordance with the terms of the law and regulations in force. No juvenile should be sanctioned unless he or she has been informed of the alleged infraction in a manner appropriate to the full understanding of the juvenile, and given a proper opportunity of presenting his or her defence, including the right of appeal to a competent impartial authority. Complete records should be kept of all disciplinary proceedings.

71. No juveniles should be responsible for disciplinary functions except in the supervision of specified social, educational or sports activities or in self-government programmes.

M. Inspection and complaints

72. Qualified inspectors or an equivalent duly constituted authority not belonging to the administration of the facility should be empowered to conduct inspections on a regular basis and to undertake unannounced inspections on their own initiative, and should enjoy full guarantees of independence in the exercise of this function. Inspectors should have unrestricted access to all persons employed by or working in any facility where juveniles are or may be deprived of their liberty, to all juveniles and to all records of such facilities.

73. Qualified medical officers attached to the inspecting authority or the public health service should participate in the inspections, evaluating compliance with the rules concerning the physical environment, hygiene, accommodation, food, exercise and medical services, as well as any other aspect or conditions of institutional life that affect the physical and mental health of juveniles. Every juvenile should have the right to talk in confidence to any inspecting officer.

74. After completing the inspection, the inspector should be required to submit a report on the findings. The report should include an evaluation of the compliance of the detention facilities with the present rules and relevant provisions of national law, and recommendations regarding any steps considered necessary to ensure compliance with them. Any facts discovered by an inspector that appear to indicate that a violation of legal provisions concerning the rights of juveniles or the operation of a juvenile detention facility has occurred should be communicated to the competent authorities for investigation and prosecution.

75. Every juvenile should have the opportunity of making requests or complaints to the director of the detention facility and to his or her authorized representative.

76. Every juvenile should have the right to make a request or complaint, without censorship as to substance, to the central administration, the judicial authority or other proper authorities through approved channels, and to be informed of the response without delay.

77. Efforts should be made to establish an independent office (ombudsman) to receive and investigate complaints made by juveniles deprived of their liberty and to assist in the achievement of equitable settlements.

78. Every juvenile should have the right to request assistance from family members, legal counsellors, humanitarian groups or others where possible, in order to make a complaint. Illiterate juveniles should be provided with assistance should they need to use the services of public or private agencies and organizations which provide legal counsel or which are competent to receive complaints.

N. Return to the community

79. All juveniles should benefit from arrangements designed to assist them in returning to society, family life, education or employment after release. Procedures, including early release, and special courses should be devised to this end.

80. Competent authorities should provide or ensure services to assist juveniles in re-establishing themselves in society and to lessen prejudice against such juveniles. These services should ensure, to the extent possible, that the juvenile is provided with suitable residence, employment, clothing, and sufficient means to maintain himself or herself upon release in order to facilitate successful reintegration. The representatives of agencies providing such services should be consulted and should have access to juveniles while detained, with a view to assisting them in their return to the community.

V. Personnel

81. Personnel should be qualified and include a sufficient number of specialists such as educators, vocational instructors, counsellors, social workers, psychiatrists and psychologists. These and other specialist staff should normally be employed on a permanent basis. This should not preclude part-time or volunteer workers when the level of support and training they can provide is appropriate and beneficial. Detention facilities should make use of all remedial, educational, moral, spiritual, and other resources and forms of assistance that are appropriate and available in the community, according to the individual needs and problems of detained juveniles.

82. The administration should provide for the careful selection and recruitment of every grade and type of personnel, since the proper management of detention facilities depends on their integrity, humanity, ability and professional capacity to deal with juveniles, as well as personal suitability for the work.

83. To secure the foregoing ends, personnel should be appointed as professional officers with adequate remuneration to attract and retain suitable women and men. The personnel of juvenile detention facilities should be continually encouraged to fulfil their duties and obligations in a humane, committed, professional, fair and efficient manner, to conduct themselves at all times in such a way as to deserve and gain the respect of the juveniles, and to provide juveniles with a positive role model and perspective.

84. The administration should introduce forms of organization and management that facilitate communications between different categories of staff in each detention facility so as to enhance cooperation between the various services engaged in the care of juveniles, as well as between staff and the administration, with a view to ensuring that staff directly in contact with juveniles are able to function in conditions favourable to the efficient fulfilment of their duties.

85. The personnel should receive such training as will enable them to carry out their responsibilities effectively, in particular training in child psychology, child welfare and international standards and norms of human rights and the rights of the child, including the present Rules. The personnel should maintain and improve their knowledge and professional capacity by attending courses of in-service training, to be organized at suitable intervals throughout their career.

86. The director of a facility should be adequately qualified for his or her task, with administrative ability and suitable training and experience, and should carry out his or her duties on a full-time basis.

87. In the performance of their duties, personnel of detention facilities should respect and protect the human dignity and fundamental human rights of all juveniles, in particular, as follows:

(a) No member of the detention facility or institutional personnel may inflict, instigate or tolerate any act of torture or any form of harsh, cruel, inhuman or degrading treatment, punishment, correction or discipline under any pretext or circumstance whatsoever;

(b) All personnel should rigorously oppose and combat any act of corruption, reporting it without delay to the competent authorities;

(c) All personnel should respect the present Rules. Personnel who have reason to believe that a serious violation of the present Rules has occurred or is about to occur should report the matter to their superior authorities or organs vested with reviewing or remedial power;

(d) All personnel should ensure the full protection of the physical and mental health of juveniles, including protection from physical, sexual and emotional abuse and exploitation, and should take immediate action to secure medical attention whenever required;

(e) All personnel should respect the right of the juvenile to privacy, and, in particular, should safeguard all confidential matters concerning juveniles or their families learned as a result of their professional capacity;

(f) All personnel should seek to minimize any differences between life inside and outside the detention facility which tend to lessen due respect for the dignity of juveniles as human beings.

4.7 UNITED NATIONS GUIDELINES FOR THE PREVENTION OF JUVENILE DELINQUENCY, 1990[8]

(The Riyadh Guidelines)

I. Fundamental principles

1. The prevention of juvenile delinquency is an essential part of crime prevention in society. By engaging in lawful, socially useful activities and adopting a humanistic orientation towards society and outlook on life, young persons can develop non-criminogenic attitudes.

---

[8] Adopted and proclaimed by General Assembly resolution 45/112 of 14 December 1990.

2. The successful prevention of juvenile delinquency requires efforts on the part of the entire society to ensure the harmonious development of adolescents, with respect for and promotion of their personality from early childhood.

3. For the purposes of the interpretation of the present Guidelines, a child-centred orientation should be pursued. Young persons should have an active role and partnership within society and should not be considered as mere objects of socialization or control.

4. In the implementation of the present Guidelines, in accordance with national legal systems, the well-being of young persons from their early childhood should be the focus of any preventive programme.

5. The need for and importance of progressive delinquency prevention policies and the systematic study and the elaboration of measures should be recognized. These should avoid criminalizing and penalizing a child for behaviour that does not cause serious damage to the development of the child or harm to others. Such policies and measures should involve:

(a) The provision of opportunities, in particular educational opportunities, to meet the varying needs of young persons and to serve as a supportive framework for safeguarding the personal development of all young persons, particularly those who are demonstrably endangered or at social risk and are in need of special care and protection;

(b) Specialized philosophies and approaches for delinquency prevention, on the basis of laws, processes, institutions, facilities and a service delivery network aimed at reducing the motivation, need and opportunity for, or conditions giving rise to, the commission of infractions;

(c) Official intervention to be pursued primarily in the overall interest of the young person and guided by fairness and equity;

(d) Safeguarding the well-being, development, rights and interests of all young persons;

(e) Consideration that youthful behaviour or conduct that does not conform to overall social norms and values is often part of the maturation and growth process and tends to disappear spontaneously in most individuals with the transition to adulthood;

(f) Awareness that, in the predominant opinion of experts, labelling a young person as "deviant", "delinquent" or "pre-delinquent" often contributes to the development of a consistent pattern of undesirable behaviour by young persons.

6. Community-based services and programmes should be developed for the prevention of juvenile delinquency, particularly where no agencies have yet been established. Formal agencies of social control should only be utilized as a means of last resort.

II. Scope of the Guidelines

7. The present Guidelines should be interpreted and implemented within the broad framework of the Universal Declaration of Human Rights, the International Covenant on Economic, Social and Cultural Rights, the International Covenant on Civil and Political Rights, the Declaration of the Rights of the Child and the Convention on the Rights of the Child, and in the context of the United Nations Standard Minimum Rules for the Administration of Juvenile Justice (The Beijing Rules), as well as other instruments and norms relating to the rights, interests and well-being of all children and young persons.

8. The present Guidelines should also be implemented in the context of the economic, social and cultural conditions prevailing in each Member State.

III. General prevention

9. Comprehensive prevention plans should be instituted at every level of Government and include the following:

(a) In-depth analyses of the problem and inventories of programmes, services, facilities and resources available;

(b) Well-defined responsibilities for the qualified agencies, institutions and personnel involved in preventive efforts;

(c) Mechanisms for the appropriate co-ordination of prevention efforts between governmental and non-governmental agencies;

(d) Policies, programmes and strategies based on prognostic studies to be continuously monitored and carefully evaluated in the course of implementation;

(e) Methods for effectively reducing the opportunity to commit delinquent acts;

(f) Community involvement through a wide range of services and programmes;

(g) Close interdisciplinary co-operation between national, State, provincial and local governments, with the involvement of the private sector, representative citizens of the community to be served, and labour, child-care, health education, social, law enforcement and judicial agencies in taking concerted action to prevent juvenile delinquency and youth crime;

(h) Youth participation in delinquency prevention policies and processes, including recourse to community resources, youth self-help, and victim compensation and assistance programmes;

(i) Specialized personnel at all levels.

IV. Socialization processes

10. Emphasis should be placed on preventive policies facilitating the successful socialization and integration of all children and young persons, in particular through the family, the community, peer groups, schools, vocational training and the world of work, as well as through voluntary organizations. Due respect should be given to the proper personal development of children and young persons, and they should be accepted as full and equal partners in socialization and integration processes.

A. Family

11. Every society should place a high priority on the needs and well-being of the family and of all its members.

12. Since the family is the central unit responsible for the primary socialization of children, governmental and social efforts to preserve the integrity of the family, including the extended family, should be pursued. The society has a responsibility to assist the family in providing care and protection and in ensuring the physical and mental well-being of children. Adequate arrangements including day-care should be provided.

13. Governments should establish policies that are conducive to the bringing up of children in stable and settled family environments. Families in need of assistance in the resolution of conditions of instability or conflict should be provided with requisite services.

14. Where a stable and settled family environment is lacking and when community efforts to assist parents in this regard have failed and the extended family cannot fulfil this role, alternative placements, including foster care and adoption, should be considered. Such placements should replicate, to the extent possible, a stable and settled family environment, while, at the same time, establishing a sense of permanency for children, thus avoiding problems associated with "foster drift".

15. Special attention should be given to children of families affected by problems brought about by rapid and uneven economic, social and cultural change, in particular the children of indigenous, migrant and refugee families. As such changes may disrupt the social capacity of the family to secure the traditional rearing and nurturing of children, often as a result of role and culture conflict, innovative and socially constructive modalities for the socialization of children have to be designed.

16. Measures should be taken and programmes developed to provide families with the opportunity to learn about parental roles and obligations as regards child development and child care, promoting positive parent-child relationships, sensitizing parents to the problems of children and young persons and encouraging their involvement in family and community-based activities.

17. Governments should take measures to promote family cohesion and harmony and to discourage the separation of children from their parents, unless circumstances affecting the welfare and future of the child leave no viable alternative.

18. It is important to emphasize the socialization function of the family and extended family; it is also equally important to recognize the future role, responsibilities, participation and partnership of young persons in society.

19. In ensuring the right of the child to proper socialization, Governments and other agencies should rely on existing social and legal agencies, but, whenever traditional institutions and customs are no longer effective, they should also provide and allow for innovative measures.

B. Education

20. Governments are under an obligation to make public education accessible to all young persons.

21. Education systems should, in addition to their academic and vocational training activities, devote particular attention to the following:

> (a) Teaching of basic values and developing respect for the child's own cultural identity and patterns, for the social values of the country in which the child is living, for civilizations different from the child's own and for human rights and fundamental freedoms;
>
> (b) Promotion and development of the personality, talents and mental and physical abilities of young people to their fullest potential;

(c) Involvement of young persons as active and effective participants in, rather than mere objects of, the educational process;

(d) Undertaking activities that foster a sense of identity with and of belonging to the school and the community;

(e) Encouragement of young persons to understand and respect diverse views and opinions, as well as cultural and other differences;

(f) Provision of information and guidance regarding vocational training, employment opportunities and career development;

(g) Provision of positive emotional support to young persons and the avoidance of psychological maltreatment;

(h) Avoidance of harsh disciplinary measures, particularly corporal punishment.

22. Educational systems should seek to work together with parents, community organizations and agencies concerned with the activities of young persons.

23. Young persons and their families should be informed about the law and their rights and responsibilities under the law, as well as the universal value system, including United Nations instruments.

24. Educational systems should extend particular care and attention to young persons who are at social risk. Specialized prevention programmes and educational materials, curricula, approaches and tools should be developed and fully utilized.

25. Special attention should be given to comprehensive policies and strategies for the prevention of alcohol, drug and other substance abuse by young persons. Teachers and other professionals should be equipped and trained to prevent and deal with these problems. Information on the use and abuse of drugs, including alcohol, should be made available to the student body.

26. Schools should serve as resource and referral centres for the provision of medical, counselling and other services to young persons, particularly those with special needs and suffering from abuse, neglect, victimization and exploitation.

27. Through a variety of educational programmes, teachers and other adults and the student body should be sensitized to the problems, needs and perceptions of young persons, particularly

those belonging to underprivileged, disadvantaged, ethnic or other minority and low-income groups.

28. School systems should attempt to meet and promote the highest professional and educational standards with respect to curricula, teaching and learning methods and approaches, and the recruitment and training of qualified teachers. Regular monitoring and assessment of performance by the appropriate professional organizations and authorities should be ensured.

29. School systems should plan, develop and implement extracurricular activities of interest to young persons, in co-operation with community groups.

30. Special assistance should be given to children and young persons who find it difficult to comply with attendance codes, and to "drop-outs".

31. Schools should promote policies and rules that are fair and just; students should be represented in bodies formulating school policy, including policy on discipline, and decision-making.

C. Community

32. Community-based services and programmes which respond to the special needs, problems, interests and concerns of young persons and which offer appropriate counselling and guidance to young persons and their families should be developed, or strengthened where they exist.

33. Communities should provide, or strengthen where they exist, a wide range of community-based support measures for young persons, including community development centres, recreational facilities and services to respond to the special problems of children who are at social risk. In providing these helping measures, respect for individual rights should be ensured.

34. Special facilities should be set up to provide adequate shelter for young persons who are no longer able to live at or who do not have s to live in.

35. A range of services and helping measures should be provided to deal with the difficulties experienced by young persons in the transition to adulthood. Such services should include special programmes for young drug abusers which emphasize care, counselling, assistance and therapy-oriented interventions.

36. Voluntary organizations providing services for young persons should be given financial and other support by Governments and other institutions.

37. Youth organizations should be created or strengthened at the local level and given full participatory status in the management of community affairs. These organizations should encourage youth to organize collective and voluntary projects, particularly projects aimed at helping young persons in need of assistance.

38. Government agencies should take special responsibility and provide necessary services for less or street children; information about local facilities, accommodation, employment and other forms and sources of help should be made readily available to young persons.

39. A wide range of recreational facilities and services of particular interest to young persons should be established and made easily accessible to them.

D. Mass media

40. The mass media should be encouraged to ensure that young persons have access to information and material from a diversity of national and international sources.

41. The mass media should be encouraged to portray the positive contribution of young persons to society.

42. The mass media should be encouraged to disseminate information on the existence of services, facilities and opportunities for young persons in society.

43. The mass media generally, and the television and film media in particular, should be encouraged to minimize the level of pornography, drugs and violence portrayed and to display violence and exploitation disfavourably, as well as to avoid demeaning and degrading presentations, especially of children, women and interpersonal relations, and to promote egalitarian principles and roles.

44. The mass media should be aware of its extensive social role and responsibility, as well as its influence, in communications relating to youthful drug and alcohol abuse. It should use its power for drug abuse prevention by relaying consistent messages through a balanced approach. Effective drug awareness campaigns at all levels should be promoted.

V. Social policy

45. Government agencies should give high priority to plans and programmes for young persons and should provide sufficient funds and other resources for the effective delivery of services, facilities and staff for adequate medical and mental health care, nutrition, housing and other relevant services, including drug and alcohol abuse prevention and treatment, ensuring that such resources reach and actually benefit young persons.

46. The institutionalization of young persons should be a measure of last resort and for the minimum necessary period, and the best interests of the young person should be of paramount importance. Criteria authorizing formal intervention of this type should be strictly defined and limited to the following situations: (a) where the child or young person has suffered harm that has been inflicted by the parents or guardians; (b) where the child or young person has been sexually, physically or emotionally abused by the parents or guardians; (c) where the child or young person has been neglected, abandoned or exploited by the parents or guardians; (d) where the child or young person is threatened by physical or moral danger due to the behaviour of the parents or guardians; and (e) where a serious physical or psychological danger to the child or young person has manifested itself in his or her own behaviour and neither the parents, the guardians, the juvenile himself or herself nor non-residential community services can meet the danger by means other than institutionalization.

47. Government agencies should provide young persons with the opportunity of continuing in full-time education, funded by the State where parents or guardians are unable to support the young persons, and of receiving work experience.

48. Programmes to prevent delinquency should be planned and developed on the basis of reliable, scientific research findings, and periodically monitored, evaluated and adjusted accordingly.

49. Scientific information should be disseminated to the professional community and to the public at large about the sort of behaviour or situation which indicates or may result in physical and psychological victimization, harm and abuse, as well as exploitation, of young persons.

50. Generally, participation in plans and programmes should be voluntary. Young persons themselves should be involved in their formulation, development and implementation.

51. Government should begin or continue to explore, develop and implement policies, measures and strategies within and outside the criminal justice system to prevent domestic violence against and affecting young persons and to ensure fair treatment to these victims of domestic violence.

VI. Legislation and juvenile justice administration

52. Governments should enact and enforce specific laws and procedures to promote and protect the rights and well-being of all young persons.

53. Legislation preventing the victimization, abuse, exploitation and the use for criminal activities of children and young persons should be enacted and enforced.

54. No child or young person should be subjected to harsh or degrading correction or punishment measures at , in schools or in any other institutions.

55. Legislation and enforcement aimed at restricting and controlling accessibility of weapons of any sort to children and young persons should be pursued.

56. In order to prevent further stigmatization, victimization and criminalization of young persons, legislation should be enacted to ensure that any conduct not considered an offence or not penalized if committed by an adult is not considered an offence and not penalized if committed by a young person.

57. Consideration should be given to the establishment of an office of ombudsman or similar independent organ, which would ensure that the status, rights and interests of young persons are upheld and that proper referral to available services is made. The ombudsman or other organ designated would also supervise the implementation of the Riyadh Guidelines, the Beijing Rules and the Rules for the Protection of Juveniles Deprived of their Liberty. The ombudsman or other organ would, at regular intervals, publish a report on the progress made and on the difficulties encountered in the implementation of the instrument. Child advocacy services should also be established.

58. Law enforcement and other relevant personnel, of both sexes, should be trained to respond to the special needs of young persons and should be familiar with and use, to the maximum extent possible, programmes and referral possibilities for the diversion of young persons from the justice system.

59. Legislation should be enacted and strictly enforced to protect children and young persons from drug abuse and drug traffickers.

VII. Research, policy development and coordination

60. Efforts should be made and appropriate mechanisms established to promote, on both a multidisciplinary and an intradisciplinary basis, interaction and coordination between economic, social, education and health agencies and services, the justice system, youth, community and development agencies and other relevant institutions.

61. The exchange of information, experience and expertise gained through projects, programmes, practices and initiatives relating to youth crime, delinquency prevention and juvenile justice should be intensified at the national, regional and international levels.

62. Regional and international co-operation on matters of youth crime, delinquency prevention and juvenile justice involving practitioners, experts and decision makers should be further developed and strengthened.

63. Technical and scientific cooperation on practical and policy-related matters, particularly in training, pilot and demonstration projects, and on specific issues concerning the prevention of youth crime and juvenile delinquency should be strongly supported by all Governments, the United Nations system and other concerned organizations.

64. Collaboration should be encouraged in undertaking scientific research with respect to effective modalities for youth crime and juvenile delinquency prevention and the findings of such research should be widely disseminated and evaluated.

65. Appropriate United Nations bodies, institutes, agencies and offices should pursue close collaboration and coordination on various questions related to children juvenile justice and youth crime and juvenile delinquency prevention.

66. On the basis of the present Guidelines, the United Nations Secretariat, in cooperation with interested institutions, should play an active role in the conduct of research, scientific collaboration, the formulation of policy options and the review and monitoring of their implementation, and should serve as a source of reliable information on effective modalities for delinquency prevention.

4.8 GUIDELINES FOR ACTION ON CHILDREN IN THE CRIMINAL JUSTICE SYSTEM, 1997[9]

1. Pursuant to Economic and Social Council resolution 1996/13 of 23 July 1996, the present Guidelines for Action on Children in the Criminal Justice System were developed at an expert group meeting held at Vienna from 23 to 25 February 1997 with the financial support of the Government of Austria. In developing the Guidelines for Action, the experts took into account the views expressed and the information submitted by Governments.

2. Twenty-nine experts from eleven States in different regions, representatives of the Centre for Human Rights of the Secretariat, the United Nations Children's Fund and the Committee on the Rights of the Child, as well as observers for non-governmental organizations concerned with juvenile justice, participated in the meeting.

---

[9] Recommended by Economic and Social Council resolution 1997/30 of 21 July 1997. In resolution 1997/30, paragraph 1, the Economic and Social Council welcomed the Guidelines for Action on Children in the Criminal Justice System annexed to the resolution and invited all parties concerned to make use of the Guidelines in the implementation of the Convention on the Rights of the Child with regard to juvenile justice.

3. The Guidelines for Action are addressed to the Secretary-General and relevant United Nations agencies and programmes, States parties to the Convention on the Rights of the Child, as regards its implementation, as well as Member States as regards the use and application of the United Nations Standard Minimum Rules for the Administration of Juvenile Justice (The Beijing Rules), the United Nations Guidelines for the Prevention of Juvenile Delinquency (The Riyadh Guidelines) and the United Nations Rules for the Protection of Juveniles Deprived of their Liberty, hereinafter together referred to as United Nations standards and norms in juvenile justice.

I. Aims, objectives and basic considerations

4. The aims of the Guidelines for Action are to provide a framework to achieve the following objectives:

(a) To implement the Convention on the Rights of the Child and to pursue the goals set forth in the Convention with regard to children in the context of the administration of juvenile justice, as well as to use and apply the United Nations standards and norms in juvenile justice and other related instruments, such as the Declaration of Basic Principles of Justice for Victims of Crime and Abuse of Power;

(b) To facilitate the provision of assistance to States parties for the effective implementation of the Convention on the Rights of the Child and related instruments.

5. In order to ensure effective use of the Guidelines for Action, improved cooperation between Governments, relevant entities of the United Nations system, non-governmental organizations, professional groups, the media, academic institutions, children and other members of civil society is essential.

6. The Guidelines for Action should be based on the principle that the responsibility to implement the Convention clearly rests with the States parties thereto.

7. The basis for the use of the Guidelines for Action should be the recommendations of the Committee on the Rights of the Child.

8. In the use of the Guidelines for Action at both the international and national levels, consideration should be given to the following:

(a) Respect for human dignity, compatible with the four general principles underlying the Convention, namely: non-discrimination, including gender-sensitivity; upholding the best interests of the child; the right to life, survival and development; and respect for the views of the child;

(b) A rights-based orientation;

(c) A holistic approach to implementation through maximization of resources and efforts;

(d) The integration of services on an interdisciplinary basis;

(e) Participation of children and concerned sectors of society;

(f) Empowerment of partners through a developmental process;

(g) Sustainability without continuing dependency on external bodies;

(f) Equitable application and accessibility to those in greatest need;

(i) Accountability and transparency of operations;

(j) Proactive responses based on effective preventive and remedial measures.

9. Adequate resources (human, organizational, technological, financial and information) should be allocated and utilized efficiently at all levels (international, regional, national, provincial and local) and in collaboration with relevant partners, including Governments, United Nations entities, non-governmental organizations, professional groups, the media, academic institutions, children and other members of civil society, as well as other partners.

II. Plans for the implementation of the Convention on the Rights of the Child, the pursuit of its goals and the use and application of international standards and norms in juvenile justice

A. Measures of general application

10. The importance of a comprehensive and consistent national approach in the area of juvenile justice should be recognized, with respect for the interdependence and indivisibility of all rights of the child.

11. Measures relating to policy, decision-making, leadership and reform should be taken, with the goal of ensuring that:

(a) The principles and provisions of the Convention on the Rights of the Child and the United Nations standards and norms in juvenile justice are fully reflected in national and local legislation policy and practice, in particular by establishing a child-oriented juvenile justice system that guarantees the rights of children, prevents the violation of the rights of children, promotes children's sense of dignity and worth, and fully respects their age, stage of development and their right to participate meaningfully in, and contribute to, society;

(b) The relevant contents of the above-mentioned instruments are made widely known to children in language accessible to children. In addition, if necessary, procedures should be established to ensure that each and every child is provided with the relevant information on his or her rights set out in those instruments, at least from his or her first contact with the criminal justice system, and is reminded of his or her obligation to obey the law;

(c) The public's and the media's understanding of the spirit, aims and principles of justice centred on the child is promoted in accordance with the United Nations standards and norms in juvenile justice.

B. Specific targets

12. States should ensure the effectiveness of their birth registration programmes. In those instances where the age of the child involved in the justice system is unknown, measures should be taken to ensure that the true age of a child is ascertained by independent and objective assessment.

13. Notwithstanding the age of criminal responsibility, civil majority and the age of consent as defined by national legislation, States should ensure that children benefit from all their rights, as guaranteed to them by international law, specifically in this context those set forth in articles 3, 37 and 40 of the Convention.

14. Particular attention should be given to the following points:

(a) There should be a comprehensive child-centred juvenile justice process;

(b) Independent expert or other types of panels should review existing and proposed juvenile justice laws and their impact on children;

(c) No child who is under the legal age of criminal responsibility should be subject to criminal charges;

(d) States should establish juvenile courts with primary jurisdiction over juveniles who commit criminal acts and special procedures should be designed to take into account the specific needs of children. As an alternative, regular courts should incorporate such procedures, as appropriate. Wherever necessary, national legislative and other measures should be considered to accord all the rights of and protection for the child, where the child is brought before a court other than a juvenile court, in accordance with articles 3, 37 and 40 of the Convention.

15. A review of existing procedures should be undertaken and, where possible, diversion or other alternative initiatives to the classical criminal justice systems should be developed to avoid recourse to the criminal justice systems for young persons accused of an offence. Appropriate steps should be taken to make available throughout the State a broad range of alternative and educative measures at the pre-arrest, pre-trial, trial and post-trial stages, in order to prevent recidivism and promote the social rehabilitation of child offenders. Whenever appropriate, mechanisms for the informal resolution of disputes in cases involving a child offender should be utilized, including mediation and restorative justice practices, particularly processes involving victims. In the various measures to be adopted, the family should be involved, to the extent that it operates in favour of the good of the child offender. States should ensure that alternative measures comply with the Convention, the United Nations standards and norms in juvenile justice, as well as other existing standards and norms in crime prevention and criminal justice, such as the United Nations Standard Minimum Rules for Non-custodial Measures (The Tokyo Rules), with special regard to ensuring respect for due process rules in applying such measures and for the principle of minimum intervention.

16. Priority should be given to setting up agencies and programmes to provide legal and other assistance to children, if needed free of charge, such as interpretation services, and, in particular, to ensure that the right of every child to have access to such assistance from the moment that the child is detained is respected in practice.

17. Appropriate action should be ensured to alleviate the problem of children in need of special protection measures, such as children working or living on the streets or children permanently deprived of a family environment, children with disabilities, children of minorities, immigrants and indigenous peoples and other vulnerable groups of children.

18. The placement of children in closed institutions should be reduced. Such placement of children should only take place in accordance with the provisions of article 37 (b) of the Convention and as a matter of last resort and for the shortest period of time. Corporal punishment in the child justice and welfare systems should be prohibited.

19. The United Nations Rules for the Protection of Juveniles Deprived of their Liberty and article 37 (d) of the Convention also apply to any public or private setting from which the child

cannot leave at will, by order of any judicial, administrative or other public authority.

20. In order to maintain a link between the detained child and his or her family and community, and to facilitate his or her social reintegration, it is important to ensure easy access by relatives and persons who have a legitimate interest in the child to institutions where children are deprived of their liberty, unless the best interests of the child would suggest otherwise.

21. An independent body to monitor and report regularly on conditions in custodial facilities should be established, if necessary. Monitoring should take place within the framework of the United Nations standards and norms in juvenile justice, in particular the United Nations Rules for the Protection of Juveniles Deprived of their Liberty. States should permit children to communicate freely and confidentially with the monitoring bodies.

22. States should consider positively requests from concerned humanitarian, human rights and other organizations for access to custodial facilities, where appropriate.

23. In relation to children in the criminal justice system, due account should be taken of concerns raised by intergovernmental and non-governmental organizations and other interested parties, in particular systemic issues, including inappropriate admissions and lengthy delays that have an impact on children deprived of their liberty.

24. All persons having contact with, or being responsible for, children in the criminal justice system should receive education and training in human rights, the principles and provisions of the Convention and other United Nations standards and norms in juvenile justice as an integral part of their training programmes. Such persons include police and other law enforcement officials; judges and magistrates, prosecutors, lawyers and administrators; prison officers and other professionals working in institutions where children are deprived of their liberty; and health personnel, social workers, peacekeepers and other professionals concerned with juvenile justice.

25. In the light of existing international standards, States should establish mechanisms to ensure a prompt, thorough and impartial investigation into allegations against officials of deliberate violation of the fundamental rights and freedoms of children. States should equally ensure that those found responsible are duly sanctioned.

C. Measures to be taken at the international level

26. Juvenile justice should be given due attention internationally, regionally and nationally, including within the framework of the United Nations system-wide action.

27. There is an urgent need for close cooperation between all bodies in this field, in particular, the Crime Prevention and Criminal Justice Division of the Secretariat, the Office of the United Nations High Commissioner for Human Rights/Centre for Human Rights, the Office of the United Nations High Commissioner for Refugees, the United Nations Children's Fund, the United Nations Development Programme, the Committee on the Rights of the Child, the International Labour Organization, the United Nations Educational, Scientific and Cultural Organization and the World Health Organization. In addition, the World Bank and other international and regional financial institutions and organizations, as well as non-governmental organizations and academic institutions, are invited to support the provision of advisory services and technical assistance in the field of juvenile justice. Cooperation should therefore be strengthened, in particular with regard to research, dissemination of information, training, implementation and monitoring of the Convention on the Rights of the Child and the use and application of existing standards, as well as with regard to the provision of technical advice and assistance programmes, for example by making use of existing international networks on juvenile justice.

28. The effective implementation of the Convention on the Rights of the Child, as well as the use and application of international standards through technical cooperation and advisory service programmes, should be ensured by giving particular attention to the following aspects related to protecting and promoting human rights of children in detention, strengthening the rule of law and improving the administration of the juvenile justice system:

(a) Assistance in legal reform;

(b) Strengthening national capacities and infrastructures;

(c) Training programmes for police and other law enforcement officials, judges and magistrates, prosecutors, lawyers, administrators, prison officers and other professionals working in institutions where children are deprived of their liberty, health personnel, social workers, peacekeepers and other professionals concerned with juvenile justice;

(d) Preparation of training manuals;

(e) Preparation of information and education material to inform children about their rights in juvenile justice;

(f) Assistance with the development of information and management systems.

29. Close cooperation should be maintained between the Crime Prevention and Criminal Justice Division and the Department of Peacekeeping Operations of the Secretariat in view of the

relevance of the protection of children's rights in peacekeeping operations, including the problems of children and youth as victims and perpetrators of crime in peace-building and post-conflict or other emerging situations.

D. Mechanisms for the implementation of technical advice and assistance projects

30. In accordance with articles 43, 44 and 45 of the Convention, the Committee on the Rights of the Child reviews the reports of States parties on the implementation of the Convention. According to article 44 of the Convention, these reports should indicate factors and difficulties, if any, affecting the degree of fulfilment of the obligations under the Convention.

31. States parties to the Convention are invited to provide in their initial and periodic reports comprehensive information, data and indicators on the implementation of the provisions of the Convention and on the use and application of the United Nations standards and norms in juvenile justice.

32. As a result of the process of examining the progress made by States parties in fulfilling their obligations under the Convention, the Committee may make suggestions and general recommendations to the State party to ensure full compliance with the Convention (in accordance with article 45 (d) of the Convention). In order to foster the effective implementation of the Convention and to encourage international cooperation in the area of juvenile justice, the Committee transmits, as it may consider appropriate, to specialized agencies, the United Nations Children's Fund and other competent bodies any reports from States parties that contain a request, or indicate a need, for advisory services and technical assistance, together with observations and suggestions of the Committee, if any, on those requests or indications (in accordance with article 45 (b) of the Convention).

33. Accordingly, should a State party report and the review process by the Committee reveal any necessity to initiate reform in the area of juvenile justice, including through assistance by the United Nations technical advice and assistance programmes or those of the specialized agencies, the State party may request such assistance, including assistance from the Crime Prevention and Criminal Justice Division, the Centre for Human Rights and the United Nations Children's Fund.

34. In order to provide adequate assistance in response to those requests, a coordination panel on technical advice and assistance in juvenile justice should be established, to be convened at least annually by the Secretary-General. The panel will consist of representatives of the Division, the Office of the United Nations High Commissioner for Human Rights/Centre for Human Rights, the United Nations Children's Fund, the United Nations Development Programme, the

Committee on the Rights of the Child, the institutes comprising the United Nations Crime Prevention and Criminal Justice Programme network and other relevant United Nations entities, as well as other interested intergovernmental, regional and non-governmental organizations, including international networks on juvenile justice and academic institutions involved in the provision of technical advice and assistance, in accordance with paragraph 39 below.

35. Prior to the first meeting of the coordination panel, a strategy should be elaborated for addressing the issue of how to activate further international cooperation in the field of juvenile justice. The coordination panel should also facilitate the identification of common problems, the compilation of examples of good practice and the analysis of shared experiences and needs, which in turn would lead to a more strategic approach to needs assessment and to effective proposals for action. Such a compilation would allow for concerted advisory services and technical assistance in juvenile justice, including an early agreement with the Government requesting such assistance, as well as with all other partners having the capacity and competence to implement the various segments of a country project, thus ensuring the most effective and problem-oriented action. This compilation should be developed continuously in close cooperation with all parties involved. It will take into account the possible introduction of diversion programmes and measures to improve the administration of juvenile justice, to reduce the use of remand s and pre-trial detention, to improve the treatment of children deprived of their liberty and to create effective reintegration and recovery programmes.

36. Emphasis should be placed on formulating comprehensive prevention plans, as called for in the United Nations Guidelines for the Prevention of Juvenile Delinquency (the Riyadh Guidelines). Projects should focus on strategies to socialize and integrate all children and young persons successfully, in particular through the family, the community, peer groups, schools, vocational training and the world of work. These projects should pay particular attention to children in need of special protection measures, such as children working or living on the streets or children permanently deprived of a family environment, children with disabilities, children of minorities, immigrants and indigenous peoples and other vulnerable groups of children. In particular, the placement of these children in institutions should be proscribed as much as possible. Measures of social protection should be developed in order to limit the risks of criminalization for these children.

37. The strategy will also set out a coordinated process for the delivery of international advisory services and technical assistance to States parties to the Convention, on the basis of joint missions to be undertaken, whenever appropriate, by staff of the different organizations and agencies involved, with a view to devising longer term technical assistance projects.

38. Important actors in the delivery of advisory services and technical assistance programmes at the country level are the United Nations resident coordinators, with significant roles to be played by the field offices of the Office of the United Nations High Commissioner for Human Rights/Centre for Human Rights, the United Nations Children's Fund and the United Nations Development Programme. The vital nature of the integration of juvenile justice technical cooperation in country planning and programming, including through the United Nations country strategy note, is emphasized.

39. Resources must be mobilized for both the coordinating mechanism of the coordination panel and regional and country projects formulated to improve observance of the Convention. Resources for those purposes (see paragraphs 34 to 38 above) will come either from regular budgets or from extrabudgetary resources. Most of the resources for specific projects will have to be mobilized from external sources.

40. The coordination panel may wish to encourage, and in fact be the vehicle for, a coordinated approach to resource mobilization in this area. Such resource mobilization should be on the basis of a common strategy as contained in a programme document drawn up in support of a global programme in this area. All interested United Nations bodies and agencies as well as non-governmental organizations that have a demonstrated capacity to deliver technical cooperation services in this area should be invited to participate in such a process.

E. Further considerations for the implementation of country projects

41. One of the obvious tenets in juvenile delinquency prevention and juvenile justice is that long-term change is brought about not only when symptoms are treated but also when root causes are addressed. For example, excessive use of juvenile detention will be dealt with adequately only by applying a comprehensive approach, which involves both organizational and managerial structures at all levels of investigation, prosecution and the judiciary, as well as the penitentiary system. This requires communication, inter alia, with and among police, prosecutors, judges and magistrates, authorities of local communities, administration authorities and with the relevant authorities of detention centres. In addition, it requires the will and ability to cooperate closely with each other.

42. To prevent further overreliance on criminal justice measures to deal with children's behaviour, efforts should be made to establish and apply programmes aimed at strengthening social assistance, which would allow for the diversion of children from the justice system, as appropriate, as well as improving the application of non-custodial measures and reintegration programmes. To establish and apply such programmes, it is necessary to foster close cooperation

between the child justice sectors, different services in charge of law enforcement, social welfare and education sectors.

III. Plans concerned with child victims and witnesses

43. In accordance with the Declaration of Basic Principles of Justice for Victims of Crime and Abuse of Power, States should undertake to ensure that child victims and witnesses are provided with appropriate access to justice and fair treatment, restitution, compensation and social assistance. If applicable, measures should be taken to prevent the settling of penal matters through compensation outside the justice system, when doing so is not in the best interests of the child.

44. Police, lawyers, the judiciary and other court personnel should receive training in dealing with cases where children are victims. States should consider establishing, if they have not yet done so, specialized offices and units to deal with cases involving offences against children. States should establish, as appropriate, a code of practice for proper management of cases involving child victims.

45. Child victims should be treated with compassion and respect for their dignity. They are entitled to access to the mechanisms of justice and to prompt redress, as provided for by national legislation, for the harm they have suffered.

46. Child victims should have access to assistance that meets their needs, such as advocacy, protection, economic assistance, counselling, health and social services, social reintegration and physical and psychological recovery services. Special assistance should be given to those children who are disabled or ill. Emphasis should be placed upon family- and community-based rehabilitation rather than institutionalization.

47. Judicial and administrative mechanisms should be established and strengthened where necessary to enable child victims to obtain redress through formal or informal procedures that are prompt, fair and accessible. Child victims and/or their legal representatives should be informed accordingly.

48. Access should be allowed to fair and adequate compensation for all child victims of violations of human rights, specifically torture and other cruel, inhuman or degrading treatment or punishment, including rape and sexual abuse, unlawful or arbitrary deprivation of liberty, unjustifiable detention and miscarriage of justice. Necessary legal representation to bring an action within an appropriate court or tribunal, as well as interpretation into the native language of the child, if necessary, should be available.

49. Child witnesses need assistance in the judicial and administrative processes. States should review, evaluate and improve, as necessary, the situation for children as witnesses of crime in their evidential and procedural law to ensure that the rights of children are fully protected. In accordance with the different law traditions, practices and legal framework, direct contact should be avoided between the child victim and the offender during the process of investigation and prosecution as well as during trial hearings as much as possible. The identification of the child victim in the media should be prohibited, where necessary to protect the privacy of the child. Where prohibition is contrary to the fundamental legal principles of Member States, such identification should be discouraged.

50. States should consider, if necessary, amendments of their penal procedural codes to allow for, inter alia, videotaping of the child's testimony and presentation of the videotaped testimony in court as an official piece of evidence. In particular, police, prosecutors, judges and magistrates should apply more child-friendly practices, for example, in police operations and interviews of child witnesses.

51. The responsiveness of judicial and administrative processes to the needs of child victims and witnesses should be facilitated by:

(a) Informing child victims of their role and the scope, timing and progress of the proceedings and of the disposition of their cases, especially where serious crimes are involved;

(b) Encouraging the development of child witness preparation schemes to familiarize children with the criminal justice process prior to giving evidence. Appropriate assistance should be provided to child victims and witnesses throughout the legal process;

(c) Allowing the views and concerns of child victims to be presented and considered at appropriate stages of the proceedings where their personal interests are affected, without prejudice to the accused and in accordance with the relevant national criminal justice system;

(d) Taking measures to minimize delays in the criminal justice process, protecting the privacy of child victims and witnesses and, when necessary, ensuring their safety from intimidation and retaliation.

52. Children displaced illegally or wrongfully retained across borders are as a general principle to be returned to the country of origin. Due attention should be paid to their safety, and they should be treated humanely and receive necessary assistance, pending their return. They

should be returned promptly to ensure compliance with the Convention on the Rights of the Child. Where the Hague Convention on the Civil Aspects of International Child Abduction of 1980 or the Hague Convention on the Protection of Children and Cooperation in respect of Inter-Country Adoption of 1993, approved by the Hague Conference on Private International Law, the Convention on Jurisdiction, Applicable Law, Recognition, Enforcement and Cooperation in Respect of Parental Responsibility and Measures for the Protection of the Child are applicable, the provisions of these conventions with regard to the return of the child should be promptly applied. Upon the return of the child, the country of origin should treat the child with respect, in accordance with international principles of human rights, and offer adequate family-based rehabilitation measures.

53. The United Nations Crime Prevention and Criminal Justice Programme, including the institutes comprising the Programme network, the Office of the United Nations High Commissioner for Human Rights/Centre for Human Rights, the United Nations Children's Fund, the United Nations Development Programme, the Committee on the Rights of the Child, the United Nations Educational, Scientific and Cultural Organization, the World Bank and interested non-governmental organizations should assist Member States, at their request, within the overall appropriations of the United Nations budgets or from extrabudgetary resources, in developing multidisciplinary training, education and information activities for law enforcement and other criminal justice personnel, including police officers, prosecutors, judges and magistrates.

4.9 GUIDELINES ON JUSTICE MATTERS INVOLVING CHILD VICTIMS AND WITNESSES OF CRIME, 2005[10]

I. Objectives

1. The present Guidelines on Justice for Child Victims and Witnesses of Crime set forth good practice based on the consensus of contemporary knowledge and relevant international and regional norms, standards and principles.

2. The Guidelines should be implemented in accordance with relevant national legislation and judicial procedures as well as take into consideration legal, social, economic, cultural and geographical conditions. However, States should constantly endeavour to overcome practical difficulties in the application of the Guidelines.

---

[10] Adopted by the Economic and Social Council in its resolution 2005/20 of 22 July 2005.

3. The Guidelines provide a practical framework to achieve the following objectives:

(a) To assist in the review of national and domestic laws, procedures and practices so that these ensure full respect for the rights of child victims and witnesses of crime and contribute to the implementation of the Convention on the Rights of the Child,1 by parties to that Convention;

(b) To assist Governments, international organizations, public agencies, nongovernmental and community-based organizations and other interested parties in designing and implementing legislation, policy, programmes and practices that address key issues related to child victims and witnesses of crime;

(c) To guide professionals and, where appropriate, volunteers working with child victims and witnesses of crime in their day-to-day practice in the adult and juvenile justice process at the national, regional and international levels, consistent with the Declaration of Basic Principles of Justice for Victims of Crime and Abuse of Power;

(d) To assist and support those caring for children in dealing sensitively with child victims and witnesses of crime.

4. In implementing the Guidelines, each jurisdiction should ensure that adequate training, selection and procedures are put in place to protect and meet the special needs of child victims and witnesses of crime, where the nature of the victimization affects categories of children differently, such as sexual assault of children, especially girls.

5. The Guidelines cover a field in which knowledge and practice are growing and improving. They are neither intended to be exhaustive nor to preclude further development, provided it is in harmony with their underlying objectives and principles.

6. The Guidelines could also be applied to processes in informal and customary systems of justice such as restorative justice and in non-criminal fields of law including, but not limited to, custody, divorce, adoption, child protection, mental health, citizenship, immigration and refugee law.

II. Special considerations

7. The Guidelines were developed:

(a) Cognizant that millions of children throughout the world suffer harm as a result of crime and abuse of power and that the rights of those children have not been adequately recognized and that they may suffer additional hardship when assisting in the justice process;

(b) Recognizing that children are vulnerable and require special protection appropriate to their age, level of maturity and individual special needs;

(c) Recognizing that girls are particularly vulnerable and may face discrimination at all stages of the justice system;

(d) Reaffirming that every effort must be made to prevent victimization of children, including through implementation of the Guidelines for the Prevention of Crime;

(e) Cognizant that children who are victims and witnesses may suffer additional hardship if mistakenly viewed as offenders when they are in fact victims and witnesses;

(f) Recalling that the Convention on the Rights of the Child sets forth requirements and principles to secure effective recognition of the rights of children and that the Declaration of Basic Principles of Justice for Victims of Crime and Abuse of Power sets forth principles to provide victims with the right to information, participation, protection, reparation and assistance;

(g) Recalling international and regional initiatives that implement the principles of the Declaration of Basic Principles of Justice for Victims of Crime and Abuse of Power, including the Handbook on Justice for Victims and the Guide for Policy Makers on the Declaration of Basic Principles, both issued by the United Nations Office for Drug Control and Crime Prevention in 1999;

(h) Recognizing the efforts of the International Bureau for Children's Rights in laying the groundwork for the development of guidelines on justice for child victims and witnesses of crime;

(i) Considering that improved responses to child victims and witnesses of crime can make children and their families more willing to disclose instances of victimization and more supportive of the justice process;

(j) Recalling that justice for child victims and witnesses of crime must be assured while safeguarding the rights of accused and convicted offenders;

(k) Bearing in mind the variety of legal systems and traditions, and noting that crime is increasingly transnational in nature and that there is a need to ensure that child victims and witnesses of crime receive equivalent protection in all countries.

III. Principles

8. As stated in international instruments and in particular the Convention on the Rights of the Child as reflected in the work of the Committee on the Rights of the Child, and in order to ensure justice for child victims and witnesses of crime, professionals and others responsible for the well-being of those children must respect the following cross-cutting principles:

(a) *Dignity*. Every child is a unique and valuable human being and as such his or her individual dignity, special needs, interests and privacy should be respected and protected;

(b) *Non-discrimination*. Every child has the right to be treated fairly and equally, regardless of his or her or the parent's or legal guardian's race, ethnicity, colour, gender, language, religion, political or other opinion, national, ethnic or social origin, property, disability and birth or other status;

(c) *Best interests of the child*. While the rights of accused and convicted offenders should be safeguarded, every child has the right to have his or her best interests given primary consideration. This includes the right to protection and to a chance for harmonious development:

(i) *Protection*. Every child has the right to life and survival and to be shielded from any form of hardship, abuse or neglect, including physical, psychological, mental and emotional abuse and neglect;

(ii) *Harmonious development*. Every child has the right to a chance for harmonious development and to a standard of living adequate for physical, mental, spiritual, moral and social growth. In the case of a child who has been traumatized, every step should be taken to enable the child to enjoy healthy development;

(d) *Right to participation*. Every child has, subject to national procedural law, the right to express his or her views, opinions and beliefs freely, in his or her own words, and to contribute especially to the decisions affecting his or her life, including those taken in any judicial processes, and to have those views taken into consideration according to his or her abilities, age, intellectual maturity and evolving capacity.

IV. Definitions

9. Throughout these Guidelines, the following definitions apply:

(a) "Child victims and witnesses" denotes children and adolescents, under the age of 18, who are victims of crime or witnesses to crime regardless of their role in the offence or in the prosecution of the alleged offender or groups of offenders;

(b) "Professionals" refers to persons who, within the context of their work, are in contact with child victims and witnesses of crime or are responsible for addressing the needs of children in the justice system and for whom these Guidelines are applicable. This includes, but is not limited to, the following: child and victim advocates and support persons; child protection service practitioners; child welfare agency staff; prosecutors and, where appropriate, defence lawyers; diplomatic and consular staff; domestic violence programme staff; judges; court staff; law enforcement officials; medical and mental health professionals; and social workers;

(c) "Justice process" encompasses detection of the crime, making of the complaint, investigation, prosecution and trial and post-trial procedures, regardless of whether the case is handled in a national, international or regional criminal justice system for adults or juveniles, or in a customary or informal system of justice;

(d) "Child-sensitive" denotes an approach that balances the child's right to protection and that takes into account the child's individual needs and views.

V. The right to be treated with dignity and compassion

10. Child victims and witnesses should be treated in a caring and sensitive manner throughout the justice process, taking into account their personal situation and immediate needs, age, gender, disability and level of maturity and fully respecting their physical, mental and moral integrity.

11. Every child should be treated as an individual with his or her individual needs, wishes and feelings.

12. Interference in the child's private life should be limited to the minimum needed at the same time as high standards of evidence collection are maintained in order to ensure fair and equitable outcomes of the justice process.

13. In order to avoid further hardship to the child, interviews, examinations and other forms of investigation should be conducted by trained professionals who proceed in a sensitive, respectful and thorough manner.

14. All interactions described in these Guidelines should be conducted in a child-sensitive manner in a suitable environment that accommodates the special needs of the child, according to his or her abilities, age, intellectual maturity and evolving capacity. They should also take place in a language that the child uses and understands.

VI. The right to be protected from discrimination

15. Child victims and witnesses should have access to a justice process that protects them from discrimination based on the child's, parent's or legal guardian's race, colour, gender, language, religion, political or other opinion, national, ethnic or social origin, property, disability and birth or other status.

16. The justice process and support services available to child victims and witnesses and their families should be sensitive to the child's age, wishes, understanding, gender, sexual orientation, ethnic, cultural, religious, linguistic and social background, caste, socio-economic condition and immigration or refugee status, as well as to the special needs of the child, including health, abilities and capacities. Professionals should be trained and educated about such differences.

17. In certain cases, special services and protection will need to be instituted to take account of gender and the different nature of specific offences against children, such as sexual assault involving children.

18. Age should not be a barrier to a child's right to participate fully in the justice process. Every child should be treated as a capable witness, subject to examination, and his or her testimony should not be presumed invalid or untrustworthy by reason of the child's age alone as long as his or her age and maturity allow the giving of intelligible and credible testimony, with or without communication aids and other assistance.

VII. The right to be informed

19. Child victims and witnesses, their parents or guardians and legal representatives, from their first contact with the justice process and throughout that process, should be promptly and adequately informed, to the extent feasible and appropriate, of, inter alia:

(a) The availability of health, psychological, social and other relevant services as well as the means of accessing such services along with legal or other advice or representation, compensation and emergency financial support, where applicable;

(b) The procedures for the adult and juvenile criminal justice process, including the role of child victims and witnesses, the importance, timing and manner of testimony, and ways in which "questioning" will be conducted during the investigation and trial;

(c) The existing support mechanisms for the child when making a complaint and participating in the investigation and court proceedings;

(d) The specific places and times of hearings and other relevant events;

(e) The availability of protective measures;

(f) The existing mechanisms for review of decisions affecting child victims and witnesses;

(g) The relevant rights for child victims and witnesses pursuant to the Convention on the Rights of the Child and the Declaration of Basic Principles of Justice for Victims of Crime and Abuse of Power.

20. In addition, child victims, their parents or guardians and legal representatives should be promptly and adequately informed, to the extent feasible and appropriate, of:

(a) The progress and disposition of the specific case, including the apprehension, arrest and custodial status of the accused and any pending changes to that status, the prosecutorial decision and relevant post-trial developments and the outcome of the case;

(b) The existing opportunities to obtain reparation from the offender or from the State through the justice process, through alternative civil proceedings or through other processes.

VIII. The right to be heard and to express views and concerns

21. Professionals should make every effort to enable child victims and witnesses to express their views and concerns related to their involvement in the justice process, including by:

(a) Ensuring that child victims and where appropriate witnesses are consulted on the matters set forth in paragraph 19 above;

(b) Ensuring that child victims and witnesses are enabled to express freely and in their own manner their views and concerns regarding their involvement in the justice process, their concerns regarding safety in relation to the accused, the manner in which they prefer to provide testimony and their feelings about the conclusions of the process;

(c) Giving due regard to the child's views and concerns and, if they are unable to accommodate them, explain the reasons to the child.

IX. The right to effective assistance

22. Child victims and witnesses and, where appropriate, family members should have access to assistance provided by professionals who have received relevant training as set out in paragraphs 40 to 42 below. This may include assistance and support services such as financial, legal, counselling, health, social and educational services, physical and psychological recovery services and other services necessary for the child's reintegration. All such assistance should address the child's needs and enable him or her to participate effectively at all stages of the justice process.

23. In assisting child victims and witnesses, professionals should make every effort to coordinate support so that the child is not subjected to excessive interventions.

24. Child victims and witnesses should receive assistance from support persons, such as child victim/witness specialists, commencing at the initial report and continuing until such services are no longer required.

25. Professionals should develop and implement measures to make it easier for children to testify or give evidence to improve communication and understanding at the pre-trial and trial stages. These measures may include:

(a) Child victim and witness specialists to address the child's special needs;

(b) Support persons, including specialists and appropriate family members to accompany the child during testimony;

(c) Where appropriate, to appoint guardians to protect the child's legal interests.

X. The right to privacy

26. Child victims and witnesses should have their privacy protected as a matter of primary importance.

27. Information relating to a child's involvement in the justice process should be protected. This can be achieved through maintaining confidentiality and restricting disclosure of

information that may lead to identification of a child who is a victim or witness in the justice process.

28. Measures should be taken to protect children from undue exposure to the public by, for example, excluding the public and the media from the courtroom during the child's testimony, where permitted by national law.

XI. The right to be protected from hardship during the justice process

29. Professionals should take measures to prevent hardship during the detection, investigation and prosecution process in order to ensure that the best interests and dignity of child victims and witnesses are respected.

30. Professionals should approach child victims and witnesses with sensitivity, so that they:

(a) Provide support for child victims and witnesses, including accompanying the child throughout his or her involvement in the justice process, when it is in his or her best interests;

(b) Provide certainty about the process, including providing child victims and witnesses with clear expectations as to what to expect in the process, with as much certainty as possible. The child's participation in hearings and trials should be planned ahead of time and every effort should be made to ensure continuity in the relationships between children and the professionals in contact with them throughout the process;

(c) Ensure that trials take place as soon as practical, unless delays are in the child's best interest. Investigation of crimes involving child victims and witnesses should also be expedited and there should be procedures, laws or court rules that provide for cases involving child victims and witnesses to be expedited;

(d) Use child-sensitive procedures, including interview rooms designed for children, interdisciplinary services for child victims integrated in the same location, modified court environments that take child witnesses into consideration, recesses during a child's testimony, hearings scheduled at times of day appropriate to the age and maturity of the child, an appropriate notification system to ensure the child goes to court only when necessary and other appropriate measures to facilitate the child's testimony.

31. Professionals should also implement measures:

(a) To limit the number of interviews: special procedures for collection of evidence from child victims and witnesses should be implemented in order to reduce the number of interviews, statements, hearings and, specifically, unnecessary contact with the justice process, such as through use of video recording;

(b) To ensure that child victims and witnesses are protected, if compatible with the legal system and with due respect for the rights of the defence, from being cross-examined by the alleged perpetrator: as necessary, child victims and witnesses should be interviewed, and examined in court, out of sight of the alleged perpetrator, and separate courthouse waiting rooms and private interview areas should be provided;

(c) To ensure that child victims and witnesses are questioned in a child-sensitive manner and allow for the exercise of supervision by judges, facilitate testimony and reduce potential intimidation, for example by using testimonial aids or appointing psychological experts.

XII. The right to safety

32. Where the safety of a child victim or witness may be at risk, appropriate measures should be taken to require the reporting of those safety risks to appropriate authorities and to protect the child from such risk before, during and after the justice process.

33. Professionals who come into contact with children should be required to notify appropriate authorities if they suspect that a child victim or witness has been harmed, is being harmed or is likely to be harmed.

34. Professionals should be trained in recognizing and preventing intimidation, threats and harm to child victims and witnesses. Where child victims and witnesses may be the subject of intimidation, threats or harm, appropriate conditions should be put in place to ensure the safety of the child. Such safeguards could include:

(a) Avoiding direct contact between child victims and witnesses and the alleged perpetrators at any point in the justice process;

(b) Using court-ordered restraining orders supported by a registry system;

(c) Ordering pre-trial detention of the accused and setting special "no contact" bail conditions;

(d) Placing the accused under house arrest;

(e) Wherever possible and appropriate, giving child victims and witnesses protection by the police or other relevant agencies and safeguarding their whereabouts from disclosure.

XIII. The right to reparation

35. Child victims should, wherever possible, receive reparation in order to achieve full redress, reintegration and recovery. Procedures for obtaining and enforcing reparation should be readily accessible and child-sensitive.

36. Provided the proceedings are child-sensitive and respect these Guidelines, combined criminal and reparations proceedings should be encouraged, together with informal and community justice procedures such as restorative justice.

37. Reparation may include restitution from the offender ordered in the criminal court, aid from victim compensation programmes administered by the State and damages ordered to be paid in civil proceedings. Where possible, costs of social and educational reintegration, medical treatment, mental health care and legal services should be addressed. Procedures should be instituted to ensure enforcement of reparation orders and payment of reparation before fines.

XIV. The right to special preventive measures

38. In addition to preventive measures that should be in place for all children, special strategies are required for child victims and witnesses who are particularly vulnerable to recurring victimization or offending.

39. Professionals should develop and implement comprehensive and specially tailored strategies and interventions in cases where there are risks that child victims may be victimized further. These strategies and interventions should take into account the nature of the victimization, including victimization related to abuse in the home, sexual exploitation, abuse in institutional settings and trafficking. The strategies may include those based on government, neighbourhood and citizen initiatives.

XV. Implementation

40. Adequate training, education and information should be made available to professionals, working with child victims and witnesses with a view to improving and sustaining specialized methods, approaches and attitudes in order to protect and deal effectively and sensitively with child victims and witnesses.

41. Professionals should be trained to effectively protect and meet the needs of child victims and witnesses, including in specialized units and services.

42. This training should include:

(a) Relevant human rights norms, standards and principles, including the rights of the child;

(b) Principles and ethical duties of their office;

(c) Signs and symptoms that indicate crimes against children;

(d) Crisis assessment skills and techniques, especially for making referrals, with an emphasis placed on the need for confidentiality;

(e) Impact, consequences, including negative physical and psychological effects, and trauma of crimes against children;

(f) Special measures and techniques to assist child victims and witnesses in the justice process;

(g) Cross-cultural and age-related linguistic, religious, social and gender issues;

(h) Appropriate adult-child communication skills;

(i) Interviewing and assessment techniques that minimize any trauma to the child while maximizing the quality of information received from the child;

(j) Skills to deal with child victims and witnesses in a sensitive, understanding, constructive and reassuring manner;

(k) Methods to protect and present evidence and to question child witnesses;

(l) Roles of, and methods used by, professionals working with child victims and witnesses.

43. Professionals should make every effort to adopt an interdisciplinary and cooperative approach in aiding children by familiarizing themselves with the wide array of available services, such as victim support, advocacy, economic assistance, counselling, education, health, legal and social services. This approach may include protocols for the different stages of the justice process to encourage cooperation among entities that provide services to child victims and witnesses, as well as other forms of multidisciplinary work that includes police, prosecutor, medical, social services and psychological personnel working in the same location.

44. International cooperation should be enhanced between States and all sectors of society, both at the national and international levels, including mutual assistance for the purpose of facilitating collection and exchange of information and the detection, investigation and prosecution of transnational crimes involving child victims and witnesses.

45. Professionals should consider utilizing the present Guidelines as a basis for developing laws and written policies, standards and protocols aimed at assisting child victims and witnesses involved in the justice process.

46. Professionals should be enabled to periodically review and evaluate their role, together with other agencies in the justice process, in ensuring the protection of the rights of the child and the effective implementation of the present Guidelines.

CHAPTER 5

WOMEN

Comments: Women have a right to legal equality with men. This right to legal equality is independent of a woman's civil status. It is absolute and must be guaranteed in all circumstances and at all times. The prohibition of discrimination based on sex includes gender-based violence. It also means that States have a duty to eliminate all legal and factual discrimination against women in both the public and private sectors. States are duty bound, as a minimum, to take all appropriate measures to modify local customs and traditions that may impede the full realization of women's right to equality. The Human Rights Committee has emphasized that non-discrimination, "together with equality before the law and equal protection of the law without any discrimination, constitutes a basic and general principle relating to the protection of human rights".[1]

While women in some countries have made great strides towards securing increased respect for their human rights, including the right to equality with men in areas such as family law and the law of succession and in access to education, adequate health care and the labour market, the majority of women still suffer violations of their most basic human rights. For instance, they are not always allowed to enter freely into marriage or to divorce on the same conditions as men, and do not enjoy equal rights with men in terms of succession. They are denied the right to education or even to the most basic health services. They may also be subjected to strict dress codes, the violation of which can result in severe corporal punishment. Women's rights to life, personal liberty and security are also frequently violated through domestic, institutional and community violence such as dowry killings, "honour" killings, trafficking, forced prostitution, and traditional practices such as female genital mutilation (FGM)[2] and child marriage. Discrimination against females occurs even before birth in some communities,

---

[1] General Comment No. 18 (Non-discrimination), *United Nations Compilation of General Comments*, p. 134, para. 1.

[2] Female genital mutilation is a practice that is widespread in certain parts of the world and may have serious implications for girls' health, even causing death through the use of unsterilized surgical tools or owing to poor general hygiene during the intervention.

in the form of pre-natal sex determination and abortion of female foetuses. Sexual assaults and the use of women as weapons of war are strategies adopted commonly during armed conflicts, and violation of the human rights of women by soldiers, international aid workers, peacekeepers and custodians of the law is the rule rather than the exception.

The only universal legal document dealing *expressis verbis* with violence against women is the Declaration on the Elimination of Violence against Women, which was adopted by the United Nations General Assembly in 1993. State responsibility is clearly mentioned in Article 4 of the Declaration, which stipulates that "States should exercise due diligence to prevent, investigate and, in accordance with national legislation, punish acts of violence against women, whether those acts are perpetrated by the State or by private persons." States should ensure that national legislation, once adopted, does not go unenforced.[3] Any approach designed to combat violence must be twofold, addressing the root causes of the problem and treating its manifestations. Society at large, including judges and police officers, must be educated to change social attitudes and beliefs that encourage violence against women.

5.1 GENERAL

The UN Charter

Article 1(3) of the Charter of the United Nations provides that one of the purposes of the Organization is "to achieve international co-operation in solving international problems of an economic, social, cultural, or humanitarian character, and in promoting and encouraging respect for human rights and for fundamental freedoms for all without distinction as to race, *sex*, language, or religion" (emphasis added). The same principle of equality between men and women is stated in articles 13 (1) (b), 55(c) and 76(c). At the universal level, the prohibition of discrimination on the basis of sex was subsequently included in article 2 of the Universal Declaration of Human Rights, articles 2(1), 4(1) and 26 of the International Covenant on Civil and Political Rights and article 2(2) of the International Covenant on Economic, Social and

---

[3] In India, the Protection of Women from Domestic Violence Act, 2005, requires each State government to appoint protection officers, register service providers and notify medical facilities for the implementation of the Act. While the Ministry of Women and Child Development and the Ministry of Home Affairs have issued advisories to State governments, with the exception of West Bengal and Delhi no State is known to have appointed independent protection officers even five years hence. Most States have fobbed off the requirement by giving "additional" responsibility to existing functionaries. Rajasthan, a high-prevalence State for domestic violence, has entrusted the already overburdened anganwadi workers who are striving to ensure the supply of nutrition to infants, children and lactating mothers, with the responsibility..... The 2005 Act is impractical and consequently non-implementable in favour of those that need protection the most. Shailaja Chandra, Towards protecting women, *THE HINDU*, 17 June 2010.

Cultural Rights. By virtue of article 3 of both Covenants, the States parties further expressly undertake to ensure the equal right of men and women to the enjoyment of all the rights guaranteed by the respective Covenant.

Convention for the Suppression of the Traffic in Persons and of the Exploitation of the Prostitution of Others, 1951

Parties that sign this Convention "agree to punish any person who, to gratify the passions of another: (1) Procures, entices or leads away, for purposes of prostitution, another person, even with the consent of that person; (2) Exploits the prostitution of another person, even with the consent of that person". In addition, the states parties promise to punish any person who keeps or manages, or knowingly finances or takes part in the financing of a brothel; and anyone who knowingly lets or rents a building or other place for the purpose of the prostitution of others.

Rights of Women in Conflict Situations

Recent conflicts have highlighted the systematic and specific targeting of women for sexual violence. Rape, sexual assault, forced prostitution, sexual slavery, forced pregnancy and other forms of sexual violence are used as a method of warfare. During armed conflict and displacement, women and girls may face sexual violence and exploitation at the hands of, or with the complicity of, their supposed protectors –peacekeepers and aid workers. The four Geneva Conventions of 1949 and their Additional Protocols of 1977 protects women both as members of the civilian population not taking part in the hostility and also as combatants, fallen into the hands of enemy. Women get protection against abuse by the parties to conflict into whose power women have fallen:

1. General: Women are protected as civilians at the time of war. Basic principle of humane treatment, respect for life and physical and moral integrity, forbidden coercion, corporal punishment, torture, collective fine, reprisal, pillage and taking of hostage. Women have right to be tried by an independent and impartial court established by law- with recognized principles of judicial procedure. Women are especially protected against any attack on their honour in particular against rape, enforced prostitution or any form of indecent assault.

2. Respect for preferential treatment of women: At the time of war special benefit is accorded to pregnant women and mothers of children under the age of seven by national laws. Countries at war generally take some measures for the benefits of persons whose weakness in one respect or another warrants special care. They generally cover;

supplementary ration, medical facilities, hospital treatment, special welfare, exemption from hard work, measures against effect of war, evacuation, transfer to third (neutral) country.

3. Interned women: A belligerent may intern people, if it has serious and legitimate reasons to think that they are the members of organization whose object is to cause disturbance, or they may resort to sabotage or espionage. In addition occupying power may also charge protected persons with infraction of penal laws which it has promulgated for its own protection. In such situations women interns shall be: (i) held in separate jails (quarters) separated from men with separate sanitary conveniences; (ii) they will be under supervision of women; (iii) if families are detained, they will be accommodated in the same place as family units; and (iv) a women intern will not be searched except by a woman.

In the cases of pregnant women and maternity cases: (i) the cases to be considered on priority; (ii) they may be repatriated, or relocated on priority in case of reciprocity; (iii) they shall be given additional food and placed at a place where additional medical care could be provided, if needed; (iv) they are not to be sent on journey detrimental to their health, unless required for their safety; and (v) death penalty may not be awarded to pregnant women or to mothers having dependent infants. The cases of mothers of young children: (i) to be decided on top priority for release, repatriation or relocation; and (ii) to be provided with additional ration.

4. Protection of women combatants: Women are protected by IHL from the moment they fall into the power of the enemy. They are entitled to the status of prisoner of war (POW), once captured. They are entitled to all benefits which are granted to men POW, and have right to same protection. Special protection accorded to women combatants are (i) pregnant women and mothers having dependent children - their cases are to be considered on utmost priority; (ii) they shall be treated with all the regards due to their sex; (iii) in camps where women and men POW are accommodated, separate dormitories and conveniences shall be provided for women; (iv) male POW shall not have access to women prisoners; (v) women POW may be put to labour who are physically fit, taking into account their age, sex, rank, physical aptitude with a view to maintain them in a good state of physical and mental health; (vi) a women POW shall not be awarded or sentenced to a punishment more serious/severe, than the men or women member of the detaining power dealt with for a similar offence; and (vii) women POW undergoing punishment shall be confined in a separate quarter than male POW and shall be under the immediate supervision of Women.

However, a number of academics maintain that IHL continues to fail women. Generally, women are valued in IHL in terms of sexual and reproductive aspects of their lives.[4] IHL in addressing humanitarian needs in armed conflict assumes a population in which there is no systemic gender inequality. The system fails to recognize the unequal situation of men and women in society generally.[5] The provisions of IHL which offer specific *additional* protection to women are either generic, such as the requirement in Article 14 of the Third Geneva Convention that "women ... be treated with all the regard due to their sex"; or more specific, such as the provisions in the Third Convention which spell out how this general obligation should be implemented in practice, for example, by the provision of separate detention quarters and sanitary facilities for female POW and the requirement that they be under the immediate supervision of women if confined.

Convention on the Rights of the Child (1989)

The Convention on the rights of the Child explicitly extends to children the protection afforded to adults through the various legal instruments. For example, States Parties agree to safeguard due judicial process for children and protect children affected by armed conflict. Four general principles are enshrined in the convention:

1. *Non-Discrimination* (Article 2): states party must ensure that all children within their Jurisdiction enjoy their rights. The essential message is equality of opportunities: girls should be given the same opportunities as boys.

2. *Best interests of the child* (Article 3): the best interests of children must be a primary consideration in all State decisions which affect children.

3. *The right to life, survival and development* (Article 6): the right-to-life article includes formulations about the right to survival and to development.

---

[4] Forty-three provisions of the Geneva Conventions and Protocols specifically deal with women and the effects of armed conflict. However, they all deal with women in their relationships with others, not as individuals in their own right. Nineteen are, in fact, designed to protect children. Those that deal with sexual offenses are couched in terms of offenses against women's honor. Women's honor, as depicted in IHL, is constituted solely on the basis of certain sexual attributes, the characterizing features of which are what is seen as important to men, namely the chastity and modesty of women. In contrast, the honor of men is a much more complex concept in IHL, encompassing both mind and bodily attributes.

[5] Gardam J. and M. Jarvis.2001. *Women, Armed Conflict and International Law*, The Hague: Kluwer Law International, p. 97.

4. *The views of the child* (Article 12): states that children should be free to have options in all matters affecting them, and those views should be given due weight "in accordance to the age and maturity of the child".

The Vienna Declaration (1993)

Although not legally binding per se, the Vienna Declaration and Programme of Action is an important statement of principles and policy that was unanimously adopted by the States participating in the World Conference on Human Rights in 1993. According to the Declaration, the "human rights of women and of the girl child are an inalienable, integral and indivisible part of universal human rights" and the "full and equal participation of women in political, civil, economic, social and cultural life, at the national, regional and international levels, and the eradication of all forms of discrimination on grounds of sex are priority objectives of the international community." The declaration calls for the elimination of gender-based violence. It recognizes the importance of joint efforts to eliminate violence against women in public and private life, and confirms that the violation of women's human rights in armed conflict situations is a violation of the fundamental principles of international human rights and humanitarian law.

Declaration on the Elimination of Violence Against Women, Asserts that violence against women is pervasive in all societies, across lines of income, class and culture, and recognizes that violence against women by private actors is a human rights violation. The Declaration reaffirmed that violence against women is the manifestation of historically unequal power relations between men and women and that it is one of the critical mechanisms by which women are forced into a subordinate status.

Beijing Platform for Action (1995)

In 1995, at the 4th International Women's Conference in Beijing, China, the "Beijing Statement" and "Beijing Platform for Action" were passed, and they set out specific actions that governments must undertake to advance equality. They also discuss actions required to reduce the suffering of women and girls living in war-torn areas, which includes the six strategic objectives: (i) Increase the participation of women in conflict resolutions at decision-making levels and protect women living in situations of armed conflicts or under foreign occupation; (ii) Reduce excessive military expenditures and control over the availability of armaments; (iii) Promote non-violent forms of conflict resolution and reduce the incidence of human rights abuse in conflict situations; (iv) Promote women's contribution to fostering a culture of peace; (v) Provide protection, assistance and training to refugee women, other displaced women in need of international protection and internally displaced women; and (vi) Provide assistance to the women in the colonies and non-self-governing territories.[6]

The Platform identifies violence against women as an obstacle to the achievement of the objectives of equality, development and peace. It includes a focus on combating violence against women as one of its strategic objectives and on promoting the status of women in war affected countries. During post-conflict and reconstruction an additional set of legal instrument must be taken into account. These instruments include:

ILO Convention 100: Equal Remuneration (1951)

States which have ratified C.100 agree to promote the principle of equal pay for work of equal value. They must ensure its application to all workers in a manner consistent with the national methods used to determine rates of pay. The Convention defines equal pay for work of equal value as a rate of pay fixed without discrimination based on sex.

Convention on Political Rights of Women (1952)

The main objective of the Convention is to implement the principle of equality of rights for men and women in the enjoyment and exercise of political rights. The Convention formulates important principles providing that women, without any discrimination, shall be (a) entitled to vote in all elections; (b) eligible for elections to all publicly elected bodies established by national law; (c) entitled to hold public office and exercise all public functions established by national law.

ILO Convention 111: Discrimination (1958)

Each ratifying state must adhere to the basic goal of promoting equality of opportunity and treatment by means of a national policy that aims to end all forms of discrimination in employment and occupation. Discrimination is defined as any distinction, exclusion or preference based on race, colour, sex, religion, political opinion, national extraction or social origin that nullifies or impairs equality of opportunity or treatment in employment or occupation.

Convention against Discrimination in Education (1960)

Adopted by the General Conference of UNESCO, this convention paves the way for equal educational opportunities for girls and women. The convention is not only directed

6 http://www.un.org/womenwatch/daw/beijing/platform/armed.htm

at the elimination of discrimination in education but also concerns the adoption of measures aimed at promoting equality of opportunity and treatment in this field.

Security Council Resolution 1325

UN Security Council Resolution 1325 passed on the 31st October 2000, recognized that women world-wide are playing an active and positive role in conflict resolution and peace building. It acknowledged that peace cannot be sustained unless women have an equal and active role in formulating political, economic and social policy and that without women's full participation in peace processes, there can be no justice or sustainable development in the reconstruction of societies.

Rehabilitation

Rehabilitation is guaranteed in many universal treaties and declarations. Article 14 (1) of the Convention Against Torture provides that 'each State Party shall ensure in its legal system that the victim of an act of torture obtains redress and has an enforceable right to fair and adequate compensation, including the means for as full rehabilitation as possible.' Article 39 CRC states that 'States Parties shall take all appropriate measures to promote physical and psychological recovery and social reintegration of a child victim….'. The Special Rapporteur on torture has recommended that states ensure 'fair and adequate compensation, including the means for the fullest rehabilitation possible'. The Committee on the Elimination of Discrimination against Women has listed rehabilitation in its General Recommendation 19 on Violence against Women.[7]

5.2 DECLARATION ON THE ELIMINATION OF DISCRIMINATION AGAINST WOMEN, 1967 [8]

Article 1

Discrimination against women, denying or limiting as it does their equality of rights with men, is fundamentally unjust and constitutes an offence against human dignity.

Article 2

All appropriate measures shall be taken to abolish existing laws, customs, regulations and practices which are discriminatory against women, and to establish adequate legal protection for equal rights of men and women, in particular:

[7] *General Recommendation 19 on Violence against Women*, 29 January 1992, A/47/38, par a 24 (a), (b).

[8] UN General Assembly resolution A/RES/2263, 7 November 1967.

(a) The principle of equality of rights shall be embodied in the constitution or otherwise guaranteed by law;

(b) The international instruments of the United Nations and the specialized agencies relating to the elimination of discrimination against women shall be ratified or acceded to and fully implemented as soon as practicable.

Article 3

All appropriate measures shall be taken to educate public opinion and to direct national aspirations towards the eradication of prejudice and the abolition of customary and all other practices which are based on the idea of the inferiority of women.

Article 4

All appropriate measures shall be taken to ensure to women on equal terms with men, without any discrimination:

(a) The right to vote in all elections and be eligible for election to all publicly elected bodies;

(b) The right to vote in all public referenda;

(c) The right to hold public office and to exercise all public functions.

Such rights shall be guaranteed by legislation.

Article 5

Women shall have the same rights as men to acquire, change or retain their nationality. Marriage to an alien shall not automatically affect the nationality of the wife either by rendering her stateless or by forcing upon her the nationality of her husband.

Article 6

1. Without prejudice to the safeguarding of the unity and the harmony of the family, which remains the basic unit of any society, all appropriate measures, particularly legislative measures, shall be taken to ensure to women, married or unmarried, equal rights with men in the field of civil law, and in particular:

(a) The right to acquire, administer, enjoy, dispose of and inherit property, including property acquired during marriage;

(b) The right to equality in legal capacity and the exercise thereof;

(c) The same rights as men with regard to the law on the movement of persons.

2. All appropriate measures shall be taken to ensure the principle of equality of status of the husband and wife, and in particular:

(a) Women shall have the same right as men to free choice of a spouse and to enter into marriage only with their free and full consent;

(b) Women shall have equal rights with men during marriage and at its dissolution. In all cases the interest of the children shall be paramount;

(c) Parents shall have equal rights and duties in matters relating to their children. In all cases the interest of the children shall be paramount.

3. Child marriage and the betrothal of young girls before puberty shall be prohibited, and effective action, including legislation, shall be taken to specify a minimum age for marriage and to make the registration of marriages in an official registry compulsory.

Article 7

All provisions of penal codes which constitute discrimination against women shall be repealed.

Article 8

All appropriate measures, including legislation, shall be taken to combat all forms of traffic in women and exploitation of prostitution of women.

Article 9

All appropriate measures shall be taken to ensure to girls and women, married or unmarried, equal rights with men in education at all levels, and in particular:

(a) Equal conditions of access to, and study in, educational institutions of all types, including universities and vocational, technical and professional schools;

(b) The same choice of curricula, the same examinations, teaching staff with qualifications of the same standard, and school premises and equipment of the same quality, whether the institutions are co-educational or not;

(c) Equal opportunities to benefit from scholarships and other study grants;

(d) Equal opportunities for access to programmes of continuing education, including adult literacy programmes;

(e) Access to educational information to help in ensuring the health and well-being of families.

Article 10

1. All appropriate measures shall be taken to ensure to women, married or unmarried, equal rights with men in the field of economic and social life, and in particular:

(a) The right, without discrimination on grounds of marital status or any other grounds, to receive vocational training, to work, to free choice of profession and employment, and to professional and vocational advancement;

(b) The right to equal remuneration with men and to equality of treatment in respect of work of equal value;

(c) The right to leave with pay, retirement privileges and provision for security in respect of unemployment, sickness, old age or other incapacity to work;

(d) The right to receive family allowances on equal terms with men.

2. In order to prevent discrimination against women on account of marriage or maternity and to ensure their effective right to work, measures shall be taken to prevent their dismissal in the event of marriage or maternity and to provide paid maternity leave, with the guarantee of returning to former employment, and to provide the necessary social services, including child-care facilities.

3. Measures taken to protect women in certain types of work, for reasons inherent in their physical nature, shall not be regarded as discriminatory.

Article 11

1. The principle of equality of rights of men and women demands implementation in all States in accordance with the principles of the Charter of the United Nations and of the Universal Declaration of Human Rights.

2. Governments, non-governmental organizations and individuals are urged, therefore, to do all in their power to promote the implementation of the principles contained in this Declaration.

5.3 DECLARATION ON THE PROTECTION OF WOMEN AND CHILDREN IN EMERGENCY AND ARMED CONFLICT, 1974[9]

The General Assembly,

Having considered the recommendation of the Economic and Social Council contained in its resolution 1861 (LVI) of 16 May 1974,

Expressing its deep concern over the sufferings of women and children belonging to the civilian population who in periods of emergency and armed conflict in the struggle for peace, self-determination, national liberation and independence are too often the victims of inhuman acts and consequently suffer serious harm,

Aware of the suffering of women and children in many areas of the world, especially in those areas subject to suppression, aggression, colonialism, racism, alien domination and foreign subjugation,

Deeply concerned by the fact that, despite general and unequivocal condemnation, colonialism, racism and alien and foreign domination continue to subject many peoples under their yoke, cruelly suppressing the national liberation movements and inflicting heavy losses and incalculable sufferings on the populations under their domination, including women and children,

Deploring the fact that grave attacks are still being made on fundamental freedoms and the dignity of the human person and that colonial and racist foreign domination Powers continue to violate international humanitarian law,

Recalling the relevant provisions contained in the instruments of international humanitarian law relative to the protection of women and children in time of peace and war,

Recalling , among other important documents, its resolutions 2444 (XXIII) of 19 December 1968, 2597 (XXIV) of 16 December 1969 and 2674 (XXV) and 2675 (XXV) of 9 December 1970, on respect for human rights and on basic principles for the protection of civilian populations in armed conflicts, as well as Economic and Social Council resolution 1515 (XLVIII) of 28 May 1970 in which the Council requested the General Assembly to consider the possibility of drafting a declaration on the protection of women and children in emergency or wartime,

---

[9] Proclaimed by UN General Assembly resolution 3318 (XXIX) of 14 December 1974.

Conscious of its responsibility for the destiny of the rising generation and for the destiny of mothers, who play an important role in society, in the family and particularly in the upbringing of children,

Bearing in mind the need to provide special protection of women and children belonging to the civilian population,

Solemnly proclaims this Declaration on the Protection of Women and Children in Emergency and Armed Conflict and calls for the strict observance of the Declaration by all Member States:

1. Attacks and bombings on the civilian population, inflicting incalculable suffering, especially on women and children, who are the most vulnerable members of the population, shall be prohibited, and such acts shall be condemned.

2. The use of chemical and bacteriological weapons in the course of military operations constitutes one of the most flagrant violations of the Geneva Protocol of 1925, the Geneva Conventions of 1949 and the principles of international humanitarian law and inflicts heavy losses on civilian populations, including defenceless women and children, and shall be severely condemned.

3. All States shall abide fully by their obligations under the Geneva Protocol of 1925 and the Geneva Conventions of 1949, as well as other instruments of international law relative to respect for human rights in armed conflicts, which offer important guarantees for the protection of women and children.

4. All efforts shall be made by States involved in armed conflicts, military operations in foreign territories or military operations in territories still under colonial domination to spare women and children from the ravages of war. All the necessary steps shall be taken to ensure the prohibition of measures such as persecution, torture, punitive measures, degrading treatment and violence, particularly against that part of the civilian population that consists of women and children.

5. All forms of repression and cruel and inhuman treatment of women and children, including imprisonment, torture, shooting, mass arrests, collective punishment, destruction of dwellings and forcible eviction, committed by belligerents in the course of military operations or in occupied territories shall be considered criminal.

6. Women and children belonging to the civilian population and finding themselves in circumstances of emergency and armed conflict in the struggle for peace, self-determination, national liberation and independence, or who live in occupied

territories, shall not be deprived of shelter, food, medical aid or other inalienable rights, in accordance with the provisions of the Universal Declaration of Human Rights, the International Covenant on Civil and Political Rights, the International Covenant on Economic, Social and Cultural Rights, the Declaration of the Rights of the Child or other instruments of international law.

5.4 THE CONVENTION ON THE ELIMINATION OF ALL FORMS OF DISCRIMINATION AGAINST WOMEN, 1979 [10]

Discrimination based on sex became the exclusive focus of the 1979 Convention on the Elimination of All Forms of Discrimination against Women (CEDAW), which entered into force on 3 September 1981. The Convention was preceded by the Declaration on the Elimination of Discrimination against Women, proclaimed by the General Assembly in 1967. The Convention has become an important legal means of promoting the protection of the equal rights of women within the framework of the United Nations. The implementation of its provisions is reviewed by the Committee on the Elimination of Discrimination against Women.

The key principles of CEDAW are substantive equality; non-discrimination and State obligation. *Substantive equality* differs from formal equality in that it mandates States to ensure: (i) Equality of opportunity through law, policy, programmes and institutional arrangements; (ii) Equality of access by (a) eliminating all obstacles that prevent access to the opportunities as well as (b) institution of positive measures/enabling conditions, including temporary special measures, to level the playing field between men and women; and (iii) Equality of results that entitles women to outcomes and social goods (education, employment etc) on an equal basis with men.

Article 1 of the Convention states:

> "the term 'discrimination against women' shall mean any distinction, exclusion or restriction made on the basis of sex which has the effect or purpose of impairing or nullifying the recognition, enjoyment or exercise by women, irrespective of their marital status, on a basis of equality of men and women, of human rights and fundamental freedoms in the political, economic, social, cultural, civil or any other field."

It is also important to point out that, contrary to the International Convention on the Elimination of All Forms of Racial Discrimination, which only refers to discrimination in the "field of public

---

[10] Adopted and opened for signature, ratification and accession by General Assembly resolution 34/180 of 18 December 1979; entry into force 3 September 1981, in accordance with article 27(1).

life", Article 1 of the 1979 Convention on the Elimination of All Forms of Discrimination against Women has a wider field of application and also covers acts falling within the private sphere. As emphasized by the Committee on the Elimination of Discrimination against Women, "discrimination under the Convention is not restricted to action by or on behalf of Governments (Articles 2(e), 2(f) and 5). For example, under article 2(e) the Convention calls on States parties to take all appropriate measures to eliminate discrimination against women by any person, organization or enterprise. Under general international law and specific human rights covenants, States may also be responsible for private acts if they fail to act with due diligence to compensation."

Under article 2 of the Convention, States parties more particularly "agree to pursue by all appropriate means and without delay a policy of eliminating discrimination against women" and to this end they undertake:

- To embody the principle of equality of men and women in their national constitutions or other appropriate legislation ... and to ensure ... the practical realization of this principle (Article 2(a));
- To adopt appropriate legislative and other measures, including sanctions where appropriate, prohibiting all discrimination against women (Article 2(b));
- To establish effective legal protection of the equal rights of women ... and to ensure through competent national tribunals and other public institutions the effective protection of women against any act of discrimination (Article 2(c));
- To refrain from engaging in any act or practice of discrimination against women and to ensure that public authorities and institutions shall act in conformity with this obligation (Article 2(d));
- To take all appropriate measures to eliminate discrimination against women by any person, organization or enterprise (Article 2(e));
- To take all appropriate measures, including legislation, to modify or abolish existing laws, regulations, customs and practices which constitute discrimination against women (Article 2(f));
- To repeal all national penal provisions which constitute discrimination against women (Article 2(g)).

The subsequent articles provide further details of States parties' obligations to eliminate discrimination against women, which include the following:

- To modify the social and cultural patterns of conduct of men and women ... which are based on the idea of the inferiority or the superiority of either of the sexes or on stereotyped roles for men and women (Article 5(a));
- To ensure that family education includes a proper understanding of maternity as a social function and the recognition of the common responsibility of men and women in the upbringing and development of their children, it being understood that the interest of the children is the primordial consideration in all cases (Article 5(b));
- To take "all appropriate measures, including legislation, to suppress all forms of trafficking in women and exploitation of prostitution of women (Article 6), to eliminate discrimination against women in the political and public life of the country (Article 7 and 8), and in education (Article 10), employment (Article 11), health care (Article 12) and other areas of economic and social life (Article 13), and to ensure the application of the Convention to women in rural areas (Article 14).

While many articles of the Convention are framed as general legal obligations of States parties to take "all appropriate measures" to eliminate discrimination against women, some set forth specific rights that must be guaranteed on a basis of equality to men and women such as:

- The right to education: women have the right, inter alia, to the same conditions for career and vocational guidance and for access to studies and to the same opportunities for access to scholarships and other grants (Article 10);
- The right to work, to the same employment opportunities, to free choice of profession and employment, to equal remuneration, to social security and to protection of health and safety in working conditions (Article 11);
- The right to family benefits, to bank loans, mortgages and other forms of financial credit and to participate in recreational facilities, sports and all aspects of cultural life (Article 13);
- The right of rural women to participate in the elaboration and implementation of development plans, to have access to adequate health care facilities, to benefit directly from social security programmes, to obtain all types of training and education, to organize self-help groups, to participate in all community activities, to have access to agricultural credit and loans, and to enjoy adequate living conditions (Article 14).

The Convention imposes a specific duty on States parties to accord to women "equality with men before the law" and a legal capacity in civil matters identical to that of men (Article 15(1) and (2)), and requires them to ensure, "on a basis of equality of men and women" a number of rights relating to marriage and the family (Article 16):

Article 15

1. States Parties shall accord to women equality with men before the law.

2. States Parties shall accord to women, in civil matters, a legal capacity identical to that of men and the same opportunities to exercise that capacity. In particular, they shall give women equal rights to conclude contracts and to administer property and shall treat them equally in all stages of procedure in courts and tribunals.

3. States Parties agree that all contracts and all other private instruments of any kind with a legal effect which is directed at restricting the legal capacity of women shall be deemed null and void.

4. States Parties shall accord to men and women the same rights with regard to the law relating to the movement of persons and the freedom to choose their residence and domicile.

Article 16

1. States Parties shall take all appropriate measures to eliminate discrimination against women in all matters relating to marriage and family relations and in particular shall ensure, on a basis of equality of men and women:

(a) The same right to enter into marriage;

(b) The same right freely to choose a spouse and to enter into marriage only with their free and full consent;

(c) The same rights and responsibilities during marriage and at its dissolution;

(d) The same rights and responsibilities as parents, irrespective of their marital status, in matters relating to their children; in all cases the interests of the children shall be paramount;

(e) The same rights to decide freely and responsibly on the number and spacing of their children and to have access to the information, education and means to enable them to exercise these rights;

(f) The same rights and responsibilities with regard to guardianship, wardship, trusteeship and adoption of children, or similar institutions where these concepts exist in national legislation; in all cases the interests of the children shall be paramount;

(g) The same personal rights as husband and wife, including the right to choose a family name, a profession and an occupation;

(h) The same rights for both spouses in respect of the ownership, acquisition, management, administration, enjoyment and disposition of property, whether free of charge or for a valuable consideration.

2. The betrothal and the marriage of a child shall have no legal effect, and all necessary action, including legislation, shall be taken to specify a minimum age for marriage and to make the registration of marriages in an official registry compulsory.

With regard to the equality of rights between women and men as provided by article 3 of the Covenant, it implies, according to the Committee, "that all human beings should enjoy the rights provided for in the Covenant, on an equal basis and in their totality. The full effect of this provision is impaired whenever any person is denied the full and equal enjoyment of any right. Consequently, States should ensure to men and women equally the enjoyment of all rights provided for in the Covenant."

The obligation to ensure the rights contained in the Covenant without discrimination "requires that States parties take all necessary steps to enable every person to enjoy those rights. These steps include the removal of obstacles to the equal enjoyment of such rights, the education of the population and of State officials to human rights, and the adjustment of domestic legislation so as to give effect to the undertakings set forth in the Covenant. The State party must not only adopt measures of protection, but also positive measures in all areas so as to achieve the effective and equal empowerment of women."

The Committee on the Elimination of Discrimination against Women has recommended that States parties to the Convention on the Elimination of All Forms of Discrimination against Women should ensure "the enactment and effective enforcement of laws that prohibit female genital mutilation".[11] It has also recommended that States parties "take appropriate and effective measures with a view to eradicating the practice of female circumcision". Such

---

[11] General Recommendation No. 24 (Article 12 – Women and health), *United Nations Compilation of General Comments,* p. 248, para. 15(d)

measures could include: (i) the collection and dissemination of basic data about such traditional practices; (ii) the support of women's organizations working for the elimination of female circumcision and other practices harmful to women; (iii) the encouragement of politicians, professionals, religious and community leaders at all levels including the media and the arts to cooperate in influencing attitudes towards the eradication of female circumcision; (iv) the introduction of appropriate educational and training programmes and seminars based on research findings about the problems arising from female circumcision; (v) the inclusion in national health policies of appropriate strategies aimed at eradicating female circumcision in public health care.[12]

The abuse of women in police custody or otherwise deprived of their liberty is another problem area needing international attention. The Human Rights Committee in General Comment No. 28, has emphasized that "States parties must provide all information relevant to ensuring that the rights of persons deprived of their liberty are protected on equal terms for men and women. In particular, States parties should report on whether men and women are separated in prisons and whether women are guarded only by female guards. States parties should also report about compliance with the rule that accused juvenile females shall be separated from adults and on any difference in treatment between male and female persons deprived of liberty, such as access to rehabilitation and education programmes and to conjugal and family visits. Pregnant women who are deprived of their liberty should receive humane treatment and respect for their inherent dignity at all times, and in particular during the birth and while caring for their newborn children."[13]

Women's Right to an Effective Remedy, including the Right of Access to the Courts

The duty to provide effective remedies for persons whose rights and freedoms are violated is contained in Article 2(3) of the International Covenant on Civil and Political Rights. Article 2(b) and (c) of the Convention on the Elimination of All Forms of Discrimination against Women contains rules about the legal duties of States parties "to adopt appropriate legislative and other measures, including sanctions where appropriate, prohibiting all discrimination against women" and "to establish legal protection of the rights of women on an equal basis with men".

---

12 General Recommendation No. 14 (Female circumcision), *United Nations Compilation of General Comments*, pp. 211-212, subparagraphs (a) and (b).

13 General Recommendation No. 28 (Article 3 – Equality of rights between men and women), *United Nations Compilation of General Comments*, p. 170, para. 15.

Article 14 of the ICCPR also contains due process guarantees which must be ensured to everyone without discrimination on any ground such as sex. The right guarantees access to the courts or access to justice. The women may in many instances be in a particularly disadvantageous position to vindicate their rights, since they may not, for instance, have access to the courts or be able to benefit from due process guarantees. The case of *Ato del Avellanal v. Peru* illustrates the dilemma that can face women who do not have equal access to justice. In this case, a Peruvian women who owned two apartment buildings in Lima and who, by final decision of the Supreme Court, was not allowed to sue the tenants in order to collect overdue rents, since, under article 168 of the Peruvian Civil Code, when a women is married, only her husband is entitled to represent the matrimonial property before the courts. According to the Human Rights Committee, this violated the following provisions of the ICCPR: (i) Article 14(1), which guarantees that all persons shall be equal before the courts and tribunals, since "the wife was not equal to her husband for purposes of suing in Court"; (ii) Article 3, which requires States parties to ensure the equal right of men and women to the enjoyment of all civil and political rights set forth in the Covenant; and (iii) Article 26, which states that "all persons are equal before the law and are entitled without any discrimination to the equal protection of the law." The Committee found that the application of article 168 of the Peruvian Civil Code to the author "resulted in denying her equality before the courts and constituted discrimination on the ground of sex".[14]

Optional Protocol to CEDAW (1999)

Optional Protocol enables individuals to raise complaints with the UN Committee for CEDAW. The Committee is empowered to probe into violation of human rights in member states. By ratifying the Optional Protocol, a State would recognize the competence of the Committee on the Elimination of Discrimination against Women.

5.5 CONVENTION ON THE PROTECTION OF THE RIGHTS OF ALL MIGRANT WORKERS AND THEIR FAMILIES, 1990[15]

Women Migrant Workers

Although both men and women migrate, migration is not a gender-neutral phenomenon. The position of female migrants is different from that of male migrants in terms of legal migration channels, the sectors into which they migrate, the forms of abuse they suffer and the

[14] Communication No. 202/1986, *G. Ato del Avellanal v. Peru* (views adopted on 28 October 1988), in UN doc. GAOR, A/44/40, p. 196, paras. 1 and 2.1.

[15] Adopted by General Assembly resolution 45/158 of 18 December 1990.

consequences thereof. The Committee on the Elimination of Discrimination against Women, in its General recommendation No. 26 on women migrant workers has emphasized that:

> 6. All women migrant workers are entitled to the protection of their human rights, which include the right to life, the right to personal liberty and security, the right not to be tortured, the right to be free of degrading and inhumane treatment, the right to be free from discrimination on the basis of sex, race, ethnicity, cultural particularities, nationality, language, religion or other status, the right to be free from poverty, the right to an adequate standard of living, the right to equality before the law and the right to benefit from the due processes of the law.
>
> 7. Women migrant workers are also entitled to protection from discrimination on the basis of the Convention, which requires States parties to take all appropriate measures without delay to eliminate all forms of discrimination against women and to ensure that they will be able to exercise and enjoy de jure and de facto rights on an equal basis with men in all fields.
>
> 20. Women migrant workers are more vulnerable to sexual abuse, sexual harassment and physical violence, especially in sectors where women predominate. Domestic workers are particularly vulnerable to physical and sexual assault, food and sleep deprivation and cruelty by their employers. Sexual harassment of women migrant workers in other work environments, such as on farms or in the industrial sector, is a problem worldwide.
>
> 21. Access to justice may be limited for women migrant workers. In some countries, restrictions are imposed on the use of the legal system by women migrant workers to obtain remedies for discriminatory labour standards, employment discrimination or sex- and gender-based violence. Further, women migrant workers may not be eligible for free government legal aid, and there may be other impediments, such as unresponsive and hostile officials and, at times, collusion between officials and the perpetrator. In some cases, diplomats have perpetrated sexual abuse, violence and other forms of discrimination against women migrant domestic workers while enjoying diplomatic immunity. In some countries, there are gaps in the laws protecting migrant women workers. For example, they may lose their work permits once they make a report of abuse or discrimination and then they cannot afford to remain in the country for the duration of the trial, if any. In addition to these formal barriers, practical barriers may prevent access to remedies.

22. Undocumented women migrant workers are particularly vulnerable to exploitation and abuse because of their irregular immigration status, which exacerbates their exclusion and the risk of exploitation. They may be exploited as forced labour, and their access to minimum labour rights may be limited by fear of denouncement. They may also face harassment by the police. If they are apprehended, they are usually prosecuted for violations of immigration laws and placed in detention centres, where they are vulnerable to sexual abuse, and then deported.[16]

Some of the recommendations made by the Committee to the State parties are as follows.

1. Common responsibilities of countries of origin and destination

Formulating a comprehensive gender-sensitive and rights-based policy: States parties should use the Convention and the general recommendations to formulate a gender-sensitive, rights-based policy on the basis of equality and non-discrimination to regulate and administer all aspects and stages of migration, to facilitate access of women migrant workers to work opportunities abroad, promoting safe migration and ensuring the protection of the rights of women migrant workers.

2. Responsibilities specific to countries of origin

Countries of origin must respect and protect the human rights of their female nationals who migrate for purposes of work. Measures that may be required include, but are not limited to, the following:

(a) Lifting of discriminatory bans or restrictions on migration: States parties should repeal sex-specific bans and discriminatory restrictions on women's migration on the basis of age, marital status, pregnancy or maternity status. They should lift restrictions that require women to get permission from their spouse or male guardian to obtain a passport or to travel.

(b) Education, awareness-raising and training.

(c) States parties should adopt regulations and design monitoring systems to ensure that recruiting agents and employment agencies respect the rights of all women migrant workers.

---

[16] Paragraphs 6, 7, 20, 21 and 22. CEDAW/C/2009/WP.1/R dated 5 December 2008.

(d) Health services: States parties should ensure the provision of standardized and authentic health certificates if required by countries of destination and require prospective employers to purchase medical insurance for women migrant workers.

(e) Travel documents: States parties should ensure that women have equal and independent access to travel documents.

(f) Legal and administrative assistance: States parties should ensure the availability of legal assistance in connection with migration for work.

(g) Safeguarding remittances of income: States parties should establish measures to safeguard the remittances of women migrant workers and provide information and assistance to women to access formal financial institutions to send money home and to encourage them to participate in savings schemes.

(h) Facilitating the right to return: States parties should ensure that women who wish to return to their countries of origin are able to do so free of coercion and abuse.

(j) Diplomatic and consular protection: States parties must properly train and supervise their diplomatic and consular staff to ensure that they fulfil their role in protecting the rights of women migrant workers abroad. Such protection should include quality support services available to women migrants, including timely provision of interpreters, medical care, counselling, legal aid and shelter when needed.

3. Responsibilities specific to countries of transit

States parties through which migrant women travel should take all appropriate steps to ensure that their territories are not used to facilitate the violation of the rights of women migrant workers. Measures that may be required include, but are not limited to, the following:

(a) Training, monitoring and supervision of Government agents: States parties should ensure that their border police and immigration officials are adequately trained, supervised and monitored for gender-sensitivity and non-discriminatory practices when dealing with women migrants (article 2 (d));

(b) Protection against violations of migrant women workers' rights that take place under their jurisdiction: States parties should take active measures to prevent, prosecute and punish all migration-related human rights violations that occur under their jurisdiction, whether perpetrated by public authorities or private actors. States parties should provide or facilitate services and assistance in situations where women travelling with an agent or escort have been abandoned, make all attempts to trace perpetrators and take legal action against them (articles 2 (c) and (e));

4. Responsibilities specific to countries of destination

States parties in countries where migrant women work should take all appropriate measures to ensure non-discrimination and the equal rights of women migrant workers, including in their own communities. Measures that may be required include, but are not limited to, the following:

(a) Lifting of discriminatory bans or restrictions on immigration: States parties should repeal outright bans and discriminatory restrictions on women's immigration. They should ensure that their visa schemes do not indirectly discriminate against women by restricting permission to women migrant workers to be employed in certain job categories where men predominate, or by excluding certain female-dominated occupations from visa schemes. Further, they should lift bans that prohibit women migrant workers from getting married to nationals or permanent residents, becoming pregnant or securing independent housing.

(b) Legal protection for the rights of women migrant workers: States parties should ensure that constitutional and civil law and labour codes provide to women migrant workers the same rights and protection that are extended to all workers in the country, including the right to organize and freely associate. They should ensure that contracts for women migrant workers are legally valid. In particular, they should ensure that occupations dominated by women migrant workers, such as domestic work and some forms of entertainment, are protected by labour laws, including wage and hour regulations, health and safety codes and holiday and vacation leave regulations. The laws should include mechanisms for monitoring workplace conditions of migrant women, especially in the kinds of jobs where they dominate.

(c) Access to remedies: States parties should ensure that women migrant workers have the ability to access remedies when their rights are violated. Specific measures include, but are not limited to, the following:

(i) Promulgate and enforce laws and regulations that include adequate legal remedies and complaints mechanisms, and put in place easily accessible dispute resolution mechanisms, protecting both documented and undocumented women migrant workers from discrimination or sex-based exploitation and abuse;

(ii) Repeal or amend laws that prevent women migrant workers from using the courts and other systems of redress. These include laws on loss of work permit, which results in loss of earnings and possible deportation by immigration authorities when a worker files a complaint of exploitation or abuse and while pending investigation. States parties should introduce flexibility into the process of changing employers or sponsors without deportation in cases where workers complain of abuse;

(iii) Ensure that women migrant workers have access to legal assistance and to the courts and regulatory systems charged with enforcing labour and employment laws, including through free legal aid;

(iv) Provide temporary shelters for women migrant workers who wish to leave abusive employers, husbands or other relatives and provide facilities for safe accommodation during trial;

(d) Legal protection for the freedom of movement: States parties should ensure that employers and recruiters do not confiscate or destroy travel or identity documents belonging to women migrants. States parties should also take steps to end the forced seclusion or locking in the homes of women migrant workers, especially those working in domestic service. Police officers should be trained to protect the rights of women migrant workers from such abuses.

(e) Non-discriminatory family reunification schemes: States parties should ensure that family reunification schemes for migrant workers are not directly or indirectly discriminatory on the basis of sex.

(f) Non-discriminatory residency regulations: when residency permits of women migrant workers are premised on the sponsorship of an employer or spouse, States parties should enact provisions relating to independent residency status. Regulations should be made to allow for the legal stay of a woman who flees her abusive employer or spouse or is fired for complaining about abuse.

(g) Training and awareness-raising: States parties should provide mandatory awareness-raising programmes concerning the rights of migrant women workers and gender sensitivity training for relevant public and private recruitment agencies and employers and relevant State employees, such as criminal justice officers, border police, immigration authorities, border police and social service and health-care providers.

(h) Monitoring systems: States parties should adopt regulations and design monitoring systems to ensure that recruiting agents and employers respect the rights of all women migrant workers. States parties should closely monitor recruiting agencies and prosecute them for acts of violence, coercion, deception or exploitation.

(i) Access to services: States parties should ensure that linguistically and culturally appropriate gender-sensitive services for women migrant workers are available, including language and skills training programmes, emergency shelters, health-care services, police services, recreational and other programmes designed especially for isolated women migrant workers, such as domestic workers and others secluded in the home, in addition to victims of domestic violence. Victims of abuse must be provided with relevant emergency and social services, regardless of their immigration status.

(j) The rights of women migrant workers in detention, whether they are documented or undocumented: States parties should ensure that women migrant workers who are in detention do not suffer discrimination or gender-based violence, and that pregnant and breastfeeding mothers as well as women in ill health have access to appropriate services. They should review, eliminate or reform laws, regulations, or policies that result in a disproportionate number of women migrant workers being detained for migration-related reasons.

(k) Social inclusion of women migrant workers: States parties should adopt policies and programmes with the aim of enabling women migrant workers to integrate into the new society. Such efforts should be respectful of the cultural identity of women migrant workers and protective of their human rights, in compliance with the Convention.

(l) Protection of undocumented women migrant workers: the situation of undocumented women needs specific attention. Regardless of the lack of immigration status of undocumented women migrant workers, States parties have an obligation to protect their basic human rights. Undocumented women migrant workers must have access to legal remedies and justice in cases of risk to life and of cruel and degrading treatment, or if they are coerced into forced labour, face deprivation of fulfilment of basic needs, including in times of health emergencies or pregnancy and maternity, or if they are abused physically or sexually by employers or others. If they are arrested or detained, the States parties must ensure that undocumented women migrant workers receive humane treatment and have access to due process of the law, including through free legal aid.

5. Bilateral and regional cooperation

States parties who are sending or receiving and transit countries should enter into bilateral or regional agreements or memorandums of understanding protecting the rights of women migrant workers. States parties should cooperate on providing information on perpetrators of violations of the rights of women migrant workers. When provided with information regarding perpetrators within their territory, States parties should take measures to investigate, prosecute and punish them.

5.6 DECLARATION ON THE ELIMINATION OF VIOLENCE AGAINST WOMEN, 1993 [17]

The General Assembly,

Recognizing the urgent need for the universal application to women of the rights and principles with regard to equality, security, liberty, integrity and dignity of all human beings,

Noting that those rights and principles are enshrined in international instruments, including the Universal Declaration of Human Rights, the International Covenant on Civil and Political Rights, the International Covenant on Economic, Social and Cultural Rights, the Convention on the Elimination of All Forms of Discrimination against Women and the Convention against Torture and Other Cruel, Inhuman or Degrading Treatment or Punishment,

Recognizing that effective implementation of the Convention on the Elimination of All Forms of Discrimination against Women would contribute to the elimination of violence against women and that the Declaration on the Elimination of Violence against Women, set forth in the present resolution, will strengthen and complement that process,

Concerned that violence against women is an obstacle to the achievement of equality, development and peace, as recognized in the Nairobi Forward-looking Strategies for the Advancement of Women, in which a set of measures to combat violence against women was recommended, and to the full implementation of the Convention on the Elimination of All Forms of Discrimination against Women,

Affirming that violence against women constitutes a violation of the rights and fundamental freedoms of women and impairs or nullifies their enjoyment of those rights and freedoms, and

---

[17] UN General Assembly resolution A/RES/48/104, 23 February 1994.

concerned about the long-standing failure to protect and promote those rights and freedoms in the case of violence against women,

Recognizing that violence against women is a manifestation of historically unequal power relations between men and women, which have led to domination over and discrimination against women by men and to the prevention of the full advancement of women, and that violence against women is one of the crucial social mechanisms by which women are forced into a subordinate position compared with men,

Concerned that some groups of women, such as women belonging to minority groups, indigenous women, refugee women, migrant women, women living in rural or remote communities, destitute women, women in institutions or in detention, female children, women with disabilities, elderly women and women in situations of armed conflict, are especially vulnerable to violence,

Recalling the conclusion in paragraph 23 of the annex to Economic and Social Council resolution 1990/15 of 24 May 1990 that the recognition that violence against women in the family and society was pervasive and cut across lines of income, class and culture had to be matched by urgent and effective steps to eliminate its incidence,

Recalling also Economic and Social Council resolution 1991/18 of 30 May 1991, in which the Council recommended the development of a framework for an international instrument that would address explicitly the issue of violence against women,

Welcoming the role that women's movements are playing in drawing increasing attention to the nature, severity and magnitude of the problem of violence against women,

Alarmed that opportunities for women to achieve legal, social, political and economic equality in society are limited, inter alia, by continuing and endemic violence,

Convinced that in the light of the above there is a need for a clear and comprehensive definition of violence against women, a clear statement of the rights to be applied to ensure the elimination of violence against women in all its forms, a commitment by States in respect of their responsibilities, and a commitment by the international community at large to the elimination of violence against women,

Solemnly proclaims the following Declaration on the Elimination of Violence against Women and urges that every effort be made so that it becomes generally known and respected:

Article 1

For the purposes of this Declaration, the term "violence against women" means any act of gender-based violence that results in, or is likely to result in, physical, sexual or psychological harm or suffering to women, including threats of such acts, coercion or arbitrary deprivation of liberty, whether occurring in public or in private life.

Article 2

Violence against women shall be understood to encompass, but not be limited to, the following:

(a) Physical, sexual and psychological violence occurring in the family, including battering, sexual abuse of female children in the household, dowry-related violence, marital rape, female genital mutilation and other traditional practices harmful to women, non-spousal violence and violence related to exploitation;

(b) Physical, sexual and psychological violence occurring within the general community, including rape, sexual abuse, sexual harassment and intimidation at work, in educational institutions and elsewhere, trafficking in women and forced prostitution;

(c) Physical, sexual and psychological violence perpetrated or condoned by the State, wherever it occurs.

Article 3

Women are entitled to the equal enjoyment and protection of all human rights and fundamental freedoms in the political, economic, social, cultural, civil or any other field. These rights include, inter alia:

(a) The right to life;

(b) The right to equality;

(c) The right to liberty and security of person;

(d) The right to equal protection under the law;

(e) The right to be free from all forms of discrimination;

(f) The right to the highest standard attainable of physical and mental health;

(g) The right to just and favourable conditions of work;

(h) The right not to be subjected to torture, or other cruel, inhuman or degrading treatment or punishment.

Article 4

States should condemn violence against women and should not invoke any custom, tradition or religious consideration to avoid their obligations with respect to its elimination. States should pursue by all appropriate means and without delay a policy of eliminating violence against women and, to this end, should:

(a) Consider, where they have not yet done so, ratifying or acceding to the Convention on the Elimination of All Forms of Discrimination against Women or withdrawing reservations to that Convention;

(b) Refrain from engaging in violence against women;

(c) Exercise due diligence to prevent, investigate and, in accordance with national legislation, punish acts of violence against women, whether those acts are perpetrated by the State or by private persons;

(d) Develop penal, civil, labour and administrative sanctions in domestic legislation to punish and redress the wrongs caused to women who are subjected to violence; women who are subjected to violence should be provided with access to the mechanisms of justice and, as provided for by national legislation, to just and effective remedies for the harm that they have suffered; States should also inform women of their rights in seeking redress through such mechanisms;

(e) Consider the possibility of developing national plans of action to promote the protection of women against any form of violence, or to include provisions for that purpose in plans already existing, taking into account, as appropriate, such cooperation as can be provided by non-governmental organizations, particularly those concerned with the issue of violence against women;

(f) Develop, in a comprehensive way, preventive approaches and all those measures of a legal, political, administrative and cultural nature that promote the protection of women against any form of violence, and ensure that the re-victimization of women does not occur because of laws insensitive to gender considerations, enforcement practices or other interventions;

(g) Work to ensure, to the maximum extent feasible in the light of their available resources and, where needed, within the framework of international cooperation, that women subjected to violence and, where appropriate, their children have specialized assistance, such as rehabilitation, assistance in child care and maintenance, treatment, counselling, and health and social services, facilities and programmes, as well as support structures, and should take all other appropriate measures to promote their safety and physical and psychological rehabilitation;

(h) Include in government budgets adequate resources for their activities related to the elimination of violence against women;

(i) Take measures to ensure that law enforcement officers and public officials responsible for implementing policies to prevent, investigate and punish violence against women receive training to sensitize them to the needs of women;

(j) Adopt all appropriate measures, especially in the field of education, to modify the social and cultural patterns of conduct of men and women and to eliminate prejudices, customary practices and all other practices based on the idea of the inferiority or superiority of either of the sexes and on stereotyped roles for men and women;

(k) Promote research, collect data and compile statistics, especially concerning domestic violence, relating to the prevalence of different forms of violence against women and encourage research on the causes, nature, seriousness and consequences of violence against women and on the effectiveness of measures implemented to prevent and redress violence against women; those statistics and findings of the research will be made public;

(l) Adopt measures directed towards the elimination of violence against women who are especially vulnerable to violence;

(m) Include, in submitting reports as required under relevant human rights instruments of the United Nations, information pertaining to violence against women and measures taken to implement the present Declaration;

(n) Encourage the development of appropriate guidelines to assist in the implementation of the principles set forth in the present Declaration;

(o) Recognize the important role of the women's movement and non-governmental organizations worldwide in raising awareness and alleviating the problem of violence against women;

(p) Facilitate and enhance the work of the women's movement and non-governmental organizations and cooperate with them at local, national and regional levels;

(q) Encourage intergovernmental regional organizations of which they are members to include the elimination of violence against women in their programmes, as appropriate.

Article 5

The organs and specialized agencies of the United Nations system should, within their respective fields of competence, contribute to the recognition and realization of the rights and the principles set forth in the present Declaration and, to this end, should, inter alia:

(a) Foster international and regional cooperation with a view to defining regional strategies for combating violence, exchanging experiences and financing programmes relating to the elimination of violence against women;

(b) Promote meetings and seminars with the aim of creating and raising awareness among all persons of the issue of the elimination of violence against women;

(c) Foster coordination and exchange within the United Nations system between human rights treaty bodies to address the issue of violence against women effectively;

(d) Include in analyses prepared by organizations and bodies of the United Nations system of social trends and problems, such as the periodic reports on the world social situation, examination of trends in violence against women;

(e) Encourage coordination between organizations and bodies of the United Nations system to incorporate the issue of violence against women into ongoing programmes, especially with reference to groups of women particularly vulnerable to violence;

(f) Promote the formulation of guidelines or manuals relating to violence against women, taking into account the measures referred to in the present Declaration;

(g) Consider the issue of the elimination of violence against women, as appropriate, in fulfilling their mandates with respect to the implementation of human rights instruments;

(h) Cooperate with non-governmental organizations in addressing the issue of violence against women.

Article 6

Nothing in the present Declaration shall affect any provision that is more conducive to the elimination of violence against women that may be contained in the legislation of a State or in any international convention, treaty or other instrument in force in a State.

5.7 PROTOCOL TO PREVENT, SUPPRESS AND PUNISH TRAFFICKING IN PERSONS, ESPECIALLY WOMEN AND CHILDREN, 2003 [18]

The trafficking of persons, particularly women and children, for forced and exploitative labour, including for sexual exploitation, is one of the most egregious violations of human rights that the United Nations now confronts. It is rooted in social and economic conditions in the countries from which the victims come, facilitated by practices that discriminate against women and driven by cruel indifference to human suffering on the part of those who exploit the services that the victims are forced to provide. The fate of these most vulnerable people is an affront to human dignity and a challenge to every State, every people and every community.

The Protocol to Prevent, Suppress and Punish Trafficking in Persons, especially Women and Children, was adopted by General Assembly resolution 55/25. It entered into force on 25 December 2003. It is the first global legally binding instrument with an agreed definition on trafficking in persons. The intention behind this definition is to facilitate convergence in national approaches with regard to the establishment of domestic criminal offences that would support efficient international cooperation in investigating and prosecuting trafficking in persons cases. An additional objective of the Protocol is to protect and assist the victims of trafficking in persons with full respect for their human rights.

The purposes of this Protocol are: (i) To prevent and combat trafficking in persons, paying particular attention to women and children; and (ii) To protect and assist the victims of such trafficking, with full respect for their human rights (Article 2). The term "trafficking in persons" as defined in Article 3(a) of the Protocol means:

---

[18] The United Nations Convention against Transnational Organized Crime, adopted by General Assembly resolution 55/ 25 of 15 November 2000, is the main international instrument in the fight against transnational organized crime. It entered into force on 29 September 2003. The Convention is further supplemented by three Protocols, which target specific areas and manifestations of organized crime: the Protocol to Prevent, Suppress and Punish Trafficking in Persons, Especially Women and Children; the Protocol against the Smuggling of Migrants by Land, Sea and Air; and the Protocol against the Illicit Manufacturing of and Trafficking in Firearms, their Parts and Components and Ammunition.

the recruitment, transportation, transfer, harbouring or receipt of persons, by means of the threat or use of force or other forms of coercion, of abduction, of fraud, of deception, of the abuse of power or of a position of vulnerability or of the giving or receiving of payments or benefits to achieve the consent of a person having control over another person, for the purpose of exploitation. Exploitation shall include, at a minimum, the exploitation of the prostitution of others or other forms of sexual exploitation, forced labour or services, slavery or practices similar to slavery, servitude or the removal of organs.

Article 6 of the Protocol relating to "assistance to and protection of victims of trafficking in persons" provides:

1. In appropriate cases and to the extent possible under its domestic law, each State Party shall protect the privacy and identity of victims of trafficking in persons, including, inter alia, by making legal proceedings relating to such trafficking confidential.

2. Each State Party shall ensure that its domestic legal or administrative system contains measures that provide to victims of trafficking in persons, in appropriate cases:

(a) Information on relevant court and administrative proceedings;

(b) Assistance to enable their views and concerns to be presented and considered at appropriate stages of criminal proceedings against offenders, in a manner not prejudicial to the rights of the defence.

3. Each State Party shall consider implementing measures to provide for the physical, psychological and social recovery of victims of trafficking in persons, including, in appropriate cases, in cooperation with non-governmental organizations, other relevant organizations and other elements of civil society, and, in particular, the provision of:

(a) Appropriate housing;

(b) Counselling and information, in particular as regards their legal rights, in a language that the victims of trafficking in persons can understand;

(c) Medical, psychological and material assistance; and

(d) Employment, educational and training opportunities.

4. Each State Party shall take into account, in applying the provisions of this article, the age, gender and special needs of victims of trafficking in persons, in particular the special needs of children, including appropriate housing, education and care.

5. Each State Party shall endeavour to provide for the physical safety of victims of trafficking in persons while they are within its territory.

6. Each State Party shall ensure that its domestic legal system contains measures that offer victims of trafficking in persons the possibility of obtaining compensation for damage suffered.

The Protocol attempts to address trafficking by a three-pronged approach of 'prevention' of the act of trafficking, 'protection' of the victims of trafficking and the 'prosecution' of the perpetrators of trafficking. Serious attention and resources and genuine political will are required to implement anti-trafficking measures. Source countries should be fully integrated in preventive efforts, both at governmental level and through civil society. In countries of destination, demand for trafficking needs serious attention. Because trafficking disproportionately affects women, gender-mainstreaming policies should form the basis of anti-trafficking strategies. Long-term policies to combat trafficking need to address poverty and pervasive gender discrimination as root causes of trafficking.

CHAPTER 6

DISABLED PERSONS

Comments: All persons with disabilities have the right to be free from discrimination in the enjoyment of their rights. This includes the right to be free from discrimination on the basis of disability, but also on any other basis such as race, colour, sex, language, religion, political or other opinion, national or social origin, property, birth or other status. Although existing human rights conventions offer considerable potential to promote and protect the rights of persons with disabilities, it became clear that this potential was not being tapped. Indeed, persons with disabilities continued being denied their human rights and were kept on the margins of society in all parts of the world. Thus, the adoption of a legally binding instrument setting out the legal obligations of States to promote and protect the rights of persons with disabilities became a necessity.

The UN Convention on the Rights of Persons with Disabilities and its Optional Protocol was adopted on 13 December 2006. The Convention marks a paradigm shift in attitudes and approaches to persons with disabilities. It takes to a new height the movement to view persons with disabilities as "subjects" who are capable of claiming their rights and making decisions for their lives based on their free and informed consent as well as being active members of society, rather than as "objects" of charity, medical treatment and social protection. The Convention reaffirms that persons with disabilities enjoy the same human rights as everyone. It is intended to be a human rights instrument with an explicit, social development dimension. It identifies the rights of persons with disabilities as well as the obligations of State parties to promote, protect and ensure those rights. The Convention also establishes two implementation mechanisms: the Committee on the Rights of Persons with Disabilities, established to monitor implementation, and the Conference of States Parties, established to consider matters regarding implementation.

The Optional Protocol to the Disability Convention is also an international treaty. It establishes two procedures aimed at strengthening the implementation and monitoring of the Convention. The first is an individual communications procedure allowing individuals to bring petitions to the Committee claiming breaches of their rights; the second is an inquiry procedure giving the Committee authority to undertake inquiries of grave or systematic violations of the Convention.

6.1 CONVENTION ON THE RIGHTS OF PERSONS WITH DISABILITIES, 2006[1]

Preamble

The States Parties to the present Convention,

(a) Recalling the principles proclaimed in the Charter of the United Nations which recognize the inherent dignity and worth and the equal and inalienable rights of all members of the human family as the foundation of freedom, justice and peace in the world,

(b) Recognizing that the United Nations, in the Universal Declaration of Human Rights and in the International Covenants on Human Rights, has proclaimed and agreed that everyone is entitled to all the rights and freedoms set forth therein, without distinction of any kind,

(c) Reaffirming the universality, indivisibility, interdependence and interrelatedness of all human rights and fundamental freedoms and the need for persons with disabilities to be guaranteed their full enjoyment without discrimination,

(d) Recalling the International Covenant on Economic, Social and Cultural Rights, the International Covenant on Civil and Political Rights, the International Convention on the Elimination of All Forms of Racial Discrimination, the Convention on the Elimination of All Forms of Discrimination against Women, the Convention against Torture and Other Cruel, Inhuman or Degrading Treatment or Punishment, the Convention on the Rights of the Child, and the International Convention on the Protection of the Rights of All Migrant Workers and Members of Their Families,

(e) Recognizing that disability is an evolving concept and that disability results from the interaction between persons with impairments and attitudinal and environmental barriers that hinders their full and effective participation in society on an equal basis with others,

---

[1] The Convention entered into force on 3 May 2008.

(f) Recognizing the importance of the principles and policy guidelines contained in the World Programme of Action concerning Disabled Persons and in the Standard Rules on the Equalization of Opportunities for Persons with Disabilities in influencing the promotion, formulation and evaluation of the policies, plans, programmes and actions at the national, regional and international levels to further equalize opportunities for persons with disabilities,

(g) Emphasizing the importance of mainstreaming disability issues as an integral part of relevant strategies of sustainable development,

(h) Recognizing also that discrimination against any person on the basis of disability is a violation of the inherent dignity and worth of the human person,

(i) Recognizing further the diversity of persons with disabilities,

(j) Recognizing the need to promote and protect the human rights of all persons with disabilities, including those who require more intensive support,

(k) Concerned that, despite these various instruments and undertakings, persons with disabilities continue to face barriers in their participation as equal members of society and violations of their human rights in all parts of the world,

(l) Recognizing the importance of international cooperation for improving the living conditions of persons with disabilities in every country, particularly in developing countries,

(m) Recognizing the valued existing and potential contributions made by persons with disabilities to the overall well-being and diversity of their communities, and that the promotion of the full enjoyment by persons with disabilities of their human rights and fundamental freedoms and of full participation by persons with disabilities will result in their enhanced sense of belonging and in significant advances in the human, social and economic development of society and the eradication of poverty,

(n) Recognizing the importance for persons with disabilities of their individual autonomy and independence, including the freedom to make their own choices,

(o) Considering that persons with disabilities should have the opportunity to be actively involved in decision-making processes about policies and programmes, including those directly concerning them,

(p) Concerned about the difficult conditions faced by persons with disabilities who are subject to multiple or aggravated forms of discrimination on the basis of race, colour, sex, language, religion, political or other opinion, national, ethnic, indigenous or social origin, property, birth, age or other status,

(q) Recognizing that women and girls with disabilities are often at greater risk, both within and outside the of violence, injury or abuse, neglect or negligent treatment, maltreatment or exploitation,

(r) Recognizing that children with disabilities should have full enjoyment of all human rights and fundamental freedoms on an equal basis with other children, and recalling obligations to that end undertaken by States Parties to the Convention on the Rights of the Child,

(s) Emphasizing the need to incorporate a gender perspective in all efforts to promote the full enjoyment of human rights and fundamental freedoms by persons with disabilities,

(t) Highlighting the fact that the majority of persons with disabilities live in conditions of poverty, and in this regard recognizing the critical need to address the negative impact of poverty on persons with disabilities,

(u) Bearing in mind that conditions of peace and security based on full respect for the purposes and principles contained in the Charter of the United Nations and observance of applicable human rights instruments are indispensable for the full protection of persons with disabilities, in particular during armed conflicts and foreign occupation,

(v) Recognizing the importance of accessibility to the physical, social, economic and cultural environment, to health and education and to information and communication, in enabling persons with disabilities to fully enjoy all human rights and fundamental freedoms,

(w) Realizing that the individual, having duties to other individuals and to the community to which he or she belongs, is under a responsibility to strive for the promotion and observance of the rights recognized in the International Bill of Human Rights,

(x) Convinced that the family is the natural and fundamental group unit of society and is entitled to protection by society and the State, and that persons with disabilities and their family members should receive the necessary protection and assistance to enable families to contribute towards the full and equal enjoyment of the rights of persons with disabilities,

(y) Convinced that a comprehensive and integral international convention to promote and protect the rights and dignity of persons with disabilities will make a significant contribution to redressing the profound social disadvantage of persons with disabilities and promote their participation in the civil, political, economic, social and cultural spheres with equal opportunities, in both developing and developed countries,

Have agreed as follows:

Article 1

Purpose

The purpose of the present Convention is to promote, protect and ensure the full and equal enjoyment of all human rights and fundamental freedoms by all persons with disabilities, and to promote respect for their inherent dignity.

Persons with disabilities include those who have long-term physical, mental, intellectual or sensory impairments which in interaction with various barriers may hinder their full and effective participation in society on an equal basis with others.

Article 2

Definitions

For the purposes of the present Convention:

"Communication" includes languages, display of text, Braille, tactile communication, large print, accessible multimedia as well as written, audio, plain-language, human-reader and augmentative and alternative modes, means and formats of communication, including accessible information and communication technology;

"Language" includes spoken and signed languages and other forms of non-spoken languages;

"Discrimination on the basis of disability" means any distinction, exclusion or restriction on the basis of disability which has the purpose or effect of impairing or nullifying the recognition, enjoyment or exercise, on an equal basis with others, of all human rights and fundamental freedoms in the political, economic, social, cultural, civil or any other field. It includes all forms of discrimination, including denial of reasonable accommodation;

"Reasonable accommodation" means necessary and appropriate modification and adjustments not imposing a disproportionate or undue burden, where needed in a particular case, to ensure to persons with disabilities the enjoyment or exercise on an equal basis with others of all human rights and fundamental freedoms;

"Universal design" means the design of products, environments, programmes and services to be usable by all people, to the greatest extent possible, without the need for adaptation or specialized design. "Universal design" shall not exclude assistive devices for particular groups of persons with disabilities where this is needed.

Article 3

General principles

The principles of the present Convention shall be:

(a) Respect for inherent dignity, individual autonomy including the freedom to make one's own choices, and independence of persons;

(b) Non-discrimination;

(c) Full and effective participation and inclusion in society;

(d) Respect for difference and acceptance of persons with disabilities as part of human diversity and humanity;

(e) Equality of opportunity;

(f) Accessibility;

(g) Equality between men and women;

(h) Respect for the evolving capacities of children with disabilities and respect for the right of children with disabilities to preserve their identities.

Article 4

General obligations

1. States Parties undertake to ensure and promote the full realization of all human rights and fundamental freedoms for all persons with disabilities without discrimination of any kind on the basis of disability. To this end, States Parties undertake:

(a) To adopt all appropriate legislative, administrative and other measures for the implementation of the rights recognized in the present Convention;

(b) To take all appropriate measures, including legislation, to modify or abolish existing laws, regulations, customs and practices that constitute discrimination against persons with disabilities;

(c) To take into account the protection and promotion of the human rights of persons with disabilities in all policies and programmes;

(d) To refrain from engaging in any act or practice that is inconsistent with the present Convention and to ensure that public authorities and institutions act in conformity with the present Convention;

(e) To take all appropriate measures to eliminate discrimination on the basis of disability by any person, organization or private enterprise;

(f) To undertake or promote research and development of universally designed goods, services, equipment and facilities, as defined in article 2 of the present Convention, which should require the minimum possible adaptation and the least cost to meet the specific needs of a person with disabilities, to promote their availability and use, and to promote universal design in the development of standards and guidelines;

(g) To undertake or promote research and development of, and to promote the availability and use of new technologies, including information and communications technologies, mobility aids, devices and assistive technologies, suitable for persons with disabilities, giving priority to technologies at an affordable cost;

(h) To provide accessible information to persons with disabilities about mobility aids, devices and assistive technologies, including new technologies, as well as other forms of assistance, support services and facilities;

(i) To promote the training of professionals and staff working with persons with disabilities in the rights recognized in this Convention so as to better provide the assistance and services guaranteed by those rights.

2. With regard to economic, social and cultural rights, each State Party undertakes to take measures to the maximum of its available resources and, where needed, within the framework of international cooperation, with a view to achieving progressively the full realization of these rights, without prejudice to those obligations contained in the present Convention that are immediately applicable according to international law.

3. In the development and implementation of legislation and policies to implement the present Convention, and in other decision-making processes concerning issues relating to persons with disabilities, States Parties shall closely consult with and actively involve persons with disabilities, including children with disabilities, through their representative organizations.

4. Nothing in the present Convention shall affect any provisions which are more conducive to the realization of the rights of persons with disabilities and which may be contained in the law of a State Party or international law in force for that State. There shall be no restriction upon or derogation from any of the human rights and fundamental freedoms recognized or existing in any State Party to the present Convention pursuant to law, conventions, regulation or custom on the pretext that the present Convention does not recognize such rights or freedoms or that it recognizes them to a lesser extent.

5. The provisions of the present Convention shall extend to all parts of federal states without any limitations or exceptions.

Article 5

Equality and non-discrimination

1. States Parties recognize that all persons are equal before and under the law and are entitled without any discrimination to the equal protection and equal benefit of the law.

2. States Parties shall prohibit all discrimination on the basis of disability and guarantee to persons with disabilities equal and effective legal protection against discrimination on all grounds.

3. In order to promote equality and eliminate discrimination, States Parties shall take all appropriate steps to ensure that reasonable accommodation is provided.

4. Specific measures which are necessary to accelerate or achieve de facto equality of persons with disabilities shall not be considered discrimination under the terms of the present Convention.

Article 6

Women with disabilities

1. States Parties recognize that women and girls with disabilities are subject to multiple discrimination, and in this regard shall take measures to ensure the full and equal enjoyment by them of all human rights and fundamental freedoms.

2. States Parties shall take all appropriate measures to ensure the full development, advancement and empowerment of women, for the purpose of guaranteeing them the exercise and enjoyment of the human rights and fundamental freedoms set out in the present Convention.

Article 7

Children with disabilities

1. States Parties shall take all necessary measures to ensure the full enjoyment by children with disabilities of all human rights and fundamental freedoms on an equal basis with other children.

2. In all actions concerning children with disabilities, the best interests of the child shall be a primary consideration.

3. States Parties shall ensure that children with disabilities have the right to express their views freely on all matters affecting them, their views being given due weight in accordance with their age and maturity, on an equal basis with other children, and to be provided with disability and age-appropriate assistance to realize that right.

Article 8

Awareness-raising

1. States Parties undertake to adopt immediate, effective and appropriate measures:

   (a) To raise awareness throughout society, including at the family level, regarding persons with disabilities, and to foster respect for the rights and dignity of persons with disabilities;

   (b) To combat stereotypes, prejudices and harmful practices relating to persons with disabilities, including those based on sex and age, in all areas of life;

   (c) To promote awareness of the capabilities and contributions of persons with disabilities.

2. Measures to this end include:

   (a) Initiating and maintaining effective public awareness campaigns designed:

      (i) To nurture receptiveness to the rights of persons with disabilities;

(ii) To promote positive perceptions and greater social awareness towards persons with disabilities;

(iii) To promote recognition of the skills, merits and abilities of persons with disabilities, and of their contributions to the workplace and the labour market;

(b) Fostering at all levels of the education system, including in all children from an early age, an attitude of respect for the rights of persons with disabilities;

(c) Encouraging all organs of the media to portray persons with disabilities in a manner consistent with the purpose of the present Convention;

(d) Promoting awareness-training programmes regarding persons with disabilities and the rights of persons with disabilities.

Article 9

Accessibility

1. To enable persons with disabilities to live independently and participate fully in all aspects of life, States Parties shall take appropriate measures to ensure to persons with disabilities access, on an equal basis with others, to the physical environment, to transportation, to information and communications, including information and communications technologies and systems, and to other facilities and services open or provided to the public, both in urban and in rural areas. These measures, which shall include the identification and elimination of obstacles and barriers to accessibility, shall apply to, inter alia:

(a) Buildings, roads, transportation and other indoor and outdoor facilities, including schools, housing, medical facilities and workplaces;

(b) Information, communications and other services, including electronic services and emergency services.

2. States Parties shall also take appropriate measures to:

(a) Develop, promulgate and monitor the implementation of minimum standards and guidelines for the accessibility of facilities and services open or provided to the public;

(b) Ensure that private entities that offer facilities and services which are open or provided to the public take into account all aspects of accessibility for persons with disabilities;

(c) Provide training for stakeholders on accessibility issues facing persons with disabilities;

(d) Provide in buildings and other facilities open to the public signage in Braille and in easy to read and understand forms;

(e) Provide forms of live assistance and intermediaries, including guides, readers and professional sign language interpreters, to facilitate accessibility to buildings and other facilities open to the public;

(f) Promote other appropriate forms of assistance and support to persons with disabilities to ensure their access to information;

(g) Promote access for persons with disabilities to new information and communications technologies and systems, including the Internet;

(h) Promote the design, development, production and distribution of accessible information and communications technologies and systems at an early stage, so that these technologies and systems become accessible at minimum cost.

Article 10

Right to life

States Parties reaffirm that every human being has the inherent right to life and shall take all necessary measures to ensure its effective enjoyment by persons with disabilities on an equal basis with others.

Article 11

Situations of risk and humanitarian emergencies

States Parties shall take, in accordance with their obligations under international law, including international humanitarian law and international human rights law, all necessary measures to ensure the protection and safety of persons with disabilities in situations of risk, including situations of armed conflict, humanitarian emergencies and the occurrence of natural disasters.

Article 12

Equal recognition before the law

1. States Parties reaffirm that persons with disabilities have the right to recognition everywhere as persons before the law.

2. States Parties shall recognize that persons with disabilities enjoy legal capacity on an equal basis with others in all aspects of life.

3. States Parties shall take appropriate measures to provide access by persons with disabilities to the support they may require in exercising their legal capacity.

4. States Parties shall ensure that all measures that relate to the exercise of legal capacity provide for appropriate and effective safeguards to prevent abuse in accordance with international human rights law. Such safeguards shall ensure that measures relating to the exercise of legal capacity respect the rights, will and preferences of the person, are free of conflict of interest and undue influence, are proportional and tailored to the person's circumstances, apply for the shortest time possible and are subject to regular review by a competent, independent and impartial authority or judicial body. The safeguards shall be proportional to the degree to which such measures affect the person's rights and interests.

5. Subject to the provisions of this article, States Parties shall take all appropriate and effective measures to ensure the equal right of persons with disabilities to own or inherit property, to control their own financial affairs and to have equal access to bank loans, mortgages and other forms of financial credit, and shall ensure that persons with disabilities are not arbitrarily deprived of their property.

Article 13

Access to justice

1. States Parties shall ensure effective access to justice for persons with disabilities on an equal basis with others, including through the provision of procedural and age-appropriate accommodations, in order to facilitate their effective role as direct and indirect participants, including as witnesses, in all legal proceedings, including at investigative and other preliminary stages.

2. In order to help to ensure effective access to justice for persons with disabilities, States Parties shall promote appropriate training for those working in the field of administration of justice, including police and prison staff.

CHAPTER 7

APARTHEID, RACIAL DISCRIMINATION AND SLAVERY

Comments: The International Convention on the Suppression and Punishment of Apartheid was adopted by the United Nations General Assembly in November 1973. The treaty was an attempt to criminalize racial separation and segregation policies such as those that had been imposed by South Africa's White minority government. Under the Convention, which now has more than 100 States parties, the crime of apartheid refers to a series of inhuman acts—including murder, torture, arbitrary arrest, illegal imprisonment, exploitation, marginalization, and persecution—committed for the purpose of establishing and maintaining the domination of one racial group by another. The Convention is particularly notable for its departure from the traditional rule of state sovereignty in that it authorizes the national courts of States parties to attribute individual criminal responsibility for the crime to both government leaders and their supporters in certain instances. In 1998, the Rome Statute of the International Criminal Court included the "crime of apartheid" as a form of crime against humanity (Article 7). The Apartheid Convention may be considered as dead as far as the original cause for its creation – apartheid in South Africa – is concerned, but it lives on as a species of the crime against humanity, under both customary international law and the Rome Statute of the International Criminal Court.

Racial discrimination, xenophobia and related intolerance occur on the grounds of race, colour, descent or national or ethnic origin and victims of such discrimination can suffer multiple or aggravated forms of discrimination based on other grounds such as sex, language, religion, political or other opinion, social origin, property, birth or other status. Any doctrine of racial superiority is scientifically false, socially unjust and dangerous, and must be rejected along with theories which attempt to determine the existence of separate human races. A global fight against racism, racial discrimination, xenophobia and related intolerance and all their abhorrent and evolving forms and manifestations is a matter of priority for the international community.

Although slavery has existed since ancient times, the 1815 Declaration Relative to the Universal Abolition of the Slave Trade was the first international instrument to condemn it. A large number of agreements dating from the early nineteenth century, both multilateral and bilateral, contain provisions prohibiting such practices in times of war and peace. It has been estimated that between 1815 and 1957 some 300 international agreements were implemented to suppress slavery. None has been totally effective. After the Second World War the United Nations continued working towards the elimination of slavery, and as a result it is now a well-established principle of international law that the "prohibition against slavery and slavery-related practices have achieved the level of customary international law and have attained *'jus cogens'* status."

7.1 **SLAVERY CONVENTION, 1926** [1]

Article 1

For the purpose of the present Convention, the following definitions are agreed upon:

(1) Slavery is the status or condition of a person over whom any or all of the powers attaching to the right of ownership are exercised.

(2) The slave trade includes all acts involved in the capture, acquisition or disposal of a person with intent to reduce him to slavery; all acts involved in the acquisition of a slave with a view to selling or exchanging him; all acts of disposal by sale or exchange of a slave acquired with a view to being sold or exchanged, and, in general, every act of trade or transport in slaves.

Article 2

The High Contracting Parties undertake, each in respect of the territories placed under its sovereignty, jurisdiction, protection, suzerainty or tutelage, so far as they have not already taken the necessary steps:

(a) To prevent and suppress the slave trade;

(b) To bring about, progressively and as soon as possible, the complete abolition of slavery in all its forms.

---

[1] Entry into force: 9 March 1927, in accordance with article 12. The Convention was amended by the Protocol on 7 December 1953; the amended Convention entered into force on 7 July 1955, the date on which the amendments, set forth in the annex to the Protocol of 7 December 1953, entered into force in accordance with article III of the Protocol.

Article 3

The High Contracting Parties undertake to adopt all appropriate measures with a view to preventing and suppressing the embarkation, disembarkation and transport of slaves in their territorial waters and upon all vessels flying their respective flags.

The High Contracting Parties undertake to negotiate as soon as possible a general Convention with regard to the slave trade which will give them rights and impose upon them duties of the same nature as those provided for in the Convention of June 17th, 1925, relative to the International Trade in Arms (Articles 12, 20, 21, 22, 23, 24 and paragraphs 3, 4 and 5 of Section II of Annex II), with the necessary adaptations, it being understood that this general Convention will not place the ships (even of small tonnage) of any High Contracting Parties in a position different from that of the other High Contracting Parties.

It is also understood that, before or after the coming into force of this general Convention, the High Contracting Parties are entirely free to conclude between themselves, without, however, derogating from the principles laid down in the preceding paragraph, such special agreements as, by reason of their peculiar situation, might appear to be suitable in order to bring about as soon as possible the complete disappearance of the slave trade.

Article 4

The High Contracting Parties shall give to one another every assistance with the object of securing the abolition of slavery and the slave trade.

Article 5

The High Contracting Parties recognise that recourse to compulsory or forced labour may have grave consequences and undertake, each in respect of the territories placed under its sovereignty, jurisdiction, protection, suzerainty or tutelage, to take all necessary measures to prevent compulsory or forced labour from developing into conditions analogous to slavery.

It is agreed that:

(1) Subject to the transitional provisions laid down in paragraph (2) below, compulsory or forced labour may only be exacted for public purposes.

(2) In territories in which compulsory or forced labour for other than public purposes still survives, the High Contracting Parties shall endeavour progressively and as soon as possible to put an end to the practice. So long as such forced or compulsory labour exists, this labour shall invariably be of an exceptional character, shall always receive

adequate remuneration, and shall not involve the removal of the labourers from their usual place of residence.

(3) In all cases, the responsibility for any recourse to compulsory or forced labour shall rest with the competent central authorities of the territory concerned.

Article 6

Those of the High Contracting Parties whose laws do not at present make adquate provision for the punishment of infractions of laws and regulations enacted with a view to giving effect to the purposes of the present Convention undertake to adopt the necessary measures in order that severe penalties may be imposed in respect of such infractions.

Article 7

The High Contracting Parties undertake to communicate to each other and to the Secretary-General of the League of Nations any laws and regulations which they may enact with a view to the application of the provisions of the present Convention.

Protocol Amending the Slavery Convention[2]

Have agreed as follows:

Article 1

The States Parties to the present Protocol undertake that as between themselves they will, in accordance with the provisions of the Protocol, attribute full legal force and effect to and duly apply the amendments to the Convention set forth in the annex to the Protocol.

Annex to the Protocol amending the Slavery Convention signed at Geneva on 25 September 1926

In article 7 "the Secretary-General of the United Nations" shall be substituted for "the Secretary-General of the League of Nations".

In article 8 "the International Court of Justice" shall be substituted for the "Permanent Court of International Justice" and "the Statute of the International Court of Justice" shall be substituted for "the Protocol of December 16th, 1920, relating to the Permanent Court of International Justice".

---

2 Approved by GA resolution 794 (VIII) of 23 October 1953.

In the first and second paragraphs of article 10 "the United Nations" shall be substituted for "the League of Nations".

The last three paragraphs of article 11 shall be deleted and the following substituted:

"The present Convention shall be open to accession by all States, including States which are not Members of the United Nations, to which the Secretary-General of the United Nations shall have communicated a certified copy of the Convention."

"Accession shall be effected by the deposit of a formal instrument with the Secretary-General of the United Nations, who shall give notice thereof to all States Parties to the Convention and to all other States contemplated in the present article, informing them of the date on which each such instrument of accession was received in deposit."

In article 12 "the United Nations" shall be substituted for "the League of Nations".

Supplementary Convention on the Abolition of Slavery, the Slave Trade, and Institutions and Practices Similar to Slavery[3]

Preamble

The States Parties to the present Convention,

Considering that freedom is the birthright of every human being,

Mindful that the peoples of the United Nations reaffirmed in the Charter their faith in the dignity and worth of the human person,

Considering that the Universal Declaration of Human Rights, proclaimed by the General Assembly of the United Nations as a common standard of achievement for all peoples and all nations, states that no one shall be held in slavery or servitude and that slavery and the slave trade shall be prohibited in all their forms,

Recognizing that, since the conclusion of the Slavery Convention signed at Geneva on 25 September 1926, which was designed to secure the abolition of slavery and of the slave trade, further progress has been made towards this end,

Having regard to the Forced Labour Convention of 1930 and to subsequent action by the International Labour Organisation in regard to forced or compulsory labour,

---

[3] Adopted by a Conference of Plenipotentiaries convened by Economic and Social Council resolution 608(XXI) of 30 April 1956 and done at Geneva on 7 September 1956,Entry into force: 30 April 1957, in accordance with article 13.

Being aware, however, that slavery, the slave trade and institutions and practices similar to slavery have not yet been eliminated in all parts of the world,

Having decided, therefore, that the Convention of 1926, which remains operative, should now be augmented by the conclusion of a supplementary convention designed to intensify national as well as international efforts towards the abolition of slavery, the slave trade and institutions and practices similar to slavery,

Have agreed as follows:

Section I. - Institutions and practices similar to slavery

Article 1

Each of the States Parties to this Convention shall take all practicable and necessary legislative and other measures to bring about progressively and as soon as possible the complete abolition or abandonment of the following institutions and practices, where they still exist and whether or not they are covered by the definition of slavery contained in article 1 of the Slavery Convention signed at Geneva on 25 September 1926:

(a) Debt bondage, that is to say, the status or condition arising from a pledge by a debtor of his personal services or of those of a person under his control as security for a debt, if the value of those services as reasonably assessed is not applied towards the liquidation of the debt or the length and nature of those services are not respectively limited and defined;

(b) Serfdom, that is to say, the condition or status of a tenant who is by law, custom or agreement bound to live and labour on land belonging to another person and to render some determinate service to such other person, whether for reward or not, and is not free to change his status;

(c) Any institution or practice whereby:

(i) A woman, without the right to refuse, is promised or given in marriage on payment of a consideration in money or in kind to her parents, guardian, family or any other person or group; or

(ii) The husband of a woman, his family, or his clan, has the right to transfer her to another person for value received or otherwise; or

(iii) A woman on the death of her husband is liable to be inherited by another person;

(d) Any institution or practice whereby a child or young person under the age of 18 years, is delivered by either or both of his natural parents or by his guardian to another person, whether for reward or not, with a view to the exploitation of the child or young person or of his labour.

Article 2

With a view to bringing to an end the institutions and practices mentioned in article 1 (c) of this Convention, the States Parties undertake to prescribe, where appropriate, suitable minimum ages of marriage, to encourage the use of facilities whereby the consent of both parties to a marriage may be freely expressed in the presence of a competent civil or religious authority, and to encourage the registration of marriages.

Section II. - The slave trade

Article 3

1. The act of conveying or attempting to convey slaves from one country to another by whatever means of transport, or of being accessory thereto, shall be a criminal offence under the laws of the States Parties to this Convention and persons convicted thereof shall be liable to very severe penalties.

2. (a) The States Parties shall take all effective measures to prevent ships and aircraft authorized to fly their flags from conveying slaves and to punish persons guilty of such acts or of using national flags for that purpose.

(b) The States Parties shall take all effective measures to ensure that their ports, airfields and coasts are not used for the conveyance of slaves.

3. The States Parties to this Convention shall exchange information in order to ensure the practical co-ordination of the measures taken by them in combating the slave trade and shall inform each other of every case of the slave trade, and of every attempt to commit this criminal offence, which comes to their notice.

Article 4

Any slave who takes refuge on board any vessel of a State Party to this Convention shall ipso facto be free.

Section III. - Slavery and institutions and practices similar to slavery

Article 5

In a country where the abolition or abandonment of slavery, or of the institutions or practices mentioned in article 1 of this Convention, is not yet complete, the act of mutilating, branding or otherwise marking a slave or a person of servile status in order to indicate his status, or as a punishment, or for any other reason, or of being accessory thereto, shall be a criminal offence under the laws of the States Parties to this Convention and persons convicted thereof shall be liable to punishment.

Article 6

1. The act of enslaving another person or of inducing another person to give himself or a person dependent upon him into slavery, or of attempting these acts, or being accessory thereto, or being a party to a conspiracy to accomplish any such acts, shall be a criminal offence under the laws of the States Parties to this Convention and persons convicted thereof shall be liable to punishment.

2. Subject to the provisions of the introductory paragraph of article 1 of this Convention, the provisions of paragraph 1 of the present article shall also apply to the act of inducing another person to place himself or a person dependent upon him into the servile status resulting from any of the institutions or practices mentioned in article 1, to any attempt to perform such acts, to being accessory thereto, and to being a party to a conspiracy to accomplish any such acts.

Section IV. - Definitions

Article 7

For the purposes of the present Convention:

(a) "Slavery" means, as defined in the Slavery Convention of 1926, the status or condition of a person over whom any or all of the powers attaching to the right of ownership are exercised, and "slave" means a person in such condition or status;

(b) "A person of servile status" means a person in the condition or status resulting from any of the institutions or practices mentioned in article 1 of this Convention;

(c) "Slave trade" means and includes all acts involved in the capture, acquisition or disposal of a person with intent to reduce him to slavery; all acts involved in the acquisition of a slave with a view to selling or exchanging him; all acts of disposal by sale or exchange of a person acquired with a view to being sold or exchanged; and, in general, every act of trade or transport in slaves by whatever means of conveyance.

Convention (No. 105) Concerning the Abolition of Forced Labour, 1957[4]

The General Conference of the International Labour Organisation,

Having been convened at Geneva by the Governing Body of the International Labour Office, and having met in its Fortieth Session on 5 June 1957, and

Having considered the question of forced labour, which is the fourth item on the agenda of the session, and

Having noted the provisions of the Forced Labour Convention, 1930, and

Having noted that the Slavery Convention, 1926, provides that all necessary measures shall be taken to prevent compulsory or forced labour from developing into conditions analogous to slavery and that the Supplementary Convention on the Abolition of Slavery, the Slave Trade and Institutions and Practices Similar to Slavery, 1956, provides for the complete abolition of debt bondage and serfdom, and

Having noted that the Protection of Wages Convention, 1949, provides that wages shall be paid regularly and prohibits methods of payment which deprive the worker of a genuine possibility of terminating his employment, and

Having decided upon the adoption of further proposals with regard to the abolition of certain forms of forced or compulsory labour constituting a violation of the rights of man referred to in the Charter of the United Nations and enunciated by the Universal Declaration of Human Rights, and

Having determined that these proposals shall take the form of an international Convention,

Adopts this twenty-fifth day of June of the year one thousand nine hundred and fifty-seven the following Convention, which may be cited as the Abolition of Forced Labour Convention, 1957:

Article 1

Each Member of the International Labour Organisation which ratifies this Convention undertakes to suppress and not to make use of any form of forced or compulsory labour:

---

[4] Adopted on 25 June 1957; Entry into force: 17 January 1959.

(a) as a means of political coercion or education or as a punishment for holding or expressing political views or views ideologically opposed to the established political, social or economic system;

(b) as a method of mobilising and using labour for purposes of economic development;

(c) as a means of labour discipline;

(d) as a punishment for having participated in strikes;

(e) as a means of racial, social, national or religious discrimination.

Article 2

Each Member of the International Labour Organisation which ratifies this Convention undertakes to take effective measures to secure the immediate and complete abolition of forced or compulsory labour as specified in Article 1 of this Convention.

7.2 CONVENTION ON THE ELIMINATION OF ALL FORMS OF RACIAL DISCRIMINATION, 1965[5]

The States Parties to this Convention,

Considering that the Charter of the United Nations is based on the principles of the dignity and equality inherent in all human beings, and that all Member States have pledged themselves to take joint and separate action, in co-operation with the Organization, for the achievement of one of the purposes of the United Nations which is to promote and encourage universal respect for and observance of human rights and fundamental freedoms for all, without distinction as to race, sex, language or religion,

Considering that the Universal Declaration of Human Rights proclaims that all human beings are born free and equal in dignity and rights and that everyone is entitled to all the rights and freedoms set out therein, without distinction of any kind, in particular as to race, colour or national origin,

Considering that all human beings are equal before the law and are entitled to equal protection of the law against any discrimination and against any incitement to discrimination,

---

[5] Adopted and opened for signature and ratification by General Assembly resolution 2106 (XX) of 21 December 1965, entry into force 4 January 1969, in accordance with Article 19.

Considering that the United Nations has condemned colonialism and all practices of segregation and discrimination associated therewith, in whatever form and wherever they exist, and that the Declaration on the Granting of Independence to Colonial Countries and Peoples of 14 December 1960 (General Assembly resolution 1514 (XV)) has affirmed and solemnly proclaimed the necessity of bringing them to a speedy and unconditional end,

Considering that the United Nations Declaration on the Elimination of All Forms of Racial Discrimination of 20 November 1963 (General Assembly resolution 1904 (XVIII)) solemnly affirms the necessity of speedily eliminating racial discrimination throughout the world in all its forms and manifestations and of securing understanding of and respect for the dignity of the human person,

Convinced that any doctrine of superiority based on racial differentiation is scientifically false, morally condemnable, socially unjust and dangerous, and that there is no justification for racial discrimination, in theory or in practice, anywhere,

Reaffirming that discrimination between human beings on the grounds of race, colour or ethnic origin is an obstacle to friendly and peaceful relations among nations and is capable of disturbing peace and security among peoples and the harmony of persons living side by side even within one and the same State,

Convinced that the existence of racial barriers is repugnant to the ideals of any human society,

Alarmed by manifestations of racial discrimination still in evidence in some areas of the world and by governmental policies based on racial superiority or hatred, such as policies of apartheid, segregation or separation,

Resolved to adopt all necessary measures for speedily eliminating racial discrimination in all its forms and manifestations, and to prevent and combat racist doctrines and practices in order to promote understanding between races and to build an international community free from all forms of racial segregation and racial discrimination,

Bearing in mind the Convention concerning Discrimination in respect of Employment and Occupation adopted by the International Labour Organisation in 1958, and the Convention against Discrimination in Education adopted by the United Nations Educational, Scientific and Cultural Organization in 1960,

Desiring to implement the principles embodied in the United Nations Declaration on the Elimination of All Forms of Racial Discrimination and to secure the earliest adoption of practical measures to that end,

Have agreed as follows:

PART I

Article 1

1. In this Convention, the term "racial discrimination" shall mean any distinction, exclusion, restriction or preference based on race, colour, descent, or national or ethnic origin which has the purpose or effect of nullifying or impairing the recognition, enjoyment or exercise, on an equal footing, of human rights and fundamental freedoms in the political, economic, social, cultural or any other field of public life.

2. This Convention shall not apply to distinctions, exclusions, restrictions or preferences made by a State Party to this Convention between citizens and non-citizens.

3. Nothing in this Convention may be interpreted as affecting in any way the legal provisions of States Parties concerning nationality, citizenship or naturalization, provided that such provisions do not discriminate against any particular nationality.

4. Special measures taken for the sole purpose of securing adequate advancement of certain racial or ethnic groups or individuals requiring such protection as may be necessary in order to ensure such groups or individuals equal enjoyment or exercise of human rights and fundamental freedoms shall not be deemed racial discrimination, provided, however, that such measures do not, as a consequence, lead to the maintenance of separate rights for different racial groups and that they shall not be continued after the objectives for which they were taken have been achieved.

Article 2

1. States Parties condemn racial discrimination and undertake to pursue by all appropriate means and without delay a policy of eliminating racial discrimination in all its forms and promoting understanding among all races, and, to this end:

(a) Each State Party undertakes to engage in no act or practice of racial discrimination against persons, groups of persons or institutions and to en sure that all public authorities and public institutions, national and local, shall act in conformity with this obligation;

(b) Each State Party undertakes not to sponsor, defend or support racial discrimination by any persons or organizations;

(c) Each State Party shall take effective measures to review governmental, national and local policies, and to amend, rescind or nullify any laws and regulations which have the effect of creating or perpetuating racial discrimination wherever it exists;

(d) Each State Party shall prohibit and bring to an end, by all appropriate means, including legislation as required by circumstances, racial discrimination by any persons, group or organization;

(e) Each State Party undertakes to encourage, where appropriate, integrationist multiracial organizations and movements and other means of eliminating barriers between races, and to discourage anything which tends to strengthen racial division.

2. States Parties shall, when the circumstances so warrant, take, in the social, economic, cultural and other fields, special and concrete measures to ensure the adequate development and protection of certain racial groups or individuals belonging to them, for the purpose of guaranteeing them the full and equal enjoyment of human rights and fundamental freedoms. These measures shall in no case en tail as a con sequence the maintenance of unequal or separate rights for different racial groups after the objectives for which they were taken have been achieved.

Article 3

States Parties particularly condemn racial segregation and apartheid and undertake to prevent, prohibit and eradicate all practices of this nature in territories under their jurisdiction.

Article 4

States Parties condemn all propaganda and all organizations which are based on ideas or theories of superiority of one race or group of persons of one colour or ethnic origin, or which attempt to justify or promote racial hatred and discrimination in any form, and undertake to adopt immediate and positive measures designed to eradicate all incitement to, or acts of, such discrimination and, to this end, with due regard to the principles embodied in the Universal Declaration of Human Rights and the rights expressly set forth in article 5 of this Convention, inter alia:

(a) Shall declare an offence punishable by law all dissemination of ideas based on racial superiority or hatred, incitement to racial discrimination, as well as all acts of violence or incitement to such acts against any race or group of persons of another colour or ethnic origin, and also the provision of any assistance to racist activities, including the financing thereof;

(b) Shall declare illegal and prohibit organizations, and also organized and all other propaganda activities, which promote and incite racial discrimination, and shall recognize participation in such organizations or activities as an offence punishable by law;

(c) Shall not permit public authorities or public institutions, national or local, to promote or incite racial discrimination.

Article 5

In compliance with the fundamental obligations laid down in article 2 of this Convention, States Parties undertake to prohibit and to eliminate racial discrimination in all its forms and to guarantee the right of everyone, without distinction as to race, colour, or national or ethnic origin, to equality before the law, notably in the enjoyment of the following rights:

(a) The right to equal treatment before the tribunals and all other organs administering justice;

(b) The right to security of person and protection by the State against violence or bodily harm, whether inflicted by government officials or by any individual group or institution;

(c) Political rights, in particular the right to participate in elections-to vote and to stand for election-on the basis of universal and equal suffrage, to take part in the Government as well as in the conduct of public affairs at any level and to have equal access to public service;

(d) Other civil rights, in particular:

(i) The right to freedom of movement and residence within the border of the State;

(ii) The right to leave any country, including one's own, and to return to one's country;

(iii) The right to nationality;

(iv) The right to marriage and choice of spouse;

(v) The right to own property alone as well as in association with others;

(vi) The right to inherit;

(vii) The right to freedom of thought, conscience and religion;

(viii) The right to freedom of opinion and expression;

(ix) The right to freedom of peaceful assembly and association;

(e) Economic, social and cultural rights, in particular:

(i) The rights to work, to free choice of employment, to just and favourable conditions of work, to protection against unemployment, to equal pay for equal work, to just and favourable remuneration;

(ii) The right to form and join trade unions;

(iii) The right to housing;

(iv) The right to public health, medical care, social security and social services;

(v) The right to education and training;

(vi) The right to equal participation in cultural activities;

(f) The right of access to any place or service intended for use by the general public, such as transport hotels, restaurants, cafes, theatres and parks.

Article 6

States Parties shall assure to everyone within their jurisdiction effective protection and remedies, through the competent national tribunals and other State institutions, against any acts of racial discrimination which violate his human rights and fundamental freedoms contrary to this Convention, as well as the right to seek from such tribunals just and adequate reparation or satisfaction for any damage suffered as a result of such discrimination.

Article 7

States Parties undertake to adopt immediate and effective measures, particularly in the fields of teaching, education, culture and information, with a view to combating prejudices which lead to racial discrimination and to promoting understanding, tolerance and friendship among nations and racial or ethnical groups, as well as to propagating the purposes and principles of the Charter of the United Nations, the Universal Declaration of Human Rights, the United Nations Declaration on the Elimination of All Forms of Racial Discrimination, and this Convention.

7.3 CONVENTION ON THE SUPPRESSION AND PUNISHMNET OF THE CRIME OF APARTHEID, 1973[6]

The States Parties to the present Convention,

Recalling the provisions of the Charter of the United Nations, in which all Members pledged themselves to take joint and separate action in co-operation with the Organization for the achievement of universal respect for, and observance of, human rights and fundamental freedoms for all without distinction as to race, sex, language or religion,

Considering the Universal Declaration of Human Rights, which states that all human beings are born free and equal in dignity and rights and that everyone is entitled to all the rights and freedoms set forth in the Declaration, without distinction of any kind, such as race, colour or national origin,

Considering the Declaration on the Granting of Independence to Colonial Countries and Peoples, in which the General Assembly stated that the process of liberation is irresistible and irreversible and that, in the interests of human dignity, progress and justice, an end must be put to colonialism and all practices of segregation and discrimination associated therewith,

Observing that, in accordance with the International Convention on the Elimination of All Forms of Racial Discrimination, States particularly condemn racial segregation and apartheid and undertake to prevent, prohibit and eradicate all practices of this nature in territories under their jurisdiction,

Observing that, in the Convention on the Prevention and Punishment of the Crime of Genocide, certain acts which may also be qualified as acts of apartheid constitute a crime under international law,

Observing that, in the Convention on the Non-Applicability of Statutory Limitations to War Crimes and Crimes against Humanity, "inhuman acts resulting from the policy of apartheid" are qualified as crimes against humanity,

Observing that the General Assembly of the United Nations has adopted a number of resolutions in which the policies and practices of apartheid are condemned as a crime against humanity,

---

[6] Adopted and opened for signature, ratification by General Assembly resolution 3068 (XXVIII) of 30 November 1973, entry into force 18 July 1976, in accordance with article XV.

Observing that the Security Council has emphasized that apartheid and its continued intensification and expansion seriously disturb and threaten international peace and security,

Convinced that an International Convention on the Suppression and Punishment of the Crime of Apartheid would make it possible to take more effective measures at the international and national levels with a view to the suppression and punishment of the crime of apartheid,

Have agreed as follows:

Article I

1. The States Parties to the present Convention declare that apartheid is a crime against humanity and that inhuman acts resulting from the policies and practices of apartheid and similar policies and practices of racial segregation and discrimination, as defined in article II of the Convention, are crimes violating the principles of international law, in particular the purposes and principles of the Charter of the United Nations, and constituting a serious threat to international peace and security.

2. The States Parties to the present Convention declare criminal those organizations, institutions and individuals committing the crime of apartheid.

Article II

For the purpose of the present Convention, the term "the crime of apartheid", which shall include similar policies and practices of racial segregation and discrimination as practised in southern Africa, shall apply to the following inhuman acts committed for the purpose of establishing and maintaining domination by one racial group of persons over any other racial group of persons and systematically oppressing them:

(a) Denial to a member or members of a racial group or groups of the right to life and liberty of person:

(i) By murder of members of a racial group or groups;

(ii) By the infliction upon the members of a racial group or groups of serious bodily or mental harm, by the infringement of their freedom or dignity, or by subjecting them to torture or to cruel, inhuman or degrading treatment or punishment;

(iii) By arbitrary arrest and illegal imprisonment of the members of a racial group or groups;

(b) Deliberate imposition on a racial group or groups of living conditions calculated to cause its or their physical destruction in whole or in part;

(c) Any legislative measures and other measures calculated to prevent a racial group or groups from participation in the political, social, economic and cultural life of the country and the deliberate creation of conditions preventing the full development of such a group or groups, in particular by denying to members of a racial group or groups basic human rights and freedoms, including the right to work, the right to form recognized trade unions, the right to education, the right to leave and to return to their country, the right to a nationality, the right to freedom of movement and residence, the right to freedom of opinion and expression, and the right to freedom of peaceful assembly and association;

(d) Any measures, including legislative measures, designed to divide the population along racial lines by the creation of separate reserves and ghettos for the members of a racial group or groups, the prohibition of mixed marriages among members of various racial groups, the expropriation of landed property belonging to a racial group or groups or to members thereof;

(e) Exploitation of the labour of the members of a racial group or groups, in particular by submitting them to forced labour;

(f) Persecution of organizations and persons, by depriving them of fundamental rights and freedoms, because they oppose apartheid.

Article III

International criminal responsibility shall apply, irrespective of the motive involved, to individuals, members of organizations and institutions and representatives of the State, whether residing in the territory of the State in which the acts are perpetrated or in some other State, whenever they:

(a) Commit, participate in, directly incite or conspire in the commission of the acts mentioned in article II of the present Convention;

(b) Directly abet, encourage or co-operate in the commission of the crime of apartheid.

Article IV

The States Parties to the present Convention undertake:

(a) To adopt any legislative or other measures necessary to suppress as well as to prevent any encouragement of the crime of apartheid and similar segregationist policies or their manifestations and to punish persons guilty of that crime;

(b) To adopt legislative, judicial and administrative measures to prosecute, bring to trial and punish in accordance with their jurisdiction persons responsible for, or accused of, the acts defined in article II of the present Convention, whether or not such persons reside in the territory of the State in which the acts are committed or are nationals of that State or of some other State or are stateless persons.

Article V

Persons charged with the acts enumerated in article II of the present Convention may be tried by a competent tribunal of any State Party to the Convention which may acquire jurisdiction over the person of the accused or by an international penal tribunal having jurisdiction with respect to those States Parties which shall have accepted its jurisdiction.

Article VI

The States Parties to the present Convention undertake to accept and carry out in accordance with the Charter of the United Nations the decisions taken by the Security Council aimed at the prevention, suppression and punishment of the crime of apartheid, and to co-operate in the implementation of decisions adopted by other competent organs of the United Nations with a view to achieving the purposes of the Convention.

Article VII

1. The States Parties to the present Convention undertake to submit periodic reports to the group established under article IX on the legislative, judicial, administrative or other measures that they have adopted and that give effect to the provisions of the Convention.

2. Copies of the reports shall be transmitted through the Secretary-General of the United Nations to the Special Committee on Apartheid.

Article VIII

Any State Party to the present Convention may call upon any competent organ of the United Nations to take such action under the Charter of the United Nations as it considers appropriate for the prevention and suppression of the crime of apartheid.

Article IX

1. The Chairman of the Commission on Human Rights shall appoint a group consisting of three members of the Commission on Human Rights, who are also representatives of States Parties to the present Convention, to consider reports submitted by States Parties in accordance with article VII.

2. If, among the members of the Commission on Human Rights, there are no representatives of States Parties to the present Convention or if there are fewer than three such representatives, the Secretary-General of the United Nations shall, after consulting all States Parties to the Convention, designate a representative of the State Party or representatives of the States Parties which are not members of the Commission on Human Rights to take part in the work of the group established in accordance with paragraph 1 of this article, until such time as representatives of the States Parties to the Convention are elected to the Commission on Human Rights.

3. The group may meet for a period of not more than five days, either before the opening or after the closing of the session of the Commission on Human Rights, to consider the reports submitted in accordance with article VII.

Article X

1. The States Parties to the present Convention empower the Commission on Human Rights:

a. To request United Nations organs, when transmitting copies of petitions under article 15 of the International Convention on the Elimination of All Forms of Racial Discrimination, to draw its attention to complaints concerning acts which are enumerated in article II of the present Convention;

b. To prepare, on the basis of reports from competent organs of the United Nations and periodic reports from States Parties to the present Convention, a list of individuals, organizations, institutions and representatives of States which are alleged to be responsible for the crimes enumerated in article II of the Convention, as well as those against whom legal proceedings have been undertaken by States Parties to the Convention;

c. To request information from the competent United Nations organs concerning measures taken by the authorities responsible for the administration of Trust and Non-Self-Governing Territories, and all other Territories to which General

Assembly resolution 1514 (XV) of 14 December 1960 applies, with regard to such individuals alleged to be responsible for crimes under article II of the Convention who are believed to be under their territorial and administrative jurisdiction.

2. Pending the achievement of the objectives of the Declaration on the Granting of Independence to Colonial Countries and Peoples, contained in General Assembly resolution 1514 (XV), the provisions of the present Convention shall in no way limit the right of petition granted to those peoples by other international instruments or by the United Nations and its specialized agencies.

Article XI

1. Acts enumerated in article II of the present Convention shall not be considered political crimes for the purpose of extradition.

2. The States Parties to the present Convention undertake in such cases to grant extradition in accordance with their legislation and with the treaties in force.

Article XII

Disputes between States Parties arising out of the interpretation, application or implementation of the present Convention which have not been settled by negotiation shall, at the request of the States parties to the dispute, be brought before the International Court of Justice, save where the parties to the dispute have agreed on some other form of settlement.

CHAPTER 8

TORTURE AND ENFORCED DISAPPEARANCE

Comments: Torture – the deliberate infliction of severe pain or suffering on a powerless victim, usually a detainee for a specific purpose, such as extraction of a confession or information constitutes one of the most brutal human rights violation and a direct attack on the core of the human personality and dignity. The international law of human rights, which is applicable both in times of peace and in times of emergency and armed conflict, absolutely prohibits torture. In 1948, the international community condemned torture and other cruel, inhuman or degrading treatment in the Universal Declaration of Human Rights (Article 5) adopted by the United Nations General Assembly. In 1975, responding to vigorous activity by non-governmental organizations (NGOs), the General Assembly adopted the Declaration on the Protection of All Persons from Being Subjected to Torture and Other Cruel, Inhuman or Degrading Treatment or Punishment.

In addition to the absolute prohibition of torture or other forms of cruel, inhuman or degrading treatment or punishment under Article 7 of the ICCPR, the prohibition of torture also has been firmly rooted in international human rights law, international criminal law and customary international law. The most important among all international instruments is the UN Convention against Torture and Other Cruel, Inhuman or Degrading Treatment or Punishment (CAT) which was adopted by the General Assembly on 10 December 1984 and entered into force on 26 June 1987. The most innovative aspect of the Convention is the obligation of States to combat impunity of perpetrators of torture by enacting torture as a crime under their domestic criminal law with appropriate penalties and by assuming the responsibility of establishing various types of jurisdiction, including for the first time in a human rights treaty the obligation of universal jurisdiction.

The General Assembly, on 18 December 2002, adopted an Optional Protocol to the Convention against Torture (OPCAT) which entered into force on 22 June 2006. It established a Sub-committee on Prevention with the task of carrying out missions to State parties and preventive visits to places of detention. The Protocol requires States to establish national bodies to make similar visits to places of detention.

The Human Rights Council in its resolution: "Torture and other Cruel, Inhuman or Degrading Treatment or Punishment: the Role and Responsibility of Judges, Prosecutors and Lawyers" of 15 April 2010,[1] has urged the States to respect and ensure respect for the critical role that judges, prosecutors and lawyers play in the prevention of torture and other cruel, inhuman or degrading treatment or punishment, including with respect to arbitrary detention, due process safeguards and fair trial standards, and bringing perpetrators to justice.

8.1 CONVENTION AGAINST TORTURE AND OTHER CRUEL, INHUMAN OR DEGRADING TREATMENT OR PUNISHMNET, 1984[2]

Part I

Article 1

1. For the purposes of this Convention, "torture" means any act by which severe pain or suffering, whether physical or mental, is intentionally inflicted on a person for such purposes as obtaining from him or a third person information or a confession, punishing him for an act he or a third person has committed or is suspected of having committed, or intimidating or coercing him or a third person, or for any reason based on discrimination of any kind, when such pain or suffering is inflicted by or at the instigation of or with the consent or acquiescence of a public official or other person acting in an official capacity. It does not include pain or suffering arising only from, inherent in or incidental to lawful sanctions.

Article 2

1. Each State Party shall take effective legislative, administrative, judicial or other measures to prevent acts of torture in any territory under its jurisdiction.

2. No exceptional circumstances whatsoever, whether a state of war or a threat or war, internal political instability or any other public emergency, may be invoked as a justification of torture.

3. An order from a superior officer or a public authority may not be invoked as a justification of torture.

---

[1] Resolution 13/19, dated 15 April 2010.

[2] General Assembly resolution 39/46 of 10 December 1984, entry into force 26 June 1987.

Article 3

1. No State Party shall expel, return (*refouler*) or extradite a person to another State where there are substantial grounds for believing that he would be in danger of being subjected to torture.

2. For the purpose of determining whether there are such grounds, the competent authorities shall take into account all relevant considerations including, where applicable, the existence in the State concerned of a consistent pattern of gross, flagrant or mass violations of human rights.

Article 4

1. Each State Party shall ensure that all acts of torture are offences under its criminal law. The same shall apply to an attempt to commit torture and to an act by any person which constitutes complicity or participation in torture.

2. Each State Party shall make these offences punishable by appropriate penalties which take into account their grave nature.

Article 5

1. Each State Party shall take such measures as may be necessary to establish its jurisdiction over the offences referred to in article 4 in the following cases:

    a. When the offences are committed in any territory under its jurisdiction or on board a ship or aircraft registered in that State;

    b. When the alleged offender is a national of that State;

    c. When the victim was a national of that State if that State considers it appropriate.

2. Each State Party shall likewise take such measures as may be necessary to establish its jurisdiction over such offences in cases where the alleged offender is present in any territory under its jurisdiction and it does not extradite him pursuant to article 8 to any of the States mentioned in Paragraph 1 of this article.

3. This Convention does not exclude any criminal jurisdiction exercised in accordance with internal law.

Article 6

1. Upon being satisfied, after an examination of information available to it, that the circumstances so warrant, any State Party in whose territory a person alleged to have committed any offence referred to in article 4 is present, shall take him into custody or take other legal measures to ensure his presence. The custody and other legal measures shall be as provided in the law of that State but may be continued only for such time as is necessary to enable any criminal or extradition proceedings to be instituted.

2. Such State shall immediately make a preliminary inquiry into the facts.

3. Any person in custody pursuant to paragraph 1 of this article shall be assisted in communicating immediately with the nearest appropriate representative of the State of which he is a national, or, if he is a stateless person, to the representative of the State where he usually resides.

4. When a State, pursuant to this article, has taken a person into custody, it shall immediately notify the States referred to in article 5, paragraph 1, of the fact that such person is in custody and of the circumstances which warrant his detention. The State which makes the preliminary inquiry contemplated in paragraph 2 of this article shall promptly report its findings to the said State and shall indicate whether it intends to exercise jurisdiction.

Article 7

1. The State Party in territory under whose jurisdiction a person alleged to have committed any offence referred to in article 4 is found, shall in the cases contemplated in article 5, if it does not extradite him, submit the case to its competent authorities for the purpose of prosecution.

2. These authorities shall take their decision in the same manner as in the case of any ordinary offence of a serious nature under the law of that State. In the cases referred to in article 5, paragraph 2, the standards of evidence required for prosecution and conviction shall in no way be less stringent than those which apply in the cases referred to in article 5, paragraph 1.

3. Any person regarding whom proceedings are brought in connection with any of the offences referred to in article 4 shall be guaranteed fair treatment at all stages of the proceedings.

Article 8

1. The offences referred to in article 4 shall be deemed to be included as extraditable offences in any extradition treaty existing between States Parties. States Parties undertake to include such offences as extraditable offences in every extradition treaty to be concluded between them.

2. If a State Party which makes extradition conditional on the existence of a treaty receives a request for extradition from another State Party with which it has no extradition treaty, it may consider this Convention as the legal basis for extradition in respect of such offenses. Extradition shall be subject to the other conditions provided by the law of the requested State.

3. States Parties which do not make extradition conditional on the existence of a treaty shall recognize such offences as extraditable offences between themselves subject to the conditions provided by the law of the requested state.

4. Such offences shall be treated, for the purpose of extradition between States Parties, as if they had been committed not only in the place in which they occurred but also in the territories of the States required to establish their jurisdiction in accordance with article 5, paragraph 1.

Article 9

1. States Parties shall afford one another the greatest measure of assistance in connection with civil proceedings brought in respect of any of the offences referred to in article 4, including the supply of all evidence at their disposal necessary for the proceedings.

2. States Parties shall carry out their obligations under paragraph 1 of this article in conformity with any treaties on mutual judicial assistance that may exist between them.

Article 10

1. Each State Party shall ensure that education and information regarding the prohibition against torture are fully included in the training of law enforcement personnel, civil or military, medical personnel, public officials and other persons who may be involved in the custody, interrogation or treatment of any individual subjected to any form of arrest, detention or imprisonment.

2. Each State Party shall include this prohibition in the rules or instructions issued in regard to the duties and functions of any such persons.

Article 11

Each State Party shall keep under systematic review interrogation rules, instructions, methods and practices as well as arrangements for the custody and treatment of persons subjected to any form of arrest, detention or imprisonment in any territory under its jurisdiction, with a view to preventing any cases of torture.

Article 12

Each State Party shall ensure that its competent authorities proceed to a prompt and impartial investigation, wherever there is reasonable ground to believe that an act of torture has been committee in any territory under its jurisdiction.

Article 13

Each State Party shall ensure that any individual who alleges he has been subjected to torture in any territory under its jurisdiction has the right to complain to and to have his case promptly and impartially examined its competent authorities. Steps shall be taken to ensure that the complainant and witnesses are protected against all ill-treatment or intimidation as a consequence of his complaint or any evidence given.

Article 14

1. Each State Party shall ensure in its legal system that the victim of an act of torture obtains redress and has an enforceable right to fair and adequate compensation including the means for as full rehabilitation as possible. In the event of the death of the victim as a result of an act of torture, his dependents shall be entitled to compensation.

2. Nothing in this article shall affect any right of the victim or other person to compensation which may exist under national law.

Article 15

Each State Party shall ensure that any statement which is established to have been made as a result of torture shall not be invoked as evidence in any proceedings, except against a person accused of torture as evidence that the statement was made.

Article 16

1. Each State Party shall undertake to prevent in any territory under its jurisdiction other acts of cruel, inhuman or degrading treatment or punishment which do not amount to torture as defined in article 1, when such acts are committed by or at the instigation of or with the consent or acquiescence of a public official or other person acting in an official capacity. In particular, the obligations contained in articles 10, 11, 12 and 13 shall apply with the substitution for references to torture or references to other forms of cruel, inhuman or degrading treatment or punishment.

2. The provisions of this Convention are without prejudice to the provisions of any other international instrument or national law which prohibit cruel, inhuman or degrading treatment or punishment or which relate to extradition or expulsion.

8.2 PRINCIPLES OF MEDICAL ETHICS RELEVANT TO THE ROLE OF HEALTH PERSONNEL, PARTICULARLY PHYSICIANS, IN THE PROTECTION OF PRISONERS AND DETAINEES AGAINST TORTURE AND OTHER CRUEL, INHUMAN OR DEGRADING TREATMENT OR PUNISHMENT, 1982[3]

Principle 1

Health personnel, particularly physicians, charged with the medical care of prisoners and detainees have a duty to provide them with protection of their physical and mental health and treatment of disease of the same quality and standard as is afforded to those who are not imprisoned or detained.

Principle 2

It is a gross contravention of medical ethics, as well as an offence under applicable international instruments, for health personnel, particularly physicians, to engage, actively or passively, in acts which constitute participation in, complicity in, incitement to or attempts to commit torture or other cruel, inhuman or degrading treatment or punishment.

---

[3] Adopted by General Assembly resolution 37/194 of 18 December 1982.

Principle 3

It is a contravention of medical ethics for health personnel, particularly physicians, to be involved in any professional relationship with prisoners or detainees the purpose of which is not solely to evaluate, protect or improve their physical and mental health.

Principle 4

It is a contravention of medical ethics for health personnel, particularly physicians:

(a) To apply their knowledge and skills in order to assist in the interrogation of prisoners and detainees in a manner that may adversely affect the physical or mental health or condition of such prisoners or detainees and which is not in accordance with the relevant international instruments;[4]

(b) To certify, or to participate in the certification of, the fitness of prisoners or detainees for any form of treatment or punishment that may adversely affect their physical or mental health and which is not in accordance with the relevant international instruments, or to participate in any way in the infliction of any such treatment or punishment which is not in accordance with the relevant international instruments.

Principle 5

It is a contravention of medical ethics for health personnel, particularly physicians, to participate in any procedure for restraining a prisoner or detainee unless such a procedure is determined in accordance with purely medical criteria as being necessary for the protection of the physical or mental health or the safety of the prisoner or detainee himself, of his fellow prisoners or detainees, or of his guardians, and presents no hazard to his physical or mental health.

Principle 6

There may be no derogation from the foregoing principles on any ground whatsoever, including public emergency.

---

[4] Particularly the Universal Declaration of Human Rights (resolution 217 A (III)), the International Covenants on Human Rights (resolution 2200 A (XXI). annex), the Declaration on the Protection of All Persons from Being Subjected to Torture and Other Cruel, Inhuman or Degrading Treatment or Punishment (resolution 3452 (XXX), annex) and the Standard Minimum Rules for the Treatment of Prisoners (First United Nations Congress on the Prevention of Crime and the Treatment of Offenders: report by the Secretariat (United Nations publication, Sales No. E.1956.IV.4, annex I.A)).

8.3 PRINCIPLES ON THE EFFECTIVE INVESTIGATION AND DOCUMENTATION OF TORTURE AND OTHER CRUEL, INHUMAN OR DEGRADING TREATMENT OR PUNISHMENT, 2000 [5]

1. The purposes of effective investigation and documentation of torture and other cruel, inhuman or degrading treatment (torture or other ill-treatment) include the following:

(i) Clarification of the facts and establishment and acknowledgement of individual and State responsibility for victims and their families;

(ii) Identification of measures needed to prevent recurrence;

(iii) Facilitating prosecution and/or, as appropriate, disciplinary sanctions for those indicated by the investigation as being responsible, and demonstrating the need for full reparation and redress from the State, including fair and adequate financial compensation and provision of the means for medical care and rehabilitation.

2. States shall ensure that complaints and reports of torture or ill-treatment shall be promptly and effectively investigated. Even in the absence of an express complaint, an investigation should be undertaken if there are other indications that torture or ill-treatment might have occurred. The investigators, who shall be independent of the suspected perpetrators and the agency they serve, shall be competent and impartial. They shall have access to, or be empowered to commission investigations by impartial medical or other experts. The methods used to carry out such investigations shall meet the highest professional standards, and the findings shall be made public.

3. (*a*) The investigative authority shall have the power and obligation to obtain all the information necessary to the inquiry. Under certain circumstances, professional ethics may require information to be kept confidential. These requirements should be respected. The persons conducting the investigation shall have at their disposal all the necessary budgetary and technical resources for effective investigation. They shall also have the authority to oblige all those acting in an official capacity allegedly involved in torture or ill-treatment to appear and testify. The same shall apply to any witness. To this end, the investigative authority shall be entitled to issue summonses to witnesses, including any officials allegedly involved, and to demand the production of evidence;

---

[5] Annexed to the Commission on Human Rights resolution 2000/43, 20 April 2000.

(*b*) Alleged victims of torture or ill-treatment, witnesses, those conducting the investigation and their families shall be protected from violence, threats of violence or any other form of intimidation that may arise pursuant to the investigation. Those potentially implicated in torture or ill-treatment shall be removed from any position of control or power, whether direct or indirect, over complainants, witnesses and their families, as well as those conducting the investigation.

4. Alleged victims of torture or ill-treatment and their legal representatives shall be informed of, and have access to any hearing as well as to all information relevant to the investigation, and shall be entitled to present other evidence.

5. (*a*) In cases in which the established investigative procedures are inadequate because of insufficient expertise or suspected bias, or because of the apparent existence of a pattern of abuse, or for other substantial reasons, States shall ensure that investigations are undertaken through an independent commission of inquiry or similar procedure. Members of such a commission shall be chosen for their recognized impartiality, competence and independence as individuals. In particular, they shall be independent of any suspected perpetrators and the institutions or agencies they may serve. The commission shall have the authority to obtain all information necessary to the inquiry and shall conduct the inquiry as provided for under these Principles;

(*b*) A written report, made within a reasonable time, shall include the scope of the inquiry, procedures and methods used to evaluate evidence as well as conclusions and recommendations based on findings of fact and on applicable law. On completion, this report shall be made public. It shall also describe in detail specific events that were found to have occurred, the evidence upon which such findings were based, and list the names of witnesses who testified with the exception of those whose identities have been withheld for their own protection. The State shall, within a reasonable period of time, reply to the report of the investigation and, as appropriate, indicate steps to be taken in response.

6. (*a*) Medical experts involved in the investigation of torture or ill-treatment should behave at all times in conformity with the highest ethical standards and in particular shall obtain informed consent before any examination is undertaken. The examination must conform to established standards of medical practice. In particular, examinations shall be conducted in private under the control of the medical expert and outside the presence of security agents and other government officials;

(*b*) The medical expert should promptly prepare an accurate written report. This report should include at least the following:

(i) Circumstances of the interview: name of the subject and name affiliation of those present at the examination; the exact time and date; the location, nature and address of the institution (including, where appropriate, the room) where the examination is being conducted (e.g. detention centre, clinic, house, etc.); the circumstances of the subject at the time of the examination (e.g. nature of any restraints on arrival or during the examination, presence of security forces during the examination, demeanour of those accompanying the prisoner, threatening statements to the examiner, etc.); and any other relevant factor;

(ii) History: a detailed record of the subject's story as given during the interview, including alleged methods of torture or ill-treatment, the times when torture or ill-treatment is alleged to have occurred and all complaints of physical and psychological symptoms;

(iii) Physical and psychological examination: a record of all physical and psychological findings on clinical examination including appropriate diagnostic tests and, where possible, colour photographs of all injuries;

(iv) Opinion: an interpretation as to the probable relationship of the physical and psychological findings to possible torture or ill-treatment. A recommendation for any necessary medical and psychological treatment and/or further examination should be given;

(v) Authorship: the report should clearly identify those carrying out the examination and should be signed;

(c) The report should be confidential and communicated to the subject or his or her nominated representative. The views of the subject and his or her representative about the examination process should be solicited and recorded in the report. It should also be provided in writing, where appropriate, to the authority responsible for investigating the allegation of torture or ill-treatment. It is the responsibility of the State to ensure that it is delivered securely to these persons. The report should not be made available to any other person, except with the consent of the subject or on the authorization of a court empowered to enforce such transfer.

8.4 DECLARATION ON THE PROTECTION OF ALL PERSONS FROM ENFORCED DISAPPEARANCE[6]

The General Assembly,

Considering that, in accordance with the principles proclaimed in the Charter of the United Nations and other international instruments, recognition of the inherent dignity and of the equal and inalienable rights of all members of the human family is the foundation of freedom, justice and peace in the world,

Bearing in mind the obligation of States under the Charter, in particular Article 55, to promote universal respect for, and observance of, human rights and fundamental freedoms,

Deeply concerned that in many countries, often in a persistent manner, enforced disappearances occur, in the sense that persons are arrested, detained or abducted against their will or otherwise deprived of their liberty by officials of different branches or levels of Government, or by organized groups or private individuals acting on behalf of, or with the support, direct or indirect, consent or acquiescence of the Government, followed by a refusal to disclose the fate or whereabouts of the persons concerned or a refusal to acknowledge the deprivation of their liberty, which places such persons outside the protection of the law,

Considering that enforced disappearance undermines the deepest values of any society committed to respect for the rule of law, human rights and fundamental freedoms, and that the systematic practice of such acts is of the nature of a crime against humanity,

Recalling its resolution 33/173 of 22 December 1978, in which it expressed concern about the reports from various parts of the world relating to enforced or involuntary disappearances, as well as about the anguish and sorrows caused by those disappearances, and called upon Governments to hold law enforcement and security forces legally responsible for excesses which might lead to enforced or involuntary disappearances of persons,

Recalling also the protection afforded to victims of armed conflicts by the Geneva Conventions of 12 August 1949 and the Additional Protocols thereto, of 1977,

Having regard in particular to the relevant articles of the Universal Declaration of Human Rights and the International Covenant on Civil and Political Rights, which protect the right to life, the

---

[6] General Assembly resolution 47/133 of 18 December 1992.

right to liberty and security of the person, the right not to be subjected to torture and the right to recognition as a person before the law,

Having regard also to the Convention against Torture and Other Cruel, Inhuman or Degrading Treatment or Punishment, which provides that States parties shall take effective measures to prevent and punish acts of torture,

Bearing in mind the Code of Conduct for Law Enforcement Officials, the Basic Principles on the Use of Force and Firearms by Law Enforcement Officials, the Declaration of Basic Principles of Justice for Victims of Crime and Abuse of Power and the Standard Minimum Rules for the Treatment of Prisoners,

Affirming that, in order to prevent enforced disappearances, it is necessary to ensure strict compliance with the Body of Principles for the Protection of All Persons under Any Form of Detention or Imprisonment contained in the annex to its resolution 43/173 of 9 December 1988, and with the Principles on the Effective Prevention and Investigation of Extra-legal, Arbitrary and Summary Executions, set forth in the annex to Economic and Social Council resolution 1989/65 of 24 May 1989 and endorsed by the General Assembly in its resolution 44/162 of 15 December 1989,

Bearing in mind that, while the acts which comprise enforced disappearance constitute a violation of the prohibitions found in the aforementioned international instruments, it is none the less important to devise an instrument which characterizes all acts of enforce disappearance of persons as very serious offences and sets forth standards designed to punish and prevent their commission,

Proclaims the present Declaration on the Protection of All Persons from Enforced Disappearance, as a body of principles for all States;

Urges that all efforts be made so that the Declaration becomes generally known and respected;

Article 1

1. Any act of enforced disappearance is an offence to human dignity. It is condemned as a denial of the purposes of the Charter of the United Nations and as a grave and flagrant violation of the human rights and fundamental freedoms proclaimed in the Universal Declaration of Human Rights and reaffirmed and developed in international instruments in this field.

2. Any act of enforced disappearance places the persons subjected thereto outside the protection of the law and inflicts severe suffering on them and their families. It constitutes a

violation of the rules of international law guaranteeing, inter alia, the right to recognition as a person before the law, the right to liberty and security of the person and the right not to be subjected to torture and other cruel, inhuman or degrading treatment or punishment. It also violates or constitutes a grave threat to the right to life.

Article 2

1. No State shall practise, permit or tolerate enforced disappearances.

2. States shall act at the national and regional levels and in cooperation with the United Nations to contribute by all means to the prevention and eradication of enforce disappearance.

Article 3

Each State shall take effective legislative, administrative, judicial or other measures to prevent and terminate acts of enforced disappearance in any territory under its jurisdiction.

Article 4

1. All acts of enforced disappearance shall be offences under criminal law punishable by appropriate penalties which shall take into account their extreme seriousness.

2. Mitigating circumstances may be established in national legislation for persons who, having participated in enforced disappearances, are instrumental in bringing the victims forward alive or in providing voluntarily information which would contribute to clarifying cases of enforced disappearance.

Article 5

In addition to such criminal penalties as are applicable, enforced disappearances render their perpetrators and the State or State authorities which organize, acquiesce in or tolerate such disappearances liable under civil law, without prejudice to the international responsibility of the State concerned in accordance with the principles of international law.

Article 6

1. No order or instruction of any public authority, civilian, military or other, may be invoked to justify an enforced disappearance. Any person receiving such an order or instruction shall have the right and duty not to obey it.

2. Each State shall ensure that orders or instructions directing, authorizing or encouraging any enforced disappearance are prohibited.

4. Training of law enforcement officials shall emphasize the provisions in paragraphs 1 and 2 of the present article.

Article 7

No circumstances whatsoever, whether a threat of war, a state of war, internal political instability or any other public emergency, may be invoked to justify enforced disappearances.

Article 8

1. No State shall expel, return (*refouler*) or extradite a person to another State where there are substantial grounds to believe that he would be in danger of enforced disappearance.

2. For the purpose of determining whether there are such grounds, the competent authorities shall take into account all relevant considerations including, where applicable, the existence in the State concerned of a consistent pattern of gross, flagrant or mass violations of human rights.

Article 9

1. The right to a prompt and effective judicial remedy as a means of determining the whereabouts or state of health of persons deprived of their liberty and/or identifying the authority ordering or carry out the deprivation of liberty is required to prevent enforced disappearances under all circumstances, including those referred to in article 7 above.

2. In such proceedings, competent national authorities shall have access to all places where persons deprived of their liberty are being held and to each part of those places, as well as to any place in which there are grounds to believe that such persons may be found.

3. Any other competent authority entitled under the law of the State or by any international legal instrument to which the State is a party may also have access to such places.

Article 10

1. Any person deprived of liberty shall be held in an officially recognized place of detention and, in conformity with national law, be brought before a judicial authority promptly after detention.

2. Accurate information on the detention of such persons and their place or places of detention, including transfers, shall be made promptly available to their family members, their counsel or

to any other persons having a legitimate interest in the information unless a wish to the contrary has been manifested by the persons concerned.

3. An official up-to-date register of all persons deprived of their liberty shall be maintained in every place of detention. Additionally, each State shall take steps to maintain similar centralized registers. The information contained in these registers shall be made available to the persons mentioned in the preceding paragraph, to any judicial or other competent and independent national authority and to any other competent authority entitled under the law of the State concerned or any international legal instrument to which a State concerned is a party, seeking to trace the whereabouts of a detained person.

Article 11

All persons deprived of liberty must be released in a manner permitting reliable verification that they have actually been released and, further, have been released in conditions in which their physical integrity and ability fully to exercise their rights are assured.

Article 12

1. Each State shall establish rules under its national law indicating those officials authorized to order deprivation of liberty, establishing the conditions under which such orders may be given, and stipulating penalties for officials who, without legal justification, refuse to provide information on any detention.

2. Each State shall likewise ensure strict supervision, including a clear chain of command, of all law enforcement officials responsible for apprehensions, arrests, detentions, custody, transfers and imprisonment, and of other officials authorized by law to use force and firearms.

Article 13

1. Each State shall ensure that any person having knowledge or a legitimate interest who alleges that a person has been subjected to enforced disappearance has the right to complain to a competent and independent State authority and to have that complaint promptly, thoroughly and impartially investigated by that authority. Whenever there are reasonable grounds to believe that an enforced disappearance has been committed, the State shall promptly refer the matter to that authority for such an investigation, even if there has been no formal complaint. No measure shall be taken to curtail or impede the investigation.

2. Each State shall ensure that the competent authority shall have the necessary powers and resources to conduct the investigation effectively, including powers to compel attendance of witnesses and production of relevant documents and to make immediate on-site visits.

3. Steps shall be taken to ensure that all involved in the investigation, including the complainant, counsel, witnesses and those conducting the investigation, are protected against ill-treatment, intimidation or reprisal.

4. The findings of such an investigation shall be made available upon request to all persons concerned, unless doing so would jeopardize an ongoing criminal investigation.

5. Steps shall be taken to ensure that any ill-treatment, intimidation or reprisal or any other form of interference on the occasion of the lodging of a complaint or during the investigation procedure is appropriately punished.

6. An investigation, in accordance with the procedures described above, should be able to be conducted for as long as the fate of the victim of enforced disappearance remains unclarified.

Article 14

Any person alleged to have perpetrated an act of enforced disappearance in a particular State shall, when the facts disclosed by an official investigation so warrant, be brought before the competent civil authorities of that State for the purpose of prosecution and trial unless he has been extradited to another State wishing to exercise jurisdiction in accordance with the relevant international agreements in force. All States should take any lawful and appropriate action available to them to bring to justice all persons presumed responsible for an act of enforced disappearance, who are found to be within their jurisdiction or under their control.

Article 15

The fact that there are grounds to believe that a person has participated in acts of an extremely serious nature such as those referred to in article 4, paragraph 1, above, regardless of the motives, shall be taken into account when the competent authorities of the State decide whether or not to grant asylum.

Article 16

1. Persons alleged to have committed any of the acts referred to in article 4, paragraph 1, above, shall be suspended from any official duties during the investigation referred to in article 13 above.

2. They shall be tried only by the competent ordinary courts in each State, and not by any other special tribunal, in particular military courts.

3. No privileges, immunities or special exemptions shall be admitted in such trials, without prejudice to the provisions contained in the Vienna Convention on Diplomatic Relations.

4. The persons presumed responsible for such acts shall be guaranteed fair treatment in accordance with the relevant provisions of the Universal Declaration of Human Rights and other relevant international agreements in force at all stages of the investigation and eventual prosecution and trial.

Article 17

1. Acts constituting enforced disappearance shall be considered a continuing offence as long as the perpetrators continue to conceal the fate and the whereabouts of persons who have disappeared and these facts remain unclarified.

2. When the remedies provided for in article 2 of the International Covenant on Civil and Political Rights are no longer effective, the statute of limitations relating to acts of enforced disappearance shall be suspended until these remedies are re-established.

3. Statutes of limitations, where they exist, relating to acts of enforced disappearance shall be substantial and commensurate with the extreme seriousness of the offence.

Article 18

1. Persons who have or are alleged to have committed offences referred to in article 4, paragraph 1, above, shall not benefit from any special amnesty law or similar measures that might have the effect of exempting them from any criminal proceedings or sanction.

2. In the exercise of the right of pardon, the extreme seriousness of acts of enforced disappearance shall be taken into account.

Article 19

The victims of acts of enforced disappearance and their family shall obtain redress and shall have the right to adequate compensation, including the means for as complete a rehabilitation as possible. In the event of the death of the victim as a result of an act of enforced disappearance, their dependents shall also be entitled to compensation.

Article 20

1. States shall prevent and suppress the abduction of children of parents subjected to enforced disappearance and of children born during their mother's enforced disappearance, and shall devote their efforts to the search for and identification of such children and to the restitution of the children to their families of origin.

2. Considering the need to protect the best interests of children referred to in the preceding paragraph, there shall be an opportunity, in States which recognize a system of adoption, for a review of the adoption of such children and, in particular, for annulment of any adoption which originated in enforced disappearance. Such adoption should, however, continue to be in force if consent is given, at the time of the review, by the child's closest relatives.

3. The abduction of children of parents subjected to enforced disappearance or of children born during their mother's enforced disappearance, and the act of altering or suppressing documents attesting to their true identity, shall constitute an extremely serious offence, which shall be punished as such.

4. For these purpose, States shall, where appropriate, conclude bilateral and multilateral agreements.

Article 21

The provisions of the present Declaration are without prejudice to the provisions enunciated in the Universal Declaration of Human Rights or in any other international instrument, and shall not be construed as restricting or derogating from any of those provisions.

8.5 CONVENTION FOR THE PROTECTION OF ALL PERSONS FROM ENFORCED DISAPPEARANCE, 2006 [7]

Preamble

The States Parties to this Convention,

Considering the obligation of States under the Charter of the United Nations to promote universal respect for, and observance of, human rights and fundamental freedoms,

Having regard to the Universal Declaration of Human Rights,

---

[7] Not yet in force.

Recalling the International Covenant on Economic, Social and Cultural Rights, the International Covenant on Civil and Political Rights and the other relevant international instruments in the fields of human rights, humanitarian law and international criminal law,

Also recalling the Declaration on the Protection of All Persons from Enforced Disappearance adopted by the General Assembly of the United Nations in its resolution 47/133 of 18 December 1992,

Aware of the extreme seriousness of enforced disappearance, which constitutes a crime and, in certain circumstances defined in international law, a crime against humanity,

Determined to prevent enforced disappearances and to combat impunity for the crime of enforced disappearance,

Considering the right of any person not to be subjected to enforced disappearance, the right of victims to justice and to reparation,

Affirming the right of any victim to know the truth about the circumstances of an enforced disappearance and the fate of the disappeared person, and the right to freedom to seek, receive and impart information to this end,

Have agreed on the following articles:

Part I

Article 1

1. No one shall be subjected to enforced disappearance.

2. No exceptional circumstances whatsoever, whether a state of war or a threat of war, internal political instability or any other public emergency, may be invoked as a justification for enforced disappearance.

Article 2

For the purposes of this Convention, "enforced disappearance" is considered to be the arrest, detention, abduction or any other form of deprivation of liberty by agents of the State or by persons or groups of persons acting with the authorization, support or acquiescence of the State, followed by a refusal to acknowledge the deprivation of liberty or by concealment of the fate or whereabouts of the disappeared person, which place such a person outside the protection of the law.

Article 3

Each State Party shall take appropriate measures to investigate acts defined in article 2 committed by persons or groups of persons acting without the authorization, support or acquiescence of the State and to bring those responsible to justice.

Article 4

Each State Party shall take the necessary measures to ensure that enforced disappearance constitutes an offence under its criminal law.

Article 5

The widespread or systematic practice of enforced disappearance constitutes a crime against humanity as defined in applicable international law and shall attract the consequences provided for under such applicable international law.

Article 6

1. Each State Party shall take the necessary measures to hold criminally responsible at least:

(a) Any person who commits, orders, solicits or induces the commission of, attempts to commit, is an accomplice to or participates in an enforced disappearance;

(b) A superior who:

(i) Knew, or consciously disregarded information which clearly indicated, that subordinates under his or her effective authority and control were committing or about to commit a crime of enforced disappearance;

(ii) Exercised effective responsibility for and control over activities which were concerned with the crime of enforced disappearance; and

(iii) Failed to take all necessary and reasonable measures within his or her power to prevent or repress the commission of an enforced disappearance or to submit the matter to the competent authorities for investigation and prosecution;

(c) Subparagraph (b) above is without prejudice to the higher standards of responsibility applicable under relevant international law to a military commander or to a person effectively acting as a military commander.

2. No order or instruction from any public authority, civilian, military or other, may be invoked to justify an offence of enforced disappearance.

Article 7

1. Each State Party shall make the offence of enforced disappearance punishable by appropriate penalties which take into account its extreme seriousness.

2. Each State Party may establish:

(a) Mitigating circumstances, in particular for persons who, having been implicated in the commission of an enforced disappearance, effectively contribute to bringing the disappeared person forward alive or make it possible to clarify cases of enforced disappearance or to identify the perpetrators of an enforced disappearance;

(b) Without prejudice to other criminal procedures, aggravating circumstances, in particular in the event of the death of the disappeared person or the commission of an enforced disappearance in respect of pregnant women, minors, persons with disabilities or other particularly vulnerable persons.

Article 8

Without prejudice to article 5,

1. A State Party which applies a statute of limitations in respect of enforced disappearance shall take the necessary measures to ensure that the term of limitation for criminal proceedings:

(a) Is of long duration and is proportionate to the extreme seriousness of this offence;

(b) Commences from the moment when the offence of enforced disappearance ceases, taking into account its continuous nature.

2. Each State Party shall guarantee the right of victims of enforced disappearance to an effective remedy during the term of limitation.

Article 9

1. Each State Party shall take the necessary measures to establish its competence to exercise jurisdiction over the offence of enforced disappearance:

(a) When the offence is committed in any territory under its jurisdiction or on board a ship or aircraft registered in that State;

(b) When the alleged offender is one of its nationals;

(c) When the disappeared person is one of its nationals and the State Party considers it appropriate.

2. Each State Party shall likewise take such measures as may be necessary to establish its competence to exercise jurisdiction over the offence of enforced disappearance when the alleged offender is present in any territory under its jurisdiction, unless it extradites or surrenders him or her to another State in accordance with its international obligations or surrenders him or her to an international criminal tribunal whose jurisdiction it has recognized.

3. This Convention does not exclude any additional criminal jurisdiction exercised in accordance with national law.

Article 10

1. Upon being satisfied, after an examination of the information available to it, that the circumstances so warrant, any State Party in whose territory a person suspected of having committed an offence of enforced disappearance is present shall take him or her into custody or take such other legal measures as are necessary to ensure his or her presence. The custody and other legal measures shall be as provided for in the law of that State Party but may be maintained only for such time as is necessary to ensure the person's presence at criminal, surrender or extradition proceedings.

2. A State Party which has taken the measures referred to in paragraph 1 of this article shall immediately carry out a preliminary inquiry or investigations to establish the facts. It shall notify the States Parties referred to in article 9, paragraph 1, of the measures it has taken in pursuance of paragraph 1 of this article, including detention and the circumstances warranting detention, and of the findings of its preliminary inquiry or its investigations, indicating whether it intends to exercise its jurisdiction.

3. Any person in custody pursuant to paragraph 1 of this article may communicate immediately with the nearest appropriate representative of the State of which he or she is a national, or, if he or she is a stateless person, with the representative of the State where he or she usually resides.

Article 11

1. The State Party in the territory under whose jurisdiction a person alleged to have committed an offence of enforced disappearance is found shall, if it does not extradite that person or

surrender him or her to another State in accordance with its international obligations or surrender him or her to an international criminal tribunal whose jurisdiction it has recognized, submit the case to its competent authorities for the purpose of prosecution.

2. These authorities shall take their decision in the same manner as in the case of any ordinary offence of a serious nature under the law of that State Party. In the cases referred to in article 9, paragraph 2, the standards of evidence required for prosecution and conviction shall in no way be less stringent than those which apply in the cases referred to in article 9, paragraph 1.

3. Any person against whom proceedings are brought in connection with an offence of enforced disappearance shall be guaranteed fair treatment at all stages of the proceedings. Any person tried for an offence of enforced disappearance shall benefit from a fair trial before a competent, independent and impartial court or tribunal established by law.

Article 12

1. Each State Party shall ensure that any individual who alleges that a person has been subjected to enforced disappearance has the right to report the facts to the competent authorities, which shall examine the allegation promptly and impartially and, where necessary, undertake without delay a thorough and impartial investigation. Appropriate steps shall be taken, where necessary, to ensure that the complainant, witnesses, relatives of the disappeared person and their defence counsel, as well as persons participating in the investigation, are protected against all ill-treatment or intimidation as a consequence of the complaint or any evidence given.

2. Where there are reasonable grounds for believing that a person has been subjected to enforced disappearance, the authorities referred to in paragraph 1 of this article shall undertake an investigation, even if there has been no formal complaint.

3. Each State Party shall ensure that the authorities referred to in paragraph 1 of this article:

(a) Have the necessary powers and resources to conduct the investigation effectively, including access to the documentation and other information relevant to their investigation;

(b) Have access, if necessary with the prior authorization of a judicial authority, which shall rule promptly on the matter, to any place of detention or any other place where there are reasonable grounds to believe that the disappeared person may be present.

4. Each State Party shall take the necessary measures to prevent and sanction acts that hinder the conduct of an investigation. It shall ensure in particular that persons suspected of having

committed an offence of enforced disappearance are not in a position to influence the progress of an investigation by means of pressure or acts of intimidation or reprisal aimed at the complainant, witnesses, relatives of the disappeared person or their defence counsel, or at persons participating in the investigation.

Article 13

1. For the purposes of extradition between States Parties, the offence of enforced disappearance shall not be regarded as a political offence or as an offence connected with a political offence or as an offence inspired by political motives. Accordingly, a request for extradition based on such an offence may not be refused on these grounds alone.

2. The offence of enforced disappearance shall be deemed to be included as an extraditable offence in any extradition treaty existing between States Parties before the entry into force of this Convention.

3. States Parties undertake to include the offence of enforced disappearance as an extraditable offence in any extradition treaty subsequently to be concluded between them.

4. If a State Party which makes extradition conditional on the existence of a treaty receives a request for extradition from another State Party with which it has no extradition treaty, it may consider this Convention as the necessary legal basis for extradition in respect of the offence of enforced disappearance.

5. States Parties which do not make extradition conditional on the existence of a treaty shall recognize the offence of enforced disappearance as an extraditable offence between themselves.

6. Extradition shall, in all cases, be subject to the conditions provided for by the law of the requested State Party or by applicable extradition treaties, including, in particular, conditions relating to the minimum penalty requirement for extradition and the grounds upon which the requested State Party may refuse extradition or make it subject to certain conditions.

7. Nothing in this Convention shall be interpreted as imposing an obligation to extradite if the requested State Party has substantial grounds for believing that the request has been made for the purpose of prosecuting or punishing a person on account of that person's sex, race, religion, nationality, ethnic origin, political opinions or membership of a particular social group, or that compliance with the request would cause harm to that person for any one of these reasons.

Article 14

1. States Parties shall afford one another the greatest measure of mutual legal assistance in connection with criminal proceedings brought in respect of an offence of enforced disappearance, including the supply of all evidence at their disposal that is necessary for the proceedings.

2. Such mutual legal assistance shall be subject to the conditions provided for by the domestic law of the requested State Party or by applicable treaties on mutual legal assistance, including, in particular, the conditions in relation to the grounds upon which the requested State Party may refuse to grant mutual legal assistance or may make it subject to conditions.

Article 15

States Parties shall cooperate with each other and shall afford one another the greatest measure of mutual assistance with a view to assisting victims of enforced disappearance, and in searching for, locating and releasing disappeared persons and, in the event of death, in exhuming and identifying them and returning their remains.

Article 16

1. No State Party shall expel, return (*refouler*), surrender or extradite a person to another State where there are substantial grounds for believing that he or she would be in danger of being subjected to enforced disappearance.

2. For the purpose of determining whether there are such grounds, the competent authorities shall take into account all relevant considerations, including, where applicable, the existence in the State concerned of a consistent pattern of gross, flagrant or mass violations of human rights or of serious violations of international humanitarian law.

Article 17

1. No one shall be held in secret detention.

2. Without prejudice to other international obligations of the State Party with regard to the deprivation of liberty, each State Party shall, in its legislation:

(a) Establish the conditions under which orders of deprivation of liberty may be given;

(b) Indicate those authorities authorized to order the deprivation of liberty;

(c) Guarantee that any person deprived of liberty shall be held solely in officially recognized and supervised places of deprivation of liberty;

(d) Guarantee that any person deprived of liberty shall be authorized to communicate with and be visited by his or her family, counsel or any other person of his or her choice, subject only to the conditions established by law, or, if he or she is a foreigner, to communicate with his or her consular authorities, in accordance with applicable international law;

(e) Guarantee access by the competent and legally authorized authorities and institutions to the places where persons are deprived of liberty, if necessary with prior authorization from a judicial authority;

(f) Guarantee that any person deprived of liberty or, in the case of a suspected enforced disappearance, since the person deprived of liberty is not able to exercise this right, any persons with a legitimate interest, such as relatives of the person deprived of liberty, their representatives or their counsel, shall, in all circumstances, be entitled to take proceedings before a court, in order that the court may decide without delay on the lawfulness of the deprivation of liberty and order the person's release if such deprivation of liberty is not lawful.

3. Each State Party shall assure the compilation and maintenance of one or more up-to-date official registers and/or records of persons deprived of liberty, which shall be made promptly available, upon request, to any judicial or other competent authority or institution authorized for that purpose by the law of the State Party concerned or any relevant international legal instrument to which the State concerned is a party. The information contained therein shall include, as a minimum:

(a) The identity of the person deprived of liberty;

(b) The date, time and place where the person was deprived of liberty and the identity of the authority that deprived the person of liberty;

(c) The authority that ordered the deprivation of liberty and the grounds for the deprivation of liberty;

(d) The authority responsible for supervising the deprivation of liberty;

(e) The place of deprivation of liberty, the date and time of admission to the place of deprivation of liberty and the authority responsible for the place of deprivation of liberty;

(f) Elements relating to the state of health of the person deprived of liberty;

(g) In the event of death during the deprivation of liberty, the circumstances and cause of death and the destination of the remains;

(h) The date and time of release or transfer to another place of detention, the destination and the authority responsible for the transfer.

Article 18

1. Subject to articles 19 and 20, each State Party shall guarantee to any person with a legitimate interest in this information, such as relatives of the person deprived of liberty, their representatives or their counsel, access to at least the following information:

(a) The authority that ordered the deprivation of liberty;

(b) The date, time and place where the person was deprived of liberty and admitted to the place of deprivation of liberty;

(c) The authority responsible for supervising the deprivation of liberty;

(d) The whereabouts of the person deprived of liberty, including, in the event of a transfer to another place of deprivation of liberty, the destination and the authority responsible for the transfer;

(e) The date, time and place of release;

(f) Elements relating to the state of health of the person deprived of liberty;

(g) In the event of death during the deprivation of liberty, the circumstances and cause of death and the destination of the remains.

2. Appropriate measures shall be taken, where necessary, to protect the persons referred to in paragraph 1 of this article, as well as persons participating in the investigation, from any ill-treatment, intimidation or sanction as a result of the search for information concerning a person deprived of liberty.

Article 19

1. Personal information, including medical and genetic data, which is collected and/or transmitted within the framework of the search for a disappeared person shall not be used or made available for purposes other than the search for the disappeared person. This is without prejudice to the use of such information in criminal proceedings relating to an offence of enforced disappearance or the exercise of the right to obtain reparation.

2. The collection, processing, use and storage of personal information, including medical and genetic data, shall not infringe or have the effect of infringing the human rights, fundamental freedoms or human dignity of an individual.

Article 20

1. Only where a person is under the protection of the law and the deprivation of liberty is subject to judicial control may the right to information referred to in article 18 be restricted, on an exceptional basis, where strictly necessary and where provided for by law, and if the transmission of the information would adversely affect the privacy or safety of the person, hinder a criminal investigation, or for other equivalent reasons in accordance with the law, and in conformity with applicable international law and with the objectives of this Convention. In no case shall there be restrictions on the right to information referred to in article 18 that could constitute conduct defined in article 2 or be in violation of article 17, paragraph 1.

2. Without prejudice to consideration of the lawfulness of the deprivation of a person's liberty, States Parties shall guarantee to the persons referred to in article 18, paragraph 1, the right to a prompt and effective judicial remedy as a means of obtaining without delay the information referred to in article 18, paragraph 1. This right to a remedy may not be suspended or restricted in any circumstances.

Article 21

Each State Party shall take the necessary measures to ensure that persons deprived of liberty are released in a manner permitting reliable verification that they have actually been released. Each State Party shall also take the necessary measures to assure the physical integrity of such persons and their ability to exercise fully their rights at the time of release, without prejudice to any obligations to which such persons may be subject under national law.

Article 22

Without prejudice to article 6, each State Party shall take the necessary measures to prevent and impose sanctions for the following conduct:

(a) Delaying or obstructing the remedies referred to in article 17, paragraph 2 (f), and article 20, paragraph 2;

(b) Failure to record the deprivation of liberty of any person, or the recording of any information which the official responsible for the official register knew or should have known to be inaccurate;

(c) Refusal to provide information on the deprivation of liberty of a person, or the provision of inaccurate information, even though the legal requirements for providing such information have been met.

Article 23

1. Each State Party shall ensure that the training of law enforcement personnel, civil or military, medical personnel, public officials and other persons who may be involved in the custody or treatment of any person deprived of liberty includes the necessary education and information regarding the relevant provisions of this Convention, in order to:

(a) Prevent the involvement of such officials in enforced disappearances;

(b) Emphasize the importance of prevention and investigations in relation to enforced disappearances;

(c) Ensure that the urgent need to resolve cases of enforced disappearance is recognized.

2. Each State Party shall ensure that orders or instructions prescribing, authorizing or encouraging enforced disappearance are prohibited. Each State Party shall guarantee that a person who refuses to obey such an order will not be punished.

3. Each State Party shall take the necessary measures to ensure that the persons referred to in paragraph 1 of this article who have reason to believe that an enforced disappearance has occurred or is planned report the matter to their superiors and, where necessary, to the appropriate authorities or bodies vested with powers of review or remedy.

Article 24

1. For the purposes of this Convention, 'victim' means the disappeared person and any individual who has suffered harm as the direct result of an enforced disappearance.

2. Each victim has the right to know the truth regarding the circumstances of the enforced disappearance, the progress and results of the investigation and the fate of the disappeared person. Each State Party shall take appropriate measures in this regard.

3. Each State Party shall take all appropriate measures to search for, locate and release disappeared persons and, in the event of death, to locate, respect and return their remains.

4. Each State Party shall ensure in its legal system that the victims of enforced disappearance have the right to obtain reparation and prompt, fair and adequate compensation.

5. The right to obtain reparation referred to in paragraph 4 of this article covers material and moral damages and, where appropriate, other forms of reparation such as:

(a) Restitution;

(b) Rehabilitation;

(c) Satisfaction, including restoration of dignity and reputation;

(d) Guarantees of non-repetition.

6. Without prejudice to the obligation to continue the investigation until the fate of the disappeared person has been clarified, each State Party shall take the appropriate steps with regard to the legal situation of disappeared persons whose fate has not been clarified and that of their relatives, in fields such as social welfare, financial matters, family law and property rights.

7. Each State Party shall guarantee the right to form and participate freely in organizations and associations concerned with attempting to establish the circumstances of enforced disappearances and the fate of disappeared persons, and to assist victims of enforced disappearance.

Article 25

1. Each State Party shall take the necessary measures to prevent and punish under its criminal law:

(a) The wrongful removal of children who are subjected to enforced disappearance, children whose father, mother or legal guardian is subjected to enforced disappearance or children born during the captivity of a mother subjected to enforced disappearance;

(b) The falsification, concealment or destruction of documents attesting to the true identity of the children referred to in subparagraph (a) above.

2. Each State Party shall take the necessary measures to search for and identify the children referred to in paragraph 1 (a) of this article and to return them to their families of origin, in accordance with legal procedures and applicable international agreements.

3. States Parties shall assist one another in searching for, identifying and locating the children referred to in paragraph 1 (a) of this article.

4. Given the need to protect the best interests of the children referred to in paragraph 1 (a) of this article and their right to preserve, or to have re-established, their identity, including their nationality, name and family relations as recognized by law, States Parties which recognize a system of adoption or other form of placement of children shall have legal procedures in place to review the adoption or placement procedure, and, where appropriate, to annul any adoption or placement of children that originated in an enforced disappearance.

5. In all cases, and in particular in all matters relating to this article, the best interests of the child shall be a primary consideration, and a child who is capable of forming his or her own views shall have the right to express those views freely, the views of the child being given due weight in accordance with the age and maturity of the child.

Part II

Article 26

1. A Committee on Enforced Disappearances (the Committee) shall be established to carry out the functions provided for under this Convention. The Committee shall consist of ten experts of high moral character and recognized competence in the field of human rights, who shall serve in their personal capacity and be independent and impartial. The members of the Committee shall be elected by the States Parties according to equitable geographical distribution. Due account shall be taken of the usefulness of the participation in the work of the Committee of persons having relevant legal experience and of balanced gender representation.

2. The members of the Committee shall be elected by secret ballot from a list of persons nominated by States Parties from among their nationals, at biennial meetings of the States Parties convened by the Secretary-General of the United Nations for this purpose. At those

meetings, for which two thirds of the States Parties shall constitute a quorum, the persons elected to the Committee shall be those who obtain the largest number of votes and an absolute majority of the votes of the representatives of States Parties present and voting.

3. The initial election shall be held no later than six months after the date of entry into force of this Convention. Four months before the date of each election, the Secretary-General of the United Nations shall address a letter to the States Parties inviting them to submit nominations within three months. The Secretary-General shall prepare a list in alphabetical order of all persons thus nominated, indicating the State Party which nominated each candidate, and shall submit this list to all States Parties.

4. The members of the Committee shall be elected for a term of four years. They shall be eligible for re-election once. However, the term of five of the members elected at the first election shall expire at the end of two years; immediately after the first election, the names of these five members shall be chosen by lot by the chairman of the meeting referred to in paragraph 2 of this article.

5. If a member of the Committee dies or resigns or for any other reason can no longer perform his or her Committee duties, the State Party which nominated him or her shall, in accordance with the criteria set out in paragraph 1 of this article, appoint another candidate from among its nationals to serve out his or her term, subject to the approval of the majority of the States Parties. Such approval shall be considered to have been obtained unless half or more of the States Parties respond negatively within six weeks of having been informed by the Secretary-General of the United Nations of the proposed appointment.

6. The Committee shall establish its own rules of procedure.

7. The Secretary-General of the United Nations shall provide the Committee with the necessary means, staff and facilities for the effective performance of its functions. The Secretary-General of the United Nations shall convene the initial meeting of the Committee.

8. The members of the Committee shall be entitled to the facilities, privileges and immunities of experts on mission for the United Nations, as laid down in the relevant sections of the Convention on the Privileges and Immunities of the United Nations.

9. Each State Party shall cooperate with the Committee and assist its members in the fulfilment of their mandate, to the extent of the Committee's functions that the State Party has accepted.

Article 27

A Conference of the States Parties will take place at the earliest four years and at the latest six years following the entry into force of this Convention to evaluate the functioning of the Committee and to decide, in accordance with the procedure described in article 44, paragraph 2, whether it is appropriate to transfer to another body - without excluding any possibility - the monitoring of this Convention, in accordance with the functions defined in articles 28 to 36.

Article 28

1. In the framework of the competencies granted by this Convention, the Committee shall cooperate with all relevant organs, offices and specialized agencies and funds of the United Nations, with the treaty bodies instituted by international instruments, with the special procedures of the United Nations and with the relevant regional intergovernmental organizations or bodies, as well as with all relevant State institutions, agencies or offices working towards the protection of all persons against enforced disappearances.

2. As it discharges its mandate, the Committee shall consult other treaty bodies instituted by relevant international human rights instruments, in particular the Human Rights Committee instituted by the International Covenant on Civil and Political Rights, with a view to ensuring the consistency of their respective observations and recommendations.

Article 29

1. Each State Party shall submit to the Committee, through the Secretary-General of the United Nations, a report on the measures taken to give effect to its obligations under this Convention, within two years after the entry into force of this Convention for the State Party concerned.

2. The Secretary-General of the United Nations shall make this report available to all States Parties.

3. Each report shall be considered by the Committee, which shall issue such comments, observations or recommendations as it may deem appropriate. The comments, observations or recommendations shall be communicated to the State Party concerned, which may respond to them, on its own initiative or at the request of the Committee.

4. The Committee may also request States Parties to provide additional information on the implementation of this Convention.

Article 30

1. A request that a disappeared person should be sought and found may be submitted to the Committee, as a matter of urgency, by relatives of the disappeared person or their legal representatives, their counsel or any person authorized by them, as well as by any other person having a legitimate interest.

2. If the Committee considers that a request for urgent action submitted in pursuance of paragraph 1 of this article:

(a) Is not manifestly unfounded;

(b) Does not constitute an abuse of the right of submission of such requests;

(c) Has already been duly presented to the competent bodies of the State Party concerned, such as those authorized to undertake investigations, where such a possibility exists;

(d) Is not incompatible with the provisions of this Convention; and

(e) The same matter is not being examined under another procedure of international investigation or settlement of the same nature;

it shall request the State Party concerned to provide it with information on the situation of the persons sought, within a time limit set by the Committee.

3. In the light of the information provided by the State Party concerned in accordance with paragraph 2 of this article, the Committee may transmit recommendations to the State Party, including a request that the State Party should take all the necessary measures, including interim measures, to locate and protect the person concerned in accordance with this Convention and to inform the Committee, within a specified period of time, of measures taken, taking into account the urgency of the situation. The Committee shall inform the person submitting the urgent action request of its recommendations and of the information provided to it by the State as it becomes available.

4. The Committee shall continue its efforts to work with the State Party concerned for as long as the fate of the person sought remains unresolved. The person presenting the request shall be kept informed.

Article 31

1. A State Party may at the time of ratification of this Convention or at any time afterwards declare that it recognizes the competence of the Committee to receive and consider communications from or on behalf of individuals subject to its jurisdiction claiming to be victims of a violation by this State Party of provisions of this Convention. The Committee shall not admit any communication concerning a State Party which has not made such a declaration.

2. The Committee shall consider a communication inadmissible where:

(a) The communication is anonymous;

(b) The communication constitutes an abuse of the right of submission of such communications or is incompatible with the provisions of this Convention;

(c) The same matter is being examined under another procedure of international investigation or settlement of the same nature; or where

(d) All effective available domestic remedies have not been exhausted. This rule shall not apply where the application of the remedies is unreasonably prolonged.

3. If the Committee considers that the communication meets the requirements set out in paragraph 2 of this article, it shall transmit the communication to the State Party concerned, requesting it to provide observations and comments within a time limit set by the Committee.

4. At any time after the receipt of a communication and before a determination on the merits has been reached, the Committee may transmit to the State Party concerned for its urgent consideration a request that the State Party will take such interim measures as may be necessary to avoid possible irreparable damage to the victims of the alleged violation. Where the Committee exercises its discretion, this does not imply a determination on admissibility or on the merits of the communication.

5. The Committee shall hold closed meetings when examining communications under the present article. It shall inform the author of a communication of the responses provided by the State Party concerned. When the Committee decides to finalize the procedure, it shall communicate its views to the State Party and to the author of the communication.

Article 32

A State Party to this Convention may at any time declare that it recognizes the competence of the Committee to receive and consider communications in which a State Party claims that another State Party is not fulfilling its obligations under this Convention. The Committee shall not receive communications concerning a State Party which has not made such a declaration, nor communications from a State Party which has not made such a declaration.

Article 33

1. If the Committee receives reliable information indicating that a State Party is seriously violating the provisions of this Convention, it may, after consultation with the State Party concerned, request one or more of its members to undertake a visit and report back to it without delay.

2. The Committee shall notify the State Party concerned, in writing, of its intention to organize a visit, indicating the composition of the delegation and the purpose of the visit. The State Party shall answer the Committee within a reasonable time.

3. Upon a substantiated request by the State Party, the Committee may decide to postpone or cancel its visit.

4. If the State Party agrees to the visit, the Committee and the State Party concerned shall work together to define the modalities of the visit and the State Party shall provide the Committee with all the facilities needed for the successful completion of the visit.

5. Following its visit, the Committee shall communicate to the State Party concerned its observations and recommendations.

Article 34

If the Committee receives information which appears to it to contain well-founded indications that enforced disappearance is being practised on a widespread or systematic basis in the territory under the jurisdiction of a State Party, it may, after seeking from the State Party concerned all relevant information on the situation, urgently bring the matter to the attention of the General Assembly of the United Nations, through the Secretary-General of the United Nations.

Article 35

1. The Committee shall have competence solely in respect of enforced disappearances which commenced after the entry into force of this Convention.

2. If a State becomes a party to this Convention after its entry into force, the obligations of that State vis-à-vis the Committee shall relate only to enforced disappearances which commenced after the entry into force of this Convention for the State concerned.

Article 36

1. The Committee shall submit an annual report on its activities under this Convention to the States Parties and to the General Assembly of the United Nations.

2. Before an observation on a State Party is published in the annual report, the State Party concerned shall be informed in advance and shall be given reasonable time to answer. This State Party may request the publication of its comments or observations in the report.

Part III

Article 37

Nothing in this Convention shall affect any provisions which are more conducive to the protection of all persons from enforced disappearance and which may be contained in:

(a) The law of a State Party;

(b) International law in force for that State.

Article 38

1. This Convention is open for signature by all Member States of the United Nations.

2. This Convention is subject to ratification by all Member States of the United Nations. Instruments of ratification shall be deposited with the Secretary-General of the United Nations.

3. This Convention is open to accession by all Member States of the United Nations. Accession shall be effected by the deposit of an instrument of accession with the Secretary-General.

Article 39

1. This Convention shall enter into force on the thirtieth day after the date of deposit with the Secretary-General of the United Nations of the twentieth instrument of ratification or accession.

2. For each State ratifying or acceding to this Convention after the deposit of the twentieth instrument of ratification or accession, this Convention shall enter into force on the thirtieth day after the date of the deposit of that State's instrument of ratification or accession.

Article 40

The Secretary-General of the United Nations shall notify all States Members of the United Nations and all States which have signed or acceded to this Convention of the following:

(a) Signatures, ratifications and accessions under article 38;

(b) The date of entry into force of this Convention under article 39.

Article 41

The provisions of this Convention shall apply to all parts of federal States without any limitations or exceptions.

Article 42

1. Any dispute between two or more States Parties concerning the interpretation or application of this Convention which cannot be settled through negotiation or by the procedures expressly provided for in this Convention shall, at the request of one of them, be submitted to arbitration. If within six months from the date of the request for arbitration the Parties are unable to agree on the organization of the arbitration, any one of those Parties may refer the dispute to the International Court of Justice by request in conformity with the Statute of the Court.

2. A State may, at the time of signature or ratification of this Convention or accession thereto, declare that it does not consider itself bound by paragraph 1 of this article. The other States Parties shall not be bound by paragraph 1 of this article with respect to any State Party having made such a declaration.

3. Any State Party having made a declaration in accordance with the provisions of paragraph 2 of this article may at any time withdraw this declaration by notification to the Secretary-General of the United Nations.

Article 43

This Convention is without prejudice to the provisions of international humanitarian law, including the obligations of the High Contracting Parties to the four Geneva Conventions of 12 August 1949 and the two Additional Protocols thereto of 8 June 1977, or to the opportunity available to any State Party to authorize the International Committee of the Red Cross to visit places of detention in situations not covered by international humanitarian law.

Article 44

1. Any State Party to this Convention may propose an amendment and file it with the Secretary-General of the United Nations. The Secretary-General shall thereupon communicate the proposed amendment to the States Parties to this Convention with a request that they indicate whether they favour a conference of States Parties for the purpose of considering and voting upon the proposal. In the event that within four months from the date of such communication at least one third of the States Parties favour such a conference, the Secretary-General shall convene the conference under the auspices of the United Nations.

2. Any amendment adopted by a majority of two thirds of the States Parties present and voting at the conference shall be submitted by the Secretary-General of the United Nations to all the States Parties for acceptance.

3. An amendment adopted in accordance with paragraph 2 of this article shall enter into force when two thirds of the States Parties to this Convention have accepted it in accordance with their respective constitutional processes.

4. When amendments enter into force, they shall be binding on those States Parties which have accepted them, other States Parties still being bound by the provisions of this Convention and any earlier amendment which they have accepted.

Article 45

1. This Convention, of which the Arabic, Chinese, English, French, Russian and Spanish texts are equally authentic, shall be deposited with the Secretary-General of the United Nations.

2. The Secretary-General of the United Nations shall transmit certified copies of this Convention to all States referred to in article 38.

8.6 SECRET DETENTION

The Human Rights Council has recently released a joint study [8] on global practices in relation to secret detention. Secret detention in the context of counter-terrorism is not a new phenomenon. Striking similarities can be identified between security measures in the 1970s and 1980s in the

---

[8]Joint study on global practices in relation to secret detention in the context of countering terrorism; undertaken by the Special Rapporteur on the promotion and protection of human rights and fundamental freedoms while countering terrorism, the Special Rapporteur on torture and other cruel, inhuman or degrading treatment or punishment, the Working Group on Arbitrary Detention and the Working Group on Enforced or Involuntary Disappearances. The study addresses the use of secret detention in the context of the "global war on terror" in the post 11 September 2001 era. A/ HRC/13/42,26 January 2010

context of Latin America and in the last century in other regions such as Africa, Asia, Europe, and the Middle East. The methods used then as now consist *inter alia* of broad emergency laws, the enhanced role of military and special courts, the practice of torture and/or ill-treatment, kidnappings (renditions), enforced disappearances and notably secret detention. The aim is always the same; to have a deterrent effect because detainees would vanish without leaving a trace and no information would be given as to their whereabouts or fate.

Secret detention is irreconcilable with international human rights law and international humanitarian law. It violates the right to liberty and security of the person and the prohibition of arbitrary arrest or detention. Article 9, paragraph 1, of the International Covenant on Civil and Political Rights affirms that everyone has the right to liberty and security of person, that no one should be subjected to arbitrary arrest or detention nor be deprived of his or her liberty except on such grounds and in accordance with such procedure as are established by law. Furthermore, article 9, paragraph 4 of the Covenant stipulates that anyone deprived of their liberty by arrest or detention should be entitled to take proceedings before a court, in order that that court may decide, without delay, on the lawfulness of their detention and order their release if the detention is not lawful.

Every instance of secret detention also amounts to a case of enforced disappearance. Article 2 of the International Convention for the Protection of All Persons from Enforced Disappearance defines "enforced disappearance" as: "the arrest, detention, abduction or any other form of deprivation of liberty by agents of the State or by persons or groups of persons acting with the authorization, support or acquiescence of the State, followed by a refusal to acknowledge the deprivation of liberty or by concealment of the fate or whereabouts of the disappeared person, which place such a person outside the protection of the law." Since secret detention amounts to an enforced disappearance, if resorted to in a widespread or systematic manner, such aggravated form of enforced disappearance can reach the threshold of a crime against humanity. In its article 7, the Rome Statute of the International Criminal Court labels the "enforced disappearance of persons" as a crime against humanity if it is committed as part of a widespread or systematic attack directed against any civilian population, with knowledge of the attack.[9] Article 5 of the International Convention for the Protection of All Persons from Enforced Disappearance, states that the widespread or systematic practice of enforced disappearance constitutes a crime against humanity as defined in applicable international law, and should attract the consequences provided for under such applicable international law, thus confirming this approach.

---

[9] *Prosecutor v. Kupreskic et al*, IT-95-16-A, judgement of trial chamber of the International Criminal Tribunal for the Former Yugoslavia, para. 566 (14 January 2000).

Secret detention amounts to a manifold human rights violation that cannot be justified under any circumstances, including during states of emergency. Every instance of secret detention is by definition *incommunicado* detention. Prolonged *incommunicado* detention may facilitate the perpetration of torture and other cruel, inhuman or degrading treatment or punishment and can in itself constitute such treatment. The suffering caused to family members of a secretly detained, i.e. disappeared person, may also amount to torture or other forms of ill-treatment, and at the same time violates the right to the protection of family life. Secret detainees are typically deprived of their right to a fair trial as State authorities do not intend to charge or try the detainee.

It is not only States whose authorities keep the detainee in secret custody that are internationally responsible for violations of international human rights law. The practice of "proxy detention", involving the transfer of a detainee from one State to another outside the realm of any international or national legal procedure (known as "rendition" or "extraordinary rendition"), often in disregard of the principle of *non-refoulement*, also involves the responsibility of the State at whose behest the detention takes place. The Geneva Conventions, applicable to all armed conflicts, also prohibit secret detention under any circumstances.

States of emergency, armed conflicts and the combat against terrorism – often framed in vaguely defined legal provisions – constitute an "enabling environment" for secret detention. As in the past, extraordinary powers are today conferred on authorities, including armed forces, law-enforcement bodies and/or intelligence agencies, under states of emergency or global war paradigms without or with very restricted control mechanisms by parliaments or judicial bodies. In many contexts, intelligence agencies operate in a legal vacuum with no law, or no publicly available law, governing their actions. Many times, although legislation does not authorize intelligence bodies to detain persons, they do so, sometimes for prolonged periods. In such situations, there are either no oversight and accountability mechanisms at all, or they are severely restricted, with limited powers and hence ineffective.

The Experts conclude with concrete recommendations regarding these practices, aimed at curbing the resort to secret detention and the unlawful treatment or punishment of detainees in the context of counter-terrorism:

1. Secret detention should be explicitly prohibited, along with all other forms of unofficial detention. Detention records should be kept (including in times of armed conflict as required by the Geneva Conventions, including the number of detainees, their nationality, and the legal basis on which they are being held, whether as prisoners of war or civilian internees). Internal inspections as well as independent mechanisms should have timely access to all places where persons are deprived of their liberty for

monitoring purposes at all times. In times of armed conflict, the location of all detention facilities should be disclosed to the International Committee of the Red Cross.

2. Safeguards for persons deprived of their liberty should be fully respected. No undue restrictions on these safeguards under counter-terrorism or emergency legislation are permissible. In particular, effective *habeas corpus* reviews by independent judicial bodies are central to ensuring respect for the right to personal liberty. Therefore domestic legislative frameworks should not allow for any exceptions from *habeas corpus*, operating independently from the detaining authority and from the place and form of deprivation of liberty. The study has shown that judicial bodies can play a crucial role in protecting people against secret detention. The law should foresee penalties for officials who refuse to disclose relevant information during *habeas corpus* proceedings.

3. All steps necessary to ensure that the immediate families of those detained are informed of their relatives' capture, location, legal status, and condition of health should be taken in a timely manner.

4. Any action by intelligence services should be governed by law, which in turn should be in conformity with international norms. To ensure accountability in intelligence cooperation, truly independent intelligence review and oversight mechanisms should be established and enhanced. Such mechanisms should have access to any information, including sensitive information. They should be mandated to undertake reviews and investigate upon their initiative, and to make public reports.

5. Institutions strictly independent from those which have been alleged of having been involved in secret detention should promptly investigate any allegations of secret detention and "extraordinary rendition". Those individuals, who are found to have participated in secretly detaining persons and any unlawful acts perpetrated during such detention, including their superiors if they ordered, encouraged or consented to secret detentions, should be prosecuted without delay and where found guilty given sentences commensurate with the gravity of the acts perpetrated.

6. The status of all pending investigations into allegations of ill-treatment and torture of detainees and detainee deaths in custody must be made public. No evidence or information that has been obtained by torture or cruel, inhuman and degrading treatment may be used in any proceedings.

7. Transfers or the facilitation of transfers from one State to the custody of authorities of another State must be carried out under judicial supervision and in line with international standards. The principle of non-refoulement of persons to countries where they would be at risk of torture or other inhuman, cruel or degrading treatment must be honoured.

8. Victims of secret detention should be provided with judicial remedies and reparation in accordance with relevant international norms. These international standards recognize the right of victims to adequate, effective and prompt reparation which should be proportionate to the gravity of the violations and the harm suffered. As families of disappeared persons have been recognized as victims under international law, they should also benefit from rehabilitation and compensation.

9. States should ratify and implement the International Covenant on Civil and Political Rights and the Convention against Torture. Given that the Optional Protocol to the Convention against Torture (OPCAT) requires the setting up of monitoring systems covering all situations of deprivation of liberty, adhering to this international instrument adds a layer of protection. States should ratify the OPCAT and create independent national preventive mechanisms that are in compliance with the Paris Principles, and ratify the International Convention for the Protection of All Persons from Enforced Disappearance. Other regional systems may wish to replicate the system put in place by the Inter-American Convention on Forced Disappearance of Persons.

10. Governments have an obligation to protect their citizens abroad and provide consular protection to ensure that foreign States comply with their obligations under international law, including international human rights law.

11. Under international human rights law, states have the obligation to provide witness protection. But doing so is also a precondition for effectively combating secret detention.

CHAPTER 9

SUMMARY EXECUTION AND DEATH PENALTY

Comments: The United Nations has continuously expressed concern over the question of capital punishment. The General Assembly, in its resolutions has urged member States to restrict the number of offences for which capital punishment may be imposed, with a view to the desirability of protection of the rights of those facing the death penalty and abolishing this punishment in all countries. In 1984, the General Assembly adopted safeguards guaranteeing protection of the rights of those facing the death penalty. It also urged States to ensure that capital punishment be imposed only for the most serious crimes. These safeguards cover, *inter alia*, the right to benefit from lighter penalties under certain conditions and to appeal and to seek pardon; exemptions from capital punishment for persons below 18 years of age, pregnant women, new mothers and persons who have become insane; necessary evidentiary requirements and suspension of executions.

In a number of countries, impunity continues to prevail and often leads to extrajudicial, summary or arbitrary executions. The States have an obligation to conduct exhaustive and impartial investigations into all suspected cases of extrajudicial, summary or arbitrary executions, to identify and bring to justice those responsible, while ensuring the right of every person to a fair and public hearing by a competent, independent and impartial tribunal established by law, to grant adequate compensation within a reasonable time to the victims or their families and to adopt all necessary measures, including legal and judicial, in order to bring an end to impunity and to prevent the recurrence of such executions, as stated in the Principles on the Effective Prevention and Investigation of Extra-legal, Arbitrary and Summary Executions.

9.1 SAFEGURADS GUARANTEEING PROTECTION OF THE RIGHTS OF THOSE FACING THE DEATH PENALTY, 1984 [1]

1. In countries which have not abolished the death penalty, capital punishment may be imposed only for the most serious crimes, it being understood that their scope should not go beyond intentional crimes with lethal or other extremely grave consequences.

2. Capital punishment may be imposed only for a crime for which the death penalty is prescribed by law at the time of its commission, it being understood that if, subsequent to the commission of the crime, provision is made by law for the imposition of a lighter penalty, the offender shall benefit thereby.

3. Persons below 18 years of age at the time of the commission of the crime shall not be sentenced to death, nor shall the death sentence be carried out on pregnant women, or on new mothers, or on persons who have become insane.

4. Capital punishment may be imposed only when the guilt of the person charged is based upon clear and convincing evidence leaving no room for an alternative explanation of the facts.

5. Capital punishment may only be carried out pursuant to a final judgement rendered by a competent court after legal process which gives all possible safeguards to ensure a fair trial, at least equal to those contained in article 14 of the International Covenant on Civil and Political Rights, including the right of anyone suspected of or charged with a crime for which capital punishment may be imposed to adequate legal assistance at all stages of the proceedings.

6. Anyone sentenced to death shall have the right to appeal to a court of higher jurisdiction, and steps should be taken to ensure that such appeals shall become mandatory.

7. Anyone sentenced to death shall have the right to seek pardon, or commutation of sentence; pardon or commutation of sentence may be granted in all cases of capital punishment.

8. Capital punishment shall not be carried out pending any appeal or other recourse procedure or other proceeding relating to pardon or commutation of the sentence.

9. Where capital punishment occurs, it shall be carried out so as to inflict the minimum possible suffering.

---

[1] ECOSOC resolution 1984/50, annex, 1984 UN ESCOR Supp. (No. 1) at 33, UN Doc. E/1984/84 (1984).

9.2 PRINCIPLES ON THE EFFECTIVE PREVENTION AND INVESTIGATION OF EXTRA-LEGAL, ARBITRARY AND SUMMARY EXECUTIONS, 1989 [2]

Prevention

1. Governments shall prohibit by law all extra-legal, arbitrary and summary executions and shall ensure that any such executions are recognized as offences under their criminal laws, and are punishable by appropriate penalties which take into account the seriousness of such offences. Exceptional circumstances including a state of war or threat of war, internal political instability or any other public emergency may not be invoked as a justification of such executions. Such executions shall not be carried out under any circumstances including, but not limited to, situations of internal armed conflict, excessive or illegal use of force by a public official or other person acting in an official capacity or by a person acting at the instigation, or with the consent or acquiescence of such person, and situations in which deaths occur in custody. This prohibition shall prevail over decrees issued by governmental authority.

2. In order to prevent extra-legal, arbitrary and summary executions, Governments shall ensure strict control, including a clear chain of command over all officials responsible for apprehension, arrest, detention, custody and imprisonment, as well as those officials authorized by law to use force and firearms.

3. Governments shall prohibit orders from superior officers or public authorities authorizing or inciting other persons to carry out any such extralegal, arbitrary or summary executions. All persons shall have the right and the duty to defy such orders. Training of law enforcement officials shall emphasize the above provisions.

4. Effective protection through judicial or other means shall be guaranteed to individuals and groups who are in danger of extra-legal, arbitrary or summary executions, including those who receive death threats.

5. No one shall be involuntarily returned or extradited to a country where there are substantial grounds for believing that he or she may become a victim of extra-legal, arbitrary or summary execution in that country.

6. Governments shall ensure that persons deprived of their liberty are held in officially recognized places of custody, and that accurate information on their custody and whereabouts, including transfers, is made promptly available to their relatives and lawyer or other persons of confidence.

---

[2] ECOSOC resolution 1989/65, annex, 1989 UN ESCOR Supp. (No. 1) at 52, UN Doc. E/1989/89 (1989)

7. Qualified inspectors, including medical personnel, or an equivalent independent authority, shall conduct inspections in places of custody on a regular basis, and be empowered to undertake unannounced inspections on their own initiative, with full guarantees of independence in the exercise of this function. The inspectors shall have unrestricted access to all persons in such places of custody, as well as to all their records.

8. Governments shall make every effort to prevent extra-legal, arbitrary and summary executions through measures such as diplomatic intersession, improved access of complainants to intergovernmental and judicial bodies, and public denunciation. Intergovernmental mechanisms shall be used to investigate reports of any such executions and to take effective action against such practices. Governments, including those of countries where extra-legal, arbitrary and summary executions are reasonably suspected to occur, shall cooperate fully in international investigations on the subject.

Investigation

9. There shall be thorough, prompt and impartial investigation of all suspected cases of extra-legal, arbitrary and summary executions, including eases where complaints by relatives or other reliable reports suggest unnatural death in the above circumstances. Governments shall maintain investigative offices and procedures to undertake such inquiries. The purpose of the investigation shall be to determine the cause, manner and time of death, the person responsible, and any pattern or practice which may have brought about that death. It shall include an adequate autopsy, collection and analysis of all physical and documentary evidence and statements from witnesses. The investigation shall distinguish between natural death, accidental death, suicide and homicide.

10. The investigative authority shall have the power to obtain all the information necessary to the inquiry. Those persons conducting the investigation shall have at their disposal all the necessary budgetary and technical resources for effective investigation. They shall also have the authority to oblige officials allegedly involved in any such executions to appear and testify. The same shall apply to any witness. To this end, they shall be entitled to issue summonses to witnesses, including the officials allegedly involved and to demand the production of evidence.

11. In cases in which the established investigative procedures are inadequate because of lack of expertise or impartiality, because of the importance of the matter or because of the apparent existence of a pattern of abuse, and in cases where there are complaints from the family of the victim about these inadequacies or other substantial reasons, Governments shall pursue investigations through an independent commission of inquiry or similar procedure. Members of such a commission shall be chosen for their recognized impartiality, competence and

independence as individuals. In particular, they shall be independent of any institution, agency or person that may be the subject of the inquiry. The commission shall have the authority to obtain all information necessary to the inquiry and shall conduct the inquiry as provided for under these Principles.

12. The body of the deceased person shall not be disposed of until an adequate autopsy is conducted by a physician, who shall, if possible, be an expert in forensic pathology. Those conducting the autopsy shall have the right of access to all investigative data, to the place where the body was discovered, and to the place where the death is thought to have occurred. If the body has been buried and it later appears that an investigation is required, the body shall be promptly and competently exhumed for an autopsy. If skeletal remains are discovered, they should be carefully exhumed and studied according to systematic anthropological techniques.

13. The body of the deceased shall be available to those conducting the autopsy for a sufficient amount of time to enable a thorough investigation to be carried out. The autopsy shall, at a minimum, attempt to establish the identity of the deceased and the cause and manner of death. The time and place of death shall also be determined to the extent possible. Detailed colour photographs of the deceased shall be included in the autopsy report in order to document and support the findings of the investigation. The autopsy report must describe any and all injuries to the deceased including any evidence of torture.

14. In order to ensure objective results, those conducting the autopsy must be able to function impartially and independently of any potentially implicated persons or organizations or entities.

15. Complainants, witnesses, those conducting the investigation and their families shall be protected from violence, threats of violence or any other form of intimidation. Those potentially implicated in extra-legal, arbitrary or summary executions shall be removed from any position of control or power, whether direct or indirect. over complainants, witnesses and their families, as well as over those conducting investigations.

16. Families of the deceased and their legal representatives shall be informed of, and have access to any hearing as well as to all information relevant to the investigation, and shall be entitled to present other evidence. The family of the deceased shall have the right to insist that a medical or other qualified representative be present at the autopsy. When the identity of a deceased person has been determined, a notification of death shall be posted, and the family or relatives of the deceased shall be informed immediately. The body of the deceased shall be returned to them upon completion of the investigation.

17. A written report shall be made within a reasonable period of time on the methods and findings of such investigations. The report shall be made public immediately and shall include the scope of the inquiry, procedures and methods used to evaluate evidence as well as conclusions and recommendations based on findings of fact and on applicable law. The report shall also describe in detail specific events that were found to have occurred and the evidence upon which such findings were based, and list the names of witnesses who testified, with the exception of those whose identities have been withheld for their own protection. The Government shall, within a reasonable period of time, either reply to the report of the investigation, or indicate the steps to be taken in response to it.

Legal proceedings

18. Governments shall ensure that persons identified by the investigation as having participated in extra-legal, arbitrary or summary executions in any territory under their jurisdiction are brought to justice. Governments shall either bring such persons to justice or cooperate to extradite any such persons to other countries wishing to exercise jurisdiction. This principle shall apply irrespective of who and where the perpetrators or the victims are, their nationalities or where the offence was committed.

19. Without prejudice to principle 3 above, an order from a superior officer or a public authority may not be invoked as a justification for extralegal, arbitrary or summary executions. Superiors, officers or other public officials may be held responsible for acts committed by officials under their authority if they had a reasonable opportunity to prevent such acts. In no circumstances, including a state of war, siege or other public emergency, shall blanket immunity from prosecution be granted to any person allegedly involved in extra-legal, arbitrary or summary executions.

20. The families and dependents of victims of extra-legal, arbitrary or summary executions shall be entitled to fair and adequate compensation within a reasonable period of time.

9.3 UNITED NATION MANUAL ON THE EFFECTIVE PREVENTION AND INVESTIGATION OF EXTRA-LEGAL, ARBITRARY AND SUMMARY EXECUTIONS, 1991[3]

Introduction

In many countries throughout the world, extra-legal, arbitrary and summary executions take place undocumented and undetected. These executions include: (a) political assassinations; (b) deaths resulting from torture or ill-treatment in prison or detention; (c) death resulting

[3] UN Doc. E/ST/CSDHA/12 (1991).

from enforced "disappearances"; (d) deaths resulting from the excessive use of force by law-enforcement personnel; (e) executions without due process; and (f) acts of genocide. The failure to detect and disclose these executions to the international community is a major obstacle to the rendering of justice for past executions and the prevention of future executions.

This Manual is the result of several years of analysis, research and drafting undertaken because of extra-legal, arbitrary and summary executions throughout the world. Its purpose is to supplement the "Principles on the effective prevention and investigation of extra-legal, arbitrary and summary executions", adopted by the Economic and Social Council in its resolution 1989/65 of 24 May 1989, on the recommendation of the Committee on Crime Prevention and Control, at its tenth session, held in Vienna, from 5 to 16 February 1990.

Model Protocol for a Legal Investigation of Extra-Legal Arbitrary and Summary Executions (Minnesota Protocol)

A. Introduction

B. Purposes of an inquiry

C. Procedures for an inquiry

1. Processing of the crime scene
2. Processing of the evidence
3. Avenues to investigation
4. Personal testimony

D. Commission of inquiry

1. Factors triggering a special investigation
2. Defining the scope of the inquiry
3. Power of the commission
4. Membership qualifications
5. Number of commissioners
6. Choosing a commission counsel

7. Choosing expert advisors
8. Choosing investigators
9. Protection of witnesses
10. Proceedings
11. Notice of inquiry
12. Receipt of evidence
13. Rights of parties
14. Evaluation of evidence
15. The report of the commission
16. Response of the Government

E. Model Autopsy Protocol

1. Introduction
2. Proposed model autopsy protocol
    (a) Scene investigation
    (b) Autopsy

F. Model Protocol for Disinterment and Analysis of Skeletal Remains

1. Introduction
2. Proposed model skeletal analysis protocol
    (a) Scene investigation
    (b) Laboratory analysis of skeletal remains
    (c) Final report
    (d) Repository for evidence

MINNESOTA PROTOCOL

A. Introduction

Suspected extra-legal, arbitrary and summary executions can be investigated under established national or local laws and can lead to criminal proceedings. In some cases, however, investigative procedures may be inadequate because of the lack of resources and expertise or because the agency assigned to conduct the investigation may be partial. Hence, such criminal proceedings are less likely to be brought to a successful outcome.

The following comments may enable those conducting investigations and other parties, as appropriate, to obtain some in-depth guidance for conducting investigations. Such guidance in a general way, has been set out in the Principles on the Effective Prevention and Investigation of Extra-Legal, Arbitrary and Summary Executions. The guidelines set forth in this proposed model protocol for a legal investigation of extra-legal, arbitrary and summary executions are not binding. Instead, the model protocol is meant to be illustrative of methods for carrying out the standards enumerated in the Principles.

By definition, this model protocol cannot be exhaustive as the variety of legal and political arrangements escapes its application. Also, investigative techniques vary from country to country and these cannot be standardized in the form of internationally adopted principles. Consequently, additional comments may be relevant for the practical implementation of the Principles.

Sections B and C of this model protocol contain guidelines for the investigation of all violent, sudden, unexpected or suspicious deaths, including suspected extra-legal, arbitrary and summary executions. These guidelines apply to investigations conducted by law enforcement personnel and by members of an independent commission of inquiry.

Section D provides guidelines for establishing a special independent commission of inquiry. These guidelines are based on the experiences of several countries that have established independent commissions to investigate alleged arbitrary executions.

Several considerations should be taken into account when a Government decides to establish an independent commission of inquiry. First, persons subject to an inquiry should be guaranteed the minimum procedural safeguards protected by international law at all stages of the investigation. Secondly, investigators should have the support of adequate technical and administrative personnel, as well as access to objective, impartial legal advice to ensure that the investigation will produce admissible evidence for later criminal proceedings. Thirdly, investigators should receive the full scope of the Government's resources and powers. Finally, investigators should have the power to seek help from the international community of experts in law, medicine and forensic sciences.

The fundamental principles of any viable investigation into the causes of death are competence, thoroughness, promptness and impartiality of the investigation, which flow from paragraphs 9 and 11 of the Principles. These elements can be adapted to any legal system and should guide all investigations of alleged extra-legal, arbitrary and summary executions.

B. Purposes of an inquiry

As set out in paragraph 9 of the Principles, the broad purpose of an inquiry is to discover the truth about the events leading to the suspicious death of a victim. To fulfil this purpose, those conducting the inquiry shall, at a minimum, seek:

(a) To identify the victim;

(b) To recover and preserve evidentiary material related to the death to aid in any potential prosecution of those responsible;

(c) To identify possible witnesses and obtain statements from them concerning the death;

(d) To determine the cause, manner, location and time of death, as well as any pattern or practice that may have brought about the death;

(e) To distinguish between natural death, accidental death, suicide and homicide;

(f) To identify and apprehend the person(s) involved in the death;

(g) To bring the suspected perpetrator(s) before a competent court established by law.

C. Procedures of an inquiry

One of the most important aspects of a thorough and impartial investigation of an extra-legal, arbitrary and summary execution is the collection and analysis of evidence. It is essential to recover and preserve physical evidence, and to interview potential witnesses so that the circumstances surrounding a suspicious death can be clarified.

1. Processing of the crime scene

Law enforcement personnel and other non-medical investigators should co-ordinate their efforts in processing the scene with those of medical personnel. Persons conducting an investigation should have access to the scene where the body was discovered and to the scene where the death may have occurred:

(a) The area around the body should be closed off. Only investigator and their staff should be allowed entry into the area;

(b) Colour photographs of the victim should be taken as these, in comparison with black and white photographs, may reveal in more detail the nature and circumstances of the victim's death;

(c) Photographs should be taken of the scene (interior and exterior) of any other physical evidence;

(d) A record should be made of the body position and condition of the clothing;

(e) The following factors may be helpful in estimating the time of death:

(i) Temperature of the body (warm, cool, cold);

(ii) Location and degree of fixation of lividity;

(iii) Rigidity of the body;

(iv) Stage of its decomposition;

(f) Examination of the scene for blood should take place. Any samples of blood, hair, fibres and threads should be collected and preserved;

(g) If the victim appears to have been sexually assaulted, this fact should be recorded;

(h) A record should be made of any vehicles found in the area;

(i) Castings should be made and preserved of pry marks, tyre or shoe impressions, or any other impressions of an evidentiary nature;

(j) Any evidence of weapons, such as guns, projectiles, bullets and cartridge cases, should be taken and preserved. When applicable, tests for gunshot residue and trace metal detection should be performed;

(k) Any fingerprints should be located, developed, lifted and preserved;

(1) A sketch of the crime scene to scale should be made showing all relevant details of the crime, such as the location of weapons, furniture, vehicles, surrounding terrain, including the position, height and width of items, and their relationship to each other;

(m) A record of the identity of all persons at the scene should be made, including complete names, addresses and telephone numbers;

(n) Information should be obtained from scene witnesses, including those who last saw the decedent alive, when, where and under what circumstances;

(o) Any relevant papers, records or documents should be saved for evidentiary use and handwriting analysis.

2. Processing of the evidence

(a) The body must be identified by reliable witnesses and other objective methods;

(b) A report should be made detailing any observations at the scene, actions of investigators and disposition of all evidence recovered;

(c) Property forms listing all evidence should be completed;

(d) Evidence must be properly collected, handled, packaged, labelled and placed in safekeeping to prevent contamination and loss of evidence.

3. Avenues to investigation

(a) What evidence is there, if any, that the death was premeditated and intentional, rather than accidental? Is there any evidence of torture?

(b) What weapon or means was used and in what manner?

(c) How many persons were involved in the death?

(d) What other crime, if any, and the exact details thereof, was committed during or associated with the death?

(e) What was the relationship between the suspected perpetrator(s) and the victim prior to the death?

(f) Was the victim a member of any political, religious, ethnic or social group(s), and could this have been a motive for the death?

4. Personal testimony

(a) Investigators should identify and interview all potential witnesses to the crime, including:

(i) Suspects;

(ii) Relatives and friends of the victim;

(iii) Persons who knew the victim;

(iv) Individuals residing or located in the area of the crime;

(v) Persons who knew or had knowledge of the suspects;

(vi) Persons who may have observed either the crime, the scene, the victim or the suspects in the week prior to the execution;

(vii) Persons having knowledge of possible motives;

(b) Interviews should take place as soon as possible and should be written and/or taped. All tapes should be transcribed and maintained;

(c) Witnesses should be interviewed individually, and assurance should be given that any possible means of protecting their safety before, during and after the proceedings will be used, if necessary.

D. Commission of inquiry

In cases where government involvement is suspected, an objective and impartial investigation may not be possible unless a special commission of inquiry is established. A commission of inquiry may also be necessary where the expertise of the investigators is called into question. This section sets out factors that give rise to a presumption of government complicity, partiality or insufficient expertise on the part of those conducting the investigation. Any one of these presumptions should trigger the creation of a special commission of inquiry. It then sets out procedures that can be used as a model for the creation and function of commissions of inquiry. The procedures were derived from the experience of major inquiries that have been mounted to investigate executions or similarly grievous cases of human rights violations.

Establishing a commission of inquiry entails defining the scope of the inquiry, appointing commission members and staff, determining the type of proceedings to be followed and selecting procedures governing those proceedings, and authorizing the commission to report on its findings and make recommendations. Each of these areas will be covered separately.

1. Factors triggering a special investigation

Factors that support a belief that the Government was involved in the execution, and that should trigger the creation of a special impartial investigation commission include:

(a) Where the political views, religious or ethnic affiliation, or social status of the victim give rise to a suspicion of government involvement or complicity in the death because of any one or combination of the following factors:

(i) Where the victim was last seen alive in police custody or detention;

(ii) Where the modus operandi is recognizably attributable to government-sponsored death squads;

(iii) Where persons in the Government or associated with the Government have attempted to obstruct or delay the investigation of the execution;

(iv) Where the physical or testimonial evidence essential to the investigation becomes unavailable.

(b) As set out in paragraph 11 of the Principles, an independent commission of inquiry or similar procedure should also be established where a routine investigation is inadequate for the following reasons:

(i) The lack of expertise; or

(ii) The lack of impartiality; or

(iii) The importance of the matter; or

(iv) The apparent existence of a pattern of abuse; or

(v) Complaints from the family of the victim about the above inadequacies or other substantial reasons.

2. Defining the scope of the inquiry

Governments and organizations establishing commissions of inquiry need to define the scope of the inquiry by including terms of reference in their authorization. Defining the commission's terms of reference can greatly increase its success by giving legitimacy to the proceedings, assisting commission members in reaching a consensus on the scope of inquiry and providing a measure by which the commission's final report can be judged. Recommendations for defining terms of reference are as follows:

(a) They should be neutrally framed so that they do not suggest a predetermined outcome. To be neutral, terms of reference must not limit investigations in areas that might uncover government responsibility for extra-legal, arbitrary and summary executions;

(b) They should state precisely which events and issues are to be investigated and addressed in the commission's final report;

(c) They should provide flexibility in the scope of inquiry to ensure that thorough investigation by the commission is not hampered by overly restrictive or overly broad terms of reference. The necessary flexibility may be accomplished, for example by permitting the commission to amend its terms of reference as necessary. It is important, however, that the commission keep the public informed of any amendments to its charge.

3. Power of the commission

The principles set out in a general manner the powers of the commission. More specifically such a commission would need the following:

(a) To have the authority to obtain all information necessary to the inquiry, for example, for determining the cause, manner and time of death, including the authority to compel testimony under legal sanction, to order the production of documents including government and medical records, and to protect witnesses, families of the victim and other sources;

(b) To have the authority to issue a public report;

(c) To have the authority to prevent the burial or other disposal of the body until an adequate postmortem examination has been performed;

(d) To have the authority to conduct on-site visits, both at the scene where the body was discovered and at the scene where the death may have occurred;

(e) To have the authority to receive evidence from witnesses and organizations located outside the country.

4. Membership qualifications

Commission members should be chosen for their recognized impartiality, competence and independence as individuals:

- Impartiality: Commission members should not be closely associated with any individual, government entity, political party or other organization potentially implicated in the execution or disappearance, or an organization or group associated with the victim, as this may damage the commission's credibility.

- Competence: Commission members must be capable of evaluating and weighing evidence, and exercising sound judgement. If possible, commissions of inquiry should include individuals with expertise in law, medicine, forensic science and other specialized fields, as appropriate.

- Independence: Members of the commission should have a reputation in their community for honesty and fairness.

5. Number of commissioners

The Principles do not contain a provision on the number of members of the commission, but it would not be unreasonable to note that objectivity of the investigation and commission's findings may, among other things, depend on whether it has three or more members rather than one or two. Investigations into extra-legal, arbitrary and summary executions should, in general, not be conducted by a single commissioner. A single, isolated commissioner will generally be limited in the depth of investigation he or she can conduct alone. In addition, a single commissioner will have to make controversial and important decisions without debate, and will be particularly vulnerable to governmental and other outside pressure.

6. Choosing a commission counsel

Commissions of inquiry should have impartial, expert counsel. Where the commission is investigating allegations of governmental misconduct, it would be advisable to appoint counsel outside the Ministry of Justice. The chief counsel to the commission should be insulated from political influence, as through civil service tenure, or status as a wholly independent member of the bar.

7. Choosing expert advisors

The investigation will often require expert advisors. Technical expertise in such areas as pathology, forensic science and ballistics should be available to the commission.

8. Choosing investigators

To conduct a completely impartial and thorough investigation, the commission will almost always need its own investigators to pursue leads and to develop evidence. The credibility of an inquiry will be significantly enhanced to the extent that the commission can rely on its own investigators.

9. Protection of witnesses

(a) The Government shall protect complainants, witnesses, those conducting the investigation, and their families from violence, threats of violence or any other form of intimidation;

(b) If the commission concludes that there is a reasonable fear of persecution, harassment, or harm to any witness or prospective witness, the commission may find it advisable:

(i) To hear the evidence in camera;

(ii) To keep the identity of the informant or witness confidential;

(iii) To use only such evidence as will not present a risk of identifying the witness;

(iv) To take any other appropriate measures.

10. Proceedings

It follows from general principles of criminal procedure that hearings should be conducted in public, unless in camera proceedings are necessary to protect the safety of a witness. In camera proceedings should be recorded and the closed, unpublished record kept in a known location. Occasionally, complete secrecy may be required to encourage testimony, and the commission will want to hear witnesses privately, informally and without recording testimony.

11. Notice of inquiry

Wide notice of the establishment of a commission and the subject of the inquiry should be given. The notice should also include an invitation to submit relevant information and/or written statements to the commission, and instructions to persons wishing to testify. Notice can be disseminated through newspapers, magazines, radio, television, leaflets and posters.

12. Receipt of evidence

Power to compel evidence: As emphasized in Principle 10, commissions of inquiry should have the power to compel testimony and production of documents: in this context, Principle 10 refers to "the authority to oblige officials" allegedly involved in extra-legal, arbitrary and summary executions. Practically, this authority may involve the power to impose fines or sentences if the Government or individuals refuse to comply.

Use of witness statements: Commissions of inquiry should invite persons to testify or submit written statements as a first step in gathering evidence Written statements may become an important source of evidence if their author become afraid to testify, cannot travel to proceedings, or are otherwise unavailable.

Use of evidence from other proceedings: Commissions of inquiry should review other proceedings that could provide relevant information. For example the commission should obtain the findings from an inquest into cause of death conducted by a coroner or medical examiner. Such inquests generally rely on postmortem or autopsy examinations. A commission of inquiry should review the inquest and the results of the autopsy presented to the inquest to determine if they were conducted thoroughly and impartially. If the inquest and autopsy were so conducted, the coroner's findings are entitled to be given great weight.

13. Rights of parties

As mentioned in Principle 16, families of the deceased and their legal representatives shall be informed of, and have access to, any hearing and to all information relevant to the investigation, and shall be entitled to present evidence. This particular emphasis on the role of the family as a party to the proceedings implies the specially important role the family's interests play in the conduct of the investigation. However, all other interested parties should also have the opportunity at being heard. As mentioned in Principle 10, the investigative body shall be entitled to issue summons to witnesses, including the officials allegedly involved and to demand the production of evidence. All these witnesses should be permitted legal counsel if they are likely to be harmed by the inquiry, for example, when their testimony could expose them to criminal charges or civil liability. Witnesses may not be compelled to testify against themselves regarding matter unrelated to the scope of inquiry. There should be an opportunity for the effective questioning of witnesses by the commission. Parties to the inquiry should be allowed to submit written questions to the commission.

14. Evaluation of evidence

The commission shall assess all information and evidence it receives to determine its relevance, veracity, reliability and probity. The commission should evaluate oral testimony based upon the demeanour and overall credibility of the witness. Corroboration of evidence from several sources will increase the probative value of such evidence. The reliability of hearsay evidence from several sources will increase the probative value of such evidence. The reliability of hearsay evidence must be considered carefully before the commission should accept it as fact. Testimony not tested by cross-examination must also be viewed with caution. In camera testimony preserved in a closed record or not recorded at all is often not subjected to cross-examination and therefore may be given less weight.

15. The report of the commission

As stated in Principle 17, the commission should issue a public report within a reasonable period of time. It may be added that where the commission is not unanimous in its findings, the minority commissioner(s) should file a dissenting opinion.

From the practical experience gathered, commission of inquiry reports should contain the following information:

(a) The scope of inquiry and terms of reference;

(b) The procedures and methods of evaluating evidence;

(c) A list of all witnesses who have testified, except for those whose identities are withheld for protection and who have testified in camera, and exhibits received in evidence;

(d) The time and place of each sitting (this might be annexed to the report);

(e) The background to the inquiry such as relevant social, political and economic conditions;

(f) The specific events that occurred and the evidence upon which such findings are based;

(g) The law upon which the commission relied;

(h) The commission's conclusions based upon applicable law and findings of fact;

(i) Recommendations based upon the findings of the commission.

16. Response of the Government

The Government should either reply publicly to the commission's report or should indicate what steps it intends to take in response to the report.

E. Model Autopsy Protocol

1. Introduction

Difficult or sensitive cases should ideally be the responsibility of an objective, experienced, well-equipped and well-trained prosector (the person performing the autopsy and preparing the written report) who is separate from any potentially involved political organization or entity. Unfortunately, this ideal is often unattainable. This proposed model autopsy protocol includes a comprehensive checklist of the steps in a basic forensic postmortem examination that should be followed to the extent possible given the resources available. Use of this autopsy protocol will permit early and final resolution of potentially controversial cases and will thwart the speculation and innuendo that are fueled by unanswered, partially answered or poorly answered questions in the investigation of an apparently suspicious death.

This model autopsy protocol is intended to have several applications and may be of value to the following categories of individuals:

(a) Experienced forensic pathologists may follow this model autopsy protocol to ensure a systematic examination and to facilitate meaningful positive or negative criticism by later observers. While -trained pathologists may justifiably abridge certain aspects of the postmortem examination or written descriptions of their findings in routine cases, abridged examinations or reports are never appropriate in potentially controversial cases. Rather, a systematic and comprehensive examination and report are required to prevent the omission or loss of important details;

(b) General pathologists or other physicians who have not been trained in forensic pathology but are familiar with basic postmortem examination techniques may supplement their customary autopsy procedures with this model autopsy protocol. It may also alert them to situations in which they should seek consultation, as written material cannot replace the knowledge gained through experience;

(c) Independent consultants whose expertise has been requested in observing, performing or reviewing an autopsy may cite this model autopsy protocol and its proposed minimum criteria as a basis for their actions or opinions;

(d) Governmental authorities, international political organizations, law enforcement agencies, families or friends of decedents, or representatives of potential defendants charged with responsibility for a death may use this model autopsy protocol to establish appropriate procedures for the postmortem examination prior to its performance;

(e) Historians, journalists, attorneys, judges, other physicians and representatives of the public may also use this model autopsy protocol as a benchmark for evaluating an autopsy and its findings;

(f) Governments or individuals who are attempting either to establish or upgrade their medico-legal system for investigating deaths may use this model autopsy protocol as a guideline, representing the procedures and goals to be incorporated into an ideal medico-legal system.

While performing any medico-legal death investigation, the proseutor should collect information that will establish the identity of the deceased, the time and place of death, the cause of death, and the manner or mode of death (homicide, suicide, accident or natural).

It is of the utmost importance that an autopsy performed following a controversial death be thorough in scope. The documentation and recording of the autopsy findings should be equally thorough so as to permit meaningful use of the autopsy results. It is important to have as few omissions or discrepancies as possible, as proponents of different interpretations of a case may take advantage of any perceived shortcomings in the investigation. An autopsy performed in a controversial death should meet certain minimum criteria if the autopsy report is to be proffered as meaningful or conclusive by the prosector, the autopsy's sponsoring agency or governmental unit, or anyone else attempting to make use of such an autopsy's findings or conclusions.

This model autopsy protocol is designed to be used in diverse situations. Resources such as autopsy rooms, X-ray equipment or adequately trained personnel are not available everywhere. Forensic pathologists must operate under widely divergent political systems. In addition, social and religious customs vary widely throughout the world; an autopsy is an expected and routine procedure in some areas, while it is abhorred in others. A prosector, therefore, may not always be able to follow all of the steps in this protocol when performing autopsies. Variation from this protocol may be inevitable or even preferable in some cases. It is suggested, however, that any major deviations, with the supporting reasons, should be noted.

It is important that the body should be made available to the prosector for a minimum of 12 hours in order to assure an adequate and unhurried examination. Unrealistic limits or conditions are occasionally placed upon the prosector with respect to the length of time permitted for the examination or the circumstances under which an examination is allowed. When conditions are imposed, the prosector should be able to refuse to perform a compromised examination and should prepare a report explaining this position. Such a refusal should not be interpreted as indicating that an examination was unnecessary or inappropriate. If the prosector decides to proceed with the examination notwithstanding difficult conditions or circumstances, he or she should include in the autopsy report an explanation of the limitations or impediments.

Certain steps in this model autopsy protocol have been emphasized by the use of **boldface type**. These represent the most essential elements of the protocol.

2. Proposed model autopsy protocol

(a) Scene investigation

The prosector(s) and medical investigators should have the right of access to the scene where the body is found. The medical personnel should be notified immediately to assure that no alteration of the body has occurred. If access to the scene was denied, if the body was altered or if information was withheld, this should be stated in the prosector's report.

A system for co-ordination between the medical and non-medical investigators (e.g. law enforcement agencies) should be established. This should address such issues as how the prosector will be notified and who will be in charge of the scene. Obtaining certain types of evidence is often the role of the non-medical investigators, but the medical investigators who have access to the body at the scene of death should perform the following steps:

(a) Photograph the body as it is found and after it has been moved;

(b) Record the body position and condition, including body warmth or coolness, lividity and rigidity;

(c) Protect the deceased's hands, e.g. with paper bags;

(d) Note the ambient temperature. In cases where the time of death is an issue, rectal temperature should be recorded and any insects present should be collected for forensic entomological study. Which procedure is applicable will depend on the length of the apparent postmortem interval;

(e) Examine the scene for blood, as this may be useful in identifying suspects;

(f) Record the identities of all persons at the scene;

(g) Obtain information from scene witnesses, including those who last saw the decedent alive, and when, where and under what circumstances. Interview any emergency medical personnel who may have had contact with the body;

(h) Obtain identification of the body and other pertinent information from friends or relatives. Obtain the deceased's medical history from his or her physician(s) and hospital charts, including any previous surgery, alcohol or drug use, suicide attempts and habits;

(i) Place the body in a body pouch or its equivalent. Save this pouch after the body has been removed from it;

(j) Store the body in a secure refrigerated location so that tampering with the body and its evidence cannot occur;

(k) Make sure that projectiles, guns, knives and other weapons are available for examination by the responsible medical personnel;

(1) If the decedent was hospitalized prior to death, obtain admission or blood specimens and any X-rays, and review and summarize hospital records;

(m) Before beginning the autopsy, become familiar with the types of torture or violence that are prevalent in that country or locale.

(b) Autopsy

The following Protocol should be followed during the autopsy:

(a) Record the date, starting and finishing times, and place of the autopsy (a complex autopsy may take as long as an entire working day);

(b) Record the name(s) of the prosector(s), the participating assistant(s), and all other persons present during the autopsy, including the medical and/or scientific degrees and professional, political or administrative affiliations(s) of each. Each person's role in the autopsy should be indicated, and one person should be designated as the principal prosector who will have the authority to direct the performance of the autopsy.

Observers and other team members are subject to direction by, and should not interfere with, the principal prosector. The time(s) during the autopsy when each person is present should be included. The use of a "sign-in" sheet is recommended;

(c) Adequate photographs are crucial for thorough documentation of autopsy findings:

(i) Photographs should be in colour (transparency or negative/ print), in focus, adequately illuminated, and taken by a professional or good quality camera. Each photograph should contain a ruled reference scale, an identifying case name or number, and a sample of standard grey. A description of the camera (including the lens "f-number" and focal length), film and the lighting system must be included in the autopsy report. If more than one camera is utilized, the identifying information should be recorded for each. Photographs should also include information indicating which camera took each picture, if more than one camera is used. The identity of the person taking the photographs should be recorded;

(ii) Serial photographs reflecting the course of the external examination must be included. Photograph the body prior to and following undressing, washing or cleaning and shaving;

(iii) Supplement close-up photographs with distant and/or immediate range photographs to permit orientation and identification of the close-up photographs;

(iv) Photographs should be comprehensive in scope and must confirm the presence of all demonstrable signs of injury or disease commented upon in the autopsy report;

(v) Identifying facial features should be portrayed (after washing or cleaning the body), with photographs of a full frontal aspect of the face, and right and left profiles of the face with hair in normal position and with hair retracted, if necessary, to reveal the ears;

(d) Radiograph the body before it is removed from its pouch or wrappings. X-rays should be repeated both before and after undressing the body. Fluoroscopy may also be performed. Photograph all X-ray films;

(i) Obtain dental X-rays, even if identification has been established in other ways;

(ii) Document any skeletal system injury by X-ray. Skeletal X-rays may also record anatomic defects or surgical procedures. Check especially for fractures of the fingers, toes and other bones in the hands and feet. Skeletal X-rays may also aid in the identification of the deceased, by detecting identifying characteristics, estimating age and height, and determining sex and race. Frontal sinus films should also be taken, as these can be particularly useful for identification purposes;

(iii) Take X-rays in gunshot cases to aid in locating-the projectile(s). Recover, photograph and save any projectile or major projectile fragment that is seen on an X-ray. Other radio-opaque objects (pacemakers, artificial joints or valves, knife fragments etc.) documented with X-rays should also be removed, photographed and saved;

(iv) Skeletal X-rays are essential in children to assist in determining age and developmental status;

(e) Before the clothing is removed, examine the body and the clothing. Photograph the clothed body. Record any jewellery present;

(f) The clothing should be carefully removed over a clean sheet or body pouch. Let the clothing dry if it is bloody or wet. Describe the clothing that is removed and label it in a permanent fashion. Either place the clothes in the custody of a responsible person or keep them, as they may be useful as evidence or for identification;

(g) The external examination, focusing on a search for external evidence of injury is, in most cases, the most important portion of the autopsy;

(i) Photograph all surfaces - 100 per cent of the body area. Take good quality, well-focused, colour photographs with adequate illumination;

(ii) Describe and document the means used to make the identification. Examine the body and record the deceased's apparent age, length, weight, sex, head hair style and length, nutritional status, muscular development and colour of skin, eyes and hair (head, facial and body);

(iii) In children, measure also the head circumference, crown-rump length and crown-heel length;

(iv) Record the degree, location and fixation of rigor and livor mortis;

(v) Note body warmth or coolness and state of preservation; note any decomposition changes, such as skin slippage. Evaluate the general condition of the body and note adipocere formation, maggots, eggs or anything else that suggests the time or place of death;

(vi) With all injuries, record the size, shape, pattern, location (related to obvious anatomic landmarks), colour, course, direction, depth and structure involved. Attempt to distinguish injuries resulting from therapeutic measures from those unrelated to medical treatment. In the description of projectile wounds, note the presence or absence of soot, gunpowder, or singeing. If gunshot residue is present, document it photographically and save it for analysis. Attempt to determine whether the gunshot wound is an entry or exit wound. If an entry wound is present and no exit wound is seen, the projectile must be found and saved or accounted for. Excise wound tract tissue samples for microscopic examination. Tape together the edges of knife wounds to assess the blade size and characteristics;

(vii) Photograph all injuries, taking two colour pictures of each, labelled with the autopsy identification number on a scale that is oriented parallel or perpendicular to the injury. Shave hair where necessary to clarify an injury, and take photographs before and after shaving. Save all hair removed from the site of the injury. Take photographs before and after washing the site of any injury. Wash the body only after any blood or material that may have come from an assailant has been collected and saved;

(viii) Examine the skin. Note and photograph any scars, areas of keloid formation, tattoos, prominent moles, areas of increased or decreased pigmentation, and anything distinctive or unique such as birthmarks. Note any bruises and incise them for delineation of their extent. Excise them for microscopic examination. The head and genital area should be checked with special care. Note any injection sites or puncture wounds and excise them to use for toxicological evaluation. Note any abrasions and excise them; microscopic sections may be useful for attempting to date the time of injury. Note any bite marks; these should be photographed to record the dental pattern, swabbed for saliva testing (before the body is washed) and excised for microscopic examination. Bite marks should also be analysed by a forensic odontologist, if possible. Note any burn marks and attempt to determine the cause (burning rubber, a cigarette, electricity, a blowtorch, acid, hot oil etc.). Excise any suspicious areas for microscopic examination, as it may be possible to distinguish microscopically between burns caused by electricity and those caused by heat;

(ix) Identify and label any foreign object that is recovered, including its relation to specific injuries. Do not scratch the sides or tip of any projectiles. Photograph each projectile and large projectile fragment with an identifying label, and then place each in a sealed, padded and labelled container in order to maintain the chain of custody;

(x) Collect a blood specimen of at least 50 cc from a subclavian or femoral vessel;

(xi) Examine the head and external scalp, bearing in mind that injuries way be hidden by the hair. Shave hair where necessary. Check for fleas and lice, as these way indicate unsanitary conditions prior to death. Note any alopecia as this may be caused by malnutrition, heavy metals (e.g. thallium), drugs or traction. Pull, do not cut, 20 representative head hairs and save them, as hair may also be useful for detecting some drugs and poisons;

(xii) Examine the teeth and note their condition. Record any that are absent, loose or damaged, and record all dental work (restorations, fillings etc.), using a dental identification system to identify each tooth. Check the gums for periodontal disease. Photograph dentures, if any, and save them if the decedent's identity is unknown. Remove the mandible and maxilla if necessary for identification. Check the inside of the mouth and note any evidence of trauma, injection sites, needle marks or biting of the lips, cheeks or tongue. Note any articles or substances in the mouth. In cases of suspected sexual assault, save oral fluid or get a swab for spermatozoa and acid phosphatase evaluation. (Swabs taken at the tooth-gum junction and samples from between the teeth provide the best specimens for identifying spermatozoa.) Also take swabs from the oral cavity for seminal fluid typing. Dry the swabs quickly with cool, blown air if possible, and preserve them in clean plain paper envelopes. If rigor mortis prevents an adequate examination, the masseter muscles may be cut to permit better exposure;

(xiii) Examine the face and note if it is cyanotic or if petechiae are present; a. examine the eyes and view the conjunctiva of both the globes and the eyelids. Note any petechiae in the upper on lower eyelids. Note any scleralicterus. Save contact lenses, if any are present. Collect at least 1 ml of vitreous humor from each eye; b. examine the nose and ears and note any evidence of trauma, haemorrhage or other abnormalities. Examine the tympanic membranes;

(xiv) Examine the neck externally on all aspects and note any contusions, abrasions or petechia. Describe and document injury patterns to differentiate manual, ligature and hanging strangulation. Examine the neck at the conclusion of the autopsy, when the blood has drained out of the area and the tissues are dry;

(xv) Examine all surfaces of the extremities: arms, forearms, wrists, hands, legs and feet, and note any "defence" wounds. Dissect and describe any injuries. Note any bruises about the wrists or ankles that may suggest restraints such as handcuffs or suspension. Examine the medial and lateral surfaces of the fingers, the anterior forearms and the backs of the knees for bruises;

(xvi) Note any broken or missing fingernails. Note any gunpowder residue on the hands, document photographically and save it for analysis. Take fingerprints in all cases. If the decedent's identity is unknown and fingerprints cannot be obtained, remove the "glove" of the skin, if present. Save the fingers if no other means of obtaining fingerprints is possible. Save finger nail clippings and any under-nail tissue (nail scrapings). Examine the fingernail and toenail beds for evidence of object having been pushed beneath the nails. Nails can be removed b, dissecting the lateral margins and proximal base, and then the undersurface of the nails can be inspected. If this is done, the hands must be photographed before and after the nails are removed. Carefully examine the soles of the feet, noting any evidence of beating. Incise the soles to delineate the extent of any injuries. Examine the palms and knees, looking especially for glass shards or lacerations;

(xvii) Examine the external genitalia and note the presence of any foreign material or semen. Note the size, location and number of any abrasions or contusions. Note any injury to the inner thighs or peri-anal area. Look for peri-anal burns;

(xviii) In cases of suspected sexual assault, examine all potentially involved orifices. A speculum should be used to examine the vaginal walls. Collect foreign hair by combing the pubic hair. Pull and save at least 20 of the deceased's own pubic hairs, including roots. Aspirate fluid from the vagina and/or rest, for acid phosphatase, blood group and spermatozoa evaluation. Take swabs from the same areas for seminal fluid typing. Dry the swabs quickly with cool, blown air if possible, and preserve them in clean plain paper envelopes;

(xix) The length of the back, the buttocks and extremities including wrists and ankles must be systematically incised to look for deep injuries. The shoulders, elbows, hips and knee joints must also be incised to look for ligamentous injury;

(h) The internal examination for internal evidence of injury should clarify and augment the external examination;

(i) Be systematic in the internal examination. Perform the examination either by body regions or by systems, including the cardiovascular, respiratory, biliary, gastrointestinal, reticuloendothelial, genitourinary, endocrine, musculoskeletal, and central nervous systems. Record the weight, size, shape, colour and consistency of each organ, and note any neoplasia, inflammation, anomalies, haemorrhage, ischemia, infarcts, surgical procedures or injuries. Take sections of normal and any abnormal areas of each organ for microscopic examination. Take samples of any fractured bones for radiographic and microscopic estimation of the age of the fracture;

(ii) Examine the chest. Note any abnormalities of the breasts. Record any rib fractures, noting whether cardiopulmonary resuscitation was attempted. Before opening, check for pneumothoraces. Record the thickness of subcutaneous fat. Immediately after opening the chest, evaluate the pleural cavities and the pericardial sac for the presence of blood or other fluid, and describe and quantify any fluid present. Save any fluid present until foreign objects are accounted for. Note the presence of air embolism, characterized by frothy blood within the right atrium and right ventricle. Trace any injuries before removing the organs. If blood is not available at other sites, collect a sample directly from the heart. Examine the heart, noting degree and location of coronary artery disease or other abnormalities. Examine the lungs, noting any abnormalities;

(iii) Examine the abdomen and record the amount of subcutaneous fat. Retain 50 grams of adipose tissue for toxicological evaluation. Note the interrelationships of the organs. Trace any injuries before removing the organs. Note any fluid or blood present in the peritoneal cavity, and save it until foreign objects are accounted for. Save all urine and bile for toxicologic examination;

(iv) Remove, examine and record the quantitative information on the liver, spleen, pancreas, kidneys and adrenal glands. Save at least 150 grams each of kidney and liver for toxicological evaluation. Remove the gastrointestinal tract and examine the contents. Note any food present and its degree of digestion. Save the contents of the stomach. If a more detailed toxicological evaluation is desired, the contents of other regions of the gastrointestinal tract may be saved. Examine the rectum and anus for burns, lacerations or other injuries. Locate and retain any foreign bodies present. Examine the aorta, inferior vena cava and iliac vessels;

(v) Examine the organs in the pelvis, including ovaries, fallopian tubes, uterus, vagina, testes, prostate gland, seminal vesicles, urethra and urinary bladder. Trace any injuries before removing the organs. Remove these organs carefully so as not to injure them artifactually. Note any evidence of previous or current pregnancy, miscarriage or delivery. Save any foreign objects within the cervix, uterus, vagina, urethra or rectum;

(vi) Palpate the head and examine the external and internal surfaces of the scalp, noting any trauma or haemorrhage. Note any skull fractures. Remove the calvarium carefully and note epidural and subdural haematomas. Quantify, date and save any haematomas that are present. Remove the dura to examine the internal surface of the skull for fractures. Remove the brain and note any abnormalities. Dissect and describe any injuries. Cerebral cortical atrophy, whether focal or generalized, should be specifically commented upon;

(vii) Evaluate the cerebral vessels. Save at least 150 grams of cerebral tissue for toxicological evaluation. Submerge the brain in fixative prior to examination, if this is indicated;

(viii) Examine the neck after the heart and brain have been removed and the neck vessels have been drained. Remove the neck organs, taking care not to fracture the hyoid bone. Dissect and describe any injuries. Check the mucosa of the larynx, pyriform sinuses and esophagus, and note any petechiae, edema or burns caused by corrosive substances. Note any articles or substances within the lumina of these structures. Examine the thyroid gland. Separate and examine the parathyroid glands, they are readily identifiable;

(ix) Dissect the neck muscles, noting any haemorrhage. Remove all organs, including the tongue. Dissect the muscles from the bones and note any fractures of the hyoid bone or thyroid or cricoid cartilages;

(x) Examine the cervical, thoracic and lumbar spine. Examine the vertebrae from their anterior aspects and note any fractures, dislocations, compressions or haemorrhages. Examine the vertebral bodies. Cerebrospinal fluid may be obtained if additional toxicological evaluation is indicated;

(xi) In cases in which spinal injury is suspected, dissect and describe the spinal cord. Examine the cervical spine anteriorly and note any haemorrhage in the paravertebral muscles. The posterior approach is best for evaluating high cervical injuries. Open the spinal canal and remove the spinal cord. Make transverse sections every 0.5 cm and note any abnormalities;

(i) After the autopsy has been completed, record which specimens have been saved. Label all specimens with the name of the deceased, the autopsy identification number, the date and time of collection, the name of the prosector and the contents. Carefully preserve all evidence and record the chain of custody with appropriate release forms;

(i) Perform appropriate toxicologic tests and retain portions of the tested samples to permit retesting;

a. Tissues: 150 grams of liver and kidney should be saved routinely. Brain, hair and adipose tissue may be saved for additional studies in cases where drugs, poisons or other toxic substances are suspected;

b. Fluids: 50 cc (if possible) of blood (spin and save serum in all or some of the tubes), all available urine, vitreous humor and stomach contents should be saved routinely. Bile, regional gastrointestinal tract contents and cerebrospinal fluid should be saved in cases where drugs, poisons or toxic substances are suspected. Oral, vaginal and rectal fluid should be saved in cases of suspected sexual assault;

(ii) Representative samples of all major organs, including areas of normal and any abnormal tissue, should be processed histologically and stained with hematoxylin and eosin (and other stains as indicated). The slides, wet tissue and paraffin blocks should be kept indefinitely;

(iii) Evidence that must be saved includes:

a. All foreign objects, including projectiles, projectile fragments, pellets, knives and fibres. Projectiles must be subjected to ballistic analysis;

b. All clothes and personal effects of the deceased, worn by or in the possession of the deceased at the time of death;

c. Fingernails and under nail scrapings;

d. Hair, foreign and pubic, in cases of suspected sexual assault;

e. Head hair, in cases where the place of death or location of the body prior to its discovery may be an issue;

(j) After the autopsy, all unretained organs should be replaced in the body, and the body should be well embalmed to facilitate a second autopsy in case one is desired at some future point;

(k) The written autopsy report should address those items that are emphasized in boldface type in the protocol. At the end of the autopsy report should be a summary of the findings and the cause of death. This should include the prosector's comments attributing any injuries to external trauma, therapeutic efforts, postmortem change, or other causes. A full report should be given to the appropriate authorities and to the deceased's family.

F. Model Protocol for Disinterment and Analysis of Skeletal Remains

1. Introduction

This proposed model protocol for the disinterment and analysis of skeletal remains includes a comprehensive checklist of the steps in a basic forensic examination. The objectives of an anthropological investigation are the same as those of a medicolegal investigation of a recently deceased person. The anthropologist must collect information that will establish the identity of the deceased, the time and place of death, the cause of death and the manner or mode of death (homicide, suicide, accident or natural). The approach of the anthropologist differs, however, because of the nature of the material to be examined. Typically, a prosector is required to examine a body, whereas an anthropologist is required to examine a skeleton. The prosector focuses on information obtained from soft tissues, whereas the anthropologist focuses on information from hard tissues. Since decomposition is a continuous process, the work of both specialists can overlap. An anthropologist may examine a fresh body when bone is exposed or when bone trauma is a factor. An experienced prosector may be required when mummified tissues are present. In some circumstances, use of both this protocol and the model autopsy protocol may be necessary to yield the maximum information. The degree of decomposition of the body will dictate the type of investigation and, therefore, the protocol(s) to be followed.

The questions addressed by the anthropologist differ from those pursued in a typical autopsy. The anthropological investigation invests more time and attention to basic questions such as the following:

(a) Are the remains human?

(b) Do they represent a single individual or several?

(c) What was the decedent's sex, race, stature, body weight, handedness and physique?

(d) Are there any skeletal traits or anomalies that could serve to positively identify the decedent?

The time, cause and manner of death are also addressed by the anthropologist, but the margin of error is usually greater than that which can be achieved by an autopsy shortly after death.

This model protocol may be of use in many diverse situations. Its application may be affected, however, by poor conditions, inadequate financial resources or lack of time. Variation from the protocol may be inevitable or even preferable in some cases. It is suggested, however, that any major deviations, with the supporting reasons, should be noted in the final report.

2. Proposed model skeletal analysis protocol

(a) Scene investigation

A burial recovery should be handled with the same exacting care given to a crime-scene search. Efforts should be co-ordinated between the principal investigator and the consulting physical anthropologist or archaeologist. Human remains are frequently exhumed by law enforcement officers or cemetery workers unskilled in the techniques of forensic anthropology. Valuable information may be lost in this manner and false information is sometimes generated. Disinterment by untrained persons should be prohibited. The consulting anthropologist should be present to conduct or supervise the disinterment. Specific problems and procedures accompany the excavation of each type of burial. The amount of information obtained from the excavation depends on knowledge of the burial situation and judgement based on experience. The final report should include a rationale for the excavation procedure.

The following procedure should be followed during disinterment:

(a) Record the date, location, starting and finishing times of the disinterment, and the names of all workers;

(b) Record the information in narrative form, supplemented by sketches and photographs;

(c) Photograph the work area from the same perspective before work begins and after it ends every day to document any disturbance not related to the official procedure;

(d) In some cases, it is necessary to first locate the grave within a given area. There are numerous methods of locating graves, depending on the age of the grave:

(i) An experienced archaeologist may recognize clues such as changes in surface contour and variation in local vegetation;

(ii) A metal probe can be used to locate the less compact soil characteristics of grave fill;

(iii) The area to be explored can be cleared and the top soil scraped away with a flat shovel. Graves appear darker than the surrounding ground because the darker topsoil has mixed with the lighter subsoil in the grave fill. Sometimes a light spraying of the surface with water may enhance a grave's outline;

(e) Classify the burial as follows:

(i) Individual or commingled. A grave may contain the remains of one person buried alone, or it may contain the commingled remains of two or more persons buried either at the same time or over a period of time;

(ii) Isolated or adjacent. An isolated grave is separate from other graves and can be excavated without concern about encroaching upon another grave. Adjacent graves, such as in a crowded cemetery, require a different excavation technique because the wall of one grave is also the wall of another grave;

(iii) Primary or secondary. A primary grave is the grave in which the deceased is first placed. If the remains are then removed and reburied, the grave is considered to be secondary;

(iv) Undisturbed or disturbed. An undisturbed burial is unchanged (except by natural processes) since the time of primary burial. A disturbed burial is one that has been altered by human intervention after the time of primary burial. All secondary burials are considered to be disturbed; archaeological methods can be used to detect a disturbance in a primary burial;

(f) Assign an unambiguous number to the burial. If an adequate numbering system is not already in effect, the anthropologist should devise a system;

(g) Establish a datum point, then block and map the burial site using an appropriate-sized grid and standard archaeological techniques. In some cases, it may be adequate simply to measure the depth of the grave from the surface to the skull and from the surface to the feet. Associated material can then be recorded in terms of their position relative to the skeleton;

(h) Remove the overburden of earth, screening the dirt for associated materials. Record the level (depth) and relative co-ordinates of any such findings. The type of burial, especially whether primary or secondary, influences the care and attention that needs to be given to this step. Associated materials located at a secondary burial site are unlikely to reveal the circumstances of the primary burial but may provide information on events that have occurred after that burial;

(i) Search for items such as bullets or jewellery, for which a metal detector can be useful, particularly in the levels immediately above and below the level of the remains;

(j) Circumscribe the body, when the level of the burial is located, and, when possible, open the burial pit to a minimum of 30 cm on all sides of the body;

(k) Pedestal the burial by digging on all sides to the lowest level of the body (approximately 30 cm). Also pedestal any associated artifacts;

(l) Expose the remains with the use of a soft brush or whisk broom. Do not use a brush on fabric, as it may destroy fibre evidence. Examine the soil found around the skull for hair. Place this soil in a bag for laboratory study. Patience is invaluable at this time. The remains may be fragile, and interrelationships of elements are important and may be easily disrupted. Damage can seriously reduce the amount of information available for analysis;

(m) Photograph and map the remains in situ. All photographs should include an identification number, the date, a scale and an indication of magnetic north;

(i) First photograph the entire burial, then focus on significant details so that their relation to the whole can be easily visualized;

(ii) Anything that seems unusual or remarkable should be photographed at close range. Careful attention should be given to evidence of trauma or pathological change, either recent or healed;

(iii) Photograph and map all associated materials (clothes, hair, coffin, artifacts, bullets, casings etc.). The map should include a rough sketch of the skeleton as well as any associated materials;

(n) Before displacing anything, measure the individual:

(i) Measure the total length of the remains and record the terminal points of the measurement, e.g. apex to plantar surface of calcaneus (note: This is not a stature measurement);

(ii) If the skeleton is so fragile that it may break when lifted, measure as much as possible before removing it from the ground;

(o) Remove all elements and place them in bags or boxes, taking care to avoid damage. Number, date and initial every container;

(p) Excavate and screen the level of soil immediately under the burial. A level of "sterile" (artifact-free) soil should be located before ceasing excavation and beginning to backfill.

(b) Laboratory analysis of skeletal remains

The following protocol should be followed during the laboratory analysis of the skeletal remains:

(a) Record the date, location, starting and finishing times of the skeletal analysis, and the names of all workers;

(b) Radiograph all skeletal elements before any further cleaning:

(i) Obtain bite-wing, apical and panoramic dental X-rays, if possible;

(ii) The entire skeleton should be X-rayed. Special attention should be directed to fractures, developmental anomalies and the effects of surgical procedures. Frontal sinus films should be included for identification purposes;

(c) Retain some bones in their original state; two lumbar vertebrae should be adequate. Rinse the rest of the bones clean but do not soak or scrub them. Allow the bones to dry;

(d) Lay out the entire skeleton in a systematic way:

(i) Distinguish left from right;

(ii) Inventory every bone and record on a skeletal chart;

(iii) Inventory the teeth and record on a dental chart. Note broken, carious, restored and missing teeth;

(iv) Photograph the entire skeleton in one frame. All photographs should contain an identification number and scale;

(e) If more than one individual is to be analysed, and especially if there is any chance that comparisons will be made between individuals, number every element with indelible ink before any other work is begun;

(f) Record the condition of the remains, e.g. fully intact and solid, eroding and friable, charred or cremated;

(g) Preliminary identification:

(i) Determine age, sex, race and stature;

(ii) Record the reasons for each conclusion (e.g. sex identity based on skull and femoral head);

(iii) Photograph all evidence supporting these conclusions;

(h) Individual identification:

(i) Search for evidence of handedness, pathological change, trauma and developmental anomalies;

(ii) Record the reasons for each conclusion;

(iii) Photograph all evidence supporting these conclusions;

(i) Attempt to distinguish injuries resulting from therapeutic measures from those unrelated to medical treatment. Photograph all injuries:

(i) Examine the hyoid bone for cracks or breaks;

(ii) Examine the thyroid cartilage for damage;

(iii) Each bone should be examined for evidence of contact with metal. The superior or inferior edges of the ribs require particular scrutiny. A dissecting microscope is useful;

(j) If the remains are to be reburied before obtaining an identification, retain the following samples for further analysis:

(i) A mid-shaft cross-section from either femur, 2 cm or more in height;

(ii) A mid-shaft cross-section from either fibula, 2 cm or more in height;

(iii) A 4-cm section from the sternal end of a rib (sixth, if possible);

(iv) A tooth (preferably a mandibular incisor) that was vital at the time of death;

(v) Several molar teeth for possible later deoxyribonucleic acid fingerprinting for identification;

(vi) A cast of the skull for possible facial reconstruction;

(vii) Record what samples have been saved, and label all samples with the identification number, date and name of the person who removed the sample.

(c) Final report

The following steps should be taken in the preparation of a final report:

(a) Prepare a full report of all procedures and results;

(b) Include a short summary of the conclusions;

(c) Sign and date the report.

(d) Repository for evidence

In cases where the body cannot be identified, the exhumed remains or other evidence should be preserved for a reasonable time. A repository should be established to hold the bodies for 5-10 years in case they can be identified at a later time.

CHAPTER 10

INTERNATIONAL HUMANITARAIN LAW

Comments: International humanitarian law (IHL) is a set of international rules, established by treaty or custom, which are specifically intended to solve humanitarian problems directly arising from international or non-international armed conflicts. It protects persons and property that are, or may be, affected by an armed conflict and limits the rights of the parties to a conflict to use methods and means of warfare of their choice. IHL is applicable in times of armed conflict, whether international or non-international. International conflicts are wars involving two or more States, and wars of liberation, regardless of whether a declaration of war has been made or whether the parties involved recognize that there is a state of war. Non-international armed conflicts are those in which government forces are fighting against armed insurgents, or rebel groups are fighting among themselves. Because IHL deals with exceptional situations of armed conflicts, no derogations whatsoever from its provisions are permitted.

Children are among the principal victims of war. In the last decade, an estimated 2 million children have died and 6 million have been wounded as a direct result of armed conflict. They have been made targets of the worst possible violence and abuse. They have been abducted, raped, recruited into armed forces and groups and forced to participate in atrocities. In times of armed conflict, children are also protected by the laws and customs of war, including general provisions relating to civilians, provisions specific to children and, for those children recruited into the armed forces, provisions specific to combatants.

IHL main treaty sources applicable in international armed conflict are the four Geneva Conventions of 1949 and their Additional Protocol I of 1977. The main treaty sources applicable in non-international armed conflict are Article 3 common to the Geneva Conventions and Additional Protocol II of 1977.

10.1 GENEVA CONVENTION (I) FOR THE AMELIORATION OF THE CONDITION OF THE WOUNDED AND SICK IN ARMED FORCES IN THE FIELD OF AUGUST 12, 1949

Chapter I: General Provisions

Respect for the Convention

Article 1

The High Contracting Parties undertake to respect and to ensure respect for the present Convention in all circumstances.

Application of the Convention

Article 2

In addition to the provisions which shall be implemented in peacetime, the present Convention shall apply to all cases of declared war or of any other armed conflict which may arise between two or more of the High Contracting Parties, even if the state of war is not recognized by one of them.

The Convention shall also apply to all cases of partial or total occupation of the territory of a High Contracting Party, even if the said occupation meets with no armed resistance.

Although one of the Powers in conflict may not be a party to the present Convention, the Powers who are parties thereto shall remain bound by it in their mutual relations. They shall furthermore be bound by the Convention in relation to the said Power, if the latter accepts and applies the provisions thereof.

Conflicts not of an International Character

Article 3

In the case of armed conflict not of an international character occurring in the territory of one of the High Contracting Parties, each Party to the conflict shall be bound to apply, as a minimum, the following provisions:

(1) Persons taking no active part in the hostilities, including members of armed forces who have laid down their arms and those placed hors de combat by sickness, wounds, detention, or

any other cause, shall in all circumstances be treated humanely, without any adverse distinction founded on race, colour, religion or faith, sex, birth or wealth, or any other similar criteria.

To this end, the following acts are and shall remain prohibited at any time and in any place whatsoever with respect to the above-mentioned persons:

(a) violence to life and person, in particular murder of all kinds, mutilation, cruel treatment and torture;

(b) taking of hostages;

(c) outrages upon personal dignity, in particular humiliating and degrading treatment;

(d) the passing of sentences and the carrying out of executions without previous judgement pronounced by a regularly constituted court, affording all the judicial guarantees which are recognized as indispensable by civilized peoples.

(2) The wounded and sick shall be collected and cared for. An impartial humanitarian body, such as the International Committee of the Red Cross, may offer its services to the Parties to the conflict.

The Parties to the conflict should further endeavour to bring into force, by means of special agreements, all or part of the other provisions of the present Convention.

The application of the preceding provisions shall not affect the legal status of the Parties to the conflict.

Application by Neutral Powers

Article 4

Neutral Powers shall apply by analogy the provisions of the present Convention to the wounded and sick, and to members of the medical personnel and to chaplains of the armed forces of the Parties to the conflict, received or interned in their territory, as well as to dead persons found.

Duration of Application

Article 5

For the protected persons who have fallen into the hands of the enemy, the present Convention shall apply until their final repatriation.

Special Agreements

Article 6

In addition to the agreements expressly provided for [in Articles 10, 15, 23, 28, 31, 36, 37 and 52], the High Contracting Parties may conclude other special agreements for all matters concerning which they may deem it suitable to make separate provision. No special agreement shall adversely affect the situation of the wounded and sick, of members of the medical personnel or of chaplains, as defined by the present Convention, nor restrict the rights which it confers upon them.

Wounded and sick, as well as medical personnel and chaplains, shall continue to have the benefit of such agreements as long as the Convention is applicable to them, except where express provisions to the contrary are contained in the aforesaid or in subsequent agreements, or where more favourable measures have been taken j with regard to them by one or other of the Parties to the conflict.

Non-renunciation of Rights

Article 7

Wounded and sick, as well as members of the medical personnel and chaplains, may in no circumstances renounce in part or in entirety the rights secured to them by the present Convention, and by the special agreements referred to in the foregoing Article, if such there be.

Chapter II: Wounded and Sick

Protection and Care

Article 12

Members of the armed forces and other persons mentioned in the following Article, who are wounded or sick, shall be respected and protected in all circumstances.

They shall be treated humanely and cared for by the Party to the conflict in whose power they may be, without any adverse distinction founded on sex, race, nationality, religion, political opinions, or any other similar criteria. Any attempts upon their lives, or violence to their persons, shall be strictly prohibited; in particular, they shall not be murdered or exterminated, subjected to torture or to biological experiments; they shall not wilfully be left without medical assistance and care, nor shall conditions exposing them to contagion or infection be created.

Only urgent medical reasons will authorize priority in the order of treatment to be administered.

Women shall be treated with all consideration due to their sex. The Party to the conflict which is compelled to abandon wounded or sick to the enemy shall, as far as military considerations permit, leave with them a part of its medical personnel and material to assist in their care.

Protected Persons

Article 13

The present Convention shall apply to the wounded and sick belonging to the following categories:

(1) Members of the armed forces of a Party to the conflict, as well as members of militias or volunteer corps forming part of such armed forces.

(2) Members of other militias and members of other volunteer corps, including those of organized resistance movements, belonging to a Party to the conflict and operating in or outside their own territory, even if this territory is occupied, provided that such militias or volunteer corps, including such organized resistance movements, fulfil the following conditions:

(a) that of being commanded by a person responsible for his subordinates;

(b) that of having a fixed distinctive sign recognizable at a distance;

(c) that of carrying arms openly;

(d) that of conducting their operations in accordance with the laws and customs of war.

(3) Members of regular armed forces who profess allegiance to a Government or an authority not recognized by the Detaining Power.

(4) Persons who accompany the armed forces without actually being members thereof, such as civil members of military aircraft crews, war correspondents, supply contractors, members of labour units or of services responsible for the welfare of the armed forces, provided that they have received authorization from the armed forces which they accompany.

(5) Members of crews, including masters, pilots and apprentices, of the merchant marine and the crews of civil aircraft of the Parties to the conflict, who do not benefit by more favourable treatment under any other provisions in international law.

(6) Inhabitants of a non-occupied territory, who on the approach of the enemy, spontaneously take up arms to resist the invading forces, without having had time to form themselves into regular armed units, provided they carry arms openly and respect the laws and customs of war.

Status

Article 14

Subject to the provisions of Article 12, the wounded and sick of a belligerent who fall into enemy hands shall be prisoners of war, and the provisions of international law concerning prisoners of war shall apply to them.

Role of the Population

Article 18

The military authorities may appeal to the charity of the inhabitants voluntarily to collect and care for, under their direction, the wounded and sick, granting persons who have responded to this appeal the necessary protection and facilities.

No one may ever be molested or convicted for having nursed the wounded or sick.

Chapter IV: Personnel

Personnel

Article 24

Medical personnel exclusively engaged in the search for, or the collection, transport or treatment of the wounded or sick, or in the prevention of disease, staff exclusively engaged in the administration of medical units and establishments, as well as chaplains attached to the armed forces, shall be respected and protected in all circumstances.

Article 28

Personnel designated in Articles 24......who fall into the hands of the adverse Party, shall be retained only in so far as the state of health, the spiritual needs and the number of prisoners of war require.

Personnel thus retained shall not be deemed prisoners of war. Nevertheless they shall at least benefit by all the provisions of the Geneva Convention relative to the Treatment of Prisoners of War of 12 August 1949. Within the framework of the military laws and regulations of the

Detaining Power, and under the authority of its competent service, they shall continue to carry out, in accordance with their professional ethics, their medical and spiritual duties on behalf of prisoners of war, preferably those of the armed forces to which they themselves belong. They shall further enjoy the following facilities for carrying out their medical or spiritual duties.

Chapter VIII: Execution of the Convention

Detailed Execution, Unforeseen cases

Article 45

Each Party to the conflict, acting through its Commanders-in-Chief, shall ensure the detailed execution of the preceding Articles, and provide for unforeseen cases, in conformity with the general principles of the present Convention.

Prohibition of Reprisal

Article 46

Reprisals against the wounded, sick, personnel, buildings or equipment protected by the Convention are prohibited.

Chapter IX: Repression of Abuses and Infractions

Penal Sanctions: I. General Observations

Article 49

The High Contracting Parties undertake to enact any legislation necessary to provide effective penal sanctions for persons committing, or ordering to be committed, any of the grave breaches of the present Convention defined in the following Article.

Each High Contracting Party shall be under the obligation to search for persons alleged to have committed, or to have ordered to be committed, such grave breaches, and shall bring such persons, regardless of their nationality, before its own courts. It may also, if it prefers, and in accordance with the provisions of its own legislation, hand such persons over for trial to another High Contracting Party concerned, provided such High Contracting Party has made out a prima facie case.

Each High Contracting Party shall take measures necessary for the suppression of all acts contrary to the provisions of the present Convention other than the grave breaches defined in the following Article.

In all circumstances, the accused persons shall benefit by safeguards of proper trial and defence, which shall not be less favourable than those provided by Article 105 and those following, of the Geneva Convention relative to the Treatment of Prisoners of War of 12 August 1949.

Penal Sanctions: II. Grave Breaches

Article 50

Grave breaches to which the preceding Article relates shall be those involving any of the following acts, if committed against persons or property protected by the Convention: wilful killing, torture or inhuman treatment, including biological experiments, wilfully causing great suffering or serious injury to body or health, and extensive destruction and appropriation of property, not justified by military necessity and carried out unlawfully and wantonly.

Penal Sanctions: III. Responsibilities of the Contracting Parties

Article 51

No High Contracting Party shall be allowed to absolve itself or any other High Contracting Party of any liability incurred by itself or by another High Contracting Party in respect of breaches referred to in the preceding Article.

Enquiry Procedure

Article 52

At the request of a Party to the conflict, an enquiry shall be instituted, in a manner to be decided between the interested Parties, concerning any alleged violation of the Convention.

If agreement has not been reached concerning the procedure for the enquiry, the Parties should agree on the choice of an umpire who will decide upon the procedure to be followed.

Once the violation has been established, the Parties to the conflict shall put an end to it and shall repress it with the least possible delay.

10.2 GENEVA CONVENTION (II) FOR THE AMELIORATION OF THE CONDITION OF THE WOUNDED, SICK AND SHIPWRECKED MEMBERS OF ARMED FORCES AT SEA OF AUGUST 12, 1949

Chapter I: General Provisions

Respect for the Convention

Article 1

Application of the Convention

Article 2

Conflicts not of an International Character

Article 3

Articles 1, 2 and 3 are common to four Geneva Conventions of 1949. Please see page 378.

Field of Application

Article 4

In case of hostilities between land and naval forces of Parties to the conflict, the provisions of the present Convention shall apply only to forces on board ship.

Forces put ashore shall immediately become subject to the provisions of the Geneva Convention for the Amelioration of the Condition of the Wounded and Sick in Armed Forces in the Field of August 12, 1949.

Application by Neutral Powers

Article 5

Neutral Powers shall apply by analogy the provisions of the present Convention to the wounded, sick and shipwrecked, and to members of the medical personnel and to chaplains of the armed forces of the Parties to the conflict received or interned in their territory, as well as to dead persons found.

Special Agreements

Article 6

In addition to the agreements expressly provided for in Articles 10, 18, 31, 38, 39, 40, 43 and 53, the High Contracting Parties may conclude other special agreements for all matters concerning which they may deem it suitable to make separate provision. No special agreement shall adversely affect the situation of wounded, sick and shipwrecked persons, of members of the medical personnel or of chaplains, as defined by the present Convention, nor restrict the rights which it confers upon them.

Wounded, sick and shipwrecked persons, as well as medical personnel and chaplains, shall continue to have the benefit of such agreements as long as the Convention is applicable to them, except where express provisions to the contrary are contained in the aforesaid or in subsequent agreements, or where more favourable measures have been taken with regard to them by one or other of the Parties to the conflict.

Non-renunciation of Rights

Article 7

Wounded, sick and shipwrecked persons, as well as members of the medical personnel and chaplains, may in no circumstances renounce in part or in entirety the rights secured to them by the present Convention, and by the special agreements referred to in the foregoing Article, if such there be.

Chapter II: Wounded, Sick and Shipwrecked

Protection and Care

Article 12

Members of the armed forces and other persons mentioned in the following Article, who are at sea and who are wounded, sick or shipwrecked, shall be respected and protected in all circumstances, it being understood that the term "shipwreck" means shipwreck from any cause and includes forced landings at sea by or from aircraft.

Such persons shall be treated humanely and cared for by the Parties to the conflict in whose power they may be, without any adverse distinction founded on sex, race, nationality, religion, political opinions, or any other similar criteria. Any attempts upon their lives, or violence to their persons, shall be strictly prohibited; in particular, they shall not be murdered or exterminated, subjected to torture or to biological experiments; they shall not wilfully be left without medical assistance and care, nor shall conditions exposing them to contagion or infection be created.

Only urgent medical reasons will authorize priority in the order of treatment to be administered.

Women shall be treated with all consideration due to their sex.

Protected Persons

Article 13

The present Convention shall apply to the wounded, sick and shipwrecked at sea belonging to the following categories:

(1) Members of the armed forces of a Party to the conflict, as well as members of militias or volunteer corps forming part of such armed forces.

(2) Members of other militias and members of other volunteer corps, including those of organized resistance movements, belonging to a Party to the conflict and operating in or outside their own territory, even if this territory is occupied, provided that such militias or volunteer corps, including such organized resistance movements, fulfil the following conditions:

(a) that of being commanded by a person responsible for his subordinates;

(b) that of having a fixed distinctive sign recognizable at a distance;

(c) that of carrying arms openly;

(d) that of conducting their operations in accordance with the laws and customs of war.

(3) Members of regular armed forces who profess allegiance to a Government or an authority not recognized by the Detaining Power.

(4) Persons who accompany the armed forces without actually being members thereof, such as civilian members of military aircraft crews, war correspondents, supply contractors, members of labour units or of services responsible for the welfare of the armed forces, provided that they have received authorization from the armed forces which they accompany.

(5) Members of crews, including masters, pilots and apprentices, of the merchant marine and the crews of civil aircraft of the Parties to the conflict, who do not benefit by more favourable treatment under any other provisions of international law.

(6) Inhabitants of a non-occupied territory who, on the approach of the enemy, spontaneously take up arms to resist the invading forces, without having had time to form themselves into regular armed units, provided they carry arms openly and respect the laws and customs of war.

Handing Over of Belligerent

Article 14

All warships of a belligerent Party shall have the right to demand that the wounded, sick or shipwrecked on board military hospital ships, and hospital ships belonging to relief societies or to private individuals, as well as merchant vessels, yachts and other craft shall be surrendered, whatever their nationality, provided that the wounded and sick are in a fit state to be moved and that the warship can provide adequate facilities for necessary medical treatment.

Wounded taken on board a Neutral Warship

Article 15

If wounded, sick or shipwrecked persons are taken on board a neutral warship or a neutral military aircraft, it shall be ensured, where so required by international law, that they can take no further part in operations of war.

Wounded falling into Enemy hands

Article 16

Subject to the provisions of Article 12, the wounded, sick and shipwrecked of a belligerent who fall into enemy hands shall be prisoners of war, and the provisions of international law concerning prisoners of war shall apply to them. The captor may decide, according to circumstances, whether it is expedient to hold them, or to convey them to a port in the captor's own country, to a neutral port or even to a port in enemy territory. In the last case, prisoners of war thus returned to their home country may not serve for the duration of the war.

Wounded landed in a Neutral Port

Article 17

Wounded, sick or shipwrecked persons who are landed in neutral ports with the consent of the local authorities, shall, failing arrangements to the contrary between the neutral and the belligerent Powers, be so guarded by the neutral Power, where so required by international law, that the said persons cannot again take part in operations of war.

The costs of hospital accommodation and internment shall be borne by the Power on whom the wounded, sick or shipwrecked persons depend.

Search for Casualties after an Engagement

Article 18

After each engagement, Parties to the conflict shall, without delay, take all possible measures to search for and collect the shipwrecked, wounded and sick, to protect them against pillage and ill-treatment, to ensure their adequate care, and to search for the dead and prevent their being despoiled.

Whenever circumstances permit, the Parties to the conflict shall conclude local arrangements for the removal of the wounded and sick by sea from a besieged or encircled area and for the passage of medical and religious personnel and equipment on their way to that area.

Recording and Forwarding of Information

Article 19

The Parties to the conflict shall record as soon as possible, in respect of each shipwrecked, wounded, sick or dead person of the adverse Party falling into their hands, any particulars which may assist in his identification. These records should if possible include:

(a) designation of the Power on which he depends;

(b) army, regimental, personal or serial number;

(c) surname;

(d) first name or names;

(e) date of birth;

(f) any other particulars shown on his identity card or disc;

(g) date and place of capture or death;

(h) particulars concerning wounds or illness, or cause of death.

As soon as possible the above-mentioned information shall be forwarded to the information bureau described in Article 122 of the Geneva Convention relative to the Treatment of Prisoners of War of August 12, 1949, which shall transmit this information to the Power on which these persons depend through the intermediary of the Protecting Power and of the Central Prisoners of War Agency.

Parties to the conflict shall prepare and forward to each other through the same bureau, certificates of death or duly authenticated lists of the dead. They shall likewise collect and forward through the same bureau one half of the double identity disc, or the identity disc itself if it is a single disc, last wills or other documents of importance to the next of kin, money and in general all articles of an intrinsic or sentimental value, which are found on the dead. These articles, together with unidentified articles, shall be sent in sealed packets, accompanied by statements giving all particulars necessary for the identification of the deceased owners, as well as by a complete list of the contents of the parcel.

Chapter IV: Personnel

Protection of the Personnel of Hospital Ships

Article 36

The religious, medical and hospital personnel of hospital ships and their crews shall be respected and protected; they may not be captured during the time they are in the service of the hospital ship, whether or not there are wounded and sick on board.

Medical and Religious Personnel of other ships

Article 37

The religious, medical and hospital personnel assigned to the medical or spiritual care of the persons designated in Articles 12 and 13 shall, if they fall into the hands of the enemy, be respected and protected; they may continue to carry out their duties as long as this is necessary for the care of the wounded and sick. They shall afterwards be sent back as soon as the Commander-in-Chief, under whose authority they are, considers it practicable. They may take with them, on leaving the ship, their personal property.

If, however, it prove necessary to retain some of this personnel owing to the medical or spiritual needs of prisoners of war, everything possible shall be done for their earliest possible landing.

Retained personnel shall be subject, on landing, to the provisions of the Geneva Convention for the Amelioration of the Condition of the Wounded and Sick in Armed Forces in the Field of August 12, 1949.

Chapter VII: Execution of the Convention

Detailed Execution

Article 46

Each Party to the conflict, acting through its Commanders-in-Chief, shall ensure the detailed execution of the preceding Articles and provide for unforeseen cases, in conformity with the general principles of the present Convention.

Prohibition of Reprisals

Article 47

Reprisals against the wounded, sick and shipwrecked persons, the personnel, the vessels or the equipment protected by the Convention are prohibited.

Chapter VIII: Repression of Abuses and Infractions

Penal Sanctions: I. General Observations

Article 50

The High Contracting Parties undertake to enact any legislation necessary to provide effective penal sanctions for persons committing, or ordering to be committed, any of the grave breaches of the present Convention defined in the following Article.

Each High Contracting Party shall be under the obligation to search for persons alleged to have committed, or to have ordered to be committed, such grave breaches, and shall bring such persons, regardless of their nationality, before its own courts. It may also, if it prefers, and in accordance with the provisions of its own legislation, hand such persons over for trial to another High Contracting Party concerned, provided such High Contracting Party has made out a prima facie case.

Each High Contracting Party shall take measures necessary for the suppression of all acts contrary to the provisions of the present Convention other than the grave breaches defined in the following Article.

In all circumstances, the accused persons shall benefit by safeguards of proper trial and defence, which shall not be less favourable than those provided by Article 105 and those following of the Geneva Convention relative to the Treatment of Prisoners of War of August 12, 1949.

Penal Sanctions: II. Grave Breaches

Article 51

Grave breaches to which the preceding Article relates shall be those involving any of the following acts, if committed against persons or property protected by the Convention: wilful killing, torture or inhuman treatment, including biological experiments, wilfully causing great suffering or serious injury to body or health, and extensive destruction and appropriation of property, not justified by military necessity and carried out unlawfully and wantonly.

Penal Sanctions: III. Responsibilities of the Contracting Parties

Article 52

No High Contracting Party shall be allowed to absolve itself or any other High Contracting Party of any liability incurred by itself or by another High Contracting Party in respect of breaches referred to in the preceding Article.

Enquiry Procedure

Article 53

At the request of a Party to the conflict, an enquiry shall be instituted, in a manner to be decided between the interested Parties, concerning any alleged violation of the Convention.

If agreement has not been reached concerning the procedure for the enquiry, the Parties should agree on the choice of an umpire, who will decide upon the procedure to be followed.

Once the violation has been established, the Parties to the conflict shall put an end to it and shall repress it with the least possible delay.

10.3 GENEVA CONVENTION (III) RELATIVE TO THE PRISONERS OF WAR OF AUGUST 12, 1949

Part I: General Provisions

Respect for Convention

Article 1

Application of the Convention

Article 2

Conflicts not of an International Character

Article 3

Articles 1, 2 and 3 are common to four Geneva Conventions of 1949. Please see page 378.

Prisoners of War

Article 4

A. Prisoners of war, in the sense of the present Convention, are persons belonging to one of the following categories, who have fallen into the power of the enemy:

(1) Members of the armed forces of a Party to the conflict, as well as members of militias or volunteer corps forming part of such armed forces.

(2) Members of other militias and members of other volunteer corps, including those of organized resistance movements, belonging to a Party to the conflict and operating in or outside their own territory, even if this territory is occupied, provided that such militias or volunteer corps, including such organized resistance movements, fulfil the following conditions:

(a) that of being commanded by a person responsible for his subordinates;

(b) that of having a fixed distinctive sign recognizable at a distance;

(c) that of carrying arms openly;

(d) that of conducting their operations in accordance with the laws and customs of war.

(3) Members of regular armed forces who profess allegiance to a government or an authority not recognized by the Detaining Power.

(4) Persons who accompany the armed forces without actually being members thereof, such as civilian members of military aircraft crews, war correspondents, supply contractors, members of labour units or of services responsible for the welfare of the armed forces, provided that they have received authorization, from the armed forces which they accompany, who shall provide them for that purpose with an identity card similar to the annexed model.

(5) Members of crews, including masters, pilots and apprentices, of the merchant marine and the crews of civil aircraft of the Parties to the conflict, who do not benefit by more favourable treatment under any other provisions of international law.

(6) Inhabitants of a non-occupied territory, who on the approach of the enemy spontaneously take up arms to resist the invading forces, without having had time to form themselves into regular armed units, provided they carry arms openly and respect the laws and customs of war.

B. The following shall likewise be treated as prisoners of war under the present Convention:

(1) Persons belonging, or having belonged, to the armed forces of the occupied country, if the occupying Power considers it necessary by reason of such allegiance to intern them, even though it has originally liberated them while hostilities were going on outside the territory it occupies, in particular where such persons have made an unsuccessful attempt to rejoin the armed forces to which they belong and which are engaged in combat, or where they fail to comply with a summons made to them with a view to internment.

(2) The persons belonging to one of the categories enumerated in the present Article, who have been received by neutral or non-belligerent Powers on their territory and whom these Powers are required to intern under international law, without prejudice to any more favourable treatment which these Powers may choose to give and with the exception of Articles 8, 10, 15, 30, fifth paragraph, 58-67, 92, 126 and, where diplomatic relations exist between the Parties to the conflict and the neutral or non-belligerent Power concerned, those Articles concerning the Protecting Power. Where such diplomatic relations exist, the Parties to a conflict on whom these persons depend shall be allowed to perform towards them the functions of a Protecting Power as provided in the present Convention, without prejudice to the functions which these Parties normally exercise in conformity with diplomatic and consular usage and treaties.

C. This Article shall in no way affect the status of medical personnel and chaplains as provided for in Article 33 of the present Convention.

Beginning and the end of Application

Article 5

The present Convention shall apply to the persons referred to in Article 4 from the time they fall into the power of the enemy and until their final release and repatriation.

Should any doubt arise as to whether persons, having committed a belligerent act and having fallen into the hands of the enemy, belong to any of the categories enumerated in Article 4, such persons shall enjoy the protection of the present Convention until such time as their status has been determined by a competent tribunal.

Special Agreements

Article 6

In addition to the agreements expressly provided for in Articles 10, 23, 28, 33, 60, 65, 66, 67, 72, 73, 75, 109, 110, 118, 119, 122 and 132, the High Contracting Parties may conclude other special agreements for all matters concerning which they may deem it suitable to make separate provision. No special agreement shall adversely affect the situation of prisoners of war, as defined by the present Convention, nor restrict the rights which it confers upon them.

Prisoners of war shall continue to have the benefit of such agreements as long as the Convention is applicable to them, except where express provisions to the contrary are contained in the aforesaid or in subsequent agreements, or where more favourable measures have been taken with regard to them by one or other of the Parties to the conflict.

Non- Renunciation of Rights

Article 7

Prisoners of war may in no circumstances renounce in part or in entirety the rights secured to them by the present Convention, and by the special agreements referred to in the foregoing Article, if such there be.

Part II: General Protection of Prisoners of War

Responsibility for the treatment of Prisoners

Article 12

Prisoners of war are in the hands of the enemy Power, but not of the individuals or military units who have captured them. Irrespective of the individual responsibilities that may exist, the Detaining Power is responsible for the treatment given them.

Prisoners of war may only be transferred by the Detaining Power to a Power which is a party to the Convention and after the Detaining Power has satisfied itself of the willingness and ability of such transferee Power to apply the Convention. When prisoners of war are transferred under such circumstances, responsibility for the application of the Convention rests on the Power accepting them while they are in its custody.

Nevertheless, if that Power fails to carry out the provisions of the Convention in any important respect, the Power by whom the prisoners of war were transferred shall, upon being notified by the Protecting Power, take effective measures to correct the situation or shall request the return of the prisoners of war. Such requests must be complied with.

Humane Treatment of Prisoners

Article 13

Prisoners of war must at all times be humanely treated. Any unlawful act or omission by the Detaining Power causing death or seriously endangering the health of a prisoner of war in its custody is prohibited, and will be regarded as a serious breach of the present Convention. In particular, no prisoner of war may be subjected to physical mutilation or to medical or scientific experiments of any kind which are not justified by the medical, dental or hospital treatment of the prisoner concerned and carried out in his interest.

Likewise, prisoners of war must at all times be protected, particularly against acts of violence or intimidation and against insults and public curiosity.

Measures of reprisal against prisoners of war are prohibited.

Respect for the Person of Prisoners

Article 14

Prisoners of war are entitled in all circumstances to respect for their persons and their honour.

Women shall be treated with all the regard due to their sex and shall in all cases benefit by treatment as favourable as that granted to men.

Prisoners of war shall retain the full civil capacity which they enjoyed at the time of their capture. The Detaining Power may not restrict the exercise, either within or without its own territory, of the rights such capacity confers except in so far as the captivity requires.

Maintenance of Prisoners

Article 15

The Power detaining prisoners of war shall be bound to provide free of charge for their maintenance and for the medical attention required by their state of health.

Equality of treatment

Article 16

Taking into consideration the provisions of the present Convention relating to rank and sex, and subject to any privileged treatment which may be accorded to them by reason of their state of health, age or professional qualifications, all prisoners of war shall be treated alike by the Detaining Power, without any adverse distinction based on race, nationality, religious belief or political opinions, or any other distinction founded on similar criteria.

Part III: Captivity

Section I: Beginning of Captivity

Questioning of Prisoners

Article 17

Every prisoner of war, when questioned on the subject, is bound to give only his surname, first names and rank, date of birth, and army, regimental, personal or serial number, or failing this, equivalent information.

If he wilfully infringes this rule, he may render himself liable to a restriction of the privileges accorded to his rank or status.

No physical or mental torture, nor any other form of coercion, may be inflicted on prisoners of war to secure from them information of any kind whatever. Prisoners of war who refuse to answer may not be threatened, insulted, or exposed to unpleasant or disadvantageous treatment of any kind.

Section II: Internment of Prisoner of War

Chapter I. General Observations

Restriction on liberty of Movement

Article 21

The Detaining Power may subject prisoners of war to internment. It may impose on them the obligation of not leaving, beyond certain limits, the camp where they are interned, or if the said camp is fenced in, of not going outside its perimeter. Subject to the provisions of the present Convention relative to penal and disciplinary sanctions, prisoners of war may not be held in close confinement except where necessary to safeguard their health and then only during the continuation of the circumstances which make such confinement necessary.

Prisoners of war may be partially or wholly released on parole or promise, in so far as is allowed by the laws of the Power on which they depend. Such measures shall be taken particularly in cases where this may contribute to the improvement of their state of health. No prisoner of war shall be compelled to accept liberty on parole or promise.

Upon the outbreak of hostilities, each Party to the conflict shall notify the adverse Party of the laws and regulations allowing or forbidding its own nationals to accept liberty on parole or promise. Prisoners of war who are paroled or who have given their promise in conformity with the laws and regulations so notified, are bound on their personal honour scrupulously to fulfil, both towards the Power on which they depend and towards the Power which has captured them, the engagements of their paroles or promises. In such cases, the Power on which they depend is bound neither to require nor to accept from them any service incompatible with the parole or promise given.

Places and conditions of Internment

Article 22

Prisoners of war may be interned only in premises located on land and affording every guarantee of hygiene and healthfulness. Except in particular cases which are justified by the interest of the prisoners themselves, they shall not be interned in penitentiaries.

Prisoners of war interned in unhealthy areas, or where the climate is injurious for them, shall be removed as soon as possible to a more favourable climate.

The Detaining Power shall assemble prisoners of war in camps or camp compounds according to their nationality, language and customs, provided that such prisoners shall not be separated from prisoners of war belonging to the armed forces with which they were serving at the time of their capture, except with their consent.

Security of Prisoners

Article 23

No prisoner of war may at any time be sent to, or detained in areas where he may be exposed to the fire of the combat zone, nor may his presence be used to render certain points or areas immune from military operations.

Prisoners of war shall have shelters against air bombardment and other hazards of war, to the same extent as the local civilian population. With the exception of those engaged in the protection of their quarters against the aforesaid hazards, they may enter such shelters as soon as possible after the giving of the alarm. Any other protective measure taken in favour of the population shall also apply to them.

Detaining Powers shall give the Powers concerned, through the intermediary of the Protecting Powers, all useful information regarding the geographical location of prisoner of war camps.

Art 41. In every camp the text of the present Convention and its Annexes and the contents of any special agreement provided for in Article 6, shall be posted, in the prisoners' own language, in places where all may read them. Copies shall be supplied, on request, to the prisoners who cannot have access to the copy which has been posted.

Regulations, orders, notices and publications of every kind relating to the conduct of prisoners of war shall be issued to them in a language which they understand. Such regulations, orders and publications shall be posted in the manner described above and copies shall be handed to the prisoners' representative. Every order and command addressed to prisoners of war individually must likewise be given in a language which they understand.

Section III: Labour of Prisoners

Working Conditions

Article 51

Prisoners of war must be granted suitable working conditions, especially as regards accommodation, food, clothing and equipment; such conditions shall not be inferior to those enjoyed by nationals of the Detaining Power employed in similar work; account shall also be taken of climatic conditions.

The Detaining Power, in utilizing the labour of prisoners of war, shall ensure that in areas in which such prisoners are employed, the national legislation concerning the protection of labour, and, more particularly, the regulations for the safety of workers, are duly applied.

Prisoners of war shall receive training and be provided with the means of protection suitable to the work they will have to do and similar to those accorded to the nationals of the Detaining Power. Subject to the provisions of Article 52, prisoners may be submitted to the normal risks run by these civilian workers.

Conditions of labour shall in no case be rendered more arduous by disciplinary measures.

Dangerous and Humiliating Labour

Article 52

Unless he be a volunteer, no prisoner of war may be employed on labour which is of an unhealthy or dangerous nature.

No prisoner of war shall be assigned to labour which would be looked upon as humiliating for a member of the Detaining Power's own forces.

The removal of mines or similar devices shall be considered as dangerous labour.

Section VI. Relations Between Prisoners of War and the Authorities

Chapter I. Complaints of Prisoners of War Respecting the Conditions of Captivity

Complaints and Request

Article 78

Prisoners of war shall have the right to make known to the military authorities in whose power they are, their requests regarding the conditions of captivity to which they are subjected.

They shall also have the unrestricted right to apply to the representatives of the Protecting Powers either through their prisoners' representative or, if they consider it necessary, direct, in order to draw their attention to any points on which they may have complaints to make regarding their conditions of captivity.

These requests and complaints shall not be limited nor considered to be a part of the correspondence quota referred to in Article 71. They must be transmitted immediately. Even if they are recognized to be unfounded, they may not give rise to any punishment.

Prisoners' representatives may send periodic reports on the situation in the camps and the needs of the prisoners of war to the representatives of the Protecting Powers.

Chapter III: Penal and Disciplinary Sanctions

I. General Provisions

Applicable Legislation

Article 82

A prisoner of war shall be subject to the laws, regulations and orders in force in the armed forces of the Detaining Power; the Detaining Power shall be justified in taking judicial or disciplinary measures in respect of any offence committed by a prisoner of war against such laws, regulations or orders. However, no proceedings or punishments contrary to the provisions of this Chapter shall be allowed.

If any law, regulation or order of the Detaining Power shall declare acts committed by a prisoner of war to be punishable, whereas the same acts would not be punishable if committed by a member of the forces of the Detaining Power, such acts shall entail disciplinary punishments only.

Choice of Disciplinary or Judicial Proceedings

Article 83

In deciding whether proceedings in respect of an offence alleged to have been committed by a prisoner of war shall be judicial or disciplinary, the Detaining Power shall ensure that the competent authorities exercise the greatest leniency and adopt, wherever possible, disciplinary rather than judicial measures.

Courts

Article 84

A prisoner of war shall be tried only by a military court, unless the existing laws of the Detaining Power expressly permit the civil courts to try a member of the armed forces of the Detaining

Power in respect of the particular offence alleged to have been committed by the prisoner of war.

In no circumstances whatever shall a prisoner of war be tried by a court of any kind which does not offer the essential guarantees of independence and impartiality as generally recognized, and, in particular, the procedure of which does not afford the accused the rights and means of defence provided for in Article 105.

Offences Committed Before capture

Article 85

Prisoners of war prosecuted under the laws of the Detaining Power for acts committed prior to capture shall retain, even if convicted, the benefits of the present Convention.

'Non bis in idem'

Article 86

No prisoner of war may be punished more than once for the same act or on the same charge.

Penalties

Article 87

Prisoners of war may not be sentenced by the military authorities and courts of the Detaining Power to any penalties except those provided for in respect of members of the armed forces of the said Power who have committed the same acts.

When fixing the penalty, the courts or authorities of the Detaining Power shall take into consideration, to the widest extent possible, the fact that the accused, not being a national of the Detaining Power, is not bound to it by any duty of allegiance, and that he is in its power as the result of circumstances independent of his own will. The said courts or authorities shall be at liberty to reduce the penalty provided for the violation of which the prisoner of war is accused, and shall therefore not be bound to apply the minimum penalty prescribed.

Collective punishment for individual acts, corporal punishment, imprisonment in premises without daylight and, in general, any form of torture or cruelty, are forbidden.

No prisoner of war may be deprived of his rank by the Detaining Power, or prevented from wearing his badges.

Execution of Penalties

Article 88

Officers, non-commissioned officers and men who are prisoners of war undergoing a disciplinary or judicial punishment, shall not be subjected to more severe treatment than that applied in respect of the same punishment to members of the armed forces of the Detaining Power of equivalent rank.

A woman prisoner of war shall not be awarded or sentenced to a punishment more severe, or treated whilst undergoing punishment more severely, than a woman member of the armed forces of the Detaining Power dealt with for a similar offence.

In no case may a woman prisoner of war be awarded or sentenced to a punishment more severe, or treated whilst undergoing punishment more severely, than a male member of the armed forces of the Detaining Power dealt with for a similar offence.

Prisoners of war who have served disciplinary or judicial sentences may not be treated differently from other prisoners of war.

II. Disciplinary Sanctions

General Observations: I. Forms of Punishment

Article 89

The disciplinary punishments applicable to prisoners of war are the following:

(1) A fine which shall not exceed 50 per cent of the advances of pay and working pay which the prisoner of war would otherwise receive under the provisions of Articles 60 and 62 during a period of not more than thirty days.

(2) Discontinuance of privileges granted over and above the treatment provided for by the present Convention.

(3) Fatigue duties not exceeding two hours daily.

(4) Confinement.

The punishment referred to under (3) shall not be applied to officers.

In no case shall disciplinary punishments be inhuman, brutal or dangerous to the health of prisoners of war.

General Observations: II. Duration of Punishment

Article 90

The duration of any single punishment shall in no case exceed thirty days. Any period of confinement awaiting the hearing of a disciplinary offence or the award of disciplinary punishment shall be deducted from an award pronounced against a prisoner of war.

The maximum of thirty days provided above may not be exceeded, even if the prisoner of war is answerable for several acts at the same time when he is awarded punishment, whether such acts are related or not.

The period between the pronouncing of an award of disciplinary punishment and its execution shall not exceed one month.

When a prisoner of war is awarded a further disciplinary punishment, a period of at least three days shall elapse between the execution of any two of the punishments, if the duration of one of these is ten days or more.

Escape: I. Successful Escape

Article 91

The escape of a prisoner of war shall be deemed to have succeeded when:

(1) he has joined the armed forces of the Power on which he depends, or those of an allied Power;

(2) he has left the territory under the control of the Detaining Power, or of an ally of the said Power;

(3) he has joined a ship flying the flag of the Power on which he depends, or of an allied Power, in the territorial waters of the Detaining Power, the said ship not being under the control of the last named Power.

Prisoners of war who have made good their escape in the sense of this Article and who are recaptured, shall not be liable to any punishment in respect of their previous escape.

Escape: II. Unsuccessful Escape

Article 92

A prisoner of war who attempts to escape and is recaptured before having made good his escape in the sense of Article 91 shall be liable only to a disciplinary punishment in respect of this act, even if it is a repeated offence.

A prisoner of war who is recaptured shall be handed over without delay to the competent military authority.

Article 88, fourth paragraph, notwithstanding, prisoners of war punished as a result of an unsuccessful escape may be subjected to special surveillance. Such surveillance must not affect the state of their health, must be undergone in a prisoner of war camp, and must not entail the suppression of any of the safeguards granted them by the present Convention.

Escape: III. Connected Offences

Article 93

Escape or attempt to escape, even if it is a repeated offence, shall not be deemed an aggravating circumstance if the prisoner of war is subjected to trial by judicial proceedings in respect of an offence committed during his escape or attempt to escape.

In conformity with the principle stated in Article 83, offences committed by prisoners of war with the sole intention of facilitating their escape and which do not entail any violence against life or limb, such as offences against public property, theft without intention of self-enrichment, the drawing up or use of false papers, or the wearing of civilian clothing, shall occasion disciplinary punishment only.

Prisoners of war who aid or abet an escape or an attempt to escape shall be liable on this count to disciplinary punishment only.

Escape: IV. Notification of Recapture

Article 94

If an escaped prisoner of war is recaptured, the Power on which he depends shall be notified thereof in the manner defined in Article 122, provided notification of his escape has been made.

Procedure: I. Confinement Awaiting Hearing

Article 95

A prisoner of war accused of an offence against discipline shall not be kept in confinement pending the hearing unless a member of the armed forces of the Detaining Power would be so kept if he were accused of a similar offence, or if it is essential in the interests of camp order and discipline.

Any period spent by a prisoner of war in confinement awaiting the disposal of an offence against discipline shall be reduced to an absolute minimum and shall not exceed fourteen days.

The provisions of Articles 97 and 98 of this Chapter shall apply to prisoners of war who are in confinement awaiting the disposal of offences against discipline.

Procedure: II. Competent Authorities and right of Defence

Article 96

Acts which constitute offences against discipline shall be investigated immediately.

Without prejudice to the competence of courts and superior military authorities, disciplinary punishment may be ordered only by an officer having disciplinary powers in his capacity as camp commander, or by a responsible officer who replaces him or to whom he has delegated his disciplinary powers.

In no case may such powers be delegated to a prisoner of war or be exercised by a prisoner of war.

Before any disciplinary award is pronounced, the accused shall be given precise information regarding the offences of which he is accused, and given an opportunity of explaining his conduct and of defending himself. He shall be permitted, in particular, to call witnesses and to have recourse, if necessary, to the services of a qualified interpreter. The decision shall be announced to the accused prisoner of war and to the prisoners' representative.

A record of disciplinary punishments shall be maintained by the camp commander and shall be open to inspection by representatives of the Protecting Power.

Execution of Punishment: I. Premises

Article 97

Prisoners of war shall not in any case be transferred to penitentiary establishments (prisons, penitentiaries, convict prisons, etc.) to undergo disciplinary punishment therein.

All premises in which disciplinary punishments are undergone shall conform to the sanitary requirements set forth in Article 25. A prisoner of war undergoing punishment shall be enabled to keep himself in a state of cleanliness, in conformity with Article 29.

Officers and persons of equivalent status shall not be lodged in the same quarters as non-commissioned officers or men.

Women prisoners of war undergoing disciplinary punishment shall be confined in separate quarters from male prisoners of war and shall be under the immediate supervision of women.

Execution of Punishment: II. Essential Safeguards

Article 98

A prisoner of war undergoing confinement as a disciplinary punishment, shall continue to enjoy the benefits of the provisions of this Convention except in so far as these are necessarily rendered inapplicable by the mere fact that he is confined. In no case may he be deprived of the benefits of the provisions of Articles 78 and 126.

A prisoner of war awarded disciplinary punishment may not be deprived of the prerogatives attached to his rank.

Prisoners of war awarded disciplinary punishment shall be allowed to exercise and to stay in the open air at least two hours daily.

They shall be allowed, on their request, to be present at the daily medical inspections. They shall receive the attention which their state of health requires and, if necessary, shall be removed to the camp infirmary or to a hospital.

They shall have permission to read and write, likewise to send and receive letters. Parcels and remittances of money however, may be withheld from them until the completion of the punishment; they shall meanwhile be entrusted to the prisoners' representative, who-will hand over to the infirmary the perishable goods contained in such parcels.

III. Judicial Proceedings

Essential Rules: I. General Principles

Article 99

No prisoner of war may be tried or sentenced for an act which is not forbidden by the law of the Detaining Power or by international law, in force at the time the said act was committed.

No moral or physical coercion may be exerted on a prisoner of war in order to induce him to admit himself guilty of the act of which he is accused.

No prisoner of war may be convicted without having had an opportunity to present his defence and the assistance of a qualified advocate or counsel.

Essential Rules: II. Death Penalty

Article 100

Prisoners of war and the Protecting Powers shall be informed as soon as possible of the offences which are punishable by the death sentence under the laws of the Detaining Power.

Other offences shall not thereafter be made punishable by the death penalty without the concurrence of the Power on which the prisoners of war depend.

The death sentence cannot be pronounced on a prisoner of war unless the attention of the court has, in accordance with Article 87, second paragraph, been particularly called to the fact that since the accused is not a national of the Detaining Power, he is not bound to it by any duty of allegiance, and that he is in its power as the result of circumstances independent of his own will.

Essential Rules: III. Delay in Execution of the Death Penalty

Article 101

If the death penalty is pronounced on a prisoner of war, the sentence shall not be executed before the expiration of a period of at least six months from the date when the Protecting Power receives, at an indicated address, the detailed communication provided for in Article 107.

Procedure: I. Conditions of Validity of Sentence

Article 102

A prisoner of war can be validly sentenced only if the sentence has been pronounced by the same courts according to the same procedure as in the case of members of the armed forces of the Detaining Power, and if, furthermore, the provisions of the present Chapter have been observed.

Procedure: II. Confinement Awaiting Trial

Article 103

Judicial investigations relating to a prisoner of war shall be conducted as rapidly as circumstances permit and so that his trial shall take place as soon as possible. A prisoner of war shall not be confined while awaiting trial unless a member of the armed forces of the Detaining Power would be so confined if he were accused of a similar offence, or if it is essential to do so in the interests of national security. In no circumstances shall this confinement exceed three months.

Any period spent by a prisoner of war in confinement awaiting trial shall be deducted from any sentence of imprisonment passed upon him and taken into account in fixing any penalty.

The provisions of Articles 97 and 98 of this Chapter shall apply to a prisoner of war whilst in confinement awaiting trial.

Procedure: III. Notification of Proceedings

Article 104

In any case in which the Detaining Power has decided to institute judicial proceedings against a prisoner of war, it shall notify the Protecting Power as soon as possible and at least three weeks before the opening of the trial. This period of three weeks shall run as from the day on which such notification reaches the Protecting Power at the address previously indicated by the latter to the Detaining Power.

The said notification shall contain the following information:

(1) Surname and first names of the prisoner of war, his rank, his army, regimental, personal or serial number, his date of birth, and his profession or trade, if any;

(2) Place of internment or confinement;

(3) Specification of the charge or charges on which the prisoner of war is to be arraigned, giving the legal provisions applicable;

(4) Designation of the court which will try the case, likewise the date and place fixed for the opening of the trial.

The same communication shall be made by the Detaining Power to the prisoners' representative.

If no evidence is submitted, at the opening of a trial, that the notification referred to above was received by the Protecting Power, by the prisoner of war and by the prisoners' representative concerned, at least three weeks before the opening of the trial, then the latter cannot take place and must be adjourned.

Procedure: IV. Rights and Means of Defence

Article 105

The prisoner of war shall be entitled to assistance by one of his prisoner comrades, to defence by a qualified advocate or counsel of his own choice, to the calling of witnesses and, if he deems necessary, to the services of a competent interpreter. He shall be advised of these rights by the Detaining Power in due time before the trial.

Failing a choice by the prisoner of war, the Protecting Power shall find him an advocate or counsel, and shall have at least one week at its disposal for the purpose. The Detaining Power shall deliver to the said Power, on request, a list of persons qualified to present the defence. Failing a choice of an advocate or counsel by the prisoner of war or the Protecting Power, the Detaining Power shall appoint a competent advocate or counsel to conduct the defence.

The advocate or counsel conducting the defence on behalf of the prisoner of war shall have at his disposal a period of two weeks at least before the opening of the trial, as well as the necessary facilities to prepare the defence of the accused. He may, in particular, freely visit the accused and interview him in private. He may also confer with any witnesses for the defence, including prisoners of war. He shall have the benefit of these facilities until the term of appeal or petition has expired.

Particulars of the charge or charges on which the prisoner of war is to be arraigned, as well as the documents which are generally communicated to the accused by virtue of the laws in force in the armed forces of the Detaining Power, shall be communicated to the accused prisoner of war in a language which he understands, and in good time before the opening of the trial. The same communication in the same circumstances shall be made to the advocate or counsel conducting the defence on behalf of the prisoner of war.

The representatives of the Protecting Power shall be entitled to attend the trial of the case, unless, exceptionally, this is held in camera in the interest of State security. In such a case the Detaining Power shall advise the Protecting Power accordingly.

Procedure: V. Appeals

Article 106

Every prisoner of war shall have, in the same manner as the members of the armed forces of the Detaining Power, the right of appeal or petition from any sentence pronounced upon him, with a view to the quashing or revising of the sentence or the reopening of the trial. He shall be fully informed of his right to appeal or petition and of the time limit within which he may do so.

Procedure: VI. Notification of Finding and Sentence

Article 107

Any judgment and sentence pronounced upon a prisoner of war shall be immediately reported to the Protecting Power in the form of a summary communication, which shall also indicate whether he has the right of appeal with a view to the quashing of the sentence or the reopening of the trial. This communication shall likewise be sent to the prisoners' representative concerned. It shall also be sent to the accused prisoner of war in a language he understands, if the sentence was not pronounced in his presence. The Detaining Power shall also immediately communicate to the Protecting Power the decision of the prisoner of war to use or to waive his right of appeal.

Furthermore, if a prisoner of war is finally convicted or if a sentence pronounced on a prisoner of war in the first instance is a death sentence, the Detaining Power shall as soon as possible address to the Protecting Power a detailed communication containing:

(1) the precise wording of the finding and sentence;

(2) a summarized report of any preliminary investigation and of the trial, emphasizing in particular the elements of the prosecution and the defence;

(3) notification, where applicable, of the establishment where the sentence will be served.

The communications provided for in the foregoing sub-paragraphs shall be sent to the Protecting Power at the address previously made known to the Detaining Power.

Execution of Penalties, Penal Regulations

Article 108

Sentences pronounced on prisoners of war after a conviction has become duly enforceable, shall be served in the same establishments and under the same conditions as in the case of members of the armed forces of the Detaining Power. These conditions shall in all cases conform to the requirements of health and humanity.

A woman prisoner of war on whom such a sentence has been pronounced shall be confined in separate quarters and shall be under the supervision of women.

In any case, prisoners of war sentenced to a penalty depriving them of their liberty shall retain the benefit of the provisions of Articles 78 and 126 of the present Convention. Furthermore, they shall be entitled to receive and dispatch correspondence, to receive at least one relief parcel monthly, to take regular exercise in the open air, to have the medical care required by their state of health, and the spiritual assistance they may desire. Penalties to which they may be subjected shall be in accordance with the provisions of Article 87, third paragraph.

Part IV. Termination of Captivity

Section I. Direct Repatriation and Accommodation in Neutral Countries

Article 115

No prisoner of war on whom a disciplinary punishment has been imposed and who is eligible for repatriation or for accommodation in a neutral country, may be kept back on the plea that he has not undergone his punishment.

Prisoners of war detained in connection with a judicial prosecution or conviction, and who are designated for repatriation or accommodation in a neutral country, may benefit by such measures before the end of the proceedings or the completion of the punishment, if the Detaining Power consents.

Parties to the conflict shall communicate to each other the names of those who will be detained until the end of the proceedings or the completion of the punishment.

10.4 GENEVA CONVENTION (IV) RELATIVE TO THE PROTECTION OF CIVILIAN PERSONS IN TIME OF WAR OF AUGUST 12, 1949

Part I: General Provisions

Respect for the Convention

Article 1

Application of the Convention

Article 2

Conflicts not of an International Character

Article 3

Articles 1, 2 and 3 are common to four Geneva Conventions of 1949. Please see page 378.

Definition of the Protected Persons

Article 4

Persons protected by the Convention are those who, at a given moment and in any manner whatsoever, find themselves, in case of a conflict or occupation, in the hands of a Party to the conflict or Occupying Power of which they are not nationals.

Nationals of a State which is not bound by the Convention are not protected by it. Nationals of a neutral State who find themselves in the territory of a belligerent State, and nationals of a co-belligerent State, shall not be regarded as protected persons while the State of which they are nationals has normal diplomatic representation in the State in whose hands they are.

The provisions of Part II are, however, wider in application, as defined in Article 13.

Persons protected by the Geneva Convention for the Amelioration of the Condition of the Wounded and Sick in Armed Forces in the Field of 12 August 1949, or by the Geneva Convention for the Amelioration of the Condition of Wounded, Sick and Shipwrecked Members of Armed Forces at Sea of 12 August 1949, or by the Geneva Convention relative to the Treatment of Prisoners of War of 12 August 1949, shall not be considered as protected persons within the meaning of the present Convention.

Derogations

Article 5

Where in the territory of a Party to the conflict, the latter is satisfied that an individual protected person is definitely suspected of or engaged in activities hostile to the security of the State, such individual person shall not be entitled to claim such rights and privileges under the present Convention as would, if exercised in the favour of such individual person, be prejudicial to the security of such State.

Where in occupied territory an individual protected person is detained as a spy or saboteur, or as a person under definite suspicion of activity hostile to the security of the Occupying Power, such person shall, in those cases where absolute military security so requires, be regarded as having forfeited rights of communication under the present Convention.

In each case, such persons shall nevertheless be treated with humanity and, in case of trial, shall not be deprived of the rights of fair and regular trial prescribed by the present Convention. They shall also be granted the full rights and privileges of a protected person under the present Convention at the earliest date consistent with the security of the State or Occupying Power, as the case may be.

Beginning and end of application

Article 6

The present Convention shall apply from the outset of any conflict or occupation mentioned in Article 2.

In the territory of Parties to the conflict, the application of the present Convention shall cease on the general close of military operations.

Non-renunciation of Rights

Article 8

Protected persons may in no circumstances renounce in part or in entirety the rights secured to them by the present Convention, and by the special agreements referred to in the foregoing Article, if such there be.

Part II. General Protection of Populations against Certain Consequences of War

Field of Application of Part II

Article 13

The provisions of Part II cover the whole of the populations of the countries in conflict, without any adverse distinction based, in particular, on race, nationality, religion or political opinion, and are intended to alleviate the sufferings caused by war.

Wounded and Sick: I. General Protection

Article 16

The wounded and sick, as well as the infirm, and expectant mothers, shall be the object of particular protection and respect.

As far as military considerations allow, each Party to the conflict shall facilitate the steps taken to search for the killed and wounded, to assist the shipwrecked and other persons exposed to grave danger, and to protect them against pillage and ill-treatment.

Measures relating to Child Welfare

Article 24

The Parties to the conflict shall take the necessary measures to ensure that children under fifteen, who are orphaned or are separated from their families as a result of the war, are not left to their own resources, and that their maintenance, the exercise of their religion and their education are facilitated in all circumstances. Their education shall, as far as possible, be entrusted to persons of a similar cultural tradition.

The Parties to the conflict shall facilitate the reception of such children in a neutral country for the duration of the conflict with the consent of the Protecting Power, if any, and under due safeguards for the observance of the principles stated in the first paragraph.

They shall, furthermore, endeavour to arrange for all children under twelve to be identified by the wearing of identity discs, or by some other means.

Part III: Status and Treatment of Protected Persons

Section I. Provisions common to the territories of the parties to the conflict and to occupied territories

Treatment: I. General Observations

Article 27

Protected persons are entitled, in all circumstances, to respect for their persons, their honour, their family rights, their religious convictions and practices, and their manners and customs. They shall at all times be humanely treated, and shall be protected especially against all acts of violence or threats thereof and against insults and public curiosity.

Women shall be especially protected against any attack on their honour, in particular against rape, enforced prostitution, or any form of indecent assault.

Without prejudice to the provisions relating to their state of health, age and sex, all protected persons shall be treated with the same consideration by the Party to the conflict in whose power they are, without any adverse distinction based, in particular, on race, religion or political opinion.

However, the Parties to the conflict may take such measures of control and security in regard to protected persons as may be necessary as a result of the war.

Treatment: II. Danger Zones

Article 28

The presence of a protected person may not be used to render certain points or areas immune from military operations.

Treatment: III. Responsibilities

Article 29

The Party to the conflict in whose hands protected persons may be, is responsible for the treatment accorded to them by its agents, irrespective of any individual responsibility which may be incurred.

Prohibition of Coercion

Article 31

No physical or moral coercion shall be exercised against protected persons, in particular to obtain information from them or from third parties.

Prohibition of Corporal Punishment, Torture, etc,.

Article 32

The High Contracting Parties specifically agree that each of them is prohibited from taking any measure of such a character as to cause the physical suffering or extermination of protected persons in their hands. This prohibition applies not only to murder, torture, corporal punishments, mutilation and medical or scientific experiments not necessitated by the medical treatment of a protected person, but also to any other measures of brutality whether applied by civilian or military agents.

Individual Responsibility, Collective Penalties, Pillage, Reprisals

Article 33

No protected person may be punished for an offence he or she has not personally committed. Collective penalties and likewise all measures of intimidation or of terrorism are prohibited.

Pillage is prohibited.

Reprisals against protected persons and their property are prohibited.

Hostages

Article 34

The taking of hostages is prohibited.

Section II. Aliens in the territory of a party to the conflict

Persons in Confinement

Article 37

Protected persons who are confined pending proceedings or serving a sentence involving loss of liberty, shall during their confinement be humanely treated.

Section III. Occupied territories

Inviolability of Rights

Article 47

Protected persons who are in occupied territory shall not be deprived, in any case or in any manner whatsoever, of the benefits of the present Convention by any change introduced, as the result of the occupation of a territory, into the institutions or government of the said territory, nor by any agreement concluded between the authorities of the occupied territories and the Occupying Power, nor by any annexation by the latter of the whole or part of the occupied territory.

Penal Legislation: I. General Observations

Article 64

The penal laws of the occupied territory shall remain in force, with the exception that they may be repealed or suspended by the Occupying Power in cases where they constitute a threat to its security or an obstacle to the application of the present Convention.

Subject to the latter consideration and to the necessity for ensuring the effective administration of justice, the tribunals of the occupied territory shall continue to function in respect of all offences covered by the said laws.

The Occupying Power may, however, subject the population of the occupied territory to provisions which are essential to enable the Occupying Power to fulfil its obligations under the present Convention, to maintain the orderly government of the territory, and to ensure the security of the Occupying Power, of the members and property of the occupying forces or administration, and likewise of the establishments and lines of communication used by them.

Penal Legislation: II. Publication

Article 65

The penal provisions enacted by the Occupying Power shall not come into force before they have been published and brought to the knowledge of the inhabitants in their own language. The effect of these penal provisions shall not be retroactive.

Penal Legislation: III. Competent Courts

Article 66

In case of a breach of the penal provisions promulgated by it by virtue of the second paragraph of Article 64 the Occupying Power may hand over the accused to its properly constituted, non-political military courts, on condition that the said courts sit in the occupied country. Courts of appeal shall preferably sit in the occupied country.

Penal Legislation: IV. Applicable Provisions

Art. 67. The courts shall apply only those provisions of law which were applicable prior to the offence, and which are in accordance with general principles of law, in particular the principle that the penalty shall be proportionate to the offence. They shall take into consideration the fact the accused is not a national of the Occupying Power.

Penal Legislation: V. Penalties: Death Penalty

Article 68

Protected persons who commit an offence which is solely intended to harm the Occupying Power, but which does not constitute an attempt on the life or limb of members of the occupying forces or administration, nor a grave collective danger, nor seriously damage the property of the occupying forces or administration or the installations used by them, shall be liable to internment or simple imprisonment, provided the duration of such internment or imprisonment is proportionate to the offence committed. Furthermore, internment or imprisonment shall, for such offences, be the only measure adopted for depriving protected persons of liberty. The courts provided for under Article 66 of the present Convention may at their discretion convert a sentence of imprisonment to one of internment for the same period.

The penal provisions promulgated by the Occupying Power in accordance with Articles 64 and 65 may impose the death penalty against a protected person only in cases where the person is guilty of espionage, of serious acts of sabotage against the military installations of the Occupying Power or of intentional offences which have caused the death of one or more persons, provided that such offences were punishable by death under the law of the occupied territory in force before the occupation began.

The death penalty may not be pronounced against a protected person unless the attention of the court has been particularly called to the fact that since the accused is not a national of the Occupying Power, he is not bound to it by any duty of allegiance.

In any case, the death penalty may not be pronounced on a protected person who was under eighteen years of age at the time of the offence.

Penal Legislation: VI. Deduction from sentence of period spent under arrest

Article 69

In all cases the duration of the period during which a protected person accused of an offence is under arrest awaiting trial or punishment shall be deducted from any period of imprisonment of awarded.

Penal Legislation: VII. Offences Committed before Occupation

Article 70

Protected persons shall not be arrested, prosecuted or convicted by the Occupying Power for acts committed or for opinions expressed before the occupation, or during a temporary interruption thereof, with the exception of breaches of the laws and customs of war.

Nationals of the occupying Power who, before the outbreak of hostilities, have sought refuge in the territory of the occupied State, shall not be arrested, prosecuted, convicted or deported from the occupied territory, except for offences committed after the outbreak of hostilities, or for offences under common law committed before the outbreak of hostilities which, according to the law of the occupied State, would have justified extradition in time of peace.

Penal Procedure: I. General Observations

Article 71

No sentence shall be pronounced by the competent courts of the Occupying Power except after a regular trial.

Accused persons who are prosecuted by the Occupying Power shall be promptly informed, in writing, in a language which they understand, of the particulars of the charges preferred against them, and shall be brought to trial as rapidly as possible. The Protecting Power shall be informed of all proceedings instituted by the Occupying Power against protected persons in respect of charges involving the death penalty or imprisonment for two years or more; it shall be enabled, at any time, to obtain information regarding the state of such proceedings. Furthermore, the Protecting Power shall be entitled, on request, to be furnished with all particulars of these and of any other proceedings instituted by the Occupying Power against protected persons.

The notification to the Protecting Power, as provided for in the second paragraph above, shall be sent immediately, and shall in any case reach the Protecting Power three weeks before the date of the first hearing. Unless, at the opening of the trial, evidence is submitted that the provisions of this Article are fully complied with, the trial shall not proceed. The notification shall include the following particulars:

(a) description of the accused;

(b) place of residence or detention;

(c) specification of the charge or charges (with mention of the penal provisions under which it is brought);

(d) designation of the court which will hear the case;

(e) place and date of the first hearing.

Penal Procedure: II. Right of Defnce

Article 72

Accused persons shall have the right to present evidence necessary to their defence and may, in particular, call witnesses. They shall have the right to be assisted by a qualified advocate or counsel of their own choice, who shall be able to visit them freely and shall enjoy the necessary facilities for preparing the defence.

Failing a choice by the accused, the Protecting Power may provide him with an advocate or counsel. When an accused person has to meet a serious charge and the Protecting Power is not functioning, the Occupying Power, subject to the consent of the accused, shall provide an advocate or counsel.

Accused persons shall, unless they freely waive such assistance, be aided by an interpreter, both during preliminary investigation and during the hearing in court. They shall have the right at any time to object to the interpreter and to ask for his replacement.

Penal Procedure: III. Right of Appeal

Article73

A convicted person shall have the right of appeal provided for by the laws applied by the court. He shall be fully informed of his right to appeal or petition and of the time limit within which he may do so.

The penal procedure provided in the present Section shall apply, as far as it is applicable, to appeals. Where the laws applied by the Court make no provision for appeals, the convicted person shall have the right to petition against the finding and sentence to the competent authority of the Occupying Power.

Penal Procedure: IV. Assistance by Protecting Power

Article 74

Representatives of the Protecting Power shall have the right to attend the trial of any protected person, unless the hearing has, as an exceptional measure, to be held in camera in the interests of the security of the Occupying Power, which shall then notify the Protecting Power. A notification in respect of the date and place of trial shall be sent to the Protecting Power.

Any judgement involving a sentence of death, or imprisonment for two years or more, shall be communicated, with the relevant grounds, as rapidly as possible to the Protecting Power. The notification shall contain a reference to the notification made under Article 71 and, in the case of sentences of imprisonment, the name of the place where the sentence is to be served. A record of judgements other than those referred to above shall be kept by the court and shall be open to inspection by representatives of the Protecting Power. Any period allowed for appeal in the case of sentences involving the death penalty, or imprisonment of two years or more, shall not run until notification of judgement has been received by the Protecting Power.

Penal Procedure: V. Death Sentence

Article 75

In no case shall persons condemned to death be deprived of the right of petition for pardon or reprieve.

No death sentence shall be carried out before the expiration of a period of a least six months from the date of receipt by the Protecting Power of the notification of the final judgment confirming such death sentence, or of an order denying pardon or reprieve.

The six months period of suspension of the death sentence herein prescribed may be reduced in individual cases in circumstances of grave emergency involving an organized threat to the security of the Occupying Power or its forces, provided always that the Protecting Power is notified of such reduction and is given reasonable time and opportunity to make representations to the competent occupying authorities in respect of such death sentences.

Treatment of detainees

Article 76

Protected persons accused of offences shall be detained in the occupied country, and if convicted they shall serve their sentences therein. They shall, if possible, be separated from other detainees and shall enjoy conditions of food and hygiene which will be sufficient to keep them in good health, and which will be at least equal to those obtaining in prisons in the occupied country.

They shall receive the medical attention required by their state of health.

They shall also have the right to receive any spiritual assistance which they may require.

Women shall be confined in separate quarters and shall be under the direct supervision of women.

Proper regard shall be paid to the special treatment due to minors.

Protected persons who are detained shall have the right to be visited by delegates of the Protecting Power and of the International Committee of the Red Cross, in accordance with the provisions of Article 143.

Such persons shall have the right to receive at least one relief parcel monthly.

Handing over of detainees at the choice of Occupation

Article 77

Protected persons who have been accused of offences or convicted by the courts in occupied territory, shall be handed over at the close of occupation, with the relevant records, to the authorities of the liberated territory.

Security Measures, Internment and assigned Residence, right of Appeal

Article 78

If the Occupying Power considers it necessary, for imperative reasons of security, to take safety measures concerning protected persons, it may, at the most, subject them to assigned residence or to internment.

Decisions regarding such assigned residence or internment shall be made according to a regular procedure to be prescribed by the Occupying Power in accordance with the provisions of the present Convention. This procedure shall include the right of appeal for the parties concerned. Appeals shall be decided with the least possible delay. In the event of the decision being upheld, it shall be subject to periodical review, if possible every six months, by a competent body set up by the said Power.

Protected persons made subject to assigned residence and thus required to leave their homes shall enjoy the full benefit of Article 39 of the present Convention.

Section IV. Regulations for the treatment of internees

Chapter VII: Administration and Discipline

Camp Administration

Article 99

Every place of internment shall be put under the authority of a responsible officer, chosen from the regular military forces or the regular civil administration of the Detaining Power. The officer in charge of the place of internment must have in his possession a copy of the present Convention in the official language, or one of the official languages, of his country and shall be responsible for its application. The staff in control of internees shall be instructed in the provisions of the present Convention and of the administrative measures adopted to ensure its application.

The text of the present Convention and the texts of special agreements concluded under the said Convention shall be posted inside the place of internment, in a language which the internees understand, or shall be in the possession of the Internee Committee.

Regulations, orders, notices and publications of every kind shall be communicated to the internees and posted inside the places of internment, in a language which they understand.

Every order and command addressed to internees individually must, likewise, be given in a language which they understand.

General Discipline

Article 100

The disciplinary regime in places of internment shall be consistent with humanitarian principles, and shall in no circumstances include regulations imposing on internees any physical exertion dangerous to their health or involving physical or moral victimization. Identification by tattooing or imprinting signs or markings on the body, is prohibited.

In particular, prolonged standing and roll-calls, punishment drill, military drill and manoeuvres, or the reduction of food rations, are prohibited.

Complaint and Petitions

Article 101

Internees shall have the right to present to the authorities in whose power they are, any petition with regard to the conditions of internment to which they are subjected.

They shall also have the right to apply without restriction through the Internee Committee or, if they consider it necessary, direct to the representatives of the Protecting Power, in order to indicate to them any points on which they may have complaints to make with regard to the conditions of internment.

Such petitions and complaints shall be transmitted forthwith and without alteration, and even if the latter are recognized to be unfounded, they may not occasion any punishment.

Periodic reports on the situation in places of internment and as to the needs of the internees may be sent by the Internee Committees to the representatives of the Protecting Powers.

Chapter IX: Penal and Disciplinary Sanctions

General Provisions, Applicable Legislation

Article 117

Subject to the provisions of the present Chapter, the laws in force in the territory in which they are detained will continue to apply to internees who commit offences during internment.

If general laws, regulations or orders declare acts committed by internees to be punishable, whereas the same acts are not punishable when committed by persons who are not internees, such acts shall entail disciplinary punishments only.

No internee may be punished more than once for the same act, or on the same count.

Penalties

Article 118

The courts or authorities shall in passing sentence take as far as possible into account the fact that the defendant is not a national of the Detaining Power. They shall be free to reduce the penalty prescribed for the offence with which the internee is charged and shall not be obliged, to this end, to apply the minimum sentence prescribed.

Imprisonment in premises without daylight, and, in general, all forms of cruelty without exception are forbidden.

Internees who have served disciplinary or judicial sentences shall not be treated differently from other internees.

The duration of preventive detention undergone by an internee shall be deducted from any disciplinary or judicial penalty involving confinement to which he may be sentenced.

Internee Committees shall be informed of all judicial proceedings instituted against internees whom they represent, and of their result.

Disciplinary Punishments

Article 119

The disciplinary punishments applicable to internees shall be the following:

(1) a fine which shall not exceed 50 per cent of the wages which the internee would otherwise receive under the provisions of Article 95 during a period of not more than thirty days.

(2) discontinuance of privileges granted over and above the treatment provided for by the present Convention

(3) fatigue duties, not exceeding two hours daily, in connection with the maintenance of the place of internment.

(4) confinement.

In no case shall disciplinary penalties be inhuman, brutal or dangerous for the health of internees.

Account shall be taken of the internee's age, sex and state of health.

The duration of any single punishment shall in no case exceed a maximum of thirty consecutive days, even if the internee is answerable for several breaches of discipline when his case is dealt with, whether such breaches are connected or not.

Escapes

Article 120

Internees who are recaptured after having escaped or when attempting to escape, shall be liable only to disciplinary punishment in respect of this act, even if it is a repeated offence.

Article 118, paragraph 3, notwithstanding, internees punished as a result of escape or attempt to escape, may be subjected to special surveillance, on condition that such surveillance does not affect the state of their health, that it is exercised in a place of internment and that it does not entail the abolition of any of the safeguards granted by the present Convention.

Internees, who aid and abet an escape or attempt to escape, shall be liable on this count to disciplinary punishment only.

Connected offences

Article 121

Escape, or attempt to escape, even if it is a repeated offence, shall not be deemed an aggravating circumstance in cases where an internee is prosecuted for offences committed during his escape.

The Parties to the conflict shall ensure that the competent authorities exercise leniency in deciding whether punishment inflicted for an offence shall be of a disciplinary or judicial nature, especially in respect of acts committed in connection with an escape, whether successful or not.

Investigations, Confinement awaiting hearing

Article 122

Acts which constitute offences against discipline shall be investigated immediately. This rule shall be applied, in particular, in cases of escape or attempt to escape. Recaptured internees shall be handed over to the competent authorities as soon as possible.

In cases of offences against discipline, confinement awaiting trial shall be reduced to an absolute minimum for all internees, and shall not exceed fourteen days. Its duration shall in any case be deducted from any sentence of confinement.

The provisions of Articles 124 and 125 shall apply to internees who are in confinement awaiting trial for offences against discipline.

Competent Authorities, Procedure

Article 123

Without prejudice to the competence of courts and higher authorities, disciplinary punishment may be ordered only by the commandant of the place of internment, or by a responsible officer or official who replaces him, or to whom he has delegated his disciplinary powers.

Before any disciplinary punishment is awarded, the accused internee shall be given precise information regarding the offences of which he is accused, and given an opportunity of explaining his conduct and of defending himself. He shall be permitted, in particular, to call witnesses and to have recourse, if necessary, to the services of a qualified interpreter. The decision shall be announced in the presence of the accused and of a member of the Internee Committee.

The period elapsing between the time of award of a disciplinary punishment and its execution shall not exceed one month.

When an internee is awarded a further disciplinary punishment, a period of at least three days shall elapse between the execution of any two of the punishments, if the duration of one of these is ten days or more.

A record of disciplinary punishments shall be maintained by the commandant of the place of internment and shall be open to inspection by representatives of the Protecting Power.

Premises for Disciplinary Punishments

Article 124

Internees shall not in any case be transferred to penitentiary establishments (prisons, penitentiaries, convict prisons, etc.) to undergo disciplinary punishment therein.

The premises in which disciplinary punishments are undergone shall conform to sanitary requirements: they shall in particular be provided with adequate bedding. Internees undergoing punishment shall be enabled to keep themselves in a state of cleanliness.

Women internees undergoing disciplinary punishment shall be confined in separate quarters from male internees and shall be under the immediate supervision of women.

Essential Safeguards

Article 125

Internees awarded disciplinary punishment shall be allowed to exercise and to stay in the open air at least two hours daily.

They shall be allowed, if they so request, to be present at the daily medical inspections. They shall receive the attention which their state of health requires and, if necessary, shall be removed to the infirmary of the place of internment or to a hospital.

They shall have permission to read and write, likewise to send and receive letters. Parcels and remittances of money, however, may be withheld from them until the completion of their punishment; such consignments shall meanwhile be entrusted to the Internee Committee, who will hand over to the infirmary the perishable goods contained in the parcels.

No internee given a disciplinary punishment may be deprived of the benefit of the provisions of Articles 107 (correspondence) and 143 (supervision) of the present Convention.

Provisions Applicable to Judicial Proceedings

Article 126

The provisions of Articles 71 to 76 inclusive shall apply, by analogy, to proceedings against internees who are in the national territory of the Detaining Power.

10.5 PROTOCOL ADDITIONAL TO THE GENEVA CONVENTIONS OF 12 AUGUST 1949, AND RELATING TO THE PROTECTION OF VICTIMS OF INTERNATIONAL ARMED CONFLICTS (PROTOCOL I) OF 8 JUNE 1977

PART I. GENERAL PROVISIONS

General principles and scope of application

Article1

1. The High Contracting Parties undertake to respect and to ensure respect for this Protocol in all circumstances.

2. In cases not covered by this Protocol or by other international agreements, civilians and combatants remain under the protection and authority of the principles of international law derived from established custom, from the principles of humanity and from dictates of public conscience.

3. This Protocol, which supplements the Geneva Conventions of 12 August 1949 for the protection of war victims, shall apply in the situations referred to in Article 2 common to those Conventions.

4. The situations referred to in the preceding paragraph include armed conflicts in which peoples are fighting against colonial domination and alien occupation and against racist regimes in the exercise of their right of self-determination, as enshrined in the Charter of the United Nations and the Declaration on Principles of International Law concerning Friendly Relations and Co-operation among States in accordance with the Charter of the United Nations.

Part. II WOUNDED, SICK AND SHIPWRECKED

Section I: General Protection

Field of application

Article 9

1. This Part, the provisions of which are intended to ameliorate the condition of the wounded, sick and shipwrecked, shall apply to all those affected by a situation referred to in Article 1, without any adverse distinction founded on race, colour, sex, language, religion or belief political or other opinion, national or social origin, wealth, birth or other status, or on any other similar criteria.

2. The relevant provisions of Articles 27 and 32 of the First Convention shall apply to permanent medical units and transports (other than hospital ships, to which Article 25 of the Second Convention applies) and their personnel made available to a Party to the conflict for humanitarian purposes:

(a) by a neutral or other State which is not a Party to that conflict;

(b) by a recognized and authorized aid society of such a State;

(c) by an impartial international humanitarian organization.

Protection and care

Article 10

1. All the wounded, sick and shipwrecked, to whichever Party they belong, shall be respected and protected.

2. In all circumstances they shall be treated humanely and shall receive, to the fullest extent practicable and with the least possible delay, the medical care and attention required by their condition. There shall be no distinction among them founded on any grounds other than medical ones.

Protection of persons

Article 11

1. The physical or mental health and integrity of persons who are in the power of the adverse Party or who are interned, detained or otherwise deprived of liberty as a result of a situation referred to in Article 1 shall not be endangered by any unjustified act or omission. Accordingly, it is prohibited to subject the persons described in this Article to any medical procedure which is not indicated by the state of health of the person concerned and which is not consistent with generally accepted medical standards which would be applied under similar medical circumstances to persons who are nationals of the Party conducting the procedure and who are in no way deprived of liberty.

2. It is, in particular, prohibited to carry out on such persons, even with their consent:

(a) physical mutilations;

(b) medical or scientific experiments;

(c) removal of tissue or organs for transplantation, except where these acts are justified in conformity with the conditions provided for in paragraph 1.

3. Exceptions to the prohibition in paragraph 2 (c) may be made only in the case of donations of blood for transfusion or of skin for grafting, provided that they are given voluntarily and without any coercion or inducement, and then only for therapeutic purposes, under conditions consistent with generally accepted medical standards and controls designed for the benefit of both the donor and the recipient.

4. Any wilful act or omission which seriously endangers the physical or mental health or integrity of any person who is in the power of a Party other than the one on which he depends and which either violates any of the prohibitions in paragraphs 1 and 2 or fails to comply with the requirements of paragraph 3 shall be a grave breach of this Protocol.

5. The persons described in paragraph 1 have the right to refuse any surgical operation. In case of refusal, medical personnel shall endeavour to obtain a written statement to that effect, signed or acknowledged by the patient.

6. Each Party to the conflict shall keep a medical record for every donation of blood for transfusion or skin for grafting by persons referred to in paragraph 1, if that donation is made under the responsibility of that Party. In addition, each Party to the conflict shall endeavour to keep a record of all medical procedures undertaken with respect to any person who is interned, detained or otherwise deprived of liberty as a result of a situation referred to in Article 1. These records shall be available at all times for inspection by the Protecting Power.

Section II. Combatants and Prisoners of War

Armed Forces

Article 43

1. The armed forces of a Party to a conflict consist of all organized armed forces, groups and units which are under a command responsible to that Party for the conduct or its subordinates, even if that Party is represented by a government or an authority not recognized by an adverse Party. Such armed forces shall be subject to an internal disciplinary system which, inter alia, shall enforce compliance with the rules of international law applicable in armed conflict.

2. Members of the armed forces of a Party to a conflict (other than medical personnel and chaplains covered by Article 33 of the Third Convention) are combatants, that is to say, they have the right to participate directly in hostilities.

3. Whenever a Party to a conflict incorporates a paramilitary or armed law enforcement agency into its armed forces it shall so notify the other Parties to the conflict.

Combatants and prisoners of war

Article 44

1. Any combatant, as defined in Article 43, who falls into the power of an adverse Party shall be a prisoner of war.

2. While all combatants are obliged to comply with the rules of international law applicable in armed conflict, violations of these rules shall not deprive a combatant of his right to be a combatant or, if he falls into the power of an adverse Party, of his right to be a prisoner of war, except as provided in paragraphs 3 and 4.

3. In order to promote the protection of the civilian population from the effects of hostilities, combatants are obliged to distinguish themselves from the civilian population while they are engaged in an attack or in a military operation preparatory to an attack. Recognizing, however, that there are situations in armed conflicts where, owing to the nature of the hostilities an armed combatant cannot so distinguish himself, he shall retain his status as a combatant, provided that, in such situations, he carries his arms openly:

(a) during each military engagement, and

(b) during such time as he is visible to the adversary while he is engaged in a military deployment preceding the launching of an attack in which he is to participate.

Acts which comply with the requirements of this paragraph shall not be considered as perfidious within the meaning of Article 37, paragraph 1 (c).

4. A combatant who falls into the power of an adverse Party while failing to meet the requirements set forth in the second sentence of paragraph 3 shall forfeit his right to be a prisoner of war, but he shall, nevertheless, be given protections equivalent in all respects to those accorded to prisoners of war by the Third Convention and by this Protocol. This protection includes protections equivalent to those accorded to prisoners of war by the Third Convention in the case where such a person is tried and punished for any offences he has committed.

5. Any combatant who falls into the power of an adverse Party while not engaged in an attack or in a military operation preparatory to an attack shall not forfeit his rights to be a combatant and a prisoner of war by virtue of his prior activities.

6. This Article is without prejudice to the right of any person to be a prisoner of war pursuant to Article 4 of the Third Convention.

7. This Article is not intended to change the generally accepted practice of States with respect to the wearing of the uniform by combatants assigned to the regular, uniformed armed units of a Party to the conflict.

8. In addition to the categories of persons mentioned in Article 13 of the First and Second Conventions, all members of the armed forces of a Party to the conflict, as defined in Article 43 of this Protocol, shall be entitled to protection under those Conventions if they are wounded or sick or, in the case of the Second Convention, shipwrecked at sea or in other waters.

Protection of persons who have taken part in hostilities

Article 45

1. A person who takes part in hostilities and falls into the power of an adverse Party shall be presumed to be a prisoner of war, and therefore shall be protected by the Third Convention, if he claims the status of prisoner of war, or if he appears to be entitled to such status, or if the Party on which he depends claims such status on his behalf by notification to the detaining Power or to the Protecting Power. Should any doubt arise as to whether any such person is entitled to the status of prisoner of war, he shall continue to have such status and, therefore, to be protected by the Third Convention and this Protocol until such time as his status has been determined by a competent tribunal.

2. If a person who has fallen into the power of an adverse Party is not held as a prisoner of war and is to be tried by that Party for an offence arising out of the hostilities, he shall have the right to assert his entitlement to prisoner-of-war status before a judicial tribunal and to have that question adjudicated. Whenever possible under the applicable procedure, this adjudication shall occur before the trial for the offence. The representatives of the Protecting Power shall be entitled to attend the proceedings in which that question is adjudicated, unless, exceptionally, the proceedings are held in camera in the interest of State security. In such a case the detaining Power shall advise the Protecting Power accordingly.

3. Any person who has taken part in hostilities, who is not entitled to prisoner-of-war status and who does not benefit from more favourable treatment in accordance with the Fourth Convention shall have the right at all times to the protection of Article 75 of this Protocol. In occupied territory, any such person, unless he is held as a spy, shall also be entitled, notwithstanding Article 5 of the Fourth Convention, to his rights of communication under that Convention.

Section III. Treatment of Persons in the Power of a Party to the Conflict

Chapter I. Field of application and protection of persons and objects

Field of application

Article 72

The provisions of this Section are additional to the rules concerning humanitarian protection of civilians and civilian objects in the power of a Party to the conflict contained in the Fourth Convention, particularly Parts I and III thereof, as well as to other applicable rules of international law relating to the protection of fundamental human rights during international armed conflict.

Fundamental guarantees

Article 75

1. In so far as they are affected by a situation referred to in Article 1 of this Protocol, persons who are in the power of a Party to the conflict and who do not benefit from more favourable treatment under the Conventions or under this Protocol shall be treated humanely in all circumstances and shall enjoy, as a minimum, the protection provided by this Article without any adverse distinction based upon race, colour, sex, language, religion or belief, political or other opinion, national or social origin, wealth, birth or other status, or on any other similar criteria. Each Party shall respect the person, honour, convictions and religious practices of all such persons.

2. The following acts are and shall remain prohibited at any time and in any place whatsoever, whether committed by civilian or by military agents:

(a) violence to the life, health, or physical or mental well-being of persons, in particular:

(i) murder;

(ii) torture of all kinds, whether physical or mental;

(iii) corporal punishment; and

(iv) mutilation;

(b) outrages upon personal dignity, in particular humiliating and degrading treatment, enforced prostitution and any form of indecent assault;

(c) the taking of hostages;

(d) collective punishments; and

(e) threats to commit any of the foregoing acts.

3. Any person arrested, detained or interned for actions related to the armed conflict shall be informed promptly, in a language he understands, of the reasons why these measures have been taken. Except in cases of arrest or detention for penal offences, such persons shall be released with the minimum delay possible and in any event as soon as the circumstances justifying the arrest, detention or internment have ceased to exist.

4. No sentence may be passed and no penalty may be executed on a person found guilty of a penal offence related to the armed conflict except pursuant to a conviction pronounced by an impartial and regularly constituted court respecting the generally recognized principles of regular judicial procedure, which include the following:

(a) the procedure shall provide for an accused to be informed without delay of the particulars of the offence alleged against him and shall afford the accused before and during his trial all necessary rights and means of defence;

(b) no one shall be convicted of an offence except on the basis of individual penal responsibility;

(c) no one shall be accused or convicted of a criminal offence on account or any act or omission which did not constitute a criminal offence under the national or international law to which he which was applicable at the time when the criminal offence was committed; if, after the commission of the offence, provision is made by law for the imposition of a lighter penalty, the offender shall benefit thereby;

(d) anyone charged with an offence is presumed innocent until proved guilty according to law;

(e) anyone charged with an offence shall have the right to be tried in his presence;

(f) no one shall be compelled to testify against himself or to confess guilt;

(g) anyone charged with an offence shall have the right to examine, or have examined, the witnesses against him and to obtain the attendance and examination of witnesses on his behalf under the same conditions as witnesses against him;

(h) no one shall be prosecuted or punished by the same Party for an offence in respect of which a final judgement acquitting or convicting that person has been previously pronounced under the same law and judicial procedure;

(i) anyone prosecuted for an offence shall have the right to have the judgement pronounced publicly; and

(j) a convicted person shall be advised on conviction or his judicial and other remedies and of the time-limits within which they may be exercised.

5. Women whose liberty has been restricted for reasons related to the armed conflict shall be held in quarters separated from men's quarters. They shall be under the immediate supervision of women. Nevertheless, in cases where families are detained or interned, they shall, whenever possible, be held in the same place and accommodated as family units.

6. Persons who are arrested, detained or interned for reasons related to the armed conflict shall enjoy the protection provided by this Article until their final release, repatriation or re-establishment, even after the end of the armed conflict.

7. In order to avoid any doubt concerning the prosecution and trial of persons accused of war crimes or crimes against humanity, the following principles shall apply: (a) persons who are accused of such crimes should be submitted for the purpose of prosecution and trial in accordance with the applicable rules of international law; and (b) any such persons who do not benefit from more favourable treatment under the Conventions or this Protocol shall be accorded the treatment provided by this Article, whether or not the crimes of which they are accused constitute grave breaches of the Conventions or of this Protocol.

8. No provision of this Article may be construed as limiting or infringing any other more favourable provision granting greater protection, under any applicable rules of international law, to persons covered by paragraph 1

Chapter II: Measures in favour of women and children

Protection of Women

Article 76

1. Women shall be the object of special respect and shall be protected in particular against rape, forced prostitution and any other form of indecent assault.

2. Pregnant women and mothers having dependent infants who are arrested, detained or interned for reasons related to the armed conflict, shall have their cases considered with the utmost priority.

3. To the maximum extent feasible, the Parties to the conflict shall endeavour to avoid the pronouncement of the death penalty on pregnant women or mothers having dependent infants, for an offence related to the armed conflict. The death penalty for such offences shall not be executed on such women.

Protection of Children

Article 77

1. Children shall be the object of special respect and shall be protected against any form of indecent assault. The Parties to the conflict shall provide them with the care and aid they require, whether because of their age or for any other reason.

2. The Parties to the conflict shall take all feasible measures in order that children who have not attained the age of fifteen years do not take a direct part in hostilities and, in particular, they shall refrain from recruiting them into their armed forces. In recruiting among those persons who have attained the age of fifteen years but who have not attained the age of eighteen years the Parties to the conflict shall endeavour to give priority to those who are oldest.

3. If, in exceptional cases, despite the provisions of paragraph 2, children who have not attained the age of fifteen years take a direct part in hostilities and fall into the power of an adverse Party, they shall continue to benefit from the special protection accorded by this Article, whether or not they are prisoners of war.

4. If arrested, detained or interned for reasons related to the armed conflict, children shall be held in quarters separate from the quarters of adults, except where families are accommodated as family units as provided in Article 75, paragraph 5.

5. The death penalty for an offence related to the armed conflict shall not be executed on persons who had not attained the age of eighteen years at the time the offence was committed.

Part V. Execution of the Conventions and of its Protocols

Section II. Repression of Breaches of the Conventions and of this Protocol

Repression of breaches of this Protocol

Article 85

1. The provisions of the Conventions relating to the repression of breaches and grave breaches, supplemented by this Section, shall apply to the repression of breaches and grave breaches of this Protocol.

2. Acts described as grave breaches in the Conventions are grave breaches of this Protocol if committed against persons in the power of an adverse Party protected by Articles 44, 45 and 73 of this Protocol, or against the wounded, sick and shipwrecked of the adverse Party who are protected by this Protocol, or against those medical or religious personnel, medical units or medical transports which are under the control of the adverse Party and are protected by this Protocol.

3. In addition to the grave breaches defined in Article 11, the following acts shall be regarded as grave breaches of this Protocol, when committed wilfully, in violation of the relevant provisions of this Protocol, and causing death or serious injury to body or health:

(a) making the civilian population or individual civilians the object of attack;

(b) launching an indiscriminate attack affecting the civilian population or civilian objects in the knowledge that such attack will cause excessive loss of life, injury to civilians or damage to civilian objects, as defined in Article 57, paragraph 2 (a)(iii);

(c) launching an attack against works or installations containing dangerous forces in the knowledge that such attack will cause excessive loss of life, injury to civilians or damage to civilian objects, as defined in Article 57, paragraph 2 (a)(iii);

(d) making non-defended localities and demilitarized zones the object of attack;

(e) making a person the object of attack in the knowledge that he is *hors de combat*;

(f) the perfidious use, in violation of Article 37, of the distinctive emblem of the red cross, red crescent or red lion and sun or of other protective signs recognized by the Conventions or this Protocol.

4. In addition to the grave breaches defined in the preceding paragraphs and in the Conventions, the following shall be regarded as grave breaches of this Protocol, when committed wilfully and in violation of the Conventions or the Protocol:

(a) the transfer by the occupying Power of parts of its own civilian population into the territory it occupies, or the deportation or transfer of all or parts of the population of the occupied territory within or outside this territory, in violation of Article 49 of the Fourth Convention;

(b) unjustifiable delay in the repatriation of prisoners of war or civilians;

(c) practices of apartheid and other inhuman and degrading practices involving outrages upon personal dignity, based on racial discrimination;

(d) making the clearly-recognized historic monuments, works of art or places of worship which constitute the cultural or spiritual heritage of peoples and to which special protection has been given by special arrangement, for example, within the framework of a competent international organization, the object of attack, causing as a result extensive destruction thereof, where there is no evidence of the violation by the adverse Party of Article 53, subparagraph (b), and when such historic monuments, works of art and places of worship are not located in the immediate proximity of military objectives;

(e) depriving a person protected by the Conventions or referred to in paragraph 2 of this Article of the rights of fair and regular trial.

5. Without prejudice to the application of the Conventions and of this Protocol, grave breaches of these instruments shall be regarded as war crimes.

Failure to Act

Article 86

The High Contracting Parties and the Parties to the conflict shall repress grave breaches, and take measures necessary to suppress all other breaches, of the Conventions or of this Protocol which result from a failure to act when under a duty to do so.

2. The fact that a breach of the Conventions or of this Protocol was committed by a subordinate does not absolve his superiors from penal or disciplinary responsibility, as the case may be, if they knew, or had information which should have enabled them to conclude in the circumstances

at the time, that he was committing or was going to commit such a breach and if they did not take all feasible measures within their power to prevent or repress the breach.

Duty of Commanders

Article 87

1. The High Contracting Parties and the Parties to the conflict shall require military commanders, with respect to members of the armed forces under their command and other persons under their control, to prevent and, where necessary, to suppress and to report to competent authorities breaches of the Conventions and of this Protocol.

2. In order to prevent and suppress breaches, High Contracting Parties and Parties to the conflict shall require that, commensurate with their level of responsibility, commanders ensure that members of the armed forces under their command are aware of their obligations under the Conventions and this Protocol.

3. The High Contracting Parties and Parties to the conflict shall require any commander who is aware that subordinates or other persons under his control are going to commit or have committed a breach of the Conventions or of this Protocol, to initiate such steps as are necessary to prevent such violations of the Conventions or this Protocol, and, where appropriate, to initiate disciplinary or penal action against violators thereof.

Mutual assistance in criminal matters

Article 88

1. The High Contracting Parties shall afford one another the greatest measure of assistance in connection with criminal proceedings brought in respect of grave breaches of the Conventions or of this Protocol.

2. Subject to the rights and obligations established in the Conventions and in Article 85, paragraph 1 of this Protocol, and when circumstances permit, the High Contracting Parties shall co-operate in the matter of extradition. They shall give due consideration to the request of the State in whose territory the alleged offence has occurred.

3. The law of the High Contracting Party requested shall apply in all cases. The provisions of the preceding paragraphs shall not, however, affect the obligations arising from the provisions of any other treaty of a bilateral or multilateral nature which governs or will govern the whole or part of the subject of mutual assistance in criminal matters.

Cooperation

Article 89

In situations of serious violations of the Conventions or of this Protocol, the High Contracting Parties undertake to act jointly or individually, in co-operation with the United Nations and in conformity with the United Nations Charter.

Responsibility

Article 91

A Party to the conflict which violates the provisions of the Conventions or of this Protocol shall, if the case demands, be liable to pay compensation. It shall be responsible for all acts committed by persons forming part of its armed forces.

Each High Contracting Party shall take measures necessary for the suppression of all acts contrary to the provisions of the present Convention other than the grave breaches defined in the following Article.

In all circumstances, the accused persons shall benefit by safeguards of proper trial and defence, which shall not be less favourable than those provided by Article 105 and those following of the Geneva Convention relative to the Treatment of Prisoners of War of 12 August 1949.

Penal Sanctions: II. Grave Breaches

Article 147

Grave breaches to which the preceding Article relates shall be those involving any of the following acts, if committed against persons or property protected by the present Convention: wilful killing, torture or inhuman treatment, including biological experiments, wilfully causing great suffering or serious injury to body or health, unlawful deportation or transfer or unlawful confinement of a protected person, compelling a protected person to serve in the forces of a hostile Power, or wilfully depriving a protected person of the rights of fair and regular trial prescribed in the present Convention, taking of hostages and extensive destruction and appropriation of property, not justified by military necessity and carried out unlawfully and wantonly.

10.6 PROTOCOL ADDITIONAL TO THE GENEVA CONVENTIONS OF 12 AUGUST 1949, AND RELATING TO THE PROTECTION OF VICTIMS OF NON-INTERNATIONAL ARMED CONFLICTS (PROTOCOL II) OF 8 JUNE 1977

Part I. Scope of this Protocol

Material field of application

Article 1

1. This Protocol, which develops and supplements Article 3 common to the Geneva Conventions of 12 August 1949 without modifying its existing conditions or application, shall apply to all armed conflicts which are not covered by Article 1 of the Protocol Additional to the Geneva Conventions of 12 August 1949, and relating to the Protection of Victims of International Armed Conflicts (Protocol I) and which take place in the territory of a High Contracting Party between its armed forces and dissident armed forces or other organized armed groups which, under responsible command, exercise such control over a part of its territory as to enable them to carry out sustained and concerted military operations and to implement this Protocol.

2. This Protocol shall not apply to situations of internal disturbances and tensions, such as riots, isolated and sporadic acts of violence and other acts of a similar nature, as not being armed conflicts.

Personal field of application

Article 2

1. This Protocol shall be applied without any adverse distinction founded on race, colour, sex, language, religion or belief, political or other opinion, national or social origin, wealth, birth or other status, or on any other similar criteria (hereinafter referred to as "adverse distinction") to all persons affected by an armed conflict as defined in Article 1.

2. At the end of the armed conflict, all the persons who have been deprived of their liberty or whose liberty has been restricted for reasons related to such conflict, as well as those deprived of their liberty or whose liberty is restricted after the conflict for the same reasons, shall enjoy the protection of Articles 5 and 6 until the end of such deprivation or restriction of liberty.

Non-intervention

Article 3

1. Nothing in this Protocol shall be invoked for the purpose of affecting the sovereignty of a State or the responsibility of the government, by all legitimate means, to maintain or re-establish law and order in the State or to defend the national unity and territorial integrity of the State.

2. Nothing in this Protocol shall be invoked as a justification for intervening, directly or indirectly, for any reason whatever, in the armed conflict or in the internal or external affairs of the High Contracting Party in the territory of which that conflict occurs.

Part II. Humane Treatment

Fundamental guarantees

Article 4

1. All persons who do not take a direct part or who have ceased to take part in hostilities, whether or not their liberty has been restricted, are entitled to respect for their person, honour and convictions and religious practices. They shall in all circumstances be treated humanely, without any adverse distinction. It is prohibited to order that there shall be no survivors.

2. Without prejudice to the generality of the foregoing, the following acts against the persons referred to in paragraph I are and shall remain prohibited at any time and in any place whatsoever:

(a) violence to the life, health and physical or mental well-being of persons, in particular murder as well as cruel treatment such as torture, mutilation or any form of corporal punishment;

(b) collective punishments;

(c) taking of hostages;

(d) acts of terrorism;

(e) outrages upon personal dignity, in particular humiliating and degrading treatment, rape, enforced prostitution and any form or indecent assault;

(f) slavery and the slave trade in all their forms;

(g) pillage;

(h) threats to commit any or the foregoing acts.

3. Children shall be provided with the care and aid they require, and in particular:

(a) they shall receive an education, including religious and moral education, in keeping with the wishes of their parents, or in the absence of parents, of those responsible for their care;

(b) all appropriate steps shall be taken to facilitate the reunion of families temporarily separated;

(c) children who have not attained the age of fifteen years shall neither be recruited in the armed forces or groups nor allowed to take part in hostilities;

(d) the special protection provided by this Article to children who have not attained the age of fifteen years shall remain applicable to them if they take a direct part in hostilities despite the provisions of subparagraph (c) and are captured;

(e) measures shall be taken, if necessary, and whenever possible with the consent of their parents or persons who by law or custom are primarily responsible for their care, to remove children temporarily from the area in which hostilities are taking place to a safer area within the country and ensure that they are accompanied by persons responsible for their safety and well-being.

Persons whose liberty has been restricted

Article 5

1. In addition to the provisions of Article 4 the following provisions shall be respected as a minimum with regard to persons deprived of their liberty for reasons related to the armed conflict, whether they are interned or detained;

(a) the wounded and the sick shall be treated in accordance with Article 7;

(b) the persons referred to in this paragraph shall, to the same extent as the local civilian population, be provided with food and drinking water and be afforded safeguards as regards health and hygiene and protection against the rigours of the climate and the dangers of the armed conflict;

(c) they shall be allowed to receive individual or collective relief;

(d) they shall be allowed to practise their religion and, if requested and appropriate, to receive spiritual assistance from persons, such as chaplains, performing religious functions;

(e) they shall, if made to work, have the benefit of working conditions and safeguards similar to those enjoyed by the local civilian population.

2. Those who are responsible for the internment or detention of the persons referred to in paragraph 1 shall also, within the limits of their capabilities, respect the following provisions relating to such persons:

(a) except when men and women of a family are accommodated together, women shall be held in quarters separated from those of men and shall be under the immediate supervision of women;

(b) they shall be allowed to send and receive letters and cards, the number of which may be limited by competent authority if it deems necessary;

(c) places of internment and detention shall not be located close to the combat zone. The persons referred to in paragraph 1 shall be evacuated when the places where they are interned or detained become particularly exposed to danger arising out of the armed conflict, if their evacuation can be carried out under adequate conditions of safety;

(d) they shall have the benefit of medical examinations;

(e) their physical or mental health and integrity shall not be endangered by any unjustified act or omission. Accordingly, it is prohibited to subject the persons described in this Article to any medical procedure which is not indicated by the state of health of the person concerned, and which is not consistent with the generally accepted medical standards applied to free persons under similar medical circumstances.

3. Persons who are not covered by paragraph 1 but whose liberty has been restricted in any way whatsoever for reasons related to the armed conflict shall be treated humanely in accordance with Article 4 and with paragraphs 1 (a), (c) and (d), and 2 (b) of this Article.

4. If it is decided to release persons deprived of their liberty, necessary measures to ensure their safety shall be taken by those so deciding.

Penal Prosecutions

Article 6

1. This Article applies to the prosecution and punishment of criminal offences related to the armed conflict.

2. No sentence shall be passed and no penalty shall be executed on a person found guilty of an offence except pursuant to a conviction pronounced by a court offering the essential guarantees of independence and impartiality.

In particular:

(a) the procedure shall provide for an accused to be informed without delay of the particulars of the offence alleged against him and shall afford the accused before and during his trial all necessary rights and means of defence;

(b) no one shall be convicted of an offence except on the basis of individual penal responsibility;

(c) no one shall be held guilty of any criminal offence on account of any act or omission which did not constitute a criminal offence, under the law, at the time when it was committed; nor shall a heavier penalty be imposed than that which was applicable at the time when the criminal offence was committed; if, after the commission of the offence, provision is made by law for the imposition of a lighter penalty, the offender shall benefit thereby;

(d) anyone charged with an offence is presumed innocent until proved guilty according to law;

(e) anyone charged with an offence shall have the right to be tried in his presence;

(f) no one shall be compelled to testify against himself or to confess guilt.

3. A convicted person shall be advised on conviction of his judicial and other remedies and of the time-limits within which they may be exercised.

4. The death penalty shall not be pronounced on persons who were under the age of eighteen years at the time of the offence and shall not be carried out on pregnant women or mothers of young children.

5. At the end of hostilities, the authorities in power shall endeavour to grant the broadest possible amnesty to persons who have participated in the armed conflict, or those deprived of their liberty for reasons related to the armed conflict, whether they are interned or detained.

Part III. Wounded, Sick and Shipwrecked

Protection and care

Article 7

1. All the wounded, sick and shipwrecked, whether or not they have taken part in the armed conflict, shall be respected and protected.

2. In all circumstances they shall be treated humanely and shall receive to the fullest extent practicable and with the least possible delay, the medical care and attention required by their condition. There shall be no distinction among them founded on any grounds other than medical ones.

Search

Article 8

Whenever circumstances permit and particularly after an engagement, all possible measures shall be taken, without delay, to search for and collect the wounded, sick and shipwrecked, to protect them against pillage and ill-treatment, to ensure their adequate care, and to search for the dead, prevent their being despoiled, and decently dispose of them.

Protection of medical and religious personnel

Article 9

1. Medical and religious personnel shall be respected and protected and shall be granted all available help for the performance of their duties. They shall not be compelled to carry out tasks which are not compatible with their humanitarian mission.

2. In the performance of their duties medical personnel may not be required to give priority to any person except on medical grounds.

General protection of medical duties

Article 10

1. Under no circumstances shall any person be punished for having carried out medical activities compatible with medical ethics, regardless of the person benefiting therefrom.

2. Persons engaged in medical activities shall neither be compelled to perform acts or to carry out work contrary to, nor be compelled to refrain from acts required by, the rules of medical ethics or other rules designed for the benefit of the wounded and sick, or this Protocol.

3. The professional obligations of persons engaged in medical activities regarding information which they may acquire concerning the wounded and sick under their care shall, subject to national law, be respected.

4. Subject to national law, no person engaged in medical activities may be penalized in any way for refusing or failing to give information concerning the wounded and sick who are, or who have been, under his care.

Part IV. Civilian Population

Protection of the civilian population

Article 13

1. The civilian population and individual civilians shall enjoy general protection against the dangers arising from military operations. To give effect to this protection, the following rules shall be observed in all circumstances.

2. The civilian population as such, as well as individual civilians, shall not be the object of attack. Acts or threats of violence the primary purpose of which is to spread terror among the civilian population are prohibited.

3. Civilians shall enjoy the protection afforded by this part, unless and for such time as they take a direct part in hostilities.

CHAPTER 11

INTERNATIONAL CRIMINAL COURT

Comments: The Rome Statute of the International Criminal Court (ICC) was adopted on 17 July 1998. The Court has been given substantial powers, as it was intended to act as a true international court, self-reliant and independent of any particular state. The jurisdiction of the Court is based on the principle of complementarity: the court would not hear any case unless the State or States that would have municipal jurisdiction were "unwilling or unable genuinely" to prosecute the offender. The ICC's powers and functions include holding individuals accountable, and subjecting the accused to investigation, arrest, detention, prosecution and if found guilty, incarceration. The Rome Statute creates obligations on the part of State parties to provide the means to enforce these powers. The Statute limits the ICC's focus to genocide, crimes against humanity, war crimes and aggression. Once as a country ratifies the Rome Statute, it becomes subject to the ICC's jurisdiction.

11.1 ROME STATUTE OF THE INTERNATIONAL CRIMINAL COURT [1]

Part I Establishment of the Court

Article 1

The Court

An International Criminal Court ('the Court") is hereby established. It shall be a permanent institution and shall have the power to exercise its jurisdiction over persons for the most serious crimes of international concern, as referred to in this Statute, and shall be complementary to national criminal jurisdictions. The jurisdiction and functioning of the Court shall be governed by the provisions of this Statute.

---

[1] The Statute entered into force on 1 July 2002.

Part II Jurisdiction, admissibility and applicable law

Article 5

Crimes within the jurisdiction of the Court

1. The jurisdiction of the Court shall be limited to the most serious crimes of concern to the international community as a whole. The Court has jurisdiction in accordance with this Statute with respect to the following crimes:

(a) The crime of genocide;

(b) Crimes against humanity;

(c) War crimes;

(d) The crime of aggression.

Article 19

Challenges to the jurisdiction of the Court or the admissibility of a case

1. The Court shall satisfy itself that it has jurisdiction in any case brought before it. The Court may, on its own motion, determine the admissibility of a case in accordance with article 17.

2. Challenges to the admissibility of a case on the grounds referred to in article 17 or challenges to the jurisdiction of the Court may be made by:

(a) An accused or a person for whom a warrant of arrest or a summons to appear has been issued under article 58;

(b) A State which has jurisdiction over a case, on the ground that it is investigating or prosecuting the case or has investigated or prosecuted; or

(c) A State from which acceptance of jurisdiction is required under article 12.

3. The Prosecutor may seek a ruling from the Court regarding a question of jurisdiction or admissibility. In proceedings with respect to jurisdiction or admissibility, those who have referred the situation under article 13, as well as victims, may also submit observations to the Court.

4. The admissibility of a case or the jurisdiction of the Court may be challenged only once by any person or State referred to in paragraph 2. The challenge shall take place prior to or at the

commencement of the trial. In exceptional circumstances, the Court may grant leave for a challenge to be brought more than once or at a time later than the commencement of the trial. Challenges to the admissibility of a case, at the commencement of a trial, or subsequently with the leave of the Court, may be based only on article 17, paragraph 1 (c).

Article 20

Ne bis in idem

1. Except as provided in this Statute, no person shall be tried before the Court with respect to conduct which formed the basis of crimes for which the person has been convicted or acquitted by the Court.

2. No person shall be tried by another court for a crime referred to in article 5 for which that person has already been convicted or acquitted by the Court. 3. No person who has been tried by another court for conduct also proscribed under article 6, 7 or 8 shall be tried by the Court with respect to the same conduct unless the proceedings in the other court:

(a) Were for the purpose of shielding the person concerned from criminal responsibility for crimes within the jurisdiction of the Court; or

(b) Otherwise were not conducted independently or impartially in accordance with the norms of due process recognized by international law and were conducted in a manner which, in the circumstances, was inconsistent with an intent to bring the person concerned to justice.

Article 21

Applicable law

1. The Court shall apply:

(a) In the first place, this Statute, Elements of Crimes and its Rules of Procedure and Evidence;

(b) In the second place, where appropriate, applicable treaties and the principles and rules of international law, including the established principles of the international law of armed conflict;

(c) Failing that, general principles of law derived by the Court from national laws of legal systems of the world including, as appropriate, the national laws of States that would normally exercise jurisdiction over the crime, provided that those principles are not inconsistent with this Statute and with international law and internationally recognized norms and standards.

2. The Court may apply principles and rules of law as interpreted in its previous decisions.

3. The application and interpretation of law pursuant to this article must be consistent with internationally recognized human rights, and be without any adverse distinction founded on grounds such as gender as defined in article 7, paragraph 3, age, race, colour, language, religion or belief, political or other opinion, national, ethnic or social origin, wealth, birth or other status.

Part III General Principles of Criminal Law

Article 22

Nullum crimen sine lege

1. A person shall not be criminally responsible under this Statute unless the conduct in question constitutes, at the time it takes place, a crime within the jurisdiction of the Court.

2. The definition of a crime shall be strictly construed and shall not be extended by analogy. In case of ambiguity, the definition shall be interpreted in favour of the person being investigated, prosecuted or convicted.

3. This article shall not affect the characterization of any conduct as criminal under international law independently of this Statute.

Article 23

Nulla poena sine lege

A person convicted by the Court may be punished only in accordance with this Statute.

Article 24

Non-retroactivity ratione personae

1. No person shall be criminally responsible under this Statute for conduct prior to the entry into force of the Statute.

2. In the event of a change in the law applicable to a given case prior to a final judgement, the law more favourable to the person being investigated, prosecuted or convicted shall apply.

Article 25

Individual criminal responsibility

1. The Court shall have jurisdiction over natural persons pursuant to this Statute.

2. A person who commits a crime within the jurisdiction of the Court shall be individually responsible and liable for punishment in accordance with this Statute.

3. In accordance with this Statute, a person shall be criminally responsible and liable for punishment for a crime within the jurisdiction of the Court if that person:

(a) Commits such a crime, whether as an individual, jointly with another or through another person, regardless of whether that other person is criminally responsible;

(b) Orders, solicits or induces the commission of such a crime which in fact occurs or is attempted;

(c) For the purpose of facilitating the commission of such a crime, aids, abets or otherwise assists in its commission or its attempted commission, including providing the means for its commission;

(d) In any other way contributes to the commission or attempted commission of such a crime by a group of persons acting with a common purpose. Such contribution shall be intentional and shall either:

(i) Be made with the aim of furthering the criminal activity or criminal purpose of the group, where such activity or purpose involves the commission of a crime within the jurisdiction of the Court; or

(ii) Be made in the knowledge of the intention of the group to commit the crime;

(e) In respect of the crime of genocide, directly and publicly incites others to commit genocide;

(f) Attempts to commit such a crime by taking action that commences its execution by means of a substantial step, but the crime does not occur because of circumstances independent of the person's intentions.

However, a person who abandons the effort to commit the crime or otherwise prevents the completion of the crime shall not be liable for punishment under this Statute for the attempt to commit that crime if that person completely and voluntarily gave up the criminal purpose.

4. No provision in this Statute relating to individual criminal responsibility shall affect the responsibility of States under international law.

Article 26

Exclusion of jurisdiction over persons under eighteen

The Court shall have no jurisdiction over any person who was under the age of 18 at the time of the alleged commission of a crime.

Article 29

Non-applicability of statute of limitations

The crimes within the jurisdiction of the Court shall not be subject to any statute of limitations.

Article 30

Mental element

1. Unless otherwise provided, a person shall be criminally responsible and liable for punishment for a crime within the jurisdiction of the Court only if the material elements are committed with intent and knowledge.

3. For the purposes of this article, 'knowledge' means awareness that a circumstance exists or a consequence will occur in the ordinary course of events. 'Know' and 'knowingly' shall be construed accordingly.

Article 35

Service of judges

1. All judges shall be elected as full-time members of the Court and shall be available to serve on that basis from the commencement of their terms of office.

2. The judges composing the Presidency shall serve on a full-time basis as soon as they are elected.[2]

3. The Presidency may, on the basis of the workload of the Court and in consultation with its members, decide from time to time to what extent the remaining judges shall be required to serve on a full-time basis. Any such arrangement shall be without prejudice to the provisions of article 40.

4. The financial arrangements for judges not required to serve on a full-time basis shall be made in accordance with article 49.

Article 40

Independence of the judges

1. The judges shall be independent in the performance of their functions.

2. Judges shall not engage in any activity which is likely to interfere with their judicial functions or to affect confidence in their independence.

3. Judges required to serve on a full-time basis at the seat of the Court shall not engage in any other occupation of a professional nature.

4. Any question regarding the application of paragraphs 2 and 3 shall be decided by an absolute majority of the judges. Where any such question concerns an individual judge, that judge shall not take part in the decision.

Article 55

Rights of persons during an investigation

1. In respect of an investigation under this Statute, a person:

---

[2] Article 36 (3) of the Rome Statute dealing with the qualifications, nomination and election of judges further provides. (a) The judges shall be chosen from among persons of high moral character, impartiality and integrity who possess the qualifications required in their respective States for appointment to the highest judicial offices; (b) Every candidate for election to the Court shall: (i) Have established competence in criminal law and procedure, and the necessary relevant experience, whether as judge, prosecutor, advocate or in other similar capacity, in criminal proceedings; or (ii) Have established competence in relevant areas of international law such as international humanitarian law and the law of human rights, and extensive experience in a professional legal capacity which is of relevance to the judicial work of the Court; and (c) Every candidate for election to the Court shall have an excellent knowledge of and be fluent in at least one of the working languages of the Court.

(a) Shall not be compelled to incriminate himself or herself or to confess guilt;

(b) Shall not be subjected to any form of coercion, duress or threat, to torture or to any other form of cruel, inhuman or degrading treatment or punishment;

(c) Shall, if questioned in a language other than a language the person fully understands and speaks, have, free of any cost, the assistance of a competent interpreter and such translations as are necessary to meet the requirements of fairness; and

(d) Shall not be subjected to arbitrary arrest or detention, and shall not be deprived of his or her liberty except on such grounds and in accordance with such procedures as are established in this Statute.

2. Where there are grounds to believe that a person has committed a crime within the jurisdiction of the Court and that person is about to be questioned either by the Prosecutor, or by national authorities pursuant to a request made under Part 9, that person shall also have the following rights of which he or she shall be informed prior to being questioned:

(a) To be informed, prior to being questioned, that there are grounds to believe that he or she has committed a crime within the jurisdiction of the Court;

(b) To remain silent, without such silence being a consideration in the determination of guilt or innocence;

(c) To have legal assistance of the person's choosing, or, if the person does not have legal assistance, to have legal assistance assigned to him or her, in any case where the interests of justice so require, and without payment by the person in any such case if the person does not have sufficient means to pay for it; and

(d) To be questioned in the presence of counsel unless the person has voluntarily waived his or her right to counsel.

Article 59

Arrest proceedings in the custodial State

1. A State Party which has received a request for provisional arrest or for arrest and surrender shall immediately take steps to arrest the person in question in accordance with its laws and the provisions of Part 9.

2. A person arrested shall be brought promptly before the competent judicial authority in the custodial State which shall determine, in accordance with the law of that State, that:

(a) The warrant applies to that person;

(b) The person has been arrested in accordance with the proper process; and

(c) The person's rights have been respected.

3. The person arrested shall have the right to apply to the competent authority in the custodial State for interim release pending surrender.

Article 60

Initial proceedings before the Court

1. Upon the surrender of the person to the Court, or the person's appearance before the Court voluntarily or pursuant to a summons, the Pre-Trial Chamber shall satisfy itself that the person has been informed of the crimes which he or she is alleged to have committed, and of his or her rights under this Statute, including the right to apply for interim release pending trial.

4. The Pre-Trial Chamber shall ensure that a person is not detained for an unreasonable period prior to trial due to inexcusable delay by the Prosecutor. If such delay occurs, the Court shall consider releasing the person, with or without conditions.

Article 61

Confirmation of the charges before trial

1. Subject to the provisions of paragraph 2, within a reasonable time after the person's surrender or voluntary appearance before the Court, the Pre-Trial Chamber shall hold a hearing to confirm the charges on which the Prosecutor intends to seek trial. The hearing shall be held in the presence of the Prosecutor and the person charged, as well as his or her counsel.

2. The Pre-Trial Chamber may, upon request of the Prosecutor or on its own motion, hold a hearing in the absence of the person charged to confirm the charges on which the Prosecutor intends to seek trial when the person has:

(a) Waived his or her right to be present; or

(b) Fled or cannot be found and all reasonable steps have been taken to secure his or her appearance before the Court and to inform the person of the charges and that a hearing to confirm those charges will be held.

In that case, the person shall be represented by counsel where the Pre-Trial Chamber determines that it is in the interests of justice.

6. At the hearing, the person may:

(a) Object to the charges;

(b) Challenge the evidence presented by the Prosecutor; and

(c) Present evidence.

Part VI The trial

Article 63

Trial in the presence of the accused

1. The accused shall be present during the trial.

2. If the accused, being present before the Court, continues to disrupt the trial, the Trial Chamber may remove the accused and shall make provision for him or her to observe the trial and instruct counsel from outside the courtroom, through the use of communications technology, if required. Such measures shall be taken only in exceptional circumstances after other reasonable alternatives have proved inadequate, and only for such duration as is strictly required.

Article 65

Proceedings on an admission of guilt

1. Where the accused makes an admission of guilt, [3] the Trial Chamber shall determine whether:

(a) The accused understands the nature and consequences of the admission of guilt;

(b) The admission is voluntarily made by the accused after sufficient consultation with defence counsel.

Article 66

Presumption of innocence

1. Everyone shall be presumed innocent until proved guilty before the Court in accordance with the applicable law.

2. The onus is on the Prosecutor to prove the guilt of the accused.

---

[3] In pursuant to paragraph 8 (a), Article 64 of the Rome Statute.

3. In order to convict the accused, the Court must be convinced of the guilt of the accused beyond reasonable doubt.

Article 67

Rights of the accused

1. In the determination of any charge, the accused shall be entitled to a public hearing, having regard to the provisions of this Statute, to a fair hearing conducted impartially, and to the following minimum guarantees, in full equality:

(a) To be informed promptly and in detail of the nature, cause and content of the charge, in a language which the accused fully understands and speaks;

(b) To have adequate time and facilities for the preparation of the defence and to communicate freely with counsel of the accused's choosing in confidence;

(c) To be tried without undue delay;

(d) Subject to article 63, paragraph 2, to be present at the trial, to conduct the defence in person or through legal assistance of the accused's choosing, to be informed, if the accused does not have legal assistance, of this right and to have legal assistance assigned by the Court in any case where the interests of justice so require, and without payment if the accused lacks sufficient means to pay for it;

(e) To examine, or have examined, the witnesses against him or her and to obtain the attendance and examination of witnesses on his or her behalf under the same conditions as witnesses against him or her. The accused shall also be entitled to raise defences and to present other evidence admissible under this Statute;

(f) To have, free of any cost, the assistance of a competent interpreter and such translations as are necessary to meet the requirements of fairness, if any of the proceedings of or documents presented to the Court are not in a language which the accused fully understands and speaks;

(g) Not to be compelled to testify or to confess guilt and to remain silent, without such silence being a consideration in the determination of guilt or innocence;

(h) To make an unsworn oral or written statement in his or her defence; and

(i) Not to have imposed on him or her any reversal of the burden of proof or any onus of rebuttal.

2. In addition to any other disclosure provided for in this Statute, the Prosecutor shall, as soon as practicable, disclose to the defence evidence in the Prosecutor's possession or control which he or she believes shows or tends to show the innocence of the accused, or to mitigate the guilt of the accused, or which may affect the credibility of prosecution evidence. In case of doubt as to the application of this paragraph, the Court shall decide.

Article 69

Evidence

7. Evidence obtained by means of a violation of this Statute or internationally recognized human rights shall not be admissible if:

(a) The violation casts substantial doubt on the reliability of the evidence; or

(b) The admission of the evidence would be antithetical to and would seriously damage the integrity of the proceedings.

Article 75

Reparations to victims

1. The Court shall establish principles relating to reparations to, or in respect of, victims, including restitution, compensation and rehabilitation. On this basis, in its decision the Court may, either upon request or on its own motion in exceptional circumstances, determine the scope and extent of any damage, loss and injury to, or in respect of, victims and will state the principles on which it is acting.

2. The Court may make an order directly against a convicted person specifying appropriate reparations to, or in respect of, victims, including restitution, compensation and rehabilitation. Where appropriate, the Court may order that the award for reparations be made through the Trust Fund provided for in article 79.[4]

---

[4] Article 79 of the Rome Statute provides for Trust Fund. It states:

1. A Trust Fund shall be established by decision of the Assembly of States Parties for the benefit of victims of crimes within the jurisdiction of the Court, and of the families of such victims. 2. The Court may order money and other property collected through fines or forfeiture to be transferred, by order of the Court, to the Trust Fund. 3. The Trust Fund shall be managed according to criteria to be determined by the Assembly of States Parties.

Article 76

Sentencing

1. In the event of a conviction, the Trial Chamber shall consider the appropriate sentence to be imposed and shall take into account the evidence presented and submissions made during the trial that are relevant to the sentence.

4. The sentence shall be pronounced in public and, wherever possible, in the presence of the accused.

Article 81

Appeal against decision of acquittal or conviction or against sentence

2. (a) A sentence may be appealed, in accordance with the Rules of Procedure and Evidence, by the Prosecutor or the convicted person on the ground of disproportion between the crime and the sentence.

Article 83

Proceedings on appeal

1. For the purposes of proceedings under article 81 and this article, the Appeals Chamber shall have all the powers of the Trial Chamber.

2. If the Appeals Chamber finds that the proceedings appealed from were unfair in a way that affected the reliability of the decision or sentence, or that the decision or sentence appealed from was materially affected by error of fact or law or procedural error, it may:

(a) Reverse or amend the decision or sentence; or

(b) Order a new trial before a different Trial Chamber.

For these purposes, the Appeals Chamber may remand a factual issue to the original Trial Chamber for it to determine the issue and to report back accordingly, or may itself call evidence to determine the issue. When the decision or sentence has been appealed only by the person convicted, or the Prosecutor on that person's behalf, it cannot be amended to his or her detriment.

3. If in an appeal against sentence the Appeals Chamber finds that the sentence is disproportionate to the crime, it may vary the sentence in accordance with Part 7.

Article 84

Revision of conviction or sentence

1. The convicted person or, after death, spouses, children, parents or one person alive at the time of the accused's death who has been given express written instructions from the accused to bring such a claim, or the Prosecutor on the person's behalf, may apply to the Appeals Chamber to revise the final judgement of conviction or sentence on the grounds that:

(a) New evidence has been discovered that:

(i) Was not available at the time of trial, and such unavailability was not wholly or partially attributable to the party making application; and

(ii) Is sufficiently important that had it been proved at trial it would have been likely to have resulted in a different verdict;

(b) It has been newly discovered that decisive evidence, taken into account at trial and upon which the conviction depends, was false, forged or falsified;

(c) One or more of the judges who participated in conviction or confirmation of the charges has committed, in that case, an act of serious misconduct or serious breach of duty of sufficient gravity to justify the removal of that judge or those judges from office under article 46.

Article 85

Compensation to an arrested or convicted person

1. Anyone who has been the victim of unlawful arrest or detention shall have an enforceable right to compensation.

2. When a person has by a final decision been convicted of a criminal offence, and when subsequently his or her conviction has been reversed on the ground that a new or newly discovered fact shows conclusively that there has been a miscarriage of justice, the person who has suffered punishment as a result of such conviction shall be compensated according to law, unless it is proved that the non-disclosure of the unknown fact in time is wholly or partly attributable to him or her.

3. In exceptional circumstances, where the Court finds conclusive facts showing that there has been a grave and manifest miscarriage of justice, it may in its discretion award compensation,

according to the criteria provided in the Rules of Procedure and Evidence, to a person who has been released from detention following a final decision of acquittal or a termination of the proceedings for that reason.

Article 108

Limitation on the prosecution or punishment of other offences

1. A sentenced person in the custody of the State of enforcement shall not be subject to prosecution or punishment or to extradition to a third State for any conduct engaged in prior to that person's delivery to the State of enforcement, unless such prosecution, punishment or extradition has been approved by the Court at the request of the State of enforcement.

11.2 ROME STATUTE
RULES OF PROCEDURE AND EVIDENCE[5]

Chapter 2. Composition and administration of the Court

Section III: The Registry

Subsection 3: Counsel for the Defence

Rule 20

Responsibilities of the Registrar relating to the rights of the defence

1. ....the Registrar shall organize the staff of the Registry in a manner that promotes the rights of the defence, consistent with the principle of fair trial as defined in the Statute. For that purpose, the Registrar shall, inter alia:

(a) Facilitate the protection of confidentiality;

(b) Provide support, assistance, and information to all defence counsel appearing before the Court and, as appropriate, support for professional investigators necessary for the efficient and effective conduct of the defence;

---

[5] The Rules of Procedure and Evidence is an instrument for the application of the Rome Statute of the International Criminal Court, to which they are subordinate. The Rules of Procedure and Evidence should be read in conjunction with and subject to the provisions of the Statute. Adopted by the Assembly of States Parties, First session; New York, 3-10 September 2002; Official Records ICC-ASP/1/3.

(c) Assist arrested persons.....in obtaining legal advice and the assistance of legal counsel;

(d) Advise the Prosecutor and the Chambers, as necessary, on relevant defence-related issues;

(e) Provide the defence with such facilities as may be necessary for the direct performance of the duty of the defence;

(f) Facilitate the dissemination of information and case law of the Court to defence counsel and, as appropriate, cooperate with national defence and bar associations or any independent representative body of counsel and legal associations referred to in sub-rule 3 to promote the specialization and training of lawyers in the law of the Statute and the Rules.

2. The Registrar shall carry out the functions stipulated in sub-rule 1, including the financial administration of the Registry, in such a manner as to ensure the professional independence of defence counsel.

3. For purposes such as the management of legal assistance in accordance with rule 21 and the development of a Code of Professional Conduct in accordance with rule 8, the Registrar shall consult, as appropriate, with any independent representative body of counsel or legal associations, including any such body the establishment of which may be facilitated by the Assembly of States Parties.

Rule 21

Assignment of legal assistance

1. .....criteria and procedures for assignment of legal assistance shall be established in the Regulations, based on a proposal by the Registrar, following consultations with any independent representative body of counsel or legal associations.

2. The Registrar shall create and maintain a list of counsel who meet the criteria set forth in rule 22 and the Regulations. The person shall freely choose his or her counsel from this list or other counsel who meets the required criteria and is willing to be included in the list.

3. A person may seek from the Presidency a review of a decision to refuse a request for assignment of counsel. The decision of the Presidency shall be final. If a request is refused, a further request may be made by a person to the Registrar, upon showing a change in circumstances.

4. A person choosing to represent himself or herself shall so notify the Registrar in writing at the first opportunity.

5. Where a person claims to have insufficient means to pay for legal assistance and this is subsequently found not to be so, the Chamber dealing with the case at that time may make an order of contribution to recover the cost of providing counsel.

Rule 22

Appointment and qualifications of Counsel for the defence

1. A counsel for the defence shall have established competence in international or criminal law and procedure, as well as the necessary relevant experience, whether as judge, prosecutor, advocate or in other similar capacity, in criminal proceedings. A counsel for the defence shall have an excellent knowledge of and be fluent in at least one of the working languages of the Court. Counsel for the defence may be assisted by other persons, including professors of law, with relevant expertise.

2. Counsel for the defence engaged by a person exercising his or her right under the Statute to retain legal counsel of his or her choosing shall file a power of attorney with the Registrar at the earliest opportunity.

3. In the performance of their duties, Counsel for the defence shall be subject to the Statute, the Rules, the Regulations, the Code of Professional Conduct for Counsel adopted in accordance with rule 8 and any other document adopted by the Court that may be relevant to the performance of their duties.

Section II: Disclosure

Rule 76

Pre-trial disclosure relating to prosecution witnesses

1. The Prosecutor shall provide the defence with the names of witnesses whom the Prosecutor intends to call to testify and copies of any prior statements made by those witnesses. This shall be done sufficiently in advance to enable the adequate preparation of the defence.

2. The Prosecutor shall subsequently advise the defence of the names of any additional prosecution witnesses and provide copies of their statements when the decision is made to call those witnesses.

3. The statements of prosecution witnesses shall be made available.

Rule 77

Inspection of material in possession or control of the Prosecutor

The Prosecutor shall, subject to the restrictions on disclosure......,permit the defence to inspect any books, documents, photographs and other tangible objects in the possession or control of the Prosecutor, which are material to the preparation of the defence or are intended for use by the Prosecutor as evidence for the purposes of the confirmation hearing or at trial, as the case may be, or were obtained from or belonged to the person.

Rule 78

Inspection of material in possession or control of the defence

The defence shall permit the Prosecutor to inspect any books, documents, photographs and other tangible objects in the possession or control of the defence, which are intended for use by the defence as evidence for the purposes of the confirmation hearing or at trial.

Chapter 4. Provisions relating to various stages of the proceedings

Section III: Victims and witnesses

Subsection 4. Reparations to victims

Rule 94

Procedure upon request

1. A victim's request for reparations under article 75 shall be made in writing and filed with the Registrar. It shall contain the following particulars:

(a) The identity and address of the claimant;

(b) A description of the injury, loss or harm;

(c) The location and date of the incident and, to the extent possible, the identity of the person or persons the victim believes to be responsible for the injury, loss or harm;

(d) Where restitution of assets, property or other tangible items is sought, a description of them;

(e) Claims for compensation;

(f) Claims for rehabilitation and other forms of remedy;

(g) To the extent possible, any relevant supporting documentation, including names and addresses of witnesses.

Rule 98

Trust Fund

1. Individual awards for reparations shall be made directly against a convicted person.

2. The Court may order that an award for reparations against a convicted person be deposited with the Trust Fund where at the time of making the order it is impossible or impracticable to make individual awards directly to each victim. The award for reparations thus deposited in the Trust Fund shall be separated from other resources of the Trust Fund and shall be forwarded to each victim as soon as possible.

3. The Court may order that an award for reparations against a convicted person be made through the Trust Fund where the number of the victims and the scope, forms and modalities of reparations makes a collective award more appropriate.

4. Following consultations with interested States and the Trust Fund, the Court may order that an award for reparations be made through the Trust Fund to an intergovernmental, international or national organization approved by the Trust Fund.

5. Other resources of the Trust Fund may be used for the benefit of victims subject to the provisions of article 79.

Chapter 6: Trial procedure

Rule 135

Medical examination of the accused

1. The Trial Chamber may, for the purpose of discharging its obligations under article 64, paragraph 8 (a), or for any other reasons, or at the request of a party, order a medical, psychiatric or psychological examination of the accused, under the conditions set forth in rule 113.

2. The Trial Chamber shall place its reasons for any such order on the record.

3. The Trial Chamber shall appoint one or more experts from the list of experts approved by the Registrar, or an expert approved by the Trial Chamber at the request of a party.

4. Where the Trial Chamber is satisfied that the accused is unfit to stand trial, it shall order that the trial be adjourned. The Trial Chamber may, on its own motion or at the request of the prosecution or the defence, review the case of the accused. In any event, the case shall be reviewed every 120 days unless there are reasons to do otherwise. If necessary, the Trial Chamber may order further examinations of the accused. When the Trial Chamber is satisfied that the accused has become fit to stand trial, it shall proceed in accordance with rule 132.

Rule 140

Directions for the conduct of the proceedings and testimony

2. (d) The defence shall have the right to be the last to examine a witness.

Chapter 8. Appeal and revision

Section II: Appeals against convictions, acquittals, sentences and reparation orders

Rule 150

Appeal

1. Subject to sub-rule 2, an appeal against a decision of conviction or acquittal under article 74, a sentence under article 76 or a reparation order under article 75 may be filed not later than 30 days from the date on which the party filing the appeal is notified of the decision, the sentence or the reparation order.

2. The Appeals Chamber may extend the time limit set out in sub-rule 1, for good cause, upon the application of the party seeking to file the appeal.

3. The appeal shall be filed with the Registrar.

Section III: Appeals against other decisions

Rule 158

Judgement on the appeal

1. An Appeals Chamber which considers an appeal referred to in this section may confirm, reverse or amend the decision appealed.

Chapter 10. Compensation to an arrested or convicted person

Rule 173

Request for compensation

1. Anyone seeking compensation on any of the grounds....shall submit a request, in writing, to the Presidency, which shall designate a Chamber composed of three judges to consider the request. These judges shall not have participated in any earlier judgement of the Court regarding the person making the request.

2. The request for compensation shall be submitted not later than six months from the date the person making the request was notified of the decision of the Court concerning:

(a) The unlawfulness of the arrest or detention under article 85, paragraph 1;

(b) The reversal of the conviction under article 85, paragraph 2;

(c) The existence of a grave and manifest miscarriage of justice under article 85, paragraph 3.

3. The request shall contain the grounds and the amount of compensation requested.

4. The person requesting compensation shall be entitled to legal assistance.

Section V: Review concerning reduction of sentence under article 110

Rule 223

Criteria for review concerning reduction of sentence

In reviewing the question of reduction of sentence pursuant to article 110, paragraphs 3 and 5, the three judges of the Appeals Chamber shall take into account the criteria listed in article 110, paragraph 4 (a) and (b), and the following criteria:

(a) The conduct of the sentenced person while in detention, which shows a genuine dissociation from his or her crime;

(b) The prospect of the resocialization and successful resettlement of the sentenced person;

(c) Whether the early release of the sentenced person would give rise to significant social instability;

(d) Any significant action taken by the sentenced person for the benefit of the victims as well as any impact on the victims and their families as a result of the early release;

(e) Individual circumstances of the sentenced person, including a worsening state of physical or mental health or advanced age.

Rule 224

Procedure for review concerning reduction of sentence

1. For the application of article 110, paragraph 3, three judges of the Appeals Chamber appointed by that Chamber shall conduct a hearing, unless they decide otherwise in a particular case, for exceptional reasons. The hearing shall be conducted with the sentenced person, who may be assisted by his or her counsel, with interpretation, as may be required. Those three judges shall invite the Prosecutor, the State of enforcement of any penalty under article 77 or any reparation order pursuant to article 75 and, to the extent possible, the victims or their legal representatives who participated in the proceedings, to participate in the hearing or to submit written observations. Under exceptional circumstances, this hearing may be conducted by way of a videoconference or in the State of enforcement by a judge delegated by the Appeals Chamber.

2. The same three judges shall communicate the decision and the reasons for it to all those who participated in the review proceedings as soon as possible.

3. For the application of article 110, paragraph 5, three judges of the Appeals Chamber appointed by that Chamber shall review the question of reduction of sentence every three years, unless it establishes a shorter interval in its decision taken pursuant to article 110, paragraph 3. In case of a significant change in circumstances, those three judges may permit the sentenced person to apply for a review within the three-year period or such shorter period as may have been set by the three judges.

4. For any review under article 110, paragraph 5, three judges of the Appeals Chamber appointed by that Chamber shall invite written representations from the sentenced person or his or her counsel, the Prosecutor, the State of enforcement of any penalty under article 77 and any reparation order pursuant to article 75 and, to the extent possible, the victims or their legal representatives who participated in the proceedings. The three judges may also decide to hold a hearing.

5. The decision and the reasons for it shall be communicated to all those who participated in the review proceedings as soon as possible.

11.3 INTERNATIONAL CRIMINAL COURT: CODE OF JUDICIAL ETHICS, 2005

The judges of the International Criminal Court; having regard to the United Nations Basic Principles on the Independence of the Judiciary (1985) and other international and national rules and standards relating to judicial conduct; have adopted a Code of Judicial Ethics[6] pursuant to regulation 126 of the Rules and the Regulations of the Court.

Article 2

Use of terms

In this Code of Judicial Ethics the terms "Court", "Statute", "Rules" and "Regulations" shall have the meaning attached to them in the Regulations of the Court.

Article 3

Judicial independence

1. Judges shall uphold the independence of their office and the authority of the Court and shall conduct themselves accordingly in carrying out their judicial functions.

2. Judges shall not engage in any activity which is likely to interfere with their judicial functions or to affect confidence in their independence.

Article 4

Impartiality

1. Judges shall be impartial and ensure the appearance of impartiality in the discharge of their judicial functions.

2. Judges shall avoid any conflict of interest, or being placed in a situation which might reasonably be perceived as giving rise to a conflict of interest.

---

[6] vide ICC-BD/02-01-05.

Article 5

Integrity

1. Judges shall conduct themselves with probity and integrity in accordance with their office, thereby enhancing public confidence in the judiciary.

2. Judges shall not directly or indirectly accept any gift, advantage, privilege or reward that can reasonably be perceived as being intended to influence the performance of their judicial functions.

Article 6

Confidentiality

Judges shall respect the confidentiality of consultations which relate to their judicial functions and the secrecy of deliberations.

Article 7

Diligence

1. Judges shall act diligently in the exercise of their duties and shall devote their professional activities to those duties.

2. Judges shall take reasonable steps to maintain and enhance the knowledge, skills and personal qualities necessary for judicial office.

3. Judges shall perform all judicial duties properly and expeditiously.

4. Judges shall deliver their decisions and any other rulings without undue delay.

Article 8

Conduct during proceedings

1. In conducting judicial proceedings, judges shall maintain order, act in accordance with commonly accepted decorum, remain patient and courteous towards all participants and members of the public present and require them to act likewise.

2. Judges shall exercise vigilance in controlling the manner of questioning of witnesses or victims in accordance with the Rules and give special attention to the right of participants to the proceedings to equal protection and benefit of the law.

3. Judges shall avoid conduct or comments which are racist, sexist or otherwise degrading and, to the extent possible, ensure that any person participating in the proceedings refrains from such comments or conduct.

Article 9

Public expression and association

1. Judges shall exercise their freedom of expression and association in a manner that is compatible with their office and that does not affect or appear to affect judicial independence or impartiality.

2. While judges are free to participate in public debate on matters pertaining to legal subjects, the judiciary or the administration of justice, they shall not comment on pending cases and shall avoid expressing views which may undermine the standing and integrity of the Court.

Article 10

Extra-judicial activity

1. Judges shall not engage in any extra-judicial activity that is incompatible with their judicial function or the efficient and timely functioning of the Court, or that may affect or may reasonably appear to affect their independence or impartiality.

2. Judges shall not exercise any political function.

Article 11

Observance of the Code

1. The principles embodied in this Code shall serve as guidelines on the essential ethical standards required of judges in the performance of their duties. They are advisory in nature and have the object of assisting judges with respect to ethical and professional issues with which they are confronted.

2. Nothing in this Code is intended in any way to limit or restrict the judicial independence of the judges.

11.4 PRINCIPLES OF INTERNATIONAL COOPERATION IN THE DETECTION, ARREST, EXTRADITION AND PUNISHMENT OF PERSONS GUILTY OF WAR CRIMES AND CRIMES AGAINST HUMANITY, 1973[7]

The General Assembly,

Recalling its resolutions 2583 (XXIV) of 15 December 1969, 2712 (XXV) of 15 December 1970, 2840 (XXVI) of 18 December 1971 and 3020 (XXVII) of 18 December 1972,

Taking into account the special need for international action in order to ensure the prosecution and punishment of persons guilty of war crimes and crimes against humanity,

Having considered the draft principles of international co-operation in the detection, arrest, extradition and punishment of persons guilty of war crimes and crimes against humanity,

Declares that the United Nations, in pursuance of the principles and purposes set forth in the Charter concerning the promotion of co-operation between peoples and the maintenance of international peace and security, proclaims the following principles of international co-operation in the detection, arrest, extradition and punishment of persons guilty of war crimes and crimes against humanity:

1. War crimes and crimes against humanity, wherever they are committed, shall be subject to investigation and the persons against whom there is evidence that they have committed such crimes shall be subject to tracing, arrest, trial and, if found guilty, to punishment.

2. Every State has the right to try its own nationals for war crimes against humanity.

3. States shall co-operate with each other on a bilateral and multilateral basis with a view to halting and preventing war crimes and crimes against humanity, and shall take the domestic and international measures necessary for that purpose.

4. States shall assist each other in detecting, arresting and bringing to trial persons suspected of having committed such crimes and, if they are found guilty, in punishing them.

5. Persons against whom there is evidence that they have committed war crimes and crimes against humanity shall be subject to trial and, if found guilty, to punishment, as a general rule in the countries in which they committed those crimes. In that connection, States shall co-operate on questions of extraditing such persons.

---

[7] Adopted by General Assembly resolution 3074 (XXVIII) of 3 December 1973.

6. States shall co-operate with each other in the collection of information and evidence which would help to bring to trial the persons indicated in para-graph 5 above and shall exchange such information.

7. In accordance with article 1 of the Declaration on Territorial Asylum of 14 December 1967, States shall not grant asylum to any person with respect to whom there are serious reasons for considering that he has committed a crime against peace, a war crime or a crime against humanity.

8. States shall not take any legislative or other measures which may be prejudicial to the international obligations they have assumed in regard to the detection, arrest, extradition and punishment of persons guilty of war crimes and crimes against humanity.

9. In co-operating with a view to the detection, arrest and extradition of persons against whom there is evidence that they have committed war crimes and crimes against humanity and, if found guilty, their punishment, States shall act in conformity with the provisions of the Charter of the United Nations and of the Declaration on Principles of International Law concerning Friendly Relations and Co-operation among States in accordance with the Charter of the United Nations.

11.5 CONVENTION ON THE PREVENTION AND PUNISHMENT OF THE CRIME OF GENOCIDE, 1948 [8]

The Contracting Parties,

Having considered the declaration made by the General Assembly of the United Nations in its resolution 96 (I) dated 11 December 1946 that genocide is a crime under international law, contrary to the spirit and aims of the United Nations and condemned by the civilized world,

Recognizing that at all periods of history genocide has inflicted great losses on humanity, and

Being convinced that, in order to liberate mankind from such an odious scourge, international co-operation is required,

Hereby agree as hereinafter provided:

---

[8] Approved and proposed for signature and ratification or accession by General Assembly resolution 260 A (III) of 9 December 1948, Entry into force: 12 January 1951, in accordance with article XIII.

Article I

The Contracting Parties confirm that genocide, whether committed in time of peace or in time of war, is a crime under international law which they undertake to prevent and to punish.

Article II

In the present Convention, genocide means any of the following acts committed with intent to destroy, in whole or in part, a national, ethnical, racial or religious group, as such:

(a) Killing members of the group;

(b) Causing serious bodily or mental harm to members of the group;

(c) Deliberately inflicting on the group conditions of life calculated to bring about its physical destruction in whole or in part;

(d) Imposing measures intended to prevent births within the group;

(e) Forcibly transferring children of the group to another group.

Article III

The following acts shall be punishable:

(a) Genocide;

(b) Conspiracy to commit genocide;

(c) Direct and public incitement to commit genocide;

(d) Attempt to commit genocide;

(e) Complicity in genocide.

Article IV

Persons committing genocide or any of the other acts enumerated in article III shall be punished, whether they are constitutionally responsible rulers, public officials or private individuals.

Article V

The Contracting Parties undertake to enact, in accordance with their respective Constitutions, the necessary legislation to give effect to the provisions of the present Convention, and, in particular, to provide effective penalties for persons guilty of genocide or any of the other acts enumerated in article III.

Article VI

Persons charged with genocide or any of the other acts enumerated in article III shall be tried by a competent tribunal of the State in the territory of which the act was committed, or by such international penal tribunal as may have jurisdiction with respect to those Contracting Parties which shall have accepted its jurisdiction.

Article VII

Genocide and the other acts enumerated in article III shall not be considered as political crimes for the purpose of extradition.

The Contracting Parties pledge themselves in such cases to grant extradition in accordance with their laws and treaties in force.

Article VIII

Any Contracting Party may call upon the competent organs of the United Nations to take such action under the Charter of the United Nations as they consider appropriate for the prevention and suppression of acts of genocide or any of the other acts enumerated in article III.

Article IX

Disputes between the Contracting Parties relating to the interpretation, application or fulfilment of the present Convention, including those relating to the responsibility of a State for genocide or for any of the other acts enumerated in article III, shall be submitted to the International Court of Justice at the request of any of the parties to the dispute.

Article X

The present Convention, of which the Chinese, English, French, Russian and Spanish texts are equally authentic, shall bear the date of 9 December 1948.

Article XI

The present Convention shall be open until 31 December 1949 for signature on behalf of any Member of the United Nations and of any non-member State to which an invitation to sign has been addressed by the General Assembly.

The present Convention shall be ratified, and the instruments of ratification shall be deposited with the Secretary-General of the United Nations. After 1 January 1950, the present Convention may be acceded to on behalf of any Member of the United Nations and of any non-member State which has received an invitation as aforesaid.

Instruments of accession shall be deposited with the Secretary-General of the United Nations.

Article XII

Any Contracting Party may at any time, by notification addressed to the Secretary-General of the United Nations, extend the application of the present Convention to all or any of the territories for the conduct of whose foreign relations that Contracting Party is responsible.

Article XIII

On the day when the first twenty instruments of ratification or accession have been deposited, the Secretary-General shall draw up a procès-verbal and transmit a copy thereof to each Member of the United Nations and to each of the non-member States contemplated in article XI.

The present Convention shall come into force on the ninetieth day following the date of deposit of the twentieth instrument of ratification or accession.

Any ratification or accession effected subsequent to the latter date shall become effective on the ninetieth day following the deposit of the instrument of ratification or accession.

Article XIV

The present Convention shall remain in effect for a period of ten years as from the date of its coming into force.

It shall thereafter remain in force for successive periods of five years for such Contracting Parties as have not denounced it at least six months before the expiration of the current period.

Denunciation shall be effected by a written notification addressed to the Secretary-General of the United Nations.

Article XV

If, as a result of denunciations, the number of Parties to the present Convention should become less than sixteen, the Convention shall cease to be in force as from the date on which the last of these denunciations shall become effective.

Article XVI

A request for the revision of the present Convention may be made at any time by any Contracting Party by means of a notification in writing addressed to the Secretary-General.

The General Assembly shall decide upon the steps, if any, to be taken in respect of such request.

Article XVII

The Secretary-General of the United Nations shall notify all Members of the United Nations and the non-member States contemplated in article XI of the following:

(a) Signatures, ratifications and accessions received in accordance with article XI;

(b) Notifications received in accordance with article XII;

(c) The date upon which the present Convention comes into force in accordance with article XIII;

(d) Denunciations received in accordance with article XIV;

(e) The abrogation of the Convention in accordance with article XV;

(f) Notifications received in accordance with article XVI.

Article XVIII

The original of the present Convention shall be deposited in the archives of the United Nations.

A certified copy of the Convention shall be transmitted to each Member of the United Nations and to each of the non-member States contemplated in article XI.

Article XIX

The present Convention shall be registered by the Secretary-General of the United Nations on the date of its coming into force.

CHAPTER 12

MILITARY TRIBUNALS

Comments: The armed forces the world over are governed by a special code of conduct designed to ensure the highest standard of discipline among the members. An independent justice system for the armed forces has been provided by a large number of democracies. The existence of military criminal tribunals raises serious issues related to the right to a fair trial. The Human Rights Committee has on several occasions recommended in its country observations that legislation be codified so that civilians are tried by civilian courts and not by military tribunals. In the case of Peru, the Committee considered that the prosecution of civilians by military tribunals was incompatible with Article 14 of the ICCPR, because it "is not consistent with the fair, impartial and independent administration of justice".[1]

The European Court of Human Rights has also referred to military judges and tribunals on numerous occasions. According to the Court, military judges cannot be considered independent and impartial due to the nature of the body they belong to. In *Findlay v. The United Kingdom*, the European Court found that the applicant's court martial was neither independent nor impartial because its members were subordinate in rank to the convening officer, who also acted as "confirming officer" and who could modify any sentence handed down.[2]

The Human Rights Committee in its General Comment No. 13[3] held that the provisions of Article 14 of the ICCPR apply to all courts and tribunals, whether ordinary or specialized. Quite often the reason for the establishment of such courts is to enable exceptional procedures to be applied which do not comply with normal standards of justice. While the Covenant does not prohibit such categories of courts, nevertheless the conditions which it lays down clearly indicate

---

[1] Concluding Observations of the Human Rights Committee on Peru, UN document CCPR/CO/70/PER, para. 11.

[2] [1997] 24 EHRR 221, ECHR.

[3] Article 14, (Administration of Justice), 1984.

that the trying of civilians by such courts should be very exceptional and take place under conditions which genuinely afford the full guarantees stipulated in Article 14. Several countries have amended their laws to ensure that members of the military accused of military offences enjoy the safeguards that are necessary for a fair trial.

12.1 PRINCIPLES GOVERNING THE ADMINISTRATION OF JUSTICE THROUGH MILITARY TRIBUNALS, 2005

The Human Rights Commission, at its sixty-first session, referred to the issue of the administration of justice through military tribunals in two mutually complementary resolutions: (i) Integrity of the judicial system (2005/30), and (ii) Independence and impartiality of the judiciary, jurors and assessors and the independence of lawyers (2005/33), and adopted both on 19 April 2005. The latter contained "the report submitted by Mr. Emmanuel Decaux to the Sub-Commission on the Promotion and Protection of Human Rights on the administration of justice through military tribunals,[4] which includes draft principles governing the administration of justice through military tribunals."

The right to a fair trial is a norm of international human rights law, designed to protect individuals from the unlawful and arbitrary curtailment or deprivation of their basic rights and freedoms, the most prominent of which are the rights to life and to liberty. It is important to situate the development of "military justice" within the framework of the general principles for the proper administration of justice. In General Comment No. 13, the Human Rights Committee stated with regard to the creation of military and other special tribunals:

> The provisions of Article 14 of the ICCPR apply to all courts and tribunals within the scope of that article whether ordinary or specialized. The Committee notes the existence, in many countries, of military or special courts which try civilians. In the case of South Asian countries, particularly Bangladesh and Pakistan, the reason for the establishment of such courts is to enable exceptional procedures to be applied which do not comply with normal standards of justice. This poses a serious problem as far as the equitable, impartial and independent administration of justice is concerned. While the Covenant does not prohibit such categories of courts, nevertheless the conditions which it lays down clearly indicate that the trying of civilians by such courts should be very exceptional and take place under conditions which genuinely afford the full guarantees stipulated in article 14 of the ICCPR.

---

[4] E/CN.4/Sub.2/2004/7.

An updated version of the draft principles submitted to the Commission at its sixty-second session is as follows.

Principles Governing the Administration of Justice Through Military Tribunals

Principle No. 1: Establishment of military tribunals by the constitution or the law. Military tribunals, when they exist, may be established only by the constitution or the law, respecting the principle of the separation of powers. They must be an integral part of the general judicial system.

Comments: The Basic Principles on the Independence of the Judiciary, adopted by the General Assembly in 1985, stipulate that "the independence of the judiciary shall be guaranteed by the State and enshrined in the constitution or the law of the country. It is the duty of all governmental and other institutions to respect and observe the independence of the judiciary." The principle of the separation of powers goes together with the requirement of statutory guarantees provided at the highest level of the hierarchy of norms, by the constitution or by the law, avoiding any interference by the executive or the military in the administration of justice.

Principle No. 2: Respect for the standards of international law. Military tribunals must in all circumstances apply standards and procedures internationally recognized as guarantees of a fair trial, including the rules of international humanitarian law.

Comments: Military tribunals, when they exist, must in all circumstances respect the principles of international law relating to a fair trial. This is a matter of minimum guarantees; even in times of crisis, particularly as regards the provisions of article 4 of the International Covenant on Civil and Political Rights, State parties' derogations from ordinary law should not be "inconsistent with their other obligations under international law" nor involve "discrimination solely on the ground of race, colour, sex, language, religion or social origin". If article 14 of the Covenant does not explicitly figure in the "hard core" of non-derogable rights, the existence of effective judicial guarantees constitutes an intrinsic element of respect for the principles contained in the Covenant, and particularly the provisions of article 4, as the Human Rights Committee emphasizes in its general comment No. 29. Without such basic guarantees, we would be faced with a denial of justice, pure and simple. These guarantees are made explicit in the principles below.

Principle No. 3: Application of martial law. In times of crisis, recourse to martial law or special regimes should not compromise the guarantees of a fair trial. Any derogation "strictly required by the exigencies of the situation" should be consistent with the principles of the proper administration of justice. In particular, military tribunals should not be substituted for ordinary courts, in derogation from ordinary law.

Comments: Its purpose is to take account of situations of internal crisis arising in the aftermath of a natural disaster or a "public emergency" within the meaning of article 4 of the International Covenant on Civil and Political Rights, when martial law or similar exceptional regimes, such as a state of siege or emergency, are declared. This is a grey area, in which serious derogations may be made from the normal guarantees associated with the rule of law yet the safeguards provided under international humanitarian law do not necessarily apply. As the Human Rights Committee has emphasized in general comment No. 29, "As certain elements of the right to a fair trial are explicitly guaranteed under international humanitarian law during armed conflict, the Committee finds no justification for derogation from these guarantees during other emergency situations. The Committee is of the opinion that the principles of legality and the rule of law require that fundamental requirements of fair trial must be respected during a state of emergency (paragraph 16)." Any derogation "strictly required by the exigencies of the situation" should be consistent with the principles of the proper administration of justice. Consequently, all the principles relating to the administration of justice by military tribunals should continue to apply in full. In particular, military tribunals should not be substituted for ordinary courts, in derogation from ordinary law, by being given jurisdiction to try civilians.

Principle No. 4: Application of humanitarian law. In time of armed conflict, the principles of humanitarian law, and in particular the provisions of the Geneva Convention relative to the Treatment of Prisoners of War, are fully applicable to military courts.

Comments: International humanitarian law also establishes minimum guarantees in judicial matters. Article 75, paragraph 4, of Protocol I to the Geneva Conventions of 12 August 1949 provides the fundamental guarantees in judicial matters that must be respected even during international conflicts, referring to an "impartial and regularly constituted court", which, as the International Committee of the Red Cross (ICRC) has stated, "emphasizes the need for administering justice as impartially as possible, even in the extreme circumstances of armed conflict, when the value of human life is sometimes small". Article 6, paragraph 2, of Protocol II refers to a "court offering the essential guarantees of independence and impartiality". According to ICRC, "this sentence reaffirms the principle that anyone accused of having committed an offence related to the conflict is entitled to a fair trial. This right can only be effective if the judgement is given by 'a court offering the essential guarantees of independence and impartiality'". If respect for these judicial guarantees is compulsory during armed conflicts, it is not clear how such guarantees could not be absolutely respected in the absence of armed conflict. The protection of rights in peacetime should be greater than, if not equal to, that recognized in wartime.

Article 84 of the Geneva Convention relative to the Treatment of Prisoners of War reads:

"A prisoner of war shall be tried only by a military court, unless the existing laws of the Detaining Power expressly permit the civil courts to try a member of the armed forces of the Detaining Power in respect of the particular offence alleged to have been committed by the prisoner of war. In no circumstances whatever shall a prisoner of war be tried by a court of any kind which does not offer the essential guarantees of independence and impartiality as generally recognized, and, in particular, the procedure of which does not afford the accused the rights and means of defence provided for in article 105." All the provisions of the Convention are designed to guarantee strict equality of treatment "by the same courts according to the same procedure as in the case of members of the armed forces of the Detaining Power" (Article 102). Should any doubt arise as to whether "persons having committed a belligerent act and having fallen into the hands of the enemy" are prisoners of war, "such persons shall enjoy the protection of the present Convention until such time as their status has been determined by a competent tribunal" (Article 5).

Moreover, under the Geneva Convention relative to the Protection of Civilian Persons in Time of War of 12 August 1949, in situations of military occupation, "in case of a breach of the penal provisions promulgated by it by virtue of the second paragraph of article 64, the Occupying Power may hand over the accused to its properly constituted, non-political military courts, on condition that the said courts sit in the occupied country. Courts of appeal shall preferably sit in the occupied country (Article 66). The Convention stipulates that "the court shall apply only those provisions of law which were applicable prior to the offence, and which are in accordance with general principles of law, in particular the principle that the penalty shall be proportionate to the offence" (Article 67).

Principle No. 5: Jurisdiction of military courts to try civilians. Military courts should, in principle, have no jurisdiction to try civilians. In all circumstances, the State shall ensure that civilians accused of a criminal offence of any nature are tried by civilian courts.

Comments: In paragraph 4 of its general comment No. 13 on article 14 of the International Covenant on Civil and Political Rights, the Human Rights Committee noted "the existence, in many countries, of military or special tribunals which try civilians. This could present serious problems as far as the equitable, impartial and independent administration of justice is concerned. Quite often the reason for the establishment of such courts is to enable exceptional procedures to be applied which do not comply with normal standards of justice. While the Covenant does not prohibit such categories of courts, nevertheless the conditions which it lays down clearly indicate that the trying of civilians by such courts should be very exceptional and take place under conditions which genuinely afford the full guarantees stipulated in article 14".

The Human Rights Committee's practice over the past 20 years, particularly in its views concerning individual communications or its concluding observations on national reports, has only increased its vigilance, in order to ensure that the jurisdiction of military tribunals is restricted to offences of a strictly military nature committed by military personnel. Many thematic or country rapporteurs have also taken a very strong position in favour of military tribunals' lack of authority to try civilians. Similarly, the jurisprudence of the European Court of Human Rights, the Inter-American Court of Human Rights, the Inter-American Commission on Human Rights and the African Commission on Human and Peoples' Rights is unanimous on this point. As the Basic Principles on the Independence of the Judiciary put it, "everyone has the right to be tried by ordinary courts or tribunals using established legal procedures. Tribunals that do not use the duly established procedures of the legal process shall not be created to displace the jurisdiction belonging to the ordinary courts or judicial tribunals".

Principle No. 6: Conscientious objection to military service. Conscientious objector status should be determined under the supervision of an independent and impartial civil court, providing all the guarantees of a fair trial, irrespective of the stage of military life at which it is invoked.

Comments: When the right to conscientious objection is not recognized by the law, the conscientious objector is treated as a deserter and the military criminal code is applied to him or her. The United Nations has recognized the existence of conscientious objection to military service as a legitimate exercise of the right to freedom of thought, conscience and religion, as laid down in the Universal Declaration of Human Rights and the International Covenant on Civil and Political Rights. The Human Rights Committee has very clearly linked conscientious objection to the principle of freedom of conscience enshrined in article 18 of the Covenant. It has expressed its concern on several occasions recently at the fact that military courts have punished conscientious objectors for failing to perform military service. It considers that a person may invoke the right to conscientious objection not only before entering military service or joining the armed forces but also once he or she is in the service or even afterwards.

When the application for conscientious objector status is lodged before entry into military service, there should be no bar to the jurisdiction of an independent body under the control of a civilian judge under the ordinary law. The matter may appear more complicated when the application is lodged in the course of military service, when the objector is already in uniform and subject to military justice. Yet such an application should not be punished ipso facto as an act of insubordination or desertion, independently of any consideration of its substance, but should be examined in accordance with the same procedure by an independent body that offers all the guarantees of a fair trial. In case conscientious objectors are civilians, they should be tried in civil courts, under the supervision of ordinary judges.

Principle No. 7: Jurisdiction of military tribunals to try minors under the age of 18. Strict respect for the guarantees provided in the Convention on the Rights of the Child and the United Nations Standard Minimum Rules for the Administration of Juvenile Justice (Beijing Rules) should govern the prosecution and punishment of minors, who fall within the category of vulnerable persons. In no case, therefore, should minors be placed under the jurisdiction of military courts.

Comments: Articles 40 and 37 (d) of the Convention on the Rights of the Child (CRC) list the specific safeguards applicable to minors under 18 on the basis of their age, in addition to the safeguards under ordinary law that have already been mentioned. These provisions allow for the ordinary courts to be bypassed in favour of institutions or procedures better suited to the protection of children. A fortiori these protective arrangements rule out the jurisdiction of military courts in the case of persons who are minors.

Young volunteers represent a borderline case, given that article 38, paragraph 3, of the CRC allows the recruitment of minors aged between 15 and 18 if States have not ratified the Optional Protocol on the involvement of children in armed conflicts. In the event of armed conflict, article 38 provides that the principles of international humanitarian law should apply. In this regard, special attention should be paid to the situation of child soldiers in the case of war crimes or large-scale violations of human rights. Only civilian courts would appear to be well placed to take into account all the requirements of the proper administration of justice in such circumstances, in keeping with the purposes of the Convention.

Principle No. 8: Functional authority of military courts. The jurisdiction of military courts should be limited to offences of a strictly military nature committed by military personnel. Military courts may try persons treated as military personnel for infractions strictly related to their military status.

Comments: The jurisdiction of military tribunals to try military personnel or personnel treated as military personnel should not constitute a derogation in principle from ordinary law, corresponding to a jurisdictional privilege or a form of justice by one's peers. Such jurisdiction should remain exceptional and apply only to the requirements of military service. This concept constitutes the "nexus" of military justice, particularly as regards field operations, when the territorial court cannot exercise its jurisdiction. Only such a functional necessity can justify the limited but irreducible existence of military justice. The national court is prevented from exercising its active or passive jurisdiction for practical reasons arising from the remoteness of the action, while the local court that would be territorially competent is confronted with jurisdictional immunities. The distinction between combatants and non-combatants and the protection of civilian persons in time of war both require special attention in the light of the 1949 Geneva Conventions and their two Additional Protocols of 1977.

Principle No. 9: Trial of persons accused of serious human rights violations. In all circumstances, the jurisdiction of military courts should be set aside in favour of the jurisdiction of the ordinary courts to conduct inquiries into serious human rights violations such as extrajudicial executions, enforced disappearances and torture, and to prosecute and try persons accused of such crimes.

Comments: Contrary to the functional concept of the jurisdiction of military tribunals, there is today a growing tendency to consider that persons accused of serious human rights violations cannot be tried by military tribunals insofar as such acts would, by their very nature, not fall within the scope of the duties performed by such persons. Moreover, the military authorities might be tempted to cover up such cases by questioning the appropriateness of prosecutions, tending to file cases with no action taken or manipulating "guilty pleas" to victims' detriment. Civilian courts must therefore be able, from the outset, to conduct inquiries and prosecute and try those charged with such violations. The initiation by a civilian judge of a preliminary inquiry is a decisive step towards avoiding all forms of impunity. The authority of the civilian judge should also enable the rights of the victims to be taken fully into account at all stages of the proceedings.

This was the solution favoured by the General Assembly when it adopted the Declaration on the Protection of All Persons from Enforced Disappearances, which stipulates that persons presumed responsible for such crimes "shall be tried only by the competent ordinary courts in each State, and not by any other special tribunal, in particular military courts". The constituent parts of the crime of enforced disappearance cannot be considered to have been committed in the performance of military duties. The Working Group on Enforced or Involuntary Disappearances mentioned this principle in its most recent report, referring to the need to have recourse to a "competent civilian court". The 1994 Inter-American Convention on Forced Disappearance of Persons establishes the same principle in article IX.

The scope of the principle has been extended in the updated Set of principles for the promotion and protection of human rights through action to combat impunity: "The jurisdiction of military tribunals must be restricted solely to specifically military offences committed by military personnel, to the exclusion of human rights violations, which shall come under the jurisdiction of the ordinary domestic courts or, where appropriate, in the case of serious crimes under international law, of an international or internationalized criminal court."

Above all, it must be observed that the doctrine and jurisprudence of the Human Rights Committee, the Committee against Torture, the Committee on the Rights of the Child, the African Commission on Human and Peoples' Rights, the Inter-American Court of Human Rights and the Inter-American Commission on Human Rights and the country-specific and thematic procedures of the United Nations Commission on Human Rights, are unanimous: military tribunals are not competent to try military personnel responsible for serious human rights violations against civilians.

Principle No. 10: Limitations on military secrecy. The rules that make it possible to invoke the secrecy of military information should not be diverted from their original purpose in order to obstruct the course of justice or to violate human rights. Military secrecy may be invoked, under the supervision of independent monitoring bodies, when it is strictly necessary to protect information concerning national defence. Military secrecy may not be invoked:

(a) Where measures involving deprivation of liberty are concerned, which should not, under any circumstances, be kept secret, whether this involves the identity or the whereabouts of persons deprived of their liberty;

(b) In order to obstruct the initiation or conduct of inquiries, proceedings or trials, whether they are of a criminal or a disciplinary nature, or to ignore them;

(c) To deny judges and authorities delegated by law to exercise judicial activities access to documents and areas classified or restricted for reasons of national security;

(d) To obstruct the publication of court sentences;

(e) To obstruct the effective exercise of habeas corpus and other similar judicial remedies.

Comments: The invocation of military secrecy should not lead to the holding incommunicado of a person who is the subject of judicial proceedings, or who has already been sentenced or subjected to any degree of deprivation of liberty. The Human Rights Committee, in its general comment No. 29 concerning states of emergency (article 4 of the Covenant), considered that "States parties may in no circumstances invoke article 4 of the Covenant as justification for acting in violation of humanitarian law or peremptory norms of international law, for instance by taking hostages..., through arbitrary deprivations of liberty..." (para. 11), and "the prohibitions against taking of hostages, abductions or unacknowledged detention are not subject to derogation. The absolute nature of these prohibitions, even in times of emergency, is justified by their status as norms of general international law" (para. 13).

In its general comment No. 20, the Human Rights Committee stressed that "to guarantee the effective protection of detained persons, provisions should be made for detainees to be held in places officially recognized as places of detention and for their names and places of detention, as well as for the names of persons responsible for their detention, to be kept in registers readily available and accessible to those concerned, including relatives and friends". The Committee adds that "provisions should also be made against incommunicado detention" (para. 11).

In times of crisis, humanitarian law provides for the possibility of communication with the outside world, in accordance with section V of the Geneva Convention relative to the Treatment of Prisoners of War, of 12 August 1949. The European Court of Human Rights has described the situation of families lacking information on the fate of their near and dear ones as "inhuman treatment" within the meaning of article 3 of the European Convention on Human Rights, in *Cyprus v. Turkey* [2001]. The Human Rights Committee and the Inter-American Court of Human Rights and Inter-American Commission on Human Rights have followed the same approach. It is important to recall that article 32 of the Protocol Additional to the Geneva Conventions of 12 August 1949, and relating to the Protection of Victims of International Armed Conflicts (Protocol I) posits, as a general principle concerning missing and dead persons, "the right of families to know the fate of their relatives".

It should also be stressed that persons deprived of their liberty should be held in official places of detention and the authorities should keep a register of detained persons. As far as communication between persons deprived of their liberty and their lawyers is concerned, it should be recalled that the Basic Principles on the Role of Lawyers stipulate that "all arrested, detained or imprisoned persons shall be provided with adequate opportunities, time and facilities to be visited by and to communicate and consult with a lawyer, without delay, interception or censorship and in full confidentiality. Such consultations may be within sight, but not within the hearing, of law enforcement officials".

Principle No. 11: Military prison regime. Military prisons must comply with international standards, including the Standard Minimum Rules for the Treatment of Prisoners, the Basic Principles for the Treatment of Prisoners, and the Body of Principles for the Protection of All Persons under Any Form of Detention or Imprisonment, and must be accessible to domestic and international inspection bodies.

Comments: Military prisons must comply with international standards in ordinary law, subject to effective supervision by domestic and international inspection bodies. In the same way that military justice must conform to the principles of the proper administration of justice, military prisons must not depart from international standards for the protection of individuals subject to detention or imprisonment. In keeping with the preceding principles and pursuant to the principle of "separation of categories" cited in the Standard Minimum Rules for the Treatment of Prisoners, it should not be possible for a civilian to be held in a military prison. This applies to disciplinary blocks as well as military prisons or other internment camps under military supervision, and to all prisoners, whether in pretrial detention or serving sentence after conviction for a military offence.

Principle No. 12: Guarantee of habeas corpus. In all circumstances, anyone who is deprived of his or her liberty shall be entitled to take proceedings, such as habeas corpus proceedings, before a court, in order that that court may decide without delay on the lawfulness of his or her detention and order his or her release if the detention is not lawful. The right to petition for a writ of habeas corpus or other remedy should be considered as a personal right, the guarantee of which should, in all circumstances, fall within the exclusive jurisdiction of the ordinary courts. In all circumstances, the judge must be able to have access to any place where the detainee may be held.

Comments: The right of access to justice - the "right to the law" - is one of the foundations of the rule of law. In the words of article 9, paragraph 4, of the International Covenant on Civil and Political Rights: "Anyone who is deprived of his liberty by arrest or detention shall be entitled to take proceedings before a court, in order that that court may decide without delay on the lawfulness of his detention and order his release if the detention is not lawful." In wartime, the guarantees under humanitarian law, including the Geneva Convention relative to the Protection of Civilian Persons in Time of War, of 12 August 1949, apply in full. In its general comment No. 29 on states of emergency (article 4 of the Covenant), the Human Rights Committee stated (paras. 14 and 16) that "article 2, paragraph 3, of the Covenant requires a State party to the Covenant to provide remedies for any violation of the provisions of the Covenant.

Principle No. 13: Right to a competent, independent and impartial tribunal. The organization and operation of military courts should fully ensure the right of everyone to a competent, independent and impartial tribunal at every stage of legal proceedings from initial investigation to trial. The persons selected to perform the functions of judges in military courts must display integrity and competence and show proof of the necessary legal training and qualifications. Military judges should have a status guaranteeing their independence and impartiality, in particular vis-à-vis the military hierarchy. In no circumstances should military courts be allowed to resort to procedures involving anonymous or "faceless" judges and prosecutors.

Comments: This fundamental right is set out in article 10 of the Universal Declaration of Human Rights: "Everyone is entitled in full equality to a fair and public hearing by an independent and impartial tribunal, in the determination of his rights and obligations and of any criminal charge against him." Article 14 of the International Covenant on Civil and Political Rights, like the regional conventions, provides details of its practical scope. Regarding the concept of an independent and impartial tribunal, a large body of case law has spelled out the subjective as well as the objective content of independence and impartiality. Particular emphasis has been placed on the English adage that "justice should not only be done but should be seen to be done". It is also important to emphasize that the Human Rights Committee has stated that "the right to be tried by an independent and impartial tribunal is an absolute right that may suffer no exception".

The statutory independence of judges vis-a-vis the military hierarchy must be strictly protected, avoiding any direct or indirect subordination, whether in the organization and operation of the system of justice itself or in terms of career development for military judges. The concept of impartiality is still more complex in the light of the above-mentioned English adage, as the parties have good reason to view the military judge as an officer who is capable of being "judge in his own cause" in any case involving the armed forces as an institution, rather than a specialist judge on the same footing as any other. The presence of civilian judges in the composition of military tribunals can only reinforce the impartiality of such tribunals.

Emphasis should also be placed on the requirement that judges called on to sit in military courts should be competent, having undergone the same legal training as that required of professional judges. The legal competence and ethical standards of military judges, as judges who are fully aware of their duties and responsibilities, form an intrinsic part of their independence and impartiality.

The system of anonymous or "faceless" military judges and prosecutors has been heavily criticized by the Human Rights Committee, the Committee against Torture, the Special Rapporteur on the independence of judges and lawyers, and others. The Human Rights Committee has ruled that in a system of trial by "faceless judges", neither the independence nor the impartiality of the judges is guaranteed, and such a system also fails to safeguard the presumption of innocence.

Principle No. 14: Public nature of hearings. As in matters of ordinary law, public hearings must be the rule, and the holding of sessions in camera should be altogether exceptional and be authorized by a specific, well-grounded decision the legality of which is subject to review.

Comments: Public hearings are one of the fundamental elements of a fair trial. The only restrictions on this principle are those laid down in ordinary law, in keeping with article 14, paragraph 1, of the International Covenant on Civil and Political Rights: "The press and the public may be excluded from all or part of a trial for reasons of morals, public order (ordre public) or national security in a democratic society, or when the interest of the private lives of the parties so requires, or to the extent strictly necessary in the opinion of the court in special circumstances where publicity would prejudice the interests of justice ... ." All these grounds must be strictly interpreted, particularly when "national security" is invoked, and must be applied only where necessary in "a democratic society". The Covenant also states that "any judgement rendered in a criminal case or in a suit at law shall be made public except where the interest of juvenile persons otherwise requires ...". This is not the case, at least in principle, where proceedings in military courts are concerned. Here, too, a statement of the grounds for a court ruling is a condition sine qua non for any possibility of a remedy and any effective supervision.

Principle No. 15: Guarantee of the rights of the defence and the right to a just and fair trial. The exercise of the rights of the defence must be fully guaranteed in military courts under all circumstances. All judicial proceedings in military courts must offer the following guarantees:

(a) Everyone charged with a criminal offence shall be presumed innocent until proved guilty according to law;

(b) Every accused person must be informed promptly of the details of the offence with which he or she is charged and, before and during the trial, must be guaranteed all the rights and facilities necessary for his or her defence;

(c) No one shall be punished for an offence except on the basis of individual criminal responsibility;

(d) Everyone charged with a criminal offence shall have the right to be tried without undue delay and in his or her presence;

(e) Everyone charged with a criminal offence shall have the right to defend himself or herself in person or through legal assistance of his or her own choosing; to be informed, if he or she does not have legal assistance, of this right; and to have legal assistance assigned to him or her, in any case where the interests of justice so require, and without payment by him or her in any such case if he or she does not have sufficient means to pay for it;

(f) No one may be compelled to testify against himself or herself or to confess guilt;

(g) Everyone charged with a criminal offence shall have the right to examine, or have examined, the witnesses against him or her and to obtain the attendance and examination of witnesses on his or her behalf under the same conditions as witnesses against him or her;

(h) No statement or item of evidence which is established to have been obtained through torture, cruel, inhuman or degrading treatment or other serious violations of human rights or by illicit means may be invoked as evidence in the proceedings;

(i) No one may be convicted of a crime on the strength of anonymous testimony or secret evidence;

(j) Everyone convicted of a crime shall have the right to have his or her conviction and sentence reviewed by a higher tribunal according to law;

(k) Every person found guilty shall be informed, at the time of conviction, of his or her rights to judicial and other remedies and of the time limits for the exercise of those rights.

Comments: In paragraph 4 of its general comment No. 13, the Human Rights Committee stated that "the provisions of article 14 of ICCPR apply to all courts and tribunals within the scope of that article whether ordinary or specialized". In its jurisprudence and in its general comment No. 29, the Committee considered that a number of procedural rights and judicial guarantees set out in article 14 of the Covenant are not subject to derogation. At its eightieth session, in 2004, the Committee decided to draft a new general comment on article 14 of the Covenant, particularly with a view to updating general comment No. 13.

International humanitarian law establishes minimum guarantees in judicial matters. Article 75, paragraph 4, of Protocol I to the Geneva Conventions reiterates the judicial guarantees set out in article 14, paragraphs 2 and 3, of the Covenant and those mentioned in article 15 of the Covenant. This article is not subject to derogation by virtue of article 4, paragraph 2, of the Covenant. It should be emphasized that, in paragraph 16 of its general comment No. 29, the Human Rights Committee stated that "as certain elements of the right to a fair trial are explicitly guaranteed under international humanitarian law during armed conflict, the Committee finds no justification for derogation from these guarantees during other emergency situations".

The provision of legal assistance by military lawyers, particularly when they are officially appointed, has been challenged as inconsistent with respect for the rights of the defence. In the light of the adage: "justice should not only be done but should be seen to be done", the presence of military lawyers damages the credibility of these jurisdictions. Yet experience shows that the trend towards the strict independence of military lawyers - if it proves to be genuine despite the fundamental ambiguity in the title - helps to guarantee to accused persons an effective defence that is adapted to the functional constraints involved in military justice, particularly when it is applied extraterritorially. Nevertheless, the principle of free choice of defence counsel should be maintained, and accused persons should be able to call on lawyers of their own choosing if they do not wish to avail themselves of the assistance of a military lawyer. For this reason, rather than advocating the simple abolition of the post of military lawyer, it seemed preferable to note the current trend, subject to two conditions: that the principle of free choice of defence counsel by the accused is safeguarded, and that the strict independence of the military lawyer is guaranteed.

Principle No. 16: Access of victims to proceedings. Without prejudice to the principles relating to the jurisdiction of military courts, such courts should not exclude the victims of crimes or their successors from judicial proceedings, including inquiries. The judicial proceedings of military courts should ensure that the rights of the victims of crimes - or their successors - are effectively respected, by guaranteeing that they:

(a) Have the right to report criminal acts and bring an action in the military courts so that judicial proceedings can be initiated;

(b) Have a broad right to intervene in judicial proceedings and are able to participate in such proceedings as a party to the case, e.g. a claimant for criminal indemnification, an *amicus curiae* or a party bringing a private action;

(c) Have access to judicial remedies to challenge decisions and rulings by military courts against their rights and interests;

(d) Are protected against any ill-treatment and any act of intimidation or reprisal that might arise from the complaint or from their participation in the judicial proceedings.

Comments: All too often, victims are still excluded from investigations when a military court has jurisdiction; this makes it easy to file cases without taking action on grounds of expediency, or to make deals or come to amicable arrangements that flout victims' rights and interests. Such blatant inequality before the law should be abolished or, pending this, strictly limited. The presence of the victim or his or her successors should be obligatory, or the victim should be represented whenever he or she so requests, at all stages of the investigation and at the reading of the judgement, with prior access to all the evidence in the file.

Principle No. 17: Recourse procedures in the ordinary courts. In all cases where military tribunals exist, their authority should be limited to ruling in first instance. Consequently, recourse procedures, particularly appeals, should be brought before the civil courts. In all situations, disputes concerning legality should be settled by the highest civil court. Conflicts of authority and jurisdiction between military tribunals and ordinary courts must be resolved by a higher judicial body, such as a Supreme Court or constitutional court, that forms part of the system of ordinary courts and is composed of independent, impartial and competent judges.

Comments: In resolution 2005/30, "Integrity of the judicial system", the Commission on Human Rights highlighted this issue with a reference to "procedures that are recognized according to international law as guarantees of a fair trial, including the right to appeal a conviction and a sentence" (para. 8). While the residual maintenance of first-degree military courts may be justified by their functional authority, there would seem to be no justification for the existence of a parallel hierarchy of military tribunals separate from ordinary law. Indeed, the requirements of proper administration of justice by military courts dictate that remedies, especially those involving challenges to legality, are heard in civil courts. In this way, at the appeal stage or, at the very least, the cassation stage, military tribunals would form "an integral part of the general judicial system". Such recourse procedures should be available to the accused and the victims; this presupposes that victims are allowed to participate in the proceedings, particularly during the trial stage. Similarly, an impartial judicial mechanism for resolving conflicts of jurisdiction or authority should be established. This principle is vital, because it guarantees that military tribunals do not constitute a parallel system of justice outside the control of the judicial authorities. It is interesting to note that this was recommended by the Special Rapporteur on the question of torture and the Special Rapporteur on extrajudicial, summary or arbitrary executions.

Principle No. 18: Due obedience and responsibility of the superior. Without prejudice to the principles relating to the jurisdiction of military tribunals:

(a) Due obedience may not be invoked to relieve a member of the military of the individual criminal responsibility that he or she incurs as a result of the commission of serious violations of human rights, such as extrajudicial executions, enforced disappearances and torture, war crimes or crimes against humanity;

(b) The fact that a serious violation of human rights, such as an extrajudicial execution, an enforced disappearance, torture, a war crime or a crime against humanity has been committed by a subordinate does not relieve his or her superiors of criminal responsibility if they failed to exercise the powers vested in them to prevent or halt their commission, if they were in possession of information that enabled them to know that the crime was being or was about to be committed.

Comments: The principle of due obedience, often invoked in courts and tribunals, particularly military tribunals, should, in the framework of this review, be subject to the following limitations: the fact that the person allegedly responsible for a violation acted on the order of a superior should not relieve him or her of criminal responsibility. At most, this circumstance could be considered as grounds not for "extenuating circumstances" but for a reduced sentence. Conversely, violations committed by a subordinate do not relieve his or her hierarchical superiors of their criminal responsibility if they knew or had reason to know that their subordinate was committing, or was about to commit, such violations, and they did not take the action within their power to prevent such violations or restrain their perpetrator.

It is important to emphasize that, where criminal proceedings and criminal responsibility are concerned, the order given by a hierarchical superior or a public authority cannot be invoked to justify extrajudicial executions, enforced disappearances, torture, war crimes or crimes against humanity, nor to relieve the perpetrators of their individual criminal responsibility. This principle is set out in many international instruments. International law establishes the rule that the hierarchical superior bears criminal responsibility for serious violations of human rights, war crimes and crimes against humanity committed by personnel under his or her effective authority and/or control. The principle of the criminal responsibility of the negligent commanding officer is recognized in many international instruments, international case law and the legislation of a number of countries.

Principle No. 19: Non-imposition of the death penalty. Codes of military justice should reflect the international trend towards the gradual abolition of the death penalty, in both peacetime and wartime. In no circumstances shall the death penalty be imposed or carried out:

(a) For offences committed by persons aged under 18;

(b) On pregnant women or mothers with young children;

(c) On persons suffering from any mental or intellectual disabilities.

Comments: The trend towards the gradual abolition of capital punishment, including in cases of international crimes, should be extended to military justice, which provides fewer guarantees than the ordinary courts since, owing to the nature of the sentence, judicial error in this instance is irreversible. Although the death penalty is not prohibited under international law, international human rights instruments clearly lean towards abolition. In particular, the application of the death penalty to vulnerable persons, particularly minors, should be avoided in all circumstances, in keeping with article 6, paragraph 5, of the International Covenant on Civil and Political Rights, which provides that "sentence of death shall not be imposed for crimes committed by persons below 18 years of age ... ". Imposition of the death penalty on pregnant women, mothers with young children and people with mental or intellectual disabilities is also prohibited, as stated in Commission resolution 2005/59 on the question of the death penalty (para. 7). In the same resolution, the Commission "urges all States that still maintain the death penalty ... to ensure that all legal proceedings, including those before special tribunals or jurisdictions, and particularly those related to capital offences, conform to the minimum procedural guarantees contained in article 14 of the International Covenant on Civil and Political Rights." Sub-Commission resolution 2004/25 recommends that the death penalty should not be imposed on civilians tried by military tribunals or by courts in which one or more of the judges is a member of the armed forces. The same should apply to conscientious objectors on trial for desertion before military tribunals.

Principle No. 20: Review of codes of military justice. Codes of military justice should be subject to periodic systematic review, conducted in an independent and transparent manner, so as to ensure that the authority of military tribunals corresponds to strict functional necessity, without encroaching on the jurisdiction that can and should belong to ordinary civil courts.

Comments: Since the sole justification for the existence of military tribunals has to do with practical eventualities, such as those related to peacekeeping operations or extraterritorial situations, there is a need to check periodically whether this functional requirement still prevails. Each such review of codes of military justice should be carried out by an independent body, which should recommend legislative reforms designed to limit any unjustified residual authority and thus return, to the greatest extent possible, to the jurisdiction of the civil courts under ordinary law, while seeking to avoid double jeopardy. More generally, this periodic review should ensure that military justice is appropriate and effective in relation to its practical justification. It would also embody the fully democratic nature of an institution that must be accountable for its operations to the authorities and all citizens. In this way, the fundamental discussion concerning the existence of military justice as such can be conducted in a completely transparent way in a democratic society.

CHAPTER 13

REGIONAL CONVENTIONS

Comments: The main regional human rights instruments are the European Convention for the Protection of Human Rights and Fundamental Freedoms (1950), the American Convention on Human Rights (1969), and the African Charter on Human and Peoples' Rights (1981). The European Convention on Human Rights was adopted by the Council of Europe in 1950, and entered into force on 3 September 1953. The Convention originally created both a European Commission and a European Court of Human Rights entrusted with the observance of the engagements undertaken by the High Contracting Parties to the Convention, but with the entry into force of Protocol No. 1137 to the Convention on 1 November 1998, the control machinery was restructured so that all allegations are now directly referred to the European Court of Human Rights in Strasbourg, France.

The American Convention on Human Rights, 1969, also commonly called the Pact of San José, entered into force on 18 July 1978. The Convention reinforced the Inter-American Commission on Human Rights, which had existed as "an autonomous entity of the Organization of American States" since 1960. It became a treaty-based organ which, together with the Inter-American Court of Human Rights, has "competence with respect to matters relating to the fulfilment of the commitments made by the States Parties" to the Convention.

The adoption of the African Charter on Human and Peoples' Rights in 1981 was the beginning of a new era in the field of human rights in Africa. It entered into force on 21 October 1986. Although strongly inspired by the Universal Declaration of Human Rights, the two International Covenants on human rights and the regional human rights conventions, the African Charter reflects a high degree of specificity due in particular to the African conception of the term "right" and the place it accords to the responsibilities of human beings. The Charter contains a long list of rights, covering a wide spectrum not only of civil and political rights, but also of economic, social and cultural rights.

Over the past few decades, regional human rights tribunals have grown in both number and activity. The European Court of Human Rights now receives tens of thousands of petitions and issues over fifteen hundred judgments each year. The Inter-American Court of Human Rights recently tripled the number of cases that it resolves annually. The African Court on Human and Peoples' Rights, which started hearing cases in 2008, has already developed a rich jurisprudence.

13.1 REGIONAL CONVENTIONS

1. European Convention on Human Rights, 1950

The European Convention on Human Rights (ECHR) was adopted by the Council of Europe in 1950, and entered into force on 3 September 1953. The Convention originally created both a European Commission and a European Court of Human Rights entrusted with the observance of the engagements undertaken by the High Contracting Parties to the Convention, but with the entry into force of Protocol No. 11 to the Convention on 1 November 1998, the control machinery was restructured so that all allegations are now directly referred to the European Court of Human Rights (ECtHR) in Strasbourg, France. This Court is the first, and so far only, permanent human rights court sitting on a full-time basis. The rights protected by the Convention have been extended by Additional Protocols Nos. 1, 4, 6, 7, 12 and 13. Protocol No. 12 concerning the prohibition of discrimination was opened for signature on 4 November 2000 and Protocol No. 13, concerning the abolition of the death penalty in all circumstances, was opened for signature on 3 May 2002.

Article 6 of the ECHR dealing with the right to a fair trial provides:

> In the determination of his civil rights and obligations or of any criminal charge against him, everyone is entitled to a fair and public hearing within a reasonable time by an independent and impartial tribunal established by law. Judgement shall be pronounced publicly by the press and public may be excluded from all or part of the trial in the interest of morals, public order or national security in a democratic society, where the interests of juveniles or the protection of the private life of the parties so require, or the extent strictly necessary in the opinion of the court in special circumstances where publicity would prejudice the interests of justice.
>
> 1. Everyone charged with a criminal offence shall be presumed innocent until proved guilty according to law.
> 2. Everyone charged with a criminal offence has the following minimum rights:

(a) to be informed promptly, in a language which he understands and in detail, of the nature and cause of the accusation against him;

(b) to have adequate time and the facilities for the preparation of his defence;

(c) to defend himself in person or through legal assistance of his own choosing or, if he has not sufficient means to pay for legal assistance, to be given it free when the interests of justice so require;

(d) to examine or have examined witnesses against him and to obtain the attendance and examination of witnesses on his behalf under the same conditions as witnesses against him;

(e) to have the free assistance of an interpreter if he cannot understand or speak the language used in court.

The achievements of the ECHR and its supreme judicial tribunal, the ECtHR, are widely acclaimed by scholars, lawyers, government officials, and human rights advocates. Since its founding over nearly 60 years ago, the Convention has expanded along three axes – jurisprudentially, institutionally, and geographically. Following the accession to the Council of Europe of former Soviet bloc states, the ECtHR's reach now extends to more than 800 million people in 47 countries stretching the length and breadth of the continent and beyond, from Azerbaijan to Iceland and from Gibraltar to Vladivostok.

2. American Convention on Human Rights, 1969

The American Convention on Human Rights, 1969, entered into force on 18 July 1978. The Convention reinforced the Inter-American Commission on Human Rights, which since 1960 had existed as "an autonomous entity of the Organization of American States (OAS)". It became a treaty-based organ which, together with the Inter-American Court of Human Rights, "shall have competence with respect to matters relating to the fulfilment of the commitments made by the States Parties" to the Convention.[1] In 1988, the General Assembly of the OAS further adopted the Additional Protocol to the American Convention on Human Rights in the Area of Economic, Social and Cultural Rights. In 1990 the General Assembly also adopted the Protocol to the American Convention on Human Rights to Abolish the Death Penalty, which entered into force on 28 August 1991. The States parties to this Protocol "shall not apply the death penalty in their territory to any person subject to their jurisdiction" (Article 1). No reservations may be

[1] Article 33, The American Convention on Human Rights, 1969.

made to this Protocol, although States parties may declare at the time of ratification or accession "that they reserve the right to apply the death penalty in wartime in accordance with international law, for extremely serious crimes of a military nature" (Article 2(1)).

As to the rights relating to administration of justice guaranteed by the Convention, they comprise the following:

(i) the right to juridical personality – art. 3;

(ii) the right to life, including careful regulation of the death penalty from an abolitionist perspective – art. 4;

(iii) the right to humane treatment, including freedom from torture and cruel, inhuman or degrading treatment or punishment – art. 5;

(iv) Freedom from slavery, servitude, forced and compulsory labour – art. 6;

(v) the right to personal liberty and security, including freedom from arbitrary arrest or detention – art. 7;

(vi) the right to a fair trial – art. 8;

(vii) the right to freedom from ex post facto laws – art. 9;

(viii) the right to compensation in the event of a miscarriage of justice – art. 10;

(ix) the right to equality before the law and equal protection of the law – art. 24; and

(x) the right to judicial protection – art. 25.

3. African Charter on Human and Peoples' Rights, 1981

The African Charter on Human and Peoples' Rights (the African Charter), is the foundational normative instrument for the protection and promotion of human rights in Africa. It has been applauded as a document which departs from the norms in that it contains civil, political, economic, social and cultural rights. In addition, it provides for "peoples' rights" and several rights not found in other instruments; and specific "third-generation" or collective rights such as the right to development, the right to a satisfactory environment, the right to peace, and the right of people to dispose of their wealth and natural resources. Unlike the International Covenant on Civil and Political Rights and the American and European Conventions on Human Rights, the African Charter does not provide for any right of derogation for the States parties in public emergencies. The right to a fair trial protected by Article 7[2] of the Charter is a pillar of the rule of law. In the African Charter, this needs be viewed in conjunction with the duty befalling states under Article 26[3] to guarantee the independence of the courts.

The African Commission has explained the nexus between Articles 7 and 26 in *Civil Liberties Organization v Nigeria,*[4] stating: "while Article 7 focuses on the individual's right to be heard, Article 26 speaks of the institutions which are essential to give meaning and content to that right. This Article clearly envisions the protection of the courts which have traditionally been the bastion of protection of the individual's right against the abuses of State power."

Recognising the need to further strengthen and supplement the provisions relating to fair trial in the African Charter and to reflect international standards, the African Commission established a Working Group in 1999 to prepare general principles and guidelines on the right to a fair trial and legal assistance under the Charter. The Principles and Guidelines on the Right to a Fair Trial and Legal Assistance in Africa were adopted at the AU Heads of State and Government Summit in Maputo, Mozambique, in 2003.

The Principles and Guidelines on the Right to a Fair Trial and Legal Assistance in Africa attempt to collate standards relevant to fair trial in one single document. The Principles and Guidelines are fairly extensive, covering a broad spectrum of issues from general principles applicable to all legal proceedings to more specific. The Principles and Guidelines protect individuals from unlawful and arbitrary infringements of their basic rights, such as the right to life and liberty. Among the general principles applicable to all legal proceedings, a fair and public hearing is given prominence. A fair hearing enshrines the principle of equality – "equality of arms between parties to a proceeding, whether they are administrative, civil, criminal or military", equality of all persons before any judicial body, equality of access by women and men to judicial bodies, as

---

[2] Article 7: 1. Every individual shall have the right to have his cause heard. This comprises: (a) the right to an appeal to competent national organs against acts of violating his fundamental rights as recognized and guaranteed by conventions, laws, regulations and customs in force; (b) the right to be presumed innocent until proved guilty by a competent court or tribunal; (c) the right to defense, including the right to be defended by counsel of his choice; (d) the right to be tried within a reasonable time by an impartial court or tribunal. 2. No one may be condemned for an act or omission which did not constitute a legally punishable offence at the time it was committed. No penalty may be inflicted for an offence for which no provision was made at the time it was committed. Punishment is personal and can be imposed only on the offender.

[3] Article 26: States parties to the present Charter shall have the duty to guarantee the independence of the Courts and shall allow the establishment and improvement of appropriate national institutions entrusted with the promotion and protection of the rights and freedoms guaranteed by the present Charter.

[4] *129/94 Civil Liberties Organization v. Nigeria,* 9th Annual Activity Report; in *Compilation 1994–2001,* IHRDA, Banjul 2002; p. 203–206, paragraph 15.

well as equality before the law in any legal proceedings. Respect for the inherent dignity of human persons is stressed, with specific mention made about the dignity of women who participate in any legal proceedings. While the Guidelines and Principles do not have the binding legal force of a treaty, they are strongly persuasive, in that they have been formally accepted by the African Union.

13.2 AFRICAN COMMISSION ON HUMAN AND PEOPLES' RIGHT: PRINCIPLES AND GUIDELINES ON THE RIGHT TO A FAIR TRIAL AND LEGAL ASSISTANCE IN AFRICA[5]

The African Commission on Human and Peoples' Rights;

Recalling its mandate under Article 45(c) of the African Charter on Human and Peoples' Rights (the Charter) "to formulate and lay down principles and rules aimed at solving legal problems relating to human and peoples' rights and fundamental freedoms upon which African states may base their legislation";

Recalling Articles 5, 6, 7 and 26 of the Charter, which contain provisions relevant to the right to a fair trial;

Recognising that it is necessary to formulate and lay down principles and rules to further strengthen and supplement the provisions relating to fair trial in the Charter and to reflect international standards;

Recalling the resolution on the Right to Recourse and Fair Trial adopted at its 11th ordinary session in March 1992, the resolution on the Respect and the Strengthening of the Independence of the Judiciary adopted at its 19th ordinary session in March 1996 and the resolution Urging States to Envisage a Moratorium on the Death Penalty adopted at its 26th ordinary session in November 1999;

Recalling also the resolution on the Right to a Fair Trial and Legal Assistance, adopted at its 26th session held in November 1999, in which it decided to prepare general principles and guidelines on the right to a fair trial and legal assistance under the African Charter;

Solemnly proclaims these Principles and Guidelines on the Right to a Fair Trial and Legal Assistance in Africa and urges that every effort is made so that they become generally known to everyone in Africa; are promoted and protected by civil society organisations, judges, lawyers,

---

[5] DOC/OS(XXX) 247, adopted 2001.

prosecutors, academics and their professional associations; are incorporated into their domestic legislation by State parties to the Charter and respected by them:

Rights, Principles and Guidelines on the Right to a Fair Trial and Legal Assistance in Africa

A. GENERAL PRINCIPLES APPLICABLE TO ALL LEGAL PROCEEDINGS

1. Fair and Public Hearing

In the determination of any criminal charge against a person, or of a person's rights and obligations, everyone shall be entitled to a fair and public hearing by a legally constituted competent, independent and impartial judicial body.

2. Fair Hearing

The essential elements of a fair hearing include:

(a) equality of arms between the parties to a proceedings, whether they be administrative, civil, criminal, or military;

(b) equality of all persons before any judicial body without any distinction whatsoever as regards race, colour, ethnic origin, sex, gender, age, religion, creed, language, political or other convictions, national or social origin, means, disability, birth, status or other circumstances;

(c) equality of access by women and men to judicial bodies and equality before the law in any legal proceedings;

(d) respect for the inherent dignity of the human persons, especially of women who participate in legal proceedings as complainants, witnesses, victims or accused;

(e) adequate opportunity to prepare a case, present arguments and evidence and to challenge or respond to opposing arguments or evidence;

(f) an entitlement to consult and be represented by a legal representative or other qualified persons chosen by the party at all stages of the proceedings;

(g) an entitlement to the assistance of an interpreter if he or she cannot understand or speak the language used in or by the judicial body;

(h) an entitlement to have a party's rights and obligations affected only by a decision based solely on evidence presented to the judicial body;

(i) an entitlement to a determination of their rights and obligations without undue delay and with adequate notice of and reasons for the decisions; and

(j) an entitlement to an appeal to a higher judicial body.

3. Public hearing

(a) All the necessary information about the sittings of judicial bodies shall be made available to the public by the judicial body;

(b) A permanent venue for proceedings by judicial bodies shall be established by the State and widely publicised. In the case of ad-hoc judicial bodies, the venue designated for the duration of their proceedings should be made public.

(c) Adequate facilities shall be provided for attendance by interested members of the public;

(d) No limitations shall be placed by the judicial body on the category of people allowed to attend its hearings where the merits of a case are being examined;

(e) Representatives of the media shall be entitled to be present at and report on judicial proceedings except that a judge may restrict or limit the use of cameras during the hearings;

(f) The public and the media may not be excluded from hearings before judicial bodies except if it is determined to be

1. In the interest of justice for the protection of children, witnesses or the identity of victims of sexual violence

2. For reasons of public order or national security in an open and democratic society that respects human rights and the rule of law.

(g) Judicial bodies may take steps or order measures to be taken to protect the identity and dignity of victims of sexual violence, and the identity of witnesses and complainants who may be put at risk by reason of their participation in judicial proceedings.

(h) Judicial bodies may take steps to protect the identity of accused persons, witnesses or complainants where it is in the best interest of a child.

(i) Nothing in these Guidelines shall permit the use of anonymous witnesses, where the judge and the defence is unaware of the witness' identity at trial.

Any judgement rendered in legal proceedings, whether civil or criminal, shall be pronounced in public.

4. Independent tribunal

(a) The independence of judicial bodies and judicial officers shall be guaranteed by the constitution and laws of the country and respected by the government, its agencies and authorities;

(b) Judicial bodies shall be established by law to have adjudicative functions to determine matters within their competence on the basis of the rule of law and in accordance with proceedings conducted in the prescribed manner;

(c) The judiciary shall have jurisdiction over all issues of a judicial nature and shall have exclusive authority to decide whether an issue submitted for decision is within the competence of a judicial body as defined by law;

(d) A judicial body's jurisdiction may be determined, inter alia, by considering where the events involved in the dispute or offence took place, where the property in dispute is located, the place of residence or domicile of the parties and the consent of the parties;

(e) Military or other special tribunals that do not use the duly established procedure of the legal process shall not be created to displace the jurisdiction belonging to the ordinary judicial bodies;

(f) There shall not be any inappropriate or unwarranted interference with the judicial process nor shall decisions by judicial bodies be subject to revision except through judicial review, or the mitigation or commutation of sentence by competent authorities, in accordance with the law;

(g) All judicial bodies shall be independent from the executive branch.

(h) The process for appointments to judicial bodies shall be transparent and accountable and the establishment of an independent body for this purpose is encouraged. Any method of judicial selection shall safeguard the independence and impartiality of the judiciary.

(i) The sole criteria for appointment to judicial office shall be the suitability of a candidate for such office by reason of integrity, appropriate training or learning and ability.

(j) Any person who meets the criteria shall be entitled to be considered for judicial office without discrimination on any grounds such as race, colour, ethnic origin, language, sex, gender, political or other opinion, religion, creed, disability, national or social origin, birth, economic or other status. However, it shall not be discriminatory for states to:

1. Prescribe a minimum age or experience for candidates for judicial office;

2. Prescribe a maximum or retirement age or duration of service for judicial officers;

3. Prescribe that such maximum or retirement age or duration of service may vary with different level of judges, magistrates or other officers in the judiciary;

4. Require that only nationals of the state concerned shall be eligible for appointment to judicial office.

(k) No person shall be appointed to judicial office unless they have the appropriate training or learning that enables them to adequately fulfil their functions.

(l) Judges or members of judicial bodies shall have security of tenure until a mandatory retirement age or the expiry of their term of office.

(m) The tenure, adequate remuneration, pension, housing, transport, conditions of physical and social security, age of retirement, disciplinary and recourse mechanisms and other conditions of service of judicial officers shall be prescribed and guaranteed by law.

(n) Judicial officers shall not be:

1. Liable in civil or criminal proceedings for improper acts or omissions in the exercise of their judicial functions;

2. Removed from office or subject to other disciplinary or administrative procedures by reason only that their decision has been overturned on appeal or review by a higher judicial body;

3. Appointed under a contract for a fixed term.

(o) Promotion of judicial officials shall be based on objective factors, in particular ability, integrity and experience.

(p) Judicial officials may only be removed or suspended from office for gross misconduct incompatible with judicial office, or for physical or mental incapacity that prevents them from undertaking their judicial duties.

(q) Judicial officials facing disciplinary, suspension or removal proceedings shall be entitled to guarantees of a fair hearing including the right to be represented by a legal representative of their choice and to an independent review of decisions of disciplinary, suspension or removal proceedings.

(r) The procedures for complaints against and discipline of judicial officials shall be prescribed by law. Complaints against judicial officers shall be processed promptly, expeditiously and fairly.

(s) Judicial officers are entitled to freedom of expression, belief, association and assembly. In exercising these rights, they shall always conduct themselves in accordance with the law and the recognized standards and ethics of their profession.

(t) Judicial officers shall be free to form and join professional associations or other organizations to represent their interests, to promote their professional training and to protect their status.

(u) States may establish independent or administrative mechanisms for monitoring the performance of judicial officers and public reaction to the justice delivery processes of judicial bodies. Such mechanisms, which shall be constituted in equal part of members the judiciary and representatives of the Ministry responsible for judicial affairs, may include processes for judicial bodies receiving and processing complaints against its officers.

(v) States shall endow judicial bodies with adequate resources for the performance of its their functions. The judiciary shall be consulted regarding the preparation of budget and its implementation.

5. Impartial Tribunal

(a) A judicial body shall base its decision only on objective evidence, arguments and facts presented before it. Judicial officers shall decide matters before them without any restrictions, improper influence, inducements, pressure, threats or interference, direct or indirect, from any quarter or for any reason.

(b) Any party to proceedings before a judicial body shall be entitled to challenge its impartiality on the basis of ascertainable facts that the fairness of the judge or judicial body appears to be in doubt.

(c) The impartiality of a judicial body could be determined on the basis of three relevant facts:

1. That the position of the judicial officer allows him or her to play a crucial role in the proceedings;

2. The judicial officer may have expressed an opinion which would influence the decision-making;

3. The judicial official would have to rule on an action taken in a prior capacity.

(d) The impartiality of a judicial body would be undermined when:

1. A former public prosecutor or legal representative sits as a judicial officer in a case in which he or she prosecuted or represented a party;

2. A judicial official secretly participated in the investigation of a case;

3. a judicial official has some connection with the case or a party to the case;

4. A judicial official sits as member of an appeal tribunal in a case which he or she decided or participated in a lower judicial body.

In any of these circumstances, a judicial official would be under an obligation to step down.

(e) A judicial official may not consult a higher official authority before rendering a decision in order to ensure that his or her decision will be upheld.

B. JUDICIAL TRAINING

(a) States shall ensure that judicial officials have appropriate education and training and should be made aware of the ideals and ethical duties of their office, of the constitutional and statutory protections for the rights of accused persons, victims and other litigants and of human rights and fundamental freedoms recognized by national and international law.

(b) States shall establish, where they do not exist, specialised institutions for the education and training of judicial officials and encourage collaboration amongst such institutions in countries in the region and throughout Africa.

(c) States shall ensure that judicial officials receive continuous training and education throughout their career including, where appropriate, in racial, cultural and gender sensitisation.

C. RIGHT TO AN EFFECTIVE REMEDY

(a) Everyone has the right to an effective remedy by competent national tribunals for acts violating the rights granted by the constitution, by law or by the Charter, notwithstanding that the acts were committed by persons in an official capacity.

(b) The right to an effective remedy includes:

1. Access to justice;

2. Reparation for the harm suffered;

3. Access to the factual information concerning the violations.

(c) Every State has an obligation to ensure that:

1. Any person whose rights have been violated, including by persons acting in an official capacity, has an effective remedy by a competent judicial body;

2. Any person claiming a right to remedy shall have such a right determined by competent judicial, administrative or legislative authorities;

3. Any remedy granted shall be enforced by competent authorities;

4. Any state body against which a judicial order or other remedy has been granted shall comply fully with such an order or remedy.

(d) The granting of amnesty to absolve perpetrators of human rights violations from accountability violates the right of victims to an effective remedy.

D. COURT RECORDS AND PUBLIC ACCESS

(a) All information regarding judicial proceedings shall be accessible to the public, except information or documents that have been specifically determined by judicial officials not to be made public.

(b) States must ensure that proper systems exist for recording all proceedings before judicial bodies, storing such information and making it accessible to the public.

(c) All decisions of judicial bodies must be published and available to everyone throughout the country.

(d) The cost to the public of obtaining records of judicial proceedings or decisions should be kept to a minimum and should not be so high as to amount to a denial of access.

E. LOCUS STANDI

States must ensure, through adoption of national legislation, that in regard to human rights violations, which are matters of public concern, any individual, group of individuals or non-governmental organization is entitled to bring an issue before judicial bodies for determination.

F. ROLE OF PROSECUTORS

(a) States shall ensure that:

1. Prosecutors have appropriate education and training and should be made aware of the ideals and ethical duties of their office, of the constitutional and statutory protections for the rights of the suspect and the victim, and of human rights and fundamental freedoms recognized by national and international law, including the Charter.

2. Prosecutors are able to perform their professional functions without intimidation, hindrance, harassment, improper interference or unjustified exposure to civil, penal or other liability.

(b) Reasonable conditions of service of prosecutors, adequate remuneration and, where applicable, tenure, housing, transport, conditions of physical and social security, pension and age of retirement and other conditions of service shall be set out by law or published rules or regulations.

(c) Promotion of prosecutors, wherever such a system exists, shall be based on objective factors, in particular professional qualifications, ability, integrity and experience, and decided upon in accordance with fair and impartial procedures.

(d) Prosecutors like other citizens are entitled to freedom of expression, belief, association and assembly. In exercising these rights, prosecutors shall always conduct themselves in accordance with the law and the recognized standards and ethics of their profession.

(e) Prosecutors shall be free to form and join professional associations or other organizations to represent their interests, to promote their professional training and to protect their status.

(f) The office of prosecutors shall be strictly separated from judicial functions.

(g) Prosecutors shall perform an active role in criminal proceedings, including institution of prosecution and, where authorized by law or consistent with local practice, in the investigation of crime, supervision over the legality of these investigations, supervision of the execution of decisions of judicial bodies and the exercise of other functions as representatives of the public interest.

(h) Prosecutors shall, in accordance with the law, perform their duties fairly, consistently and expeditiously, and respect and protect dignity and uphold human rights, thus contributing to ensuring due process and the smooth functioning of the criminal justice system.

(i) In the performance of their duties, prosecutors shall:

1. Carry out their functions impartially and avoid all political, social, racial, ethnic, religious, cultural, sexual, gender or any other kind of discrimination;

2. Protect the public interest, act with objectivity, take proper account of the position of the suspect and the victim, and pay attention to all relevant circumstances, irrespective of whether they are to the advantage or disadvantage of the suspect;

3. Keep matters in their possession confidential, unless the performance of duty or needs of justice require otherwise;

4. Consider the views and concerns of victims when their personal interests are affected and ensure that victims are informed of their rights in accordance with the provisions below relating to victims.

(j) Prosecutors shall not initiate or continue prosecution, or shall make every effort to stay proceedings, when an impartial investigation shows the charge to be unfounded.

(k) Prosecutors shall give due attention to the prosecution of crimes committed by public officials, particularly corruption, abuse of power, grave violations of human rights and other crimes recognized by international law and, where authorized by law or consistent with local practice, the investigation of such offences.

(l) When prosecutors come into possession of evidence against suspects that they know or believe on reasonable grounds was obtained through recourse to unlawful methods, which constitute a grave violation of the suspect's human rights, especially involving torture or cruel, inhuman or degrading treatment or punishment, or other abuses of human rights, they shall refuse to use such evidence against anyone other than those who used such methods, or inform the judicial body accordingly, and shall take all necessary steps to ensure that those responsible for using such methods are brought to justice.

(m) In order to ensure the fairness and effectiveness of prosecution, prosecutors shall strive to cooperate with the police, judicial bodies, the legal profession, paralegals, non-governmental organisations and other government agencies or institutions.

(n) Disciplinary offences of prosecutors shall be based on law or lawful regulations. Complaints against prosecutors, which allege that they acted in a manner that is inconsistent with professional standards, shall be processed expeditiously and fairly under appropriate procedures prescribed by law. Prosecutors shall have the right to a fair hearing including the right to be represented by a legal representative of their choice. The decision shall be subject to independent review.

(o) Disciplinary proceedings against prosecutors shall guarantee an objective evaluation and decision. They shall be determined in accordance with the law, the code of professional conduct and other established standards and ethics.

G. ACCESS TO LAWYERS AND LEGAL SERVICES

(a) States shall ensure that efficient procedures and mechanisms for effective and equal access to lawyers are provided for all persons within their territory and subject to their jurisdiction, without distinction of any kind, such as discrimination based on race, colour, ethnic origin, sex, gender, language, religion, political, or other opinion, national or social origin, property, disability, birth, economic or other status.

(b) States shall ensure that an accused person or a party to a civil case is permitted representation by a lawyer of his or her choice, including a foreign lawyer duly accredited to the national bar.

(c) States and professional associations of lawyers shall promote programmes to inform the public about their rights and duties under the law and the important role of lawyers in protecting their fundamental rights and freedoms.

H. LEGAL AID AND LEGAL ASSISTANCE

(a) The accused or a party to a civil case has a right to have legal assistance assigned to him or her in any case where the interest of justice so require, and without payment by the accused or party to a civil case if he or she does not have sufficient means to pay for it.

(b) The interests of justice should be determined by considering:

1. In criminal matters:

(i) the seriousness of the offence;

(ii) the severity of the sentence.

2. In civil cases:

(i) the complexity of the case and the ability of the party to adequately represent himself or herself;

(ii) the rights that are affected;

(iii) the likely impact of the outcome of the case on the wider community.

(c) The interests of justice always require legal assistance for an accused in any capital case, including for appeal, executive clemency, commutation of sentence, amnesty or pardon.

(d) An accused person or a party to a civil case has the right to an effective defence or representation and has a right to choose his or her own legal representative at all stages of the case. They may contest the choice of his or her court-appointed lawyer.

(e) When legal assistance is provided by a judicial body, the lawyer appointed shall:

1. Be qualified to represent and defend the accused or a party to a civil case;

2. Have the necessary training and experience corresponding to the nature and seriousness of the matter;

3. Be free to exercise his or her professional judgement in a professional manner free of influence of the State or the judicial body;

4. Advocate in favour of the accused or party to a civil case;

5. Be sufficiently compensated to provide an incentive to accord the accused or party to a civil case adequate and effective representation.

(f) Professional associations of lawyers shall co-operate in the organisation and provision of services, facilities and other resources, and shall ensure that:

1. When legal assistance is provided by the judicial body, lawyers with the experience and competence commensurate with the nature of the case make themselves available to represent an accused person or party to a civil case;

2. Where legal assistance is not provided by the judicial body in important or serious human rights cases, they provide legal representation to the accused or party in a civil case, without any payment by him or her.

(g) Given the fact that in many States the number of qualified lawyers is low, States should recognize the role that para-legals could play in the provision of legal assistance and establish the legal framework to enable them to provide basic legal assistance.

(h) States should, in conjunction with the legal profession and non-governmental organizations, establish training, the qualification procedures and rules governing the activities and conduct of para-legals. States shall adopt legislation to grant appropriate recognition to para-legals.

(i) Para-legals could provide essential legal assistance to indigent persons, especially in rural communities and would be the link with the legal profession.

(j) Non-governmental organizations should be encouraged to establish legal assistance programmes and to train para-legals.

(k) States that recognize the role of para-legals should ensure that they are granted similar rights and facilities afforded to lawyers, to the extent necessary to enable them to carry out their functions with independence.

I. INDEPENDENCE OF LAWYERS

(a) States, professional associations of lawyers and educational institutions shall ensure that lawyers have appropriate education and training and be made aware of the ideals and ethical duties of the lawyer and of human rights and fundamental freedoms recognized by national and international law.

(b) States shall ensure that lawyers:

1. Are able to perform all of their professional functions without intimidation, hindrance, harassment or improper interference;

2. Are able to travel and to consult with their clients freely both within their own country and abroad;

3. Shall not suffer, or be threatened with, prosecution or administrative, economic or other sanctions for any action taken in accordance with recognized professional duties, standards and ethics.

(c) States shall recognize and respect that all communications and consultations between lawyers and their clients within their professional relationship are confidential.

(d) It is the duty of the competent authorities to ensure lawyers access to appropriate information, files and documents in their possession or control in sufficient time to enable lawyers to provide effective legal assistance to their clients. Such access should be provided at the earliest appropriate time.

(e) Lawyers shall enjoy civil and penal immunity for relevant statements made in good faith in written or oral pleadings or in their professional appearances before a judicial body or other legal or administrative authority.

(f) Where the security of lawyers is threatened as a result of discharging their functions, they shall be adequately safeguarded by the authorities.

(g) Lawyers shall not be identified with their clients or their clients' causes as a result of discharging their functions.

(h) Lawyers shall at all times maintain the honour and dignity of their profession as essential agents of the administration of justice.

(i) Lawyers, in protecting the rights of their clients and in promoting the cause of justice, shall seek to uphold human rights and fundamental freedoms recognized by national and international law and shall at all times act freely and diligently in accordance with the law and recognized standards and ethics of the legal profession.

(j) Lawyers shall always loyally respect the interests of their clients.

(k) Lawyers like other citizens are entitled to freedom of expression, belief, association and assembly. In particular, they shall have the right to take part in public discussion of matters concerning the law, the administration of justice and the promotion and the protection of human rights and to join or form local, national or international organizations and attend their meetings, without suffering professional restrictions by reason of their lawful action or their membership in a lawful organization. In exercising these rights, lawyers shall always conduct themselves in accordance with the law and the recognized standards and ethics of the legal profession.

(l) Lawyers shall be entitled to form and join self-governing professional associations to represent their interests, promote their continuing education and training and protect their professional integrity. The executive body of the professional association shall be elected by its members and shall exercise its functions without external interference.

(m) Codes of professional conduct for lawyers shall be established by the legal profession through its appropriate organs, or by legislation, in accordance with national law and custom and recognized international standards and norms.

(n) Charges or complaints made against lawyers in their professional capacity shall be processed expeditiously and fairly under appropriate procedures. Lawyers shall have the right to a fair hearing, including the right to be assisted by a lawyer of their choice.

(o) Disciplinary proceedings against lawyers shall be brought before an impartial disciplinary committee established by the legal profession, before an independent statutory authority, or even before a judicial body, and shall be subject to an independent judicial review.

(p) All disciplinary proceedings shall be determined in accordance with the code of professional conduct, other recognized standards and ethics of the legal profession and international standards.

J. CROSS BORDER COLLABORATION AMONGST LEGAL PROFESSIONALS

(a) States shall ensure that national legislation does not prevent collaboration amongst legal professionals in countries in their region and throughout Africa.

(b) States shall encourage the establishment of agreements amongst states and professional legal associations in their region that permit cross-border collaboration amongst lawyers including legal representation, training and education, and exchange of information and expertise.

K. ACCESS TO JUDICIAL SERVICES

(a) States shall ensure that judicial bodies are accessible to everyone within their territory and jurisdiction, without distinction of any kind, such as discrimination based on race, colour, disability, ethnic origin, sex, gender, language, religion, political or other opinion, national or social origin, property, birth, economic or other status.

(b) States must take special measures to ensure that rural communities and women have access to judicial services. States must ensure that law enforcement and judicial officials are adequately trained to deal sensitively and professionally with the special needs and requirements of women.

(c) In countries where there exist groups, communities or regions whose needs for judicial services are not met, particularly where such groups have distinct cultures, traditions or languages or have been the victims of past discrimination, States shall take special measures to ensure that adequate judicial services are accessible to them.

(d) States shall ensure that access to judicial services is not impeded including by the distance to the location of judicial institutions, the lack of information about the judicial system, the imposition of unaffordable or excessive court fees and the lack of assistance to understand the procedures and to complete formalities.

L. RIGHT OF CIVILIANS NOT TO BE TRIED BY MILITARY COURTS

(a) The only purpose of Military Courts shall be to determine offences of a purely military nature committed by military personnel.

(b) While exercising this function, Military Courts are required to respect fair trial standards enunciated in the African Charter and in these guidelines.

(c) Military courts should not in any circumstances whatsoever have jurisdiction over civilians. Similarly, Special Tribunals should not try offences which fall within the jurisdiction of regular courts.

M. PROVISIONS APPLICABLE TO ARREST AND DETENTION

1. Right to liberty and security

(a) States shall ensure that the right of everyone on its territory and under its jurisdiction to liberty and security of person is respected.

(b) States must ensure that no one shall be subject to arbitrary arrest or detention, and that arrest, detention or imprisonment shall only be carried out strictly in accordance with the provisions of the law and by competent officials or persons authorized for that purpose, pursuant to a warrant, on reasonable suspicion or for probable cause.

(c) Each State shall establish rules under its national law indicating those officials authorized to order deprivation of liberty, establishing the conditions under which such orders may be given, and stipulating penalties for officials who, without legal justification, refuse to provide information on any detention.

(d) Each State shall likewise ensure strict supervision, including a clear chain of command, of all law enforcement officials responsible for apprehensions, arrests, detentions, custody, transfers and imprisonment, and of other officials authorized by law to use force and firearms.

(e) Unless there is sufficient evidence that deems it necessary to prevent a person arrested on a criminal charge from fleeing, interfering with witnesses or posing a clear and serious risk to others, States must ensure that they are not kept in custody pending their trial. However, release may be subject to certain conditions or guarantees, including the payment of bail.

(f) Expectant mothers and mothers of infants shall not be kept in custody pending their trial, but their release may be subject to certain conditions or guarantees, including the payment of bail.

(g) States shall ensure, including by the enactment of legal provisions, that officials or other persons who arbitrarily arrest or detain any person are brought to justice.

(h) States shall ensure, including by the enactment of legal provisions and adoption of procedures, that anyone who has been the victim of unlawful arrest or detention is enabled to claim compensation.

2. Rights upon arrest

(a) Anyone who is arrested shall be informed, at the time of arrest, of the reasons for his or her arrest and shall be promptly informed, in a language he or she understands, of any charges against him or her.

(b) Anyone who is arrested or detained shall be informed upon arrest, in a language he or she understands, of the right to legal representation and to be examined by a doctor of his or her choice and the facilities available to exercise this right.

(c) Anyone who is arrested or detained has the right to inform, or have the authorities notify, their family or friends. The information must include the fact of their arrest or detention and the place the person is kept in custody.

(d) If the arrested or detained person is a foreign national, he or she must be promptly informed of the right to communicate with his or her embassy or consular post. In addition, if the person is a refugee or stateless person or under the protection of an inter-governmental organization, he or she must be notified without delay of the right to communicate with the appropriate international organization.

(e) States must ensure that any person arrested or detained is provided with the necessary facilities to communicate, as appropriate, with his or her lawyer, doctor, family and friends, and in the case of a foreign national, his or her embassy or consular post or an international organization.

(f) Any person arrested or detained shall have prompt access to a lawyer and, unless the person has waived this right in writing, shall not be obliged to answer any questions or participate in any interrogation without his or her lawyer being present.

(g) Anyone who is arrested or detained shall be given reasonable facilities to receive visits from family and friends, subject to restriction and supervision only as are necessary in the interests of the administration of justice and of security of the institution.

(h) Any form of detention and all measures affecting the human rights of a person arrested or detained shall be subject to the effective control of a judicial or other authority. In order to prevent arbitrary arrest and detention or disappearances, states should establish procedures that require police or other officials with the authority to arrest and detain to inform the appropriate judicial official or other authority of the arrest and detention. The judicial official or other authority shall exercise control over the official detaining the person.

3. Right to be brought promptly before a judicial officer

(a) Anyone who is arrested or detained on a criminal charge shall be brought before a judicial officer authorized by law to exercise judicial power and shall be entitled to trial within a reasonable time or to release.

(b) The purpose of the review before a judicial or other authority includes to:

1. Assess whether sufficient legal reason exists for the arrest;

2. Assess whether detention before trial is necessary;

3. Determine whether the detainee should be released from custody, and the conditions, if any, for such release;

4. Safeguard the well-being of the detainee;

5. Prevent violations of the detainee's fundamental rights;

6. Give the detainee the opportunity to challenge the lawfulness of his or her detention and to secure release if the arrest or detention violates his or her rights.

4. Right of arrested or detained person to take proceedings before a judicial body

Anyone who is deprived of his or her liberty by arrest or detention shall be entitled to take proceedings before a judicial body, in order that that judicial body may decide without delay on the lawfulness of his or her detention and order release if the detention is not lawful.

5. Right to habeas corpus

(a) States shall enact legislation, where it does not exist, to ensure the right to habeas corpus, amparo or similar procedures.

(b) Anyone concerned or interested in the well-being, safety or security of a person deprived of his or her liberty has the right to a prompt and effective judicial remedy as a means of determining the whereabouts or state of health of such a person and/or identifying the authority ordering or carrying out the deprivation of liberty.

(c) In such proceedings, competent national authorities shall have access to all places where persons deprived of their liberty are being held and to each part of those places, as well as to any place in which there are grounds to believe that such persons may be found.

(d) Any other competent authority entitled under law of the State or by any international legal instrument to which the State is a party may also have access to such places.

(e) Judicial bodies shall at all times hear and act upon petitions for habeas corpus, amparo or similar procedures. No circumstances whatever must be invoked as a justification for denying the right to habeas corpus, amparo or similar procedures.

6. Right to be detained in a place recognised by law

(a) Any person deprived of liberty shall be held in an officially recognised place of detention.

(b) Accurate information shall be recorded regarding any person deprived of liberty including:

1. His or her identity;

2. The reasons for arrest;

3. The time of arrest and the taking of the arrested person to a place of custody;

4. The time of his first appearance before a judicial or other authority;

5. The identity of the law enforcement officials concerned;

6. Precise information concerning the place of custody;

7. Details of the judicial official or other authority informed of the arrest and detention.

(c) Accurate information on the detention of such persons and their place or places of detention, including transfers, shall be promptly available to their family members, their legal representative or to any other persons having a legitimate interest in the information.

(d) An official up-to-date register of all persons deprived of liberty shall be maintained in every place of detention and shall be made available to any judicial or other competent and independent national authority seeking to trace the whereabouts of the a detained person.

7. Right to humane treatment

(a) States shall ensure that all persons under any form of detention or imprisonment are treated in a humane manner and with respect for the inherent dignity of the human person.

(b) In particular States must ensure that no person, lawfully deprived of his or her liberty is subjected to torture or to cruel, inhuman or degrading treatment or punishment. States shall ensure that special measures are taken to protect women detainees from ill-treatment, including making certain that their interrogation is conducted by women police or judicial officials.

(c) Women shall at all times be detained separately from men and while in custody they shall receive care, protection and all necessary individual assistance – psychological, medical and physical – that they may require in view of their sex and gender.

(d) It shall be prohibited to take undue advantage of the situation of a detained or imprisoned person for the purpose of compelling him or her to confess, to incriminate himself or herself or to testify against any other person.

(e) No detained person while being interrogated shall be subject to violence, threats or methods of interrogation which impair his or her capacity of decision or his or her judgement.

(f) No detained person shall, even with his or her consent, be subjected to any medical or scientific experimentation which could be detrimental to his or her health.

(g) A detained person or his or her legal representative or family shall have the right to lodge a complaint to the relevant authorities regarding his or her treatment, in particular in case of torture or other cruel, inhuman or degrading treatment.

(h) States shall ensure that effective mechanisms exist for the receipt and investigation of such complaints. The right to lodge complaints and the existence of such mechanisms should be promptly made known to all arrested or detained persons.

(i) States shall ensure, including by the enactment of legal provisions, that officials or other persons who subject arrested or detained persons to torture or to cruel, inhuman or degrading treatment are brought to justice.

(j) States shall ensure, including by the enactment of legal provisions and adoption of procedures, that anyone who has been the victim of torture or cruel, inhuman or degrading treatment or punishment is enabled to claim compensation.

8. Supervision of places of detention

(a) In order to supervise strict observance of relevant laws and regulations and international standards applicable to detainees, places of detention shall be visited regularly by qualified and experienced persons appointed by, and responsible to, a competent authority distinct from the authority directly in charge of the administration of the place of detention.

(b) A detained person shall have the right to communicate freely and in full confidentiality with the persons who visit the places of detention or imprisonment in accordance with the above principle, subject to reasonable conditions to ensure security and good order in such places.

N. PROVISIONS APPLICABLE TO PROCEEDINGS RELATING TO CRIMINAL CHARGES:

1. Notification of charge

(a) Any person charged with a criminal offence shall be informed promptly, as soon as a charge is first made by a competent authority, in detail, and in a language, which he or she understands, of the nature and cause of the charge against him or her.

(b) The information shall include details of the charge or applicable law and the alleged facts on which the charge is based sufficient to indicate the substance of the complaint against the accused.

(c) The accused must be informed in a manner that would allow him or her to prepare a defence and to take immediate steps to secure his or her release.

2. Right to counsel

(a) The accused has the right to defend him or herself in person or through legal assistance of his or her own choosing. Legal representation is regarded as the best means of legal defence against infringements of human rights and fundamental freedoms.

(b) The accused has the right to be informed, if he or she does not have legal assistance, of the right to defend him or herself through legal assistance of his or her own choosing.

(c) This right applies during all stages of any criminal prosecution, including preliminary investigations in which evidence is taken, periods of administrative detention, trial and appeal proceedings.

(d) The accused has the right to choose his or her own counsel freely. This right begins when the accused is first detained or charged. A judicial body may not assign counsel for the accused if a qualified lawyer of the accused's own choosing is available.

3. Right to adequate time and facilities for the preparation of a defence

(a) The accused has the right to communicate with counsel and have adequate time and facilities for the preparation of his or her defence.

(b) The accused may not be tried without his or her counsel being notified of the trial date and of the charges in time to allow adequate preparation of a defence.

(c) The accused has a right to adequate time for the preparation of a defence appropriate to the nature of the proceedings and the factual circumstances of the case. Factors which may affect the adequacy of time for preparation of a defence include the complexity of the case, the defendant's access to evidence, the length of time provided by rules of procedure prior to particular proceedings, and prejudice to the defence.

(d) The accused has a right to facilities which assist or may assist the accused in the preparation of his or her defence, including the right to communicate with defence counsel and the right to materials necessary to the preparation of a defence.

(e) All arrested, detained or imprisoned persons shall be provided with adequate opportunities, time and facilities to be visited by and to communicate with a lawyer, without delay, interception or censorship and in full confidentiality.

1. The right to confer privately with one's lawyer and exchange confidential information or instructions is a fundamental part of the preparation of a defence. Adequate facilities shall be provided that preserve the confidentiality of communications with counsel.

2. States shall recognize and respect that all communications and consultations between lawyers and their clients within their professional relationship are confidential.

3. The accused or the accused's defence counsel has a right to all relevant information held by the prosecution that could help the accused exonerate him or herself.

4. It is the duty of the competent authorities to ensure lawyers access to appropriate information, files and documents in their possession or control in sufficient time to enable lawyers to provide effective legal assistance to their clients. Such access should be provided at the earliest appropriate time.

5. The accused has a right to consult legal materials reasonably necessary for the preparation of his or her defence.

6. Before judgement or sentence is rendered, the accused and his or her defence counsel shall have the right to know and challenge all the evidence which may be used to support the decision. All evidence submitted must be considered by the judicial body.

7. Following a trial and before any appellate proceeding, the accused or the defence counsel has a right of access to (or to consult) the evidence which the judicial body considered in making a decision and the judicial body's reasoning in arriving at the judgement.

4. The right to an interpreter

(a) The accused has the right to the free assistance of an interpreter if he or she cannot understand or speak the language used before the judicial body.

(b) The right to an interpreter does not extend to the right to express oneself in the language of one's choice if the accused or the defence witness is sufficiently proficient in the language of the judicial body.

(c) The right to an interpreter applies at all stages of the proceedings, including pre-trial proceedings.

(d) The right to an interpreter applies to written as well as oral proceedings. The right extends to translation or interpretation of all documents or statements necessary for the defendant to understand the proceedings or assist in the preparation of a defence.

(e) The interpretation or translation provided shall be adequate to permit the accused to understand the proceedings and for the judicial body to understand the testimony of the accused or defence witnesses.

(f) The right to interpretation or translation cannot be qualified by a requirement that the accused pay for the costs of an interpreter or translator. Even if the accused is convicted, he or she cannot be required to pay for the costs of interpretation or translation.

5. Right to trial without undue delay

(a) Every person charged with a criminal offence has the right to a trial without undue delay.

(b) The right to a trial without undue delay means the right to a trial which produces a final judgement and, if appropriate a sentence without undue delay.

(c) Factors relevant to what constitutes undue delay include the complexity of the case, the conduct of the parties, the conduct of other relevant authorities, whether an accused is detained pending proceedings, and the interest of the person at stake in the proceedings.

6. Rights during a trial

(a) In criminal proceedings, the principle of equality of arms imposes procedural equality between the accused and the public prosecutor.

1. The prosecution and defence shall be allowed equal time to present evidence.

2. Prosecution and defence witnesses shall be given equal treatment in all procedural matters.

(b) The accused is entitled to a hearing in which his or her individual culpability is determined. Group trials in which many persons are involved may violate the person's right to a fair hearing.

(c) In criminal proceedings, the accused has the right to be tried in his or her presence.

1. The accused has the right to appear in person before the judicial body.

2. The accused may not be tried in absentia. If an accused is tried in absentia, the accused shall have the right to petition for a reopening of the proceedings upon a showing that inadequate notice was given, that the notice was not personally served on the accused, or that his or her failure to appear was for exigent reasons beyond his or her control. If the petition is granted, the accused is entitled to a fresh determination of the merits of the charge.

3. The accused may voluntarily waive the right to appear at a hearing, but such a waiver shall be established in an unequivocal manner and preferably in writing.

(d) The accused has the right not to be compelled to testify against him or herself or to confess guilt.

1. Any confession or other evidence obtained by any form of coercion or force may not be admitted as evidence or considered as probative of any fact at trial or in sentencing. Any confession or admission obtained during incommunicado detention shall be considered to have been obtained by coercion.

2. Silence by the accused may not be used as evidence to prove guilt and no adverse consequences may be drawn from the exercise of the right to remain silent.

(e) Everyone charged with a criminal offence shall have the right to be presumed innocent until proved guilty according to law.

1. The presumption of innocence places the burden of proof during trial in any criminal case on the prosecution.

2. Public officials shall maintain a presumption of innocence. Public officials, including prosecutors, may inform the public about criminal investigations or charges, but shall not express a view as to the guilt of any suspect.

3. Legal presumptions of fact or law are permissible in a criminal case only if they are rebuttable, allowing a defendant to prove his or her innocence.

(f) The accused has a right to examine, or have examined, witnesses against him or her and to obtain the attendance and examination of witnesses on his or her behalf under the same conditions as witnesses against him or her.

1. The prosecution shall provide the defence with the names of the witnesses it intends to call at trial within a reasonable time prior to trial which allows the defendant sufficient time to prepare his or her defence.

2. The accused's right to examine witnesses may be limited to those witnesses whose testimony is relevant and likely to assist in ascertaining the truth.

3. The accused has the right to be present during the testimony of a witness. This right may be limited only in exceptional circumstances such as when a witness reasonably fears reprisal by the defendant, when the accused engages in a course of conduct seriously disruptive of the proceedings, or when the accused repeatedly fails to appear for trivial reasons and after having been duly notified.

4. If the defendant is excluded or if the presence of the defendant cannot be ensured, the defendant's counsel shall always have the right to be present to preserve the defendant's right to examine the witness.

5. If national law does not permit the accused to examine witnesses during pre-trial investigations, the defendant shall have the opportunity, personally or through defence counsel, to cross-examine the witness at trial. However, the right of a defendant to cross-examine witnesses personally may be limited in respect of victims of sexual violence and child witnesses, taking into consideration the defendant's right to a fair trial.

6. The testimony of anonymous witnesses during a trial will be allowed only in exceptional circumstances, taking into consideration the nature and the circumstances of the offence and the protection of the security of the witness and if it is determined to be in the interests of justice.

(g) Evidence obtained by illegal means constituting a serious violation of internationally protected human rights shall not be used as evidence against the accused or against any other person in any proceeding, except in the prosecution of the perpetrators of the violations.

7. Right to benefit from a lighter sentence or administrative sanction

(a) No one shall be held guilty of any criminal offence on account of any act or omission which did not constitute a criminal offence, under national or international law, at the time when it was committed. Nor shall a heavier penalty be imposed than the one that was applicable at the time when the criminal offence was committed. If, subsequent to the commission of the offence, provision is made by law for the imposition of a lighter penalty, the offender shall benefit therefrom.

(b) A lighter penalty created any time before an accused's sentence has been fully served should be applied to any offender serving a sentence under the previous penalty.

(c) Administrative tribunals conducting disciplinary proceedings shall not impose a heavier penalty than the one that was applicable at the time when the offending conduct occurred. If, subsequent to the conduct, provision is made by law for the imposition of a lighter penalty, the person disciplined shall benefit thereby.

8. Second trial for same offence prohibited

No one shall be liable to be tried or punished again for an offence for which he or she has already been finally convicted or acquitted in accordance with the law and penal procedure of each country.

9. Sentencing and punishment

(a) Punishments constituting a deprivation of liberty shall have as an essential aim the reform and social re-adaptation of the prisoners.

(b) In countries that have not abolished the death penalty, sentence of death may be imposed only for the most serious crimes in accordance with the law in force at the time of the commission of the crime.

(c) Sentence of death shall not be imposed or carried out on expectant mothers and mothers of infants and young children.

(d) States that maintain the death penalty are urged to establish a moratorium on executions, and to reflect on the possibility of abolishing capital punishment.

(e) States shall provide special treatment to expectant mothers and to mothers of infants and young children who have been found guilty of infringing the penal law and shall in particular:

1. Ensure that a non-custodial sentence will always be first considered when sentencing such mothers;

2. Establish and promote measures alternative to institutional confinement for the treatment of such mothers;

3. Establish special alternative institutions for holding such mothers;

4. Ensure that a mother shall not be imprisoned with her child;

5. The essential aim of the penitentiary system will be the reformation, the integration of the mother to the family and social rehabilitation.

10. Appeal

(a) Everyone convicted in a criminal proceeding shall have the right to review of his or her conviction and sentence by a higher tribunal.

1. The right to appeal shall provide a genuine and timely review of the case, including the facts and the law. If exculpatory evidence is discovered after a person is tried and convicted, the right to appeal or some other post-conviction procedure shall permit the possibility of correcting the verdict if the new evidence would have been likely to change the verdict, unless it is proved that the non-disclosure of the unknown fact in time is wholly or partly attributable to the accused.

2. A judicial body shall stay execution of any sentence while the case is on appeal to a higher tribunal.

(b) Anyone sentenced to death shall have the right to appeal to a judicial body of higher jurisdiction, and States should take steps to ensure that such appeals become mandatory.

(c) When a person has by a final decision been convicted of a criminal offence and when subsequently his or her conviction has been reversed or he or she has been pardoned on the ground that a new or newly discovered fact shows conclusively that there has been a miscarriage of justice, the person who has suffered punishment as a result of such conviction shall be compensated according to law.

(d) Every person convicted of a crime has a right to seek pardon or commutation of sentence. Clemency, commutation of sentence, amnesty or pardon may be granted in all cases of capital punishment.

O. CHILDREN AND THE RIGHT TO A FAIR TRIAL

(a) In accordance with the African Charter on the Rights and Welfare of the Child, a child is any person under the age of 18. States must ensure that domestic legislation recognises any person under the age of 18 as a child.

(b) Children are entitled to all the fair trial guarantees applicable to adults and to some additional special protection.

(c) States must ensure that law enforcement and judicial officials are adequately trained to deal sensitively and professionally with children who interact with the criminal justice system whether as suspects, accused, complainants or witnesses.

(d) States shall establish laws and procedures which set a minimum age below which children will be presumed not to have the capacity to infringe the criminal law. The age of criminal responsibility should not be fixed below 15 years of age. No child below the age of 15 shall be arrested or detained on allegations of having committed a crime.

(e) No child shall be subjected to arbitrary arrest or detention.

(f) Law enforcement officials must ensure that all contacts with children are conducted in a manner that respects their legal status, avoids harm and promotes the well-being of the child.

(g) When a child suspected of having infringed the penal law is arrested or apprehended, his or her parent, guardians or family relatives should be notified immediately.

(h) The child's right to privacy shall be respected at all times in order to avoid harm being caused to him or her by undue publicity and no information that could identify a child suspected or accused of having committed a criminal offence shall be published.

(i) States shall consider, wherever appropriate, with the consent of the child and his or parents or guardians, dealing with a child offender without resorting to a formal trial, provided the rights of the child and legal safeguards are fully respected. Alternatives to criminal prosecution, with proper safeguards for the protection of the well-being of the child, may include:

1. The use of community, customary or traditional mediation;

2. Issuing of warnings, cautions and admonitions accompanied by measures to help the child at home with education and with problems and difficulties.

3. Arranging a conference between the child, the victim and members of the community;

4. Making use of community programmes such as temporary supervision and guidance, restitution and compensation to victims.

(j) Detention pending trial shall be used only as a measure of last resort and for the shortest possible period of time. Any child who has been arrested for having committed a crime shall be released into the care of his or her parents, legal guardians or family relatives unless there are exceptional reasons for his or her detention. The competent authorities shall ensure that children are not held in detention for any period beyond 48 hours.

(k) Children who are detained pending trial shall be kept separate from adults and shall be detained in a separate institution or in a separate part of an institution also holding adults.

(l) Every child arrested or detained for having committed a criminal offence shall have the following guarantees:

1. To be treated in a manner consistent with the promotion of the child's dignity and worth;

2. To have the assistance of his or her parents, a family relative or legal guardians from the moment of arrest;

3. To be provided by the State with legal assistance from the moment of arrest;

4. To be informed promptly and directly, in a language he or she understands, of the reasons for his or her arrest and of any charges against his or her, and if appropriate, through his or her parents, other family relative, legal guardians or legal representative;

5. To be informed of his or her rights in a language he or she understands;

6. Not to be questioned without the presence of his or her parents, a family relative or legal guardians, and a legal representative;

7. Not to be subjected to torture or any other cruel, inhuman or degrading treatment or punishment or any duress or undue pressure;

8. Not to be detained in a cell or with adults detainees.

(m) States shall establish separate or specialized procedures and institutions for dealing with cases in which children are accused of or found responsible for having committed criminal offences. The establishment of such procedures and institutions shall be based on respect for the rights of the child, shall take into account the vulnerability of children and shall promote the child's rehabilitation.

(n) Every child accused of having committed a criminal offence shall have the following additional guarantees:

1. To be presumed innocent until proven guilty according to the law;

2. Charges, and if appropriate, through his or her parents or legal guardians;

3. To be provided by the State with legal or other appropriate assistance in the preparation and presentation of his or her defence;

4. To have the case determined expeditiously by a competent, independent and impartial authority or judicial body established by law in a fair hearing;

5. To have the assistance of a legal representative and, if appropriate and in the best interests of the child, his or her parents, a family relative or legal guardians, during the proceedings;

6. Not to be compelled to give testimony or confess guilt; to examine or have examine adverse witnesses and to obtain the participation of witnesses on his or her behalf under conditions of equality;

7. If considered to have infringed the penal law, to have this decision and any measures imposed in consequence thereof reviewed by a higher competent, independent and impartial authority or judicial body according to law;

8. To have the free assistance of an interpreter if he or she cannot understand or speak the language used;

9. To have his or her privacy fully respected at all stages of the proceedings.

(o) In disposing of a case involving a child who has been found to be in conflict with the law, the competent authority shall be guided by the following principles:

1. The action taken against the child shall always be in proportion not only to the circumstances and gravity of the offence but also the best interest of the child and the interests of society;

2. Non-custodial options which emphasise the value of restorative justice should be given primary consideration and restrictions on the personal liberty of a child shall only be imposed after careful consideration and shall be limited to the possible minimum. Non-custodial measures could include:

(i) Care, guidance and supervision orders;

(ii) Probation;

(iii) Financial penalties, compensation and restitution;

(iv) Intermediate treatment and other treatment orders

(v) Orders to participate in group counselling and similar activities;

(vi) Orders concerning foster care, living communities or other educational settings

3. A child shall not be sentenced to imprisonment unless the child is adjudicated of having committed a serious act involving violence against another person or of persistence in committing other serious offences and unless there is no other appropriate response;

4. Capital punishment shall not be imposed for any crime committed by children and children shall not be subjected to corporal punishment.

(p) States shall ensure that child witnesses are able to give their best evidence with the minimum distress. Investigation and practices of judicial bodies should be adapted to afford greater protection to children without undermining the defendant's right to a fair trial. States are required, as appropriate, to adopt the following measures in regard to child witnesses:

1. Child witnesses shall not be questioned by the police or any investigating official without the presence of his or her parents, a family relative or legal guardians, or where the latter are not traceable in the presence of a social worker;

2. Police and investigating officials shall conduct their questioning of child witnesses in a manner that avoids any harm and promotes the well-being of the child;

3. Police and investigating officials shall ensure that child witnesses, especially those who are victims of sexual abuse, do not come into contact with or made to confront the alleged perpetrator of the crime;

4. The child's right to privacy shall be respected at all times and no information that could identify a child witness shall be published;

5. Where necessary, a child witness shall be questioned by law enforcement officials through an intermediary;

6. A child witness should be permitted to testify before a judicial body through an intermediary, if necessary;

7. Where resources and facilities permit, video-recorded pre-trial interviews with child witnesses should be presented;

8. Screens should be set up around the witness box to shield the child witness from viewing the defendant;

9. The public gallery should be cleared, especially in sexual offence cases and cases involving intimidation, to enable evidence to be given in private;

10. Judicial officers, prosecutors and lawyers should wear ordinary dress during the testimony of a child witness;

11. Defendants should be prevented from personally cross-examination child witnesses;

12. The circumstances in which information about the previous sexual history of alleged child victims may be sought or presented as evidence in trials for sexual offences must be restricted.

P. VICTIMS OF CRIME AND ABUSE OF POWER

(a) Victims should be treated with compassion and respect for their dignity. They are entitled to have access to the mechanisms of justice and to prompt redress, as provided for by national legislation and international law, for the harm that they have suffered.

(b) States must ensure that women who are victims of crime, especially of a sexual nature, are interviewed by women police or judicial officials.

(c) Sates shall take steps to ensure that women who are complainants, victims or witnesses are not subjected to any cruel, inhumane or degrading treatment.

(d) Judicial and administrative mechanisms should be established and strengthened where necessary to enable victims to obtain redress through formal or informal procedures that are expeditious, fair, inexpensive and accessible. Victims should be informed of their rights in seeking redress through such mechanisms.

(e) States are required to investigate and punish all complaints of violence against women, including domestic violence, whether those acts are perpetrated by the state, its officials or agents or by private persons. Fair and effective procedures and mechanisms must be established and be accessible to women who have been subjected to violence to enable them to file criminal complaints and to obtain other redress for the proper investigation of the violence suffered, to obtain restitution or reparation and to prevent further violence.

(f) Judicial officers, prosecutors and lawyers, as appropriate, should facilitate the needs of victims by:

1. Informing them of their role and the scope, timing and progress of the proceedings and the final outcome of their cases;

2. Allowing their views and concerns to be presented and considered at appropriate stages of the proceedings where their personal interests are affected, without prejudice to the accused and consistent with the relevant national criminal justice system;

3. Providing them with proper assistance throughout the legal process;

4. Taking measures to minimize inconvenience to them, protect their privacy, when necessary, and ensure their safety, as well as that of their families and witnesses on their behalf, from intimidation and retaliation;

5. Avoiding unnecessary delay in the disposition of cases and the execution of orders or decrees granting awards to victims.

(g) Informal mechanisms for the resolution of disputes, including mediation, arbitration and traditional or customary practices, should be utilized where appropriate to facilitate conciliation and redress for victims.

(h) Offenders or third parties responsible for their behaviour should, where appropriate, make fair restitution to victims, their families or dependants. Such restitution should include the return of property or payment for the harm or loss suffered, reimbursement of expenses, the provision of services and the restoration of rights.

(i) States should review their practices, regulations and laws to consider restitution as an available sentencing option in criminal cases, in addition to other criminal sanctions.

(j) Where public officials or other agents acting in an official or quasi-official capacity have violated national criminal laws or international law, the victims should receive restitution from the State whose officials or agents were responsible for the harm inflicted.

(k) When compensation is not fully available from the offender or other sources, States should endeavour to provide financial compensation to:

1. Victims who have sustained significant bodily injury or impairment of physical or mental health as a result of serious crimes;

2. The family, in particular dependants of persons who have died or become physically or mentally incapacitated.

(l) States are encouraged to establish, strengthen and expand national funds for compensation to victims.

(m) States must ensure that:

1. Victims receive the necessary material, medical, psychological and social assistance through state, voluntary, non-governmental and community-based means.

2. Victims are informed of the availability of health and social services and other relevant assistance and be readily afforded access to them.

3. Police, justice, health, social service and other personnel concerned receive training to sensitize them to the needs of victims, and guidelines are adopted to ensure proper and prompt aid.

Q. TRADITIONAL COURTS

(a) Traditional courts, where they exist, are required to respect international standards on the right to a fair trial.

(b) The following provisions shall apply, as a minimum, to all proceedings before traditional courts:

1. Equality of persons without any distinction whatsoever as regards race, colour, sex, gender, religion, creed, language, political or other opinion, national or social origin, means, disability, birth, status or other circumstances;

2. Respect for the inherent dignity of human persons, including the right not to be subject to torture, or other cruel, inhuman or degrading punishment or treatment;

3. Respect for the right to liberty and security of every person, in particular the right of every individual not to be subject to arbitrary arrest or detention;

4. Respect for the equality of women and men in all proceedings;

5. Respect for the inherent dignity of women, and their right not to be subjected to cruel, inhuman or degrading treatment or punishment;

6. Adequate opportunity to prepare a case, present arguments and evidence and to challenge or respond to opposing arguments or evidence;

7. An entitlement to the assistance of an interpreter if he or she cannot understand or speak the language used in or by the traditional court;

8. An entitlement to seek the assistance of and be represented by a representative of the party's choosing in all proceedings before the traditional court;

9. An entitlement to have a party's rights and obligations affected only by a decision based solely on evidence presented to the traditional court;

10. An entitlement to a determination of their rights and obligations without undue delay and with adequate notice of and reasons for the decisions;

11. An entitlement to an appeal to a higher traditional court, administrative authority or a judicial tribunal;

12. All hearings before traditional courts shall be held in public and its decisions shall be rendered in public, except where the interests of children require or where the proceedings concern matrimonial disputes or the guardianship of children;

(c) The independence of traditional courts shall be guaranteed by the laws of the country and respected by the government, its agencies and authorities:

1. They shall be independent from the executive branch;

2. There shall not be any inappropriate or unwarranted interference with proceedings before traditional courts.

(d) States shall ensure the impartiality of traditional courts. In particular, members of traditional courts shall decide matters before them without any restrictions, improper influence, inducements, pressure, threats or interference, direct or indirect, from any quarter.

1. The impartiality of a traditional court would be undermined when one of its members has:

1.1 Expressed an opinion which would influence the decision-making;

1.2 Some connection or involvement with the case or a party to the case;

1.3 A pecuniary or other interest linked to the outcome of the case.

2. Any party to proceedings before a traditional court shall be entitled to challenge its impartiality on the basis of ascertainable facts that the fairness any of its members or the traditional court appears to be in doubt.

(e) The procedures for complaints against and discipline of members of traditional courts shall be prescribed by law. Complaints against members of traditional courts shall be processed promptly and expeditiously, and with all the guarantees of a fair hearing, including the right to be represented by a legal representative of choice and to an independent review of decisions of disciplinary, suspension or removal proceedings.

R. NON-DEGORABILITY CLAUSE

No circumstances whatsoever, whether a threat of war, a state of international or internal armed conflict, internal political instability or any other public emergency, may be invoked to justify derogations from the right to a fair trial.

S. USE OF TERMS

For the purpose of these Principles and Guidelines:

(a) "Arrest" means the act of apprehending a person for the alleged commission of an offence or by the action of an authority.

(b) "Criminal charge" is defined by the nature of the offence and the nature and degree of severity of the penalty incurred. An accusation may constitute a criminal charge although the offence is not classified as criminal under national law.

(c) "Detained person" or "detainee" means any individual deprived of personal liberty except as a result of conviction for an offence.

(d) "Detention" means the condition of a detained person.

(e) "Imprisoned person" or "prisoner" means any individual deprived of personal liberty as a result of conviction for an offence.

(f) "Imprisonment" means the condition of imprisoned persons.

(g) "Suspect" means a person who has been arrested but not arraigned or charged before a judicial body.

(h) "Judicial body" means a dispute resolution or adjudication mechanism established and regulated by law and includes courts and other tribunals.

(i) "Judicial office" means a position on a judicial body.

(j) "Judicial officer" means a person who sits in adjudication as part of a judicial body.

(k) "Legal proceeding" means any proceeding before a judicial body brought in regard to a criminal charge or for the determination of rights or obligations of any person, natural or legal.

(l) "Traditional court" means a body which, in a particular locality, is recognised as having the power to resolve disputes in accordance with local customs, cultural or ethnic values, religious norms or tradition.

(m) "Habeas corpus", "amparo" is a legal procedure brought before a judicial body to compel the detaining authorities to provide accurate and detailed information regarding the whereabouts and conditions of detention of a person or to produce a detainee before the judicial body.

(n) "Victim" means persons who individually or collectively have suffered harm, including physical or mental injury, emotional suffering, economic loss or substantial impairment of their fundamental rights, through acts or omissions that are in violation of criminal laws or that do not yet constitute violations of national criminal laws but of internationally recognized norms relating to human rights. The term "victim" also includes, where appropriate, the immediate family or dependants of the direct victim and persons who have suffered harm in intervening to assist victims in distress.

CHAPTER 14

REPARATIONS

Comments: International human rights law not only recognizes the human rights of every human being, it also puts an obligation on States to ensure, secure or guarantee the effective enjoyment of human rights within its jurisdiction. The duty to ensure human rights also means that human rights impose a multidimensional obligation on States. In addition to the duty to adopt all necessary legislative and other measures, there are four main components of the State's obligation: the State has a duty to prevent violations and to respect, protect, and promote human rights. Moreover, all human rights always have a procedural component, such as the obligation of States to provide adequate remedies and procedures of protection against human rights violations and to undertake the investigation of these violations.

All victims of human rights violations also have a right to an effective remedy and to reparation.[1] It has been held by the Human Rights Committee that States have a duty to: (i) take legislative and other measures to give effect to rights, (ii) investigate human rights violations, (iii) provide effective remedies against violations, (iv) bring perpetrators of certain violations to justice, and (v) provide reparation to victims. The different obligations of the State are complementary and they cannot be substituted for one another. The obligations of the State are also unconditional: they do not depend on one another, nor are they conditional on an individual complaint. They cannot be renounced by victims. While victims may, of course, renounce the individual reparation that is due to them, the state cannot, for instance, forego its obligation to investigate and make public the truth on gross human rights violations and to punish the perpetrators.

The Rome Statute of the International Criminal Court includes provisions on reparations, while the UN General Assembly Resolution on the Right to a Remedy and Reparation for Victims of

---

[1] General Comment No 31 on Article 2 of the Covenant: The Nature of the General Legal Obligation Imposed on States Parties to the Covenant, 21 April 2004, CCPR/C/74/CRP.4/Rev.6.

Violations of International Human Rights and Humanitarian Law clarify current international legal principles and emerging norms on reparation, and discuss the scope of the State's obligations to prevent, investigate, punish and remedy infractions of human rights. UN Principles on Reparation stipulate that reparation includes the following forms: restitution, compensation, rehabilitation, satisfaction and guarantees of non-repetition.

14.1 DECLARATION OF BASIC PRINCIPLES OF JUSTICE FOR VICTIM OF CRIME AND ABUSE OF POWER, 1985[2]

A. VICTIMS OF CRIME

1. "Victims" means persons who, individually or collectively, have suffered harm, including physical or mental injury, emotional suffering, economic loss or substantial impairment of their fundamental rights, through acts or omissions that are in violation of criminal laws operative within Member States, including those laws proscribing criminal abuse of power.

2. A person may be considered a victim, under this Declaration, regardless of whether the perpetrator is identified, apprehended, prosecuted or convicted and regardless of the familial relationship between the perpetrator and the victim. The term "victim" also includes, where appropriate, the immediate family or dependants of the direct victim and persons who have suffered harm in intervening to assist victims in distress or to prevent victimization.

3. The provisions contained herein shall be applicable to all, without distinction of any kind, such as race, colour, sex, age, language, religion, nationality, political or other opinion, cultural beliefs or practices, property, birth or family status, ethnic or social origin, and disability.

Access to justice and fair treatment

4. Victims should be treated with compassion and respect for their dignity. They are entitled to access to the mechanisms of justice and to prompt redress, as provided for by national legislation, for the harm that they have suffered.

5. Judicial and administrative mechanisms should be established and strengthened where necessary to enable victims to obtain redress through formal or informal procedures that are expeditious, fair, inexpensive and accessible. Victims should be informed of their rights in seeking redress through such mechanisms.

---

2 UN G.A. 40/34, annex, 40 U.N. GAOR Supp. (No. 53) at 214, U.N. Doc. A/40/53 (1985).

6. The responsiveness of judicial and administrative processes to the needs of victims should be facilitated by:

(a) Informing victims of their role and the scope, timing and progress of the proceedings and of the disposition of their cases, especially where serious crimes are involved and where they have requested such information;

(b) Allowing the views and concerns of victims to be presented and considered at appropriate stages of the proceedings where their personal interests are affected, without prejudice to the accused and consistent with the relevant national criminal justice system;

(c) Providing proper assistance to victims throughout the legal process;

(d) Taking measures to minimize inconvenience to victims, protect their privacy, when necessary, and ensure their safety, as well as that of their families and witnesses on their behalf, from intimidation and retaliation;

(e) Avoiding unnecessary delay in the disposition of cases and the execution of orders or decrees granting awards to victims.

7. Informal mechanisms for the resolution of disputes, including mediation, arbitration and customary justice or indigenous practices, should be utilized where appropriate to facilitate conciliation and redress for victims.

Restitution

8. Offenders or third parties responsible for their behaviour should, where appropriate, make fair restitution to victims, their families or dependants. Such restitution should include the return of property or payment for the harm or loss suffered, reimbursement of expenses incurred as a result of the victimization, the provision of services and the restoration of rights.

9. Governments should review their practices, regulations and laws to consider restitution as an available sentencing option in criminal cases, in addition to other criminal sanctions.

10. In cases of substantial harm to the environment, restitution, if ordered, should include, as far as possible, restoration of the environment, reconstruction of the infrastructure, replacement of community facilities and reimbursement of the expenses of relocation, whenever such harm results in the dislocation of a community.

11. Where public officials or other agents acting in an official or quasi-official capacity have violated national criminal laws, the victims should receive restitution from the State whose officials or agents were responsible for the harm inflicted. In cases where the Government under whose authority the victimizing act or omission occurred is no longer in existence, the State or Government successor in title should provide restitution to the victims.

Compensation

12. When compensation is not fully available from the offender or other sources, States should endeavour to provide financial compensation to:

(a) Victims who have sustained significant bodily injury or impairment of physical or mental health as a result of serious crimes;

(b) The family, in particular dependants of persons who have died or become physically or mentally incapacitated as a result of such victimization.

13. The establishment, strengthening and expansion of national funds for compensation to victims should be encouraged. Where appropriate, other funds may also be established for this purpose, including in those cases where the State of which the victim is a national is not in a position to compensate the victim for the harm.

Assistance

14. Victims should receive the necessary material, medical, psychological and social assistance through governmental, voluntary, community-based and indigenous means.

15. Victims should be informed of the availability of health and social services and other relevant assistance and be readily afforded access to them.

16. Police, justice, health, social service and other personnel concerned should receive training to sensitize them to the needs of victims, and guidelines to ensure proper and prompt aid.

17. In providing services and assistance to victims, attention should be given to those who have special needs because of the nature of the harm inflicted or because of factors such as those mentioned in paragraph 3 above.

B. VICTIMS OF ABUSE OF POWER

18. "Victims" means persons who, individually or collectively, have suffered harm, including physical or mental injury, emotional suffering, economic loss or substantial impairment of

their fundamental rights, through acts or omissions that do not yet constitute violations of national criminal laws but of internationally recognized norms relating to human rights.

19. States should consider incorporating into the national law norms proscribing abuses of power and providing remedies to victims of such abuses. In particular, such remedies should include restitution and/or compensation, and necessary material, medical, psychological and social assistance and support.

20. States should consider negotiating multilateral international treaties relating to victims, as defined in paragraph 18.

21. States should periodically review existing legislation and practices to ensure their responsiveness to changing circumstances, should enact and enforce, if necessary, legislation proscribing acts that constitute serious abuses of political or economic power, as well as promoting policies and mechanisms for the prevention of such acts, and should develop and make readily available appropriate rights and remedies for victims of such acts.

14.2 UPDATED SET OF PRINCIPLES FOR THE PROTECTION AND PROMOTION OF HUMAN RIGHTS THROUGH ACTION TO COMBAT IMPUNITY, 2005[3]

PREAMBLE

Recalling the Preamble to the Universal Declaration of Human Rights, which recognizes that disregard and contempt for human rights have resulted in barbarous acts which have outraged the conscience of mankind,

Aware that there is an ever-present risk that such acts may again occur,

Reaffirming the commitment made by Member States under Article 56 of the Charter of the United Nations to take joint and separate action, giving full importance to developing effective international cooperation for the achievement of the purposes set forth in Article 55 of the Charter concerning universal respect for, and observance of human rights and fundamental freedoms for all,

Considering that the duty of every State under international law to respect and to secure respect for human rights requires t hat effective measures should be taken to combat impunity,

---

[3] E/CN.4/2005/102/Add.1, 8 February 2005, recommended by Commission on Human Rights resolution E/CN.4/RES/2005/81of 21 April 2005.

Aware that there can be no just and lasting reconciliation unless the need for justice is effectively satisfied,

Equally aware that forgiveness, which may be an important element of reconciliation, implies, insofar as it is a private act, that the victim or the victim's beneficiaries know the perpetrator of the violations and that the latter has acknowledged his or her deeds,

Recalling the recommendation set forth in paragraph 91 of Part II of the Vienna Declaration and Programme of Action, wherein the World Conference on Human Rights (June 1993) expressed its concern about the impunity of perpetrators of human rights violations and encouraged the efforts of the Commission on Human Rights to examine all aspects of the issue,

Convinced, therefore, that national and international measures must be taken for that purpose with a view to securing jointly, in the interests of the victims of violations, observance of the right to know and, by implication, the right to the truth, the right to justice and the right to reparation, without which there can be no effective remedy against the pernicious effects of impunity,

Pursuant to the Vienna Declaration and Programme of Action, the following principles are intended as guidelines to assist States in developing effective measures for combating impunity.

Definitions

A. Impunity

"Impunity" means the impossibility, de jure or de facto, of bringing the perpetrators of violations to account - whether in criminal, civil, administrative or disciplinary proceedings since they are not subject to any inquiry that might lead to their being accused, arrested, tried and, if found guilty, sentenced to appropriate penalties, and to making reparations to their victims.

B. Serious crimes under international law

As used in these principles, the phrase "serious crimes under international law" encompasses grave breaches of the Geneva Conventions of 12 August 1949 and of Additional Protocol I thereto of 1977 and other violations of international humanitarian law that are crimes under international law, genocide, crimes against humanity, and other violations of internationally protected human rights that are crimes under international law and/or which international law requires States to penalize, such as torture, enforced disappearance, extrajudicial execution, and slavery.

C. Restoration of or transition to democracy and/or peace

This expression, as used in these principles, refers to situations leading, within the framework of a national movement towards democracy or peace negotiations aimed at ending an armed conflict, to an agreement, in whatever form, by which the actors or parties concerned agree to take measures against impunity and the recurrence of human rights violations.

D. Truth commissions

As used in these principles, the phrase "truth commissions" refers to official, temporary, non-judicial fact-finding bodies that investigate a pattern of abuses of human rights or humanitarian law, usually committed over a number of years.

E. Archives

As used in these principles, the word "archives" refers to collections of documents pertaining to violations of human rights and humanitarian law from sources including (a) national governmental agencies, particularly those that played significant roles in relation to human rights violations; (b) local agencies, such as police stations, that were involved in human rights violations; (c) State agencies, including the office of the prosecutor and the judiciary, that are involved in the protection of human rights; and (d) materials collected by truth commissions and other investigative bodies.

I. COMBATING IMPUNITY: GENERAL OBLIGATIONS

PRINCIPLE 1. GENERAL OBLIGATIONS OF STATES TO TAKE EFFECTIVE ACTION TO COMBAT IMPUNITY

Impunity arises from a failure by States to meet their obligations to investigate violations; to take appropriate measures in respect of the perpetrators, particularly in the area of justice, by ensuring that those suspected of criminal responsibility are prosecuted, tried and duly punished; to provide victims with effective remedies and to ensure that they receive reparation for the injuries suffered; to ensure the inalienable right to know the truth about violations; and to take other necessary steps to prevent a recurrence of violations.

II. THE RIGHT TO KNOW

A. General principles

PRINCIPLE 2. THE INALIENABLE RIGHT TO THE TRUTH

Every people has the inalienable right to know the truth about past events concerning the perpetration of heinous crimes and about the circumstances and reasons that led, through massive or systematic violations, to the perpetration of those crimes. Full and effective exercise of the right to the truth provides a vital safeguard against the recurrence of violations.

PRINCIPLE 3. THE DUTY TO PRESERVE MEMORY

A people's knowledge of the history of its oppression is part of its heritage and, as such, must be ensured by appropriate measures in fulfilment of the State's duty to preserve archives and other evidence concerning violations of human rights and humanitarian law and to facilitate knowledge of those violations. Such measures shall be aimed at preserving the collective memory from extinction and, in particular, at guarding against the development of revisionist and negationist arguments.

PRINCIPLE 4. THE VICTIMS' RIGHT TO KNOW

Irrespective of any legal proceedings, victims and their families have the imprescriptible right to know the truth about the circumstances in which violations took place and, in the event of death or disappearance, the victims' fate.

PRINCIPLE 5. GUARANTEES TO GIVE EFFECT TO THE RIGHT TO KNOW

States must take appropriate action, including measures necessary to ensure the independent and effective operation of the judiciary, to give effect to the right to know. Appropriate measures to ensure this right may include non-judicial processes that complement the role of the judiciary. Societies that have experienced heinous crimes perpetrated on a massive or systematic basis may benefit in particular from the creation of a truth commission or other commission of inquiry to establish the facts surrounding those violations so that the truth may be ascertained and to prevent the disappearance of evidence. Regardless of whether a State establishes such a body, it must ensure the preservation of, and access to, archives concerning violations of human rights and humanitarian law.

B. Commissions of inquiry

PRINCIPLE 6. THE ESTABLISHMENT AND ROLE OF TRUTH COMMISSIONS

To the greatest extent possible, decisions to establish a truth commission, define its terms of reference and determine its composition should be based upon broad public consultations in which the views of victims and survivors especially are sought. Special efforts should be made to ensure that men and women participate in these deliberations on a basis of equality. In recognition of the dignity of victims and their families, investigations undertaken by truth commissions should be conducted with the object in particular of securing recognition of such part s of the truth as were formerly denied.

PRINCIPLE 7. GUARANTEES OF INDEPENDENCE, IMPARTIALITY AND COMPETENCE

Commissions of inquiry, including truth commissions, must be established through procedures that ensure their independence, impartiality and competence. To this end, the terms of reference of commissions of inquiry, including commissions that are international in character, should respect the following guidelines:

(a) They shall be constituted in accordance with criteria making clear to the public the competence and impartiality of their members, including expertise within their membership in the field of human rights and, if relevant, of humanitarian law. They shall also be constituted in accordance with conditions ensuring their independence, in particular by the irremovability of their members during their terms of office except on grounds of incapacity or behaviour rendering them unfit to discharge their duties and pursuant to procedures ensuring fair, impartial and independent determinations;

(b) Their members shall enjoy whatever privileges and immunities are necessary for their protect ion, including in the period following their mission, especially in respect of any defamation proceedings or other civil or criminal action brought against them on the basis of facts or opinions contained in the commissions' reports;

(c) In determining membership, concerted efforts should be made to ensure adequate representation of women as well as of other appropriate groups whose members have been especially vulnerable to human rights violations.

PRINCIPLE 8. DEFINITION OF A COMMISSION'S TERMS OF REFERENCE

To avoid conflicts of jurisdiction, the commission's terms of reference must be clearly defined and must be consistent with the principle that commissions of inquiry are not intended to act as substitutes for the civil, administrative or criminal courts. In particular, criminal courts alone have jurisdiction to establish individual criminal responsibility, with a view as appropriate to passing judgment and imposing a sentence. In addition to the guidelines set forth in principles 12 and 13, the terms of reference of a commission of inquiry should incorporate or reflect the following stipulations:

(a) The commission's terms of reference may reaffirm its right: to seek the assistance of law enforcement authorities, if required, including for the purpose, subject to the terms of principle 10 (a), of calling for testimonies; to inspect any places concerned in its investigations; and/or to call for the delivery of relevant documents;

(b) If the commission has reason to believe that the life, health or safety of a person concerned by its inquiry is threatened or that there is a risk of losing an element of proof, it may seek court action under an emergency procedure or take other appropriate measures to end such threat or risk;

(c) Investigations undertaken by a commission of inquiry may relate to all persons alleged to have been responsible for violations of human rights and/or humanitarian law, whether they ordered them or actually committed them, acting as perpetrators or accomplices, and whether they are public officials or members of quasi-governmental or private armed groups with any kind of link to the State, or of nongovernmental armed movements. Commissions of inquiry may also consider the role of other actors in facilitating violations of human rights and humanitarian law;

(d) Commissions of inquiry may have jurisdiction to consider all forms of violations of human rights and humanitarian law. Their investigations should focus as a matter of priority on violations constituting serious crimes under international law, including in particular violations of the fundamental rights of women and of other vulnerable groups;

(e) Commissions of inquiry shall endeavour to safeguard evidence for later use in the administration of justice;

(f) The terms of reference of commissions of inquiry should highlight the importance of preserving the commission's archives. At the outset of their work, commissions should clarify the conditions that will govern access to their documents, including conditions aimed at preventing disclosure of confidential information while facilitating public access to their archives.

PRINCIPLE 9. GUARANTEES FOR PERSONS IMPLICATED

Before a commission identifies perpetrators in its report, the individuals concerned shall be entitled to the following guarantees:

(a) The commission must try to corroborate information implicating individuals before they are named publicly;

(b) The individuals implicated shall be afforded an opportunity to provide a statement set ting forth their version of the facts either at a hearing convened by the commission while conducting its investigation or through submission of a document equivalent to a right of reply for inclusion in the commission's file.

PRINCIPLE 10. GUARANTEES FOR VICTIMS AND WITNESSES TESTIFYING ON THEIR BEHALF

Effective measures shall be taken to ensure the security, physical and psychological well-being, and, where requested, the privacy of victims and witnesses who provide information to the commission.

(a) Victims and witnesses testifying on their behalf may be called upon to testify before the commission only on a strictly voluntary basis;

(b) Social workers and/or mental health-care practitioners should be authorized to assist victims, preferably in their own language, both during and after their testimony, especially in cases of sexual assault;

(c) All expenses incurred by those giving testimony shall be borne by the State;

(d) Information that might identify a witness who provided testimony pursuant to a promise of confidentially must be protected from disclosure.

Victims providing testimony and other witnesses should in any event be informed of rules that will govern disclosure of information provided by them to the commission. Requests to provide information to the commission anonymously should be given serious consideration, especially in cases of sexual assault, and the commission should establish procedures to guarantee anonymity in appropriate cases, while allowing corroboration of the information provided, as necessary.

PRINCIPLE 11. ADEQUATE RESOURCES FOR COMMISSIONS

The commission shall be provided with:

(a) Transparent funding to ensure that its independence is never in doubt;

(b) Sufficient material and human resources to ensure that its credibility is never in doubt.

PRINCIPLE 12. ADVISORY FUNCTIONS OF THE COMMISSIONS

The commission's terms of reference should include provisions calling for it to include in its final report recommendations concerning legislative and other action to combat impunity. The terms of reference should ensure that the commission incorporates women's experiences in its work, including its recommendations. When establishing a commission of inquiry, the Government should undertake to give due consideration to the commission's recommendations.

PRINCIPLE 13. PUBLICIZING THE COMMISSION'S REPORTS

For security reasons or to avoid pressure on witnesses and commission members, the commission's terms of reference may stipulate that relevant portions of its inquiry shall be kept confidential. The commission's final report, on the other hand, shall be made public in full and shall be disseminated as widely as possible.

C. Preservation of and access to archives bearing witness to violations

PRINCIPLE 14. MEASURES FOR THE PRESERVATION OF ARCHIVES

The right to know implies that archives must be preserved. Technical measures and penalties should be applied to prevent any removal, destruction, concealment or falsification of archives, especially for the purpose of ensuring the impunity of perpetrators of violations of human rights and/or humanitarian law.

PRINCIPLE 15. MEASURES FOR FACILITATING ACCESS TO ARCHIVES

Access to archives shall be facilitated in order to enable victims and their relatives to claim their rights. Access shall be facilitated, as necessary, for persons implicated, who request it for their defence. Access to archives should also be facilitated in the interest of historical research, subject to reasonable restrictions aimed at safeguarding the privacy and security of victims and other individuals. Formal requirements governing access may not be used for purposes of censorship.

PRINCIPLE 16. COOPERATION BETWEEN ARCHIVE DEPARTMENTS AND THE COURTS AND NON-JUDICIAL COMMISSIONS OF INQUIRY

Courts and non-judicial commissions of inquiry, as well as investigators reporting to them, must have access to relevant archives. This principle must be implemented in a manner that respects applicable privacy concerns, including in particular assurances of confidentiality provided to victims and other witnesses as a precondition of their testimony. Access may not be denied on grounds of national security unless, in exceptional circumstances, the restriction has been prescribed by law; the Government has demonstrated that the restriction is necessary in a democratic society to protect a legitimate national security interest; and the denial is subject to independent judicial review.

PRINCIPLE 17. SPECIFIC MEASURES RELATING TO ARCHIVES CONTAINING NAMES

(a) For the purposes of this principle, archives containing names shall be understood to be those archives containing information that makes it possible, directly or indirectly, to identify the individuals to whom they relate;

(b) All persons shall be entitled to know whether their name appears in State archives and, if it does, by virtue of their right of access, to challenge the validity of the information concerning them by exercising a right of reply. The challenged document should include a cross-reference to the document challenging its validity and both must be made available together whenever the former is requested. Access to the files of commissions of inquiry must be balanced against the legitimate expectations of confidentiality of victims and other witnesses testifying on their behalf in accordance with principles 8 (f) and 10 (d).

PRINCIPLE 18. SPECIFIC MEASURES RELATED TO THE RESTORATION OF OR TRANSITION TO DEMOCRACY AND/OR PEACE

(a) Measures should be taken to place each archive centre under the responsibility of a specifically designated office;

(b) When inventorying and assessing their liability of stored archives, special attention should be given to archives relating to places of detention and other sites of serious violations of human rights and/or humanitarian law such as torture, in particular when the existence of such places was not officially recognized;

(c) Third countries shall be expected to cooperate with a view to communicating or restituting archives for the purpose of establishing the truth.

III. THE RIGHT TO JUSTICE

A. General principles

PRINCIPLE 19. DUTIES OF STATES WITH REGARD TO THE ADMINISTRATION OF JUSTICE

States shall undertake prompt, thorough, independent and impartial investigations of violations of human rights and international humanitarian law and take appropriate measures in respect of the perpetrators, particularly in the area of criminal justice, by ensuring that t hose responsible for serious crimes under international law are prosecuted, tried and duly punished.

Although the decision to prosecute lies primarily within the competence of the State, victims, their families and heirs should be able to institute proceedings, on either an individual or a collective basis, particularly as *parties civiles* or as persons conducting private prosecutions in States whose law of criminal procedure recognizes these procedures. States should guarantee broad legal standing in the judicial process to any wronged part y and to any person or non-governmental organization having a legitimate interest therein.

B. Distribution of jurisdiction between national, foreign, international and internationalized courts

PRINCIPLE 20. JURISDICTION OF INTERNATIONAL AND INTERNATIONALIZED CRIMINAL TRIBUNALS

It remains the rule that States have primary responsibility to exercise jurisdiction over serious crimes under international law. In accordance with the terms of their statutes, international and internationalized criminal tribunals may exercise concurrent jurisdiction when national courts cannot offer satisfactory guarantees of independence and impartiality or are materially unable or unwilling to conduct effective investigations or prosecutions.

States must ensure that they fully satisfy their legal obligations in respect of international and internationalized criminal tribunals, including where necessary through the enactment of domestic legislation that enables States to fulfil obligations that arise through their adherence to the Rome Statute of the International Criminal Court or under other binding instruments, and through implementation of applicable obligations to apprehend and surrender suspects and to cooperate in respect of evidence.

PRINCIPLE 21. MEASURES FOR STRENGTHENING THE EFFECTIVENESS OF INTERNATIONAL LEGAL PRINCIPLES CONCERNING UNIVERSAL AND INTERNATIONAL JURISDICTION

States should undertake effective measures, including the adoption or amendment of internal legislation, that are necessary to enable their courts to exercise universal jurisdiction over serious crimes under international law in accordance with applicable principles of customary and treaty law.

States must ensure that they fully implement any legal obligations they have assumed to institute criminal proceedings against persons with respect to whom there is credible evidence of individual responsibility for serious crimes under international law if they do not extradite the suspects or transfer them for prosecution before an international or internationalized tribunal.

C. Restrictions on rules of law justified by action to combat impunity

PRINCIPLE 22. NATURE OF RESTRICTIVE MEASURES

States should adopt and enforce safeguards against any abuse of rules such as those pertaining to prescription, amnesty, right to asylum, refusal to extradite, *non bis in idem*, due obedience, official immunities, repentance, the jurisdiction of military courts and the irremovability of judges that fosters or contributes to impunity.

PRINCIPLE 23. RESTRICTIONS ON PRESCRIPTION

Prescription - of prosecution or penalty - in criminal cases shall not run for such period as no effective remedy is available. Prescription shall not apply to crimes under international law that are by their nature imprescriptible.

When it does apply, prescription shall not be effective against civil or administrative actions brought by victims seeking reparation for their injuries.

PRINCIPLE 24. RESTRICTIONS AND OTHER MEASURES RELATING TO AMNESTY

Even when intended to establish conditions conducive to a peace agreement or to foster national reconciliation, amnesty and other measures of clemency shall be kept within the following bounds:

(a) The perpetrators of serious crimes under international law may not benefit from such measures until such time as the State has met the obligations to which principle 19 refers or the perpetrators have been prosecuted before a court with jurisdiction – whether international, internationalized or national - outside the State in question;

(b) Amnesties and other measures of clemency shall be without effect with respect to the victims' right to reparation, to which principles 31 through 34 refer, and shall not prejudice the right to know;

(c) Insofar as it may be interpreted as an admission of guilt, amnesty cannot be imposed on individuals prosecuted or sentenced for acts connected with the peaceful exercise of their right to freedom of opinion and expression. When they have merely exercised this legitimate right, as guaranteed by articles 18 to 20 of the Universal Declaration of Human Rights and 18, 19, 21 and 22 of the International Covenant on Civil and Political Rights, the law shall consider any judicial or other decision concerning them to be null and void; their detention shall be ended unconditionally and without delay;

(d) Any individual convicted of offences other than those to which paragraph (c) of this principle refers who comes within the scope of an amnesty is entitled to refuse it and request a retrial, if he or she has been tried without benefit of the right to a fair hearing guaranteed by articles 10 and 11 of the Universal Declaration of Human Rights and articles 9, 14 and 15 of the International Covenant on Civil and Political Rights, or if he or she was convicted on the basis of a statement established to have been made as a result of inhuman or degrading interrogation, especially under torture.

PRINCIPLE 25. RESTRICTIONS ON THE RIGHT OF ASYLUM

Under article 1, paragraph 2, of the Declaration on Territorial Asylum, adopted by the General Assembly on 14 December 1967, and article 1 F of the Convention relating to the Status of Refugees of 28 July 1951, States may not extend such protective status, including diplomatic asylum, to persons with respect to whom there are serious reasons to believe that they have committed a serious crime under international law.

PRINCIPLE 26. RESTRICTIONS ON EXTRADITION/NON BIS IN IDEM

(a) Persons who have committed serious crimes under international law may not, in order to avoid extradition, avail themselves of the favourable provisions generally relating to political offences or of the principle of non-extradition of nationals. Extradition should always be denied, however, especially by abolitionist countries, if the individual concerned risks the death penalty in the requesting country.

Extradition should also be denied where there are substantial grounds for believing that the suspect would be in danger of being subjected to gross violations of human rights such as torture; enforced disappearance; or extra-legal, arbitrary or summary execution. If extradition is denied on these grounds, the requested State shall submit the case to its competent authorities for the purpose of prosecution;

(b) The fact that an individual has previously been tried in connection with a serious crime under international law shall not prevent his or her prosecution with respect to the same conduct if the purpose of the previous proceedings was to shield the person concerned from criminal responsibility, or if those proceedings otherwise were not conducted independently or impartially in accordance with the norms of due process recognized by international law and were conducted in a manner that, in the circumstances, was inconsistent with an intent to bring the person concerned to justice.

PRINCIPLE 27. RESTRICTIONS ON JUSTIFICATIONS RELATED TO DUE OBEDIENCE, SUPERIOR RESPONSIBILITY, AND OFFICIAL STATUS

(a) The fact that the perpetrator of violations acted on the orders of his or her Government or of a superior does not exempt him or her from responsibility, in particular criminal, but may be regarded as grounds for reducing the sentence, in conformity with principles of justice;

(b) The fact that violations have been committed by a subordinate does not exempt that subordinate's superiors from responsibility, in particular criminal, if they knew or had at the time reason to know that the subordinate was committing or about to commit such a crime and they did not take all the necessary measures within their power to prevent or punish the crime;

(c) The official stat us of the perpetrator of a crime under international law - even if acting as head of State or Government - does not exempt him or her from criminal or other responsibility and is not grounds for a reduction of sentence.

PRINCIPLE 28. RESTRICTIONS ON THE EFFECTS OF LEGISLATION ON DISCLOSURE OR REPENTANCE

The fact that a perpetrator discloses the violations that he, she or others have committed in order to benefit from the favourable provisions of legislation on disclosure or repentance cannot exempt him or her from criminal or other responsibility. The disclosure may only provide grounds for a reduction of sentence in order to encourage revelation of the truth. When disclosures may subject a perpetrator to persecution, principle 25 notwithstanding, the person making the disclosure may be granted asylum – not refugee stat us - in order to facilitate revelation of the truth.

PRINCIPLE 29. RESTRICTIONS ON THE JURISDICTION OF MILITARY COURTS

The jurisdiction of military tribunals must be restricted solely to specifically military offences committed by military personnel, to the exclusion of human rights violations, which shall come under the jurisdiction of the ordinary domestic courts or, where appropriate, in the case of serious crimes under international law, of an international or internationalized criminal court.

PRINCIPLE 30. RESTRICTIONS ON THE PRINCIPLE OF THE IRREMOVABILITY OF JUDGES

The principle of irremovability, as the basic guarantee of the independence of judges, must be observed in respect of judges who have been appointed in conformity with the requirements of the rule of law. Conversely, judges unlawfully appointed or who derive their judicial power from an act of allegiance may be relieved of their functions by law in accordance with the principle of parallelism. They must be provided an opportunity to challenge their dismissal in proceedings that meet the criteria of independence and impartiality with a view toward seeking reinstatement.

IV. THE RIGHT TO REPARATION/GUARANTEES OF NON-RECURRENCE

A. The right to reparation

PRINCIPLE 31. RIGHTS AND DUTIES ARISING OUT OF THE OBLIGATION TO MAKE REPARATION

Any human rights violation gives rise to a right to reparation on the part of the victim or his or her beneficiaries, implying a duty on the part of the State to make reparation and the possibility for the victim to seek redress from the perpetrator.

PRINCIPLE 32. REPARATION PROCEDURES

All victims shall have access to a readily available, prompt and effective remedy in the form of criminal, civil, administrative or disciplinary proceedings subject to the restrictions on prescription set forth in principle 23. In exercising this right, they shall be afforded protection against intimidation and reprisals.

Reparations may also be provided through programmes, based upon legislative or administrative measures, funded by national or international sources, addressed to individuals and to communities. Victims and other sectors of civil society should play a meaningful role in the design and implementation of such programmes. Concerted efforts should be made to ensure that women and minority groups participate in public consultations aimed at developing, implementing, and assessing reparations programmes. Exercise of the right to reparation includes access to applicable international and regional procedures.

PRINCIPLE 33. PUBLICIZING REPARATION PROCEDURES

Ad hoc procedures enabling victims to exercise their right to reparation should be given the widest possible publicity by private as well as public communication media. Such dissemination should take place both within and outside the country, including through consular services, particularly in countries to which large numbers of victims have been forced into exile.

PRINCIPLE 34. SCOPE OF THE RIGHT TO REPARATION

The right to reparation shall cover all injuries suffered by victims; it shall include measures of restitution, compensation, rehabilitation, and satisfaction as provided by international law.

In the case of forced disappearance, the family of the direct victim has an imprescriptible right to be informed of the fate and/or whereabouts of the disappeared person and, in the event of decease, that person's body must be returned to the family as soon as it has been identified, regardless of whether the perpetrators have been identified or prosecuted.

B. Guarantees of non-recurrence of violations

PRINCIPLE 35. GENERAL PRINCIPLES

States shall ensure that victims do not again have to endure violations of their rights. To this end, States must undertake institutional reforms and other measures necessary to ensure respect for the rule of law, foster and sustain a culture of respect for human rights, and restore or establish public trust in government institutions. Adequate representation of women and minority groups in public institutions is essential to the achievement of these aims. Institutional reforms aimed at preventing a recurrence of violations should be developed through a process of broad public consultations, including the participation of victims and other sectors of civil society. Such reforms should advance the following objectives:

(a) Consistent adherence by public institutions to the rule of law;

(b) The repeal of laws that contribute to or authorize violations of human rights and/or humanitarian law and enactment of legislative and other measures necessary to ensure respect for human rights and humanitarian law, including measures that safeguard democratic institutions and processes;

(c) Civilian control of military and security forces and intelligence services and disbandment of parastatal armed forces;

(d) Reintegration of children involved in armed conflict into society.

PRINCIPLE 36. REFORM OF STATE INSTITUTIONS

States must take all necessary measures, including legislative and administrative reforms, to ensure that public institutions are organized in a manner that ensures respect for the rule of law and protection of human rights. At a minimum, States should undertake the following measures:

(a) Public officials and employees who are personally responsible for gross violations of human rights, in particular those involved in military, security, police, intelligence and judicial sectors, shall not continue to serve in State institutions. Their removal shall comply with the requirements of due process of law and the principle of non-discrimination. Persons formally charged with individual responsibility for serious crimes under international law shall be suspended from official duties during the criminal or disciplinary proceedings;

(b) With respect to the judiciary, States must undertake all other measures necessary to assure the independent, impartial and effective operation of courts in accordance with international standards of due process. Habeas corpus, by whatever name it may be known, must be considered a non-derogable right;

(c) Civilian control of military and security forces as well as of intelligence agencies must be ensured and, where necessary, established or restored. To this end, States should establish effective institutions of civilian oversight over military and security forces and intelligence agencies, including legislative oversight bodies;

(d) Civil complaint procedures should be established and their effective operation assured;

(e) Public officials and employees, in particular those involved in military, security, police, intelligence and judicial sectors, should receive comprehensive and ongoing training in human rights and, where applicable, humanitarian law standards and in implementation of those standards.

PRINCIPLE 37. DISBANDMENT OF PARASTATAL ARMED FORCES/ DEMOBILIZATION AND SOCIAL REINTEGRATION OF CHILDREN

Parastatal or unofficial armed groups shall be demobilized and disbanded. Their position in or links with State institutions, including in particular the army, police, intelligence and security forces, should be thoroughly investigated and the information thus acquired made public.

States should draw up a reconversion plan to ensure the social reintegration of the members of such groups.

Measures should be taken to secure the cooperation of third countries that might have contributed to the creation and development of such groups, particularly through financial or logistical support.

Children who have been recruited or used in hostilities shall be demobilized or otherwise released from service. States shall, when necessary, accord these children all appropriate assistance for their physical and psychological recovery and their social integration.

PRINCIPLE 38. REFORM OF LAWS AND INSTITUTIONS ONTRIBUTING TO IMPUNITY

Legislation and administrative regulations and institutions that contribute to or legitimize human rights violations must be repealed or abolished. In particular, emergency legislation and courts of any kind must be repealed or abolished insofar as they infringe the fundamental rights and freedoms guaranteed in the Universal Declaration of Human Rights and the International Covenant on Civil and Political Rights. Legislative measures necessary to ensure protection of human rights and to safeguard democratic institutions and processes must be enacted.

As a basis for such reforms, during periods of restoration of or transition to democracy and/or peace States should undertake a comprehensive review of legislation and administrative regulations.

14.3 BASIC PRINCIPLES AND GUIDELINES ON THE RIGHT TO A REMEDY AND REPARATIONS FOR VICTIMS OF GROSS VIOLATIONS OF INTERNATIONAL HUMAN RIGHTS LAW AND SERIOUS VIOLATIONS OF INTERNATIONAL HUMANITARIAN LAW, 2005[4]

The General Assembly,

Guided by the Charter of the United Nations, the Universal Declaration of Human Rights, the International Covenants on Human Rights, other relevant human rights instruments and the Vienna Declaration and Programme of Action,

Affirming the importance of addressing the question of remedies and reparation for victims of gross violations of international human rights law and serious violations of international humanitarian law in a systematic and thorough way at the national and international levels,

---

[4] UN General Assembly Res. 60/147, U.N. Doc. A/RES/60/147, December 16, 2005.

Recognizing that, in honouring the victims' right to benefit from remedies and reparation, the international community keeps faith with the plight of victims, survivors and future human generations and reaffirms international law in the field,

Recalling the adoption of the Basic Principles and Guidelines on the Right to a Remedy and Reparation for Victims of Gross Violations of International Human Rights Law and Serious Violations of International Humanitarian Law by the Commission on Human Rights in its resolution 2005/35 of 19 April 2005 and by the Economic and Social Council in its resolution 2005/30 of 25 July 2005, in which the Council recommended to the General Assembly that it adopt the Basic Principles and Guidelines,

1. Adopts the Basic Principles and Guidelines on the Right to a Remedy and Reparation for Victims of Gross Violations of International Human Rights Law and Serious Violations of International Humanitarian Law annexed to the present resolution;

2. Recommends that States take the Basic Principles and Guidelines into account, promote the respect thereof and bring them to the attention of members of the executive bodies of government, in particular law enforcement officials and military and security forces, legislative bodies, the judiciary, victims and their representatives, human rights defenders and lawyers, the media and the public in general;

3. Requests the Secretary-General to take steps to ensure the widest possible dissemination of the Basic Principles and Guidelines in all the official languages of the United Nations, including by transmitting them to Governments and intergovernmental and non-governmental organizations and by including the Basic Principles and Guidelines in the United Nations publication entitled Human Rights: A Compilation of International Instruments.

Basic Principles and Guidelines on the Right to a Remedy and Reparation for Victims of Gross Violations of International Human Rights Law and Serious Violations of International Humanitarian Law

Preamble

The General Assembly,

Recalling the provisions providing a right to a remedy for victims of violations of international human rights law found in numerous international instruments, in particular article 8 of the Universal Declaration of Human Rights, article 2 of the International Covenant on Civil and Political Rights, article 6 of the International Convention on the Elimination of All Forms of Racial Discrimination, article 14 of the Convention against Torture and Other Cruel, Inhuman or

Degrading Treatment or Punishment, and article 39 of the Convention on the Rights of the Child, and of international humanitarian law as found in article 3 of the Hague Convention respecting the Laws and Customs of War on Land of 18 October 1907 (Convention IV), article 91 of the Protocol Additional to the Geneva Conventions of 12 August 1949, and relating to the Protection of Victims of International Armed Conflicts (Protocol I) of 8 June 1977, and articles 68 and 75 of the Rome Statute of the International Criminal Court,

Recalling the provisions providing a right to a remedy for victims of violations of international human rights found in regional conventions, in particular article 7 of the African Charter on Human and Peoples' Rights, article 25 of the American Convention on Human Rights, and article 13 of the Convention for the Protection of Human Rights and Fundamental Freedoms,

Recalling the Declaration of Basic Principles of Justice for Victims of Crime and Abuse of Power emanating from the deliberations of the Seventh United Nations Congress on the Prevention of Crime and the Treatment of Offenders and General Assembly resolution 40/34 of 29 November 1985 by which the Assembly adopted the text recommended by the Congress,

Reaffirming the principles enunciated in the Declaration of Basic Principles of Justice for Victims of Crime and Abuse of Power, including that victims should be treated with compassion and respect for their dignity, have their right to access to justice and redress mechanisms fully respected, and that the establishment, strengthening and expansion of national funds for compensation to victims should be encouraged, together with the expeditious development of appropriate rights and remedies for victims,

Noting that the Rome Statute of the International Criminal Court requires the establishment of "principles relating to reparations to, or in respect of, victims, including restitution, compensation and rehabilitation", requires the Assembly of States Parties to establish a trust fund for the benefit of victims of crimes within the jurisdiction of the Court, and of the families of such victims, and mandates the Court "to protect the safety, physical and psychological well-being, dignity and privacy of victims" and to permit the participation of victims at all "stages of the proceedings determined to be appropriate by the Court",

Affirming that the Basic Principles and Guidelines contained herein are directed at gross violations of international human rights law and serious violations of international humanitarian law which, by their very grave nature, constitute an affront to human dignity,

Emphasizing that the Basic Principles and Guidelines contained herein do not entail new international or domestic legal obligations but identify mechanisms, modalities, procedures and methods for the implementation of existing legal obligations under international human rights law and international humanitarian law which are complementary though different as to their norms,

Recalling that international law contains the obligation to prosecute perpetrators of certain international crimes in accordance with international obligations of States and the requirements of national law or as provided for in the applicable statutes of international judicial organs, and that the duty to prosecute reinforces the international legal obligations to be carried out in accordance with national legal requirements and procedures and supports the concept of complementarity,

Noting that contemporary forms of victimization, while essentially directed against persons, may nevertheless also be directed against groups of persons who are targeted collectively,

Recognizing that, in honouring the victims' right to benefit from remedies and reparation, the international community keeps faith with the plight of victims, survivors and future human generations and reaffirms the international legal principles of accountability, justice and the rule of law,

Convinced that, in adopting a victim-oriented perspective, the international community affirms its human solidarity with victims of violations of international law, including violations of international human rights law and international humanitarian law, as well as with humanity at large, in accordance with the following Basic Principles and Guidelines,

Adopts the following Basic Principles and Guidelines:

I. Obligation to respect, ensure respect for and implement international human rights law and international humanitarian law

1. The obligation to respect, ensure respect for and implement international human rights law and international humanitarian law as provided for under the respective bodies of law emanates from:

(a) Treaties to which a State is a party;

(b) Customary international law;

(c) The domestic law of each State.

2. If they have not already done so, States shall, as required under international law, ensure that their domestic law is consistent with their international legal obligations by:

(a) Incorporating norms of international human rights law and international humanitarian law into their domestic law, or otherwise implementing them in their domestic legal system;

(b) Adopting appropriate and effective legislative and administrative procedures and other appropriate measures that provide fair, effective and prompt access to justice;

(c) Making available adequate, effective, prompt and appropriate remedies, including reparation, as defined below;

(d) Ensuring that their domestic law provides at least the same level of protection for victims as that required by their international obligations.

II. Scope of the obligation

3. The obligation to respect, ensure respect for and implement international human rights law and international humanitarian law as provided for under the respective bodies of law, includes, inter alia, the duty to:

(a) Take appropriate legislative and administrative and other appropriate measures to prevent violations;

(b) Investigate violations effectively, promptly, thoroughly and impartially and, where appropriate, take action against those allegedly responsible in accordance with domestic and international law;

(c) Provide those who claim to be victims of a human rights or humanitarian law violation with equal and effective access to justice, as described below, irrespective of who may ultimately be the bearer of responsibility for the violation; and

(d) Provide effective remedies to victims, including reparation, as described below.

III. Gross violations of international human rights law and serious violations of international humanitarian law that constitute crimes under international law

4. In cases of gross violations of international human rights law and serious violations of international humanitarian law constituting crimes under international law, States have the duty to investigate and, if there is sufficient evidence, the duty to submit to prosecution the person allegedly responsible for the violations and, if found guilty, the duty to punish her or him. Moreover, in these cases, States should, in accordance with international law, cooperate

with one another and assist international judicial organs competent in the investigation and prosecution of these violations.

5. To that end, where so provided in an applicable treaty or under other international law obligations, States shall incorporate or otherwise implement within their domestic law appropriate provisions for universal jurisdiction. Moreover, where it is so provided for in an applicable treaty or other international legal obligations, States should facilitate extradition or surrender offenders to other States and to appropriate international judicial bodies and provide judicial assistance and other forms of cooperation in the pursuit of international justice, including assistance to, and protection of, victims and witnesses, consistent with international human rights legal standards and subject to international legal requirements such as those relating to the prohibition of torture and other forms of cruel, inhuman or degrading treatment or punishment.

IV. Statutes of limitations

6. Where so provided for in an applicable treaty or contained in other international legal obligations, statutes of limitations shall not apply to gross violations of international human rights law and serious violations of international humanitarian law which constitute crimes under international law.

7. Domestic statutes of limitations for other types of violations that do not constitute crimes under international law, including those time limitations applicable to civil claims and other procedures, should not be unduly restrictive.

V. Victims of gross violations of international human rights law and serious violations of international humanitarian law

8. For purposes of the present document, victims are persons who individually or collectively suffered harm, including physical or mental injury, emotional suffering, economic loss or substantial impairment of their fundamental rights, through acts or omissions that constitute gross violations of international human rights law, or serious violations of international humanitarian law. Where appropriate, and in accordance with domestic law, the term "victim" also includes the immediate family or dependants of the direct victim and persons who have suffered harm in intervening to assist victims in distress or to prevent victimization.

9. A person shall be considered a victim regardless of whether the perpetrator of the violation is identified, apprehended, prosecuted, or convicted and regardless of the familial relationship between the perpetrator and the victim.

VI. Treatment of victims

10. Victims should be treated with humanity and respect for their dignity and human rights, and appropriate measures should be taken to ensure their safety, physical and psychological well-being and privacy, as well as those of their families. The State should ensure that its domestic laws, to the extent possible, provide that a victim who has suffered violence or trauma should benefit from special consideration and care to avoid his or her re-traumatization in the course of legal and administrative procedures designed to provide justice and reparation.

VII. Victims' right to remedies

11. Remedies for gross violations of international human rights law and serious violations of international humanitarian law include the victim's right to the following as provided for under international law:

(a) Equal and effective access to justice;

(b) Adequate, effective and prompt reparation for harm suffered;

(c) Access to relevant information concerning violations and reparation mechanisms.

VIII. Access to justice

12. A victim of a gross violation of international human rights law or of a serious violation of international humanitarian law shall have equal access to an effective

judicial remedy as provided for under international law. Other remedies available to the victim include access to administrative and other bodies, as well as mechanisms, modalities and proceedings conducted in accordance with domestic law. Obligations arising under international law to secure the right to access justice and fair and impartial proceedings shall be reflected in domestic laws. To that end, States should:

(a) Disseminate, through public and private mechanisms, information about all available remedies for gross violations of international human rights law and serious violations of international humanitarian law;

(b) Take measures to minimize the inconvenience to victims and their representatives, protect against unlawful interference with their privacy as appropriate and ensure their safety from intimidation and retaliation, as well as that of their families and witnesses, before, during and after judicial, administrative, or other proceedings that affect the interests of victims;

(c) Provide proper assistance to victims seeking access to justice;

(d) Make available all appropriate legal, diplomatic and consular means to ensure that victims can exercise their rights to remedy for gross violations of international human rights law or serious violations of international humanitarian law.

13. In addition to individual access to justice, States should endeavour to develop procedures to allow groups of victims to present claims for reparation and to receive reparation, as appropriate.

14. An adequate, effective and prompt remedy for gross violations of international human rights law or serious violations of international humanitarian law should include all available and appropriate international processes in which a person may have legal standing and should be without prejudice to any other domestic remedies.

IX. Reparation for harm suffered

15. Adequate, effective and prompt reparation is intended to promote justice by redressing gross violations of international human rights law or serious violations of international humanitarian law. Reparation should be proportional to the gravity of the violations and the harm suffered. In accordance with its domestic laws and international legal obligations, a State shall provide reparation to victims for acts or omissions which can be attributed to the State and constitute gross violations of international human rights law or serious violations of international humanitarian law. In cases where a person, a legal person, or other entity is found liable for reparation to a victim, such party should provide reparation to the victim or compensate the State if the State has already provided reparation to the victim.

16. States should endeavour to establish national programmes for reparation and other assistance to victims in the event that the parties liable for the harm suffered are unable or unwilling to meet their obligations.

17. States shall, with respect to claims by victims, enforce domestic judgements for reparation against individuals or entities liable for the harm suffered and endeavour to enforce valid foreign legal judgements for reparation in accordance with domestic law and international legal obligations. To that end, States should provide under their domestic laws effective mechanisms for the enforcement of reparation judgements.

18. In accordance with domestic law and international law, and taking account of individual circumstances, victims of gross violations of international human rights law and serious violations of international humanitarian law should, as appropriate and proportional to the

gravity of the violation and the circumstances of each case, be provided with full and effective reparation, as laid out in principles 19 to 23, which include the following forms: restitution, compensation, rehabilitation, satisfaction and guarantees of non-repetition.

19. *Restitution* should, whenever possible, restore the victim to the original situation before the gross violations of international human rights law or serious violations of international humanitarian law occurred. Restitution includes, as appropriate: restoration of liberty, enjoyment of human rights, identity, family life and citizenship, return to one's place of residence, restoration of employment and return of property.

20. *Compensation* should be provided for any economically assessable damage, as appropriate and proportional to the gravity of the violation and the circumstances of each case, resulting from gross violations of international human rights law and serious violations of international humanitarian law, such as:

(a) Physical or mental harm;

(b) Lost opportunities, including employment, education and social benefits;

(c) Material damages and loss of earnings, including loss of earning potential;

(d) Moral damage;

(e) Costs required for legal or expert assistance, medicine and medical services, and psychological and social services.

21. *Rehabilitation* should include medical and psychological care as well as legal and social services.

22. *Satisfaction* should include, where applicable, any or all of the following:

(a) Effective measures aimed at the cessation of continuing violations;

(b) Verification of the facts and full and public disclosure of the truth to the extent that such disclosure does not cause further harm or threaten the safety and interests of the victim, the victim's relatives, witnesses, or persons who have intervened to assist the victim or prevent the occurrence of further violations;

(c) The search for the whereabouts of the disappeared, for the identities of the children abducted, and for the bodies of those killed, and assistance in the recovery, identification and reburial of the bodies in accordance with the expressed or presumed wish of the victims, or the cultural practices of the families and communities;

(d) An official declaration or a judicial decision restoring the dignity, the reputation and the rights of the victim and of persons closely connected with the victim;

(e) Public apology, including acknowledgement of the facts and acceptance of responsibility;

(f) Judicial and administrative sanctions against persons liable for the violations;

(g) Commemorations and tributes to the victims;

(h) Inclusion of an accurate account of the violations that occurred in international human rights law and international humanitarian law training and in educational material at all levels.

23. *Guarantees of non-repetition* should include, where applicable, any or all of the following measures, which will also contribute to prevention:

(a) Ensuring effective civilian control of military and security forces;

(b) Ensuring that all civilian and military proceedings abide by international standards of due process, fairness and impartiality;

(c) Strengthening the independence of the judiciary;

(d) Protecting persons in the legal, medical and health-care professions, the media and other related professions, and human rights defenders;

(e) Providing, on a priority and continued basis, human rights and international humanitarian law education to all sectors of society and training for law enforcement officials as well as military and security forces;

(f) Promoting the observance of codes of conduct and ethical norms, in particular international standards, by public servants, including law enforcement, correctional, media, medical, psychological, social service and military personnel, as well as by economic enterprises;

(g) Promoting mechanisms for preventing and monitoring social conflicts and their resolution;

(h) Reviewing and reforming laws contributing to or allowing gross violations of international human rights law and serious violations of international humanitarian law.

X. Access to relevant information concerning violations and reparation mechanisms

24. States should develop means of informing the general public and, in particular, victims of gross violations of international human rights law and serious violations of international humanitarian law of the rights and remedies addressed by these Basic Principles and Guidelines and of all available legal, medical, psychological, social, administrative and all other services to which victims may have a right of access. Moreover, victims and their representatives should be entitled to seek and obtain information on the causes leading to their victimization and on the causes and conditions pertaining to the gross violations of international human rights law and serious violations of international humanitarian law and to learn the truth in regard to these violations.

XI. Non-discrimination

25. The application and interpretation of these Basic Principles and Guidelines must be consistent with international human rights law and international humanitarian law and be without any discrimination of any kind or on any ground, without exception.

XII. Non-derogation

26. Nothing in these Basic Principles and Guidelines shall be construed as restricting or derogating from any rights or obligations arising under domestic and international law. In particular, it is understood that the present Basic Principles and Guidelines are without prejudice to the right to a remedy and reparation for victims of all violations of international human rights law and international humanitarian law. It is further understood that these Basic Principles and Guidelines are without prejudice to special rules of international law.

XIII. Rights of others

27. Nothing in this document is to be construed as derogating from internationally or nationally protected rights of others, in particular the right of an accused person to benefit from applicable standards of due process.

Bibliography

Bayefsky Anne F. 2003. *How to Complain to the United Nations Human Rights Treaty System*, The Hague: Kluwer Law International.

Bajpai Asha. 2006. *Child Rights in India: Law, Policy and Practice*, New Delhi: OUP

Bekou Olympia and Robert Cryer, The International Criminal Court and Universal Jurisdiction: A Close Encounter, *International and Comparative Law Quarterly*, Vol. 56, January 2007, pp. 49-68.

Brownlie, Ian. & Guy, S Goodwin-Gill. 2000. *Basic Documents on Human Right.* New York: Oxford University Press.

Clayton Richard and Hugh Tomlinson. 2010. *Fair Trial Rights*, Oxford: Oxford University Press.

Conte Alex, Scott Davidson and Richard Burchill. 2004. *Defining Civil and Political Rights: Jurisprudence of the United Nations Human Rights Committee*, USA: Ashgate.

Cryer R., H Frimain, and D Robinson. 2008. *An Introduction to International Law*, Cambridge: Cambridge University Press.

Damgaard Ciara. 2008. *Individual Criminal responsibility for Core International Crimes*, Berlin: Springer-Verlag.

Daniel Moeckli, Sangeeta Shah, and Sandesh Sivakumaran (ed.). 2010. *International Human Rights Law*, Oxford: Oxford University Press.

Darrow, M., Arbour, L. 2009. The Pillar of Glass: Human Rights in the Development Operations of the United Nations. 103 *American Journal of International Law* 446. Available at: http://www.asil.org/ajil/July2009_2selectedpiece.pdf.

Davidson, Michael J. 1999. *Military Criminal Law: A Practical Guide for All the Services*, USA, Annapolis: Naval Institute Press.

Donnelly Jack. 2007. *International Human Rights*, USA: West View Press.

Felice D Gaer. 2004. The UN High Commissioner for Human Rights: The Challenges of International Protection, (Book Review), *American Journal of International Law*, April 2004, p. 391-397.

Feria Tinta, Monica. 2008. *Landmark Rulings of the Inter-American Court of Human Rights*, Leiden: Martinus Nijhoff.

Fleck Dieter (ed). 2008. *The Handbook of International Humanitarian Law*, Oxford: Oxford University Press.

Gardam Judith G. and Michelle J. Jarvis. 2001. *Women, Armed Conflict and International Law*, The Hague: Kluwer Law International.

Gunzman, Andrew T. 2008. *How International Law Works*, Oxford: Oxford University Press.

Handbook on Human Rights and Fundamental Freedoms of Armed Forces Personnel. 2008. Poland: OSCE Office for Democratic Institution and Human Rights (ODIHR).

Hwyns Christof and frans Viljoen. 2002. *The Impact of United Nations Human Rights Treaties on the Domestic Level*, The Hague: Kluwer Law International.

Human Rights in the Administration of Justice: A Manual on Human Rights for Judges, Prosecutors and Lawyers, PROFESSIONAL TRAINING SERIES No. 9, United Nations 2003. Available at http://www.ohchr.org/Documents/Publications/training9Titleen.pdf

Joseph Sarah, Jenny Schultz and Melissa Castan. 2000. *The International Covenant on Civil and Political Rights: Cases, Material and Commentary.* New York: Oxford University Press.

Kofi Annan, *Strengthening of the UN: An Agenda for Further Change*, GA Document A/57/387, 9 September 2002.

Lenaerts Koen. 2010. The Contribution of the European Court of Justice to the Area of Freedom, Security and Justice, *International & Comparative Law Quarterly*, Vol. 59, Part 2, April 2010, p. 255-310.

Mertus Julie A. 2009. *The United Nations and Human Rights: A Guide for a New Era*, UK: Routledge.

Mole, Nuala and Catharina Harby. 2006. *'The right to a fair trial, A guide to the implementation of Article 6 of the European Convention on Human Rights'*, Published by the Directorate General of Human Rights Council of Europe F-67075, Strasbourg Cedex.

Nowak Manfred. 2008. *The United Nations Convention Against Torture: A Commentary*, Oxford: Oxford University Press.

Morsink Johannes. 1999. *The Universal Declaration of Human Rights: Origin, Drafting and Intent*, Pennsylvania: University of Pennsylvania Press.

Muller L. 2006. *The First 365 days of the UN Human Rights Council*, published by the Swiss Government.

Ouguergouz Fatsah. 2003. *The African Charter on Human and Peoples' Rights*, The Hague: Martinus Nijhoff Publishers.

Ramcharan B G. 2008. *The Protection Role of the Human Rights Special Procedures*, Martinus Nijhoff.

Risse Thomas, Stephen C. Ropp and Kathryn Sikkink (ed.). 1999. *The Power of Human Rights: International Norms and Domestic Change*, Cambridge: Cambridge University Press.

Rohl Klaus F. and Stefan Machura (ed.). 1997. *Procedural Justice*. USA: Ashgate.

Sano Hans-Otto and Gudmundur Alfredsson (ed). 2002. *Human Rights and Good Governance*. The Hague: Martinus Nijhoff Publishers.

Scorazzi Tullio. 2007. *The Struggle Against Enforced Disappearance and the 2007 UN Convention*, Leiden: Martinus Nijhoff.

Shelton, Dinah L. 2008. *Regional Protection of Human Rights*, Oxford: Oxford University Press.

Sinha Manoj Kumar (ed.). 2010. *International Criminal Law and Human Rights*, New Delhi: Manak Publications Pvt Ltd.

The Right to a Remedy and to Reparation for Gross Human Rights Violations – A Practitioners' Guide, Switzerland: International Commission of Jurists, 2006.

Trechsel Stefan. 2005. *Human Rights in Criminal Proceedings*, Oxford: Oxford University Press.

United Nations Economic and Social Council, Commission on Human Rights; *International Standard Principles Governing the Administration of Justice Through Military Tribunals*, Geneva Centre for the Democratic Control of Armed Forces (DCAF), 2009.

United Nations, report of the Committee on the Elimination of Discrimination against Women 1998 A/53/38/Rev1 available at: <http://www.un.org/womenwatch/daw/cedaw/reports/18report.pdf> accessed 30 June 2010.

What is a fair trial? A Basic Guide to Legal Standards and Practice. 2000. Lawyers Committee for Human Rights, USA: New York. Available at: <http://www.humanrightsfirst.org/pubs/descriptions/fair_trial.pdf>

Zappala Salvatore. 2003. *Human Rights in International Criminal Proceedings*, New York: Oxford University Press.

www.achpr.org

www.icrc.org

www.ilo.org

www.ohchr.org

www.undp.org

www.unhchr.ch

Index

D

E

F

G

R

S

T

U

V

W

X